Advances in Intelligent Sys[

Volume 729

Series editor

Janusz Kacprzyk, Polish Academy of Sciences, Warsaw, Poland
e-mail: kacprzyk@ibspan.waw.pl

The series "Advances in Intelligent Systems and Computing" contains publications on theory, applications, and design methods of Intelligent Systems and Intelligent Computing. Virtually all disciplines such as engineering, natural sciences, computer and information science, ICT, economics, business, e-commerce, environment, healthcare, life science are covered. The list of topics spans all the areas of modern intelligent systems and computing such as: computational intelligence, soft computing including neural networks, fuzzy systems, evolutionary computing and the fusion of these paradigms, social intelligence, ambient intelligence, computational neuroscience, artificial life, virtual worlds and society, cognitive science and systems, Perception and Vision, DNA and immune based systems, self-organizing and adaptive systems, e-Learning and teaching, human-centered and human-centric computing, recommender systems, intelligent control, robotics and mechatronics including human-machine teaming, knowledge-based paradigms, learning paradigms, machine ethics, intelligent data analysis, knowledge management, intelligent agents, intelligent decision making and support, intelligent network security, trust management, interactive entertainment, Web intelligence and multimedia.

The publications within "Advances in Intelligent Systems and Computing" are primarily proceedings of important conferences, symposia and congresses. They cover significant recent developments in the field, both of a foundational and applicable character. An important characteristic feature of the series is the short publication time and world-wide distribution. This permits a rapid and broad dissemination of research results.

More information about this series at http://www.springer.com/series/11156

M. U. Bokhari · Namrata Agrawal
Dharmendra Saini
Editors

Cyber Security

Proceedings of CSI 2015

Springer

Editors
M. U. Bokhari
Department of Computer Science
Aligarh Muslim University
Aligarh, Uttar Pradesh
India

Dharmendra Saini
Bharati Vidyapeeth's College of Engineering (BVCOE)
New Delhi
India

Namrata Agrawal
National Institute of Financial Management
Faridabad, Haryana
India

ISSN 2194-5357 ISSN 2194-5365 (electronic)
Advances in Intelligent Systems and Computing
ISBN 978-981-10-8535-2 ISBN 978-981-10-8536-9 (eBook)
https://doi.org/10.1007/978-981-10-8536-9

Library of Congress Control Number: 2018932995

Printed on acid-free paper

This Springer imprint is published by the registered company Springer Nature Singapore Pte Ltd.
part of Springer Nature
The registered company address is: 152 Beach Road, #21-01/04 Gateway East, Singapore 189721, Singapore

Preface

The last decade has witnessed remarkable changes in the IT industry, virtually in all domains. The 50th Annual Convention, CSI-2015, on the theme "Digital Life" was organized as a part of CSI@50, by CSI at Delhi, the national capital of the country, during December 2–5, 2015. Its concept was formed with an objective to keep ICT community abreast of emerging paradigms in the areas of computing technologies and more importantly looking at its impact on the society.

Information and Communication Technology (ICT) comprises of three main components: infrastructure, services, and product. These components include the Internet, infrastructure-based/infrastructure-less wireless networks, mobile terminals, and other communication mediums. ICT is gaining popularity due to rapid growth in communication capabilities for real-time-based applications. New user requirements and services entail mechanisms for enabling systems to intelligently process speech- and language-based input from human users. CSI-2015 attracted over 1500 papers from researchers and practitioners from academia, industry, and government agencies, from all over the world, thereby making the job of the Programme Committee extremely difficult. After a series of tough review exercises by a team of over 700 experts, 565 papers were accepted for presentation in CSI-2015 during the 3 days of the convention under ten parallel tracks. The Programme Committee, in consultation with Springer, the world's largest publisher of scientific documents, decided to publish the proceedings of the presented papers, after the convention, in ten topical volumes, under ASIC series of the Springer, as detailed hereunder:

1. Volume 1: ICT Based Innovations
2. Volume 2: Next Generation Networks
3. Volume 3: Nature Inspired Computing
4. Volume 4: Speech and Language Processing for Human-Machine Communications

5. Volume 5: Sensors and Image Processing
6. Volume 6: Big Data Analytics
7. Volume 7: Systems and Architecture
8. Volume 8: Cyber Security
9. Volume 9: Software Engineering
10. Volume 10: Silicon Photonics & High Performance Computing

We are pleased to present before you the proceedings of Volume 8 on "Cyber Security." The title "Cyber Security" is devoted primarily to enhance the awareness about cyber security. It brings together much learning from skilled industry experts, academicians, and researchers. The title also covers national and international collaborations and cooperation in cyber security as an essential element of overall security of the system.

The technology in general and Internet in particular are being used widely for various kinds of transactions, information, and communications. It is really a huge challenge to stay secured on the 'open and un-trusted Internet,' and there are potential security risks presented by the Internet. The title uncovers the various nuances of information security, cyber security, and its various dimensions.

The title "Cyber Security" also covers latest security trends, ways to combat cyber threats including the detection and mitigation of security threats and risks. This volume is designed to bring together researchers and practitioners from academia and industry to focus on extending the understanding and establishing new collaborations in these areas. It is the outcome of the hard work of the editorial team, who have relentlessly worked with the authors and steered up the same to compile this volume. It will be a useful source of reference for the future researchers in this domain. Under the CSI-2015 umbrella, we received over 200 papers for this volume, out of which 48 papers are being published, after a rigorous review process, carried out in multiple cycles.

On behalf of organizing team, it is a matter of great pleasure that CSI-2015 has received an overwhelming response from various professionals from across the country. The organizers of CSI-2015 are thankful to the members of *Advisory Committee, Programme Committee, and Organizing Committee* for their all-round guidance, encouragement, and continuous support. We express our sincere gratitude to the learned *Keynote Speakers* for support and help extended to make this event a grand success. Our sincere thanks are also due to our *Review Committee Members* and the *Editorial Board* for their untiring efforts in reviewing the manuscripts, giving suggestions and valuable inputs for shaping this volume. We hope that all the participated delegates will be benefitted academically and wish them for their future endeavors.

We also take the opportunity to thank the entire team from Springer, who have worked tirelessly and made the publication of the volume a reality. Last but not least, we thank the team from Bharati Vidyapeeth's Institute of Computer Applications and Management (BVICAM), New Delhi, for their untiring support, without which the compilation of this huge volume would not have been possible.

Aligarh, India M. U. Bokhari
Faridabad, India Namrata Agrawal
New Delhi, India Dharmendra Saini
December 2017

The Organization of CSI-2015

Chief Patron

Padmashree Dr. R. Chidambaram
Principal Scientific Advisor, Government of India

Patrons

Prof. S. V. Raghavan
Department of Computer Science, IIT Madras, Chennai
Prof. Ashutosh Sharma
Secretary, Department of Science and Technology, Ministry of Science of Technology, Government of India

Chair, Programme Committee

Prof. K. K. Aggarwal
Founder Vice Chancellor, GGSIP University, New Delhi

Secretary, Programme Committee

Prof. M. N. Hoda
Director, Bharati Vidyapeeth's Institute of Computer Applications and Management (BVICAM), New Delhi

Advisory Committee

Editorial Board

Nitish Pathak, BVICAM, New Delhi
Shivendra Goel, BVICAM, New Delhi
Shalini Singh Jaspal, BVICAM, New Delhi
Vaishali Joshi, BVICAM, New Delhi

Contents

Editors and Contributors

About the Editors

Prof. M. U. Bokhari is working as a Professor in the Department of Computer Science at Aligarh Muslim University (AMU), Aligarh. He has published more than 110 research papers in reputed journals and conference proceedings. He has also authored five books on different fields of computer science. His current research interests include requirement engineering, cryptography, software reliability, wireless network security, information retrieval, soft computing, adaptive multi-modal retrieval, E-learning, and databases.

Dr. Namrata Agrawal is working as a Professor at National Institute of Financial Management (NIFM), an Institute of the Ministry of Finance, Government of India. She has formerly been a member of the MMNIT faculty at Allahabad. She has more than 25 years of teaching, research, and consultancy experience. She has published more than 25 papers in national and international journals. She has presented 40 papers at national and international conferences and received the Best Paper Award at an international conference organized by the University of Maryland Eastern Shore (UMES), USA. She has also authored many best-selling books.

Dr. Dharmender Saini is working as the Principal and a Professor in the Department of Computer Science and Engineering at Bharati Vidyapeeth's College of Engineering (BVCOE), New Delhi. He has 8 years of industry experience in the field of patent research and 8 years of academic experience. He is also a registered Indian patent agent, principal investigator with DESIDOC, DRDO, and in a data mining project, and a consultant in the field of patent research.

Contributors

Neha Agarwal Amity University, Noida, Uttar Pradesh, India

Gaurav Anand Faridabad, Haryana, India

C. Aka Assoua Anne-Marie AIIT, Amity University, Noida, Uttar Pradesh, India

Basit Ansari Marathwada Institute of Technology, Aurangabad, India

Anupam Baliyan Bharati Vidyapeeth's Institute of Computer Applications (BVICAM), New Delhi, India

Monika Bansal Rukmini Devi Institute of Advanced Studies, Delhi, India

Tosal Bhalodia Atmiya Institute of Technology and Science, Rajkot, India

M. U. Bokhari Department of Computer Science, Aligarh Muslim University, Aligarh, India

Varun Chauhan Knowledge Graph Department, Binary Semantics Pvt. Ltd., Gurgaon, India

Krishna Keerthi Chennam Gitam University, Computer Science Engineering, Hyderabad, Telangana, India

Kiran Chhabra Computer Science and Engineering, Dr. C.V. Raman University, Bilaspur, CG, India

Prachi Dewal C-DAC, Noida, India

Nilanjan Dey Department of Information Technology, Techno India College of Technology, Kolkata, India

Sangeeta Dhall Faridabad, Haryana, India

Bhawna Dhruv Amity University Noida, Noida, India

G. Dileep Kumar Bharathiar University, Coimbatore, India

Amit Doegar Department of CS NITTTR, Chandigarh, India

Avijit Dutta NIC, New Delhi, India

Ekta Department of CSE and IT, Bhagat Phool Singh Mahila Vishwavidyalaya, Sonipat, India

Princy George Department of Computer Science and Engineering, SCMS School of Engineering and Technology, Ernakulam, Kerala, India

Sakshi Goel Amity School of Engineering and Technology, Amity University, Noida, India

B. B. Gupta Department of Computer Engineering, National Institute of Technology Kurukshetra, Kurukshetra, Haryana, India

Himanshu Gupta AIIT, Amity University, Noida, Uttar Pradesh, India

Hina Gupta Amity School of Engineering and Technology, Amity University, Noida, India

Ruchika Gupta Department of Computer Engineering, Sardar Vallabhbhai National Institute of Technology, Surat, India

Shashank Gupta Department of Computer Science and Information System, Birla Institute of Technology and Science, Pilani, Pilani, Rajasthan, India

Shabbir Hassan Department of Computer Science, Aligarh Muslim University, Aligarh, India

Navjyotsinh Jadeja Faculty of Engineering, Information Technology, Marwadi Education Foundation's Group of Institutions, Rajkot, Gujarat, India

Ankit Kumar Jain National Institute of Technology Kurukshetra, Kurukshetra, Haryana, India

Vipin Jain Department of Computer Science and Engineering, S.K.I.T., Jaipur, Rajasthan, India

Vishal Jain Bharati Vidyapeeth's Institute of Computer Applications (BVICAM), New Delhi, India

Yamini Jain Faridabad, Haryana, India

Meenu Mary John Department of Computer Science and Engineering, SCMS School of Engineering and Technology, Ernakulum, Kerala, India

Chandani Kathad Ilaxo.Com, Rajkot, India

Neeraj Kaushik Amity University, Noida, Uttar Pradesh, India

Nidhi Kaushik Amity University, Noida, Uttar Pradesh, India

Anu Khosla SAG, DRDO, Metcalfe House, New Delhi, India

Mehak Khurana The NorthCap University, Gurgaon, India

C. Rama Krishna NITTTR, Chandigarh, India

Manali Kshirsagar Yashwantrao Chawan College of Engineering, Nagpur, MS, India

Mukesh Kumar H.P. University, Shimla, India

Pardeep Kumar Department of Computer Science and Applications, Kurukshetra University, Kurukshetra, Haryana, India

Praveen Kumar Amity University Noida, Noida, India

Sunil Kumar Swami Vivekanand Subharti University, Meerut, Uttar Pradesh, India

Meena Kumari Department of Computer Science and Applications, Kurukshetra University, Kurukshetra, Haryana, India; The NorthCap University, Gurgaon, India

Rana Majumdar Amity School of Engineering and Technology, Amity University, Noida, India

Kamini Malhotra SAG, DRDO, Metcalfe House, New Delhi, India

Swati Maurya Department of Computer Science and Engineering, DCRUST, Murthal, India

Sangheeta Mishra Department of Computer Applications, BSSS, Bhopal, India

Sumit Mittal M.M. Institute of Computer Technology and Business Management, Maharishi Markandeshwar (Deemed to be University), Mullana, Ambala, Haryana, India

Yogendra Mohan CSED, NERIST, Nirjuli, Arunachal Pradesh, India

Akka Laskhmi Muddana Gitam University, Information Technology, Hyderabad, Telangana, India

Tahseen Munnavara M.J.C.E.T, Information Technology, Hyderabad, Telangana, India

Jaiprakash Nagar School of Information and Communication Technology, Gautam Buddha University, Greater Noida, Uttar Pradesh, India

Deepak Narula Department of Computer Science and Applications, Kurukshetra University, Kurukshetra, Haryana, India

Gagandeep Singh Narula C-DAC, Noida, India

Mamta Narwaria School of Computer Science and Engineering, Galgotias University, Greater Noida, India

Rajender Nath Department of Computer Science and Applications, Kurukshetra University, Kurukshetra, Haryana, India

A. B. Nimbalkar A.M. College, Pune, Maharashtra, India

Priya Oberoi M.M. Institute of Computer Technology and Business Management, Maharishi Markandeshwar (Deemed to be University), Mullana, Ambala, Haryana, India

Rudra Pratap Ojha Galgotias College of Engineering and Technology, Greater Noida, India; National Institute of Technology, Durgapur, India

Disha H. Parekh Faculty of Computer Applications, Marwadi Education Foundation's Group of Institutions, Rajkot, Gujarat, India; Computer Science Department, Bharathiar University, Coimbatore, Tamilnadu, India

S. N. Panda Chitkara University, Rajpura, Punjab, India

J. P. Pandey KNIT Sultanpur, Sultanpur, India

Deepika Parashar Department of Computer Science and Engineering, S.K.I.T., Jaipur, Rajasthan, India

Monika Poriye Department of Computer Science and Applications, Kurukshetra University, Kurukshetra, Haryana, India

R. Praveen Sam Department of CSE, GPREC, Kurnool, India

K. V. Prema Department of CSE, Manipal Institute of Technology, MAHE, Manipal, Karnataka, India

Shilpa Pund-Dange Department of Computer Science, Modern College, Pune, India

Dharm Raj Galgotias College of Engineering and Technology, Greater Noida, India

K. Raja Alpha College of Engineering, Chennai, Tamilnadu, India

Ajay Rana Amity University, Noida, Uttar Pradesh, India

Udai Pratap Rao Department of Computer Engineering, Sardar Vallabhbhai National Institute of Technology, Surat, India

Seema Rawat Amity University Noida, Noida, India

U. S. Rawat Department of Computer Science and Engineering, Manipal University Jaipur, Jaipur, Rajasthan, India

Satyabrata Roy Department of Computer Science and Engineering, Manipal University Jaipur, Jaipur, Rajasthan, India

Pranav Saini Department of Information Technology, Bharati Vidyapeeth's College of Engineering, GGSIPU, New Delhi, India

Goutam Sanyal National Institute of Technology, Durgapur, India

Sonal Sarnaik Marathwada Institute of Technology, Aurangabad, India

Ankur Saxena Amity University, Noida, Uttar Pradesh, India

Aditi Sharma Department of CS NITTTR, Chandigarh, India

Gaurav Sharma Faridabad, Haryana, India

Naveen Kumar Sharma SAG, DRDO, Metcalfe House, New Delhi, India

Sandeep Sharma School of Information and Communication Technology, Gautam Buddha University, Greater Noida, Uttar Pradesh, India

Jayant Shekhar Computer Science Department, Swami Vivekanand Subharti University, Meerut, Uttar Pradesh, India

Reena P. Shinde Department of Computer Science, Sinhgad College of Science, Pune, India

Sahebrao N. Shinde Department of Computer Science, C.M.C.S. College, Nashik, India

Ajit Singh Department of CSE and IT, Bhagat Phool Singh Mahila Vishwavidyalaya, Sonipat, India

Jatinder Paul Singh Shobhit University, Meerut, India

Karan Singh School of Computer and Systems Sciences, Jawaharlal Nehru University, New Delhi, India

Shailendra Singh School of Computer and Systems Sciences, Jawaharlal Nehru University, New Delhi, India

Anita Singhrova Department of Computer Science and Engineering, DCRUST, Murthal, India

Subhranil Som Amity Institute of Information Technology, Amity University, Uttar Pradesh, India

Chetan Soni National Informatics Centre, Ministry of Defense, New Delhi, India

S. Srinivasan Research Development Center, Bharathiar University, Coimbatore, Tamilnadu, India; Department of M.C.A, K.C.G College of Technology, Chennai, Tamilnadu, India

R. Sridaran Faculty of Computer Applications, Marwadi Education Foundation's Group of Institutions, Rajkot, Gujarat, India

Abhishek Srivastava Amity School of Engineering and Technology, Amity University, Noida, India

Pramod Kumar Srivastava Galgotias College of Engineering and Technology, Greater Noida, India

Sarvesh Tanwar Department of CSE FET, Mody University of Science and Technology, Laxmangarh, India

Anupam Tiwari National Informatics Centre, Ministry of Defense, New Delhi, India

Richa Tyagi SAG, DRDO, Metcalfe House, New Delhi, India

Akanksha Upadhyaya Rukmini Devi Institute of Advanced Studies, Delhi, India

Shuchita Upadhyaya Department of Computer Science and Applications, Kurukshetra University, Kurukshetra, Haryana, India

Madhuri Vaghasia Faculty of Engineering, Information Technology, Marwadi Education Foundation's Group of Institutions, Rajkot, Gujarat, India

P. Vinod Department of Computer Science and Engineering, SCMS School of Engineering and Technology, Ernakulum, Kerala, India

Ruby Yadav The NorthCap University, Gurgaon, India

Arun Zadgaonkar Dr. C.V. Raman University, Bilaspur, CG, India

Keyur Zala Ilaxo.Com, Rajkot, India

Privacy Protection Through Hiding Location Coordinates Using Geometric Transformation Techniques in Location-Based Services Enabled Mobiles

Ruchika Gupta and Udai Pratap Rao

Abstract Mobile gadgets today are swaggering computing potential and memory at par or at times even higher to that found in desktop personal computers. A wireless interconnection has turned out to be considerably more readily accessible these days. As individuals are growing mobile with regard to the fast lifestyle and working pattern, a new, smarter system came into existence that is termed as "location-based service" (LBS). Such a system amalgamates the location data of a user with smart applications to deliver demanded services. Although LBSs provide major openings for a large variety of markets and remarkable convenience to the end user, it also presents subtle privacy attack to user's location information. Threat to the privacy sneaks into the system due to the prerequisite of sending user's current location to the LBS provider to attain related services. Since the volume of data gathered from dynamic or stationary mobile users using LBS can be high, it is vital to outline the frameworks and systems in a manner that is secure and keep the location information private. This can be portrayed as a big mobile data challenge in LBSs setting. This paper aims to explore the issues related to privacy involved in LBSs. In the paper, we introduce framework structure outline for preventing location-based vicinity inference of users who issue a query and also proposed *VIC-PRO* algorithm which helps to overcome the gaps of well-established K-anonymity approach in the existing system. The suggested approach strengthens the privacy of query initiating vicinity information.

Keywords Location-based services · Privacy · User identity and location privacy preservation · Mobility · Big mobile data

---

R. Gupta (✉) · U. P. Rao
Department of Computer Engineering, Sardar Vallabhbhai National Institute of Technology, Surat, India
e-mail: ruchika.gupta.2015@ieee.org

U. P. Rao
e-mail: upr@coed.svnit.ac.in

M. U. Bokhari et al. (eds.), *Cyber Security*, Advances in Intelligent Systems and Computing 729, https://doi.org/10.1007/978-981-10-8536-9_1

1 Introduction

The fiery escalation of location-detection enabled gadgets along with growing wireless interconnections and mobile databases results in materializing location-based applications which conveys requested information to the clients based on their present location. Location-based store finder, location-based weather forecast information, location-based traffic reports, location-based advertisements, promotions, and location-based geo-fencing are few examples of such applications.

A conventional localization arrangement based on the fundamental communications network comprises of two main elements: a mobile device carried by the end user and the base station or beacon node representing the infrastructure of the communication network (along with LBS provider). Pull LBS (Reactive), Push LBS (Proactive), and tracking LBS are three main types of LBSs (Fig. 1).

In LBS, we incline to use positioning technology to register mobile location movement. There are quite a lot of abstract approaches and real implementations of systems to resolve the place of a cell phone. The most outstanding example of such a positioning system is the GPS [1]. Although LBSs offer major openings for a large variety of markets and remarkable convenience to end user, but at the same time it also presents subtle privacy attack. Privacy of the system is threatened due to the requirement of the current location of the user in order to provide related services. Sharing the location information with service provider actually makes user's physical geographical location on the globe and user's virtual location over the World Wide Web precisely identical.

There are two major obfuscation aspects in the LBS namely (i) Obfuscate user identification and (ii) Obfuscate location identification. This paper focuses on

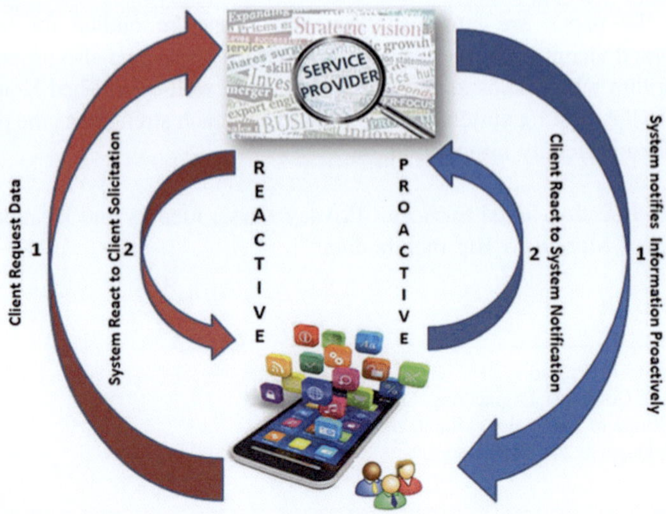

Fig. 1 Types of LBS

strengthening privacy of vicinity identification along with the privacy of location and user identification information.

2 Motivation

With the continual reduction in the price of mobile devices, it is noticed that not only the use of the location-aware gadgets raises in a growing number of civilian and military applications, additionally a developing interest for regularly being informed while out on the road for innumerable purposes. Keeping track of the traffic condition, route information, on the fly parking information, en route grocery store information, meeting a friend on way back home, and catching new movie in theaters are few of such applications. Considering the metropolitan zone with hundreds and thousands of vehicles (especially in a profoundly populated continent like Asia) where every driver or passenger is interested in such information relevant to their trips to plan visits more smartly and save their time in wasteful driving. Such era of voluminous data can be viewed as big mobile data challenge in LBSs-enabled mobiles.

Another major motivation behind writing the paper on this subject is the news of November, 2014, where New York City Mayor declared that an association of four companies named City Bridge will develop and manage up to 10,000 IEEE 802.11 access points for New York City's LinkNYC [2]. It agrees to be the biggest free municipal Wi-Fi operation in the world. In the same motion, the Prime Minister of India announced to develop intelligent cities having geo-spatial mapping, Wi-Fi hotspots, and intelligent transit system with GPS features. In both the mentioned declarations, sharing user's location information would play a major role in order to access the demanded services. Clearly, LBS will be having a sweeping impact of the digital world in the future as pointed out by the market analysis [3] and would reach $63 billion by 2019.

3 Related Work

A survey of literature in the related field has brought forth several architectures, algorithms and techniques that have been proposed by many authors in which they have discussed about anonymity based, different cloaking mechanisms based and trusted third party based privacy preservation models. A location estimation enabled smart mobile device allows users to submit location-based queries to web-based LBSs. Once the mobile apparatus throws the service request, the sender has no control over the facts contained by the submitted query. An observer with a right to access the information included in the query may utilize that information to guess the user's location. This makes a profound challenge of location privacy protection that must be ponder upon. In this concern, most of the previous work relies on trusted third party called as Anonymizer that works as an intermediary amidst user and LBS provider [4].

Location anonymity is vastly discussed by Mokbel et al. and others [5–7]. These techniques are based on hiding the position data before conveying them to the LBS provider. *K*-anonymity operates by hiding the position of the end user within a set of "*K*" members. Anonymizer includes additional $K - 1$ users from same vicinity and then forwards the anonymized query to LBS provider. It is now difficult for the LBS provider to distinguish the correct user from a set of *K* anonymous users. It keeps client recognizable proof private yet bargains the user location's vicinity information. To request a desirable level of privacy assurance, a client required to select the value of *K* cautiously. Regrettably, specifying an apt value of *K* is not easy. A user would always choose a bigger *K* value to ensure sufficiently large privacy preservation, yet this in turn will result in an unnecessary reduction of location accuracy [8]. Trusting third party and choosing an optimal value of *K* is a critical issue in this situation.

In [9], authors Chow et al. provide a clear and interesting system for avoiding identification inference based on location of users who issue spatial queries to LBS. Background knowledge attacks, when the adversary has extra data regarding specific user's preferences, are still possible.

Authors of paper [9] have taken it to the next level where mobile user forms a group and randomly select a peer from the group as agent to initiate a query. But this approach in proactive mode incurs high communication overhead and low quality of service. Bettini et al. [10] have categorized privacy problem in LBS on the basis of attack and existing defense mechanisms. In [11], authors have discussed a novel approach for privacy using encryption method for location and trajectory path which shows remarkable improvement in computational speed. This work fails to protect the current location in certain cases.

Damiani, Bertino, and Silvestri presented PROBE framework for the customized shrouding for the protection of sensitive locations using a greedy strategy [12]. They have discussed the privacy issue based on a privacy profile which also unable to keep user location private when the adversary is aware of multiple attributes of the user. No authors to our knowledge have actually discussed privacy preservation of user's vicinity information.

4 Problem Formulation

4.1 Problem Statement

Preserving the privacy of originating query vicinity information of the user by including additional $K - 1$ users from diverse directions.

The addressed setup as depicted in Fig. 2 incorporates an admirable focus on *K*—anonymity concept. The main focus is on the inclusion of additional $K - 1$ clients from diverse directions. The fundamental objective of this proposed

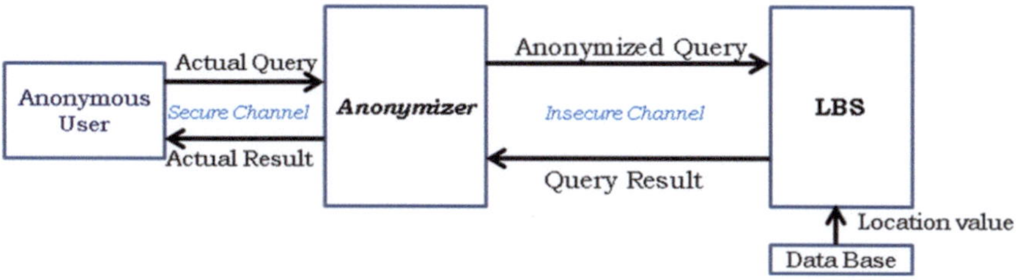

Fig. 2 General framework

approach is to obfuscate the vicinity information of an end client submitting an inquiry to LBS by including additional users from diverse directions as part of the query.

5 Proposed Approach

In our proposed framework, after accepting the location information from the sender, anonymizer runs proposed algorithm (*VIC-PRO*) and instead of including $K - 1$ more users of same vicinity, this algorithm computes K users after performing the following geometric transformation techniques and produces a final anonymized query set Q:

a. Translation
b. Reflection

Figure 3 shows the instance after computation of suggested geometric transformations.

The algorithm computes diverse $K - 1$ values assuming the nearest beacon node as the center of origin. Each new direction is now having the same probability considered to be the query initiator vicinity by an adversary. Anonymizer forwards this anonymized query to LBS provider and after processing, the result set is communicated back to anonymizer. Now, anonymizer has the actual result and some false hits. Anonymizer filters out the incorrect results and sends the genuine result to the end client.

6 Vic-Pro Algorithm

The *VICinity-PROtection (VIC-PRO)* algorithm (Fig. 4) obfuscates the query initiator vicinity information by making use of the fundamental geometric transformation techniques [13].

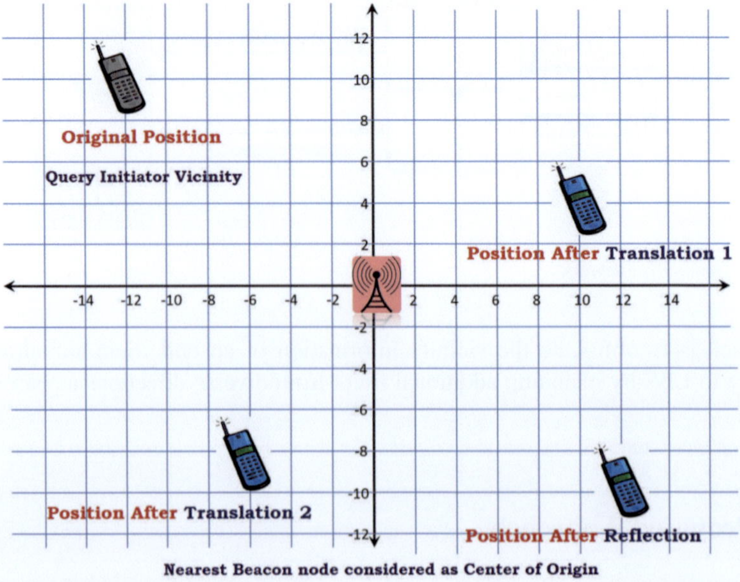

Fig. 3 An instance after transformations

Fig. 4 *VIC-PRO* pseudocode

VIC-PRO

Input: Current location coordinates *(x, y)* of the mobile client submitting query request

Output: Anonymized Query Set *Q* (consisting K users)

Initially K=0

1. *Anonymized_query_set Q = Empty Set*
   Let, current_loc = (x, y)
2. $x' = Reflection(x)$ and $y' = Reflection(y)$
   //Reflection method computes reflection geometric
   //transformation for the given input point
3. *Anonymized_query_set* $Q = Q \cup \{x', y'\}$
4. **while** (K<=18) // as K= 20 is assumed
5. {Select random translation factors δt_x and δt_y
6. $new\_x = x + \delta t_x$
7. $new\_y = y + \delta t_y$
8. *Anonymized_query_set* $Q = Q \cup \{new\_x, new\_y\}$
9. Increment K by 1}
10. *Anonymized_query_set* $Q = Q \cup \{current\_loc\ (x, y)\}$
11. **return** *Anonymized_query_set Q*

Considerations and Assumptions:

a. The utilized mobile devices are LBSs enabled and have the ability to determine their approximate location (i.e., can determine their longitude and latitude).
b. Mobile devices are being used for outside searches and utilizing Global Positioning System.
c. Coordinate representation of location is used by the algorithm to keep the explanation simple and easy to understand.
d. Proposed algorithm runs at anonymizer.
e. The value of $K = 20$ is assumed and random translation factors generated could be either homogeneous or heterogeneous.
f. Service provider is efficient enough to handle mass query requests.

This anonymized query set Q further is sent to LBS provider.

7 Example

The example shows the research gap in K-anonymity concept. SVNIT is taken as the query originating region. Consider the geographical context as depicted in Fig. 5.

Considering the case where a SVNIT student is generating a query asking for a "Nearby 34 in. by 48 in. poster printing shop". In K-anonymity principle, K users become the part of anonymized query. Anonymizer includes K-1 more client from the same vicinity and after that advances the anonymized inquiry to a service

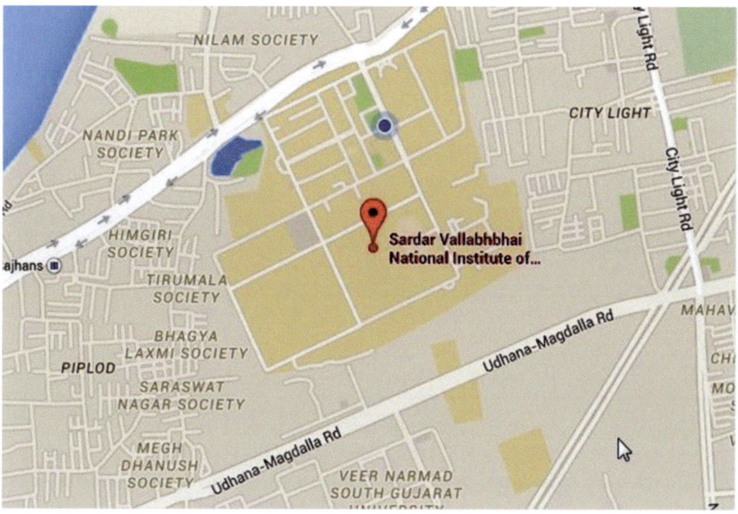

Fig. 5 Query originating location: SVNIT, Surat

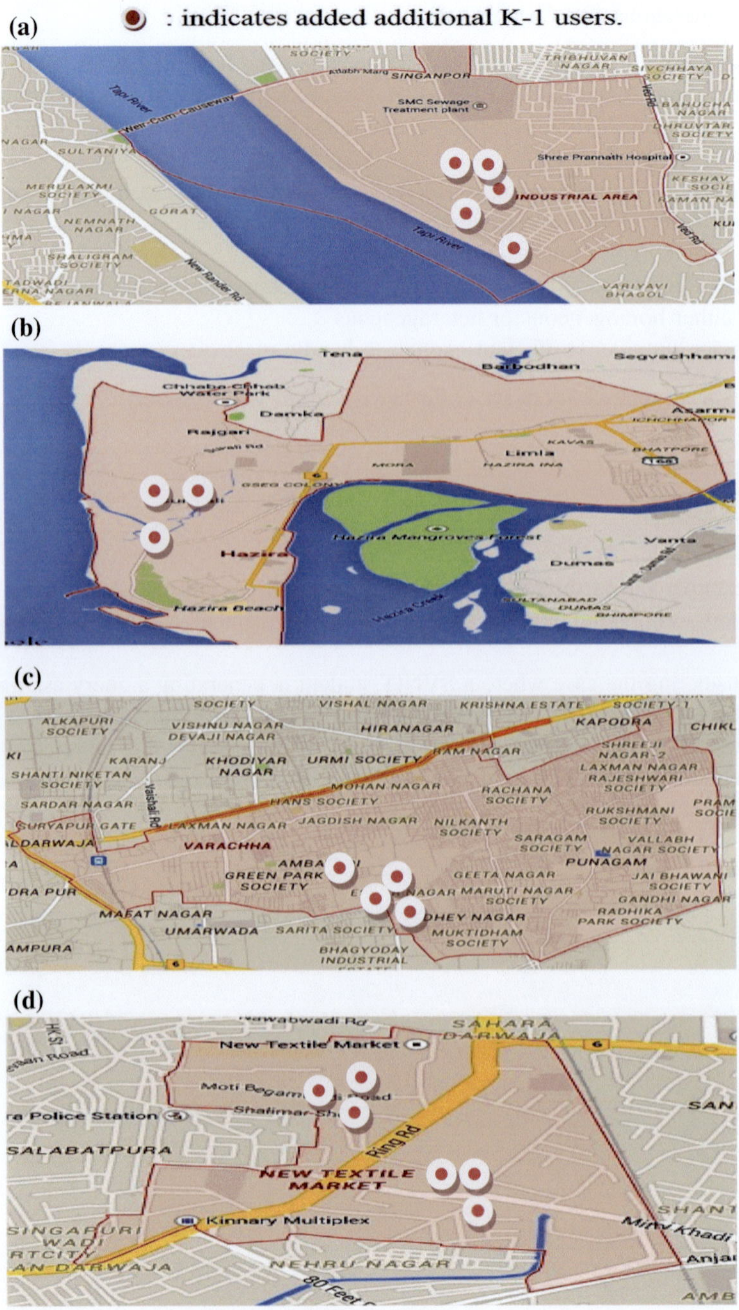

Fig. 6 **a** Vicinity—industrial area, **b** vicinity—Hazira, **c** vicinity—Varachha, **d** vicinity-new textile market

provider. Here, in this situation, though the location and user information are preserved, but breach of vicinity information privacy can be registered by an adversary.

Following TWO cases, adversary may use to estimate region information:

Case1: Adversary staying informed with client's social networking status If an adversary knows that SVNIT is the only technical institute in the vicinity and he is also keeping track of client's social networking whereabouts in which client mentioned that she is going to attend "Security & Privacy symposium-2015" and later would also introduce a publication on a certain date at certain place. For an adversary, with the help of other promotional information shared by the tagged institute, which is organizing the mentioned event on other social connecting sites, it would not be troublesome to discover that the student-initiated nearest poster printing shop search query indeed belong to SVNIT.

Case2: Adversary staying educated with demographics Considering adversary is now aware about the fact that Surat is a place known more for businesses and individuals do not go for advanced education much. In such a case, it is not difficult for an adversary with legitimate access to query information to figure out that the query initiating region is SVNIT. If an adversary further probe with the help of social networking connection, then user identification is also possible. This identification breach makes this framework susceptible to background knowledge attack.

Figure 6a–d depicts few diverse regions produced after the suggested geometric transformations at anonymizer.

8 Conclusions

This paper proposes a strategy and an algorithm *VIC-PRO* that computes the anonymized query with K users present in diverse directions unlike the existing approaches where the focus was on the inclusion of K clients from the same vicinity. Suggested approach strengthens the framework and deals with preserving vicinity privacy along with user identification privacy as each new direction now has the same probability considered to be a query initiator vicinity.

References

1. Hofmann-Wellenhof B, Lichtenegger H, Wasle E (2007) GNSS–global navigation satellite systems: GPS, GLONASS, Galileo, and more. Springer, Berlin
2. Popular Science News (November 2014) Available: http://www.popsci.com/nycs-payphones-will-become-gigabit-wi-fi-access-points
3. Market Survey News (2014) Available: http://www.dailywireless.org/category/location-services

4. Mokbel MF, Chow CY, Aref WG (2006) The new Casper: query processing for location services without compromising privacy. In: Proceedings of the 32nd international conference on very large data bases: VLDB endowment, pp 763–774
5. Mokbel MF (2007) Privacy in location-based services: state-of-the-art and research directions. In: Proceedings of international conference on mobile data management IEEE, pp 228–228
6. Ghinita G, Kalnis P, Skiadopoulos S (2007) MOBIHIDE: a mobile peer-to-peer system for anonymous location-based queries. In: Proceedings of 10th international symposium on advances in spatial and temporal databases, Springer, Berlin, Heidelberg, pp 221–238
7. Gruteser M, Grunwald D (2003) Anonymous usage of location-based services through spatial and temporal cloaking. In: Proceedings of the 1st international conference on mobile systems, applications and services ACM, pp 31–42
8. Kalnis P, Ghinita G, Mouratidis K, Papadias D (2007) Preventing location-based identity inference in anonymous spatial queries. IEEE Trans Knowl Data Eng 19(12):1719–1733
9. Chow CY, Mokbel MF, Liu X (2006) A Peer-to-Peer Spatial Cloaking Algorithm for Anonymous Location-based Service. In: Proceedings of the 14th annual ACM international symposium on advances in geographic information systems ACM, pp 171–178
10. Bettini C, Mascetti S, Wang XS, Freni D, Jajodia S (2009) Anonymity and historical-anonymity in location-based services, in privacy in location-based applications. Springer, Berlin Heidelberg, pp 1–30
11. Buchanan WJ, Kwecka Z, Ekonomou E (2013) A privacy preserving method using privacy enhancing techniques for location based services. Mobile Netw Appl 18(5):728–737
12. Damiani ML, Bertino E, Silvestri C (2010) The probe framework for the personalized cloaking of private locations. Trans Data Priv 3(2):123–148
13. Hein GW, Kneissl F, Avila-Rodriguez J-A, Wallner S (2005) Authenticating GNSS—global navigation satellite systems—proofs against spoofs

Advanced RSA Cryptographic Algorithm for Improving Data Security

Mukesh Kumar

Abstract Data security is a method which is used to cover the important information. Data security methods control the privacy and integrity of the important information. The access to the database of the companies has improved. Now companies store their business data more on computer than before. Most of the company data is for internal use and not for the general public because business data is highly confidential. At present, cryptographic block cipher is being used with some logical operation and the main drawback in this method is the generation of the secret key which is totally based on the alphabets. So with the help of loop concept, there is a chance for the hackers to find out the secret key. But I propose advanced algorithm for cryptography which is totally dependent on hashing function technique to generate a secret key which is further used to encrypt and decrypt the important information. The secret key will be generated by using different key generation algorithms which will be of higher sets of alphanumeric characters. I am using a hashing technique for cryptography along with a new quantum-bit generation method.

Keywords Cryptography · Ciphertext · Data security · Key generation algorithms

1 Introduction

Cryptography is the technique which is used to secure important information and sends it over channel which is secured and only recipient receives the message. At present, data security becomes a very important aspect of computing system. Due to easy access of the Internet today, virtually all the computer system are connected to each other. Due to advancement in the Internet, there is easy access of all the data all over the world, but it also created new risks for those users who want to remain

M. Kumar (✉)
H.P. University, Shimla, India
e-mail: mukesh.kumarphd2014@gmail.com

M. U. Bokhari et al. (eds.), *Cyber Security*, Advances in Intelligent Systems and Computing 729, https://doi.org/10.1007/978-981-10-8536-9_2

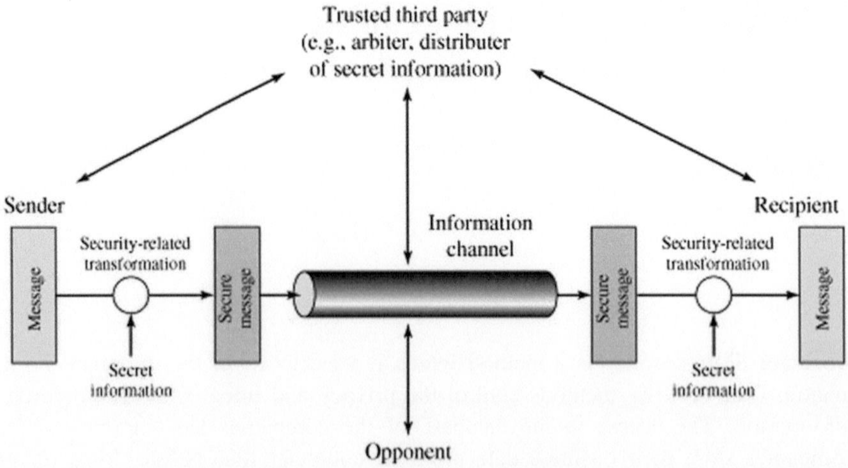

Fig. 1 Network security model

their data secret. At present, hackers are using a variety of techniques in order to break into computer system and steal information or change important data of any organizations (Fig. 1).

At present, cryptography has many applications area. Cryptography provides a high level of privacy by covering confidential data of any individuals or groups. Cryptography is used for the purpose of providing access to data in restricted way, data integrity, and authentication. At present, a lot of research work is going on to find out the new cryptographic algorithms based on security and complexity [1]. Simply talking about data security, then the following features come to our mind like privateness, validation, wholeness, disownment, access control, and availability of data.

2 Literature Review

For generating the starting key for the purpose of encryption and decryption of the information/ message provided to use, they generally used the random key generator algorithm [2]. In that particular technique, a replacement technique is used where they can take four words set from given input message and after getting the encrypted data, the equivalent words in the random key matrix can be identified. A technique is suggested by Nath in multiple sequence alignment algorithm for searching characters from a random key matrix [3]. In this technique, they provide arrangement for encrypting data. The random key matrix contains all possible characters set whose value lies between 0 and 255 (ASCII code). Text/ word key used by the end user is used for the design of the random key matrix. From the starting word/text key used by user, they are providing a new encryption/decryption steps to find the random and encryption number. The author unexpectedly finds it very difficult to meet the two variables from two unlike input. At this stage, it is very difficult to crack the encryption techniques which are provided by the author, but if anybody wants to crack the techniques then they must know all the possible pattern of the word/text key used by the user. If anybody tries to decrypt the data, then they must know the exact key matrix used and if anybody tries theoretically to make the random matrix then they almost have to try 65,536! attempts. Different researcher have applied this technique on possible data files and they have observed that it gives 100% results while applying cryptography on data.

In paper [4], a newly advanced algorithm outline symmetric algorithm is proposed which is in resemblance to Rijndael algorithm. In Rijndael technique, 128 bits block for encryption are used but in AES technique, 200 bits block are used.

3 Rivest–Shamir–Adleman Algorithm

RSA algorithm was suggested by Rivest–Shamir–Adleman of the Massachusetts Institute of Technology in 1977. Rivest–Shamir–Adleman algorithm is a cryptosystem which is used for encryption with public key, and is further used for securing secret message details, which is transmitted over an uncertain computer network. Public-key cryptography uses two different keys like one public and one private key. Both the keys are used for the encryption of secret message; and in the another case, opposite keys are used to decrypt of secret message. Due to this attribute, Rivest–Shamir–Adleman algorithm has become the most widely used algorithm. In Rivest–Shamir–Adleman algorithm, the security of the secret message is implemented through web service. In Rivest–Shamir–Adleman algorithm, public-key encryptions techniques are used. The certainty of the Rivest–Shamir–Adleman algorithm depends on the problems for factoring [3, 5]. Rivest–Shamir–Adleman algorithm is isolated or divided into two different parts:

Encryption of Secret Data: During the process of encryption of data files, different session keys for encryption are generated. These generated keys are further used for encryption with an algorithm as compared to encryption of data files as whole. A moderate public encryption of data files is further used for encryption of session.

Decryption of Encrypted Secret Data: The confidential data is changed into their ciphertext before sending from sender X to recipient Y. Then, Y extracts the session key which is further used for decryption with private key to get the confidential information. The encryption and decryption keys should be kept secret always.

Session Key: A session key of any cryptography algorithm is a decryption and an encryption key that is randomly generated to maintain the security of a transmission session between a sender and receivers.

Quantum-bits Production: For the secret data of the user, first of all, find the secret key for that data to encrypt. After getting the secret key, change the data into hexadecimal code and after that change it into binary to get the least bits as Quantum bits of 0 and 1.

4 Proposed Work

I proposed a block-based symmetric algorithm for cryptography techniques. To generate the initial key by using session key method, a pseudorandom prime number and their exponential values were used, further this key was used for encrypting the given secret data using RSA algorithm. To encrypt a secret data, I introduced a system which using 512-bit key size with some combination of alphanumeric method. But one drawback of this method is to find out two similar data. To decrypt any data file, receiver may know the same key block and then find the combination with the alphanumeric number, but theoretically if you want to decrypt the data, user has to apply 2256 trail on data. So, practically this is not possible and the data still remains traceable.

Different steps for Session Key Generation:

- This is the jointly used secret key for encryption/decryption.
- For generating session key, pseudorandom prime number and their exponential values were used.
- The session key used for encryption and decryption is 512 bits with a combination of alphanumeric values.

Proposed Algorithm for encryption and decryption:
Below are the following steps:

- First of all, get the secret key for your data. After that change into hexadecimal to binary values again.
- After the completion of first step, two binary values are obtained, which are further used for finding quantum bits.
- After getting the quantum bits, find the quantum key with the help of quantum key production.
- If the quantum bit value is 0 for both binary value, then ($1/\sqrt{2}$ (a [0] + a [1])).
- If the quantum bit value is 1 and 0 for binary value, respectively, then ($1/\sqrt{2}$ (a [0] − a [1])).
- If the quantum bit value is 0 and 1 for binary value, respectively, then a [0].
- If the value is 1 for both binary value, then a [1].
- By applying master key, the next session key is encrypted and then reserves all the important information.
- Now, key administration center issues all actual session key to the user.
- Key administration center also issues quantum bits to the use.
- Key administration center also issues session key/ quantum bits to the receiver to decrypt the messages.

5 Conclusion

This presented algorithm is mainly used for block cipher techniques and possibly this technique will take less time to encrypt a data of large size. It is not possible to crack the encryption algorithm if you do not know the exact key value and this is the main advantage of presented algorithm. I have used this algorithm for both encryption and decryption while sending or receiving important message.

References

1. A Text book by William Stallings, data and computer communications, 6e William 6e 2005
2. Chatterjee D, Nath J, Dasgupta S, Nath A (2005) A new symmetric key cryptography algorithm using extended MSA method: DJSA symmetric key algorithm, accepted for publication in IEEE CSNT2011 to be held at SMVDU (Jammu) 03–06 June 2011
3. Nath A, Das S, Chakrabarti A (2010) Data hiding and retrieval. In: Proceedings of IEEE international conference on computer intelligence and computer network held at Bhopal from 26–28 Nov 2010
4. Muhammad F, Chowdhury I, Matin MA Effect of security increment to symmetric data encryption through AES methodology, 9th ACIS international conference on software engineering, artificial intelligence, networking, and parallel/distributed computing. Phuket, Thailand. 6–8 Aug 2008. https://doi.org/10.1109/SNPD.2008.101
5. Felten K An algorithm for symmetric cryptography with a wide range of scalability. In published by 2nd international workshop on embedded systems, internet programming and industial IT
6. Wang Y, Hu M (2009) Timing evaluation of the known cryptographic algorithms. International conference on computational intelligence and security. Beijing, China, 11–14 Dec 2009. https://doi.org/10.1109/CIS.2009.81
7. Nath A, Ghosh S, Malik MA Symmetric key cryptography using random key generator, vol 2, pp 239–244

Author Biography

Mukesh Kumar (10/04/1982) has pursuing Ph.D. in Computer Science from Himachal Pradesh University, Summer-Hill Shimla-5. India. My research interest includes Data Mining, Educational Data Mining, Big Data and Image Cryptography.

Different Security Mechanisms in Two-Factor Authentication for Collaborative Computing Environment

G. Dileep Kumar and R. Praveen Sam

Abstract The main aim of this paper is to provide the security for accessing the collaborative computing environment. Main thing here is using authentication method, users can access their collaborative environments. So normal authentication is not sufficient for collaborative environment, that is why here I am proposing two-factor authentication for collaborative environment.

Keywords Security · Collaborative computing environment · Authentication Two-factor authentication

1 Introduction

Collaborative computing environment is the best suitable environment for group communications and data sharing in group manner. If the user wants to access the collaborative computing environment, the main challenging scenario is here to provide the security of this type of environments. Mainly by using the authentication method, users can access their workspace.

1.1 Authentication

Authentication is the security mechanism, using this method, we can provide security to the users work environments and users data [1].

G. Dileep Kumar (✉)
Bharathiar University, Coimbatore, India
e-mail: dileep.gopaluni@gmail.com

R. Praveen Sam
Department of CSE, GPREC, Kurnool, India
e-mail: Praveen_sam75@yahoo.com

M. U. Bokhari et al. (eds.), *Cyber Security*, Advances in Intelligent Systems and Computing 729, https://doi.org/10.1007/978-981-10-8536-9_3

For accessing the collaborative environment, only authentication is insufficient. Because this environment needs more security and so many groups can share their sensitive data in this space. So only authentication is insufficient, so here we are using two-factor authentication mechanism to provide security to collaborative environment.

1.2 Two-Factor Authentication

Something authentication is not enough for some type of environments, and then we are using two-factor authentication mechanism. Main example for this one is collaborative environment. First by using passwords, we can authenticate then the environment cannot be connected here again we will authenticate by using the advance techniques to access environments. Users having these two authentication information only can access the data via environment [2].

1.3 Different Two-Factor Authentication Mechanisms

- Face recognition
- Fingerprint recognition
- Smart cards
- Secret message
- One-time password (OTP)

1.3.1 Face Recognition

It utilizes the dimensional calculation of recognizing elements in the face. It is a type of PC vision that uses the face to distinguish or to validate a man [3].

A critical distinction with other biometric arrangements is that faces can be caught from some separation away, with for instance observation cameras. Thusly, confront acknowledgment can be connected without the subject realizing that he is being watched. This makes face acknowledgment suitable for discovering missing kids or finding outlaw culprits utilizing observation cameras (Fig. 1).

Autonomous of the arrangement seller, face acknowledgment is proficient as takes after:

- An advanced camera procures a picture of the face.
- Programming finds the face in the picture; this is additionally called face recognition. Face discovery is one of the more troublesome strides in face

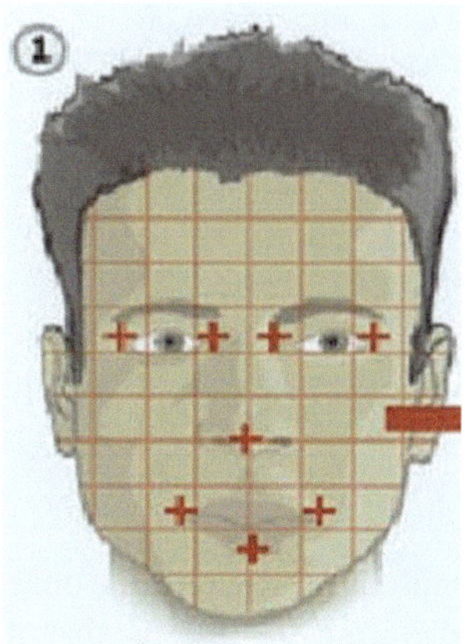

Fig. 1 Finding the elements in face recognition

acknowledgment, particularly when utilizing reconnaissance cameras for checking a whole horde of individuals.

- At the point when a face has been chosen in the picture, the product breaks down the spatial geometry. The procedures used to concentrate distinguishing elements of a face are merchant ward. When all is said in done, the product creates a layout, this is a lessened situated of information which particularly recognizes an individual taking into account the elements of his face [4].
- The created format is then contrasted and an arrangement of known layouts in a database (ID) or with one particular format (confirmation) [5].
- The product creates a score which demonstrates how well two layouts match. It relies on upon the product how high a score must be for two formats to be considered as coordinating, for instance a confirmation application obliges low FAR and in this way, the score must be sufficiently high before layouts can be proclaimed as coordinating. In a reconnaissance application, anyway you would not have any desire to pass up a major opportunity for any outlaw crooks hence obliging a low FRR, so you would set a lower coordinating score and security operators will deal with the false positives [6].

1.3.2 Fingerprint Recognition

Fingerprint recognition alludes to the computerized system for identifying or affirming the character of a person in lightweight of the comparison of two fingerprints. Distinctive finger impression acknowledgment could be a standout among the foremost understood statistics, and it is by a good margin that the foremost utilized biometric declares verification on machine-controlled frameworks. The need behind distinctive mark acknowledgment being subsequent thought of square measure the effortlessness of procurance, designed up utilization

Fig. 2 Recognition of fingerprints

and acknowledgment once contrasted with completely different statistics, and therefore the means that there square measure varied (ten) wellsprings of this biometric on every one (Fig. 2).

There exist four main types of fingerprint reader hardware:

Optical readers:
Optical readers are the most well-known sort of unique mark readers. The kind of sensor in an optical reader is an advanced camera that gains a visual picture of the unique mark. Favorable circumstances are that optical readers begin at exceptionally modest costs. Disservices are that readings are affected by grimy or stamped fingers, and this sort of unique mark reader is simpler to trick than others.
Capacitive readers:
Additionally, it is known as CMOS readers; do not read the unique mark utilizing light. Rather a CMOS reader utilizes capacitors and consequently electrical current to shape a picture of the unique mark. CMOS readers are more extravagant than optical readers, in spite of the fact that despite everything they come moderately shoddy with costs beginning great beneath 100 euros.
Ultrasound readers:
Ultrasound perusers are the most recent sort of one of a kind imprint perusers; they use high repeat sound waves to penetrate the epidermal (outside) layer of the skin. They read the exceptional imprint on the dermal skin layer, which discards the necessity for a clean, unscarred surface. Each and every other kind of one-of-a-kind imprint perusers gets a photo of the outside surface, thusly obliging hands to be cleaned and free of scars before readout. This sort of one of a kind finger impression peruser is altogether more luxurious than the starting two; however as a result of their accuracy and the way that they are difficult to trap the ultrasound perusers are starting now to a great degree standard.
Thermal readers:
Warm perusers sense, on a contact surface, the qualification of temperature amidst interesting imprint edges and valleys. Warm novel imprint perusers have different hindrances, for instance, higher power use and an execution that depend on upon nature temperature.

1.3.3 Smart Cards

It is a charge card measured card with embedded consolidated circuits, which can handle and recollect data. To validate, the client must swipe or physically embed the card in a unique per user (Fig. 3).

Fig. 3 Smart card for user physical authentication

1.3.4 Secret Message

Secret message authentication is the most useful technique. In this method, we are using some secret message to access the data. Once the environment established, some secret message created by using this message the credentials can be authenticated.

1.3.5 One-Time Password (OTP)

Where stamping into PC systems and destinations is concerned, it for the most part incorporates entering a superfluous mystery word, which is genuine just once and changes every time you sign in. This is known as a one-time secret word and another is delivered new every time you get to the system. Commonly a one-time mystery word [7] is a movement of useful in vain numbers or characters or it might be around six or something like that short, unpredictable words. How might you know your one-time mystery word if it keeps developing? It is not something you are obliged to remember that: it is delivered actually and sent to you by some system other than online transmission. It might be sent to your wireless (cell phone) as a SMS text [8]; it could be delivered by an application running on your phone or by a conferred, handheld electronic contraption called a security token; it may even be printed out and sent to you on paper, the colossal outdated way (Fig. 4).

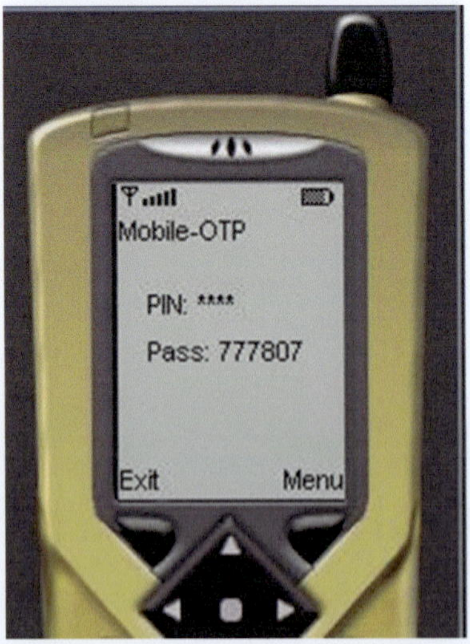

Fig. 4 Device to get the OTP information

2 Conclusion

In this paper, just we have mentioned what all are the mechanisms available in the collaborative environment accessing authentication methods. In future papers, we have to discuss the particular two-factor authentication method and how the method is implemented.

3 Future Work

Here, we mentioned the different two-factor authentication methods available for collaborative computing environment. In this particular area, extended work belongs to develop a particular two-factor authentication framework for collaborative environment.

References

1. Li Q, Cao G (2011) Multicast authentication in the smart grid with one-time signature. IEEE Trans Smart Grid 2(4)
2. www.explainthatstuff.com-how-security-tokens-work.html
3. Nguyen MD, Bui QM Your face is NOT your password
4. Marcel S, Rodriguez Y Biometric face authentication using pixel-based weak classiers
5. Woodward JD Jr, Horn C, Gatune J, Thomas A A look at facial recognition

6. FRVT 2006 and ICE 2006 Large-scale results. National Institute of Standards
7. Aloul F, Zahidi S, El-Hajj W Two factor authentication using mobile phones
8. Corella F, Lewison K Strong and convenient multi-factor authentication on mobile devices

Author Biographies

Mr. G. Dileep Kumar, is Assistant Professor of CSE department at KITS, Guntur, AP; is a scholar of Computer science at Bharathiar University, Coimbatore. His research interests are collaborative computing, network security, grid and cloud computing, and big data. The recent trends in developing real-time applications for the effective utilization of natural resources in which the society benefited mostly are enabling his research interests to focus more on the top end technologies available these days. He is life member of IACSIT and IAENG.

Dr. R. Praveen Sam received his Ph.D. in Computer Science and Engineering from JNT University, Anantapur. He is currently working as Professor in Computer Science & Engineering, G. Pulla Reddy Engineering College (Autonomous): Kurnool. His research interests are mobile and ad hoc networks, network security, computer organization, design and analysis of algorithms, big data, and cloud computing. He has around 15 years of experience in Teaching and Research. His research projects are sanctioned by UGC. He has presented papers at National and International Conferences and published articles in National & International Journals. He is life member in CSI, ISTE, IAENG, and IE.

‘Changing Trend in Network Security Measures: A Review’

Swati Maurya and Anita Singhrova

Abstract The growing connectivity across the globe has been made possible due to Internet and web applications. Social networking and e-commerce web applications are dominating the cyberspace. Cybersecurity tends to secure the computer system, information and the connecting network from the attackers whose intention is to misuse the information and damage the resources. Network security is a bit complex mechanism as compared to information security as it does not only require securing end systems but also ensure the security of entire network system. This paper discusses the network security measures and the change in trend in application of these measures.

Keywords Cybersecurity · Network security · Mission centricity
Resilient system

1 Introduction

With the latest innovations in the communication technologies, public networks are now relied for sharing personal and financial information. Earlier, security protocols were not developed for Internet to secure itself and were not even implemented in TCP/IP. This left computer systems vulnerable to attacks. Cybersecurity consists of measures for securing computer system, data and the associated network. The major intention is to secure the network for communication.

Network security implements policies that prevent unauthorized access by checking unique ID and password and monitors the requests for network resources to prevent misuse of computer network and denial of genuine user requests.

S. Maurya (✉) · A. Singhrova
Department of Computer Science and Engineering, DCRUST, Murthal, India
e-mail: swatimaurya@hotmail.com

M. U. Bokhari et al. (eds.), *Cyber Security*, Advances in Intelligent Systems and Computing 729, https://doi.org/10.1007/978-981-10-8536-9_4

1.1 Security Attributes

The attributes that assure security in a network and the respective attack methods that are used by the attackers to compromise the security of the network are listed in Table 1.

1.2 Preparedness

In the recent past, many discussions have led to recognizing the potential threats related to cyberspace and their impact on the information infrastructure and their connecting network. These threats and the nature of attackers vary according to problem domain and application area network and hence the consequences. The impact varies from target system to the network ranging from nominal to severe. Thus, preparedness against threats in cyberspace is mandatory and integral to mission assurance [2].

2 Security Management

The precautions and planning to handle the attacks should be done at all levels through long vision strategies which can be done by characterizing the threats that are expected and the risks can be detected at the preliminary stages.

2.1 Level of Threats

Cyberthreats for the network are oriented in five levels of preparedness as shown in Fig. 1. The intent of damage increases with the level. The lower levels implement the already existing security frameworks [3–6] and the higher levels follow mission assurance strategy where the assets or the resources are preserved from attacks on mission capabilities.

Table 1 Common attacks on security attributes [1]

Security attributes	Attack methods
Confidentiality	Hacking, Phishing, DoS, Eavesdropping and IP spoofing
Integrity	Viruses, Worms, Trojans, DoS and IP spoofing
Privacy	Email bombing, Spamming, Hacking, DoS and cookies
Availability	DoS, Email bombing and System boot record infectors

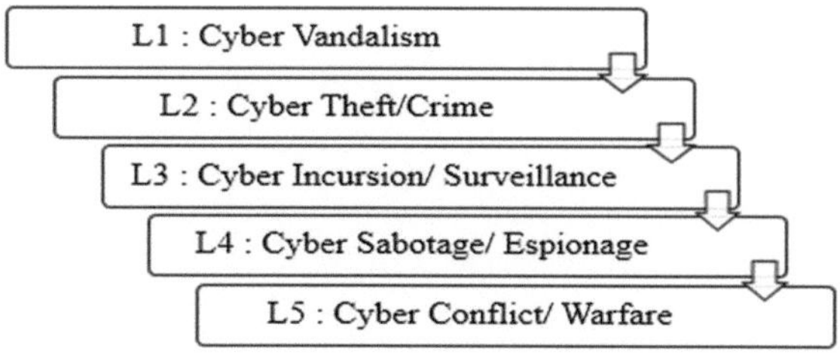

Fig. 1 Cyberthreat levels [2]

The cyberthreat levels are characterized by the following factors:

- Calibre of threat for which preparedness needs to be done.
- Technical and operational requirements for providing counter to the threats.
- Structural capabilities to handle the after effects.

2.2 *Security Measures*

The security measures as a countermeasure for the techniques used by attackers for respective cyberthreat levels are summarized in Table 2.

2.3 *Secure Information Sharing Over Network*

The cyberattacks are mainly focused for stealing or hacking the secure information. The information that is available in cyberspace is present for knowledge sharing. It is desired to be shared among authorized or allowed group of users and needs to be protected from the unwanted and harmful adversaries. Saltzer–Schroeder [7] recognized the need for providing control on the access of information by the users. Sandhu-White [8] discussed the limitations of already existing models for secure information sharing, such as discretionary access control, mandatory access control and role-based access control. They explained how these models are effective in handling the issues what their main motive is but are not capable of responding in scenarios where monitoring of life events related to cybersecurity is needed. They proposed group-centric SIS models to address the limitations of traditional models for such cases. Zhao-White [9] realized the importance of information sharing and classified threat alert levels for cybersecurity. The proposal was to form a 'Collaborative Information Sharing Framework' that would enhance the preparedness for cybersecurity. Zhao-White [10] also proposed a group-centric collaborative information sharing framework that aims to improve community cybersecurity by analysing information sharing requirements in the community through the designed formal policy model for the framework.

Table 2 Security measures for attacks according to cyberthreat levels [2]

Cyberthreat level	Techniques for attack by adversaries	Security measures
1. Cyber vandalism	–Unauthorized access –Socially engineered Trojans –Malwares	–Properly configured firewalls –Well-monitored intrusion detection system –Strong identification and authentication measures
2. Cyber theft/ crime	–Impersonation –Phishing and socially engineered attacks for gaining security credentials that facilitate data breaching	–Safe transmission of information by encrypting the data –Implementing secure protocols like SSL/TLS for transmission –Monitoring remote accesses
3. Cyber incursion/ surveillance	–Sniffing and luring internal networks of the organization –Non-targetted attacks	–Regular check and monitoring of network traffic –Quick analysis and immediate response for any abnormality noticed
4. Cyber sabotage/ espionage	–Monitoring information coming in and going out of the network –Insider-based session hijacking –Targeted attacks	–Unusual behaviour in the traffic to be monitored –Regular checks on internal information infrastructure
5. Cyber conflict/ warfare	–Destruction of information system by hampering the Network infrastructure	–Expert integration of cyber and physical penetration testing

3 Mission Centricity

A few years ago, the computer security was based on confidentiality, integrity and availability (CIA) of IT assets. The network security combines authorization with CIA triad to ensure security of the overall network. Network security elements like honeypots and darknet analysers are used to control attacks trying to gain unauthorized access and misuse and manipulate network resources. They do so by attracting harmful traffic away from the main computer resources and in the meantime analysts get to track the attacker and as a result improve network security. However, traditional systems have limited operability, and are not able to protect the network in most of the cases as nowadays attackers have sufficient knowledge to avoid getting trapped in the darknets and bypass the CIA triad for security. Considering its loopholes and the failure in providing completely secure infrastructure, the need for 'Mission Centric' paradigm increased which should be able to manage the rapid changes in the operational context and dynamic time and space bound behaviour of missions [11].

3.1 Resilient Systems

To provide security through mission centricity, a framework that supports system resilience was described by Mostashari [12]. For being a resilient system, a system is expected to have

- Preparedness from adversary attacks
- Survival during the attack event
- Ability to recover from the damage caused.

The resilient systems are mainly based on fault tolerance, intrusion tolerance and adaptiveness. ‘Fault-tolerant computing’ has provided the architectures that are having fault-tolerant features like redundancies, dynamic reconfiguration [13]. ‘Intrusion tolerant systems’ provide detailed analysis of system vulnerability and assessment and evaluation of the damage [14]. Survival of missions based on ‘reinforcement learning’ provided the concept of task distribution to maintain continuity in case of attacks or failures and to learn the patterns as the preparedness approach [15].

The Defense Advanced Research Projects Agency (DARPA), the US Department of Defense’s advanced research department, in its project called mission-oriented resilient clouds (MRC), elaborated an approach to build resiliency into existing cloud networks to preserve mission effectiveness during a cyberattack [16].

3.2 Adaptation

In case of cyberattack, to perform the role of resilient system, adaptation is needed by missions and the cyber terrain and collectively both should behave as ‘Multi-agent systems’. The scenarios where control and commanding of missions and security implementation are needed, flexibility and self-awareness about the structure and attributes of the system are the key requirements. The adaptable system comprises of the following features:

- Structural adaptation: Ability adapt to structural changes occurring internal to the system, e.g., node connectivity failure
- Functional adaptation: Ability to detect the changes in the functionality
- Resource adaptation: Flexibility to manage resource failure scenarios and work smoothly in such situation.

4 Network Security Measures

Network security measures focus on securing both private and public network. Wireless network security, IP security, firewalls and physical security are the major concerns of network security. Wireless security aims at preventing unauthorized access or damage to computers through wireless networks. The most common types of wireless security are Wi-Fi protected access (WPA) and wired equivalent privacy (WEP) which are based on the concept of 'Secure Connection' and 'Secure Session' [17]. Internet protocol security (IPsec) is a protocol for securing communications by authenticating and encrypting each IP packet of a session. IPsec includes protocols for establishing mutual authentication between agents at the beginning of the session and negotiation of cryptographic keys to be used during the session. A firewall acts like a barrier through which the traffic going in and out

Table 3 Description of advance network security measures

Author	Year	Description
Zubair Rafique et al. [19]	2014	–Network dialog contains the information needed for exchange of data between two networks and can be misused for cyberattack if manipulated by adversaries –'Network dialog minimization' through 'Network delta debugging' focuses on reducing the information shared in a dialog and providing only the needed sufficient information for transmission –'Network dialog diffing' is used to identify the similar dialogs and arrange them in proper alignment for monitoring any tampering while exchange
Lu et al. [20]	2014	–Uses network simulation by utilizing packet forwarding to monitor and analyse logs of the network which helps in predicting and forecasting any unusual behaviour in the traffic –'Statistical Bayesian techniques' and 'grey relational model' are used for monitoring the past behaviours and keeping check on current network scenario
Wang et al. [21]	2014	–Network security metrics provide an insight into how efficient the security solution is for securing the system. Traditional metrics were dependent on known vulnerabilities and hence used to fail against zero-day attacks –k-zero-day safety metric is dependent on the count of zero-day vulnerabilities that are needed for successful attack –Heuristic algorithms are used for analysing the complexity for generating the metric –Utilizes network hardening
Memari et al. [22]	2015	–Utilizes honeynets to secure the real Information systems from the intruders by pretending themselves to be the actual systems. The attackers are befooled and kept busy while the security mechanisms detect the authenticity of the client –If the client is an attacker, honeynets get sufficient time while this delay to detect the attack mechanism used by the attacker by analysing the patter and attack techniques

of the network must pass. A firewall security allows only the traffic that is authorized to pass. Packet filtering router, application-level gateway and circuit-level gateway are the three types of firewalls implemented to secure the network [18].

Table 3 lists the advanced network security measure improvements that have proven to prevent the network system from latest attacks.

5 Conclusion

The network security combines authorization with CIA triad to ensure security of the overall network. But the traditional measures have failed in providing completely secure infrastructure from the modern attackers. Hence, the need for 'Mission Centric' paradigm increased which is capable in managing the rapid changes in the operational context and dynamic time and space bound behaviour of missions. The resilient network systems that are adaptive in nature are the need of the time that should implement latest network security measures with advance implementations and modifications.

References

1. Adeyinka O (2008) Internet attack methods and internet security technology, In: Second Asia international conference on modeling & simulation, AICMS 08, pp 77–82, 13–15 May 2008
2. Bodeau DJ, Graubart R, Fabius-Greene J (2010) Improving cyber security and mission assurance via cyber preparedness (cyber prep) levels, In: IEEE second international conference on social computing (socialcom), pp 1147–1152, 20–22 Aug 2010
3. National Institute of Standards and Technology (NIST) (2009) Recommended Security Controls for Federal Information Systems and Organizations, NIST Special Publication 800-53, Rev. 3, August 2009 (updated with errata May 1, 2010)
4. NIST (2010) Guide for applying the risk management framework to Federal information systems: a security life cycle approach, NIST SP 800-37 Revision 1, February 2010
5. Information Technology (IT) Governance Institute (ITGI), COBIT (Control Objectives for IT and Related Technology) (2007) V4.1
6. International Standards Organization (ISO) and International Electrotechnical Commission (IEC), ISO/IEC 17799:2005 (2005) Information technology—security techniques—code of practice for information security management
7. Saltzer JH, Schroeder MD (1975) The protection of information in computer systems. Proc IEEE 63(9):1278–1308
8. Sandhu R, Krishnan R, White GB (2010) Towards secure information sharing models for community cyber security. In: 6th international conference on collaborative computing: networking, applications and worksharing (collaboratecom), pp 1–6, 9–12 Oct 2010
9. Zhao W, White G (2012) A collaborative information sharing framework for community cyber security. In: IEEE conference on technologies for homeland security (HST), pp 457–462, 13–15 Nov 2012
10. Zhao W, White G (2014) Designing a formal model facilitating collaborative information sharing for community cyber security. In: 47th Hawaii international conference on system sciences (HICSS), 2014, pp 1987–1996, 6–9 Jan 2014

11. Jakobson G (2013) Mission-centricity in cyber security: architecting cyber-attack resilient missions. In: 5th international conference on cyber conflict (CyCon), pp 1–18, 4–7 June 2013
12. Mostashari A (2010) Resilient critical infrastructure systems and enterprises. Imperial College Press
13. Rennels DA (1999) Fault-tolerant computing, Encyclopedia of Computer Science. In: Ralston A, Reilly E, Hemmendinger D (eds)
14. Verissimo P, Neves N, Correia M (2003) Intrusion-tolerant architectures: concepts and design. In: Lemos R, Gacek C, Romanovsky A (eds) Architecting dependable systems, LNCS 2677, Springer, Berlin
15. Carvalho M (2009) A distributed reinforcement learning approach to mission survivability in tactical MANETs, In: ACM conference CSIIRW 2009, Oak Ridge TN, 2009
16. Mission-Oriented Resilient Clouds (2011) DARPA, Information Innovation Office. http://www.darpa.mil/Our-Work/I2O/Programs/Mission-oriented-Resilient-Clouds-(MRC).aspx
17. http://dis-dpcs.wikispaces.com/Different_types_of_Network_Security
18. Kumar NS (2015) Review on network security and cryptography. Int Trans Electr Comput Eng Syst 3(1):1–11
19. Zubair Rafique M, Caballero J, Huygens C, Joosen W (2014) Network dialog minimization and network dialog diffing: two novel primitives for network security applications. In: Proceedings of the 30th annual computer security applications conference (ACSAC'14). ACM, New York, NY, USA, pp 166–175
20. Lu SS, Wang X-F, Mao L (2014) Network security situation awareness based on network simulation. In: IEEE workshop on electronics, computer and applications, 2014, pp 512–517, 8–9 May 2014
21. Wang L, Jajodia S, Singhal A, Cheng P, Noel S (2014) k-zero day safety: a network security metric for measuring the risk of unknown vulnerabilities. IEEE Trans Dependable Secur Comput 11(1):30–44
22. Memari N, Hashim SJ, Samsudin K (2015) Container based virtual honeynet for increased network security. In: 5th National symposium on information technology: towards new smart world (NSITNSW), 2015, pp 1–6, 17–19 Feb 2015

Author Biographies

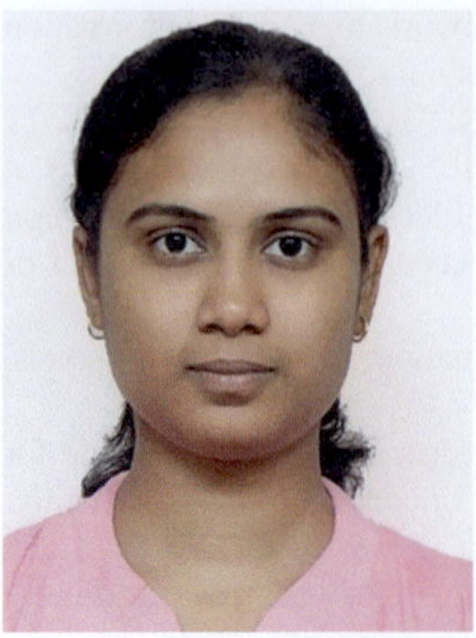

Swati Maurya obtained her M.Tech (Computer Science and Engineering) from DCR University of Science and Technology, Murthal, India. She has completed B.Tech (Computer Science and Engineering) from U.I.E.T., Kurukshetra University, India. She is presently pursuing her Ph.D. Her research area is Cyber Security

Anita Singhrova holds a Ph.D. degree from GGS Indraprastha University, Delhi, India. She has completed M.E (Computer Science and Engineering) from Punjab Engineering College, Chandigarh, India and B.Tech (Computer Science) from T.I. T&S, Bhiwani, India 2006 and 1993 respectively. She has also been certified as Java Programmer by Sun Microsystems. She possesses seventeen years of teaching experience and is presently working as Professor and Dean in the department of Computer Science and Engineering at DCR University of Science and Technology, Murthal, India. She has many research papers to her credit in reputed journals.

An Improved RED Algorithm with Input Sensitivity

Kiran Chhabra, Manali Kshirsagar and Arun Zadgaonkar

Abstract Random Early Detection (RED) is a recommended scheme of Active Queue Management (AQM) to avoid network congestion by Internet Engineering Task Force (IETF). RED being sensitive to its control parameters setting and traffic load behaves differently during different phases of scenarios and its performance degrades. To solve the above problems, we have proposed an improved algorithm LTRED, L stands for queue length and T stands for threshold, which incorporates the impact of load variation in early congestion notification along with tuning of threshold parameter of RED. Our approach is validated by doing extensive simulations on ns-2 (network simulator) and comparisons are done with RED, ARED, and AVQ well-known AQMs. Our approach has shown its superiority in terms of packet loss, early congestion indication, better link utilization, and improved goodput. In this work, mismatch between macroscopic and microscopic behavior of queue length of RED is also addressed and reduction in mismatch is achieved. In addition, LTRED makes very few changes to the original RED without making the system complex.

Keywords Random early detection (RED) · Active Queue Management (AQM) IETF (Internet Engineering Task Force) · ns-2 network simulator

K. Chhabra (✉)
Computer Science and Engineering, Dr. C.V. Raman University, Bilaspur, CG, India
e-mail: grk108@rediffmail.com

M. Kshirsagar
Yashwantrao Chawan College of Engineering, Nagpur, MS, India
e-mail: manali_kshirsagar@yahoo.com

A. Zadgaonkar
Dr. C.V. Raman University, Kargi Raod, Bilaspur, CG, India
e-mail: arunzad28@hotmail.com

M. U. Bokhari et al. (eds.), *Cyber Security*, Advances in Intelligent Systems and Computing 729, https://doi.org/10.1007/978-981-10-8536-9_5

1 Introduction

Due to the gigantic growth of the Internet, it faces the challenge of congestion [1, 2]. AQM is the solution to this congestion control. Its two main objectives are high link utilization with low packet loss and low packet queuing delay. Recommended by IETF [3] RED was first AQM, proposed by Sally Floyd and Jacobson in 1993 [4].

In RED algorithm, Exponential Weighted Moving Average (EWMA) filter as given by Eq. (1) is used for averaging of current queue size. For detection of actual congestion not transient one, averaging procedure is used. Here, two thresholds $\mathrm{TH}_{\mathrm{min}}$ minimum threshold and $\mathrm{TH}_{\mathrm{max}}$ maximum threshold are used and the average queue size is compared with these thresholds. If the average queue size is less than $\mathrm{TH}_{\mathrm{min}}$ no packet is dropped and if it is greater than $\mathrm{TH}_{\mathrm{max}}$ every incoming packet is dropped. When it lies between two thresholds, packets are randomly dropped using drop probability calculated by Eqs. (2) and (3).

$$\mathrm{avg}_{i+1} \leftarrow (1-w_{\mathrm{q}})\mathrm{avg}_i + w_{\mathrm{q}} q_i \quad (1)$$

$$P_{\mathrm{b}} \leftarrow P_{\mathrm{max}}(\mathrm{avg} - \mathrm{TH}_{\mathrm{min}})/(\mathrm{TH}_{\mathrm{max}} - \mathrm{TH}_{\mathrm{min}}) \quad (2)$$

$$P_{\mathrm{a}} \leftarrow P_{\mathrm{b}}/(1 - \mathrm{count} \times \mathrm{Pb}), \quad (3)$$

where

avg_{i+1}	average queue size at $(i + 1)$th time
avg_i	average queue size at ith time
w_{q}	moving weighted average constant
q_{i}	current queue size
$\mathrm{TH}_{\mathrm{min}}$	minimum threshold for queue
$\mathrm{TH}_{\mathrm{max}}$	maximum threshold for queue
P_{max}	maximum value for $\mathrm{P_b}$
P_{a}	current packet marking probability
P_{b}	temporary probability used in calculation
count	packets since last discarded packet

Being simple in its approach, RED achieves goal of congestion avoidance, removes global synchronization, and overcomes drawback of Drop tail [3]. Despite having been widely used in combination with TCP for several years, RED has not found acceptance in the Internet research community [1]. It has some disadvantages like hard parameter setting, congestion depends on parameters, insensitivity toward input traffic and there is no matching between average queue length and current queue length [1]. After RED's proposal, lot of research is carried out to find its suitability. Many variants of RED [2, 5–9] were proposed to overcome shortcomings of it with different congestion notification approaches used like the average queue size, packet loss and link utilization and control theory, etc.

The remainder of this paper is organized as follows. Section 2 gives the proposed work along with approach used, Sect. 3 gives simulation results and Sect. 4 deals with conclusions and the final section gives all the references used.

2 Proposed Work

Due to the exponential growth of the Internet, AQM fails to respond fast to traffic changes or to adapt to time-varying TCP dynamics. This motivated us for our proposed work. We have tuned the threshold parameter of RED that is threshold upper limit and lower limit of the average size in terms of router buffer size. Setting TH_{min} to an appropriate value could help router to make good link utilization. Improper setting of TH_{max} also causes more packets losses once the average queue size exceeds it. We have tuned TH_{min} to 40% of maximum queue size and TH_{max} to 70% of it. This tuning has given us good results as well as it helps to achieve the link utilization by properly keeping router buffer efficiently utilized. Since RED's performance degrades heavily shown by wild oscillations when the traffic load becomes bursty indicating it is insensitive to input. We have incorporated this problem in our approach. A little amount work is already done in [10]. LTRED algorithm is shown in Fig. 1.

2.1 Working of Algorithm

For each packet arrival, average value for the queue size is calculated using EWMA as in original RED. To have impact of input traffic the current queue size is compared with a threshold which is 75% value of maximum buffer value (q_{t1}) and depending upon that average value is updated by 5% of the current queue size. This step has impact of input sensitivity. Then it proceeds as RED algorithm. In order to find out if the congestion is sustained once again two checks are made. First, the current queue size is compared with another threshold (85% value of maximum buffer value—q_{t2}) for bursty input and the average queue value is compared with a reference value which is mid value of upper and lower threshold value. If this comparison is found to be true, then packets are dropped earlier as compared to RED algorithm and this is early congestion indication to sources so that they should slow down their rate of sending packets. In rest part, it will continue to work as in original RED.

```
for each packet arrival
        calculate  avg
        if  (q_i > q_t1)
                {  avg ← avg + 0.05* q_i }
          if (avg < TH_min )
                {  forward the packet }
        if (q_i > q_t2)
         {
            if ( avg ≥ mid_th )
              {  drop the packet }
             else
                 { if ( avg > TH_min)
                      { drop the packet according to RED algorithm }
                   }
          }
     if  (avg ≥ TH_max )
           { drop the packet }

Where
     avg        :  average queue size
     q_i        :  current queue size
     B          :  maximum buffer size
     q_t1       :  First threshold for  q_i
     q_t2       :  Second threshold for  q_i
     TH_min     :  Minimum Threshold value for avg
     TH_max     :  Maximum Threshold value for avg
     mid_th     :  Reference Threshold value for avg
```

Fig. 1 LTRED algorithm

3 Simulation Results and Discussion

We have implemented the proposed scheme using network simulator ns-2 [11]. To evaluate the improvements network topology is shown in Fig. 2. Bandwidth and delay associated with links are also given in the diagram and Gs to Gr is bottleneck link. We have compared proposed scheme LTRED with RED [4], ARED [7] and AVQ [2], standard AQMs and plotted graphs for various cases.

Total simulation time period is 30 s for the topology shown Two FTP sessions randomly start in between 0 and 0.01 s and lasts till the end. In the middle of simulation, another "m" FTP session would randomly start in between 10.0 and 10.1 s which is to simulate changes of network conditions. TCP Reno is used for all AQMs (RED, ARED, AVQ and LTRED). Parameters used are, for RED and ARED are $TH_{max} = 15$, $TH_{min} = 5$, queue size $q = 30$, Maxp = 0.1, $w_q = 0.002$, and for ARED and AVQ other parameters are set as per default value as in ns-2. In case of LTRED $TH_{min} = 12$ and $TH_{max} = 21$, $q_{t1} = 22.5$, $q_{t2} = 25.5$, and $mid_{th} = 16.5$ rest settings are similar to RED. We have observed results for sources varying "m" from 30 to 60 (Tables given) and drawn different graphs for 60 sources

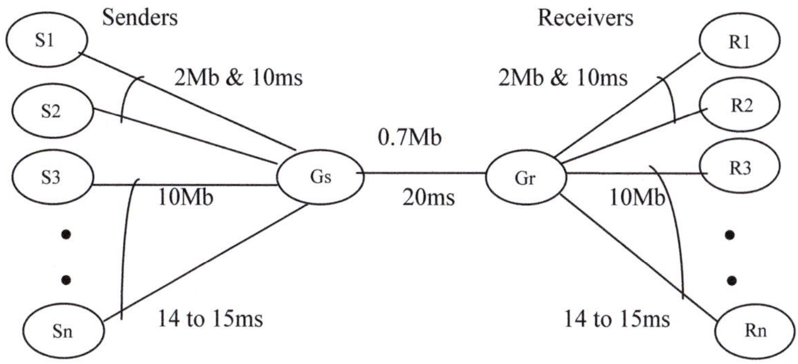

Fig. 2 Simulation network topology

for all the approaches used. We have observed performance in case of packet loss, packet arrival ratio, the average queue size, and the current queue size.

Figure 3 shows the graph for comparison of packet loss for all the four cases showing minor differences during initial period of less traffic. After 10 s when traffic increases that is during congestion period LTRED shows less number of packet losses overall, and shows improvement by 2.3–4.3%. Figure 4 shows total number of packets received for all cases, it shows that packets delivered number is largest in case of LTRED, showing improvement in throughput by 2.19–3.48%. In Fig. 5, the graph shows effective congestion notification to sources in terms of packet arrival rate. Sources are earlier informed about congestion and they reduce their sending rate here also LTRED outperforms other AQMs.

Figure 6 depicts current queue changes, showing more variation in transient congestion and later on in highly congestion area, AVQ uses less buffer size Wild oscillations in RED and ARED show unstable behavior and in case of LTRED nearly stable behavior. Figure 7 illustrates bandwidth utilization which shows that

Fig. 3 Packet loss ratio

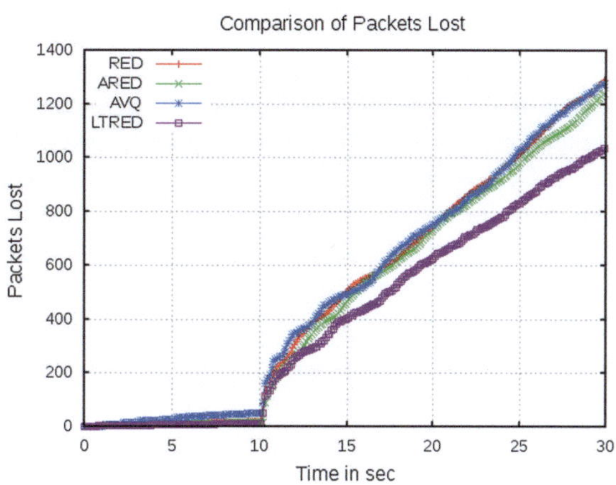

Fig. 4 Packet delivery ratio

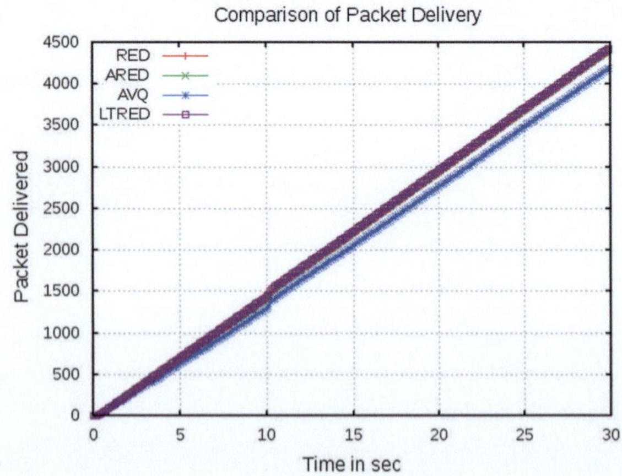

Fig. 5 Packet arrival ratio

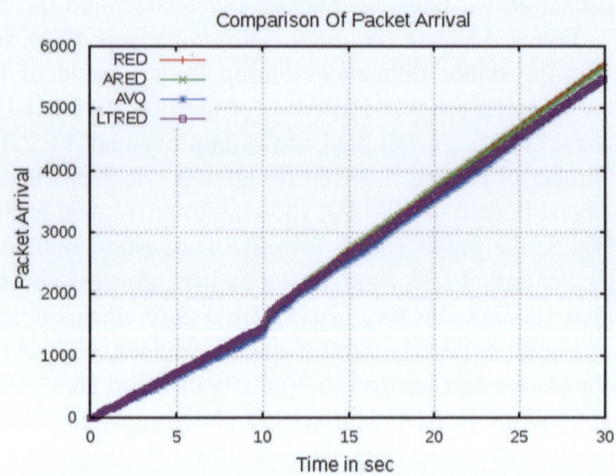

LTRED outperforms other AQMs. Figure 8 shows average queue variation for RED, ARED, and LTRED, EWMA approach is used in these cases to calculate the average queue size. In this case also LTRED outperforms RED and ARED by being within its reference limit and depicts stable behavior. Figures 9, 10, and 11 show comparison of the average and the current queue size for RED, ARED, and LTRED cases. Out of these in LTRED case, mismatch behavior of the average and the current queue size is reduced a lot. Tables 1, 2, 3, and 4 give simulation results for number of sources varying from 30 to 60, showing superiority of LTRED.

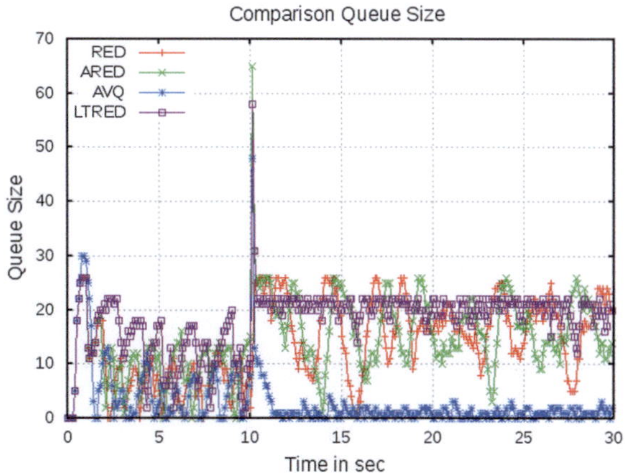

Fig. 6 Queue size variation

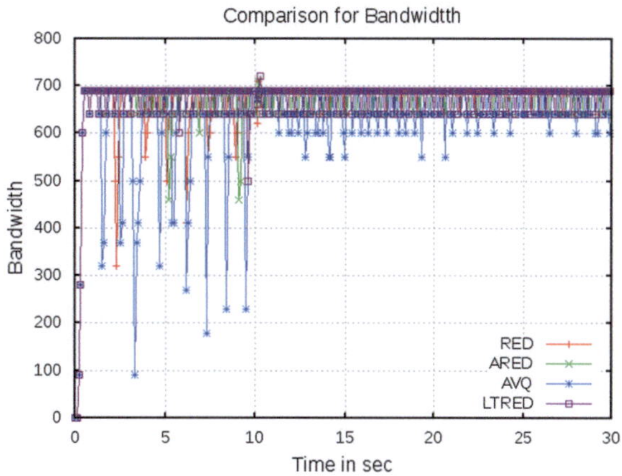

Fig. 7 Bandwidth utilization

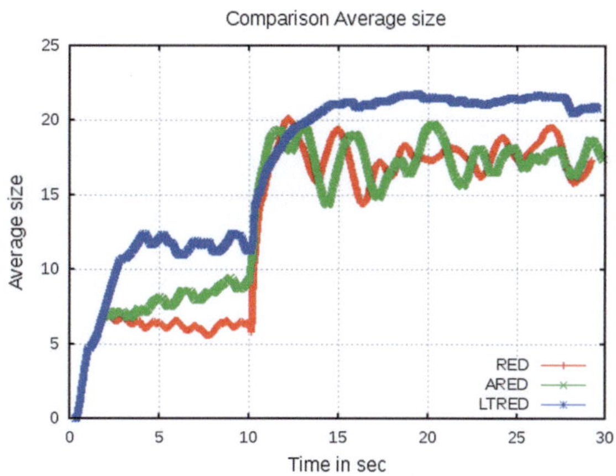

Fig. 8 Average queue size variation

Fig. 9 RED queue sizes

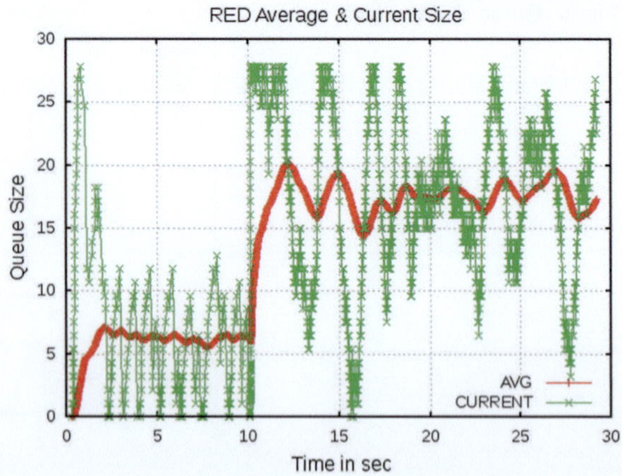

Fig. 10 ARED queue sizes

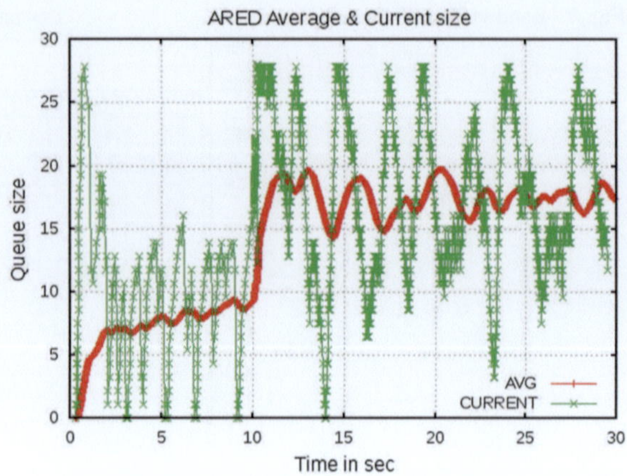

Fig. 11 LTRED queue sizes

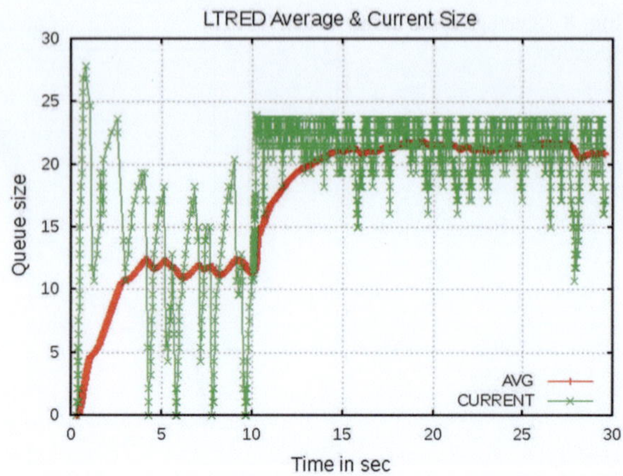

Table 1 Various simulation results for 30 sources

AQM scheme	Packets lost (%)	Packets delivered (%)	Goodput (%)	Retransmitted packets (%)	Still to be retransmitted (%)
RED	15.56	84.19	76.79	47.52	52.47
ARED	15.56	84.14	73.75	66.74	33.25
AVQ	17.73	82.23	71.31	61.58	38.42
LTRED	13.43	86.15	76.09	72.11	27.88

Table 2 Various simulation results for 40 sources

AQM scheme	Packets lost (%)	Packets delivered (%)	Goodput (%)	Retransmitted packets (%)	Still to be retransmitted (%)
RED	18.34	81.36	73.52	42.74	57.25
ARED	17.42	82.13	73.97	46.84	53.15
AVQ	20.40	79.49	70.91	42.05	57.94
LTRED	15.60	83.98	75.26	55.92	44.08

Table 3 Various simulation results for 50 sources

AQM scheme	Packets lost (%)	Packets delivered (%)	Goodput (%)	Retransmitted packets (%)	Still to be retransmitted (%)
RED	19.74	80.15	73.60	33.20	66.79
ARED	19.76	80.00	71.85	41.24	58.75
AVQ	22.01	77.93	67.75	46.23	53.77
LTRED	17.40	82.24	71.78	60.10	39.89

Table 4 Various simulation results for 60 sources

AQM scheme	Packets lost (%)	Packets delivered (%)	Goodput (%)	Retransmitted packets (%)	Still to be retransmitted (%)
RED	22.51	77.23	68.62	38.25	61.75
ARED	21.37	78.41	69.70	40.69	59.30
AVQ	23.34	76.62	67.48	39.15	60.84
LTRED	19.03	80.60	70.34	53.92	46.08

4 Conclusion

In this work, we have proposed an AQM, LTRED which is sensitive to input traffic and also tuned threshold parameter in terms of buffer size, comparing it with RED, ARED and AVQ have demonstrated better performance in terms of less number of packet loss, effective congestion indication, high throughput, reduction in mismatch behavior of the average size and the current size and high goodput values due to which retransmission of packets also reduces a lot, and effective buffer utilization at router. An adaption mechanism based on input traffic is designed to drop the packet. The key concept is that as traffic load changes and queue length deviates from a threshold, dropping of packet occur.

References

1. Ryu S, Rump C, Qiao TC (2003) Advances in internet congestion control. IEEE Commun Surv Tutorials 5(1):28–39. https://doi.org/10.1109/COMST.2003.5342228
2. Kunniyur S, Srikant R (2004) An adaptive virtual queue [AVQ] algorithm for active queue management. IEEE/ACM Trans Networking 12(2):286–299
3. Braden B, Clark D et al. (1998) Recommendations on queue management and congestion avoidance in the Internet. IETF Request for Comments RFC 2309
4. Floyd S, Jacobson V (1993) Random early detection gateway for Congestion avoidance. IEEE/ACM Trans Netw 1(4):397–413
5. Sun J, Ko K, Chen G, Zukermam M (2003) PD-RED: to improve the performance of RED. IEEE Commun Lett 7(8):406–408
6. Athuraliya S, Li V et al. (2001) REM: active queue management. IEEE Netw 15(3):48–53. https://doi.org/10.1109/65.923940
7. Floyd S, Gummadi R, Shenkar S (2001) Adaptive RED: an algorithm for increasing the robustness of RED's active queue management. Berkely CA [online]. http://www.icir.org/floyd/red.html
8. Li M, Zhao W (2010) Representation of a stochastic traffic bound. IEEE Trans Parallel Distrib Syst 21(9):1368–1372
9. Wang H, Ye Z, Wang B (2011) Using auto-tuning proportional integral probability to improve random early detection. IEEE 13th international conference on communication technology (ICCT)
10. Chhabra K, Kshirsagar M, Zadgaonkar A (2015) Effect of load and threshold variation on performance of RED: random early detection. Int J Sci Res 4(6):2319–7064. ISSN (online)
11. NS [network simulator] (1999) [online]. Available http://www.isi.edu/nsnam/ns

Author Biographies

Kiran Chhabra received her B.E. in Computer Science from Nagpur University in 1995 and M.E. in Computer Technology and Applications from Chhattisgarh Swami Vivekanand Technical University, Bhilai in 2009. She is pursuing her Ph.D. in Computer Science and Engineering in congestion avoidance area. Currently, she is working as Associate Professor in Computer Science Department at MM College of Technology, Raipur.

Dr. Manali Kshirsagar received her B.E. in Computer Technology from Nagpur University in 1992, M.E. in Computer Science and Engineering from Amravati University in 2001. She was awarded Ph.D. in 2009 by Allahabad University for her work on the Data Mining Strategy to explore Cotton Genome. Currently, she is working as Professor and Head of the Computer Technology Department at Yashwantrao Chavan College of Engineering, Nagpur. She has many papers to her credit in various international journals, the international conference, and national conference. Her areas of interest include Data Mining, Biometrics, and Computer Networks. She is also a member of professional bodies like MIE, ISTE, and ACM.

Dr. A. S. Zadgaonkar has obtained B.E. in Electrical Engineering from Pt. Ravishankar Shukla University, studying at Govt. Engineering College, Raipur in 1965. He obtained M.E. in 1978 from Nagpur University. His research paper for M.E. was awarded "Best paper" by the Institution of Engineers [India] in the year 1976 and 1977 respectively. The testing technique for the quality of wood developed by him was included in ISI in 1979. He was awarded Ph.D. in 1985 by Indira Gandhi Kala & Sangeet University, Khairagah for his work on "Acoustical and Mechanical Properties of Wood for Contemporary Indian Musical Instrument Making." He was awarded Ph.D. in 1986 by Pt. Ravishankar Shukla University on "Investigation of Dynamic Properties of Non-Conducting Materials Using Electrical Analogy." He has 47 years of teaching experience. He has published more than 500 technical papers in various journals, and National and International conferences. He has written four books on Engineering and five on "Science and Technology in Indian Mythology." He is currently adding glory to the post of Vice Chancellor of Dr. C. V. Raman University, Bilaspur[Chhattisgarh]. He is life member of Acoustical Society of India, Biomedical Society of India, Linguistic Society of India, Indian Society for Technical Education and many social bodies

Security Attacks in Wireless Sensor Networks: A Survey

Prachi Dewal, Gagandeep Singh Narula, Vishal Jain and Anupam Baliyan

Abstract Security is one of the major concerns in sensor networks. Wireless sensor network comprises of huge amount of nodes called as tiny sensor nodes. The nodes are required to exchange information with different nodes via wireless links in short intervals. The information may be potentially private regarding people and business processes. These networks suffer from adversary due to distributed behavior and deployment in distant areas. The networks are governed by some constraints at sensor node level like less battery power, less memory capacity, and low transmission range while at network level, they are governed by ad hoc networking and irregular connectivity. The paper analyzes the challenges, main security issues, security breaches in wireless sensor networks and lists their defensive measures.

Keywords Wireless sensor networks (WSN) · Protocols · Security breaches
Security mechanism

1 Introduction

Wireless sensor networks (WSN) are self-configured network with tiny sensor nodes. Each wireless node possesses low energy, memory space, and computational power. Components of sensor node include front end of radio, microcontroller,

---

P. Dewal (✉) · G. S. Narula
C-DAC, Noida, India
e-mail: prachidewal123@gmail.com

G. S. Narula
e-mail: gagan.narula87@gmail.com

V. Jain · A. Baliyan
Bharati Vidyapeeth's Institute of Computer Applications (BVICAM),
New Delhi, India
e-mail: vishaljain83@ymail.com

A. Baliyan
e-mail: anupam_hod1976@yahoo.co.in

M. U. Bokhari et al. (eds.), *Cyber Security*, Advances in Intelligent Systems and Computing 729, https://doi.org/10.1007/978-981-10-8536-9_6

main power supply, and sensors. The task of sensors is to monitor physical and environmental conditions such as humidity, pressure, sound, temperature, and many more. After monitoring, they send data to their main location. The data is requested on basis of these parameters in sensor networks (Fig. 1).

Wireless sensor network has resource constraints that act as hindrance in using existing security approaches. In fact, threats in sensor networks in context of routing are susceptible due to simple routing protocols. There are many obstacles in security for example, limited resources, unreliable communication, and unattended operation.

This paper is organized as follows: In Sect. 2, literature survey is presented. Section 3 discusses various protocols for wireless sensor networks. Section 4 gives the security framework discussing standard goals, constraints, obstacles, security breaches, and security mechanism. Finally, concluding the paper in Sect. 5 with conclusion and security threats in different protocol layer along with their defensive measure.

2 Literature Review

The nature of wireless sensor networks includes multiple nodes that make system vulnerable to adverse effects and loss of information. It has led to look into security and privacy aspects of networking by introducing new insistent technologies like wireless sensor networks [1]. Author proposed a security framework for wireless sensor networks, i.e., adaptive security architecture. It includes low-, medium-, and high-level security modes. SENP protocol is used which aims at securing patterns providing authenticity, confidentiality, and integrity. Agent-based secure routing scheme involves use of trusted neighbors that is proposed in [2] which employs use of probability and MAC model for identifying trustworthy neighbors, through which secure routes are set up. The work given in [3] presents a group-based security scheme for wireless sensor networks which includes sequential procedure: Cryptographic key pre-distribution, group-based deployment, secure data aggregation and rekeying. The author in [4] employs use of virtual grid connection to secure data from end to end at multiple base stations. In revocation scheme, random

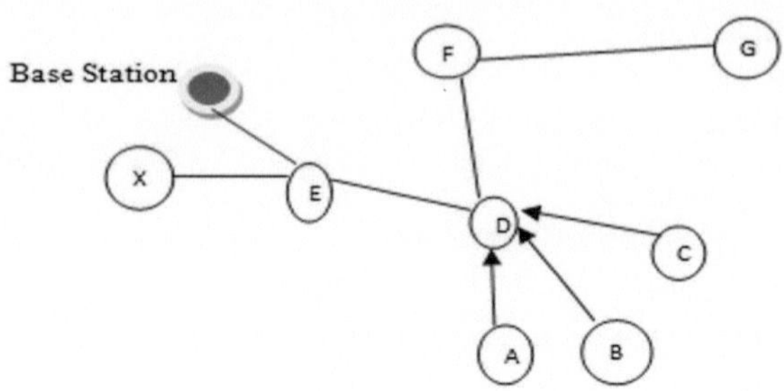

Fig. 1 Sensor network (all other nodes are sensor nodes except base station)

polynomial is used. The author in [5] proposed security protocol for verifying model, i.e., TinySec + LEAP. TinySec holds binary operations, viz., authentication and semantic secured encryption. In [6], author proposed improved fiestal based ciphers for WSN. All of WSN's block ciphers are designed using a 16 round fiestal data block. Author proposes to use controlled permutation boxes for implementation of a fiestal scheme. The author in [7] proposed two secure and efficient data transmission(SET) protocols for cluster-based wireless sensor networks, called SET-IBS and SET-IBOOS, y using the identity-based digital signature(IBS) scheme and the identity-based online/offline digital signature scheme, respectively. In [8], the author presented an architecture utilizing concept of autonomic computing and a simple object access protocol (SOAP) based interface to metadata access points (IF-MAP) external communication layer to create a network security sensor. A flexible two-level communication layer based on autonomic computing and service oriented architecture is presented. In [9], the author proposed an adaptive specification based intrusion detection system (IDS) for detecting malicious unmanned air vehicles (UAVs). An IDS audits UAVs in a distributed system to determine if the UAVs are functioning normally or are operating under malicious attacks. In [10], the author proposed a realistic and reliable IDS architecture for the advanced metering infrastructure (AMI). An AMI system is responsible for collecting, measuring, and analyzing energy usage data and transmitting this information from a smart meter to a data concentrator and then to a headend system in the utility side.

3 WSN Protocols

Protocols are the set of rules and communication standards that must be followed by source and destination in order to communicate with each other. There are several types of communication protocols which can be grouped into the lower level, high-level, and application-based protocols. Example includes TCP/IP that is set of protocols consisting of more than 65,000 protocols (Tables 1 and 2).

Table 1 Protocols associated with different network layers [11]

Layer	Protocol
Physical layer	Sonet, ISDN, SDH
Data link layer	Frame relay, FDDI, Ethernet
Network layer	RIP, OSPF, EGP, IPX, IPV6, ARP
Transport layer	TCP, UDP, SPX
Session layer	NFS, NCP, SMB
Presentation layer	MIME, HTTP, FTP, NNTP
Application layer	DNS, HTTP, POP3, BOOTP, SSH, TELNET

Table 2 Classification of protocols [11]

TCP/IP	IP, TCP, UDP, SMTP, POP3, RIP, FIP, DHCP
Cellular	GPRS, GSM, WAP AND CDMA
VOIP	SPX, RIP, MEGACO, MGCP AND H.323
General	Frame relay, ATM, X.25, PPP

4 Security in WSN

Dimensions of security includes: Goals, obstacles, constraints, security breaches, and security mechanism. All these dimensions are described below.

4.1 Standard Goals

(a) Confidentiality: Confidentiality implies that message or data is not understood by unauthorized personnel, i.e., for security, the information needs to be hidden from unauthorized access. In wireless environment, information is easily available that makes difficult to enforce confidentiality.
(b) Integrity: Unwanted changes can also be created by an interruption in the system. It is not necessarily the result of a malicious act.
(c) Availability: It ensures that the information and the network services need to be available to authorized entities.

4.2 Constraints

In comparison to traditional computer networks, wireless sensor network has many constraints. To develop security mechanisms, it is necessary to understand the resource constraint as given below:

Resource constraint:

(1) Limited Storage: This constraint leads to less storage of data as well as cryptographic keys. It is a challenge to design security protocol that uses at most number of encryption keys for secured network.
(2) Limited Computational power: Computations are based on available amount of power. Due to limited amount of power, computations are constrained. This constraint reduces the computation power of RSA public cryptographic algorithm and makes it expensive to use [11].
(3) Limited Power: Due to lack of wires and small size of sensor nodes, power restriction is there in WSNs. Sensor nodes are battery driven. Power limitation affects security, since encryption algorithm causes communication overhead.

4.3 Obstacles

Obstacles in WSNS include limited resources, untrusted communication, and unattended operation.

(1) Limited Resources: Resource limitation is a big concern is wireless sensor networks. As discussed above there are limited storage, computational power, and power in WSNs.
(2) Untrusted Communication: An untrusted wireless communication channel leads to generation of packet loss and insecurity.
(3) Idle nature of nodes: It may be possible that sensor nodes are left idle for long time depending on the function of a given network. Due to this, these nodes are exposed to attacks.

4.4 Security Breaches

Security in sensor networks posses numerous challenges due to resource and computation constraints. Type of attacks is discussed below:

Attacks based on the protocol layer:

(1) Physical layer: This layer includes the following attacks:

- Jamming: It includes transmission of signal by attacker at base stations with same frequency as of transmitter. It disrupts the radio communication and causes radio interference in the network.

  Defensive measures: A prominent measure to mitigate jamming is use of spread spectrum communication, i.e., frequency hopping spread spectrum (FHSS). It forwards given data by performing swapping of carrier data among different frequency channels [12].

- Tampering: Attacker tries to access hardware apparatus like chips. It involves handling of motes and derives secret information from shared nodes (Fig. 2).

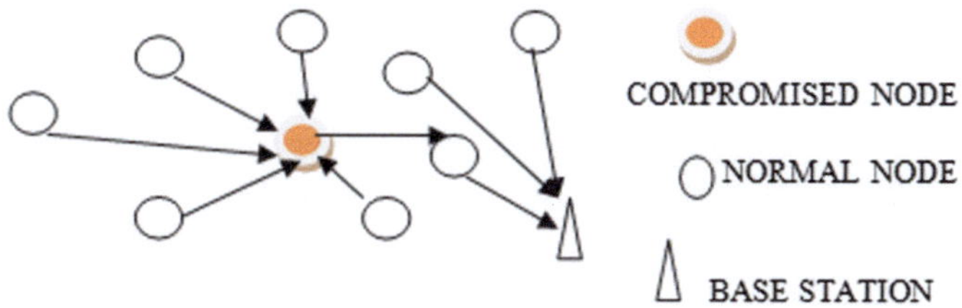

Fig. 2 Tampering attack

Defensive measures: It includes accessing of secret data that lies between external memory chip and microcontroller. This process is called as eavesdropping.

(2) Data link layer: This layer includes the following attacks:

- Collision: When an attacker listens a node transmitting a message, it forwards its own signals to make interferences. It leads to collision when multiple nodes transmit data with same frequency and data rate. It can alter the data and hence data packet can be treated as invalid.

  Defensive measures: Measures applied to jamming attacks can be applied to this attack.

- Exhaustion: Attacker continuously sends data or request over the channel which leads to starvation. The source of origination of attack can be pc or laptop.

  Defensive measures: According to [12], it is possible to reduce the MAC sending rate in order to ignore excessive request from sensor network. It prevents loss of energy as well as allows sensor node to transmit data in shorter time. In this way, nodes get attached to MAC channel for long time.

(3) Network layer: This layer consists of the following attacks:

- Selective forwarding: It includes dropping of packets by malicious node and forward most of the messages.

  Defensive measures: To counterattack multipath routing can be used. This reduces the probability of an attack by adversary. To supervise the system watchdog can be used.

- Acknowledge spoofing: Attacker may spoofs link layer acknowledgements. False error messages are generated by the attacker. Routing loops are created. As a result, end to end latency is increased and network is portioned (Fig. 3).

  Defensive measures: To counterattack all the packets must be encrypted.

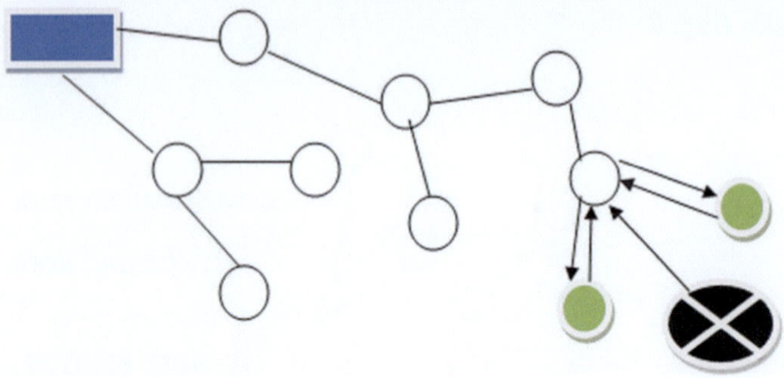

Fig. 3 Acknowledgement spoofing

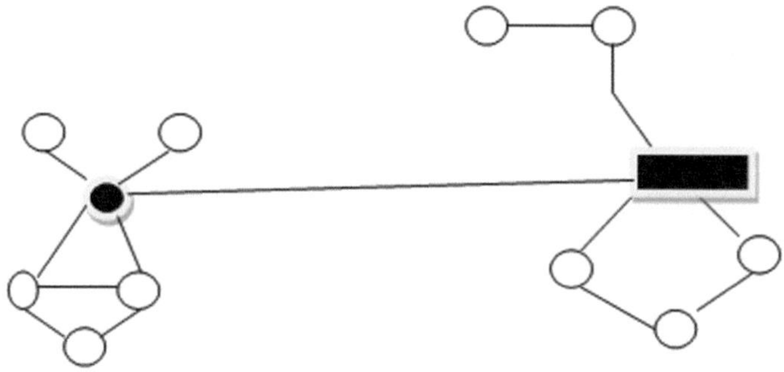

Fig. 4 Black hole attack

- Blackhole attack: Attacker intends to occupy available traffic in a network to a particular node called a black hole which is created in centre. A metaphorical sinkhole is created. All the traffic is directed to fake sinkhole (Fig. 4).

  Defensive measures: A scheme must be implemented so that all the nodes in network must comply with corrupt information produced by invalid nodes. Cryptographic methods can be used.

- Wormhole attack: According to [13], the packets are being received by attacker at specific position, transfers them to different positions and then sending back them into network from that point. The main aim of attacker is to challenge cryptography protection (Fig. 5).

  Defensive measure: To counterattack a four-way handshaking message exchange mechanism is used. Private channel can also be used for protection.

- Sybil: According to [14], self-duplicity property is attached with single node that keeps presence of node in multiple locations. Third parties target these multiple locations and cause problems in distributed storage access, multi-path routing and distortion in topology (Fig. 6).

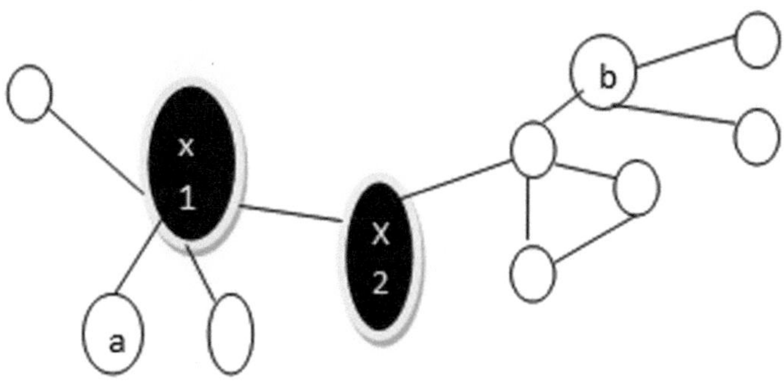

Fig. 5 Wormhole attack

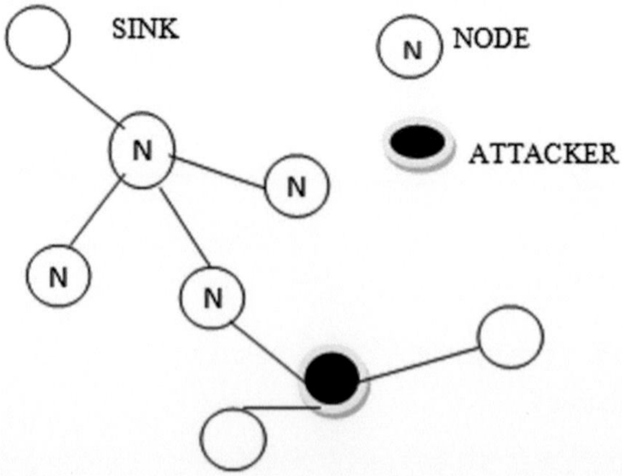

Fig. 6 Sybil attack

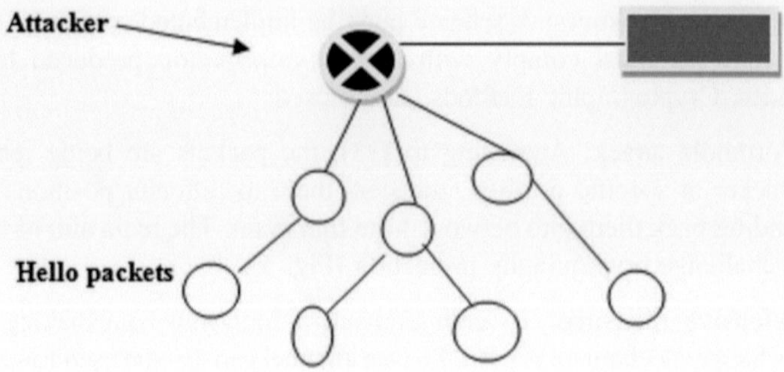

Fig. 7 Hello flood attack

Defensive measures: To counterattack validation technique must be used.

- Hello [15] flood: Attacker sends hello packets from one node to another. Attacker advertises cheap routes which lead to forwarding of messages to attacker (Fig. 7).

  Defensive measure: HELLO FLOOD can be counterattacked by using profile authentication protocol.

4.5 Security Mechanisms in WSN

See Fig. 8.

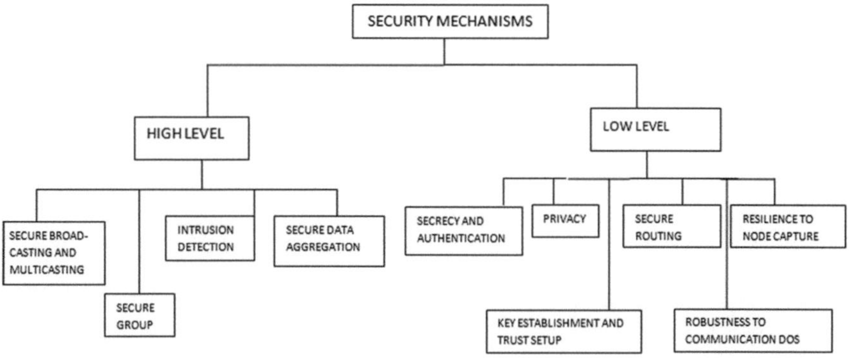

Fig. 8 Taxonomy of security mechanisms in WSN [16–22]

5 Conclusion

There is a need for effective security mechanisms in wireless sensor networks. The paper describes constraints, goals, obstacles, and security breaches based on different protocol layers, defensive measures, and security mechanism for wireless sensor networks. The attacks in protocol layer and their measures are shown in Table 3.

Table 3 Security threats in different protocol layers along with their defensive measures

Protocol layer	Security breaches	Defensive measures
Physical layer	Jamming Tampering	Spread spectrum (FHSS) Eavesdrop on the wire which is between memory chip and microcontroller
Data link layer	Collision Exhaustion	Spread spectrum Limit the mac admission control rate
Network layer	Selective forwarding Acknowledgement spoofing Black hole Wormhole Hello flood Sybil	Multipath routing Encryption Cryptographic methods Four-way handshaking scheme Identity verification protocol Validation technique
Transport layer	Flooding Desynchronization	Bidirectional verification Authentication
Application layer	Data aggregation Distortion Clock skewing	Encryption Confidentiality protection Synchronization protocols

References

1. Prasad NR, Alam M (2006) Security framework for wireless sensor networks, Springer
2. Devanagavi GD, Nalini N, Biradar RC (2014) Trusted neighbour based secured routing scheme in wireless sensor networks using agents. Springer, New York
3. Hamid MA, Sarkar AMJ (2011) A group based security scheme in wireless sensor networks. Springer
4. Ferng H-W, Nurhakim J, Horng S-J (2013) Key management protocol with end to end data security and key revocation for a multi-BS wireless sensor network. Springer, New York
5. Tobarra L, Cazorla D, Cuartero F, Diaz G, Cambronero E, Model checking Wireless sensor network security protocols: TinySec + LEAP*, Spain
6. Pazynyuk T, Li J-Z, Oreku GS (2008) Improvrd Feistal based ciphers for wireless sensor network security. J Zhejiang Univ 9(8):1111–1117
7. Huang L, Li J, Guizani M (2014) Secure and efficient data transmission for cluster-based wireless sensor networks. IEEE Trans Parallel Distrib Syst 25(3):750–761
8. Vollmer T, Manic M, Linda O (2014) Autonomic intelligent cyber-sensor to support industrial control network awareness. IEEE Trans Ind Inf 10(2):1647–1658
9. Mitchell R, Chen I-R (2014) Adaptive intrusion detection of malicious unmanned air vehicles using behavior rule specifications. IEEE Trans Syst Man Cybern Syst 44(5):593–606
10. Faisal MA, Aung Z, Williams JR, Sanchez A (2015) Data-stream-based intrusion detection system for advanced metering infrastructure in smart grid: a feasibility study. IEEE Syst J 9 (1):31–44
11. Stavron E, Wireless sensor network, part 2: limitations. http://webhosting.devshed.com/c/a/Web-Hosting-Articles/Wireless-Sensor-Networks-part-2-Limitations/
12. Fatema N, Brad R (2013) Attacks and counterattacks on wireless sensor networks. Int J Ad-Hoc Sens Ubiquit Comput 4(6):1–15
13. Hu Y-C, Perrig A, Johnson DB (2006) Wormhole attacks in wireless senor networks. IEEE J Sel Areas Commun 24(2):370–380
14. Padmavathi G, Shanmugapriya D (2009) A survey of attacks, security mechanisms and challenges in Wireless sensor networks. Int J Comput Sci Inf Secur 4(1 & 2):1–9
15. Xiong NN, Cheng H, Hussain S, Qu Y (2013) Fault tolerant and ubiquotous computing in sensor networks. Int J Distrib Sens Netw 2013:2. Article ID 524547
16. Christin D, Rosskopf C, Hollick M, Martucci L, Kanhere S (2012) IncogniSense: an anonymity-preserving reputation framework for participatory sensing applications. In: Proceedings of the IEEE international conference on pervasive computing and communications, pp. 135–143
17. Akyildiz I, Su W, Sankarasubramaniam Y, Cayirci E (2002) A survey on sensor networks. IEEE Commun Mag 40:102–114
18. Cristofaro E, Soriente C (2013) Participatory privacy: enabling privacy in participatory sensing. IEEE Netw 27:32–36
19. Erfani S, Karunasekera S, Leckie C, Parampalli U (2013) Privacy-preserving data aggregation in participatory sensing networks. In: Proceedings of the 8th IEEE international conference on intelligent sensors, sensor networks and information processing, pp. 165–170
20. Sharifnejad M, Shari M, Ghiasabadi M, Beheshti S (2007) A survey on wireless sensor networks security. SETIT
21. Cardenas AA, Berthier R, Bobba RB, Huh JH, Jetcheva JG, Grochocki D, Sanders WH (2014) A framework for evaluating intrusion detection architectures in advanced metering infrastructures. IEEE Trans Smart Grid 5(2):906–915
22. Vollmer T, Manic M (2014) Cyber-physical system security with deceptive virtual hosts for industrial control networks. IEEE Trans Industr Inf 10(2):1337–1347

Author Biographies

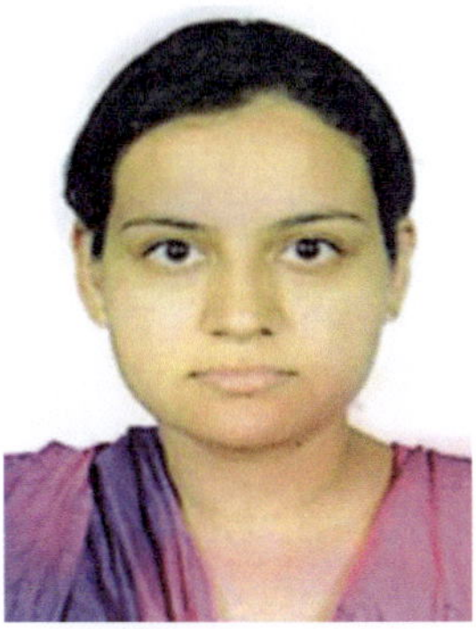

Prachi Dewal has completed her B.Tech. in Computer Science and Engineering from Rajiv Gandhi Proudyogiki Vishwavidyalaya (RGPV) University, Bhopal. Now, she is pursuing M.Tech. in Computer Science and Engineering from CDAC, Noida affiliated to GGSIPU. Her research areas include networked systems and algorithms, mobile networking, and wireless sensor networks.

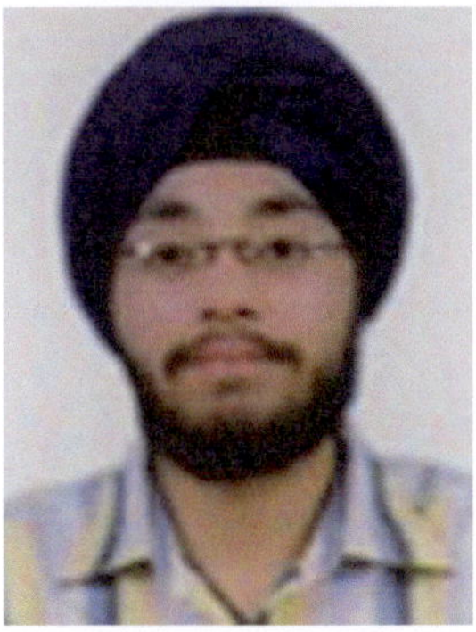

Gagandeep Singh Narula received his B.Tech. in Computer Science and Engineering from Guru Tegh Bahadur Institute of Technology (GTBIT) affiliated to Guru Gobind Singh Indraprastha University (GGSIPU), New Delhi. Now, he is pursuing M.Tech. in Computer Science from CDAC Noida affiliated to GGSIPU. He has published various research papers in various national, international journals, and conferences. His research areas include Semantic Web, information retrieval, data mining, cloud computing, and knowledge management. He is also a member of IEEE Spectrum.

Vishal Jain has completed his M.Tech. (CSE) from USIT, Guru Gobind Singh Indraprastha University, Delhi and doing Ph.D. in Computer Science and Engineering Department, Lingaya's University, Faridabad. Presently, he is working as Assistant Professor in Bharati Vidyapeeth's Institute of Computer Applications and Management, (BVICAM), New Delhi. His research area includes Web technology, Semantic Web, and information retrieval. He is also associated with CSI, ISTE.

Dr. Anupam Baliyan has completed his Ph.D. in Computer Science & Engineering from Banasthali University and M.Tech. in Computer Science & Engineering. His research area includes wireless network, routing in ad hoc network, and quality of services in delay-tolerant network. He published more than 10 research papers in various international journals and guided more than 100 students for their M.Tech. Dissertation. Presently, he is working as Associate Professor in Bharati Vidyapeeth's Institute of Computer Applications and Management, (BVICAM), New Delhi. He is also associated with CSI and ISTE.

Symmetric Key Encryption Technique: A Cellular Automata Based Approach

Deepika Parashar, Satyabrata Roy, Nilanjan Dey, Vipin Jain and U. S. Rawat

Abstract A cellular automaton is one of the most engrossing fields of studies. At the present digital world where almost every communication is being done via the Internet, requirement of security and privacy of information is a must. For securing big or small data over Internet, cryptographic techniques are essential. Usage of cellular automata characteristics in the field of cryptography is still not much explored. Here, the paper presents a symmetric key cryptographic technique of block cipher using cellular automata (CA) rules. Proposed methodology has been implemented in *C*. This cryptographic technique uses non-complemented cellular automata rules and hybrid CA rule vector to form group cellular automata that would be used to encrypt and decrypt the data.

Keywords Cryptographic technique · Cellular automata · Encryption Decryption · Plaintext · Ciphertext

D. Parashar (✉) · V. Jain
Department of Computer Science and Engineering, S.K.I.T., Jaipur, Rajasthan, India
e-mail: Deepikaparashar@27gmail.com

V. Jain
e-mail: ervipin.skit@gmail.com

S. Roy · U. S. Rawat
Department of Computer Science and Engineering, Manipal University Jaipur, Jaipur, Rajasthan, India
e-mail: satya2k6ster@gmail.com

U. S. Rawat
e-mail: umashankar.rawat@jaipur.manipal.edu

N. Dey
Department of Information Technology, Techno India College of Technology, Kolkata, India

M. U. Bokhari et al. (eds.), *Cyber Security*, Advances in Intelligent Systems and Computing 729, https://doi.org/10.1007/978-981-10-8536-9_7

1 Introduction

Secure transaction of data in real time is always needed for various confidential business operations or many other private data sharing operations. For keeping these transactions and communications safe from the intruders, cryptography is one of the most approached techniques. There are two types of techniques that are used for encryption and decryption—the first one is a symmetric key cryptography and the second one is asymmetric key cryptography. Encryption may be achieved by two types of ciphering schemes—stream cipher and block cipher as mentioned in [1].

First of all, the concept cellular automata (CA) was proposed by von Neumann [2]. In the past two decades, many areas of applications of cellular automata (CA) have been explored by many researchers as mentioned in [3–6]. Applications of cellular automata are used in different fields like—physics, chemistry, mathematics, biology, computer science, communication and engineering, etc. Recently, it has been applied in BioHash code generation [7], image encryption [8] and ECG-Hash code generation [9], watermarking [10], and authentication.

Cellular automata (CA) have some specific characteristics like—balancedness, correlation immunity, nonlinearity, easy to implement, etc. These characteristics satisfy the essential cryptographic properties. In this paper, a new idea is represented in which a CA-based cryptosystem is generated. This cryptosystem shows the high quality of randomness of the patterns which have similar significances regarding the older computational techniques of cryptography [11]. And further enhancement of quality of randomness can be embedded with the help of using programmable cellular automata (PCA) [11, 12]. The suggested cryptographic technique in this paper uses a single block of 1-D PCA.

The draft of the paper is organized as follows. In the current section, discussion is on how CA and PCA can be corresponded with important cryptographic features. Section 2 contains some basics of cellular automata (CA) and important terminologies of CA. Section 3 presents the proposed encryption and decryption algorithms using PCA theory. Section 4 shows experimental results. Section 5 concludes our work and suggests the future scope of the work.

2 Cellular Automata Basics

Cellular automata are dynamical system in which space and time are discrete that operate according to local interaction rules [2].

Here in our experiment, an example of a 1-D cellular automata (CA) is considered. It has two possible states per cell, i.e., $S = (0, 1)$ and 3 neighborhoods [3]. Each cell in a CA is updated based on its old state and the state of its left and right neighbors. The basic model of a CA is shown above in Fig. 1. In general, state of a CA at any time instant t is represented as a vector as

$$s^t = (x_1, x_2, \ldots, x_n), \tag{1}$$

where x_i denotes the bit in the ith cell x_i at time instant t and n denotes the length of the bit string. The bit in ith cell at the "next" time instant $t + 1$ is given by f^i. It is known as transition function. For elementary CA transition function for next state of each cell is denoted as

$$x_i^{t+1} = f^i\left(x_{i-1}^t, x_i^t, x_{i+1}^t\right) \quad \text{where } i = 2, 3, \ldots, n-1$$

For a two-state and three-neighborhood CA, there are $2^3 = 8$ distinct neighborhood combinations and $2^8 = 256$ distinct next states. Each mapping represents a CA rule. The number of such rule is 256 as mentioned in [1]. For representing these rules in decimal numbering, Wolfram's decimal numbering convention is used. According to this, each number from 0 to 255 can be represented by a 3 variable Boolean function as shown in [6]. Example $f(111) = 1$, $f(110) = 0$, $f(101) = 1$, $f(100) = 0$, $f(011) = 1$, $f(010) = 0$, $f(001) = 1$, $f(000) = 0$ is denoted as rule 170. Some other examples are shown in Table 1.

The corresponding combinational logics for the rules used in proposed work are

$$\text{Rule 90}: x_i^{t+1} = x_{i-1}^t \oplus x_{i+1}^t \tag{2}$$

$$\text{Rule 102}: x_i^{t+1} = x_i^t x_{i+1}^t \tag{3}$$

$$\text{Rule 150}: x_i^{t+1} = x_{i-1}^t x_i^t x_{i+1}^t \tag{4}$$

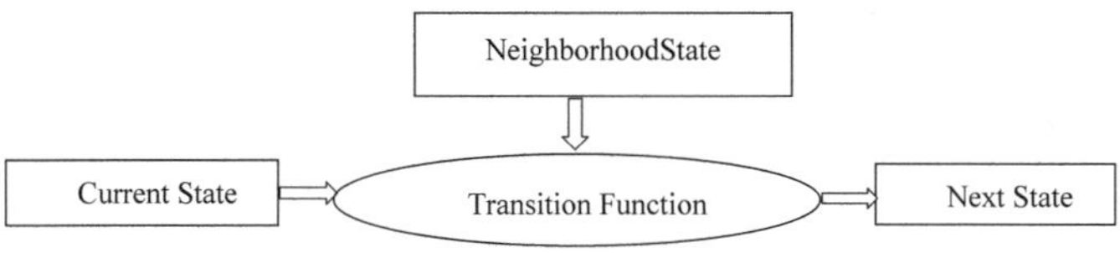

Fig. 1 Model of CA

Table 1 CA numbering rules for next state update

Rule name	7	6	5	4	3	2	1	0
	111	110	101	100	011	010	001	000
90	0	1	0	1	1	0	1	0
102	0	1	1	0	0	1	1	0
150	1	0	0	1	0	1	1	0

2.1 Additive and Nonadditive CA

When a cellular automata (CA) rule is based on EXOR/EXNOR combinational logic, then it is called additive CA and it depends on AND/OR combinational logic then it is called nonadditive CA.

2.2 Null Boundary and Periodic Boundary CA

A binary cellular automata (CA) containing n cells as x_1, x_2, …, x_n is null boundary when the left neighbor of leftmost cell and right neighbor of rightmost cell is taken as “0”. The CA is called periodic boundary CA when the neighbor of the extreme cells is considered as adjacent to each other.

2.3 Programmable Cellular Automata (PCA)

Concepts of PCA were introduced into [1] and its hardware implementation was realized into [11]. A PCA is an altered cellular automata (CA) that contains control signals and applied combinational logic in it is indefinite. Each cell in PCA is controlled by these control signals. With the help of these control signals, different rules can be applied on a single 1-D structure dynamically. Figure 2 shows the model of a PCA, which consists of three control signals. By using these signals, any possible combination of complemented and non-complemented additive CA rules [1] can be implemented. A PCA has high degree of flexibility, parallelism, and complexity, which redefines cellular automata (CA) as more appropriate and robust for cryptographic applications.

3 Proposed Encryption and Decryption Algorithms

In this paper, a symmetric key cryptographic technique using PCA has been implemented. In this experiment, non-complemented rule 150 and rule 102 are used to form a group cellular automata [1] of cycle length 12. These cycles of even length are used for encryption and decryption. Block of plain text is loaded into PCA and after six cycles, the ciphertext is generated and after next six cycles, the ciphertext is decrypted to retrieve plain text. Permutation group representations of

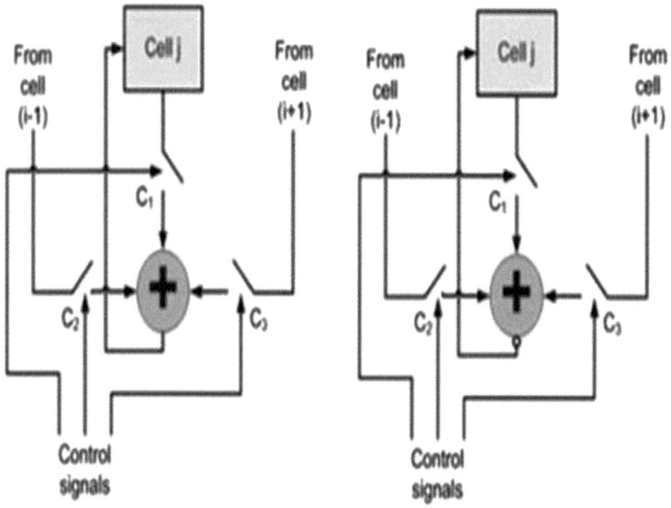

Fig. 2 Model of a single cell of PCA [11]

CA having even cycles of even length are mentioned in [1, 13]. The procedure for cryptography, which has been followed in the proposed work is formulated as

$$\text{Ciphertext, } C = K(P) \quad \text{Plaintext, } P = K(C),$$

where P is a block of plaintext, C is a block of ciphertext, K is a secret key which is used in encryption and decryption.

Out of all combinations of eight-cell CA, a hybrid CA rule vector of rule 150(90) and 102 has been selected. The combination which is used here can be represented as $\langle 11110000 \rangle$, where 0 denotes rule 150 and 1 denotes rule 102 for 8 bits. The whole procedure of proposed cryptographic technique is described through the following algorithms.

3.1 Rule Scheduler Algorithm for PCA

Input: Rule 90, 102, and 150 are applied on each cell of PCA and selection of these rules depends on the selection lines of multiplexer (Fig. 3).

Step 1: When selection lines S_0S_1 are logic "00" then rule 90 is selected.

Step 2: When selection lines S_0S_1 are logic "01" then rule 150 is selected.

Step 3: When selection lines S_0S_1 are logic "10" or "11" then rule 102 is selected.

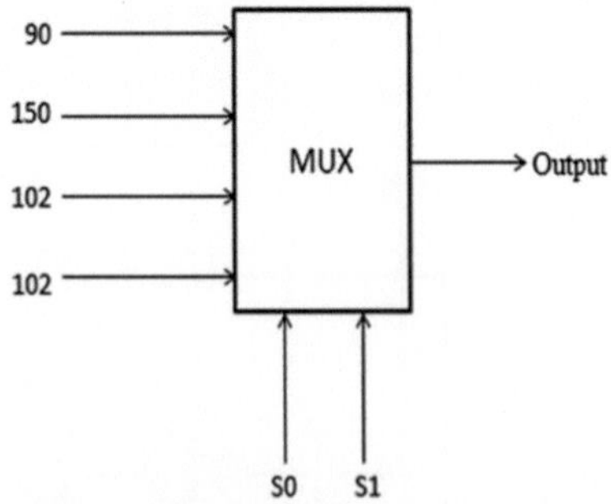

Fig. 3 A 4 × 1 multiplexer for scheduling rules

3.2 Algorithm for Encryption

Input: String of plaintext block up to length *L*.
Step 1: Store binary values of plain text in an array and the array is divided into 8-bit blocks.
Step 2: Load a single 8-bit block into PCA. Apply selected rule combination to each cell of PCA. Rule selection is performed using rule scheduler algorithm.
Step 3: Run PCA for six clock cycles.
Step 4: Generate one byte of encrypted message as output.
Step 5: Repeat Step 2 to 4 until the whole block of plaintext string of length *L* is encrypted.

3.3 Algorithm for Decryption

Input: String of ciphertext block up to length *L*.
Step 1: Store binary values of ciphertext in an array and divide the array into 8-bit blocks.
Step 2: Load a single 8-bit block into PCA. Apply selected rule combination to each cell of PCA. Rule selection is again performed using rule scheduler algorithm.
Step 3: Now run PCA for next six clock cycles.
Step 4: Generate one byte of decrypted message as output.
Step 5: Repeat Step 2 to 4 until the whole block of ciphertext string of length *L* is decrypted.

4 Result and Analysis

The above cryptographic technique has been implemented in *C*. A total of 256 combinations of CA rules can be generated [9]. Out of these, one rule arrangement is selected as the key for the proposed process of cryptography. Basic technique used in this proposed system is, when the rule combination is applied as key on every plaintext block, various results have been generated. After completing total 12 rounds with these results, same plaintext block is received. These 12 rounds have been divided into two cycles of same length. First six rounds perform the process of encryption and generated result is taken as ciphertext block. Next six rounds perform the process of decryption and generate the same plaintext block. If the entered plaintext and received plaintext is same, it ensures that the algorithm is correct. Pictographic representation by using a single 8-bit block for encryption and decryption scheme is shown in Fig. 4 and the final tested result of our proposed technique which is implemented in *C* is shown in Fig. 5.

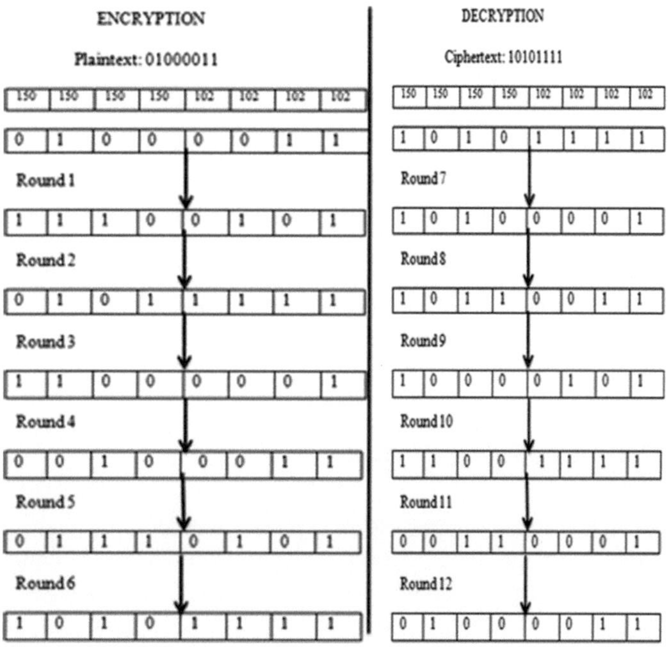

Fig. 4 Process of encryption and decryption

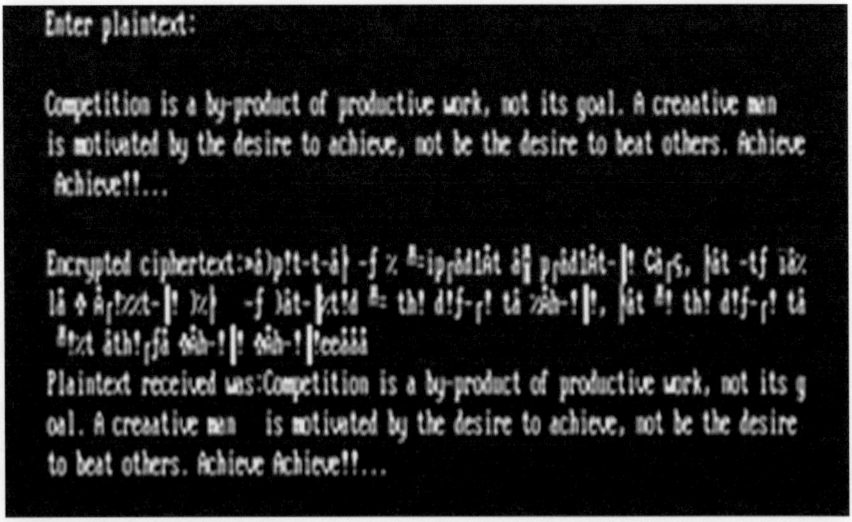

Fig. 5 Final tested result

4.1 *Statistical Analysis*

To check the quality of randomness of generated ciphertext in our experiment, the proposed algorithm has gone through a statistical test. This test is known as runs test [14]. In this test procedure, the value of normal variate, denoted as Z has to be calculated and the obtained value of Z must be closer to 1.96, which means the hypothesis of randomness of ciphertext is not rejected. Here in this experiment, the value of normal variate Z is -2.120. So the test for randomness of "0" and "1" in generated ciphertext is successful.

5 Conclusion and Future Scope

In this paper, 1-D cellular automata were explored in order to recognize the use of cellular automata in the field of cryptography. A PCA-based symmetric key cryptographic technique is proposed which uses the block cipher scheme. It can provide a good level of security and safety of data over Internet. In future, more cellular automata rule combinations can be explored in order to identify more applications in various fields of technology. Furthermore, in future this work can be used to implement the image encryption technique using MATLAB. It can also be used in 2-D cellular automata and parallel programming, which can reduce the complexity than that of the proposed scheme. This work can be used in steganography as well. The hardware implementation of this technique is easy and economical. This makes the technique also applicable in embedded system designs and other computer science technologies.

References

1. Nandi S, Kar BK, Chaudhuri Pabitra Pal (1994) Theory and applications of cellular automata in cryptography. IEEE Trans Comput 43(12):1346–1356
2. von Neumann J (1966) In: Burks AW (ed) Theory of self reproducing automata. Univ. of Illinois Press, London
3. Kotoulas L, Tsarouchis D, Sirakoulis GC, Andreadis I (2006) 1-d cellular automata for pseudo random number generation and its reconfigurable hardware implementation. In: Proceedings of IEEE international symposium on circuits and systems
4. Choudhury PP, Sahoo S, Chakraborty M, Bhandari S, Pal A (2009) Investigation of the global dynamics of cellular automata using boolean derivatives. Int J Comput Math Appl 57:1337–1351
5. Wolfram S (2002) A new kind of science. Wolfram Media Inc. ISBN: 1-57955-008-8
6. Wolfram S (1986) Theory and applications of cellular automata. Wolfram Scientific
7. Dey N, Nandi B, Dey M, Das A, Chaudhuri SS (2013) BioHash code generation from electrocardiogram features. In: 3rd IEEE international advance computing conference
8. Nandi S, Roy S, Dey N, Nath S, Chakraborty S, Kaara WBA (2014) 1-D group cellular automata based image encryption technique. In: IEEE international conference on control, instrumentation, communication and computational technologies (ICCICCT), pp 578–583
9. Nandi S, Roy S, Dansana J, Kaara WBA, Ray R, Chowdhury SR, Chakraborty S, Dey N (2014) Int J Comput Netw Inf Secur
10. Acharjee S, Chakraborty S, Ray R, Nath S, Dey N (2014) Watermarking in motion vector for security enhancement of medical videos. In: International conference on control, instrumentation, communication and computational technologies (2014)
11. Anghelescu P (2012) Hardware implementation of programmable cellular automata encryption algorithm. In: IEEE international conference on telecommunication and signal processing, Prague, pp 18–21
12. Anghelescu P, Sofron E, Rîncu C, Iana V (2008) Programmable cellular automata based encryption algorithm. Semicond Conf 2:351–354
13. Wolfram S (1985) Cryptography with cellular automata. In: Proceedings of the conference, CRTPTO'85 on advances in cryptography. Lecture notes in computer science, vol 218, pp 429–432
14. Ross SM (2010) Introductory statistics, 3rd edn. Academic Press, Elsevier, pp 676–681

A Comparative Study on Lightweight Cryptography

M. U. Bokhari and Shabbir Hassan

Abstract The traditional cryptosystem only fulfills the requirements of desktop computing epoch. Renewable lightweight cryptography algorithms are developing to beat the constraints of traditional cryptosystem, which provide tradeoff among cipher sort, attack immune, key size, plaintext length, and performance. The implementation of LWC algorithms is carried out on retaining in the mind that it will be implemented in minimal power consumption, fewer area requirement and also enough efficiency so it turns out to be ideal for such a resource confine devices such as RFID tags and wireless sensor node. In this, we are trying to emerge with frequent LWC algorithms which are grouped into stream cipher, block cipher, and hybrid model, and also reveal them, at the last a comparison is conducted on the effective parameters.

Keywords Stream cipher · Hummingbird · ECC · WG · Sober
PUF · HITAG2 · Grain

1 Introduction

As the current scenario, use of smart devices such as credit card, smart card, personal digital assistant (PDA), RFID tags, wireless sensor nodes, etc., is gaining equipotent role in our daily life. Their use is much ubiquitous. On the other hand, security and performance is one of the severe issues for such devices. So, we can need considerable security as well as performance of these devices, owning minimal storage space, and computational capabilities. This results in raising a research area known as lightweight cryptography. The aim of LWC is to provide the secured information on highly constrain relevant devices owning minimal sources. LWC

M. U. Bokhari (✉) · S. Hassan
Department of Computer Science, Aligarh Muslim University, Aligarh 202002, India
e-mail: mubokhari@gmail.com

S. Hassan
e-mail: hassan.analyst@gmail.com

M. U. Bokhari et al. (eds.), *Cyber Security*, Advances in Intelligent Systems
and Computing 729, https://doi.org/10.1007/978-981-10-8536-9_8

algorithms have got certain common features like they must possess low power consumption, lesser communication cost, low area, low energy, as well as little processing time. The implementation of LWC is done in such a way that it increases throughput and efficiency. The ubiquitous use of RFID tags rise concern about equipotent security in RFID system. Since low-cost tags are extremely resource-constrained device, common security approach is no longer applicable to them. Hence, one challenging topic is to purpose a secure lightweight cipher that is suited for RFID tags. This paper describes a comparative study among some well-known lightweight ciphers (Table 1).

2 Stream Cipher

Stream cipher was introduced in 1917 by "Gilbert Vernam". Vernam studies Electrical Engineering at Worcester Polytechnic Institute (WPI) in Massachusetts. Stream cipher sometime refers to Vernam cipher. Stream cipher is a symmetric key cipher where the plaintext digits are combined with a stream of pseudorandom cipher digit is called keystream. Stream cipher encrypts bits individually with a corresponding digit of keystream to obtain the ciphertext digit, i.e., encrypted bit. The pseudorandom keystream is generated from a primary random integer value (is called a seed) using digital shift register and the same seed value is served as a key for decryption of ciphertext stream [1].

3 Lightweight Stream Cipher

A lightweight stream cipher is used in a device (smartphones, tabs, sensor networks) due to the limitation of resources and power consumption. The lightweight stream ciphers are work better and in efficient manner in such situations and are design for targeted to resource-constrained devices like RFID (Radio Frequency Identification) smart cards, and wireless sensor nodes.

Table 1 Types of various cryptographic algorithms

Stream cipher	Block cipher		Hybrid cipher	
BSF-128, Bokhari stream cipher	Symmetric	Asymmetric	Hamming bird 1	Hamming bird 2
GRAIN, RC4	DESL	ECC	–	–
WG-7, WG-8, WG-16	–	–	–	–
HITAG2, Sober t-16/ family	–	–	–	–
PUF, Snow, Edon80	–	–	–	–

3.1 BSF-128

The BSF-128 stream cipher is designed on the basis of grain. It has designed for 128-bit secret key applications. BSF-128 consists two shift registers, one FCSR and one LFSR of 128-bit length each. It also uses an S-Box of 8 × 16, i.e., it takes 8-bit input and produced output of 16-bit. The S-Box is a combination of Skipjack and an S-Box designed by ISRC at QUT, which has also been used in SOBER t-16 cipher. On the basis of cryptanalysis, we assume that this cipher is secure against many cryptanalysis attacks [2].

3.2 Grain

For the resource constrain environment, grain cryptographic stream cipher is designed. It seems to be much pretty on the situation where there is a limitation of gates, memory space, processing time, low power consumption, etc., there are several stream ciphers that are based on LFSR to produce an arbitrary sequence of numbers. There are mainly three building blocks of grain stream cipher.

- A nonlinear feedback shift registers.
- Two linear feedback shift register.
- A nonlinear filter functions for offering the ideal security.

As we know that an LFSR with feedback chosen from a primitive polynomial can produce a well-balanced sequence of streams, whereas the NLFSR is used to achieve nonlinearity in the ciphers. Due to the inherent weakness of LFSR's, several cryptanalytic attacks [3–6] were reported against grain stream cipher. The size of LFSR, NFSR and key is 80 bits and the size of initial vector is 64 bits. A polynomial of degree 80 is used to provide the feedback to the shift registers LFSR and NFSR, where $\boldsymbol{f}(\boldsymbol{x})$ and $\boldsymbol{g}(\boldsymbol{x})$ represent the feedback function. At first, the LFSR is seeded with a 64-bit initialization vector, and NFSR is seeded with 80 bits of key. Left 16 bits are loaded with ones in order to avoid zero shift registers. At the end, input of NLFSR are masked with the output of LFSR to obtain a stable condition for NLFSR. The nonlinear filtration function $\boldsymbol{h}(\boldsymbol{x})$ needs as an input and the desired bits from both the feedback shift registers. Thereafter, a XOR operation with modulo2 is performed with all of the 7 specific bits of NFSR and then their output is further included with the filter function $\boldsymbol{h}(\boldsymbol{x})$.

3.3 Ron's Code (RC4)

RC4 designed by Ron Rivest in 1987. In the history of cryptography, RC4 has been one of the most popular stream ciphers. Its internal state contains a permutation of bits overall possible bytes sequence ranging from 0 to 255. Its design analysis and approach are quite different as compared to LFSR-based stream ciphers. The internal state consists a table of $N = 2^n$, n-bit words and two n-bit pointer [7, 8]. There are some attacks on RC4 based on the relationships between the internal states of the S-Boxes [9].

3.4 *Welch-Gong (WG-7)*

WG-7 [10] stream cipher is based on the primitive WG stream cipher [11]. It is designed by Y. Luo, "Q. Chai", "G. Gong", and "X. Lai" in 2010. WG-7 is a very fast stream cipher for the lightweight devices (for example smart mobile phone, RFID tags, as well as wireless sensor node) WG-7 is design. Both WG and WG-7 are hardware-oriented stream cipher that uses a word-oriented LFSR and a filter function based on WG. WG works on GF(2^{29}) but WG-7 in GF(2^7). WG-7 uses 80-bit secret key and 81-bit IV and the LFSR is clocked 46 times, the internal state consists of 161 bits and the security level claimed by the designer is 80-bits [4, 12].

3.4.1 Algebraic Attack on WG-7

Recently, a distinguishing attack was discovered against the WG-7 stream cipher. Within the time complexity of $O(2^{27})$, an attacker can recover both the secret key and internal state of the cipher [13].

3.5 *Welch-Gong (WG-8)*

WG-8 is a lightweight discrepancy of the well-known WG stream cipher family and was submitted to eSTREAM project. It inherits excellent randomness properties of WG such as exact linear complexity, balance, ideal tuple distribution, period, and ideal two-level autocorrelations. On AT mega 128 (8-bit) from Atmel and MSP430 (16 bit) from Texas low power microcontroller, WG-8 is able to achieve a throughput of 185.5 and 95.9 kbps on both microcontroller with energy efficiency of 458 and 125 nJ/bit respectively. As compared to other LWC implementation, the throughput of WG-8 is about $2 \approx 15$ times higher and energy consumption is about $2 \approx 220$ times smaller [14].

3.6 HITAG2

A secure version of Crypto-1 cipher has been developed by "Philips/NXP". It is also widely used in RFID cars lock for immobilizers and door opening systems. It has played a great role in the functioning and security of Alfa Romeo 156 and 166 models, Opel, Numerous Nissan, Ford Galaxy and Transit, GM Corsa and Zafira, Peugeot, and also in Volvo models. HITAG2 also seems to be playing a vital role for the access control of buildings. It has 48-bit internal state and 48-bit secret key, due to short length of secret key, the ciphers seems to be vulnerable to brute force attack. It is a lightweight LFSR-based stream cipher [15].

3.6.1 Attack on HITAG2

A cryptanalysis against HITAG2 was founded [15], which easily broke HITAG2 by a SAT solver within several hours. Besides the brute force attack, this is only a unique cryptanalysis on HITAG2 that break the security of cipher. This attack comprises of three phases [16].

- To extract 32 bit of secret key a black box attacks is vulnerable.
- To achieve other key bits the white-box attack seems also vulnerable.
- Brute force searches for the remaining key bits.
- Cost-optimized parallel code-breaker COPACOBANA is able to reveal the secret key of a HITAG2 transponder in less than 2 h (103.5 min) in the worst case [17].

3.7 SOBER

SOBER is a popular family of stream ciphers that are widely used in embedded devices. It was first proposed by G. Rose in 1998. Their family includes several stream ciphers: Sober t-16, sober t-32 [18], sober t-128 [19], and many more. The synchronous stream cipher sober t-16 and sober t-32 were submitted to NESSIE program [12] with 128-bit key and 256-bit key strength, respectively. Almost all ciphers, which belong, to sober are depending on similar principle and virtually have equivalent model structure. Most of the sober family ciphers consist of three basic components [19].

- Linear feedback shift registers (LFSR)
- Nonlinear function
- Stutter control.

3.8 Lightweight Secure PUF

The physical unclonable function (PUF) [20] is promising solution to mitigate the effect of physical attacks. PUF is the physical entity that generates output based on their input and intrinsic physical properties of embedding hardware. It exploits only those physical properties of embedding devices.

3.8.1 Drawback on PUF

Due to small hardware requirement to building a PUF, it is widely used in lightweight applications such as RFID tags. To achieve the feature of low-cost implementation, composite PUFs are developed and are introduced in HOST2014 and RECONFIG 2013. The building of composite PUFs is based on several small primitives; on the basis of cryptanalysis, the introduced PUFs RECONFIG 2013 are not secure and can be penetrated [21].

4 Block Cipher (BC)

A block cipher works on two pair of algorithms, one for encryption e and other for decryption d. A group of plain text namely P of size $L > 1$ are encrypted together by the encryption function $C = e(k, P), C$ yield cipher text under the enciphering function e with key k. A whole block of size L is encrypted with a single key k at a time. The key k is a composition of several values $k_i k_{i-1} \ldots k_1 k_0$. After encryption, the ciphertext C is decrypted by the set of composite key k under the correspondence $P = d(k, C)$. In this cipher, the ciphertext block is totally depends upon the key k. In mathematical terminology, we can also say that

$$e(k, P) = d^{-1}(k, P) = C$$
$$d(k, P) = e^{-1}(k, C) = P$$

By following transitivity can we have?

$$e^{-1}(k, e(k, P)) = P = d\left(k, d^{-1}(k, P)\right)$$
$$d^{-1}(k, d(k, C)) = C = e\left(k, e^{-1}(k, C)\right)$$

It is a deterministic algorithm that operates on a fixed length of data of size L. It is widely used to implements a cryptographic protocol and the encryption of bulk of data. Hence, block cipher encrypts bits slowly than stream cipher.

The modern architecture of block cipher is based on the concept of iteration is called product cipher; data are spitted into several boxes, and then permuted with different sub-keys derived from the main key k to enhance the security and randomization.

5 DESL

The algorithms tend to make use of inside this cipher are the DESL (build up extension of DES) & ECC, DESL is the enhanced lightweight version of DES. The microchip size of DESL is considerably reduced as individual S-Box is utilized frequently for eight times. Which can make DESL compact, tough, efficient, and prevented from linear and also differential cryptanalysis attacks. The DESL is proficient to enciphering 64 bit of plain text in 144 clock rounds while it is working with a frequency of 100 kHz and gaining current of 0.89 μA [22]. The DESL structure involves mainly the building blocks controller, mem-left, mem-right, key program, and S-Box.

6 Elliptic Curve Cryptography (ECC)

In 1985, two American mathematicians Vector Miller and Neal Koblitz proposed the concept of elliptic curve cryptography. Their theory is completely based on elliptic curve discrete logarithms and NP hard problem that requires a complete exponent time. The application of ECC involves information security, personal digital assistant (PDA), wireless communication network, wireless sensor nodes, image encryption, smart cards, e-commerce, and also in economic-based communication protocols. ECC makes use of 162-bit public key by the assist of picking points on elliptic curves, and afford a security strength that is corresponding to 1024-bit key in RSA [23].

6.1 Advantages of ECC Over RSA

- Smaller key size for equivalent security
- Provide higher security per bit.
- Provide higher security for same amount of computation.

- For higher security (Largest ECC & RSA system broken to date are 108-bit 512-bit)
- Largest effort ever expanded in PKC challenge for solving 108-bit ECC. Amount of work required was about 50 times of 512-bit RSA.

7 Hybrid Cipher (HC)

By providing tradeoff between speed [24], size, cost of implementation, efficiency, in a hybrid model of hummingbird ciphers was invented by "ALEXANDRIA" and Viswanath Ananth of Valencia, Calif in 2011. It achieves the characteristic of both stream cipher and block cipher. Their implementation is done on keeping in mind that they are efficiently adopted in low-cost sensible devices and also within microcontroller environment. Hummingbird persistently opposes to most frequent attacks on stream and blocks ciphers such as birthday attack, cube attack, side channel attack, key recovery attack, brute force attack, algebraic attack, correlation attack, timing attack, linear and differential cryptanalysis, time–memory–data tradeoff attack, distinguishing attack, passive attack, and acoustic cryptanalysis. Due to their complex internal state and 256-bit key size, it attains more security and hence it is most suited for embedded applications that are discussed above. The hybrid model of hummingbird is even categorized into two modules namely, Hummingbird-1 and Hummingbird-2. Hummingbird-1 is a nice combination of stream and block cipher [3], with 16-bit block size, 256-bit key, and 80-bit internal states.

8 Conclusion

In this comparative study, we analyzed different lightweight cryptographic algorithms including hybrid model (of Hummingbird1 and Hummingbird2), several lightweight stream ciphers have been discussed with their technologies, attack immune, features as well as drawbacks. Table 2 depicts a comparative study of several stream ciphers by tending their crucial parameters. Obviously, it is a promising work for the better analysis and design of a lightweight stream cipher for resource-constrained devices. Thus, the objective of this comparative study is to propose an efficient modification on enciphering algorithms, which eliminate most common attacks on cipher and provide highest throughput.

Table 2 Summarized comparison to depict the differences among various LWC algorithms

	Cipher type	Block size	Key size	IV	Attacks immune	S-Box	Throughput	Registers	Operator
DESL	Block cipher	64	56		Resist LC and DMA	6 × 4 single	Least among other algorithms	No	XOR and Shift
Grain	Stream cipher	1	80	64	No better KRA beside BFA	No	High but less than Hummingbird	LFSR + NFSR	XOR
ECC	Asymmetric block cipher	No	162	–	Resist SCA and TA	No	Better but less than Hummingbird	No	Point addition and point multiplications
BSF 128	Stream cipher	–	128	128	Resist COA, GDA,DA, DGA	8 × 16	High but less than Hummingbird	NFSR + FCSR	XOR
WG-7	LW stream cipher	–	80	81	Suffer from DGA, AA	No	–	Word-oriented LFSR	XOR and multiplication
WG-8	LW stream cipher	–	80	80	Able to resist AA, COA, DFA, CUA, DGA, DFTA, TMDA	No	High throughput	20 stage LFSR	XOR and multiplication
WG 16	LW stream cipher	–	128	128	Able to resist AA, COA, DFA, CUA, DGA, DFTA, TMDA	No	–	32 stage LFSR	XOR and multiplication
RC4	Stream cipher	No	128	–	Some attack based on relationship between internal state and S-Boxes	Yes	Best	No	XOR
Sober t-32	Stream cipher	–	256	–	Secure, have a good immune	Yes	–	LFSR	XOR
HC	Hybrid cipher	16	128–256	–	Most secure, and immune to most of LA, DA, CUA, BDA, AA etc.	4 × 4	Maximum	LFSR	XOR

AA Algebraic attack; *BDA* Birthday attack; *BFA* Brute force attack; *COA* Correlation attack; *CUA* Cube attack; *DA* Determine attack; *DFA* Differential attack; *DFTA* Discrete Fourier transformation attack; *DGA* Distinguish attack; *DMA* Davies Murphy attack; *GDA* Guess &determine attack; *HB* Hummingbird; *IV* Initialization vector; *KRA* Key recovery attack; *LA* Linear attack; *LC* Linear cryptanalysis; *LW* Lightweight; *SCA* Side channel attack; *TA* Timing attack; *TMDA* Time–memory–data attack

References

1. Online reference from http://en.wikipedia.org/wiki/Stream_cipher
2. Bokhari MU, Alam S (2013) BSF-128: a new synchronous stream cipher design. In: Proceeding of international conference on emerging trends in engineering and technology, pp 541–545
3. Maximov A (2006) Cryptanalysis of the grain family of stream ciphers. In: Proceedings of ACM symposium on information, computer and communications security, pp 283–288
4. Dinur I, Shamir A (2011) Breaking grain-128 with dynamic cube attacks. In Fast software encryption. Springer Berlin Heidelberg, pp 167–187
5. Bjøstad TE (2013) Cryptanalysis of grain using time/memory/data tradeoffs
6. Banik S, Maitra S, Sarkar S (2012) A differential fault attack on the grain family of stream ciphers. Proceeding of 14th international workshop on cryptographic hardware and embedded systems. Springer, Berlin Heidelberg, Leuven, Belgium, pp 122–139
7. Gupta Sen S (2014) (Non-)random sequences from (Non-)random permutations analysis of RC4 stream cipher. J Cryptol 27(1):67–108
8. Lv J, Zhang B, Lin D (2014) Some new weaknesses in the RC4 stream cipher. Inf Secur Appl 27(1):8–38
9. Xie J, Pan X (2010) An improved RC4 stream cipher. Proc Int Conf Comput Appl Syst Model 7:156–159
10. Orumiehchiha AM, Pieprzyk J, Steinfeld R (2012) Cryptanalysis of WG-7: a lightweight stream cipher. Crypt Commun 4(3–4):277–285
11. Nawaz Y, Gong G (2008) WG-7: a family of stream ciphers with designed randomness properties. Int J Inf Sci 178(7):1903–1916
12. Babbage S, Lano J (2011) Probabilistic factors in the Sober-t stream ciphers. In: Proceeding of 3rd NESSIE workshop, pp 1–12
13. Luo Y (2010) A lightweight stream cipher WG-7 for RFID encryption and authentication. In: Proceeding of IEEE global telecommunications conference, pp 1–6
14. Fan X, Mandal K, Gong G (2013) WG-8: a lightweight stream cipher for resource-constrained smart devices. Springer Berlin Heidelberg, pp 617–632
15. Courtois NT, Sean ON, Quisquater JJ (2009) Practical algebraic attacks on the Hitag2 stream cipher. In: Information security. Springer Berlin Heidelberg, pp 167–176
16. Sun S (2011) Cube cryptanalysis of Hitag2 stream cipher. In: Proceeding of 10th international conference cryptology and network security. Springer Berlin Heidelberg, CANS, pp 15–25
17. Stembera P, Novotny M (2011) Breaking Hitag2 with reconfigurable hardware. In: Proceeding on 14th IEEE Euromicro conference on digital system design, pp 558–563
18. Rose G (1998) SOBER II: a stream cipher based on linear feedback over GF (28). In: Proceeding on 3rd Australasian conference, pp 135–146
19. Hawkes P, Rose GG (2003) Primitive specification for SOBER-128. IACR cryptology ePrint archive
20. Nguyen PH, Sahoo DP (2014) Lightweight and secure PUFs: a survey. In: 4th international conference on security, privacy, and applied cryptography engineering. Springer International Publishing, pp 1–13
21. Nguyen HP (2014) Cryptanalysis of composite PUFs (extended abstract-invited talk). In: Proceeding of 18th international symposium on VLSI design and test, pp 1–2
22. John J (2012) Cryptography for resource constrained devices: a survey. Proc Int J Comput Sci Eng 1766–1770

23. Malhotra K, Gardner S, Patz R (2007) Implementation of elliptic-curve cryptography on mobile healthcare devices. In: Proceeding of IEEE international conference on networking, sensing and control, pp 239–244
24. Shende RS, Deshpande MAY (2013) VLSI design of secure cryptographic algorithm. Proc Int J Eng Res Appl 3(2):742–746

GPS Hash Table Based Location Identifier Algorithm for Security and Integrity Against Vampire Attacks

S. N. Panda

Abstract Wireless sensor networks are associated with assorted functional aspects including battery or energy, power, log of neighboring nodes, cache, and number of services. In a network attack, the malicious node or packet attempts to temporarily or permanently halt these parameters so that the authentic and realistic communication can be damaged. Such attacks were previously associated with DDoS attacks which do not allow the authentic user to access the services. Number of algorithms devised against DDoS attacks but very less treatment to the vampire attacks which is more hazardous as it is very difficult for the authentic user to confirm whether there is any attack on network. It consumes battery of node very rapidly which is not identified by the network node. In our proposed algorithm, a unique and effective algorithm for location-based key generation is devised and implemented which makes use of dynamic key exchange based on the location.

Keywords Vampire attacks · Wireless sensor network security
Reliable communication · Energy optimization in wireless sensor network

1 Introduction—Vampire Attacks

Vampire attack [1] alludes to making and transmission of information parcels by pernicious hub that causes tremendous vitality utilization by the system prompting moderate exhaustion of node's battery life (Fig. 1).

S. N. Panda (✉)
Chitkara University, Rajpura, Punjab, India
e-mail: panda.india@gmail.com

M. U. Bokhari et al. (eds.), *Cyber Security*, Advances in Intelligent Systems and Computing 729, https://doi.org/10.1007/978-981-10-8536-9_9

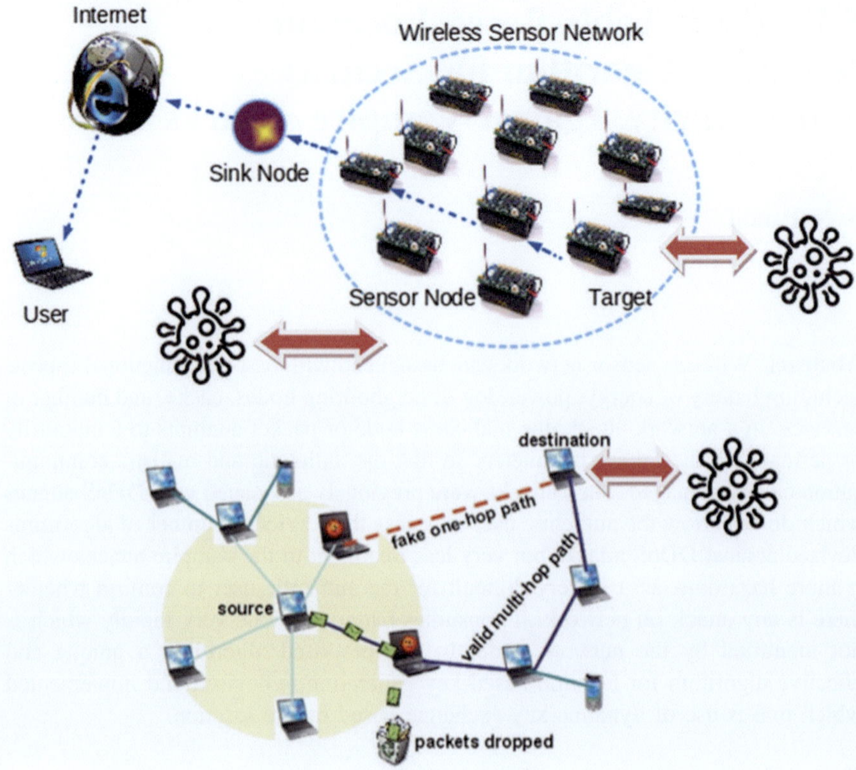

Fig. 1 Vampire attack

2 Features

Vampire attack is not definite to any specific protocol or topology or port. Such attacks do not interrupt the services directly. It affects the resources using the services. The vampires make use of protocol compatible or compliant messages vampire attacks transmit data that drain the energy level of nodes. Vampires do not change or interrupt altering discovered paths or routes.

Resource Draining Attacks—Such attacks create and send the assaults or attacks which means the creation and sending the messages by spiteful node by which the energy consumption is taken a lot by the assault.

Carousal Attack—These attack drastically increases the routing path and length which creates delay in the networks and also inadequate by the number of allowable entries in the resource route [2] (Figs. 2 and 3).

Stretch Attack [3]—Such attacks creates the artificial or fake routes using which the packet can be disguised. The attack forces the data packet to choose the fake path so that there is huge delay and battery consumption increases. Stateless

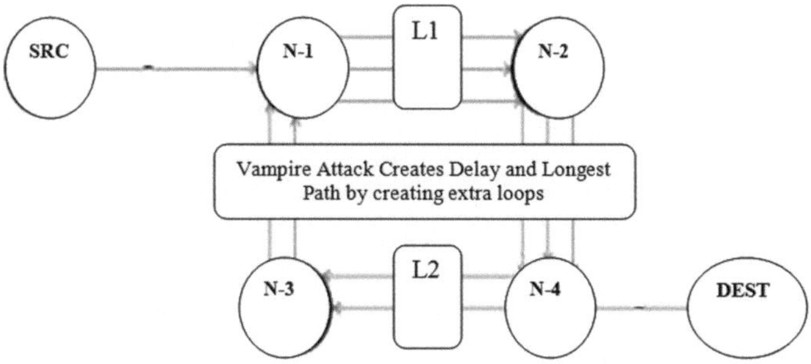

Fig. 2 Carousal attack

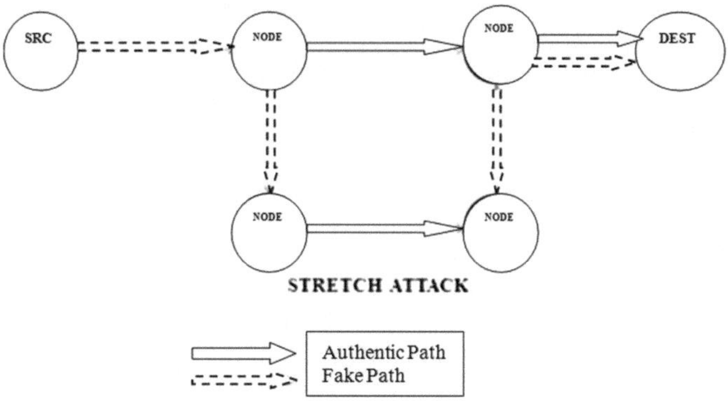

Fig. 3 Stretch attack—a scenario of vampire assault

protocols are source routing protocols that keep track of the communication in the network infrastructure [4]. Here, the source node mentions the complete and whole route to the destination that is inside the packet header. Intermediaries do not create the independent or arbitrary forwarding decisions. In stateful protocols, the nodes have advance information of state, topology, forwarding techniques and routes. Network nodes create the local forwarding decisions on that stored state.

3 Related Works and Literature Review

The issue of security has gotten significant consideration via specialists in impromptu systems [5]. Vulnerabilities in WSN could happen in light of specific measurements as per the qualities of element topology and absence of focal base station. There are a wide range of sorts of attacks that happen in remote impromptu sensor systems [6]. There are preventive measures for these attacks in the MAC layer. A percentage of the strategies are depicted beneath.

3.1 Path-Based Attacks

These attacks are basic in remote wireless sensor systems. They are normally alluded as way-based Denial of Service (DoS) attacks [6]. Restricted hash chains can keep these attacks by constraining the rate at which hubs transmit packets.

3.2 Rushing Attack

Rushing attack happens in on-interest directing conventions like DSR, ad hoc on-demand distance vector routing (AODV) where course disclosure is finished by sending REQUEST messages to the neighboring hubs [7].

3.3 Wormhole Attack

In wormhole attack, the vindictive hub builds a passage (way) to the destination in such a path, to the point that all the bundles from the source are exchanged by means of the assailant which can change substance of the bundle before sending it to the destination. To keep this attack, parcel rope system is utilized [8]. A chain is data added to the bundle in order to confine the parcel's voyaging separation.

3.4 Routing Infrastructure Attacks

Routing infrastructure concentrates on insignificant vitality steering, which intends to utilize negligible vitality to transmit and get parcels and by utilizing insignificant vitality ways to transmit bundles [9]. However, utilizing such plans may lessen the system network and lifetime of the system. To dodge such issues, a vitality mindful directing convention, which uses sub-ideal ways, was presented [10]. Numerous steering ways are available where the convention picks one taking into account probabilistic qualities. For this situation, each steering way is given an opportunity to exchange bundles along these lines improving the system lifetime.

3.5 Asset Exhaustion Attacks

Resource consumption attacks concentrate on lessening the amount of assets utilized by hubs like battery force, stockpiling, memory and so forth therefore diminishing the general limit of the system [11].

To propose and defend the research work, a number of research papers are analyzed. Following are the excerpts from the different research work performed by number of academicians and researchers.

Rong Du et al. [12]—In this paper, the work considers the issue of building a safe system against hub connivance assault taking into account system division. In this paper, the work examined the topology outline and system division issue for pitifully secure against hub trick assault.

Chris Karlof [13]—This work proposes security objectives for steering in sensor systems, indicates how assaults against specially appointed and shared systems can be adjusted into effective assaults against sensor systems.

Wenliang Du [14]—This work demonstrates that the execution (counting integration, memory use, and system versatility against hub catch) of sensor systems would be able to significantly enhance with the utilization of our proposed plan. The plan and its nitty-gritty execution assessment are exhibited in this paper.

Roberto Di Pietro [15]—This paper portrays a probabilistic model and two conventions to build up a protected pairwise correspondence channel between any pair of sensors in the WSN, by appointing a little arrangement of arbitrary keys to every sensor.

A. Liu [16]—This paper reports the test assessment of TinyECC on a few basic sensor stages, including MICAz, Tmote Sky, and Imotel. The assessment results demonstrate the effects of individual advancements on the execution time and asset utilizations.

Ben Othman, S. [17]—The reason for this paper is to introduce our starting exertion in building an adaptable system to accomplish secure information transmission in therapeutic remote sensor systems.

A. C. Jayasudha [18]—In this paper, exploiting so as to group-based restricted expectation plan is proposed spatial and fleeting connection to have precise information collection and vitality effective system.

Jun Zhao [19]—This work shows that the number of nodes with an arbitrary degree asymptotically converges to a Poisson distribution, presenting the asymptotic probability distribution for the minimum node degree of the network.

4 Proposed Algorithmic Steps

```
1. Initialize WSN[n] => Array of Sensor Nodes {n<reqdNodesRandom} in the
   Simulation Scenario
2. Energy Vector[k] Initialization and Activation
      a. EV[i] Vector is associated with each sensor node. EV[i] shall be
         investigated before and after vampire attack.
3. Activation of Mobile Nodes and Network Communication
4. Set Source SRC and Destination DEST nodes
5. LGPS := Location Sensor Investigates the Location from Satellite
6. Initialize l=random rounds () [Random Rounds Activated]
7. Initiate and Generate a Vampire Node Vi
8. for (v=0;v<=si;v++)   [si -> Simulation Iterations]
      a. Create TS -> TimeStamp Module, LGPS -> Longitude/Latitude of the
         Sensor Node, Generate the Dynamic Hash Key with LGPS,
         Communication starts, KeyMatching for SRC and DEST
      b. if (KeyMatch = True)
            Communication Successful
         else
            Packet Drop [Unsuccessful Matching deemed as Vampire]
9. Calculate MV[WSN[i][j]) Movement and Energy Vector
10.     Update EV [Energy Vector]
11.     Measure Energy Vector of Each Node
12.     If (EV <> OptimalSolution) Then Recursion Occurs and Retransmit
   the Packets
13.     Generate Vectors of Energy Consumed, Energy Throughput and related
   parameters
```

5 Implementation, Results, and Discussion

We have simulated the following scenarios in MATLAB for the implementation of vampire attacks avoidance using GPS sensor locators and timestamp-based key generation. It is found in the results that the overall integrity and reliability are improved and battery power consumption is huge (Figs. 4 and 5; Table 1).

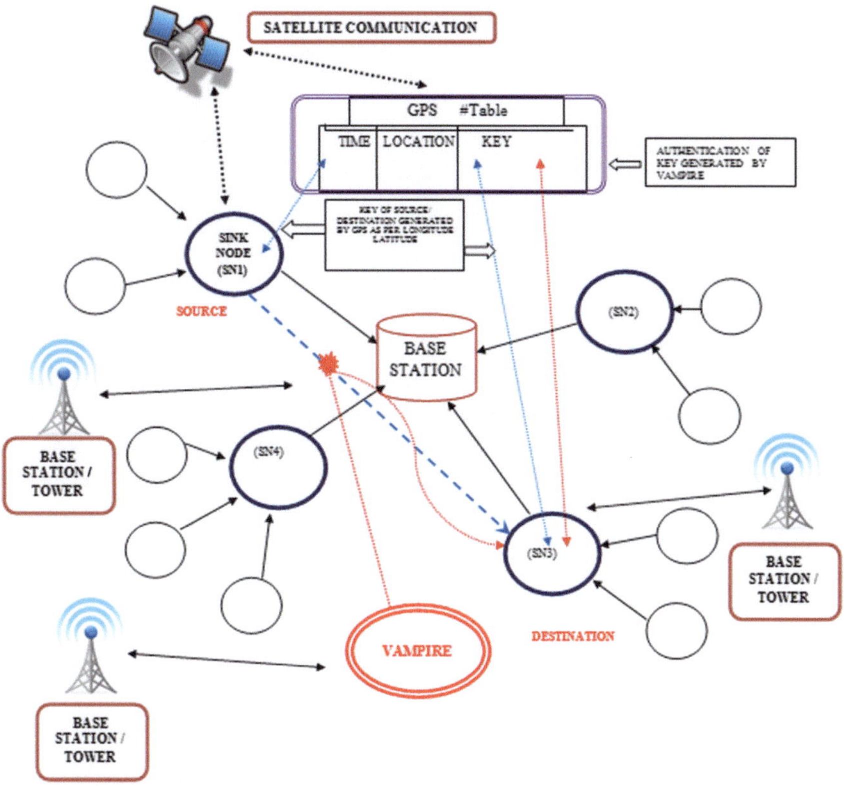

Fig. 4 Proposed model for avoidance of vampire attacks in wireless sensor networks

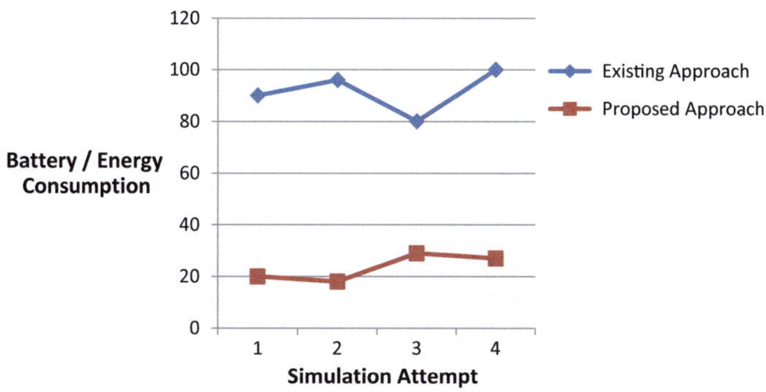

Fig. 5 Comparison between and classical and proposed in terms of energy consumption

Table 1 Energy consumed in the classical and proposed approach

Number of wireless nodes	Existing approach	Proposed approach	Simulation iterations
50	90	20	10
50	96	18	20
20	80	29	50
20	100	27	50

6 Conclusion

In the proposed work, to avoid and detract the vampire attacks, an effective location-based identifier is integrated in the network that will generate a dynamic key based on the GPS location and current timestamp. Using this approach, the genuine packets shall not be lost. The packet loss is associated with the malicious node. In the simulation scenario, the overall integrity and reliability of the network are improved using the proposed algorithmic approach.

References

1. Vasserman EY, Hopper N (2013) Vampire attacks: draining life from wireless ad hoc sensor networks. IEEE Trans Mob Comput 12(2):318–332
2. Vijayanand G, Muralidharan R (2014) Overcome vampire attacks problem in wireless ad-hoc sensor network by using distance vector protocols. Int J Comput Sci Mob Appl 2(1):115–120
3. Manimala S, Devapriya AT (2014) Detection of vampre attack using EWMA in wireless ad hoc sensor networks. IJISET Int J Innovative Sci Eng Technol 1(3):450–550
4. Khanna MMR, Divya S, Rengarajan A (2007) Securing data packets from vampire attacks in wireless ad-hoc sensor network. Int J Innov Res Comput Commun Eng 2 (An ISO 3297: 2007 Certified Organization)
5. Kaul S, Samuel H, Anand J (2014) Defending against vampire attacks in wireless sensor networks. Int J Commun Eng Appl IJCEA 5, Artical C084, March
6. Anand J, Sivachanda K (2014) Vampire attack detection in wireless sensor network. Int J Eng Sci Innov Technol (IJESIT), 3(4), July
7. Channawar PM, Chavan YV (2015) Vampire attack: energy efficient trust based solution. 3 (7), July
8. Chandekar MRS, Nayyar V (2014) Defending against energy draining attack in ad-hoc sensing network. 1(V1), November
9. Chumble MSC, Ghonge MM, Mitigation of vampire attack in wireless ad-hoc sensor network
10. Guptha NS, Lavanya NL, Detection and mitigation of vampire attacks in wireless ad-hoc sensor networks
11. Raikar MR (2014) Prevention of vampire attacks to control routing behavior in wireless ad hoc sensor networks
12. Du R, Chen C, Yang B, Lu N, Guan X, Shen X (2015) Effective urban traffic monitoring by vehicular sensor networks. IEEE Trans Vehicul Technol 64(1):273–286
13. Karlof C, Wagner D (2003) Secure routing in wireless sensor networks: attacks and countermeasures. Ad hoc networks 1(2–3):293–315

14. Du W, Deng J, Han YS, Chen S, Varshney PK (2004). A key management scheme for wireless sensor networks using deployment knowledge. In: INFOCOM 2004. Twenty-third Annual Joint Conference of the IEEE computer and communications societies (vol 1). IEEE, March
15. Conti M, Di Pietro R, Mancini L, Mei A (2011) Distributed detection of clone attacks in wireless sensor networks. IEEE T Depen Sec Comput 8(5):685–698
16. Liu A, Ning P (2008) TinyECC: A configurable library for elliptic curve cryptography in wireless sensor networks. In: Proceedings of the 7th international conference on Information processing in sensor networks (pp 245–256). IEEE Computer Society, April
17. Othman SB, Bahattab AA, Trad A, Youssef H (2014) Secure data transmission protocol for medical wireless sensor networks. In: Advanced Information Networking and Applications (AINA), 2014 IEEE 28th International Conference on (pp 649–656). IEEE, May
18. Jayasudha AC, Venkatesh V (2014) Energy competent cluster based prediction framework for wireless sensor network
19. Zhao J, Yagan O, Gligor V (2014) On topological properties of wireless sensor networks under the q-composite key pre-distribution scheme with on/off channels. In: Information Theory (ISIT), 2014 IEEE International Symposium on (pp 1131–1135). IEEE, June

Dr. S. N. Panda was born in Odisha, India, in 19/08/1969. He received the B.Sc (Hons.) with distinction from Sambalpur University, Odisha (India) and the M.Sc and Ph.D. degree in Computer Science and Engineering from Kurukshetra University, Kurukshetra, Haryana (India).

Data Security Model in Cloud Computing Environment

Meena Kumari and Rajender Nath

Abstract Cloud computing (CC) has emerged as the next generation of computing in IT Enterprise. Earlier, IT services are under proper physical and personnel control, CC migrates the application softwares and databases to the huge data centers, where the management of data along with services is done by the cloud provider. However, this characteristic poses many security challenges which have not been well understood. This paper focuses on security of data at cloud storage, which has always been a most important issue in CC security. Many approaches have been proposed to protect data in cloud which are not sufficient to meet the requirements of a cloud user. So in this paper, a model for data security at cloud storage site has been proposed.

Keywords Confidentiality · Integrity · Availability · Protection
Priority

1 Introduction

Cloud computing (CC) is a general term refers to outsourcing of hosted services and computing resources over the Internet. Here, resources refer to network resources, virtualized servers, platforms, computing infrastructures, etc. Business professionals routinely face several business-related problems. CC adopts concepts from service-oriented architecture (SOA) that can help the business professionals to outsource resources and application software's in the form of services. CC provides its resources as services using well-established standards and best practices to allow on-demand and broad network access to cloud services.

M. Kumari (✉) · R. Nath
Department of Computer Science and Applications,
Kurukshetra University, Kurukshetra, Haryana, India
e-mail: sanger.meena@gmail.com

R. Nath
e-mail: rnath@kuk.ac.in

M. U. Bokhari et al. (eds.), *Cyber Security*, Advances in Intelligent Systems and Computing 729, https://doi.org/10.1007/978-981-10-8536-9_10

Various Internet-based online services like Amazon EC2, Amazon S3, etc., do provide tremendous amounts of storage space and computing resources. Storing data into the cloud storage offers great advantage to its tenants since they do not have to worry about the complexities involved in management of hardware or software. Since all the data maintenance tasks are done by cloud storage provider, this eliminates the burden of local machines. Although CC is a promising service platform for the Internet technologies, this new computing environment brings about many challenging issues which had profound influence on its adoption. One of the biggest issues is cloud data storage security. As the amount of data is growing, as are the growing need for security. Biggest concerns with cloud data storage is that of data integrity, confidentiality, and availability at untrusted servers.

The main aim of this paper is to extend/improve the existing three-dimensional algorithms [1, 2]. Prasad et al. [1] had not included integrity constraint in their proposed formula for classification and data stored on cloud storage is not in encrypted form. Authors titled their work as three-dimensional but only two dimensions (confidentiality and availability) were involved in their proposed work. In [2], there was no mechanism for addressing the issue of data integrity and user authorization is done by the cloud provider, due to which there was data owner's loss of control issue. This paper is an attempt to overcome these limitations.

The rest of the paper is organized as follows. Section 2 summarizes related work, Sect. 3 provides the detailed motivation behind this work and Sect. 4 discusses the data security model for cloud, Sect. 5 provides a comparative analysis of proposed technique with the existing techniques and Sect. 6 gives some concluding remarks.

2 Related Work

Kulkarni et al. [3] had proposed a CC framework which works in two phases namely data classification and 3D accessibility. During data classification phase, user's data is classified based on CIA (Confidentiality, Integrity, and Availability) parameters specified by the user during storage. After classification and using their proposed formula, the priority rating of data is computed. The data having higher rating is considered as critical and hence 3D security is recommended for that data. In accessibility phase, authors had used OTP and two-factor password techniques to avoid data leakage and impersonation. The author does not provide basis for proposed formula and value of integrity constraint is not used anywhere in the proposed formula.

Prasad et al. [1] and Deokar et al. [4] had proposed the similar technique for classification of data as proposed in [3]. After classification of data in [1], the user who wants to retrieve data needs to register first and for every data access user's identity is authenticated for certain authorizations whereas in [4], different password scheme for distinct category of data were proposed. Same problems were identified in the proposed work as in [3] along with the limitation that the data stored at cloud storage site is unencrypted form and if the username and password are compromised, the data can easily be retrieved by any malicious entity.

Wang et al. [5] had proposed a data integrity verification scheme using homomorphic token and erasure codes which facilitate the integrity checking of data stored at distributed sites. The proposed methodology also supports dynamic data operations of updation, insertion, and deletion. Their experimental analysis illustrates that the proposed scheme is secure against Byzantine failure and can identify inadvertent data modifications.

Wang et al. [6] had proposed to introduce a third-party auditor (TPA) to check the integrity of stored data on behalf of cloud user. The client leverages its few privileges to TPA to audit the correctness of its data due to lack of computational power. In prior works, most data integrity checking schemes fail to verify data correctness after performing data modification operations (update, insert, and delete). Their proposed scheme allows facility to check integrity of updated data also.

Lijo et al. [7] had presented a user-centric solution for data security. According to this scheme, a client agent is incorporated to manage the activities of data auditing on behalf of Cloud user. One of the main limitations of this scheme was that cloud provider's approval is required to incorporate client agent in cloud application. If there is lot of inter-cloud communications involved, then this solution could not be applied because it further requires consent of other cloud providers also. As data stored is in encrypted form, the client must be equipped with some computational power to do encryption and decryption tasks.

In [2], Tirodkar et al. had presented a scheme for data categorization as proposed in [1], and afterwards, for different category of data a distinct user authentication scheme was used.

3 Motivation

In the work done by Prasad et al. [1], the following limitations were observed. They had calculated criticality rating of data on the basis of values passed by user for respective CIA parameters. The proposed formula was $s[i] = (C[i] + (A[i] * 10)/2$, which do not incorporate integrity parameter. They had also not provided any basis to derive formula. Further data stored at cloud storage site is in unencrypted form and if the username and password are lost, the data could easily be accessed by any malicious user. The formula is supposed to derive CIA parameters in order to be called as three-dimensional but formula uses two parameters of confidentiality and availability only. In the work done by Tirodkar et al. [2], they implemented three different user authentication mechanisms for different categories of data but there is no provision for addressing the issue of data integrity. Once data is stored at cloud storage, data owner lost its control over it and cloud storage provider can manage data leakage to help rival parties.

4 Proposed Data Security Model for Clouds

To address the limitations mentioned in Sect. 3, this paper presents a model for data security for effective data security in CC. The paper presents improved mechanism of data handling. The improved technique works in three phases—categorization, storage, and retrieval. In the following sections, abovementioned phases were discussed in detail.

4.1 Categorization Phase

As all data sent to the cloud for storage is not equally sensitive, hence a uniform level of security is not advantageous. Therefore, the data should be categorized based upon the level of its sensitivity.

When a client wants to upload data for storage in the cloud, he has to provide the values of confidentiality (C), integrity (I), and availability (A) parameters in the scale of 1–10. The value of C parameter is based on extent of secrecy required, value of I parameter is based degree of assurance of accuracy is needed and value of A is based on how often data is accessed.

The sensitivity rating of the data is computed using the following equation:

$$\mathrm{SR}[x] = (C[x] + (1/A[x]) * 10 + I[x])/2 \tag{1}$$

Depending upon the value of SR, data are classified into three categories—public, confidential, and sensitive. If SR value lies between 1 and 3 (1 and 3 inclusive) then data is labeled as public. If SR value lies between 4 and 6 (4 and 6 inclusive) then data is labeled as confidential and if SR value is greater than 6 then data is labeled as sensitive.

Algorithm for Categorization of Data

```
1. Input: D[ ] of n integer size /*data to be uploaded on cloud for storage*/,
   C [ ],                        /*Confidentiality Parameter value*/
   I [ ],                        /*Integrity Parameter value */
   A [ ]                         /*Availability Parameter value */

2. For x = 1 to n                          /* n is the no. of data sets*/
        SR[x] = (C[x] + (1/A[x])*10 + I[x])/2
                         /*data security and confidentiality are directly
             proportional to integrity and data security is inversely
             proportional to availability [5]*/
      IF (SR[x] > = 1 OR SR[x] < = 3)
                  Data_Label[x] = "Public"
      ELSEIF (SR[x] > = 4 OR SR[x] < = 6)
```

```
                        Data_Label[x] = "Confidential"
        ELSE
                    Data_Label[x] = "Sensitive"
        End If
    End For
3. Output: D [ ], Data_Label [].
```

4.2 Storage Phase

After the data is categorized successfully, it has to undergo another processing mechanism for storage. Figure 1 shows the categories of data along with the kind of security approach applied at the cloud storage. Public data require minimal security hence can be secured using login id and password. Confidential data require moderate level of security hence it is secured by using both the mechanisms of encryption and user id and password. If data is labeled as sensitive then security level should be higher which is provided through encryption and MAC.

To keep a check on data integrity Message Authentication Code (MAC) is attached with the sensitive data. MAC is basically a Hash code which is appended to the message to have a check on the integrity of data during transmission. If data is tampered during transmission MAC will not match with the message and one can ascertain that data is corrupted. With the generation of MAC, the data owner now sends data to the cloud for storage as shown in Fig. 2.

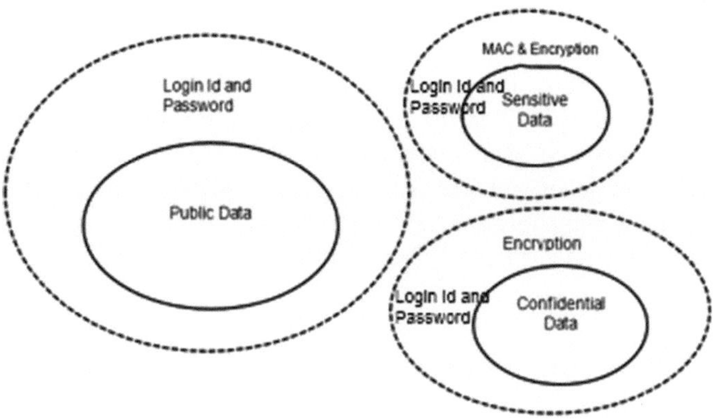

Fig. 1 Security mechanisms for different category of data

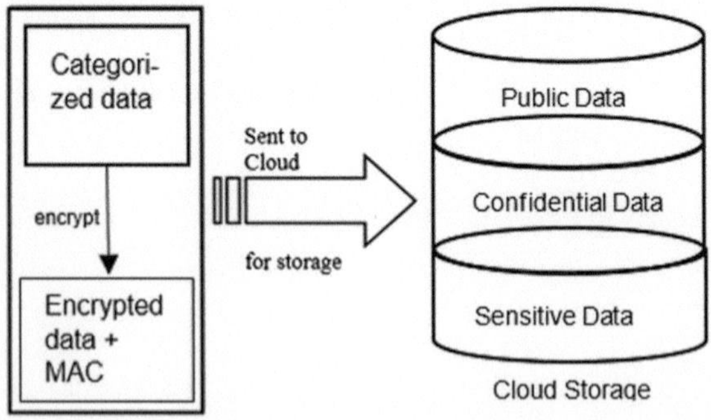

Fig. 2 Data sent to cloud for storage

4.3 Retrieval Phase

After successful storage of data by cloud provider, there must be secure procedures for retrieval as well. When a user wants to retrieve data, it has to make a request to cloud storage provider and needs to register with the owner/organization. After successful registration user gets a username and a password. This generated username and password are necessary for retrieval of data and at the same time this username is forwarded to cloud storage to store into its directory for future transactions.

Table 1 shows the authentication mechanism for a client to have access to a different category of data [2] depending upon the sensitivity level as characterized by categorization phase.

The following paragraphs discuss the mechanism of retrieval of data belonging to different categories, viz., public, confidential, and sensitive.

a. **Retrieval of Public Data**
   When a user wants to retrieve data which belongs to public data category then user has to register itself if he is already not registered.
   User has to send a request along with its registered username to have access to data. The cloud provider first checks in, to which category requested data belongs. The cloud provider first checks the username into its stored directory, if the username does not match with any entry it asks the user for registration. If the username matches with one entry in directory then it redirects the request to data owner for authentication as depicted in Fig. 3. After successful authentication, user will be allowed to access public data.

Table 1 User authentication mechanisms

S. No.	Data sensitivity	Authentication mechanism
1	Public data	Password
2	Confidential data	Graphical password
3	Sensitive data	E-mail or SMS one-time password (OTP)

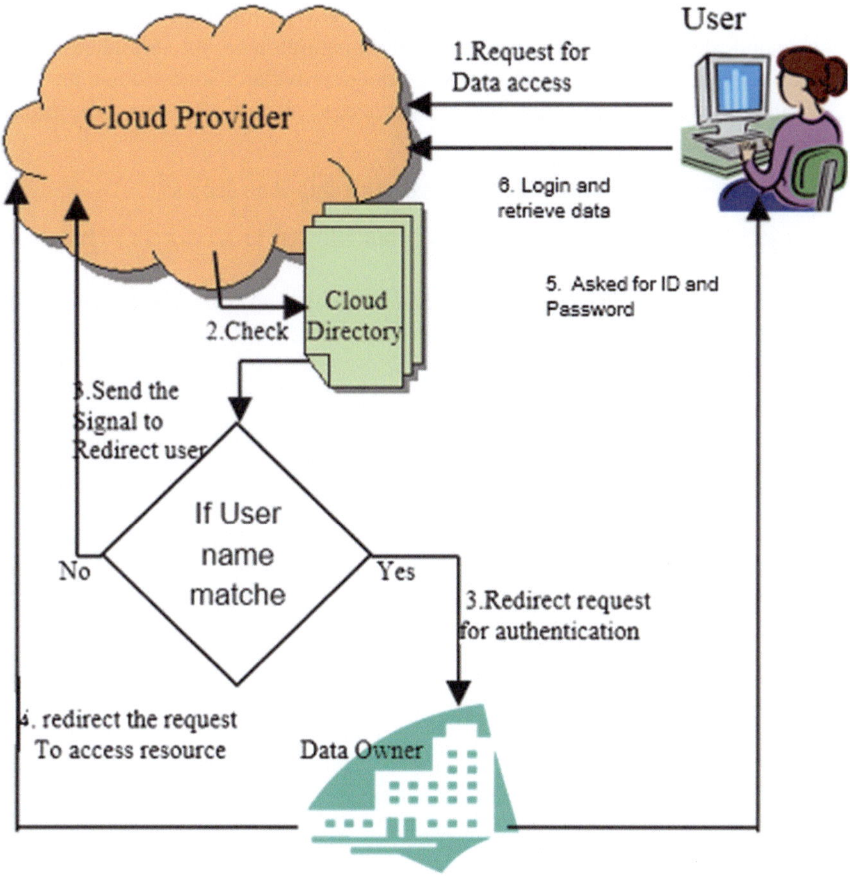

Fig. 3 Retrieval process for public data

b. **Retrieval of Confidential Data**
For retrieval of confidential data, user is authenticated using graphical password [2]. After successful authentication, data owner first sends associated decryption key to the user and redirects cloud provider to allow access to a particular user. Encrypted data is sent to the user by cloud storage provider. Using decryption key user can decrypt data. After this, the user would be able to access data.

c. **Retrieval of Sensitive Data**
For retrieval of sensitive data, user is authenticated using one-time password (OTP) through E-mail or SMS [2, 3]. Afterwards data owner send MAC digital signature and decryption key to the user and redirects cloud storage provider to allow access. Decryption keys and digital signature associated with data were kept secret by the data owner itself and issued to user after successful authentication without cloud service provider intervention. Even if data is compromised, it cannot be used as it is encrypted and cloud provider does not have the

decryption keys and associated digital signature. User transmits digital signature to cloud storage provider. These digital signatures also act as authentication means to authenticate the user to cloud storage provider. Cloud storage provider verifies the digital signature and allows access to data. By using the issued decryption key user can access data.

The following guidelines were followed regarding data access:

- A user granted access on public data is not allowed to access confidential and sensitive data.
- A user granted access on sensitive data is allowed to access confidential and public data.

5 Comparison with Existing Approaches

The latest two approaches reported in the literature are [1] and [2]. The proposed approach is compared with the existing two approaches proposed by Prasad et al. [1] and Tirodkar et al. [2]. The comparison has been made on the following parameters—identification and authentication, confidentiality, integrity, availability, non-repudiation, encryption, and security if user identity and password are compromised and security from cloud provider.

The comparison shows that the proposed model fulfills all the parameters listed in Table 2, while Prasad et al. [1] approach fulfills only four parameters and Tirodkar et al. [2] fulfills only five parameters.

Table 2 Comparative analysis

Functionality	Prasad et al. [1]	Tirodkar et al. [2]	Proposed work (2015)
Identification and authentication	Yes	Yes	Yes
Confidentiality	Yes	Yes	Yes
Integrity	No	No	Yes
Availability	Yes	Yes	Yes
Encryption	No	Optional	Yes
Non-repudiation	Yes	Yes	Yes
Secure if user identity and password is compromised	No	No	Yes
Security from cloud provider	No	No	Yes

6 Conclusion

This paper has presented a data security model based on the data sensitivity level. The model has classified the entire data to be stored in the cloud into three categories—public, confidential, and sensitive. Depending upon the category, different kinds of security mechanisms are applied. The proposed model has been compared with the existing two approaches and has been found much better than other approaches. In addition, as the user authentication is done by the data owner itself, it mitigates the issue of loss of control to a much extent and data owner can keep track of who has accessed its data.

References

1. Prasad P et al (2011) 3 Dimensional security in cloud computing. In: 3rd International conference on computer research and development, pp 198–201
2. Tirodkar S et al (2014) Improved 3-Dimensional security in cloud computing. Int J Comput Trends Technol (IJCTT) 9(5)
3. Kulkarni DA et al (2013) 3 Dimensional security in cloud computing. Int J Adv Comput Theory Eng (IJACTE) 2(2)
4. Deokar V et al (2013) Password generation techniques for accessing cloud services. Int J Inventive Eng Sci (IJIES) 1(1)
5. Wang C et al (2009) Ensuring data storage security in cloud computing. In: IEEE 17th International workshop on quality of service (IWQoS 2009), pp 1–9
6. Q Wang et al (2011) Enabling public auditability and data dynamics for storage security in cloud computing. IEEE Trans Parallel Distrib Syst 22(5):847–858
7. Lijo VP et al (2011) Cloud computing privacy issues and user-centric solution. In: ICIP 2011, Springer, pp 448–456
8. Carvalho FD et al (2006) Cyberwar-netwar: security in the information age. In: Network security through science series D: information and communication security, vol 4, p 70

Author Biographies

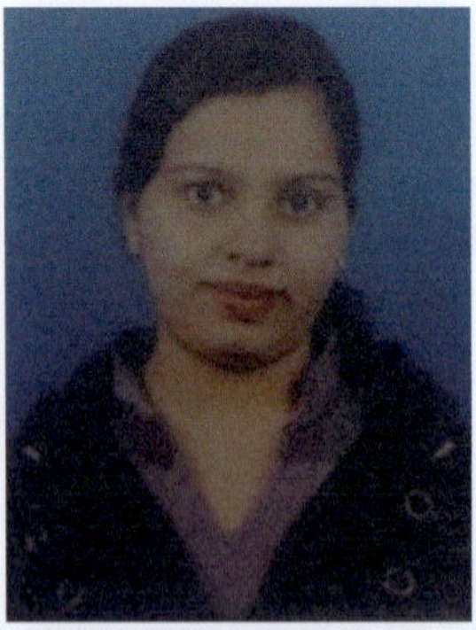

Meena Kumari received her MCA degree from Kurukshetra University, Kurukshetra, Haryana, India in 2012. She is pursuing her Ph.D. degree in Computer Science from the department of computer science and applications of Kurukshetra University, Kurukshetra. Currently she is teaching as an assistant professor in Kurukshetra University. Her research area include Cloud Computing Security, Hashing, Cryptography and Networking.

Rajender Nath is working as a Professor in the Department of Computer Science and Applications of Kurukshetra University, Kurukshetra, Haryana, India. His areas of specialization includes Computer Architecture, Object Oriented Modelling & Programming, UML, Cloud Computing, Search Engines, Biometrics, and Security in MANETS.

Review of CIDS and Techniques of Detection of Malicious Insiders in Cloud-Based Environment

Priya Oberoi and Sumit Mittal

Abstract Cloud computing has gained an extreme importance nowadays. Every organization is getting attracted toward the Cloud computing due to its attractive features like cost saving, adaptability, etc. Although it offers the attractive features but still Cloud threats need great consideration. The insider threat is critically challenging in the Cloud-based environments. In order to mitigate from insider attacks in Clouds, the use of Intrusion detection system (IDS) is quite challenging. Every type of IDS has different methods of attack detection. So, single IDS cannot guarantee the protection from all types of attacks. Thus, in this paper, we have studied the various types of IDS and their features which made them either suitable or unsuitable for cloud computing. Also on the basis of review, required features for the Cloud-based IDS are identified.

Keywords Intrusion detection system · Cloud computing · Cloud security CIDS

1 Introduction

In recent times, the IT infrastructure is outsourced by the companies to the Cloud in order to get the benefits offered by the Clouds like scalability, rapid provisioning, and reduced cost. In spite of the advantages offered by Clouds, security in general and malicious insider threats in particular has been the most critical area of concern of the organizations. Thus, gaining the trust of the Cloud users' security from the insider threats is important to achieve [1, 2]. The traditional mechanisms of intrusion detection are not flexible enough to manage with the needs of Clouds,

P. Oberoi (✉) · S. Mittal
M.M. Institute of Computer Technology & Business Management, Maharishi Markandeshwar (Deemed to be University), Mullana, Ambala, Haryana, India
e-mail: priya.hrt@gmail.com

S. Mittal
e-mail: sumit.mittal@mmumullana.org

M. U. Bokhari et al. (eds.), *Cyber Security*, Advances in Intelligent Systems and Computing 729, https://doi.org/10.1007/978-981-10-8536-9_11

such as frequent changes in infrastructure. In this paper, we study the problem of insider threats within the domain of Cloud computing. Also, we have studied the various intrusion detection systems available for the Cloud environments and identified the characteristics which are offered by the existing systems and the needs for the future improvements.

2 Cloud Computing: A Security Perspective

The security remains the biggest issue in Cloud computing, as Cloud provides services which are located on a remote location and it is the trust of consumer on Cloud service providers that their data will be secured. The integrity and confidentiality of the user's data are at risk as they do not have physical control over the data [3]. This is because of the fact that the Cloud server is at different location and client is located at different locations. Therefore, the server cannot be trusted completely for managing details of users and access rights. The data of user is at risk due to insider attacks or compromised servers. This can be overcome if the users trust Cloud service providers to secure and properly manage their data [4]. Due to the fact that the insiders are very well familiar with the infrastructure, procedures of operation and terms and conditions of the organization the attack of malicious insiders are more severe [4]. Insider attacks are done by malicious employees at any location, i.e., provider's or user's. The attacks caused by the insiders have an adverse effect on the trust of the Cloud user on the provider. Passwords, cryptographic keys, and files can easily obtained by the malicious insider. These attackers not only damage the financial value but also the reputation of an organization [4].

3 Intrusion Detection System (IDS)

Intrusion detection is the process of monitoring computers or networks for unauthorized entry, activity, or file modification.

3.1 Classification of IDS According to Source of Data [5, 6]

1. **Host-based intrusion detection system (HIDS)**: in which sensors are responsible for detecting intrusions. Intrusions are found on single host. These operate on host side and monitors as well as detects malicious activities in system calls, application logs, etc.
2. **Network intrusion detection systems (NIDS)**: sensors are focused on network segment only. NIDS monitor the attacks in networks and detect the variation in the transmissions in the networks.

3. **Distributed intrusion detection systems (DIDS)**: combine both the types of sensors. It further has three types: (a) Mobile agent IDS (MA-IDS), (b) Grid-based IDS (GIDS), and (c) Cloud-based IDS (CIDS).

3.2 Limitations of Various IDSs

HIDS cannot be used as attackers may not leave traces in the operating system of the host where the IDS are residing. NIDS cannot detect the attack if the communication is encrypted. In clouds, distinct users share various resources. The attacks can migrate from and be intended for any of the Cloud resources. Thus only DIDs can be used. But, the challenges in the adoption of the DIDS in Clouds are (i) Distinct types of users and user requirements; (ii) Complex architecture; and (iii) Different requirement of security. MA-based IDS are not suitable as (i) Hierarchical structure poses problem of reliability and scalability, and (ii) Not flexible to protect from the attacks on IDS itself. GIDS are not suitable as (i) Every service model (SaaS, IaaS and PaaS) has different set of threats, users, and requirements; (ii) Clouds are highly scalable; (iii) GIDS solution cannot correlate the alerts from the different nodes; (iv) Performance and load balancing are needed more in Clouds than Grid [6].

4 Literature Review

Rule-based learning for the identification of insiders and a solution for the detection of wrong insider activities have been given by the authors [7]. Some of the threats identified include insecure shared technology vulnerabilities, application programming interfaces, and malicious insiders. When an attack occurs, machine learning techniques are used to raise an alarm. The seven common activities of the insiders are (Table 1):

For activity classification purposes, the following machine learning techniques are used (Table 2).

It has been found by the analysis that decision tree C4.5 and multilayer perception are better for activity classification in Cloud-based environment. The result of the confusion matrix reveals C4.5 as the best classifier.

Authors in [8] have used technique of multithreading for improving the performance of the IDS. NIDS proposed sensitizes as well as monitors the network traffic using the sensors. In this model, the Cloud user accesses the remote servers over the Cloud network. The monitoring and logging of the requests and the actions of the user are done by a multi-threaded NIDS, which has large data handling capacity and also reduces the packet loss.

Table 1 Common activities of insiders

S. No.	Activity
1	No activity
2	Reboot physical machine
3	Malicious insider cloning
4	Malicious insider copying everything from a VM
5	Malicious insider taking snapshots of VM
6	Installing new guest VM on the same physical hardware
7	Turn on any guest VM on to same physical hardware

Table 2 Machine learning techniques

S. No.	Technique	Basis
1	Naive Bayes	Probability-based technique
2	Multilayer Perception	Function estimated based technique
3	Support Vector Machine	
4	Decision Tree	Rule-based technique
5	PART	

A combined approach for malware detection and root kit prevention used in [9] in virtualized Cloud environment. The IDS is intended to execute on VM instances with a backend Cloud to share out malware scanning operations among numerous back ends. Flexible, distributed security solution is given with a minimal overall resource footprint on the end host. The traditional signature checks are performed for the detection of known as all as the novel malware. An integrity check of authorized Kernel modules is given which can prevent the installation of root kits through the corrupted kernel modules. This approach is easy to maintain as only change is to be made in the kernel of the system. Infrastructural security is focused not the attacks against VM monitors.

Authors [5] in their research presented a review of various methods and tools used for detection and prevention of intruders in Cloud computing. Four concepts for the development of the CIDS identified are (a) automatic computing; (b) oncology; (c) risk management; and (d) fuzzy theory. The taxonomy gives two layers functional layer and structural layer. The requirements identified for CIDPS on the basis of review are (i) large-scale handling of multi tiered autonomous computing and data processing environments; (ii) detection of variety of attacks with least positive rates; (iii) super fast detection and prevention; (iv) self-adaptive automatically; (v) CIDPS Scalability; (vi) deterministic; (vii) synchronization of autonomous CIDPS; (viii) resistance to compromise. A Cloud intrusion detection and prevention system which meets all the requirements is considered to be good one.

A framework of CIDS is presented in [6], which has a module to review the alerts and notify the administrator of the Cloud. The features identified are (i) point-to-point solution which is applicable to various platforms and expandable; (ii) as there is no central coordinator, so single point of failure is not there; (iii) distribution of processing to different Cloud locations protects the CIDS from the threats which can organize a job in the VM and alter its workings if it was executed in monitored VM; (iv) installing middleware where the framework resides increases the flexibility and portability; (v) it uses knowledge base combined with the behavior base which increases attack coverage; (vi) every node has audit system for monitoring of the messages and logging. It gives the benefit that every node has the capability to detect the masqueraders. The following three models have been given as CIDS detection models:

1. **Audit Exchange Model (Model A)**: The nodes Cloud swap over audit data. It has high detection efficiency and the low survival of the masquerader. Its limitations include need of rapid cyclic updates of audit data at the CNs.
2. **Audit Exchange Model with a neural network (Model B)**: Combines model A to neural networks. It offers the benefit of less survival of masquerader than Model A and C. Also the hit rate is high with lower false positive and false negative alarms than Model A and C. Other than limitations of model A; it has a limitation of low performance due to overhead to update neural network.
3. **The Independent Model (Model C)**: Every node of Cloud calculates its own audit data without swapping data with Cloud nodes. The benefits offered are no need of periodic update and less burden for Cloud network, as no swapping of data is there. Also there are low processing overheads than model A and C. Limitations include longer survival of masquerader than model A & B and low hit rate than model B as neural cannot be used.

The applications of the three proposed models are to be done to find the best one. Also the summarizer and parser algorithms are to be parallelized in order to reduce the corresponding overhead.

An Insider threat detection model to detect despiteful insiders has been proposed in [10]. An observational system to test this possibility was implemented to sustain the applicability in a SaaS Cloud deployment model. This method uses the sequential rule mining approach to discover malicious utilization patterns for a particular profile.

Authors in [11] have given an ICAS (IDS Cloud analysis system). MapReduce algorithm of Hadoop is used for the analysis of intrusion detection system in log files. It creates a user-friendly output view in which user can easily and clearly monitor the behavior of the attack. In experimental study, it has been found that the calculation speed is increased by 80%. IDP8200, NK7 Admin and Snort logs are used as ICAS analysis object record in this paper. The main advantage of ICAS is the scalability and reliability offered by it. ICAS can be improved for the processing large-scale data.

A framework which is an open source solution has been given in [12]. APIs and interfaces are given which are used in the development of the security components in a distributed manner and building of customized event correlation rules. The framework consists of a collection of components which are organized in a hierarchical manner. The three main components of the framework are probes, agents, and security engines.

According to the three architectural layers, the security engines are organized in a hierarchical manner. At the lowest layer, the raw security data collected by the security engines. It can be offered by the Cloud provider as service which includes IDSs; Log analyzers; and specific security mechanisms provided by the Cloud platform. It is the responsibility of the Cloud provider, at the higher level, to enable additional IDSs and attack them to independent VMs. The provider is able to recognize the compromised virtual components of the clients by correlating the information provided by the higher layer with the data collected by the lower layer. Attack Evaluation Tree (AET) is used to represent the attack in a tree like structure. The goal of the attacker is the root node while the access path is through the offsprings.

Authors in the research [13] introduced three concrete MI attacks with a proof of concept implementation based on existing tools. Three introduced MI attacks in this paper are: memory scanning, template poisoning, and snapshot cracking.

Authors [14] described the differences between the traditional insider and insider in the Cloud. The two types of insider threats identified in Cloud computing, viz., (a) at the Cloud providers end, and (b) at the Cloud clients end. Both have different set of problems and area of attacks. The countermeasures of the insider threat in the Cloud provider are:-At client side: Cryptographic techniques, geo-redundancy are used; and At provider side: Separation of duties, logging, legal binding, and insider detection models. The problems in various methods are: (a) IDS/IPS: in IaaS host-based IDS can be used, (b) Separation of duties: As in Clouds, same person has multiple roles, it is difficult to implement it in Clouds; (c) Attack origin identification: (i) In case of Clouds, the access is usually done by some remote computer. So there are no physical evidence for the attack, only digital evidence like IP etc can be used and (ii) In case of shared credentials, it is difficult to fix the responsibly; (d) Single point of failure and data leakage: Access to console of administrator can cause heavy loss of that, that without any sign of intrusion. The countermeasures of the insider threat in the Cloud outsourcer are (a) At client side: Log auditing, host-based IDS/IPS are used and (b) At provider side: Anomaly detection, separation of duties, and multifactor authentication are used.

5 Comparative Study

The various techniques being used for the detection of the intruders revealed by review are proactive forensics, graph-based analysis, honey pots (based on network sensors), IDS (based on network sensors), system call analysis (host based user profiling), command sequences and windows usage events, file system, memory, I/O, and hardware monitoring, metrics about user sophistication (Usage Anomalies), insider threat specification language, knowledge graphs, customized minimal attack trees, technological, social and educational and psychological parameters [15–21].

Selecting the best one is quite challenging. The characteristics desired in a CIDS are (i) Scalable and distributed IDS for Clouds without the failure points, (ii) Combination of Knowledge base and behavior base in order to detect the known as well as the unknown attacks with reasonable false alarm rates, (iii) Avoid single point of failure, (iv) the IDS should be protected from the attacks by isolating it, (v) flexible architecture, (vi) take into consideration various service models and requirements of user, (vii) dynamic policies as the security needs of each VM are varied, (viii) reduction in data transfer cost by reducing the network bandwidth, (ix) easy to adapt.

6 Future Scope

In this paper, we studied the insider attacks in the Cloud-based environments. An insider can easily attack in the Cloud environment. The effect of the attack is more severe than the traditional environments. Also the entity that physically performed the attack is difficult to detect and identify. The literature review has revealed the fact that in order to secure Cloud environment from the insiders a new insider prediction and detection models is needed. Also to evade the false estimations and generate correct user profiling new CIDS is required. Moreover, it appears that there is an adorning necessity for developing transparent network in Clouds. Also application intrusion detection systems (IDS) for Clouds are required. These systems can be given as a service to their clients who want to protect their infrastructure which has been outsourced. In future, model for predicting and detecting insider threats will be developed.

References

1. https://en.wikipedia.org/wiki/Cloud_computing
2. Forrester-2012, Cloud survey. http://www.bmc.com/industryanalysts/reports/forrester-2012-cloud-survey.html (accessed May 2012)
3. Yusop ZM, Abawajy JH (2014) Analysis of insiders attack mitigation strategies. Procedia Soc Behav Sci 129:581–591
4. Ren K, Wang C, Wang Q (2012) Security challenges for the public cloud. IEEE Internet Comput 16(1):69–73. https://doi.org/10.1109/MIC.2012.14
5. Patel A, Taghavi M, Bakhtiyari K, Júnior JC (2013) An intrusion detection and prevention system in cloud computing: a systematic review. J Netw Comput Appl 36(1):25–41

6. Kholidy HA, Baiardi F (2012) CIDS: a framework for intrusion detection in cloud, systems. In: 2012 ninth international conference on information technology—new Generations, 978-0-7695-4654-4/12 $26.00 © 2012 IEEE
7. Khorshed MT, Ali ABMS, Wasimi SA (2011) Monitoring insiders activities in cloud computing using rule based learning. In: IEEE 10th international conference on trust, security and privacy in computing and communications (TrustCom-2011), 16–18 Nov 2011
8. Gul I, Hussain M (2011) Distributed cloud intrusion detection model. Int J Adv Sci Technol 34
9. Schmidt M, Baumgartner L, Graubner P, Bock D, Freisleben B (2011) Malware detection and kernel rootkit prevention in cloud computing environments. In: 19th Euromicro international conference on parallel, distributed and network-based processing (PDP-2011), pp 603–610, 9–11 Feb 2011
10. Nkosi L, Tarwireyi P, Adigun M (2013) Insider threat detection model for the cloud. 978-1-4799-0808-0/13/$31.00 ©2013 IEEE
11. Yang S-F, Chen W-Y, Wang Y-T (2011) ICAS: an inter-VM IDS log cloud analysis system. In: IEEE international conference on cloud computing and intelligence systems (CCIS-2011), 15–17 Sept 2011
12. Ficco M, Tasquier L, Aversa R (2013) Intrusion detection in cloud computing. In: 18th international conference on P2P, parallel, grid, cloud and internet computing (3PGCIC-2013), pp 276–283, 28–30 Oct 2013
13. Nguyen M-D, Chau N-T, Jung S, Jung S (2014) A demonstration of malicious insider attacks inside cloud IaaS vendor. Int J Inf Educ Technol 4(6). https://doi.org/10.7763/ijiet.2014.v4.455
14. Kandias M, Virvilis N, Gritzalis D (2013) The insider threat in cloud computing. In: Critical information infrastructure security. Lecture notes in computer science, vol 6983. Springer, Berlin, pp 93–103
15. Mehmood Y, Habiba U, Muhammad AS, Masood R (2013) Intrusion detection system in cloud computing: challenges and opportunities. In: 2nd national conference on information assurance (NCIA), pp 59–66, 978-1-4799-1288-9/13©2013 IEEE
16. Gupta S, Kumar P, Sardana A, Abraham A, A fingerprinting system calls approach for intrusion detection in cloud environment. In: 4th international conference computational aspects of social networks (CASoN-2012), published by IEEE, pp 309–314
17. Martinez-Moyano IJ, Rich E, Conrad S, Andersen DF, Stewart TR (2008) A behavioral theory of insider threat risks: a system dynamics approach. ACM Trans Modeling Comput Simul 18(2):7.1–7.27
18. Dileep Kumar G, Morarjee K (2014) Insider data theft detection using decoy and user behavior profile. Int J Res Comput Appl Robot 2(2):51–55. ISSN: 2320-7345. www.ijrcar.in
19. Young WT, Goldberg HG, Memory A, Sartain JF, Senator TE (2013) Use of domain knowledge to detect insider threats in computer activities. IEEE security and privacy workshops
20. Wongthai W, Rocha F, Van Moorsel A (2013) Logging solutions to mitigate risks associated with threats in infrastructure as a service cloud. In: International conference on cloud computing and big data, pp 163–170
21. Claycomb WR, Nicoll A (2012) Insider threats to cloud computing directions for new research challenges. In: Proceedings of the 2012 IEEE 36th annual computer software and applications conference, pp 387–394. IEEE Computer Society, Washington, DC, USA ©2012

Author Biographies

Ms. Priya Oberoi received her Master's degree from Maharishi Dayanad University, Rohtak. Presently, pursuing Ph.D. from M.M. (Deemed to be University), Mullana, Ambala, Haryana, India. She is working as Assistant Professor in Department of Computer Science, D.A.V Centenary College, Faridabad. She has 10 publications in International/National Journals and Conferences.

Dr. Sumit Mittal received his Ph.D. degree & Master's degree from Department of Computer Science & Applications, Kurukshetra University, Kurukshetra. Presently, he is working as Professor & Principal, M.M. Institute of Computer Technology & Business Management, M.M. (Deemed to be University), Mullana, Ambala, Haryana, India. He is a life member of Computer Society of India and member of various professional societies of India & Abroad. He is also a member of various academics bodies of M.M. University, Mullana. He has more than 35 publications in International/National Journals and Conferences. His research area includes Cloud Computing, Wireless communication and Distributed Environments.

DNA-Based Cryptography for Security in Wireless Sensor Networks

Monika Poriye and Shuchita Upadhyaya

Abstract Wireless sensor networks (WSNs) employ tiny nodes which accumulate information in various applications and security is essential for sensor network applications, such as military target movement, etc. To impart security and privacy to tiny sensor nodes is challenging task due to the restricted capabilities of sensor nodes in terms of computation, communication, memory/storage, and battery power. This paper proposes DNA-based cryptography with the use of secure socket layer. It is exploratory research of biological based cryptosystem. As in conventional cryptography public/private key, pair is used for encryption/decryption process, we herein propose a DNA-based system in which the key pair is generated with the use of RSA algorithm and shared with SSL protocol. So, this proposed system resolves some of the problems related with sensor nodes and here we attain security in three stages, i.e., information security, computation security, and biological security.

Keywords DNA · Cryptology · Digital certificate · Biological cryptosystem

1 Introduction

Security of data is the most significant concern over the last few decades. Cryptography is one such technique widely manifested in an array of security system. It is a promising approach toward security of data transmission over public networks by encrypting the original data or messages. Cryptography has a close relation to the disciplines of cryptology and cryptanalysis, which gives the hiding text so that data cannot be read or modified by intruder. However, as security is the main concern in every type of networks thus cryptography is usually associated with disorganizing the original information (plaintext) into hiding information

M. Poriye (✉) · S. Upadhyaya
Department of Computer Science and Applications,
Kurukshetra University, Kurukshetra 136119, Haryana, India
e-mail: monikaporiye@gmail.com

M. U. Bokhari et al. (eds.), *Cyber Security*, Advances in Intelligent Systems and Computing 729, https://doi.org/10.1007/978-981-10-8536-9_12

(ciphertext) and then the complete process is reversed for getting the original information. The whole task is done by cryptographer [1, 2]. In wireless sensor networks, sensor nodes are associated with many problems like small storage capacity, low battery power, etc., and are also prone to various undesirable attacks. As many sensor networks are assigned crucial tasks such as in military applications, etc. Thus, security becomes the main issue that requires the consideration at the time of designing the sensor networks [3–6]. So a new emerging technique, i.e., DNA computing (Biological Computing) has profound applications toward decoding the problem related with sensor nodes. In the past decade, DNA computing has gained prominence, particularly in developing sustainable medium for large-scale computation system [7]. The pioneering and revolutionary work on the implementing DNA concept is in the solutions of applications like cryptography, clustering, scheduling, forecasting, and even trying to apply this in signal and image processing application. In this context, L. Adleman decoded the complex computational problem in the year of 1994 [8]. He reported a simple and straightforward result that DNA has high storage and computational capability. This convergent and versatile method presents broad substrate scope and excellent functionality tolerance as a result of which using DNA computing tries to solve the problem related with sensor nodes. However, many DNA algorithms have also been proposed and still the research is going on [9, 10]. Here, in this paper, DNA-based algorithm has been proposed by using the concept of SSL. SSL is secure socket layer protocol used for sharing the public key and digital certificates between the sensor nodes, and for key generation, RSA algorithm is used which is very secure algorithm as the key pair is generated with the help of two randomly selected prime numbers. Thus, the problem with sensor nodes is anticipated to be solved in some sense.

In this paper, Sect. 2 provides a brief overview of DNA concept, Sect. 3 describes the proposed work, Sect. 4 gives an illustration with example of proposed work and in Sect. 5 an analytical review is done considering the different aspects of security.

2 Components of DNA

DNA is known as deoxyribonucleic acid which provides heritable information of all living things. A DNA molecule has four types of nucleotides (or Bases) which lies on two antiparallel DNA strands. These molecules are adenine (A), guanine (G), thymine (T), and cytosine (C). The double-helix structure of DNA was first discovered by Watson and Crick. It is basically the greatest scientific discovery in twentieth century and places an origination of current biological research [11]. Figure 1 shows the simple structure of DNA [12].

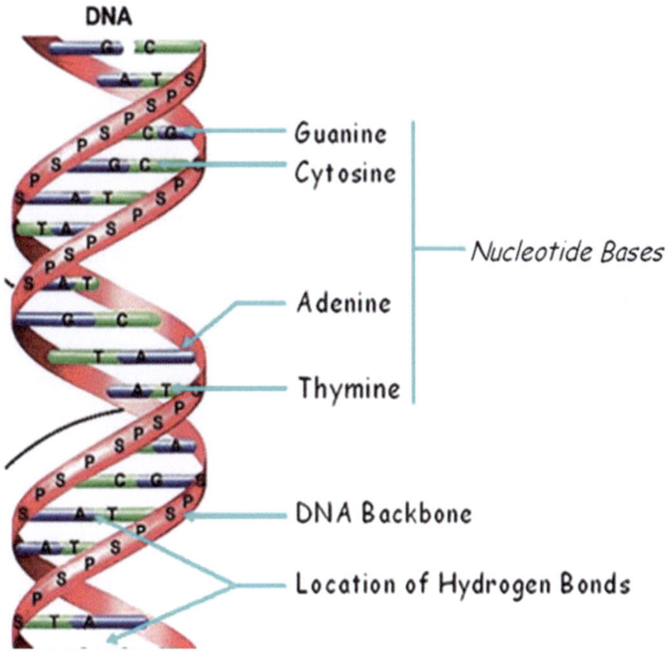

Fig. 1 DNA structure

3 Proposed Work

The proposed algorithm is specified in the following three sections.

3.1 Key Generation and Distribution

In the proposed work, RSA system is used for key generation. RSA is one of the first practical public-key cryptosystems and is widely used for secure communication. In RSA, the encryption key is public and differs from the decryption key which is kept secret [13, 14]. In RSA, the key pair is generated with the help of two prime numbers which are randomly selected.

SSL protocol is used for key sharing. SSL is secure socket layer protocol which is basically used for securely exchanging the keys and digital certificate between two sensor nodes [15, 16]. Thus, this protocol provides the functionality of confidentiality and authenticity.

3.2 Encryption

1. If two sensor nodes A and B want to communicate to each other then they should have key pairs (public key and private key). The private key will be with the sensor node. The sharing of public key among the nodes will be through SSL.
2. Encryption Process: if node A sends a message to node B then first that particular message is converted into ASCII values. After that these ASCII values are encrypted using public key of node B (which is shared by using SSL). Then convert the encrypted message (mini cipher) to base-4 equivalent which is in the form of 0, 1, 2, and 3. The next process is getting binary data from previous values and finally converting these binary values into DNA base equivalent. Table 1 shows the binary equivalent of nucleotide bases as taken in the encryption process.

3.3 Authentication and Confirmation

Both node A and node B authenticate each other by means of digital certificate which are being assigned to every node before deploying in any environment. The digital certificate is shared by both nodes A and B with secure socket layer protocol. Thus, both sensor nodes confirm each other's identity that they are not any adversary.

4 Illustration Through Example

1. First select the encryption/decryption key pair using RSA algorithm. These keys are generated using two prime numbers that must be randomly selected.
2. Table 2 shows the encryption process.

To recover the original data, the intended recipient uses its private key and the rest of the process is just reversed of the encryption. Thus, the description can be

Table 1 Binary values of nucleotide bases

Nucleotide bases	Binary values
A	00
C	01
G	10
T	11

Table 2 Encryption process

Plain text (PT)	P
ASCII value of PT	80
Encrypt with public key of sensor node which is 7 (generating by using RSA) for getting mini cipher, i.e., CT1	20971520000000
Convert CT1 into base 4 equivalent	1103302320020
Binary form	00010001000000 1100110000001 0001100100000 000000100000
Convert above binary form into DNA bases	ACACAAATA TAAAGATAG AAAAAGAA

done successfully. The proposed algorithm was implemented in Java for both encryption and decryption process and the correctness of the proposed procedure was verified.

5 Analytical Review W.R.T. Various Security Aspects

Level of Security: In our proposed system, security has been achieved in the form of information security (accomplished by RSA), computation security (in form of binary data), and biological security (as DNA bases).

Security against attacks: Security is the main issue in wireless sensor networks because of many attacks. Thus for getting the security, the seven security principles [17, 18] should be abided by any network. Our proposed system promotes all these seven security principles:

1. Confidentiality: It specifies that only sender and intended receiver can access the original message. This is achieved by our proposed system as the public key is shared via the secure socket layer. Thus, the encrypted message by public key of another node (in terms of mini cipher) is completely secure. So the interception attack is not possible here (Fig. 2).
2. Authentication: It helps to establish the proof of identities. By sharing of digital certificate between sensor nodes no adversary node can pose the other node's identity. In the Fig. 3, node C (adversary node) sends a message to node B posing as node A. This type of attack is fabrication which cannot be possible in our system.
3. Integrity: Content of message cannot be manipulated before it reaches the intended recipient. As our DNA cryptosystem acquires security in three stages. So there is no chance of modification attack by any adversary node C (Fig. 4).
4. Non-repudiation: There may be the situation that node A sends a message to node B and later on refuses that message is not sent by it. This situation cannot

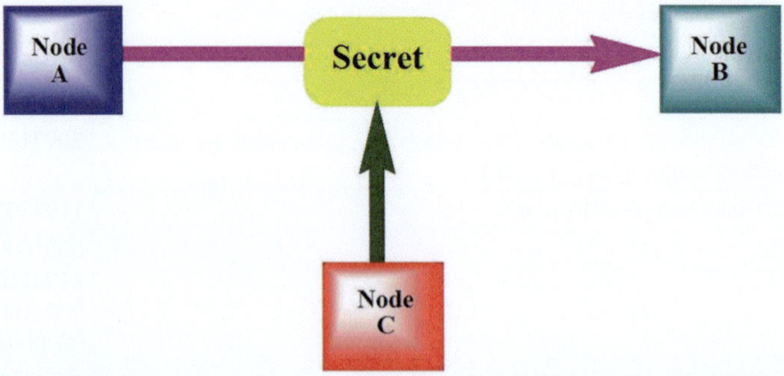

Fig. 2 Confidentiality

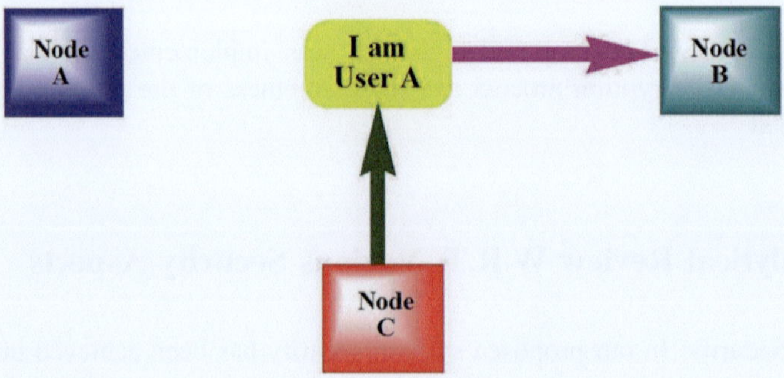

Fig. 3 Authentication

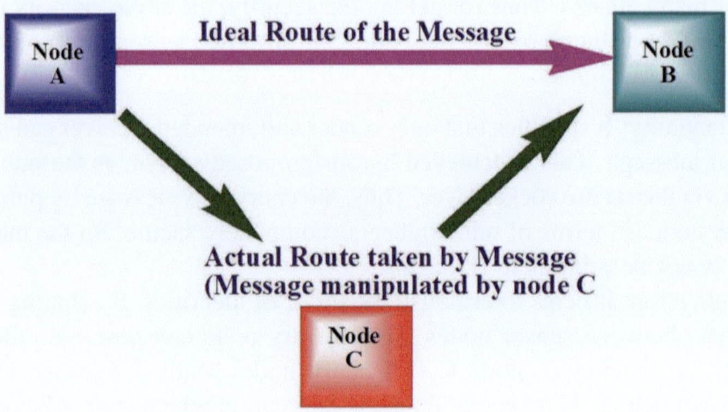

Fig. 4 Integrity

happen in our designed DNA cryptosystem because every node is having the digital certificate of every other node. Thus, no one can deny something after having done it (Fig. 5).

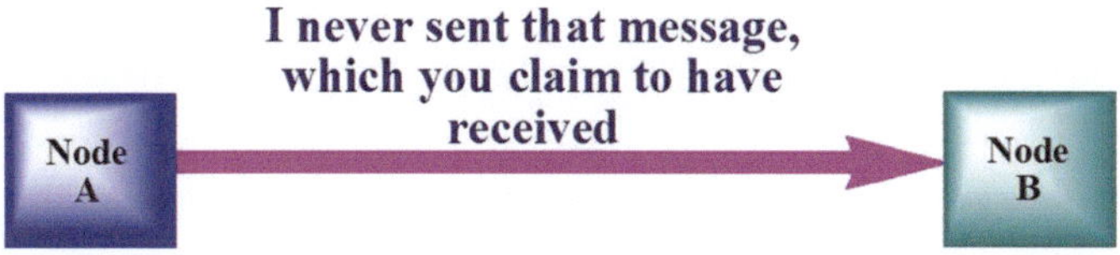

Fig. 5 Non-repudiation

5. Access Control, Availability and Signature: Access control means who can access what. Because the two nodes verify their identities via SSL, they may not be able to access any information without each other's permission.

Node C may try to interrupt the two nodes A and B by some intentional action but here it cannot be possible because node C should have their digital certificate to make a connection with node B. So interruption attack is not possible.

6 Conclusion

In this paper, a peculiar method of implementation of cryptography using the concept of biological DNA has been proposed. Here, the procedure of encryption/decryption is done with help of RSA algorithm (for key generation) and the process of confirmation/authentication is done by SSL protocol (for public key sharing). In the conventional system of asymmetric cryptology, the key generation and distribution are done after the deployment of sensor nodes which consume lots of energy of sensor nodes for computation of keys and generation of digital certificate as they have limited storage capacity and less power. However, in the proposed DNA-based cryptography, keys and digital certificates are distributed before deployment of the sensor nodes in any network which saves innumerous energy of sensor nodes. The proposed algorithm was implemented in Java and the results were verified with the presented example.

References

1. Devi TR (2013) Importance of Cryptography in Network Security. In: 2013 international conference on communication systems and network technologies (CSNT), 6–8 April, pp 462–467. https://doi.org/10.1109/csnt.2013.102
2. Diffie W, Hellman ME (1976) New directions in cryptography. IEEE Trans Inf Theory 22:644–654
3. Wang Y, Attebury G, Ramamurthy B (2006) A survey of security issues in wireless sensor networks. In: IEEE communication surveys 2nd quarter 8, pp 2–23. https://doi.org/10.1109/comst.2006.315852

4. Akyildiz IF, Su W, Sankarasubramaniam Y, Cayirci E (2012) A survey on sensor networks. IEEE Commun Mag 40:102–114. https://doi.org/10.1109/MCOM.2002.1024422
5. Chen X, Makki K, Yen K, Pissinou NS (2009) Sensor network security: a survey. IEEE Commun Surv Tutor 11:52–73. https://doi.org/10.1109/SURV.2009.090205
6. Patel MM, Aggarwal A (2013) Security attacks in wireless sensor networks: a survey. In: IEEE intelligent systems and signal processing (ISSP), Gujarat, India, 1–2 Mar 2013, pp 329–333. https://doi.org/10.1109/issp.2013.6526929
7. Pramanik S, Setua SK (2012) DNA cryptography. In: 7th international conference on electrical and computer engineering Dhaka, Bangladesh, 20–22 Dec 2012, pp 551–554. https://doi.org/10.1109/icece.2012.6471609
8. Adleman LM (1994) Molecular computation of solutions to combinatorial problems. Science 266:1021–1025. https://doi.org/10.1126/science.7973651
9. Rivest RL, Shamir A, Adleman LM (1978) A method for obtaining digital signatures and public-key cryptosystems. Commun ACM 21:120–126. https://doi.org/10.1145/359340.359342
10. Cui G, Qin L, Wang Y, Zhang X (2008) An encryption scheme using DNA technology. In: IEEE bio-inspired computing: theories and applications, Adelaide, SA, Sept 28–Oct 1 2008, pp 37–42. https://doi.org/10.1109/bicta.2008.4656701
11. Wang X, Zhang Q (2009) DNA computing-based cryptography. In: Fourth international conference on bio-inspired computing, BIC-TA'09, pp 1–3. https://doi.org/10.1109/bicta.2009.5338153
12. http://keltoncheyennepowell.weebly.com/stucture-of-dna.html (DNA structure)
13. Zhou X, Tang X (2011) Research and implementation of RSA algorithm for encryption and decryption. In: 2011 6th international forum on strategic technology (IFOST), pp 1118–1121. https://doi.org/10.1109/ifost.2011.6021216
14. https://en.wikipedia.org/wiki/RSA_(cryptosystem)
15. Zhao L, Iyer R, Makineni S, Bhuyan L (2005) Anatomy performance of SSL. In: IEEE international symposium on processing in performance analysis of systems and software ISPASS 2005, pp 197–206. https://doi.org/10.1109/ispass.2005.1430574
16. Lee HK, Malkin T, Nahum E (2007) Cryptographic strength of SSL/TLS servers: current and recent practices. In: IMC'07, San Diego, California, USA, 24–26 Oct 2007
17. Kahate A (2014) Cryptography techniques. Cryptography and network security (3rd edn). McGraw Hill Education (India) Private Limited, New Delhi, India, pp 8–12
18. Monika (2015) A comparative study on modern cryptography and DNA cryptography. In: National conference on emerging computing technologies and ICT for development, 2015

Privacy Preservation Using Various Anonymity Models

Deepak Narula, Pardeep Kumar and Shuchita Upadhyaya

Abstract Need of collection and sharing of data is increasing day by day as it is the requirement of today's society. While publishing data, one has to guarantee that sensitive information should be made secret so that no one is able to misuse it. For this purpose, one can use various methods and techniques of anonymization. A number of recent researchers are focusing on proposing different anonymity algorithms and techniques to keep published data secret. In this paper, a review of various methods of anonymity with different anonymity operators and various types of linkage attacks has been done. An analysis of the performance of various anonymity algorithms on the basis of various parameters on different data sets using ARX data anonymity software has been done in the end.

Keywords Generalization · *k*-Anonymity · *l*-Diversity · Suppression

1 Introduction

Data mining is a process of determining useful, unknown information and to summarize it for different purposes. As in today's environment, both government and private sector are publishing information so that better information will be provided for social and human progress. Therefore, most of the information is easily available. Although the information is provided for good cause, yet attackers link the available data from different data sets. By using their background details, the sensitive information can be deduced by the attackers, thus affecting the society. According to the study, approximately 87% population in the US can be identified uniquely by the data set which is published by the government of US [1]. Thus to protect such sort of leakage of data, the process of data anonymization is used. The basic aim of privacy preservation techniques is to reduce the leakage of data about

D. Narula (✉) · P. Kumar · S. Upadhyaya
Department of Computer Science and Applications,
Kurukshetra University, Kurukshetra 136119, Haryana, India
e-mail: dnarula123@yahoo.com

M. U. Bokhari et al. (eds.), *Cyber Security*, Advances in Intelligent Systems and Computing 729, https://doi.org/10.1007/978-981-10-8536-9_13

the particular record while publishing data. A lot of work has been done on data anonymization technique in recent years. The aim of these techniques is to allow retrieval of useful information from huge available data while protecting sensitive information.

The prime aim of adversary is to obtain the information about sensitive attribute that can be determined by linking various attributes of relation with each other in the published data [2]. In a relation, there are a variety of attributes which are classified as key attribute, quasi-attribute, sensitive attribute, and insensitive attribute.

Key attributes which are meant for unique identification of records and these attributes are generally removed while publishing the information. Examples of key attributes are roll no, name, phone no, etc.

Quasi-attributes are those which are used for linkage of anonymized data set with the aim to reach to sensitive information, e.g., birth date, age, gender, zip code, etc.

Sensitive attributes are those which need not be disclosed, and the aim of an attacker is to determine these, e.g., disease of person, salary, etc.

Insensitive attributes are those which can never be useful for attacker.

Any anonymization technique removes identifiers for the data set and aim is to produce anonymized data set. The present techniques and methods restrict sensitive information in published data but result in huge information loss or data distortion that affects the efficiency of data mining process.

Meanwhile, method development for data publication is utmost important; thus, the generated data remains useful, and sensitive information will be kept secret. The emphasis of this paper is on various privacy-preserving models, anonymity operation, etc.

2 Related Works

Evolution of various methods for secrecy of sensitive data is the main intent of privacy-preserving data publishing. In past years, research communities worked on these issues and have proposed various approaches. There are various operations which are applied to the data sets to make data anonymized. The operators which are frequently used for the purpose of anonymization are operation of generalization, suppression, perturbation, etc. The model for data anonymization uses these approaches, and the idea of algorithm for anonymization is based on specific anonymity operations.

1. **Generalization** is a process of substituting the substantive value against less specific but semantically consistent value. It is achieved using the purpose of hierarchy tree and associated with attribute of category quasi-identifiers. In Fig. 1a the nodes PGT, TGT, or PRT are more specific as compared with node

teaching, whereas it can be seen the node School Employee is at the top of hierarchal level with highest level of generalization.

The reverse process of generalization is called specification. Typically there are five types of generalization with difference in their scope: Full-domain generalization, subtree generalization, sibling generalization, cell generalization, and multidimensional generalization.

Full-domain generalization: This type of operation has the rarest search area among all rather it leads to highest data distortion. The basic idea behind this approach is to generate all attribute values to a common level of certain hierarchy [3] (e.g., Fig. 1a); if PGT, TGT generalized to teaching, then other attributes such as clerk, peon, etc., are also to be generalized to nonteaching.

Subtree generalization is smaller in boundary than the above said. In this, all nodes rooted at intermediate level are generalized to same level or none are generalized [4, 5], for example. If PGT which is at the lowest level of hierarchy is to be generalized to teaching, then any of its siblings, i.e., TGT or PRT, are also to be generalized, whereas other nodes at the same level will not be changed to their generalized level.

Sibling generalization: The boundary of this process is smaller than full-domain and sub-tree generalization. In this, among all intermediate nodes, some are to be generalized whereas nodes from rest set remain unchanged [3], e.g., PGT is generalized to teaching whereas other TGT remains unchanged. Commonly, in process of global recording, if one of the values of the root level is generalized, the rest will also be generalized.

Cell generalization: This approach is a little bit different as compared to other generalization techniques as this is meant only for a single record. In this

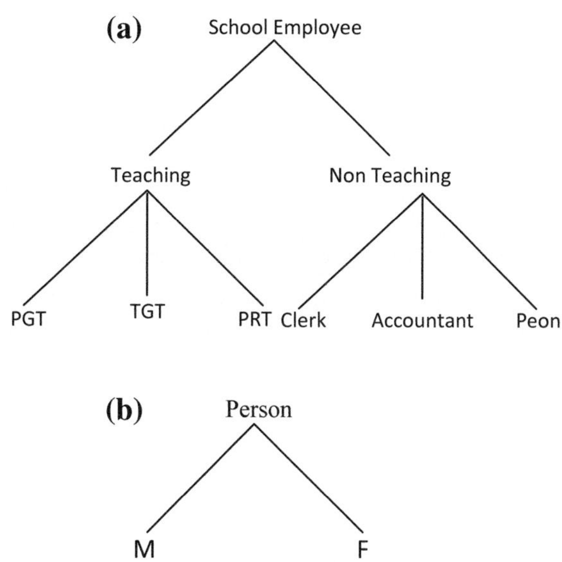

Fig. 1 **a** Example of generalization using hierarchy tree. **b** Example of generalization using hierarchy tree

scheme of local recording, if one of the values at the root level is generalized, the rest will remain unaffected [3, 6, 7], e.g., in Fig. 1a when node PGT generalizes to its parent node teaching, it can maintain the PGT value in data set. **Multidimensional generalization:** This generalization emphasizes different generalization for different combinations of values of quasi-identifiers [3, 7], e.g., in Fig. 1a, b [PGT, M] can be generalized to [Teaching, Person], while [PGT, F] generalized to [School Employee, F]. This scheme has less data distortion compared to full-domain generalization.

2. **Suppression:** This is another flavor of generalization. In this the original values of attribute generally quasi-attribute is replaced by special symbol (e.g., #,*) and makes the value of that attribute meaningless, e.g., in Fig. 2 the zip code of the city attribute is suppressed up to different levels and due to suppression at different levels will make data more anonymous.
3. **Randomization:** This works with an ability to anonymize the whole data set for certain semantic preservation. In the existing privacy-preserving data mining techniques, randomization is considered as of important technique. This method always provides the knowledge discovery and a balance between privacy and utility [8]. When the randomized data is transmitted to the recipient, recipient would receive it using distribution reconstruction algorithm.
4. **Bucketization:** The basic aim is partitioning tuples of table into buckets and further separate the quasi-identifiers with reference to sensitive attribute by arbitrary permitting values for sensitive attribute in every bucket and set of buckets with permuted sensitive attribute values as anonymized data [8]. The process of bucketization is used to anonymize high-dimensional data.

3 Privacy Models

In 1977, Dalenius [9] provided a severe explanation of privacy preservation as:

"Access to the published data should not enable the adversary to learn anything extra about any target victim compared to no access to data base, even with the presence of any adversary's background knowledge obtained from other sources." So to achieve privacy preservation different privacy models are used such as *K*-anonymity, *l*-diversity, *t*-closeness, etc.

1. ***k-anonymity method*** prevents record linkage proposed by Samarati and Sweeney [10] that each record in data set should not be distinguished with at

Fig. 2 Example of suppression

Zipcode	Suppression		
Level X	Level Y	Level Z	Level W
600231	60023*	6002**	600***
600221	60022*	6002**	600***
600210	60021*	6002**	600***

least [$k-1$] other records under quasi-identifiers which are projected. This is achieved after a series of anonymity operations such as generalization, suppression, etc. k-Anonymity assures that the probability of uniquely representing an individual in released data set will not be greater than $1/k$. When the method of k-anonymity is applied to a specific data set (created by researcher) the result with 2-anonymity is shown in Table 1. The attributes zip code and age are treated as quasi-attribute showing at least 2-tuples, which are similar.
Moreover, when we convert data to anonymous to 3 by keeping the value of k as 3, zip code is suppressed to one more level so that at least three records are similar and cannot be identified uniquely; results are shown in Table 2.

2. ***l-diversity***: For upgradation, consequences of k-anonymity and to prevent attribute linkage, Machnavajjhala et al. [11, 12] propose another model of privacy preserving called l-diversity for preventing attribute linkage attack. l-Diversity requires for every indistinguishable category of records and their exist at least l different values for a given sensitive attribute [13]. The result after applying l-diversity is shown in Table 3; from the shown result, each group of

Table 1 Example of k-anonymity with k = 2

	Age	Gender	ZiP Code	SALARY
1	*	F	60000*	30000
2	*	M	60000*	400000
3	*	M	60000*	5000000
4	*	M	60000*	650000
5	*	F	60000*	400000
6	*	M	60000*	400000
7	*	F	60000*	900000
8	*	M	60001*	200000
9	*	M	60001*	300000
10	*	M	70000*	30000
11	*	F	70000*	300000
12	*	M	70000*	400000
13	*	M	70000*	400000
14	*	M	70001*	900000
15	*	M	70001*	650000
16	*	M	70001*	300000
17	*	M	72000*	200000
18	*	M	72000*	5000000
19	*	M	72000*	650000

Table 2 Example of *k*-anonymity with $k = 3$

		Age	Gender	ZiP Code	SALARY
1	☑	*	F	6000**	30000
2	☑	*	M	6000**	400000
3	☑	*	M	6000**	5000000
4	☑	*	M	6000**	650000
5	☑	*	F	6000**	400000
6	☑	*	M	6000**	400000
7	☑	*	F	6000**	900000
8	☑	*	M	6000**	200000
9	☑	*	M	6000**	300000
10	☑	*	M	7000**	30000
11	☑	*	F	7000**	300000
12	☑	*	M	7000**	400000
13	☑	*	M	7000**	400000
14	☑	*	M	7000**	900000
15	☑	*	M	7000**	650000
16	☑	*	M	7000**	300000
17	☑	*	M	7200**	200000
18	☑	*	M	7200**	5000000
19	☑	*	M	7200**	650000

record shows the value of sensitive attribute as 3. That is, it contains three multiple values so if one identifies the group, then unable to determine the value of sensitive attribute as it is multiple in no's. In our example, we have taken salary as sensitive attribute and applied *l*-diversity on it.

l-diversity prevents the linkage attack but it suffers from the problem of skewness attack and similarity attack. When attacker is able to determine the value of sensitive attribute, moreover, this is based on frequency distribution. But similarity attack occurs when the value of sensitive attribute are different but semantically similar quasi-group.

3. ***t-closeness***: *l*-diversity never puts a check on attribute linkage when the overall distribution of sensitive attribute is skewed, let us consider an example by assuming a table containing sensitive attribute as disease and 95% of the records are suffering from Flu whereas only 5% are suffering from Cancer. Now let us suppose a qid group exists in two exactly equal half. The first half represents Flu, whereas the other equal half represents Cancer. Now, if a tuple owner is

Table 3 Example of *l*-diversity with $l = 3$

	Age	Gender	ZiP Code	SALARY
1	*	F	6000**	30000
2	*	M	6000**	400000
3	*	M	6000**	5000000
4	*	M	6000**	650000
5	*	F	6000**	400000
6	*	M	6000**	400000
7	*	F	6000**	900000
8	*	M	6000**	200000
9	*	M	6000**	300000
10	*	M	7000**	30000
11	*	F	7000**	300000
12	*	M	7000**	400000
13	*	M	7000**	400000
14	*	M	7000**	900000
15	*	M	7000**	650000
16	*	M	7000**	300000
17	*	M	7200**	200000
18	*	M	7200**	5000000
19	*	M	7200**	650000

falling in the second half of the qid group (which represents Cancer) then the chances of threat are high, because it comes under 50% confidence level as compared to 5% [9].

So for the sake of preventing skewness attack [14], *t*-closeness had been proposed, which pertains that in any group sensitive attribute distribution on identifying attribute be closer to the distribution of attribute in the overall table. *t*-Closeness algorithm is based on the concept of earth mover distance function which is used to measure the closeness between two distributions of sensitive values and closeness to be within t. The result after applying *t*-closeness algorithm is shown in Table 4. *t*-Closeness also suffers from the limitation of not suitable selection of EMD function for numerical sensitive attributes and degradation of data utility [9].

Table 4 Example of t-closeness with $T = 0.001$

		Age	Gender	ZiP Code	SALARY
1	☑	*	F	******	30000
2	☑	*	M	******	400000
3	☑	*	M	******	5000000
4	☑	*	M	******	650000
5	☑	*	F	******	400000
6	☑	*	M	******	400000
7	☑	*	F	******	900000
8	☑	*	M	******	200000
9	☑	*	M	******	300000
10	☑	*	M	******	30000
11	☑	*	F	******	300000
12	☑	*	M	******	400000
13	☑	*	M	******	400000
14	☑	*	M	******	900000
15	☑	*	M	******	650000
16	☑	*	M	******	300000
17	☑	*	M	******	200000
18	☑	*	M	******	5000000
19	☑	*	M	******	650000

4 Analysis and Experimental Results of Various Anonymity Models

In this section, ARX data anonymity software has been used for determining the values of various parameters such as minimum, maximum information loss, lowest re-identification risk, individuals affected by lowest risk, and average re-identification risk. k-Anonymity algorithm, combination of k-anonymity and l-diversity algorithm, and combination of k-anonymity algorithm with t-closeness have been applied on three different data sets. Their explanation is specified as under.

Explanation and Results of Data Set I

The first data set contains sno, name, pincode, sex, age, and disease. For the purpose of anonymization, sno and name will be treated as identifying attributes so

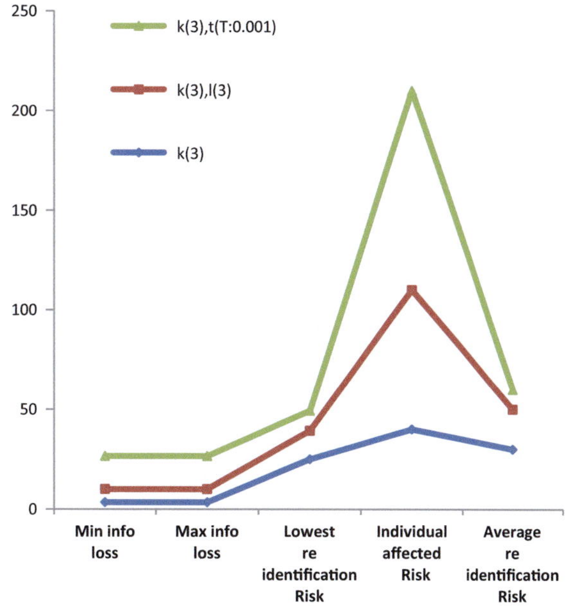

Fig. 3 A stacked line graph representing various factors with different anonymity algorithms on data set I

will not be disclosed. Attribute disease will be treated as sensitive. After applying the experimental settings for various quasi-attributes and applying anonymization algorithms as discussed in Fig. 3 shows the results for various parameters graphically.

Explanation and Results of Data Set II

The second data set contains age, education, place, and occupation. For the purpose of anonymization, attribute disease will be treated as sensitive. After applying the experimental settings for various quasi-attributes and applying anonymization algorithms as discussed, Fig. 4 shows the results for various parameters graphically.

Explanation and Results of Data Set III

The third data set contains age, designation, gender, zip code, and salary. For the purpose of anonymization, attribute salary will be treated as sensitive, after applying various hierarchical settings for quasi-attributes and applying anonymization algorithms as discussed. Figure 5 shows the results for various parameters graphically.

Fig. 4 A stacked line graph representing various factors with different anonymity algorithms on data set II

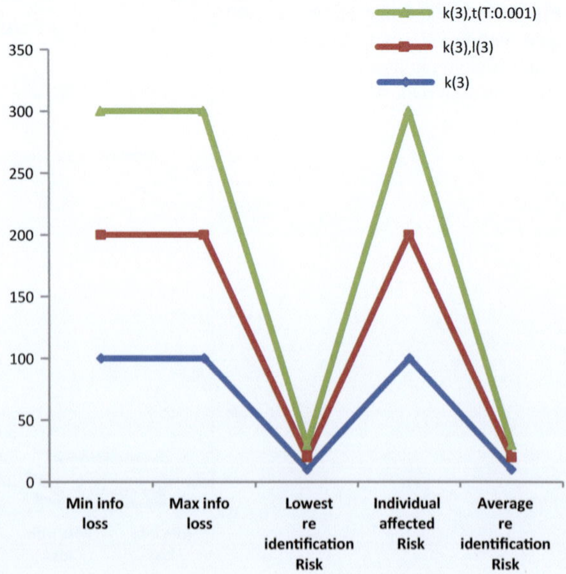

Fig. 5 A stacked line graph representing various factors with different anonymity algorithms on data set III

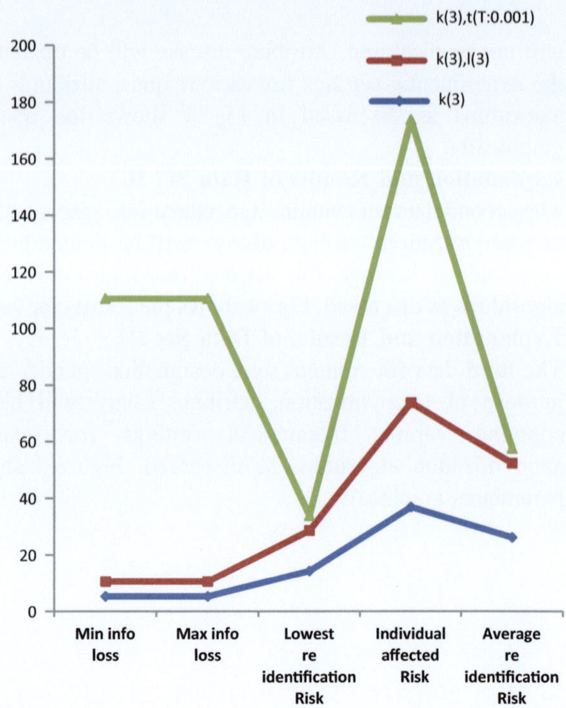

5 Conclusion

Data sharing is an essential part for many organizations as data is spread at various sites and available in different formats; data about the individual in its original form must contain some attributes which need not be disclosed, i.e., sensitive in nature and cannot be published directly. So, with the help of various privacy data models, data should be anonymized and preserved. In this paper, various models for privacy preserving have been discussed along with various linkage attacks and anonymity operations. In the last segment of this paper, it has been analyzed that no one model for anonymization gives a consistent result. Thus, one can say that not only the technique but the data set also plays an important role as values of various parameters varies from one data set to other. So, privacy-preserving methods needs to be further researched. It can also be inferred that there is a need of hybrid algorithm that can handle different scenarios.

References

1. Yang X, Ma T, Tang M, Tian W (2014) A survey of privacy preserving data publishing using generalization and suppression. An Int J Appl Math Inf Sci 8(3):1103–1116
2. Byun J-W, Kamra A, Li N (2007) Effiecient *k*-anonymization using clutering techniues, DASFAA 2007, LNCS 4443. Springer, Berlin, pp 188–200
3. LevFevre K, Dewitt DJ, Raghu R (2005) Incognito: efficient full-domain *k*-anonymity. In Proceeding of ACM SIGMOD, pp 49–60, New York, 2005
4. Bayardo RJ (2005) Data privacy through optimal *k*-anonymization. In: International conference on data engineering, pp 217–228, Washington, DC, USA, 2005
5. Fung, BCM, Wang K, Yu PS (2005) Top–down specification for information and privacy preservation, In: Proceeding of 21th IEEE international conference on data engineering, ICDE'05, pp 205–216, Tokyo, Japan 2005
6. Wong RCW, Li J, Fu AWC, Wang K (2006) (α, k)-Anonymity: an enhanced *k*-anonymity model for privacy preserving data publishing. In: Proceeding of 12th international conference on knowledge discovery and data mining, pp 754–759, Philadelphia, PA, 2006
7. Xu J, Wang W, Pei J, Wang X, Shi B, Fu AWC (2006) Utility-base anonymization using local recoding. In: Proceedings of 12th international conference on knowledge discovery and data mining, pp 785–790, Philadelphia, PA, USA, 2006
8. Mirashe MS, Hande KN (2015) Survey on efficient technique for annonymized microdata preservation. Int J Emerg Dev 2(5):97–103, ISSN 2249-6149
9. Fung BCM, Wang, K, Fu AWC, Yu PS (2011) Introduction to privacy preserving data publishing concepts and techniques. CRC Press, Taylor and Francis Group, New York, p 13, ISBN 978-1-4200-9148-9
10. Sweeney L (2002) *k*-Anonymity: a model for protecting privacy. Int J Uncertan Fuzziness, Knowl-Based Syst 10:557–570
11. Machanavajjhala A, Gehrke J, Kifer D, Venkitasubramaniam M (2006) *l*-Diversity: privacy beyond *k*-anonymity. In: Proceedings of the 22nd IEEE international conference on data engineering (ICDE), Atlanta, GA, 2006

12. Ashoka K, Poornima B (2014) A survey of latest developments in privacy preserving data publishing. Int J Adv Inf Sci Technol 32(32):1–10, ISSN 319:2682
13. Machanavajjhala A, Kifer D, Gehrke J, Venkitasaubramaniam M (2007) *l*-Diversity: privacy beyond *k*-anonymity. ACM Trans Knowl Discov Data 1(1): 1–57
14. Li N, Li T (2007) *t*-Closeness: privacy beyond *k*-anonymity and *l*-diversity. In: Proceedings of 21st IEEE international conference on data engineering ICDE), Istanbul, Turkey, April 2007

A Hybrid Security Mechanism Based on DCT and Visual Cryptography for Data Communication Networks

Yamini Jain, Gaurav Sharma, Gaurav Anand and Sangeeta Dhall

Abstract To provide security in communication networks, various cryptographic and steganographic algorithms have been proposed. Cryptography converts the data into a form understood only by the receiver node whereas steganography hides the data behind a cover file; generally, an image file is used. To provide better security, the use of hybrid mechanisms has been proposed. In this paper, we try to combine visual cryptography coupled with DCT to provide better security for communication networks. The proposed technique is implemented in MATLAB-12, and the overheads of mixing the two mechanisms are evaluated using several performance metrics such as PSNR, Mean Square Error (MSE), time complexity and Mean Absolute Error (MAE) of the mechanism. The result shows that the proposed technique is far better in terms of security but with some overheads when compared to stand-alone technique DCT.

Keywords Cryptography · Networks · Steganography

Y. Jain (✉) · G. Sharma · G. Anand · S. Dhall
Faridabad 121006, Haryana, India
e-mail: jain.yamini34@gmail.com

G. Sharma
e-mail: sharma.grv69@gmail.com

G. Anand
e-mail: gauravanand58@gmail.com

S. Dhall
e-mail: sangeeta_dhall@yahoo.co.in

M. U. Bokhari et al. (eds.), *Cyber Security*, Advances in Intelligent Systems and Computing 729, https://doi.org/10.1007/978-981-10-8536-9_14

1 Introduction

The threat of leakage of confidential data during data transmission is an utmost concern for data communication networks. To provide security against attack by hacker's one mechanism is cryptography. The main aim of cryptographic algorithms [1] is to convert the data into another form, only understood by the intended recipient. Various forms of cryptographic algorithms [2] have been proposed that may use key or not. The algorithms using key are prone to attacks while the algorithms or mechanisms that do not employ the use of key for encryption [3] and decryption are quite secured as, unless the intruder knows the algorithm, the decryption is impossible. If the intruder identifies the algorithm, data can be decrypted; otherwise, it continues to be a mystery to him.

Another mechanism to secure data communication is steganography [4]. It is basically, the art of hiding [5] the existence of data behind a cover image. The main objectives of steganography techniques are to make correlation between original and stego image nearly unity, robust against attacks, high PSNR and low time complexity of the process. Various mechanisms have been developed that tries to inculcate these objectives but still, steganalysis remains a threat. Steganalysis [6] is an art of extracting secret information from the stego media.

Both the techniques mentioned above are secure but are vulnerable to attacks. Therefore, researchers tried to combine these techniques with the aim to provide better security. Various researchers combined LSB steganography [7] technique with some sort of cryptographic algorithm. No doubt, the technique improves security but the hybrid mechanism can be further improved by using robust, less time complex steganography technique such as DCT.

In this paper, we try to make a secured mechanism and also study what are the overheads of combining the keyless mechanism with the robust mechanism like DCT. This paper is organised into different sections: Sect. 2 gives the literature survey and problem identification. Section 3 gives the proposed technique block diagram. Section 4 gives the simulation set up parameters and performance metrics used. Section 5 gives the overheads and advantages of combining the two mechanisms along with their reasons. At last, we conclude in Sect. 6 followed by references.

2 Literature Survey and Problem Identification

Researchers have focused their attention towards transform domain steganographic techniques like DCT and DWT since they are more robust to statistical attacks and provide good security than LSB steganography. LSB steganography [8] is used mostly because of its high payload capacity and less time complexity but it has following disadvantages:

1. It does not offer immunity and is very much prone to attacks.
2. It fails visual inspection.
3. It is less robust and is highly prone to statistical attacks.
4. It offers large payload capacity but often offsets the statistical properties of the image.

Stand-alone DCT is prone to steganalysis and hence needs further security, and hence a cryptographic technique should also be coupled with it. Therefore, this paper couples DCT with visual cryptography [9]. The cryptographic algorithm does not use any key for encryption hence is not vulnerable to attacks and at the same time provides very good security. Gokul M. et al. [10] proposed a hybrid technique with visual cryptography and LSB steganography. Shailender Gupta et al. [11] proposed a hybrid system of security using RSA cryptography and LSB steganography. R. Nivedhitha et al. [12] proposed the use of DES cryptography and LSB steganography. PyePye Aung et al. [13] used AES cryptography and DCT steganography technique. Shingote Parshuram N. et al. [14] in 2014 proposed AES cryptography and LSB steganography for the network security. The above works had several advantages like higher PSNR value, good security, usability for large messages, etc. and disadvantages like high time complexity, limited embedding capacity, etc. Hence, in this paper, we look forward to provide lower time complexity, very high security, higher perceptual quality and eventually higher robustness.

3 The Proposal

Figure 1 depicts the whole procedure carried out at sender and receiver side. First, the encryption is done on the secret textusing visual cryptography [15], and then, it is hidden behind a cover image using DCT steganography [16] and the stego image finally created is transmitted over the network. The reversed process is carried out at the receiver side to extract the message again.

The different techniques used in the proposal have been described as follows.

3.1 Cryptographic Technique Used

In this proposal, the cryptographic technique used is secret key visual cryptography. In this particular technique, the secret message is divided into n shares. Presence of all the n shares can only help in extracting the message as n-1 shares cannot reveal any information about the message. This technique is favoured over other

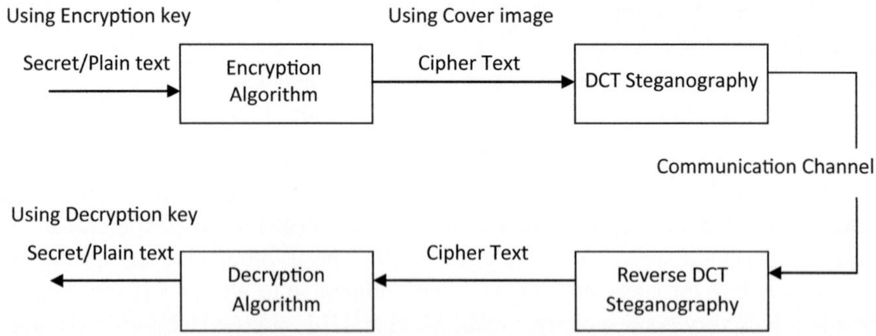

Fig. 1 Block diagram of the proposal

techniques because of its lower time complexity and this feature is a result of its simple algorithm at receiver side. Only an XOR operation is needed at receiver side to extract the message in this technique.

At the sender side, the input data string to be encrypted is represented by *inp*. Share1 and Share2 are two encrypted data strings which are created by considering value of input *inp*. In the end, these two data strings(Share1 and Share2) are combined and transmitted for further operations. *Share_Comb* represents the encrypted form of *inp*.

Algorithm for Visual Cryptography(Sender Side)

```
Len=length(inp);
for i=1 to Len
        Share1(i)=randi([0,1]);
end
for i=1 to Len
        if(a(i)==0)
                Share2(i)=Share1(i);
        else
                Share2(i)=not(Share1(i));
        end
end
for i=1 to (2*Len)
        if(i<=Len)
                Share_Comb(i)=Share1(i);
        else
                Share_Comb(i)=Share2(i-Len);
        end
end
Transmit(Share_Comb);
```

In the following algorithm, *f* represents the encrypted data. The input *f* is broken into shares (Share1 and Share2), and then, exclusive-OR is performed on shares to retrieve the original data. Here, *msg* stores the decrypted data.

Algorithm for Visual Cryptography(Receiver Side)

```
Len= length(f);
for j=1 to Len
        if(j<=Len/2)
                Share1(j)=f(j);
        else
                Share2(j-(Len/2)) = f(j);
        end
end
for i=1 to Len/2
        msg(i)= xor(Share1(i),Share2(i));
end
return (msg);
```

3.2 Steganographic Technique Used

The steganographic technique used in the proposed mechanism is transform domain DCT. The advantage of using this technique is its security and robustness. In DCT, the cover image is split into 8*8 pixels blocks. From top to bottom and left to right, DCT is applied to each and every block. DCT coefficient is then calculated and is used to store the secret message. The reverse of this is performed at the receiver side to get the message again.

Algorithm to embed text message into a cover image

INPUT: Cover image cover.jpg of WxH size and secret message stored in text.txt file
OUTPUT: A stego image
Step 1: img=imread('cover.jpg');
Step 2: temp=fopen('text.txt','r';)
Step 3: msg=fread(temp);
Step 4: msg_bin=dec2bin(msg);
Step 5: break img into 8x8 sized blocks of pixels
Step 6: Perform DCT on each block using dct2() function.
Step 7: Compress each block through quantization table.
Step 8: **while** (data left to embed) do
getLSB of next DCT coefficient from cover image
get next LSB from msg_bin
replaceLSB of DCTcoefficient with message bit
end while.
Step 9: Inverse DCT is performed using idct2() function on each block.
Step 10: All the blocks are combined to form a stego image named stego_img.

Algorithm to retrieve secret message from a stego image

INPUT: A stego image
OUTPUT: Original message
Step 1: img1=imread(stego_img);
Step 2: Break img1 into 8x8 sized blocks of pixels.
Step 3: Perform DCT on each block using dct2() function.
Step 4: Compress each block using quantization table.
Step 5: Calculate LSB of each DCT coefficient.
Step 6: Concatenate the bits obtained from above step to obtain the secret message.

---

4 Performance Metrics

For complete analysis of the proposed scheme, different parameters are used, which are divided into following categories:

4.1 *Robustness Analysis*

The parameters under this category measure the picture quality. Widely used parameters are as follows.

4.1.1 Mean Absolute Error (MAE)

The MAE represents the mean absolute error between the original image and the stego image.

$$\sum_{i=1}^{n}\sum_{j=1}^{m}|f(i,j) - y(i,j)|$$

In the above formula, the mean absolute error is a mean value of the absolute errors,. where f is the pixel value of original image and y is the true value of stego image. Size of image is $m \times n$ monochrome image. For coloured images, size of image will be $m \times n \times 3$.

4.1.2 Mean Square Error (MSE)

MSE stands for cumulative squared error between the stego image and the original image. Lower value of MSE suggests lower error. It is defined by the relation given below any m x n monochrome image.

$$\mathrm{MSE} = \frac{1}{mn}\sum_{i=0}^{m-1}\sum_{j=0}^{n-1}[I(i,j) - K(i,j)]^2$$

For coloured image size of image will be $m \times n \times 3$.

4.1.3 Peak Signal Noise Ratio (PSNR)

It is defined as the ratio of peak square value of pixels by Mean Square Error (MSE). It is expressed in decibel. The PSNR is defined as

$$\mathrm{PSNR} = 10.\log_{10}\left(\frac{MAX_I^2}{MSE}\right)$$

where MAX_I represents maximum value of pixel of the image. In the images with pixel having 8 bits per sample, its value is 255.

4.2 Efficiency Analysis

The parameters under this category give the Qualitative measure of image and time required to accomplish the process. Widely used parameters are as follows.

4.2.1 Time Complexity

It is defined as the total processing time on receiver side or receiver and transmitter side. In this paper, comparison of time consumption by all receiver side processes is taken.

4.2.2 Qualitative Analysis

The cover image may undergo change in pixel values during embedding operation as a result of which the difference maybe observed in both the images. Hence, in order to observe any change in visual quality, the qualitative visual analysis is helpful.

5 Analysis and Results

5.1 Robustness Analysis

For the text of size 16×8 bits:

Fig. 2 PSNR value comparison

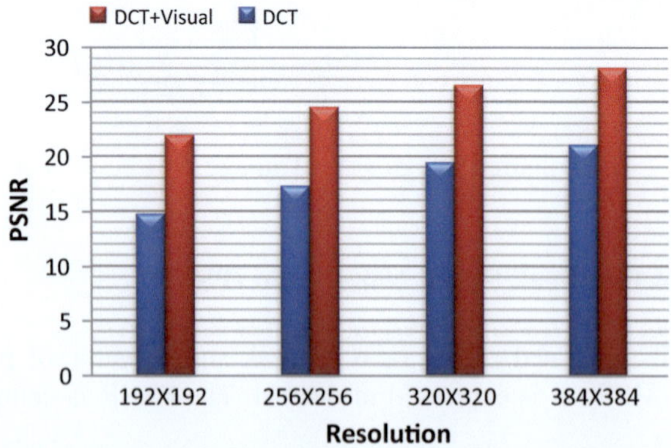

Fig. 3 MSE value comparison

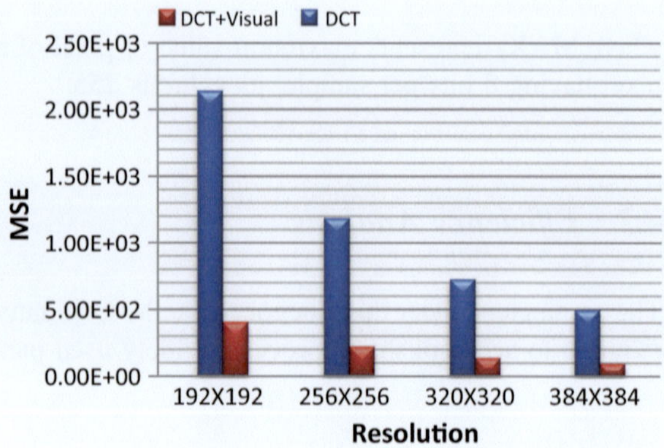

1. Figure 2 shows PSNR value comparison of stand-alone technique with the proposed one using different sizes of images,
   The PSNR value for the proposed technique is higher than stand-alone DCT. It can also be seen that PSNR value increases with increase in image size as the size of plain text is constant.
2. Figure 3 shows MSE value comparison of stand-alone technique with the proposed one using different sizes of images,
   Lower MSE and MAE value shows greater similarity between the cover image and stego image. DCT stand-alone shows higher MSE value, making its detection easier compared to our proposed technique.
3. Figure 4 shows MAE value comparison of stand-alone technique with the proposed one using different sizes of images,
   The lower MAE value of the proposed technique indicates good characteristic here compared to stand-alone DCT technique. It is observed that the proposed technique is much more robust than the stand-alone DCT.

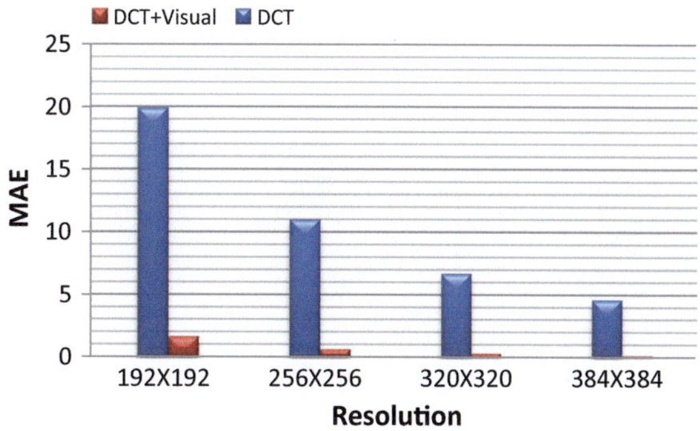

Fig. 4 MAE value comparison

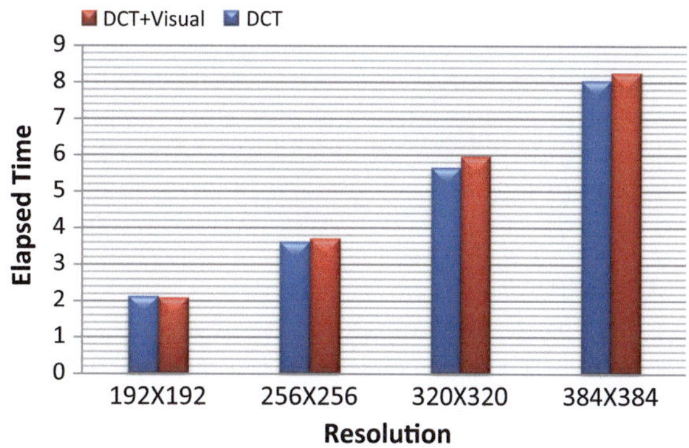

Fig. 5 Elapsed time value comparison

5.2 Efficiency Analysis

1. Figure 5 shows elapsed time value comparison of stand-alone technique with the proposed one using different sizes of images,
   The above comparison shows that time complexity is almost comparable of both techniques. Use of visual cryptography keeps the time complexity in tolerable limits.

6 Conclusion

In this paper a secure and robust hybrid mechanism has been proposed which uses DCT steganography and visual cryptography. Comparison results in Table 1 clearly depict that the proposed technique is better than stand-alone DCT in terms of various parameters as can be seen from the table below.

Table 1 Overall Comparison

Parameters	Stand-alone DCT	Proposed technique
Robustness	Low	Higher
Perceptual quality	Low	Moderate
Embedding capacity	Low	Low
Time complexity	High	Moderate
Security	Moderate	Highly secure

1. PSNR results clearly show that the proposed mechanism has a good picture quality.
2. DCT has high time complexity. Since proposed mechanism uses visual cryptography having low time complexity, therefore, the combination has moderate time complexity.
3. Proposed mechanism provides a very good security.

References

1. William S (2003) Cryptography and network security: principles and practices. Pearsons education, first Indian reprint
2. Preneel B Cryptographic algorithms: basic concepts and application to multimedia security. Katholieke University, Belgium
3. Sadkhan SB (2004) Cryptography: current status and future trends. In: Proceedings of IEEE international conference on information and communication technologies: from theory to applications, Damascus, Syria, 19–23 Apr 2004, pp 417–418
4. Moskowitz I, Longdon G, Chang L (2000) A new paradigm hidden in Steganography. In: Proceeding of the 2000 Workshop on new security paradigms, Ireland, pp 41–50
5. Bendor W, Gruhl D, Morimoto N, Lu A (1996) Techniques for data hiding. IBM Syst J 35(3 & 4)
6. Kharrazi M, Sencar HT, Memon N (2006) A performance study of common image steganography and steganalysis techniques. J Electron Imaging 15:041104
7. Ker A (2004) Improved detection of LSB steganography in grayscale images. In: Proceedings of information hiding workshop, vol 3200, Springer LNCS, pp 97–115
8. Raphael AJ, Sundaram V (2012) Cryptography and steganography—a survey. Int J Comput Technol Appl 223–231
9. Jena D (2009) A novel visual cryptography scheme. In: IEEE international conference on advanced computer control
10. Gokul M, Umeshbabu R, Vasudevan Shriram K, Karthik D (2012) Hybrid steganography using visual cryptography and LSB encryption method. Int J Comput Appl 59:5–8

11. Gupta S, Goyal A, Bhushan B (2012) Information hiding using least significant bit steganography and cryptography. I.J. Modern Education and Computer Science 6:27–34
12. Nivedhita R, Meyyappan Dr T (2012) Image security using steganography and cryptographic techniques. Int J Eng Trends Technol 3:366–371
13. Aung PP, Naing TM (2014) A novel secure combination technique of steganography and cryptography. Int J Inf Technol Model Comput (IJITMC) 2:55–62
14. Shingote PN, Syed AH, Bhujpal PM (2014) Advanced Security using Cryptography and LSB Matching Steganography. Int J Comput Electron Res 3:52–55
15. Nakajima M Extended use of visual cryptography for natural images, department of graphics and computer sciences. Graduate School of Arts and Sciences, The University of Tokyo
16. Morkel T, Eloff JHP, Olivier MS (2005) An overview of image steganography. In: New knowledge today conference, Sandton, pp 1–11

Author Biographies

Yamini jain is M.tech in Electronics and instrumentation from Y.M.C.A university of science and technology, faridabad. Her research interests includes image processing and data security.

Gaurav Sharma is currently pursuing B.tech in Electronics and instrumentation from Y.M.C.A university of science and technology, faridabad. He has 6 papers in international journals/ publications.

Gaurav Anand is currently working as an engineer in Samsung Research Institute, Noida. He is B.tech in Computer Science from Y.M.C.A university of science and technology, faridabad. His research areas includes data security.

Sangeeta Dhall is currently working as a professor in Y.M.C.A university of science and technology, faridabad. She is M.tech in Electronics and Communication and is currently pursuing her P. hd. Her research areas includes image processing.

An Advanced Dynamic Authentic Security Method for Cloud Computing

S. Srinivasan and K. Raja

Abstract Cloud computing delivers a broad range of services and resources like computational power, storage, computational platforms, and applications to cloud consumers through the Internet by on demand, pay-per-usage basics. With a growing number of cloud service providers resorting to using and sharing resources in the cloud environment, there is a necessity for protecting the data of various users from unauthorized access of information between network and cloud. However, the security and privacy of an open-ended, reasonably sharing of accessible resources is still uncertainty and present a major complication for cloud consumers to acclimatize interested in cloud environment. This manuscript initiates and deeply examines the cloud security problem. This paper deals with the protection concern that includes many of the cloud attacks, data integrity, data leakage, privacy, confidentiality, vulnerabilities during sharing of resources, services, and information. This method deals with securing the cloud information without data loss from malicious users, hackers, and attackers of a real-time environment. This method verifies user authentication and authorization management. It assures security on the transmission of data, quality of service, and prevents vital information from various active and passive attacks. This proficient method preserves the cloud environment with better performance evaluation. Furthermore, security and privacy analysis know the ability of the proposed method for cloud computing and extend productive efficiency with safe cloud computing environments.

Keywords Cloud security · Data integrity · Authentication · Vulnerabilities Attacks

S. Srinivasan (✉)
Research Development Center, Bharathiar University, Coimbatore, Tamilnadu, India
e-mail: effectivemail@yahoo.com

S. Srinivasan
Department of M.C.A, K.C.G College of Technology, Chennai, Tamilnadu, India

K. Raja
Alpha College of Engineering, Chennai, Tamilnadu, India
e-mail: raja_koth@yahoo.co.in

M. U. Bokhari et al. (eds.), *Cyber Security*, Advances in Intelligent Systems and Computing 729, https://doi.org/10.1007/978-981-10-8536-9_15

1 Introduction to Cloud Environment

Presently, cloud environment is a rapidly increasing novel information technology of computer industry, which has produced the concern of the entire world. It is the derivative of a large-scale distributed computing with Internet-based technology [1]. Cloud computing environment is also a novel approach to computational business computing, in which software, hardware, services, other resources are shared and provided to computers by a pay-per-usage computed service through the internetwork. It facilitates users to access storage, information, and resources online via Internet [2]. Moreover, cloud computing offering fault-tolerant services with improved better performance and provides an identity management mechanism for millions of users simultaneously [3].

The cloud service providers have Infrastructure as a Service, Platform as a Service, Software as Service, and several services to present. A cloud environment has several characteristics such as on-required service, resource collections, elasticity, and calculated measured service. The significant features of cloud environment are elasticity, scalability, multi-tenancy, self-provisioning of resources, and on-demand self-service [4].

A cloud can be public, private, community, and hybrid cloud. According to new information technologies (IT) and business models, the cloud computing infrastructures and applications have been developed rapidly and the security is the major consideration for the customer to adopt cloud computing. Cloud environment focuses on sharing consumers data, information, and calculations over the Internet computing clients such as computers, data storage centers, and cloud computing services. It allows efficient computing capabilities by centralizing global storage,

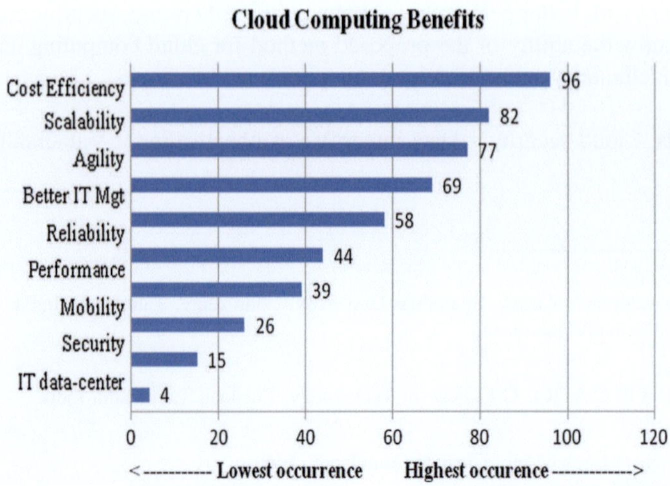

Fig. 1 Benefits of cloud computing

processing, and bandwidth. The benefits [4, 5] of cloud environment are shown in Fig. 1.

In a cloud environment, security and privacy are shared between the cloud service providers and consumers. The main problem of the cloud environment is a large number of security threats, cloud attacks, hijacking of network information on outsourcing of resources as well as business-critical process and data. Some security issues in the cloud are data integrity, information confidentiality, data leakage, vulnerability, and data intrusion. To ensure facts' confidentially, information integrity and availability, the cloud provider provides that at a minimum, include the following:

- Cryptographic method to guarantee that the shared and global data centers secured all information.
- Strong user access technique and user authentication methods to protect against illegal contact to the data.

Cloud computing security [5] is a large set of security controls, strong policies, recent technologies, and methods set to safeguard the data and applications of the cloud environment. The rest of this chapter is ordered as follows: Sect. 2 discusses cloud security risks and issues. Section 3 gives a detailed description of the proposed exciting advanced dynamic authentic security method for cloud computing. Section 4 shows the performance of experimental and their interpretation outcome. Finally, Sect. 5 concludes the paper and further improvements.

2 Security Risks and Challenges in Cloud

Security and privacy concerns indicate in the implementation of cloud computing technologies for sharing of information, resources, services, and data storage. Protecting the cloud data such as sharing of resources, user identification like credit and debit card details from the malicious insider is a foremost impact in cloud. Garfinkel [6] identified data intrusion may happen with the cloud service providers, like Amazon service, is data intrusion. A cloud security [7] is the most responding in the percentage of the challenge of nine issues recognized to cloud environment as shown in Fig. 2.

In cloud, security and privacy events are observed and mentioned below [7]:

- A salesforce.com employee fell prey to a phishing attack, which leads to loss of data that produced further during the year 2007.

According to Akhil Behl [4], Data loss is major security challenges raised by the users. When the IT companies or organizations transfer their confidential information to cloud, the cloud service provider is not able to undertake the security and data integrity as they would in their location, that cause data leakage and loss of control due to multi-tenant strategy maintained in cloud computing.

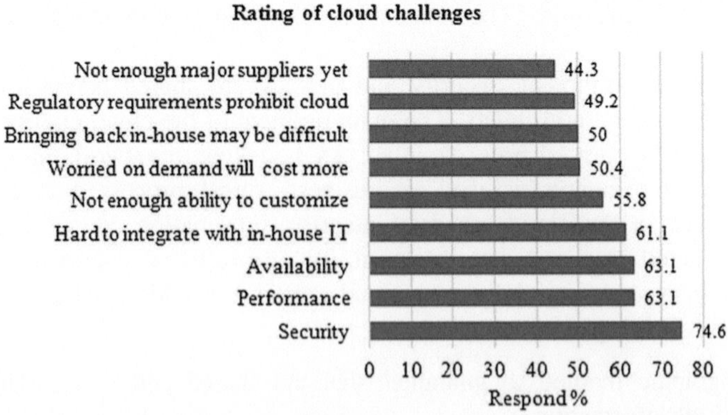

Fig. 2 Ranking of cloud environment challenges

The important problem on the cloud is data integrity. The confidential information stored in the cloud storage may suffer from harm or damage during transition actions from or to the cloud service provider such as the recently assaulted Linux's servers [8, 9].

Recent approaches for preserving the privacy and secrecy of users information stored in the cloud storages mainly include cryptographic encryption method (HMAC). Proof of Retrievability (POR) [10] is cryptography method for remotely checking the data integrity and confidential information stored on the cloud server. Information confidentiality and validity of data can be assured through cryptographic methods.

Bernd et al. [11] investigate vulnerabilities that are also a major security concern in a cloud. The control issue is a matter of vulnerabilities, which explore two examples as listed below:

- Virtualized networks offer inadequate network-based controls.
- Poor key management events

There are several areas of risks that could be identified, in which data and information security was the rate by 91.7% [12] as exposed in Table 1.

Table 1 Risk divisions with respect to cloud

Areas of risk	Critical (%)	Important (%)	Not so important (%)
Data and information security	91.7	8.3	0.0
Change control management	41.7	50.0	8.3
Third-party authentication management	41.7	41.7	16.7
Service-level agreement, regulations, and legislation	33.3	41.7	25.0
Disaster recovery	66.7	33.3	0.0

Some of the major cloud computing issues and different attacks [13] are mentioned below:

- Data confidentiality
- Vulnerability
- Leakage and loss of control
- Insider threats and malicious attacks
- Data intrusion
- Service hijacking
- Availability
- Hypervisor viruses
- Injection attack
- Denial of service
- Man-in-the-middle attack
- IP spoofing

3 Advanced Dynamic Authentic Security Method for Cloud Computing

The advanced dynamic authentic security method for cloud computing assesses the problem of security and privacy from the cloud architecture standpoint, cloud delivery model, and cloud deployment model perspective. This method appraises the problem of various attacks, data integrity, data leakage, information privacy, confidentiality, and vulnerability during the sharing of resources in cloud computing. It prevents scam, error, misuse of illegal access and rights in cloud computing environment. Cloud environment allows authenticated and authorized users' to access the confidential information and sharing of resources, which leads to developing effective and efficient security framework in the cloud computing environment. The need of filtering is enforced on the secure communication channel between cloud service provider and cloud user. To construct the self-directed security of protected cloud environment through an alliance with safety services such as authentication, privacy, and confidentiality.

To make sure of allocation of distribution information and availability of service by integrating cryptographic encryption method and protective sharing algorithm with authentication method [14]. This method strengthens the security which helps to control privileged user access and monitor activities of malicious users in a cloud environment. The advanced dynamic authentic security model for cloud computing is shown in Fig. 3.

This model applied a layered protective structure with different layers and ensures information security, eliminate various attacks, vulnerable file in this cloud environment.

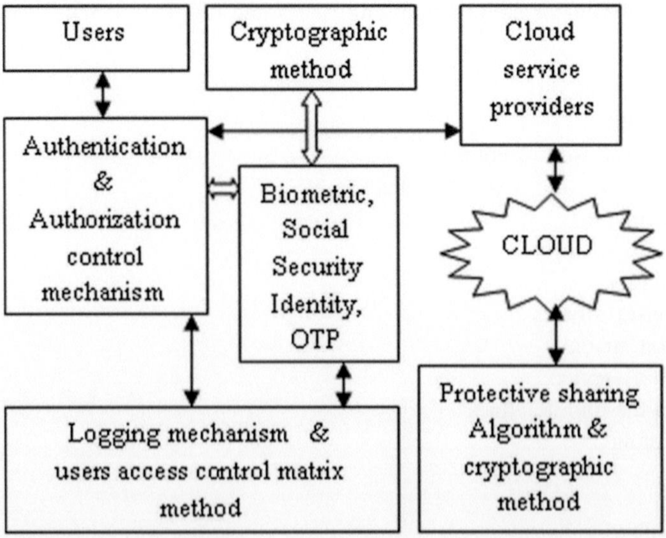

Fig. 3 An advanced dynamic authentic security model

The authentication and audit control method layer enforces user identity and validation mechanism through biometric authentic signature verification of users, one-time password method via mobile-based access security, social security identity card like Aadhaar card and separate user secret key. It controls and eliminates malicious users, attachers, and hackers with the help of centralized logging mechanism.

This dynamic security method also manages user access permission matrix method and keeps track of user activities via logging mechanism. This protective cloud computing environment provides an integrated extensive variety security solution, which ensures information confidentiality and data integrity.

In this method, protective sharing algorithm together with cryptographic methods to develop protective and sharing of resources and information in cloud computing environment [14]. The advanced dynamic authentic security model adopts multidimensional security architecture in cloud computing environment.

4 Performance and Evaluation

It is noticeable that a huge number of attacks like cross-scripting attacks, phishing attacks, threats are crashed the confidential data or reducing size, retreating sharing of services and resources, that would further enlarge the computational and communication expenses of improving services in cloud environment. The experimental results and analysis of the advanced dynamic authentic security method for reducing various vulnerabilities, attacks in cloud computing environment have been described as follows.

The main aim is to reduce various attacks, threats, and vulnerabilities in cloud computing and it should maintain expenditure and standard consistent precision, which leads to develop and improve the high performance of cloud security systems.

Figure 4 shows that better audit frequency can be achieved throughout entire audit cycle by the sampling-based audit, which eliminates the load on the cloud servers and different attacks, raise the audit effectiveness under different detection probabilities on proportion of uncertain blocks in the whole file blocks. It supports a complete integrity verification and reduces computational and communication expenses of an audit service.

Figure 5 shows the time cost to select the peak-*k* resources or vulnerable documents on various sizes among set of resources through top-*k* select algorithm [15]. For example, it costs 1 ms to select the peak-500 resources or vulnerable files from a huge deposit of 1000 resources, while it costs 5 ms for the peak-1000 from 5000 resources or vulnerable files. Even though the cost of time is less, there is space for the decrease in case of huge *k*.

Figure 6 depicts that the time with respect to the cost of this point is autonomous to the quantity of enquired words on single or various resources or possible vulnerable files.

In order to decrease attacks, vulnerability, risk, threats in a cloud environment of any organization, present advanced dynamic authentic security method exploits better and is highly secure to safeguard the information, sharing of services and resources in the cloud environment. This method still guarantees practical competence with better performance while system robustness and security are notably improved.

Fig. 4 Audit frequency with respect to proportion of uncertain blocks in the whole file blocks is shown

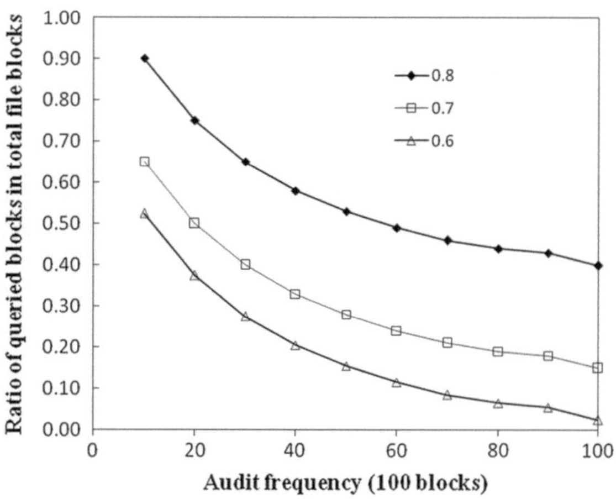

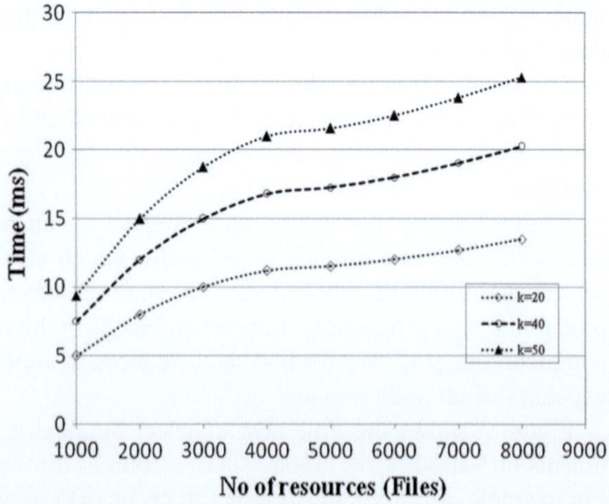

Fig. 5 The time required to select the peak-*k* resources or vulnerable documents on different resource sets is shown

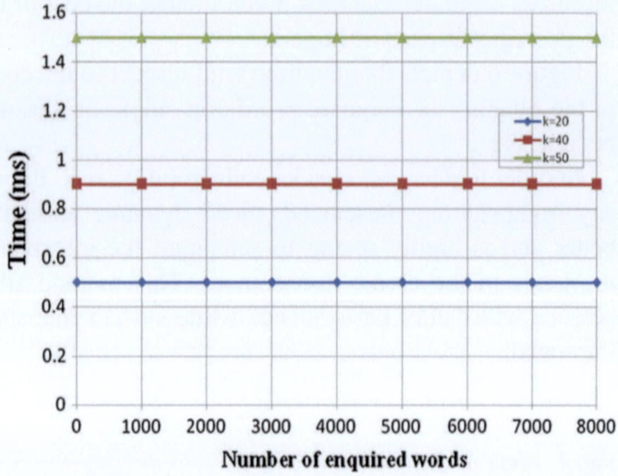

Fig. 6 The time needed to select the peak-*k* resources or vulnerable documents for several quantities of enquired words is shown

5 Conclusion and Future Work

Obviously, the present growth of cloud computing has quickly increased day-by-day, but cloud attacks, security, and privacy are still measured and it has been the most important key concern in the cloud computing. To protect confidential information and sharing of services and resources in cloud environment against threats and vulnerability a safer cloud environment is required, and therefore a suitable advanced dynamic authentic security is proposed for cloud technique and it should be enforced. This paper deals various security risks and challenges in terms of privacy, data intrusion, data integrity, data leakage, and confidentiality of cloud environment. This paper verifies user authentication and authorization management and keeps track of user activities through logging mechanism. This paper proposes a strong dynamic security structure for cloud environment with many safety features such as shielding sharing of resources through cryptographic encryption mechanism with authentication techniques.

Future research on this work will include to develop a better auditing technique with specific standard interfaces and protocols that can maintain high confidentiality, security, integrity, and to meet more secure protected cloud environment.

References

1. Lin G (2012) Research on electronic data security strategy based on cloud computing. In: 2012 IEEE second international conference on consumer electronics, ISBN: 978-1-4577-1415-3, pp 1228–1231
2. Behl A, Behl K (2012) An analysis of cloud computing security issues. In: 2012 IEEE proceedings world congress on information and communication technologies, ISBN: 978-1-4673-4805-8, pp 109–114
3. Uma S, Kanika L, Manish M (2011) Implementing digital signature with RSA encryption algorithm to enhance the data security of cloud in cloud computing. In: 2010 IEEE 1st international conference on parallel, distributed and grid computing (PDGC—2010), ISBN: 978-1-4244-7674-9, pp 211–216
4. Behl A (2011) Emerging security challenges in cloud computing. In: 2011 IEEE, ISBN: 978-1-4673-0126-8, pp 217–222
5. Chen D, Zhao H (2012) Data security and privacy protection issues in cloud computing. In: 2012 IEEE proceedings of international conference on computer science and electronics engineering, ISBN: 978-0-7695-4647-6, pp 647–651
6. Garfinkel SL (2007) An evaluation of amazon's grid computing services: EC2, S3, and SQS. Technical Report TR-08-07, Computer Science Group, Harvard University, Citeseer, pp 1–15
7. Zhou M, Zhang R, Xie W, Qian W, Zhou A (2010) Security and privacy in cloud computing: a survey. In: 2010 proceedings of sixth international conference on semantics, knowledge and grids, ISBN: 978-0-7695-4189-1, pp 105–112, 2010 IEEE
8. Cachin C, Keidar I, Shraer A (2009) Trusting the cloud. ACM SIGACT News 40:81–86
9. RedHat. https://rhn.redhat.com/errata/RHSA-2008-0855.html
10. Xu J, Chang E-C, Towards Efficient Proofs of Retrievability in Cloud Storage, National University of Singapore Department of Computer Science
11. Bernd G, Tobias (2011) Understanding cloud computing vulnerabilities. In: Co published by IEEE computer and reliabilities societies, IEEE April 2011, pp 50–57
12. Carroll M, van der Merwe A, Kotz P (2011) Secure cloud computing benefits, risks and controls. In: 2011 IEEE
13. Denz R, Taylor S (2013) A survey on securing the virtual cloud. J Cloud Comput Adv Syst Appl 2:17
14. Srinivasan S, Raja K (2014) Security challenges in cloud computing. Int J Emerg Technol Adv Eng 4(4):01–06, ISSN 2250–2459
15. Yu J, Lu P, Zhu Y, Xue G, Li M (2013) Towards secure multikeyword top-*k* retrieval over encrypted cloud data. In: IEEE Trans Dependable Secure Comput 10(4):239–250. July/August 2013

Author Biographies

S. Srinivasan is currently pursuing research at the Bharathiar University, Coimbatore, Tamil Nadu, India and is also working as Associate Professor at KCG College of Technology, Tamil Nadu, India. He received MCA from Bharathidasan University, India, in 1997 and M.E. from Sathyabama University, India, in 2009. His research interests include cloud computing. He is a member of CSI, ISTE, and IAENG.

K. Raja received Ph.D. from Sathyabama University, India, in 2006 and M.E. from Madras University, India, in 2001. Presently, he is the Principal and Dean (Academics) at Alpha College of Engineering, Tamil Nadu, India. He is a member of CSI, IEEE, ISTE, IETE, and IAENG. He has published in 25 international journals, 3 national journals, and 54 national and international conferences. He is a reviewer for national and international journals. His research interests include cloud computing and knowledge management.

Security in CryptDB Using Fine-Grained Access Controls with ECDHE-ZeroVi's Framework

Krishna Keerthi Chennam, Akka Laskhmi Muddana and Tahseen Munnavara

Abstract Cloud Computing is a vast technology with high economic benefits, with low cost, many industries planning to store their information on cloud maintained by a third party are Third-Party Storage provider (TSP). Sometimes curious or malicious administrators may leak data in the TSP. CryptDB provides confidentiality works by executing the user SQL queries about encrypted data using Onion Encryption. Another threat is from cloud users, where they try to secure the systems against external adversaries with a secured user login and secure end-to-end encrypted connections. Though, the internal adversaries remain also the biggest threat from this case. The proposed security method of applying Elliptic Curve Diffie–Hellman Ephemeral in CP-ABE (Cipher Text Attribute-Based Encryption) technique for Key Exchange Policy. CP-ABE is a fine-grained access control with the policy of Attribute Authority (AA) to a user is having Secret Key (SK) based on the set of character attributes. Elliptic Curve Diffie–Hellman Ephemeral is a well-known technique in key exchange policy. Combining CP-ABE with Elliptic Curve Diffie–Hellman Ephemeral is proposed for the ECDHE-ZeroVi's framework.

Keywords Confidentiality · Ciphetext · Fine-grained access control
Cloud · CryptDB · Elliptic curves · Diffie–Hellman ephemeral

K. K. Chennam (✉)
Gitam University, Computer Science Engineering, Hyderabad, Telangana, India
e-mail: krishnakeerthich@gmail.com

A. L. Muddana
Gitam University, Information Technology, Hyderabad, Telangana, India
e-mail: lakshmi.muddana@gitam.edu

T. Munnavara
M.J.C.E.T, Information Technology, Hyderabad, Telangana, India
e-mail: taseh05@gmail.com

M. U. Bokhari et al. (eds.), *Cyber Security*, Advances in Intelligent Systems and Computing 729, https://doi.org/10.1007/978-981-10-8536-9_16

1 Introduction

A legal agreement which stores data in public clouds, hybrid cloud, or community cloud give the advantage of TSP and may change the data on demand, where the cost of TSP is reduced control on data security. TSP is an untrusted environment. Traditional access controls are not suitable for the TSP-hosted database. The major target is to provide security in untrusted domains. Since different clients may have different queries, the access to the data must be based on individual and for particular authorized clients. A basic common method to protect the data onto the cloud environment is encryption before sending it from trusted environment. Traditional data encryption requires a single key or pair of keys to encrypt or decrypt the data. The database requires a key separately for each cell (means each column in a row) using fine-grained access, to generate the key or to store the key or to manage keys require a trusted key store.

Another approach is to decrypt all protected data cells with a single key or a key pair. CryptDB has two threats: First threat, the adversary wants to get access to the DBMS server and trying to snoop on private data onto the cloud. The DB administrator is not a trusted one. To prevent this, Onion Encryption is giving security on Cloud, where the data stored in Onion Encryption given in [1].

Second Threat is decrypting the data onto proxy servers the authenticated user and transferring data there is no guarantee of internal adversaries or logged in users. The framework ECDHE-ZeroVi's propose the use of CP-ABE with Elliptic Curves Diffie–Hellman Ephemeral to control access to data based on the data consumer attributes. Data consumers with attributes that can satisfy the policy and has authorized key to decrypt data (Fig. 1).

Two goals for these threats: the First one is executing a different number of queries with a reduced amount of secured information revealed to the cloud server.

Another one data should be encrypted with perfect and strong crypto systems with AES that avoids the cloud server by executing many SQL queries. To solve this case practically, the server needs to access the decryption key, and the adversary may access all data.

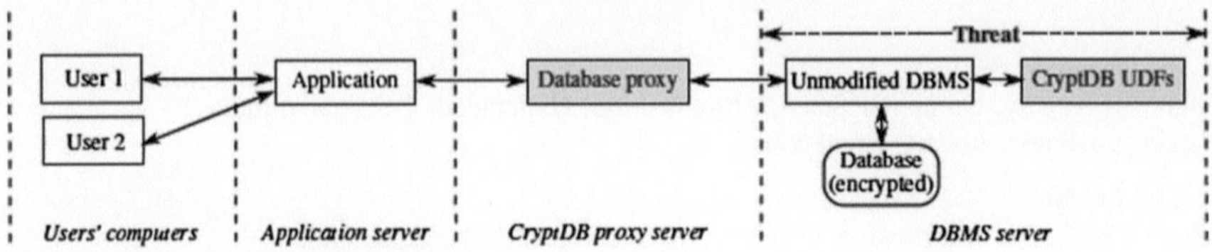

Fig. 1 CryptDB architecture [1]

Another challenge is to reduce data leaking when adversaries compromise the application server along with cloud servers. Even if application server is comprised and leaks the data then adversary will get the original data to over this problem a solution is by generating separate encryption key for each user for to retrieve data.

CryptDB using ECDHE-Zero framework has different key ideas.

- First one is executing SQL Queries on encrypted data. CryptDB implements this as discussed in [1], where all different SQL Queries like operators, comparisons, sums, and equi joins. CryptDB uses symmetric-key encryption on the DBMS software with the user-defined functions.
- The second technique is to avoid the leakage from DBMS server or Cloud Server using Onion Encryption implemented in [1], where Onions have compactly stored a variety of ciphertext with Database and reduces the cost on re-encryptions.
- Third technique is providing the chain of keys to user passwords, where the keys are produced based on ECDHE (Elliptic Curves Diffie–Hellman Ephemeral). The Database can be decrypted with the help of pair or chain of keys rooted to the password with the users to access the data. If the user has not logged in application and adversary does not know the password and secret key where public key is provided by the ECDHE and cannot decrypt the user's private data, even by the internal adversaries or by External adversaries. At the end, the DBMS or Cloud Server and application Server are fully compromised for leakage of Data.

2 Related Work

The ECDHE-ZeroVi's frameworks relates to searchable encryption and encrypted distributed key management. Sending secured transmission [5] is proposed in Broadcast encryption. Elliptic curve Diffie–Hellman Ephemeral is a different key agreement protocol; where this allows two parties to exchange, have elliptic curve public–private key allowing data access insecure channel.

The first proposed encryption to solve the problem in transferring data in a secure way from one site to any different recipients is Broad Cast Encryption [5]. Similarly extending [5] the work, increasing scalability [7, 8] and ABE (Attribute-Based Encryption) technique is used with high utility.

ABE [6] addresses the encryption problem for arbitrary number of recipients'. ABE extension work proposed by Goyal to Identity-Based Encryption in [4] by using access policy with attributes of non-distinct identities for encrypting and decrypting the data. The two important methods in ABE are CP-ABE (Cipher Text Attribute-Based Encryption) and KP-ABE (Key Policy Attribute-Based Encryption). The KP-ABE set securely the access policy and secret key of user [6]. KP-ABE gives control to whom can access or to decrypt data [2], where

CP-ABE embedded the access policy in cipher text [3] and CP-ABE secures that the owner who encrypts the data have full control and have information about the descriptors' [3]. CP-ABE generates the secret key to the user to allow the data access and data decryption when the subset of attributes are matched according to the cipher policy. Still the CP-ABE and KP-ABE both are semi-trusted techniques. Their proposed frame work includes the Multi-Authority ABE (MA-ABE) allows a different attribute authority with a different data need to generate the secret keys for user to decrypt the data based on different attribute sets.

CryptDB [1] is software that can access the encrypted data stored in cloud database and each encrypted column in tables are stored using different encryption algorithms. CryptDB works by executing SQL Queries over encrypted data on cloud database server. The database administrator never gets decrypted data access. But the CryptDB cannot provide one too many encryptions.

Our proposed framework approach builds on selected concepts from above and provides data security for the data provider with better efficient access control and overcome the problems from distributed access control. Elliptic Curve Crypto Protocol [17]: An equation shown below is a solution for an elliptic curve.

$$y^2 + axy + by = x^3 + cx + dx + e \quad (1)$$

where *a*, *b*, *c*, *d*, *e* are real numbers.

The intrusion point *O* and elliptic curve addition operation is called as point at infinity. If any three points are intersecting line on elliptic curve, then amount is equal to point at infinity *O*.

Weierstrass equation is

$$y^2 + a_1xy + a_3y = x^3 + a_2x^2 + a_4x + a_6 \quad (2)$$

K is and arbitrary constant and a_1, a_2, a_3, a_4, a_6 are constants in *K*

To use elliptic curves in cryptography the main constraint is that the curve is nonsingular.

$$f(x) = x^3 + ax + b : \quad 4a^3 + 27b^2 \neq 0 \quad (3)$$

The two elliptic curves shown in Figs. 2 and 3 are

$$y^2 = x^3 + 2x + 5 \quad (4)$$

$$y^2 = x^3 - 2x + 1 \quad (5)$$

Equations (4) and (5) should meet now. An elliptic group the Galois Field E_p (*a*, *b*) with $x^3 + ax + b \bmod p$ for $0 \leq x \leq p$ where *a* and *b* are positive integers, but less than p where mod p substitutes as in Eq. (3).

Fig. 2 Elliptic curve for $y^2 = x^3 + 2x + 5$ [17]

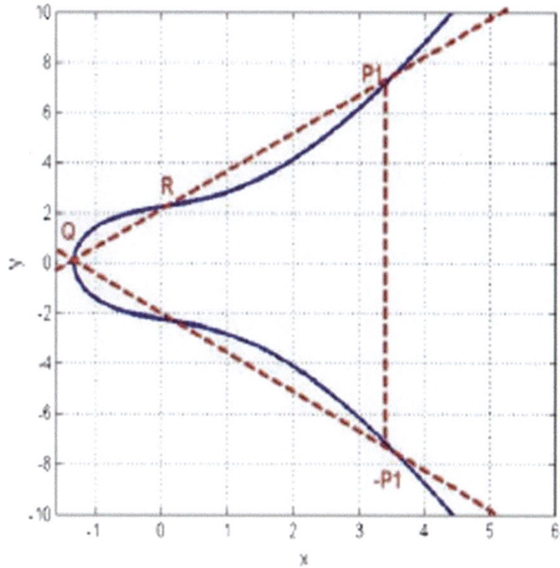

Fig. 3 Elliptic curve for $y^2 = x^3 - 2x + 5$ [17]

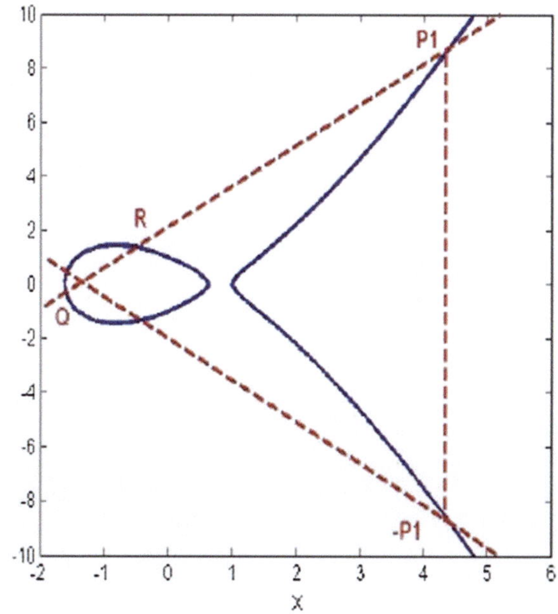

$$4a^3 + 27b^2 \bmod p \neq 0$$

A fixed prime numbers p with Galois Field Ep (a, b) group for a and b non-variable constants.

Example: Let us assume the points P = (x_1, y1) and Q = (x_2,y_2) in elliptic curve group E_p (a, b) and O is the point at infinity.

Addition rules of Elliptic group E_p (a, b) are

(1) $P + O = O + P = P$
(2) If $x_2 = x_1$ and $y_2 = -y_1$ means $P = (x_1, y_1)$ and $Q = (x_2, y_2) = (x_1 - y_1) = -P$ then $P + Q = O$
(3) If $Q \neq -P$ then $P + Q = (x_3, y_3)$

Where $x_3 = \lambda - x_1 - x_2 \bmod p$

$$y_3 = \lambda(x_1 - x_3) - y_1 modp$$

Diffie–Hellman Key Exchange: A secret communication like personal data or important data by exchanging over a public channel familiar for this is Diffie–Hellman Key Exchange. Figure 4 shows the general idea of key exchange by colors example instead of a large prime number.

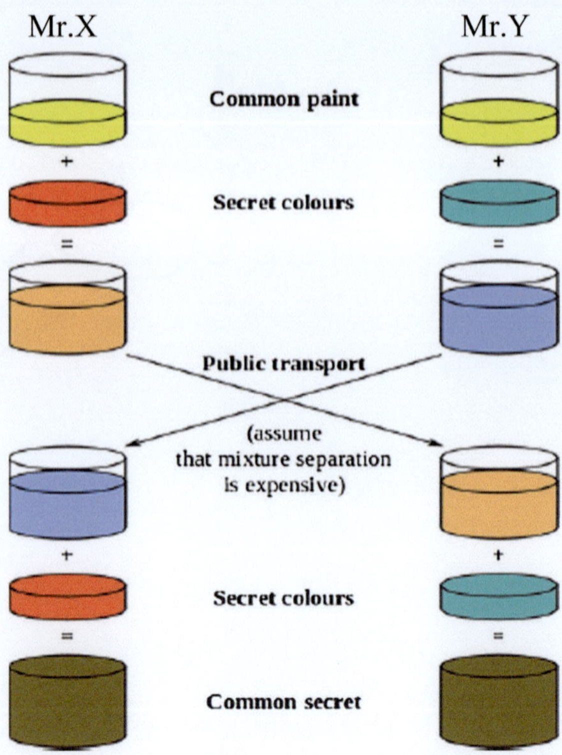

Fig. 4 Key exchange

The key is exchanged between Mr. X and Mr. Y with mixed colors. At the end the secret key is generated to encrypt and decrypt. Let us assume that yellow color is known by Mr. X and Mr. Y on agreement as shown in the figure.

3 Problem Definition: ECDHE

Initially, RSA-RC4-SH4 were used, the client randomly selects a secret key and encrypts and send it to server whoever have the secret key can decrypt the data at any time. If the adversary got the secret key while sharing they can decrypt the data ECDHE-ZeroVi means elliptic curve, Diffie–Hellman Ephemeral signed by RSA key with zero visibility of adversaries with CP-ABE. Where Diffie–Hellman Ephemeral means server generates a different public key for every new query requested by the client even though the adversaries breaks one public key can get decrypt of only one query related data and already the tables are secured Onion Encryption by CryptDB. The Elliptic curve using (P-256) is almost equal with 3248-bit RSA key so the adversary will ever never can break the key.

Proposed Performance:

Let E is an elliptic curve over the finite filed F_p is given in the following form:

$$Y^2 = X^2 + aX + b,$$
$$a, b \in F_p \text{and} -(4a^3 + 27b^2) \neq 0$$

As discussed above when Mr. X and Mr. Y agree on a key (Yellow Color) then they first fix a finite field F_q, an elliptic curve E and base point $B \in E$ (with high order). To generate key first Mr. X chooses a random number a € F_q and keep it as secret. Next Mr. X calculates a_B € E is a public and shares with Mr. Y. Where he also performs same steps and calculates b_B and shares with Mr. X. Their secret common key is $P = ab_B \in E$

Definition: An elliptic curve E over the field F is a smooth curve.

$$Y^2 + a_1XY + a_3Y = X^3 + a_2X^2 + a_4X + a_6, a_i \in F$$
$$E(F) \text{ is a set of points, } (x, y) \in F_2 \text{satisfies point at infinity } O.$$

Using ECDHE a secret key is shared between X and Y, with agreement on Elliptic Curve parameters, where X and Y have the key pair contains a Secret Key SK (Selected integer randomly less than n and where n is the order of curve) and Public Key PK = SK * G (Where G is generate point). Let (SK_X, PK_X) be the private public key pair of X and (SK_Y, PK_Y) be the private public key pair of Y.

1. The end X computers $KEY_X = (A_X, B_X) = SK_X * PK_Y$
2. Compute $KEY_Y = (A_Y, B_Y) = SK_Y * PK_X$

3. Since $SK_X * PK_Y = SK_X SK_Y G = SK_Y SK_X G = SK_Y * PK_X$
   Therefore $KEY_X = KEY_Y$ and $A_X = B_Y$
4. The Secret Key shared is KEY_X which is practically impossible to find the private key SK_X or SK_Y from the Public Key KEY_X.

As shown in Fig. 5, the proposed approach is to reduce the identified problems with the proposed framework, access the data by multiple data consumers for stored data in untrusted environment and without decrypting the data in cloud by CryptDB and CP-ABE where the security providing for the login users by providing key pair with Elliptic Curve Diffie–Hellman Ephemeral policy by transferring public key and from the public key users get the Secret Key. The core of framework is the ECDHE-ZeroVi's proxy that is responsible for encrypting the data and queries and decrypting query results. Data Provider submits the data with access policy through ECDHE ZeroVi's framework which encrypts the data CP-ABE and the key produced through ECDHE and Searchable encryption and stores the encrypted data in Cloud Server (Fig. 6).

Data Consumer requests a query along with the Secret Key that is generated from Elliptic Curve Diffie–Hellman Ephemeral through the ECDHE-ZeroVi's proxy which encrypts the query. The Cloud Server encrypted results of the query to the ECDHE-ZeroVi's proxy which decrypts the results and gives the decrypted data to the data consumer. The proposed framework depends on Attribute Authority (AA) to supply the authenticated attributes for authenticated users and avoid adversaries from requesting queries with the proposed framework. Any user can request the query to the cloud server; no user can decrypt the data without AA by

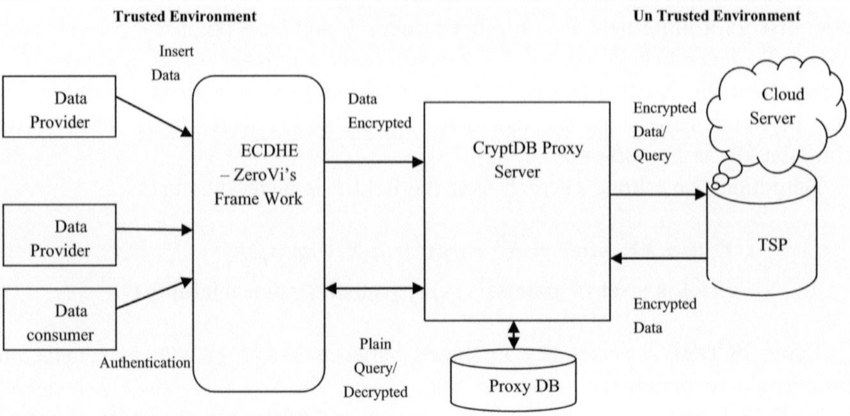

Fig. 5 ECDHE-ZeroVi's with CP-ABE architecture

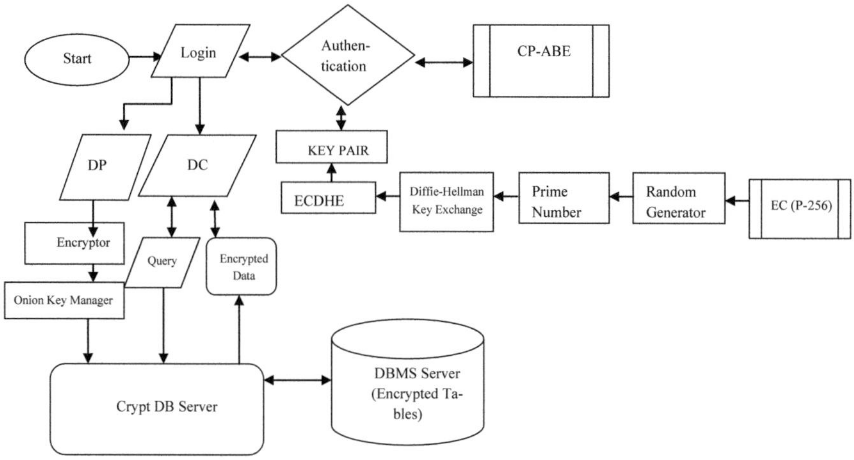

Fig. 6 Flow diagram of the proposed architecture

CP-ABE and key pair (SK, PK) by ECDHE. And even though the adversaries attack and break the key the adversaries can see the data which is related to query because the data stored in Cloud Server is encrypted using Onion Encryption where it gives high protection layers through Onion Encryption.

4 Conclusion and Future Work

In this paper, a privacy-preserving and secure information sharing scheme in cloud computing by exploiting CP-ABE and consolidating it with method of Elliptic Curve Diffie–Hellman Ephemeral Key Exchange in CryptDB server. The Diffie–Hellman Ephemeral is the key exchange cryptosystem that involves a secret key, by using Elliptic Curve Cryptography for Encryption and Decryption and CP-ABE used for user authentication. The proposed scheme guarantees fine-grained data access control, retrogressive secrecy and security against the collusion of users with the cloud and supports client expansion, denial, and characteristic alterations. Besides, proposed scheme does not unveil any elements of users to the cloud and it keeps the privacy of the users away from the cloud. Likewise, access the execution of the proposed scheme about computation complexity. The proposed scheme when implemented gives better performance in Database Query time when compared with the works included in [2] and there are no eavesdropping as the result given to the consumer is encrypted form.

References

1. Popa RA, Redfield CMS, Zeldovich N, Balakrishnan H (20111) Cryptdb: protecting confidentiality with encrypted query processing. In: Proceedings of the twenty-third ACM symposium on operating systems principles, SOSP 2011, ACM, New York, pp 85–100
2. Solomon MG, Sunderam V, Xiong L (2014) Towards secure cloud database with fine-grained access control. In: Department of Mathematics & Computer Science Emory University Atlanta, Georgia 30322, USA
3. Bethencourt J, Sahai A, Waters B (2007) Cipher text-policy attribute-based encryption. In: IEEE symposium on security and privacy, IEEE Computer Society, pp 321–334
4. Boneh D, Franklin M (2001) Identity-based encryption from the weil pairing. In: Kilian J (ed) CRYPTO 2001, vol 2139. LNCS. Springer, Heidelberg, pp 213–229
5. Fiat A, Naor M (1994) Broadcast encryption. In: Stinson DR (ed) CRYPTO 1993, LNCS, vol 773, Springer, Heidelberg, pp 480–491
6. Goyal V, Pandey O, Sahai A, Waters B (2006) Attribute-based encryption for fine grained access control of encrypted data. In: Proceedings of the 13th ACM conference on computer and communications security, CCS 2006, ACM, New York, pp 89–98
7. Kim J, Susilo W, Au MH, Seberry J (2014) Efficient semi-static secure broadcast encryption scheme. In: Cao Z, Zhang F (eds) Pairing 2013, vol 8365. LNCS. Springer, Heidelberg, pp 62–76
8. Phan D-H, Pointcheval D, Shahandashti SF, Strefler M (2013) Adaptive cca broadcast encryption with constant-size secret keys and ciphertexts. Int J Inf Secur 12(4):251–265
9. Armbrust M et al (2009) Above the clouds: a berkeley view of cloud computing [Technical report]. EECS Department, University of California, Berkeley
10. Arrington M (2006) Gmail disaster: reports of mass email deletions.http://www.techcrunch.com/2006/12/28/gmail-disasterreports-ofmassemail-deletions
11. Erway C et al (2009) Dynamic provable data possession. In: Proceedings of the 16th ACM conference on computer and communications security (CCS). ACM, pp 213–222
12. Boneh D et al (2005) Hierarchical identity based encryption with constant size cipher text. In: Advances in cryptology eEUROCRYPT, Springer
13. Ostrovsky R (2007) Attribute-based encryption with non-monotonic access structures. In: Proceedings of the 14th ACM conference on computer and communications security (CCS), pp 195–203
14. Samarati P, De Capitani di Vimercati S (2010) Data protection in outsourcing scenarios: issues and directions. In: Proceedings of the 5th ACM Symposium on information, computer and communications security (ASIACCS). ACM, pp 1–14
15. Lewko A, Waters B (2011) Decentralizing attribute-based encryption. In: Advances in cryptology EUROCRYPT. Springer, pp 568–588
16. Difo M (2012) Diffie-Hellman and its application security policies, IJESIT
17. Neha J, Brajesh P (2012) Forward secrecy for Google HTTPS using elliptic curve Diffie-Hellman key exchange algorithm. Int J Adv Res Comput Eng Technol (IJARCET) 1(9) November 2012
18. Ciphertext-policy attribute-based encryption: an expressive, E_cient, and provably secure realization: Brent Waters: University of Texas at Austin

Author Biographies

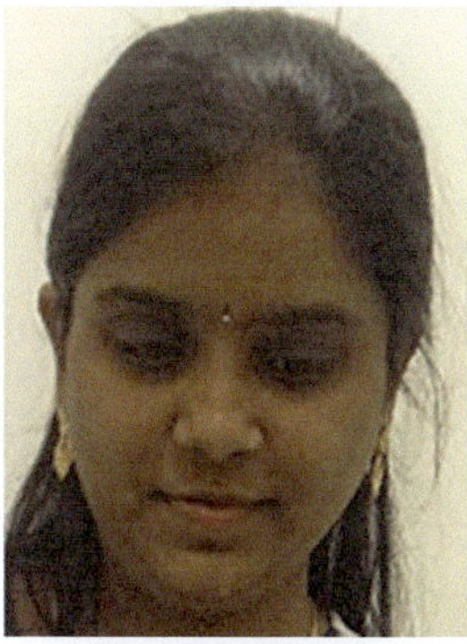

Krishna Keerthi Chennam obtained Bachelor's degree in computers science engineering from JNTU, Hyderabad in 2005, received the Masters Degree in Embedded Systems from JNTUH, in 2012 and pursuing Ph.D. in CSE from Gitam University, Hyderabad campus. Research interests include Cloud Computing, Cloud security. Currently working as Assistant Professor in Computer Science & Engineering Department at Muffakham Jah College of Engineering & Technology, Banjarahills, and Hyderabad.

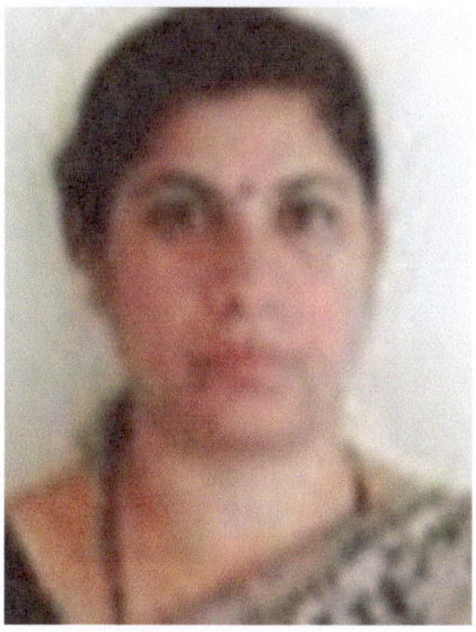

Dr. M. Akka Lakshmi received Ph.D. from Osmania University in 2008. Her research focus in Network Security, Cloud Computing, Cloud Security, Big Data. She is presently working as Professor and IT-HOD in Gitam University, Hyderabad Campus. She is the author of several research papers in the area of Network Security and Cloud computing.

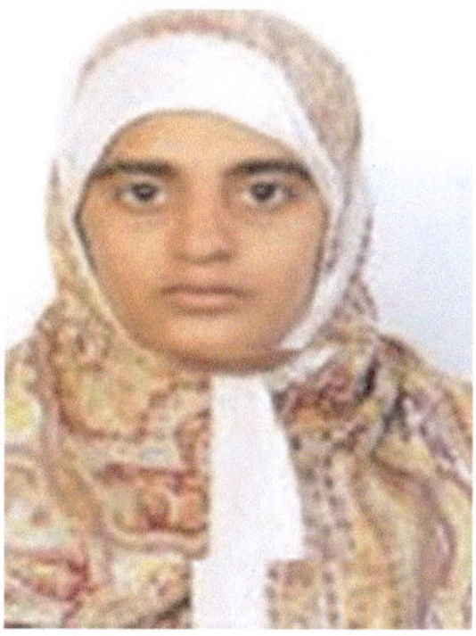

MunavvaraTahaseen working as Asst. Prof. in MJCET, Hyderabad.

Mitigating Cloud Security Threats Using Public-Key Infrastructure

Disha H. Parekh and R. Sridaran

Abstract Cloud computing is a very huge entity, as a technology, in recent era, evolving at a very rapid pace. There is a wide progress from mainframe computers toward the client/server infrastructures, including cloud computing deployment models with rudiments from autonomic computing, grid computing, and utility computing. This transition has brought tremendous effects on areas of information security and communications. These effects are majorly viewed positively, but there are some critical issues to be concerned. Due to this major transition toward cloud, various risks and challenges, identified and unidentified, have been discovered weakening the traditional security approaches. For this reason, that paper is aimed twofold: First to evaluate the requirements for cloud security and second is to propose a viable solution which would eradicate major potential threats. The model introduced in this paper will help to demolish network-related threats that arise due to trusted third party. The proposed solution will also enhance cryptography with Public-Key Infrastructure and helps in mitigating security threats. The solution presents a broad way of trusting services that realizes any security threats.

Keywords Cloud computing security · Confidentiality · Integrity Availability · Trusted third party · Information security · Public-key infrastructure · Mitigating security threats · RD model · Scramble Unscramble · AES · DES · 3DES

D. H. Parekh (✉) · R. Sridaran
Faculty of Computer Applications, Marwadi Education Foundation's Group of Institutions, Rajkot, Gujarat, India
e-mail: disha.hparekh213@gmail.com

R. Sridaran
e-mail: sridaran.rajagopal@gmail.com

D. H. Parekh
Computer Science Department, Bharathiar University, Coimbatore, Tamilnadu, India

M. U. Bokhari et al. (eds.), *Cyber Security*, Advances in Intelligent Systems and Computing 729, https://doi.org/10.1007/978-981-10-8536-9_17

1 Introduction

Computing has bloomed and expanded horizontally and vertically with lots of innovations in the field. There has been a wavy graph with a nudge in the information and communication age. The computing era initiated with mainframe computers, traversing toward minicomputers to personal computers later and now we have reached to the most noteworthy era, i.e., cloud computing era. Cloud computing services are offered by identified Cloud Service Providers (CSP) across the globe. The CSP is considered to be simply an extension from Internet Service Provider (ISP) and Application Service Provider (ASP). At the very initial level, ISP 1.0 was implemented where Internet was provided locally to the institute. Later it got transformed to ISP 2.0 and ISP 3.0, where now the Internet services were available globally and users were able to connect with telecommunications and other service providers thru associated data centers. These further got evolved to ASP (ISP 4.0), where not only the computing infrastructure but also specialized applications were provided with a greater ease. But considering the problem of ASP where only dedicated infrastructures were implemented, a newer version of ISP, ISP 5.0, called CSP got evolved, where the computing infrastructure along with applications are available on a shared basis. Cloud computing characterizes a model transition—a transfer from product-based computing to a service orientated computing [1]. The US National Institute of Standards and Technology has defined that cloud computing is a technology that facilitates well-situated, need-based network admission to a communal group of computing resources, e.g., servers, networks, applications, and offerings that can be quickly given and free with negligible management attempt or service supplier interaction [2]. The cloud encourages ease of use and is collected of five necessary distinctiveness, three delivery models, and four deployment models [3]. Services offered by cloud computing are supplied with dynamism to the customer who owns their data on cloud. As per their demand and their need, the customer can easily access the data from cloud, as it is shared across the network, from any location at a very high speed. Apart from this, cloud also provides a very greater space for each individual to store data. Its benefits like multi-tenancy, i.e., sharing of resources at the network level, high scalability, elasticity, and pay-as-you-go facility have made cloud computing a promising and swiftly budding model.

These elementary taxonomies are usually known as the "SPI Model", where it stands for Software services, Platform services, and Infrastructure services respectively [4].

- **Software as a Service (SaaS)**

An application hosted for its clients and who can use the services offered via the Internet is generally what SaaS does. A customer does not sustain or support the software; rather the software provider will only take care of its support and maintenance. Moreover, customers do not make any upgradation in the software and do not require integration of other systems also. The provider only does the patching and necessary improvements. SaaS provides clients with network-based access to the commercially available software which is kept centrally.

- **Platform as a Service (PaaS)**

The second type of delivery model is PaaS, which supplies the necessary resources that are required to create applications and offerings online, with no need of downloading or installing any software. It includes services like the integration of web services, integration of database, scalability, protection, designing, testing, deployment, and hosting.

- **Infrastructure as a Service (IaaS)**

The last service model, IaaS, is the succeeding kind of service in which the hardware or the computing infrastructure is provided to the clients to put their data or applications on network. The infrastructure provided can be scaled up and down on demand, dynamically. Additionally, it even provides the feature of multi-tenancy on the same infrastructure. It is in other terms also known as Hardware as a Service (HaaS).

Regardless of the above service models exploited, there are four models that are deployed and implemented for cloud with derived disparities which need address specific requirements.

- **Public Cloud**

In this type of cloud, the service is obtainable by the general public or to any bigger organization. The cloud provided, is usually under the ownership of an organization that sells cloud services.

- **Private Cloud**

Over here, the cloud is open only to the single client, or a solitary organization. These types of cloud can be supervised either by the organization or any third party. It varies in 2 different forms, i.e., off-premise and on-premise. In off-premise, the cloud used is generally managed by any third party while in on-premise; the cloud is managed and owned by the organization that uses it.

- **Community Cloud**

In community cloud, the cloud is mutually used in numerous organizations and it supports an explicit community that has shared anxieties. It could be under the supervision of the organizations or of an intermediate party and may be situated on-premise or off-premise.

- **Hybrid Cloud**

This cloud is a combination of more than one cloud, i.e., private, public, or community which will exist as exclusive entities but are leaped mutually by the proprietary skill that allows data and application transportability.

The cloud computing security and related work done on security issues with either encryption technique or cryptography is mentioned in the first half. The next part describes the needs for cloud computing security with respect to Confidentiality, Infrastructure, and Availability (CIA) is discussed. This paper has also proposed a model that shows the use of DES algorithm in encrypting and decrypting process but involving scrambler and unscrambler. The proposed model ensures all major needs that cloud security requires. It enhances integrity assurance and confidentiality as well as the availability of data on cloud.

2 Related Work

It is observed that a large amount work has been carried out in the vicinity of cloud security. A major portion of the work focuses on the reliability verification the saved data in the cloud. Tangowan et al. [6] have depicted cloud computing security anxieties that are specifically related to security of data and privacy-based guard issues which has remained as a chief restraint for the implementation of services provided by cloud computing. They have offered with summarizing but thorough analysis on data security and privacy protection issues. But the disadvantage is that it does not show any practical implementation of the security policy or mechanism.

Somani et al. [7] state that in cloud computing problems like data security, file system, backup, and host security persists to a greater extent. They have projected a notion of the digital signature with the use of RSA algorithms to encrypt the sensitive data while shifting it over the network. This technique has tried to solve the problem of authentication and confidentiality. But as observed, the problem of integrity still persists.

Similarly, Rafique et al. [8] have shown a secure data transfer based on identity in cloud using a method called Group Digital Signature (GDS). In this, a group manager will commune with the service giver by using a secret key that will get produced by the Diffie–Hillman key exchange algorithm. Group manager obtains the member public key of all the users in the group. The user in the group sends the data to the cloud server and will sign the message with the assigned (d, n) private key. This message is acknowledged by the group manager who authenticates the group member and then gathers the necessary detail and further attaches the secret group id and sign and sends it to the cloud provider. Cloud provider will authenticate the message and will allow the encrypted message to be stored in private cloud. But as observed, one needs to trust the group manager, which might not be feasible at every instance [5].

Moreover, Fernandes et al. [9], has shown in their paper that security related to data in the cloud can be assured with the use of digital signature with help of CFX_MF algorithms. In this digital signature is used for the verification and non-repudiation of the message, where the uniqueness of sender and the reliability of the message are preserved. According to the paper, the integrity check over the cloud computing is performed by an intermediate party which inspects the data from client and hauls out the request of unauthorized user. Some researchers do not trust the third party as there is no guarantee of mutual and equal trust.

After surveying various papers, and flaws with the usage of encryption techniques in the papers, this paper is aimed to focus on guaranteed cloud security model. This model will use Data Encryption Standard (DES) algorithm with scrambling and unscrambling of data and is also ensuring the mechanism to assure data integrity and authentic data availability at the end once the encrypted data is decrypted.

3 Cloud Computing Security

Securing data on the web involves recognizing exceptional threats and challenges which necessarily has to be attended with greater impact by applying proper countermeasures. Eventually, the required security services and controls are set up with the typical systems engineering procedure in order to efficiently amalgamate the defense controls with the information systems practical and equipped requirements, plus other significant system requirements like reliability, maintainability, and supportability [10]. Usually, the architecture of cloud computing provides a single data center for data storage and computation [11]. There can be various security benefits in utilizing the cloud environment. But, a single malfunctioning should not be alleged for any data loss. It generally is very difficult to track down the security measures in a cloud environment. The current cloud service providers have introduced and placed many complicated methods and trained staff for sustaining their systems. Due to this, there are various security benefits like data centralization, data backup, incident response, logging, etc., available. Though it shows the presence of many security features, cloud computing still addresses major key security issues and challenges, like data segregation, usage of compromised servers, certificates and auditing security, investigating an illegal undertaking, and many more.

Cloud computing has become a most important development in IT. Enterprises should acclimatize to the diversifications it brings to maximize the return on investment. To assist organizations worldwide, International System Audit and Control Association (ISACA) has identified critical issues which need operational methods like effectively organizing risks, being transparent with the third party about the enterprise policies, handling myriad regulations and adapting competently [12]. In spite of several measures and steps for cloud security, the cloud has exclusive features that involve endangering evaluation in fields like availability issues, data integrity, reliability problems, data recovery, and privacy and auditing, as stated in Gartner [13].

Cloud computing, thus, as concluded, has a huge number of security issues and challenges [14]. An elaborated record of security threats on the basis of the deployment and service models of cloud computing is presented and discussed in detail in [15]. Security, in general, to technology, is broadly standardized for evaluation of data systems security, focusing on three central goals of CIA, essentially known as, Confidentiality, Integrity, and Availability.

- **Confidentiality**

Confidentiality refers the access of restricted data only to authorized users and ceasing access of such protected data from unauthorized users. Confidentiality aims at authentication procedures like user-ids and passwords that solely recognize data users and sustaining procedures that hamper each recognized user's get access to the system's resources. But as there is augmented the quantity of parties, devices, and applications occupied on cloud, the threat compromised data grow substantially as the multiple access points come into existence. Such an increase in data usage leads to problems with multi-tenancy, applications security, data remnants, and privacy [16].

Cloud service providers usually are using a weak authentication mechanism that involves username and password and the access controls, i.e., authorization, is at a very coarse level, which results in significant security threats. To address these security threats and to answer the cloud protection, in essence, there is a use of encryption technique [17]. Encryption of data is carried out based on encryption algorithm and is dependent on key strength. The encryption carried out even depends on the cloud service providers; for example, EMC provides encryption facility to the customer data while Amazon's S3 does not provide any kind of encryption to customer data but instead customer's before uploading the data can encrypt the data on their own.

The encryption of data for the purpose of providing confidentiality to customer data primarily involves use of encryption algorithm. There are many encryption algorithms present but not all are fashioned equal [18]. Cryptographically, many algorithms are insufficient to provide the desired security. Algorithms that are evaluated by formal standard bodies like NIST or informally by the cryptographic community must be used. Next, the key length for encrypting data must be considered. It is essential to know that larger the key length, stronger is the encryption. For the NIST-approved algorithms like 3 DES (Triple Data Encryption Standard) minimum length should be of 112 bits, which will be shown in the proposed model.

- **Integrity**

Integrity is the next security aspect required for confidentiality. Integrity simply means that consumer assets can be customized only by the authenticated users and in an authorized way only. When it comes to data storage, maintaining data integrity aspect is the obvious requirement. Data integrity ensures that no illicit or illegal modification, deletion, or fabrication of data is allowed and originality of data remains intact [19]. By keeping a check on the unauthorized access, organization attains greater confidentiality in terms of data integrity. Moreover, integrity also helps in accountability of data modification, data deletion or any constructed data, to find the potential source of such intrusion.

Data encryption is a solution for confidentiality but there should be a mechanism to assure and verify the data that is decrypted by the recipient. This is taken care of data integrity which uses message authentication codes tagged with the encrypted data. These message authentication codes work as a hash function which will ensure that the data that gets decrypted in the original sent message of the sender [20].

- **Availability**

The huge accessibility computing community has pursued a mantra that no particular source of failure should be observed, yet the administration of a cloud examine by a lone company is, in fact, a distinct point of failure [21]. Availability refers to every entity that comes when we talk about cloud. It targets the availability of data in cloud, states the availability of the cloud service provider, system availability and even talks about the availability of network level security mechanism to ensure data security. Hence, availability is not only about data presence in the cloud. Network is now getting highly congested and, therefore, need to assure clients that the data will be available to them dynamically at any point of instance.

System availability involves the ability of system to continue with functioning in a proper and accurate manner even when there is any kind of authority misbehaves noticed. In spite of any security breach is identified, system should be able to carry its operations as though normal. Cloud services show a severe reliance on the resource infrastructures and network accessibility at all times [22].

Business critical applications generally rely on continuous and constant delivery of services without a gap of any time. A simple service outage only for few minutes can have a serious impact on the productivity of the enterprise. It can also result in customer dissatisfaction and service-level disobedience. According to the Cloud Computing Incidents Database (CCID) [23], which trails cloud service outages, chief cloud service providers have undergone downtime ranging from just minutes to hours. Moreover, relying on the rigorousness of the occurrence and the extent of the exaggerated infrastructure, outages may involve all or a few of clients. During a cloud service commotion, harmed clients will not be in condition to contact the services and in a few cases can even experience tainted presentation [24].

Apart from security concerns based on CIA, there are still many more other concerns like privacy, data segregation, data storage, reliability, security, and data leakage. But out of all, security is the major one where most of the researchers work in the direction to secure cloud more day by day. To ensure the best security, generally data transfer from host to server and vice versa happens with encryption algorithms. Let us take a close look at few of the encryption algorithms.

4 Encryption Algorithms Used to Ensure Cloud Security

Earlier when data was stored on-premise, security measures were levied across the institute, as the data used to be always on the traditional server residing in the organization itself. But gradually, when we have started migrating on the cloud, which is global, an essential security check to ensure data integrity, privacy, and availability have become a major concern. To avoid the flaws, strong encryption techniques are being implemented [25]. Below mentioned are kinds of encryption algorithms used to ensure data security on cloud.

- RSA Algorithm:

This is the most commonly known algorithm, named after Rivest, Shamir, and Adleman, the discoverer. It is a kind of asymmetric algorithm where an encryption key is shared publicly to all but for encrypting a message, but the decryption key is kept private and not publically. Moreover, RSA is a block cipher where each message is charted in an integer. When used on the cloud, a cloud service provider does the encryption of data, place the key publically and the user who accesses this data from cloud, will decrypt it through a private key. RSA algorithm is found to be secure only for the users, but doesn't provide scalability and uses more of memory space which is basic problems with RSA [26].

- DES Algorithm:

DES stands for Data Encryption Standard. It is a symmetric block cipher algorithm. In this, data is encrypted in 64 bits of block size. Hence, 64 bits of data is input and encrypted to 64 bits of cipher text. DES also ensures security at both the ends and is scalable also. But it requires more memory space as compared to AES algorithm [27].

- 3DES Algorithm:

3DES utilizes three occurrences of DES with different keys. It is deemed to be secure because it needs operations enumerated to 2^112 to break it and none of the recent technologies make it possible within the harmful duration of time. It is inherently slow in case of of implementations, as it was premeditated to perform on-chip rather than by chip [28]. Block diagram of Triple DES implementation is as shown in Fig. 1 [29].

Fig. 1 Block diagram of TDES

TDEA Encryption Operation:

$$I \rightarrow \boxed{\text{DES } E_{K1}} \rightarrow \boxed{\text{DES } D_{K2}} \rightarrow \boxed{\text{DES } E_{K3}} \rightarrow O$$

TDEA Decryption Operation:

$$I \rightarrow \boxed{\text{DES } D_{K3}} \rightarrow \boxed{\text{DES } E_{K2}} \rightarrow \boxed{\text{DES } D_{K1}} \rightarrow O$$

- AES Algorithm:

AES stands for Advanced Encryption Standard, and is a symmetric block cipher kind of algorithm, used maximum nowadays. AES follows 128-bit key length for encryption. In this type of algorithm, a data when is about to be stored on cloud by the data generator, it is encrypted first and then this encrypted data is stored on cloud. When any end users would like to use this data, the decryption takes place at the data generator's end and then only the users will be able to read data on their side. AES is found to be highly scalable and is also providing security at both the ends, i.e., users and the providers. Even the memory usage for AES kind of encryption is found very low [30].

- Blowfish Algorithm:

Blowfish is a symmetric key cryptographic algorithm. It encrypts blocks of size 64 bits with a changeable length key of size 128–448 bits. Blowfish is suitable for those applications where the key does not change frequently but remains constant for a very long time. Blowfish is also secured for both the users and the providers, and is also scalable. It is providing with good authenticity but is less used than AES [31].

The encryption algorithms are very essential and provide a better mechanism to secure data on cloud. As data security on cloud is the major concern, and as CIA are very essential for cloud security, a model proposed below, known as RD Model, is designed in such a way that it ensures all three very diligently.

5 Proposed RD Model

An RD Model is proposed with its architecture, depicted in Fig. 2, for communication between client and server, from client side. A similar reverse channel would exist from server to client communication. The model takes the data from the client in respective protocol as chosen by the client, and takes it into the defined encryption stages as below:

Step 1: Encryption Stage 1:

A random or pseudorandom pattern is generated to be used as key for the first time only. Later on, in the next cycles this key can be provided by the other party and may also be used to acknowledge previous communication. It will also check integrity of the complete path.

Step 2: Scrambling of data:

In this step, the key and the data are scrambled together which would generate another set of pseudorandom stream.

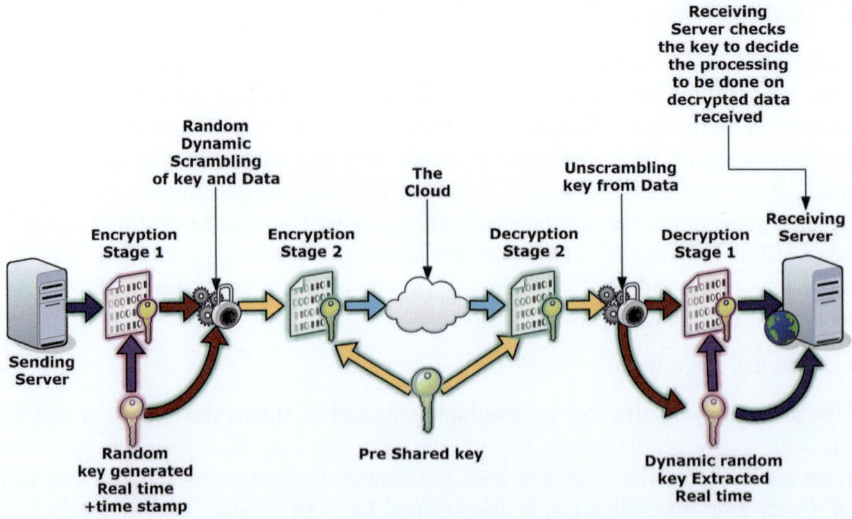

Fig. 2 Proposed RD model

Step 3: Encryption stage 2:

This is the normally used Public-Key Infrastructure (PKI), which uses a symmetric or an asymmetric keying technique as available in the network.

Step 4: Data stream in the cloud:

After the encryption stage 1 of the sender's data, scrambled data with further encryption using PKI will now be transmitted over the cloud.

Step 5: Decryption stage 2:

This stage is the corresponding complementary stage for encryption stage 2 as depicted in step 3.

Step 6: Unscrambling of data and key:

The unscrambling will be in perfect coordination to the pseudorandom scrambling of the data and the key done in step 2. In this stage, the scrambled key is extracted and retrieved accurately.

Step 7: Decryption stage 1:

It contains the exact complementary decryption algorithm as discussed in step 1 and it retrieves the data sent using the key extracted in previous step.

Step 8: Guarantee check on CIA Rules:

Using the key extracted in the step 6, the receiver will check the integrity and authenticity of the received data. This will ensure that only proper data is processed further. If the receiver, based on the preset rules decides that the received data is objectionable, the data is discarded to avoid further processing. If such a case occurs, a certain set of actions can be levied upon by the receiver which may include a retransmission request or in a worse-case request to login again by session termination.

The security deployed by this algorithm in terms of CIA of the communication far surpasses the disadvantage it suffers from, a comparatively larger overhead in terms of time. The choice of several algorithms in encryption and decryption in the stages and usage of different scrambling mechanisms further ensure the CIA of the communication stream. The process is transparent to the end users making it hard to decipher the algorithm sequence due to the most common security threat, the users themselves. The response sequence can be reutilized as keys for next sequence of data streams as encryption key in Step 1 which also ensures the increased efficiency over a communication and this in turn also works as the logical link between sending and receiving machines to optimize the data flow as well as detection of hidden threats.

6 Conclusion and Future Work

In this paper, an RD model is proposed which uses the first-level encryption followed by scrambling and second-level encryption is carried out. As data security in cloud computing is the most sensitive issue and is seeking utmost attention by researchers, this paper aims at finding a solution for data security implementing second-level encryption and scrambling of data. It also has depicted that the 2-level data decryption ensures data confidentiality integrity and availability at a successful results. The model is designed in MATLAB with implementation of 3DES algorithm at present. It also shows the use of scrambling and unscrambling of data, which ensures integrity and authenticity of transmitted data. In future, this model will be demonstrated on Java platform to implement a real time model, so that data security is guaranteed on cloud computing world without any doubts on the vulnerabilities of cloud.

References

1. Murugesan S (2011) Cloud computing gives emerging markets a lift. IT Pro, IEEE, pp 60–62
2. National Institute of Standards and Technology (2008) Guide for mapping types of information and information systems to security categories. NIST 800-60
3. Hashizume K et al (2013) An analysis of security issues for cloud computing. J Internet Serv Appl 4(1):1–13

4. Zhu W, Luo C, Wang J, Li S (2011) Multimedia cloud computing. IEEE Signal Process Mag 59–69
5. Rimal BP, Choi E, Lumb I (2009) A taxanomy and survey of cloud computing. In: 2009 fifth international joint conference on INC, IMS and IDC, IEEE, pp 44–51
6. Tangwongsan S, Itthisombat V (2014) A highly effective security model for privacy preserving on cloud storage. Cloud Comput Intell Syst (CCIS). In: IEEE 3rd international conference
7. Somani U, Lakhani K, Mundra M (2010) Implementing digital signature with RSA encryption algorithms to enhance the data security of cloud in cloud computing. IEEE
8. Rafique S et al (2015) Web application security vulnerabilities detection approaches: a systematic mapping study. In: 16th IEEE/ACIS international conference on software engineering, artificial intelligence, networking and parallel/distributed computing (SNPD). IEEE
9. Fernandes DAB et al (2014) Security issues in cloud environments: a survey. Int J Inf Secur 13(2):113–170
10. GroBauer B, Walloschek T, Stocker E (2011) Understanding cloud computing vulnerabilities. IEEE, pp 50–57
11. Schneiderman R (2011) For cloud computing, the sky is the limit. IEEE Signal Process Mag 15–17
12. Heier H, Borgman HP, Bahli B (2012) Cloudrise: opportunities and challenges for IT governance at the dawn of cloud computing. In: 45th Hawaii international conference on system science (HICSS). IEEE
13. Gartner (2008) Assessing the security risks of cloud computing. Gartner
14. Parekh DH, Sridaran R (2013) An analysis of security challenges in cloud computing. In: IJACSA
15. Cloud Security Alliance (2010) Top threats to cloud computing, Cloud Security Alliance
16. Harauz J, Kaufman LM, Potter B (2009) Data security in the world of cloud computing, IEEE, pp 61–64
17. Aazam M et al (2014) Cloud of things: integrating internet of things and cloud computing and the issues involved. 2014 11th international Bhurban conference on applied sciences and technology (IBCAST)
18. Yu S, Wang C, Ren K, Lou W (2010) Achieving secure, scalable, and fine-grained data access control in cloud computing
19. Yu S, Ren K, Lou W, Li J (2009) Defending against key abuse attacks in kp-abe enabled broadcast systems, In: Proceedings of SECURECOMM’09
20. Wang C et al (2010) Privacy-preserving public auditing for data storage security in cloud computing. In: Proceedings of INFOCOM. IEEE
21. Wang Q et al (2009) Enabling public verifiability and data dynamics for storage security in cloud computing. In: Computer Security—ESORICS 2009. Springer, Berlin, pp 355–370
22. Armbrust M et al (2010) A view of cloud computing. Commun ACM 53(4):50–58
23. Zhang Q, Cheng L, Boutaba R (2010) Cloud computing: state-of-the-art and research challenges. J Internet Serv Appl 1(1):7–18
24. Popović K (2010) Cloud computing security issues and challenges. In: MIPRO, proceedings of the 33rd international convention. IEEE
25. Subashini S, Kavitha V (2011) A survey on security issues in service delivery models of cloud computing. J Network Comput Appl. Elsevier, pp 1–11
26. Sun D et al (2011) Surveying and analyzing security, privacy and trust issues in cloud computing environments. Proc Eng 15:2852–2856
27. Buyya R et al (2009) Cloud computing and emerging IT platforms: vision, hype, and reality for delivering computing as the 5th utility. Fut Gener Comput Syst 25(6):599–616
28. Shao J, He Z (2004) High-speed implementation of 3DES encryption algorithm based on FPGA. Mod Electron Technol
29. National Institute of Standard and Technology (1999) Data encryption standard (DES)[EB/OL]. http://www.csrc.nist.gov/publications/fips/fips46-3/fips46-3.pdf

30. Sanaei Z et al Heterogeneity in mobile cloud computing: taxonomy and open challenges. Commun Surv Tutorials 16(1):369–392
31. Xiao Z, Xiao Y (2013) Security and privacy in cloud computing. Commun Surv Tutorials 15 (2):843–859

Author Biographies

Prof. Disha H. Parekh, M.Phil., MCA, PGDBA (Human Resource), is presently an Assistant Professor of Faculty of Computer Applications at Marwadi Education Foundation's Group of Institutions, Rajkot, Gujarat. She has completed her M.Phil. in Computer Science from Bharathiar University and is at present pursuing Ph.D. in computer science on cloud computing. She did her MCA from Ganpat University, Gujarat. She even completed PGDBA with a specialization in HR from Symbiosis University. She has published 3 papers in the International Journal and has presented 1 paper at National conference. She has attended many workshops and seminars. Her areas of interest are Software Engineering and Web Technologies.

Dr. R. Sridaran, is currently the Dean, Faculty of Computer Applications, Marwadi Education Foundation's Group of Institutions, Rajkot, Gujarat. He did his postgraduation in Computer Applications and Management. He was awarded Ph.D. in Computer Applications in 2010. Having started his career as an Entrepreneur, he has offered his consultancy services to various service sectors. He designed and delivered various training programs in the areas of IT and Management. He has published 15 research papers in foremost Journals and Conferences and is currently guiding five research scholars. He has got 22 years of academic experience and has served in principal educational institutions at diverse capacities.

Analysis and Impact of Different Mechanisms of Defending Pass-the-Hash Attacks

Navjyotsinh Jadeja and Madhuri Vaghasia

Abstract Pass-the-hash attack has been around more than 18 years, and founded roots of its first existence were around 1997. The reason for discussing it again now is that it has come into forefront in recent times. And with the usage of Internet and World Wide Web like never before and given the ever increasing use of the Internet (2 billion users in 2011 with forecasts of another billion users coming online in the recent 4 years) and excessive use of ubiquitous devices and computing it has capabilities of affecting the most now. There are always certain machines which are unpatched or those which can have easy to find opening and to get the different privileged accesses through them, and now that cloud-based services are used and major chunk of computers still working on Windows platform, which is most prone to this kind of attack. It becomes a big threat for cloud services providers as well. In this paper, we are trying to focus and understand pass-the-hash attack and also discuss various pros and cons of some of the different approaches. Here, we present results and approaches proposed by various researchers, and also address the strengths and weaknesses of the solutions. Albeit extensive advancement has been made, more research should be done to address this issue. We propose several defense mechanisms here which are first of their kind and if implemented may reduce the repercussions of the attack.

Keywords Pass-the-hash attack · Hash attack · Network security
Cloud security

N. Jadeja (✉) · M. Vaghasia
Faculty of Engineering, Information Technology,
Marwadi Education Foundation's Group of Institutions,
Rajkot, Gujarat, India
e-mail: navjyotsinh.jadeja@marwadieducation.edu.in

M. Vaghasia
e-mail: madhuri.vaghasia@marwadieducation.edu.in

M. U. Bokhari et al. (eds.), *Cyber Security*, Advances in Intelligent Systems and Computing 729, https://doi.org/10.1007/978-981-10-8536-9_18

1 Introduction

More and more computers, BYOD (Bring Your Own Device), and clouds expand, it invites huge number of people accessing Internet. By current numbers, it is already in billions as per one of the statistics [15]. Before we talk on different approaches or methods to defend against and reduce the mitigation of pass-the-hash attack (PTH), "There are two types of companies today, those that have been hacked and those that don't know they've been hacked" [16]. Generally, passwords are the most usually utilized security apparatus in the world today. Solid passwords are the absolutely most imperative part of data security, and weak passwords are the single biggest disappointments.

As the devices and strategies for credential theft and reuse attacks like the PTH attack enhance, malignant clients are discovering it to be less demanding to accomplish their objectives. The PTH attack is a standout among the most prevalent sorts of qualification theft and reuse attack seen by Microsoft to date. Other personal information theft attacks incorporate key logging and plaintext secret key capture, passing tickets, token mimic, and man-in-the-middle attacks. As mentioned earlier also, there are always certain machines which are unpatched or those which can have easy to find opening to get the different privileged accesses through them. This does not mean that we should surrender to attackers or hackers.

But issues with the other types of attacks are also reason for hackers preferring PTH attack. Password attacks, for example, watchword speculating or watchword breaking is time-consuming attacks. Devices that make utilization of pre-computed hashes diminish the time expected to acquire passwords incredibly. Nonetheless, there is capacity cost and time utilization identified with the era of those precompiled tables; this is particularly genuine if the calculation used to create these passwords is generally solid, and the passwords are mind boggling and long (more noteworthy than 10 characters) [12].

In a PTH attack, the objective is to utilize the hash straightforwardly without splitting it. This eradicates the need for password cracking or guessing algorithms and procedures.

1.1 What Is a Hash?

Before we can investigate the PTH attack, it is key to characterize a hash. For every client and head account on a framework, the working framework stores the username and a password with a specific end goal to perform authentication. On the other hand, of putting away the password in clear content, the working framework utilizes cryptographic hash capacities to make a hash esteem that it stores [20].

At the point when a client tries to authenticate to the framework, the framework takes the password info by the client, registers its hash esteem, and looks at the figured hash against the put away hash. On the off chance that the hashes match, the client is permitted access to the framework.

All the hashes are stored in computers Security Account Manager (SAM) file on computer. This includes all the values such as individual accounts, administrator accounts, or in that case any account details on the system.

1.2 What Is a Pass-the-Hash (PTH) Attack?

In this attack, an attacker gets entrance to a client's nearby regulatory hash and afterward tries to utilize the hashes traded off from that framework to authenticate to different frameworks on the system, conceivably obtaining entrance to extra hashes along the way. The attacker then proceeds with this parallel development of trading off distinctive frameworks inside of the system, increasing more hashes on each bargained framework. A definitive objective is to obtain entrance to a special domain account that can be utilized to get to discriminating servers and information (Fig. 1).

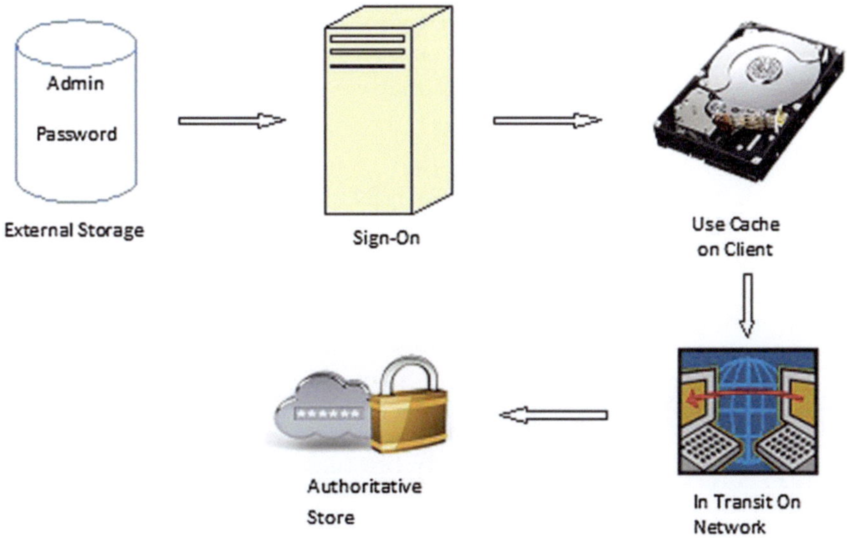

Fig. 1 Password cracking mechanism using PTH

1.3 Overview of Challenges

Overview of various challenges is discussed below:

- **Credential theft**: Most associations do not perceive when hackers/crackers are inside of the system and have admittance to data. For example, messages, private records, and other licensed innovation. Social designing and phishing plans are utilized to trap staff and get their security credentials.
- **Control level theft**: Once traded off, an assailant has complete control over a whole system. All data, assets, protected innovation, physical property, and individual data are in danger. A definitive objective of the hacker/cracker may be to get entrance to the system.
- **Data theft**: This does not stop or end with data theft. Step-by-step hierarchy of authority is also tried to be cracked. As soon as this is achieved, whole systems security is highly compromised which includes, data, critical information, etc. (Fig. 2).

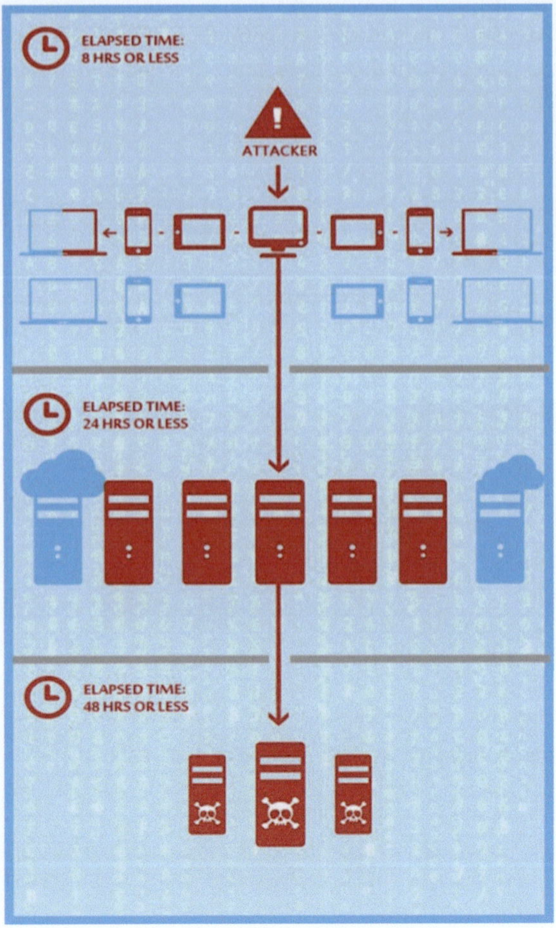

Fig. 2 Problems faced and time to reach the server levels after the theft [12]

2 Related Work

PTH is an attack that allows an attacker to use LM and NTLM hashes for authentication remote (and local) station without knowing the password and without breaking these hashes [14]. PTH attacks are no longer limited to only certain functionalities [13]. They have evolved and are causing the problems in not only client server environment but also are affecting the cloud networks as well. Cloud computing is a service-based model, and hence lot of BYOD devices are used to get the services which makes it vulnerable to the PTH form of attack.

Basic matrices can be utilized to evaluate the danger of presentation to potential cybersecurity dangers, for example, PTH. It has further demonstrated that on a fundamental level it is conceivable to process this metric continuously amid the approval period of network security, hence giving network overseers the capacity to design a network to minimize, or possibly wipe out introduction to these sorts of attacks [7].

The attacks themselves are dependable, hard to uncover, and frequently utilize exceptionally propelled hacking methods. Since they are propelled in nature, delayed, and constant, the associations behind them need to have an abnormal state of learning, propelled apparatuses, and skilled faculty to execute them. The attacks are normally preformed in a few stages—observation, readiness, execution, getting entrance, data social affair, and association upkeep. In each of the stages, attacks can be recognized with diverse probabilities. There are a few approaches to expand the level of security of an association keeping in mind the end goal to counter these occurrences. Above all else, it is important to instruct clients and framework chairmen on diverse assault vectors and furnish them with learning and assurance so that the attacks are unsuccessful. Second, actualize strict security strategies, which incorporate access control and confinements (to data or network), encrypting so as to ensure data and introducing most recent security overhauls. At last, it is conceivable to utilize programming IDS tools to identify such peculiarities [18]. There is also approach of defense in depth which can be used to reduce the threat to overall system. Dynamic defenses must also be enabled, which change attack surfaces to proactively defend a network [6].

3 Working of Pass-the-Hass Attack

There are certain set of rules, and requirements shall be met in order for PTH attack to be successful. On a very basic level, a PTH attack depends on three principles that are considered as follows:

1. The capacity to pick up administrative rights on the system putting away the required hashes,

2. Utilization of the same password on various systems, and
3. Managerial passwords that are infrequently changed.

The capacity to increase local administrative access—An intruder can pick up local administrative access to a PC by misusing vulnerability on the framework, by tempting a client into executing malicious code or through different methods.

Normal regulatory passwords—Utilizing the same password for various managerial accounts is a typical scenario for two reasons. To begin with, when frameworks are sent in a venture organizes, a base picture is made for both a workstation also, a server, and that picture is then utilized for each workstation or server that is sent. Accordingly, the greater part of the standard managerial accounts inside of the picture—also, their passwords—is engendered to each workstation or server sent on the system. Second, changing the password for every gadget would present administration complexities, including the difficulties of keeping up a record of each diverse password in a safe place and empowering IT staff to get to those passwords at the point when required.

Static passwords—Because most organizations have an extensive number of both local and server administrative accounts which numerous individuals need to access consistently, they frequently keep the authoritative passwords the same, transforming them just on the off chance that somebody in IT leaves the association. What is more, even all things considered, they may change just the passwords for the servers and not those for every individual workstations or systems [10].

There are various security frameworks already suggested to ensure security for the organizations [5]. But we would like to discuss different approaches to them. PTH attacks are normally coordinated against Windows frameworks; however, they can be found in different frameworks, for instance, vulnerable web applications and mobile applications. For list of such applications, refer SANS, 2008. In Windows operating environment, PTH attack depends on the Single Sign-On (SSO) functionality in authentication protocols like NTLM and Kerberos [2]. With SSO, users can enter their passwords once to be able to use resources they have been given rights to, without prompting them for their passwords again. This requires the system to have the users' credentials cached within the system. By replacing this credential with a password hash (or a ticket), further authentication will be done using this hash instead of the original credential [8].

SSO with Kerberos is still secure and will work fine and dandy without being helpless against this PTH attack. This is because this attack has nothing to do with Kerberos and everything to do with Windows' finished absence of security as to put away accreditations [3].

On a Unix/Linux framework, when you get a Kerberos ticket-allowing ticket store (TGT), it is scrambled utilizing a key that is allotted by the KDC when you perform a kinit. The ticket reserve is put away in/tmp and claimed/clear just by the client that made it and root, on the off chance that you let another client read that document they can mimic you. That is an extremely old issue and it is basically a tradeoff for some comfort [9] (Fig. 3).

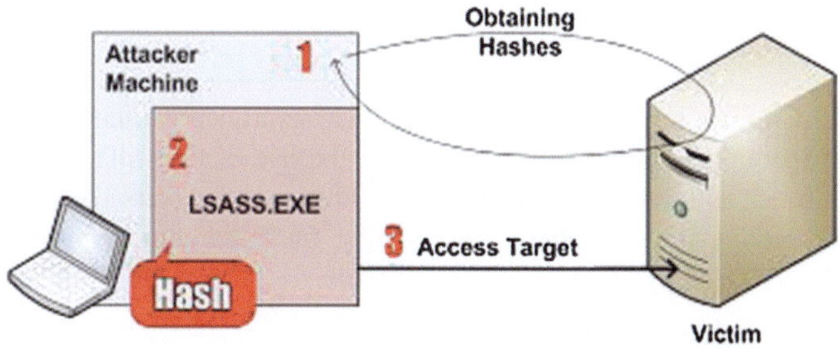

Fig. 3 Pass-the-hash attack in action [14]

3.1 Defending/Preventing Pass-the-Hash Attack

There is no single activity an association can take to keep a PTH attack. Both Microsoft and the NSA recommend the "Guard in-Depth" approach—they encourage associations to confine and ensure neighborhood and domain regulatory accounts through such procedures as making extraordinary local administrative passwords and executing least privileged access [1]. Moreover, they both prescribe confining inbound activity what s more, horizontal development on the system with firewall rule (Fig. 4).

There are several mitigations which can be applied. We have named this as Defense Mechanism 1, Defense Mechanism 2, and Defense Mechanism 3. They are the defensive measures we can apply to the system in order to reduce the amount of influence PTH can cause. After discussing this strategy, we have also suggested additional measures to avoid compromising of security due to PTH attack, especially in a cloud-based environment where access of resources and management of resources are done using various kinds of BYOD devices as well.

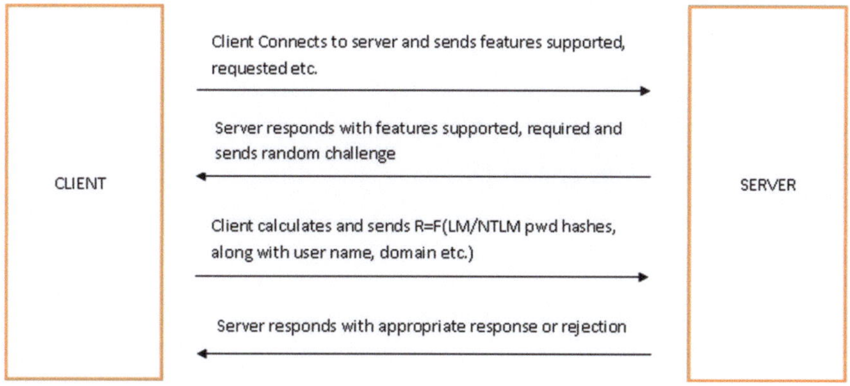

Fig. 4 Simplified diagram of NTLM challenge–response authentication protocol

3.2 Defense Mechanism 1

This mechanism is simple yet very effective. As mentioned earlier, we will have to restrict the incoming traffic to our servers, by the use of firewalls and other tools. Tools which act as layer 8 technologies in addition to 7 layers are also available such as Cyberoam firewall. Many other similar firewalls cum monitoring devices are available. These devices can play major role.

- What is the aim of this defense mechanism?

The aim is to limit the capacity of hacker/cracker from starting side long development from a traded off workstation by blocking or scanning incoming traffic.

- What methods will be deployed?

Confine every single stream of incoming traffic with all workstations aside from those with expected movement beginning from trusted sources, for example, helpdesk workstation, etc.

- Resultant Output

Even if the hacker/cracker finds access to any system, he cannot get access to the any other system in the network or cloud.

- Technical changes if any:

Not required.

3.3 Defense Mechanism 2

This mechanism works on restricting the high privileged account access if any.

- What is the aim of this defense mechanism?

This defense mechanism decreases the danger of admin level people by dividing the authority levels among several different types.

- What methods will be deployed?

Restrict the access of servers and critical accounts from limited number of systems. Also, avoid access of such critical accounts or servers from BYOD devices. Dedicated systems and computers can be assigned to admins. Also, different tasks of admin can be divided into multilevel authorities. No configuration of services or task scheduling should be done from other than the assigned systems.

- Resultant Output.

No compromise will be made for the attacker to get an access as dedicated systems are assigned and used. Also, multilevel authorities will reduce the risk.

- Technical changes if any

No technical changes are required just rephrasing and creating the various policies related to authentication and authority.

3.4 Defense Mechanism 3

This mechanism works on restricting the local accounts from getting administrative privileges. This means on local workstation; also, the user will not login using administrator account but will use with his personal login ids.

- What is the aim of this defense mechanism?

This defense mechanism confines the capacity of hacker/cracker to utilize nearby local systems or their reciprocals for parallel development PTH assaults.

- What methods will be deployed?

Restrict the access of systems from remote location or remote devices. Windows operating system above vista have this functionality inbuilt. Create different passwords for administrative accounts wherever necessary.

- Resultant Output

Even if the hacker/cracker gets the access, rights or passwords will not be able to login into the network or travel in the network parallely.

- Technical changes if any

Use of security identifiers along with different privileges can be done.

Other than this, various other defense mechanisms can also be applied in order to reduce the repercussion of the attack. The following are the more defense mechanisms.

– **Chunk the Pass**:

As we know, there is not eventually any guard against this attack, but that will not mean that we cannot do anything at all about it. It is not highly contrasting. It is just a different variant of gray. As we have seen the system of handicapping powerless password hashes conflict with APTs (progressed constant dangers), notwithstanding when the intruders own device work shall right and dandy utilizing more grounded password hashing function. The intruders or crackers did not realize that the weaker hashing function was debilitated, so intruders surrendered trying these attacks.

The finest guard against these attacks is to keep the intruders from getting super admin rights to use in any case. Tragically, that includes about each conventional PC security barrier: slightest benefit client logons, antimalware programming, white listing, firewalls, etc. Extracting the hashes from the memory can be made a bit harder. Specifically, in Windows-based system, the hashing function of passwords can be hauled out of memories for the accompanying logon sorts: intelligent, cluster, administration, open, remote intuitive, and stored intuitive. That may appear like each kind of logon you can consider, yet it does exclude system logons.

Likewise, log off procedure on regular basis expels the hash function of password from memory, in spite of the fact that it can be missing in place by applications and APIs, so you never know. One way to clear your password hashes out of memory is to log off from system.

– **Disjoin those ties**:

We request users to utilize non-intelligent approaches to oversee PCs. Rather than utilizing RDP (Remote Desktop Protocol), run with a support instrument that permits you to interface with remote PCs. A large portion of the Microsoft Management Console (MMC) apparatuses can be re-focused to remote access PCs. Use PowerShell scripts rather—at any point in time does not ask for sending the passwords.

A suggestion is disposing of all SuperAdmin from the system or at least reducing the amount of privileges they have. In active directory setup of Windows system, "delegation" can be used to give administrators simply the privileges they require without giving those highest level privileges, for example, with administrator. None of enterprises or domains prefers this to be done by a single admin handling these high-level critical operations. Rather, utilize designation and hand out only the authorizations and benefits important to handle the errands needed for those people. In case of password hash getting stolen for one of the admins, the level of threat is still very less comparatively, as the user is not super admin [4].

Other option is to work with OTPs, i.e., one-time passwords or very frequent change in passwords. So even if the intruder does get the hash for the password, but the time period to use will be reduced drastically. There are several different types of tools that can help you in these both tasks. Also, a suggestion is to avoid the recycle of the passwords on regular basis so the security remains intact [11].

Platform updates are regularly available and are generally automatically on. This can be represented in summarized form as in Table 1.

4 Conclusion and Future Work

Although PTH attacks proceed to represent a genuine danger for enterprises and firms, by obtaining entrance to a client's local administrative hash and traveling through different workstations all through the network, an attacker can gain access to a privileged domain account and use it to access critical servers and data. Still if

Table 1 Restrictions NTLM

Policy	Objective	Setting
Restrict NTLM: Inbound protocol NTLM	Allows you to enable or deny all network NTLM traffic	Deny all accounts
Restrict NTLM: Outbound protocol NTLM to remote servers	Allows you to enable or deny NTLM traffic is routed remote authentication server	Deny everything
Restrict NTLM: Authentication protocol NTLM in this domain	Allows you to enable or deny authentication Protocol NTLM within the domain of specific domain	Deny All accounts
Restrict NTLM: Audit authentication protocol NTLM in this domain	Enable or disable checking and recording authentication process on the domain controller	Prohibit
Restrict NTLM: Audit incoming traffic NTLM	Impossible to allow or disallow checking and recording incoming NTLM traffic	Prohibit

Table 2 Platform updates and features to reduce effect of PTH attack [17]

Features	Description	Available on Win—7/ Windows Server 2008 R2	Available on Win—8/ Windows Server 2012	Available on Windows 8.1/Server 2012 R2	Req. domain upgrade Windows Server 2012 R2 domain functional level
Remove LAN manager (LM) hashes and plaintext credentials from LSASS	LAN manager legacy hashes and (reversibly encrypted) plaintext passwords are no longer stored in LSASS	✓	✓	✓	
Enforce credential removal after logoff	New mechanisms have been implemented to eliminate session leaks in LSASS, thereby preventing credentials from remaining in memory	✓	✓	✓	
Logon restrictions with new well-known security identifiers (SIDs)	Use the new SIDs to block network logon for local users and groups by account type, regardless of what the local accounts are named	✓	✓	✓	

(continued)

Table 2 (continued)

Features	Description	Available on Win—7/ Windows Server 2008 R2	Available on Win—8/ Windows Server 2012	Available on Windows 8.1/Server 2012 R2	Req. domain upgrade Windows Server 2012 R2 domain functional level
Restricted admin mode for remote desktop connection	The remote desktop application and service have been updated to support authentication without providing credentials to the remote host	✓	✓	✓	
Protected users security group	The new protected users security group enables administrators to restrict authentication to the Kerberos protocol only for group members within a domain	✓	✓	✓	✓
Authentication policy and authentication policy silos	New authentication policies provide the ability to restrict account authentication to specific hosts and resources			✓	✓

proper care and right tools are used, then the defense mechanisms can be applied and the repercussions are reduced [19]. The aim of this research was to get acquainted with the attack "pass the hash" and working, then demonstrate it. This is an attack that allows an attacker to misuse hashes credentials and usage errors in the design of authentication protocols in order gaining access to high privileged accounts. Our suggested defense mechanisms reduce the risk and also protect the critical data and accounts.

As part of future work, we would like to test these mechanisms and approaches in different environments. We would like to compare results with existing methods and our approach for better accuracies and efficiency. Also, we would like to test these mechanisms in cloud-based environment as well.

Here are some of the inbuilt and available features of Windows operating system which can help reduce effect of the attack (Table 2).

References

1. Audit Collection Services (ACS) updated on 22 May 2009. Ref: http://technet.microsoft.com/en-us/library/bb381258.aspx
2. Auditing and restricting NTLM usage guide published on 29 Nov 2012. Ref: http://technet.microsoft.com/en-us/library/jj865674(v=ws.10).aspx

3. Authentication Policies and Authentication Policy Silos published on 27 Nov 2013. Ref: http://technet.microsoft.com/en-us/library/dn486813.aspx
4. Collecting Security Events Using Audit Collection Services in Operations Manager Ref: http://technet.microsoft.com/en-us/library/hh212908.aspx
5. Framework for Improving Critical Infrastructure Cybersecurity by National Institute of Standards and Technology February 12, 2014. Ref: http://www.nist.gov/cyberframework/upload/cybersecurity-framework-021214.pdf
6. Groat S, Tront J, Marchany R (2012) Advancing the defense in depth model, In: 7th international conference on system of systems engineering (SoSE), pp 285–290, 16–19 July 2012
7. Johnson JR, Hogan EA (2013) A graph analytic metric for mitigating advanced persistent threat. In: IEEE international conference on intelligence and security informatics (ISI), vol no, pp 129–133, 4–7 June 2013
8. McClure S, Scambray J, Kurtz G (2008) Hacking exposed 6: network security secrets & solutions. McGraw-Hill, New York
9. Microsoft Security Compliance Manager originally published on 6 April 2010 and updated January 28, 2013. Ref: http://technet.microsoft.com/en-us/library/cc677002.aspx
10. Microsoft Security Advisory 2871997 published on 9 Oct 2014. Ref: https://technet.microsoft.com/en-us/library/security/2871997.aspx
11. Mitigating Pass -the-Hash (PtH) Attacks and Other Credential Theft Techniques by Microsoft corporation, Published on 7 July 2014. http://download.microsoft.com/download/7/7/A/77ABC5BD-8320-41AF-863C-6ECFB10CB4B9/Mitigating%20Pass-the-Hash%20(PtH)%20Attacks%20and%20Other%20Cred-ential%20Theft%20Techniques_English.pdf
12. Pass the Hash attack, Microsoft Research as on August 12, 2015. Ref: http://www.microsoft.com/PTH
13. Pass-The-Hash Toolkit for Windows Implementation & use by Hernan Ocha published on 29 Oct 2008. Ref: www.coresecurity.com/system/files/Ochoa_2008-Pass-The-Hash.pdf
14. Secrets of America's Top Pen testers by Ed Skoudis Published in 2008. Ref: www.inguardians.com/research/docs/Skoudis_pentestsecrets.pdf
15. Source: World Internet Stats: Usage and Population Statistics, 30 June 2010. Ref: http://www.internetworldstats.com/stats.htm
16. The Year in Hacking, by the Numbers by NICOLE PERLROTH. Ref: http://bits.blogs.nytimes.com/2013/04/22/the-year-in-hacking-by-the-numbers
17. TWC: Pass-the-Hash and Credential Theft Mitigation Architectures published by Mark Simos, Nicholas DiCola published in TechEd North America on 14 May 2014. http://channel9.msdn.com/Events/TechEd/NorthAmerica/2014/DCIM-B213
18. Vukalovic J, Delija D (2015) Advanced persistent threats—detection and defense. In: 38th international convention on information and communication technology, electronics and microelectronics (MIPRO), pp 1324–1330, 25–29 May 2015
19. What's New in Remote Desktop Services in Windows Server updated on 28 May 2014. http://technet.microsoft.com/en-us/library/dn283323.aspx
20. Why Crack When You Can Pass the Hash? By Chris Hummel published on 12 Oct 2009. Ref: https://www.sans.org/reading-room/whitepapers/testing/ crack-pass-hash-33219

Data Security and Encryption Technique for Cloud Storage

Sunil Kumar, Jayant Shekhar and Jatinder Paul Singh

Abstract In the last few years, we have seen that cloud computing model has been developed as a promising business model of the fastest growing IT sector. Most of the IT companies, organizations, and educational institutes are now realizing that they can put on fast access to daily used computer applications and significantly boost up with infrastructure resources by simply moving to the cloud, at the very negligible cost. But they are also worried about privacy and security of their data, which is placed on the server of service providers. In this paper, we proposed a data security and encryption technique to provide privacy and security to our dynamic cloud data.

Keywords Secure cloud storage · Cloud data security · Cloud data encryption

1 Introduction

Today, we are living in an era, where technology plays an extremely vital role in our daily lives and business. New technologies always bring greater ease and convenience with them for us. Cloud computing is an endowed and evolving technology in the field of network-based computing that takes place over the Internet. It has become a well-known catchphrase nowadays. Cloud computing is a model that facilitates the software developers to deploy their own applications,

S. Kumar (✉)
Swami Vivekanand Subharti University, Meerut, Uttar Pradesh, India
e-mail: sunilcloudresearch@gmail.com

J. Shekhar
Computer Science Department, Swami Vivekanand Subharti University, Meerut, Uttar Pradesh, India
e-mail: jayant_shekhar@hotmail.com

J. P. Singh
Shobhit University, Meerut, India
e-mail: jatinderdavinder@gmail.com

M. U. Bokhari et al. (eds.), *Cyber Security*, Advances in Intelligent Systems and Computing 729, https://doi.org/10.1007/978-981-10-8536-9_19

client to use software, hardware or platform as a service. Cloud computing provides us reliable, secure, fault-tolerant, and scalable computational service. These services are the major magnetism of the cloud computing for the users those are from academic or IT industry, across the world. Using the Internet, anyone around the world can avail the cloud computing services on a pay-as-per uses basis that means how much they consume the cloud services; they have to pay only for that. There are lots of definitions that can be found on the Internet of cloud computing, but most accepted definition is provided by the National Institute of Science and Technology (NIST) Laboratory. Cloud computing can be defined as a technology that enables ubiquitous access to a collective group of configurable computing network assets or services that can be easily provisioned and free with least managing attempt or service provider communication [1]. Cloud computing is power-driven by virtualization technique that was offered only for mainframe systems in past years, in which, a host computer has to run an application program called the hypervisor that will create virtual machine, which simulate our computer hardware so realistically to execute any program, from an operating system to user-specific applications [2]. Cloud computing storage features attract users as well as enterprises to use a variety of capability to store and process the data on arbitrator data centers.

While cloud users move their data over the cloud that offers great ease and they do not need to take care about the management of hardware and software complexities, cloud database has been categorized as relational/SQL and non-relational/NoSQL. The pioneers of cloud data service products are IBM DB2, Microsoft Azure SQL Database, Amazon Simple, and Elastic Compute Cloud (EC2) that provide the massive amount of storage space and the facility to customize computing resources. Cloud computing model has eliminated the dependability of local machines for data protection. Cloud users are on the kindness of their service providers for the confidentiality, integrity, and availability (CIA) service of their data. From the viewpoint of cloud security, which has always been the key characteristic of better service, cloud users certainly face various security threats. First, conventional cryptographic techniques of data security protection cannot be directly used because of the user's loss control of data, while using the cloud services over the Internet. So, proper authentication of data storage on the cloud must be conducted without precise information of the whole data. The data stored on the cloud usually updated by the owner that includes insertion, modification, deletion, or reordering. Therefore, to guarantee storage security beneath data update dynamically is a very big challenge. This feature makes conventional integrity assurance technique ineffective and required a better solution. As the employment of cloud computing is power-driven by various data centers those are consecutively in the distributed style, there is a need to develop an efficient security technique for cloud storage.

2 Cloud Storage System

Using the cloud storage system, users can easily store their personal or official data (image, text, video, or audio) on the distributed cloud servers and this data will be accessible anywhere, anytime through the use of the Internet. The availability, security, and integrity of cloud data must be guaranteed by the service providers. As data of an organization or an individual user is copied to several different sites to minimize the data security threats from the hackers, therefore, an efficient and optimized cloud data security technique plays the significant role in the cloud computing. Many security techniques have been developed that give robust and secure cloud storage and also give assurance of protecting the important data of cloud users. As users frequently access or update their data from the different locations using variety of devices like mobile, laptop, etc., in every aspects, security to cloud data should be given. As a result, cloud storage is not only a third-party warehouse but also there are many issues associated with them such as protecting from unauthorized data access or modification and corruption of data, probably due to the lack of server security. Many solutions have been given by the researchers so that cloud storage can become trustworthy and users can use the cloud storage service and store their data without any worry.

3 Related Works

In [3], authors have given a competent technique to illustrate the integrity of storage data using hash index hierarchy and homomorphism verifiable response. They present with the help of provable data possession concept, which supports a good service and migration of data in the cloud environment.

In [4], authors proposed architecture with the approach for key exchange that uses Diffie–Hellman key exchange along with the authentication step for each part of the controller and the server instances. They suggest that data encryption using RSA algorithm provides strong security over insecure medium. In their method, they split the user data and encrypt, then send to the server instances for computation.

In [5], authors highlight the various cloud data security issues and also give the implementation of digital signature security technique using the elliptic curve P-192 in C language.

In [6], IBM discovers an encryption technique to improve cloud data security. They also give the capability of spam filtering.

In [7], they propose one homomorphic encryption system that uses Residue Number System (RNS), called HORNS. In that, they split the secret into multiple sources to perform independent computations so that efficiency as well as security can be increased.

In [8], authors proposed an authentication and encryption techniques based on a binary tree diagram that contains alphabet values. They gave an algorithm that converts the entered alphabets into binary values according to the position in the binary tree, and then some redundancy bits are added and converting value is sent to receiver.

There are many limitations founded in this approach. First, it takes only alphabets and does not take numbers or special character. Second, it does not compress the data after adding the redundancy bits because data will become lengthy.

Therefore, in this paper, we have removed all the limitations with the proposal of an improved algorithm technique.

4 Proposed Methodology

We have proposed a mechanism that uses a binary tree in that each node holds an alphabet, number, and special character, and each link has a binary value 0 or 1.

Figure 1 depicts a binary tree with the values of numbers, special characters, and alphabets. Depending upon their positions in the binary tree, **a** has 0, right sub-tree node of **a** is **c,** that has 01, and left node of **a** will be **b** with having 00. Same as **e position** is 001 and further elements of tree are depicted in the pair in Table 1.

4.1 Data Calculation for Security

Input the text that has to be stored on the cloud server:

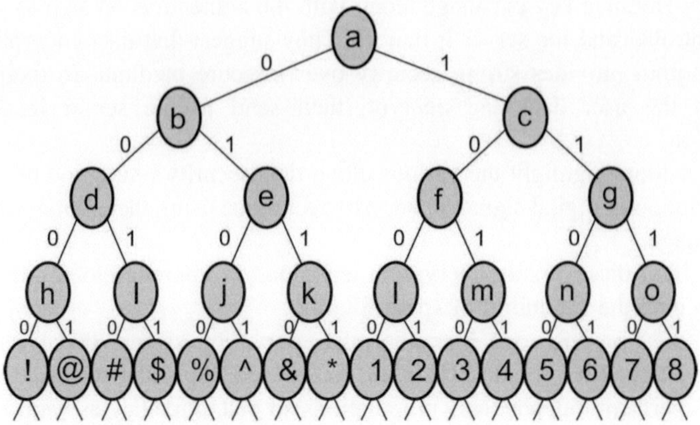

Fig. 1 A binary tree diagram along with alpha-numeric values

Table 1 Key and value pair

Key	Value
A	0
C	01
B	00
D	000
G	001
@	00001
8	01111

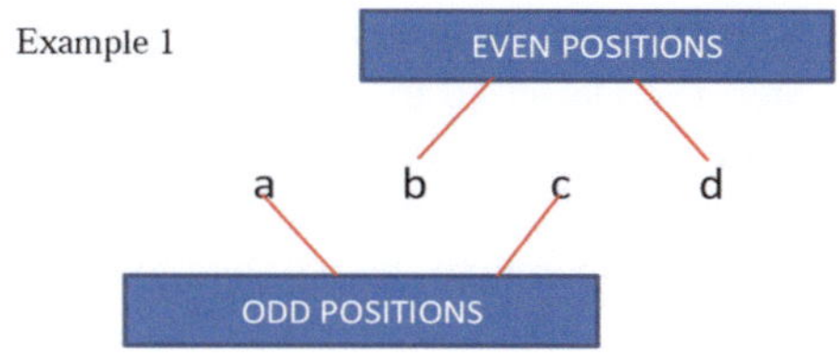

Fig. 2 Even and odd positions in input text abcd

Example 1: For the abcd input data (Fig. 2).
Example 2: Suppose our input text is a@bc.
First, we assign binary value according to Fig. 1.

a	@	**b**	**c**
0	00001	00	00

Second, mix up the odd and even position characters.

a	**b**	@	**c**
0	00	00001	01

Then, to make secure, put some bits like 1111 (Four times 1), after each bit.

01111 001111 00001 011111

In last step, apply the compression technique and send it to the cloud server for storage.

5 Encryption Algorithm on Sender Side

Step I Devise a tree with alpha-numeric values as given in Fig. 1.
Step II Input some value.
Step III Arrange the input, according to odd and even positions of input.
Step IV In that, odd position inputs will be paired first, then after even position inputs will be paired.

Step V Assign binary value (0 or 1) to the given input.
Step VI Add some redundancy bits after the value of the each input.
Step VII Compress the input data and send to the cloud server for storage.

6 Decryption Algorithm on Receiver Side

Step I Receive compressed data from the cloud server.
Step II Uncompress the data.
Step III Start assigning binary value to the data according to Fig. 1.
Step IV Detect all the redundancy bits in the received uncompressed data.
Step V Remove the redundancy bit values.
Step VI Replace the numeric values with text of the data.
Step VII Rearrange the odd and even position character's values for takeout the worth of received message.

7 Conclusion

We have developed a data security and encryption technique for providing security to cloud users. Our proposed mechanism is unique and simple, but not easy for hackers to crack because numbers increase the security while accessing the data. In future, we will provide the cloud implementation of this technique, so that data of cloud users can become more secure and cloud environment can become more trustworthy.

References

1. Naone E (2009) Technology overview, conjuring clouds. MIT Technol Rev
2. Subashini S, Kavitha V (2011) A survey on security issues in service delivery models of cloud computing. J Network Comput Appl 34:1–11
3. Merlin Shirly T, Johnson M (2014) Improved security measures for data in key exchanges in cloud environment. Int J Res Comput Appl Robot 2(3):153–158 (ISSN:2320-7345)
4. Singh K et al (2010) Implementation of elliptic curve digital signature algorithm. Int J Comput Appl (IJCA) 2(2):21–27 (ISSN: 0975–8887)
5. Tripathi A, Parul Y (2012) Enhancing security of cloud computing using elliptic curve cryptography. Int J Comput Appl 1
6. IBM Discovers Encryption Scheme That Could Improve Cloud Security, Spam Filtering. www.eweek.com/c/a/Security/IBMUncovers-Encryption-Scheme-That-Could-Improve-Cloud-Security-Spam-Filtering-135413

7. Gomathisankaran M et al (2011) HORNS: a homomorphic encryption scheme for cloud computing using residue number system. In: 45th annual conference on information sciences and systems (CISS), pp 1–5. Print ISBN: 978-1-4244-9846-8
8. Singh JP, Kumar S, Dr. Mamta (2015) Authentication and encryption in cloud computing. In: International conference on smart technologies and management for computing, communication, controls, energy and materials (ICSTM), Chennai, May 2015, p 230. ISBN: 978-1-4-4799-9854-8

Author Biography

Dr. Sunil Kumar has completed Ph.D. (CSE) from Swami Vivekanand Subharti University (NAAC 'A' grade), Meerut in 2017. He obtained his M.Tech (CS) degree from the Shobhit University, Meerut in 2011 and MCA from JRN Rajasthan Vidyapeeth Deemed University, Udaipur in 2007. He has total 10 years of IT experience and 2 year of research experience. His area of interest is Cryptography, Cloud computing, Java programming, Artificial Intelligence and Web technologies. He is associated as a consultant with Zombie softwares, Delhi and BitsMobile, Noida. Currently, he is working as a Assistant Professor in College of Computer Science and Applications of IIMT University, Meerut. He has published 10+ research papers in reputed journals like ACM, IEEE and Elsevier etc. He is also the professional member of ACM (Association of Computing Machinery), India. He is also Sun Certified Java Programmer (SCJP).

Fine-Grained Access Control and Secured Data Sharing in Cloud Computing

Neha Agarwal, Ajay Rana and J. P. Pandey

Abstract In cloud computing data, outsourcing is one of the most convenient, cost–efficient, and cheapest ways for users to share their data with remote clients. However, the main problem is that the owner loses its physical control on data and so the main challenge is how to secure and share the data efficiently and maintaining fine-grained access control on it. Several approaches have been proposed including attribute-based encryption and proxy re-encryption for secured data sharing through cloud service providers. In this paper, we have given a survey and comparison of different attribute-based encryption and proxy re-encryption techniques. We have also proposed that threshold cyptosystem can be used for secured and efficient data sharing in cloud.

Keywords Cloud computing · Fine-grained access control · Confidentiality Attribute-based encryption · Proxy re-encryption

1 Introduction

Cloud computing is a new computer science paradigm which provides access to shared pool of resources in an efficient and scalable manner over Internet on demand basis. These services may involve application, network, data, computation, infrastructure, and so on [1–5]. The customer pays for the services as per usage which leads to great advantage to customers as well as service providers (Fig. 1).

N. Agarwal (✉) · A. Rana
Amity University, Noida, Uttar Pradesh, India
e-mail: agarwalnehajain@gmail.com

A. Rana
e-mail: ajay_rana@amity.edu

J. P. Pandey
KNIT Sultanpur, Sultanpur, India
e-mail: tojppandey@rediffmail.com

M. U. Bokhari et al. (eds.), *Cyber Security*, Advances in Intelligent Systems and Computing 729, https://doi.org/10.1007/978-981-10-8536-9_20

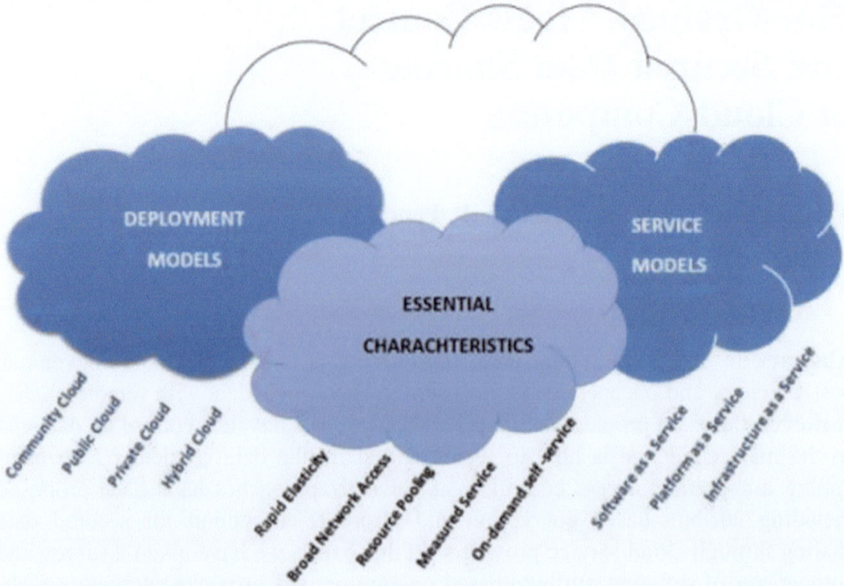

Fig. 1 Model of cloud computing

The main deployment models in cloud are public cloud, private cloud and hybrid cloud. Public cloud is cheapest of all deployment models and is owned by third party; however, they are highly insecure, for example, AWS. Private cloud is owned by individual party and so is highly secure but at the same time they are costliest, for example, Badaal Cloud. Hybrid cloud is owned partially by service providers and partially by individual party and so are partially secured and is used in mainly critical places like they are used in Union Bank of India.

Cloud computing several services are mainly categorized into three main types: Infrastructure as a Service (IaaS), Platform as a Service (Paas), and Software as a Service (SaaS). However, recently several types of service XaaS models are defined; one of the such models is Data as a Service (DaaS) [6].

2 Security Issues in Cloud Computing

Among the several services, cloud storage service enables the owner of data to store and share his important data with trusted clients which has freed the owner from worry of storage and resource management. But at the same time since the owner looses the physical control on stored data there are several security concerns related to confidentiality, security, and privacy of data-like authentication [7]. These security issues [8] are preventing the companies or people from adopting cloud which are mainly classified as follows [9]:

(i) Traditional security—There are several number of traditional risks [6, 10–13]. Gartner [14] suggested few of them which data owner should discuss with vendor beforehand. Some of the general issues and attacks include security issues like cloud malware injection attack, related to virtual machines VM-level attacks [15], cloud provider vulnerabilities [16], malicious insider, cookie poisoning, phishing attack on cloud provider such as the Salesforce phishing incident [17], SQL injection attack, authentication and authorization [18], sniffer attack, man-in-middle attack, and forensics in the cloud [19]. There are number of guidelines provided to ensure security of data to the user while storing and sharing it in cloud [20–23]; however, the data owners may not completely trust the cloud service provider. Availability of critical data is another main concern [24]. There are several issues like single-point failure, server down issues, and owner is unable to ensure that cloud service provider will not be colluding with unauthorized users and results are valid. A real-life example is an incidence in which cloud outage of Amazon S3 was down for 7 h on July 20, 2008 [25].

(ii) Third-party data control—In order to optimize the utilization of available resources in cloud, the data owner stores their data at remote site. However, security of data is a major concern since the data can reside anywhere in cloud. At the same time, the owner needs to ensure that he should have a complete control on its outsourced data rather than it being controlled by service provider [9].

As mentioned above, the major security concern of data owner is how the third service provider handles his data since architecture of storage services in cloud is bit complex so it becomes difficult for him to understand it [15, 26]. Researchers and industry people are working to address security models [7, 12, 27] by developing standards but there is still lots of work need to be done [28]. However, trusted computing and applied cryptographic techniques may offer new tools to solve these problems [29, 30].

Cryptography helps in maintaining the confidentiality of critical data by encrypting the data; yet, there are certain issues like revoking users privileges without re-encrypting data and re-distributing the new keys to the authorized users, handling collusion between users and revoked users, handling collusion between revoked users, and cloud service providers. In addition, there are several issues related to secure query processing over encrypted data [31].

3 Main Features Required for Secure Data Sharing in Cloud Computing

The main features to be achieved for securing data while outsourcing it on cloud are as follows:

1. Data Confidentiality: Any unauthorized user or even the service provider must not have an access to the data. Even if they steal the data, they must not be able to decrypt it.
2. Fine-Grained Access Control: Each and every authorized user will be associated with some access rights. This enhances the efficiency and reliability in system.
3. Improved Scalability: The system must be able to work efficiently with increased number of users.
4. User Accountability: It should be maintained so that he can be charged accordingly.
5. Efficient User Revocation: If the user is revoked, then the data owner need not have to redistribute the keys to authorized user.
6. Efficient and Secure User Rejoin: If a revoked user rejoins with same or different access rights, then he must rejoin without affecting the system or users.
7. Collusion Resistant: There must be no collusion between the revoke user and other authorized user or cloud service provider.
8. Ciphertext Size: The size of encrypted file must not be too big.
9. Support for Secured Query Processing: The encrypted query of authorized user can be executed over an encrypted data and only the result of executed query must be sent to authorized user.
10. Stateless Cloud: The cloud should not be in need to retain the state of revoked and active users.

4 Related Work

For secured data sharing in cloud through CSP, many encryption schemes have been introduced. The owner encrypts his data and sends it to third party called cloud service provider. Along with encrypted data, owner also sends the access control list specifying the authorization for accessing the attributes corresponding to users. The cloud service provider converts the ciphertext of one authorized user to another authorized user and provides it to him. In this way, data is securely shared among authorized users using concept called fine-grained access control in order to limit the access of encrypted data in cloud.

4.1 Attribute-Based Encryption (ABE)

In the traditional approach, if the owner wants to share some messages with others, he should know public key authorized user in order to encrypt the data. Identity-based encryption has changed the concept and allowed the public key to be of random string, e.g., email id of recipient. One of the main issues arises from sharing keys is user revocation where a user is needed to be revoked from accessing his data. The usual solution followed by owners is to re-encrypt the whole dataset with new generated key and redistribute the re-encrypted data to all authorized users.

Sahai and waters presented attribute-based encryption in 2005 [32] for secured data sharing based on the concept of public-key cryptography in which authorized users are allowed to decrypt the data only if they satisfy certain attributes. The main feature of this approach is that it is collusion resistant but since it uses access of monotonic attributes in order to control users access, it is restricted in real environment. Attribute-Based Encryption (ABE) was further classified as KP-ABE and CP-ABE.

In 2006, Goyal [33] proposed KP-ABE in which users' private key is used to store access control policy and encrypted data stores additional attributes. An authorized user can decrypt data if the access policy defined in users' private key satisfies attribute of data. However, the main issue with KP-ABE is owner (one who has encrypted data) cannot take a decision on who can decrypt the data.

In 2007, Bethencourt et al. [31] introduced CP-ABE in which the access policy is stored with encrypted data and attributes are stored in users' secret key; as a result, the user can access only the attributes associated with his private key. The concept supports access control in real-time environment; however, it requires flexibility and efficiency and its decryption key only supports user attributes that are logically organized as a single set; as a result, user has to use a combination of all attributes. To overcome this problem, ciphertext-policy attribute-set-based encryption is introduced. It organizes user attributes into a recursive set-based structure and user combines these attributes dynamically in order to satisfy a policy without sacrificing the flexibility. The main challenge is allowing users to combine attributes dynamically within a given key and avoiding collusion at the same time.

Earlier, ABE was based on monotonic access structure. Ostrovsky et al. in 2007 [34] proposed ABE that supports non-monotonic formulas on access policies to express any access formula. Tang et al. in 2008 [35] put forward verifiable ABE.

Muller in 2009 [36] proposed an extension of CPABE, DABE (Distributed Attribute-Based Encryption) that supports random number of parties to maintain the attributes along with their corresponding secret keys; however, the access policy has to be in DNF form.

Boneh and Franklin [37] proposed an identity-based encryption scheme, in which data is encrypted using a random string as the key and for decryption; a decryption key is mapped to the random encryption key-by-key authority.

Hierarchical Identity-Based Encryption (HIBE) [38] is the tree-like form of a single IBE; the main disadvantage of this system is key management overhead. Wang et al. [39] embedded a hierarchical structure in the CPABE. They delegated most of the computation workloads to the cloud and provided compatibility with complex applications. But the scheme does not support compound attributes.

Wan et al. [40] in 2012 proposed scalable and flexible HASBE scheme and considered that root level authority is responsible for managing top-level domain authorities. It supports flexible compound attribute set combinations and achieves efficient user revocation because of multiple values assigned to attributes (Table 1).

4.2 *Proxy Re-encryption*

The main security concern while sharing the data using cloud is to prevent it from semi-trusted cloud service providers. In order to maintain confidentiality, several proxy re-encryption techniques are available. Proxy encryption is a primitive which helps in translating ciphertext from one encryption form to another encryption form without any information leaked to third party or cloud service provider. Application of proxy re-encryption is sharing public health records online, social media, and email forwarding.

4.2.1 Type-Based Proxy Re-encryption

The scheme proposed by Tang [41] enables owner to categorize ciphertext into subsets and uses one key pair in order to simplify key management problem. These subsets are re-encrypted to ciphertext using public key of specified authorized user. The main advantage of this scheme is that every authorized user can use a particular proxy.

4.2.2 Key Private Proxy Re-encryption

It was introduced by Ateniese [42] in 2009 under this scheme that it is impossible for proxy server to identify the recipient of the message.

4.2.3 Identity-Based Proxy Re-encryption

Identity-based proposed by Shamir [43] uses string of arbitrary length such as email id for creating public key of authorized users. The proxy server will translate the ciphertext of Alice to ciphertext of Bob without being able to retrieve any information.

Table 1 Comparison of attribute-based encryption

Techniques	ABE	KP-ABE	CP-ABE	IBE	HABE	DABE	MA-ABE
Fine-grained access control	Low	High if there is re-encryption, low	Avg, high if there is re-encryption	Avg	Good	Good	Good
Efficiency	Avg	High for broadcast type system average	Avg	Low	Flexible	Avg	High
Confidentiality	Low	High	High	High	High	High	High
User accountability	Not maintain	Not maintain	Well maintain	Well maintain	Well maintain	Well maintain	Well maintain
Computation overhead	High	High	Avg	Low	Low	Avg	Avg
Collusion resistant	Avg	Good	Good	Low	Good	Good	High

4.2.4 Conditional Proxy Re-encryption

Under this scheme, the owner specifies the conditions along with ciphertext and the proxy can transform the ciphertext of data owner to encrypted form of recipient if and only if ciphertext satisfies the condition specified by the owner. This scheme is not sufficient to implement fine-grained access control [44].

4.2.5 Time-Based Proxy Re-encryption

The scheme introduced by Liu [45] has achieved user revocation and fine-grained access control in the absence of data owner. In it, each user is associated with time period for validity of user access rights so if he wants to access the data he needs to have the access rights on attributes as well as access time must satisfy the validity. Major limitation in it is for a user; the access time for all the attributes is same.

4.2.6 Threshold Proxy Re-encryption

This scheme integrates encrypting, encoding, and forwarding [46] and exhibits homomorphism, proxy re-encryption, and threshold decryption properties. Homomorphism states that for ciphertexts c1 and c2 defined on plain text p1 and p2, one can use c1 and c2 to obtain ciphertext on the plain text p1 · p2 or p1 + p2. Proxy re-encryption allows encrypted form of data of user1 to be transformed into encrypted for another user without any information leaked to third party. Threshold encryption lets the private keys to be divided into several pieces and distributed to clients and all clients must together decrypt the file.

4.3 Hybrid Approach of Attribute-Based Encryption and Proxy Re-encryption

Yu et al. [47] proposed a technique by combining KP-ABE, proxy re-encryption, and lazy re-encryption; he managed to push the task of data re-encryption and decryption to cloud. The main issue is cloud has to be stateful to retain history of user revocation.

Blaze et al. [48] proposed a proxy re-encryption which allows the encrypter to ask a third party to re-encrypt his encrypted message and deliver it to the decrypter.

Yang et al. [49] proposed a generic solution for implementing fine-grained data sharing. His technique enables cloud to be stateless and need not have to maintain state of user revocation. However, the scheme is not able to handle scenarios when a revoked user rejoins the system and is authorized with different access privileges.

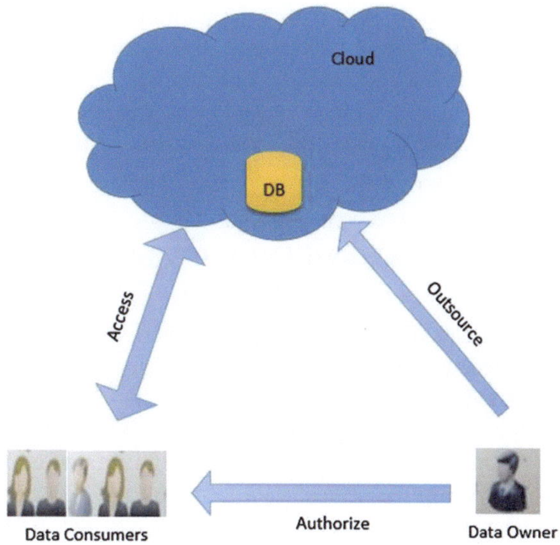

Fig. 2 Data sharing between owner and clients

The scheme also fails to handle collusion between revoked and authorized user and revoked user and untrusty cloud service provider.

Bharath et al. [50] proposed framework using proxy re-encryption and additive homomorphic encryption in order to give a solution. He has implemented the concept of federation of clouds in order to prevent collusion. However, there is a limitation in their work that they have assumed that if revoked user colludes with authorized user; then, the revoked user shares information available to authorized user only (Figure 2).

4.4 *Secured Query Processing*

One of the problems while outsourcing the data to cloud is that the query must be executed and output should be given to only authorized users who have initiated the query. While the query is being sent and processed and output generated, the process should not be accessible to any unauthorized user or cloud service provider. Boneh et al. [51] have presented a general framework for analyzing security of searching on encrypted data systems. Under this framework, they have constructed public-key systems that support comparison queries on encrypted data as well as more general queries such as subset queries.

Hakan et al. [52] have introduced an algebraic framework in which they have deployed coarse index which allows query to be partially executed on encrypted data at providers end and then decrypted at client end and remaining query executes.

Hore et al. [53] have developed a bucketization procedure for answering multidimensional range queries on multidimensional data and allow the data owner to control the tradeoff between risk and cost.

Wang et al. [54] have ensured data confidentiality both at storage and at access time and also supports different queries and data updates.

5 Conclusion and Future Work

Sharing data on cloud is widely accepted and is increasing rapidly. The data owners are interested in outsourcing the data on cloud in order to avoid storage management and capital expenditure in infrastructure but there are several issues associated with it and one of the major issues is confidentiality and security. In this paper, we have discussed on how to increase confidentiality and maintain privacy and security while sharing the critical data through third party named cloud service providers. We have explained encryption technique like ABE and PRE, when combined altogether enable us to share the data securely maintaining confidentiality along with fine-grained access control. However, the information can be leaked if there exists collusion between cloud service provider and revoked user or between authorized user and revoked users. Our proposed approach is to implement multi-party computation-based homomorphic threshold cryptosystem under this approach; private key of authorized user will be shared among n number of clouds and the secret can be revealed if x out of total n participants work together. This approach will prevent the data as the revoked user cannot collude with x number of users altogether.

References

1. Armbrust M, Fox A, Griffith R, Joseph AD, Katz R, Konwinski A, Lee G, Patterson D, Rabkin A, Stoica I, Zaharia M (2010) A view of cloud computing. Commun ACM 53:50–58
2. Mell P, Grance T (2009) The NIST definition of cloud computing. Technical report, National Institute of Standards and Technology, Information Technology Laboratory, July 2009. http://www.csrc.nist.gov/groups/sns/cloud-computing/
3. Qian L, Luo Z, Du Y, Guo L (2009) Cloud computing: an overview. In: Proceedings of the 1st international conference on cloud computing, CLOUDCOM'09. Springer, Berlin, pp 626–631
4. Rimal B, Choi E, Lumb I (2009) A taxonomy and survey of cloud computing systems. In: IEEE fifth international joint conference on INC, IMS and IDC, pp 44 –51, Aug 2009
5. Zhang Q, Cheng L, Boutaba R (2010) Cloud computing: state-of-the-art and research challenges. J Internet Serv Appl 1(1):7–18
6. Hanna S. Cloud computing: finding the silver lining. http://www.ists.dartmouth.edu/events/abstract-hanna.html

7. Kantarcioglu M, Clifton C (2005) Security issues in querying encrypted data. In: Proceedings of the 19th annual working conference on data and applications security, DBSEC'05. Springer, Berlin, pp 325–337
8. Cantor S, Sigaba JM, Philpott R, Maler E (2005) Metadata for the OASIS security assertion markup language (SAML) v2.0", copyright © OASIS open
9. Chow R, Golle P, Jakobsson M, Shi E, Staddon J, Masuoka R, Molina J (2009) Controlling data in the cloud: Outsourcing computation without outsourcing control. In: Proceedings of the 2009 ACM workshop on cloud computing security (CCSW), pp 85–90
10. Dahbur K, Mohammad B, Tarakji AB (2011) Security issues in cloud computing: a survey of risks, threats and vulnerabilities. Int J Cloud Appl Comput (IJCAC) 1
11. Dhage SN, Meshram BB, Rawat R, Padawe S, Paingaokar M, Misra A (2011) Intrusion detection system in cloud computing environment. In: Proceedings of the international conference & workshop on emerging trends in technology, ICWET'11, pp 235–239
12. Kandukuri B, Paturi V, Rakshit A (2009) Cloud security issues. In: IEEE International conference on services computing, pp 517–520
13. Singh G, Sharma A, Lehal MS (2011) Security apprehensions in different regions of cloud captious grounds. Int J Network Secur Its Appl (IJNSA) 3
14. Brodkin J. Gartner: seven cloud-computing security risks. http://www.infoworld.com/d/security-central/gartner-seven-cloud-computing-security-risks-853
15. Ristenpart T, Tromer E, Shacham H, Savage S (2009) Hey, you, get off of my cloud: exploring information leakage in third—party compute clouds. In: Proceedings of the 16th ACM conference on computer and communications security, CCS'09. ACM, New York, pp 199–212
16. Wang C, Wang Q, Ren K, Lou W (2009) Ensuring data storage security in cloud computing. In: International workshop on quality of service, pp 1 –9, July 2009
17. Salesforce.com. warns customers of phishing scam. http://www.pcworld.com/article/139353/article.html
18. Yan L, Rong C, Zhao G (2009) Strengthen cloud computing security with federal identity management using ierarchical identity-based cryptography. In: Proceedings of the 1st international conference on cloud computing, CLOUDCOM'09. Springer, Berlin, pp 167–177
19. Lu R, Lin X, Liang X, Shen XS (2010) Secure provenance: the essential of bread and butter of data forensics in cloud computing. In: Proceedings of the 5th ACM symposium on information, computer and communications security, ASIACCS'10. ACM, New York
20. Lin D, Squicciarini A (2010) Data protection models for service provisioning in the cloud. In: Proceeding of the 15th ACM symposium on access control models and technologies, SACMAT'10, pp 183–192
21. Nyre AA, Jaatun M (2009) Privacy in a semantic cloud: whats trust got to do with it? In: Cloud computing, volume 5931 of lecture notes in computer science. Springer, Berlin, pp 107–118
22. Pearson S, Shen Y, Mowbray M (2009) A privacy manager for cloud computing. In: Proceedings of the 1st international conference on cloud computing, CLOUDCOM'09. Springer, Berlin, pp 90–106
23. Thuraisingham B, Khadilkar V, Gupta A, Kantarcioglu M, Khan L (2010) Secure data storage and retrieval in the cloud. In: Collaborative computing: networking, applications and worksharing (collaboratecom), pp 1–8, Oct 2010
24. Uemura T, Dohi T, Kaio N (2009) Availability analysis of a scalable intrusion tolerant architecture with two detection modes. In: Proceedings of the 1st international conference on cloud computing, CLOUDCOM'09. Springer, Berlin, pp 178–189
25. A. S. A. event. July 20, 2008. http://status.aws.amazon.com/s3-0080720.html
26. Takabi H, Joshi J, Ahn G (2010) Security and privacy challenges in cloud computing environments. IEEE Secur Privacy 8(6):24–31
27. Jansen W, Grance T (2011) Draft special publication 800-144: guidelines on security and privacy in public cloud computing. National Institute of Standards and Technology, U.S. Department of Commerce

28. Andrei T (2009) Cloud computing challenges and related security issues
29. Agudo I, Nuez D, Giammatteo G, Rizomiliotis P, Lambrinoudakis C (2011) Cryptography goes to the cloud. in secure and trust computing, data management, and applications, vol 187 of communications in computer and information science. Springer, Berlin, pp 190–197
30. Santos N, Gummadi KP, Rodrigues R (2009) Towards trusted cloud computing. In: Proceedings of the 2009 conference on hot topics in cloud computing, HOTCLOUD'09, Berkeley, CA, USA. Usenix Association
31. Bethencourt J, Sahai A, Waters B (2007)Ciphertext-policy attribute-based encryption. In: Proceedings of IEEE symposium on security and privacy
32. Sahai A, Waters B (2005) Fuzzy identity-based encryption. In: Cramer R (ed) Advances in cryptology—EUROCRYPT 2005. Springer, Berlin, pp 457–473
33. Goyal V, Pandy O, Sahai A, Waters B (2006) Attribute based encryption for fine-grained access control of encrypted data. In: Proceedings of ACM computer and communications security conference, CCS'06
34. Ostrovsky R, Sahai A, Waters B (2007) Attribute-based encryption with non-monotonic access structures. In: Proceeding of ACM conference on computer and communications security, pp 195–203
35. Tang Q, Ji D (2010) Verifiable attribute-based encryption. Int J Network Secur 10(2):114–120
36. Müller S, Katzenbeisser S, Eckert C (2009) Distributed attribute-based encryption. In: Proceedings of 11th international conference on information security and cryptology (ICISC 08), pp 20–36
37. Boneh D, Franklin MK (2003) Identity-based encryption from the weil pairing. SIAM J Comput 32(3):586–615
38. Boneh D, Boyen X, Goh E-J (2005) Hierarchical identity based encryption with constant size ciphertext. In: Cramer R (ed) Eurocrypt, volume 3494 of lecture notes in computer science. Springer, Berlin, pp 440–456
39. Wang G, Liu Q, Wu J (2010) Hierarhical attribute-based encryption for fine-grained access control in cloud storage services. In: Proceedings of ACM conference on computer and communications security, CCS' 10
40. Wan Z, Liu J, Deng RH (2012) HASBE: a hierarchical attribute-based solution for flexible and scalable access control in cloud computing. IEEE Trans Inf Forensics Secur 7(2):743–754
41. Tang Q (2008) Type-based proxy re-encryption and its construction. In: Proceedings of ninth international conference on cryptology in India, pp 130–144
42. Ateniese G, Benson K, Hohenberger S (2009) Key-private proxy re-encryption. In: Proceedings topics in cryptology, pp 279–294
43. Shamir A (1984) Identity-based cryptosystems and signatures schemes. Adv Cryptol 47–53
44. Libert B, Vergnaud D (2008) Tracing malicious proxies in proxy re-encryption. In: Proceedings of PAIRING'08. LNCS 5209. Springer, Berlin, pp 332–353
45. Liu Q, Wang G, Wu J (2012) Time-based proxy re-encryption scheme for secure data sharing in a cloud environment. Information sciences (in press)
46. Asharov G, Jain A, Lopez-Alt A, Tromer E, Vaikuntanathan V, Wichs D (2012) Multiparty computation with low communication, computation and interaction via threshold FHE. In: Proceeding of eurocrypt'12. Springer, Berlin, pp 483–501
47. Yu S, Wang C, Ren K, Lou W (2010) Achieving secure, scalable, and fine-grained data access control in cloud computing. In: Proceedings of IEEE international conference on computer communications, INFOCOM'10
48. Blaze M, Bleumer G, Strauss M (1998) Divertible protocols and atomic proxy cryptography. In: Proceedings of advances in cryptology, eurocrypt'98
49. Yang Y, Zhang Y (2011) A generic scheme for secure data sharing in cloud. In: 40th international conference on parallel processing workshops, pp 145–153, Sept 2011
50. Samanthula BK et al (2015) A secure data sharing and query processing framework via federation of cloud computing. Inf Syst 48:196–212

51. Boneh D, Waters B (2007) Conjunctive, subset, and range queries on encrypted data. In: Proceedings of the 4th conference on theory of cryptography, TCC'07. Springer, Berlin, pp 535–554
52. Hakan H, Iyer B, Li C, Mehrotra S (2002) Executing Sql over encrypted data in the database-service provider model. In: Proceedings of the 2002 ACM sigmod international conference on management of data, SIGMOD'02. ACM, pp 216–227
53. Hore B, Mehrotra S, Canim M, Kantarcioglu M (2012) Secure multidimensional range queries over outsourced data. VLDB J 21(3):333–358
54. Wang S, Agrawal D, El Abbadi A (2011) A comprehensive framework for secure query processing on relational data in the cloud. In: Proceedings of the 8th VLDB international conference on secure data management, SDM'11. Springer, Berlin, pp 52–69

Author Biographies

Neha Agarwal is currently working as an Assistant Professor in Amity School of Engineering and Technology, Amity University, Uttar Pradesh. She is pursuing her Ph.D. from Dr. A. P.J. Abdul Kalam Technical University (APJAKTU) (UP) in the area of Cloud Computing. She received her M.Tech in Computer Science Engineering from Amity University Noida, Uttar Pradesh.

Ajay Rana is a director at Amity University. He received his M.Tech degree in Computer Science Engineering from Kurukshetra University, Haryana, India. He obtained his Ph.D. from UP Technical University, Lucknow (UP) India. He has published more than 200 Research Papers in reputed Journals and Proceedings of International and National Conferences. He has co-authored 06 Books and co-edited 36 Conference Proceedings. He is Editor in Chief, Technical Committee Member, Advisory Board Member for 18 Plus Technical Journals and Conferences at National and International Levels.

Jai Prakash Pandey is currently working as Professor and Director in the Department of Electrical Engineering at Kamala Nehru Institute of Technology, Sultanpur, (UP), India. He has received his B. Tech and M. Tech in Electrical Engineering from Kamala Nehru Institute of Technology, Sultanpur (UP), India. He obtained his Ph.D. degree from UP Technical University, Lucknow (UP) India. His research interests include applications of artificial techniques to electrical engineering problems in power system, estate estimation and power quality.

Comparative Study of Security Risk in Social Networking and Awareness to Individual

Tosal Bhalodia, Chandani Kathad and Keyur Zala

Abstract Nowadays, social networking sites are very greatly used and are continuously growing at its peak. The extraordinary use of all the social networking sites mainly Facebook, Twitter, LinkedIn, and Google Plus involve huge amount of data transferred to public daily. This data transfer involves public information such as personal information, education, professional, etc. which leads to security at personal level. Let us see the comparative study of Facebook, Twitter, LinkedIn, and Google Plus for security risk and how effective it is for well-being to society.

Keywords Social · Facebook · Twitter · Gplus · Linkedin · Security Public · Private · Government regulation · Information · Security Optimization security measures · Vulnerability

1 Introduction

Social networking implementation explores the way to communicate in public, and this leads to sharing of information to known and unknowns. Implementation of any tool to live involves great amount of security involvement and needs to concern about risk of personal/company data. Of above four social networking sites mentioned, Facebook and Gplus are very informal and easy to use for all the public. Linkedin and Twitter are very professional and generally used for connection to CEO's and other related professional users. Twitter creates followers and makes connection through users following.

T. Bhalodia (✉)
Atmiya Institute of Technology & Science, Rajkot, India
e-mail: tosalbhalodia@gmail.com

C. Kathad · K. Zala
Ilaxo.Com, Rajkot, India
e-mail: kathadchandni@gmail.com

K. Zala
e-mail: keyurzala2010@gmail.com

M. U. Bokhari et al. (eds.), *Cyber Security*, Advances in Intelligent Systems and Computing 729, https://doi.org/10.1007/978-981-10-8536-9_21

Business nowadays depends on information system. But due to vulnerability, the enterprise information system is under the attack of viruses and hackers which causes great loss to organization on reputation, information leakage, etc. Information security awareness is very important for each and every individual [5]. This awareness mainly needs to implement in all the universities in form of information security subject. This leads to educate the individual about the threat occurred due to social networking attacks. Malicious software, hacking tutorials, and other resources intended to help conduct cybercrime can be commonly found within hacker communities, often available for free or traded within black markets [9].

1.1 Facebook/GPlus

There are main three usual features for Facebook like capability to adding friends, to change or modify status, and last one is implement application for execution applications such as games and quizzes. A "Friend" means anyone on the Facebook system whom you allow to see very different levels of personal and public information, such as comments, birth date, jobs, photos, member of groups, and list of other friends and relatives. An individual can play games online and update others in day-to-day life.

Everyone can also notice friend's friend, i.e., individuals, whom you have officially became friend and may not met before, may have visualization keen on everyone's private situations and information.

There is update field which is at the pinnacle of the everyone's Facebook, but the main use of that field is that it allows the abuser to place anything similar to snippet as regards several topics at any point. It has very parallel field, although it does not agree to extra passage, and LinkedIn is not allowed for connecting associations/images/videos with the keep posted. A little example of every user's update is posted by your any social networking site like Facebook friend. These all are extremely classic:

- "Presently established a plane ticket proffer."
- "Someone is tired of every one this cold winter."

Even though that strength looks comparatively undamaging, the third position could raise a little be anxious. Every user can tell all their friends and connected links, i.e., all of your friends, which we do not be there at home used for a half year [12]. This is like to attaching an indication on the main road and infusing something.

Although the applications on social network may seem to be safe, along with in actuality a good number probably it is safe and harmless, it is forever something that can send harmful content to your computer/laptops. It is not right just to Facebook, but there are same as like Facebook, additional social networking sites which are associated with the Internet in universal situation, when you start downloading the web form or opening documents in email communications. So, you need to make sure that every user's computer has a correct and efficient antivirus or firewall, which means updated antivirus and install or run antivirus software if all are starting from a trust resource or accepted by the admin or group of IT department.

1.2 Twitter

It is a live application like to Facebook and LinkedIn which allows you to post comments which we say these days to tweet on some topics. Special users on the network of Twitter can grow to be supporters of someone's tweets related, like everyone can receive the updates regarding the data or information which are sent by them.

Study over the business ecosystems in Hungary by monitoring 6000 out of 20,000 Facebook users who publically displayed their employers. Then, they represented the complexity of connections graphically through a simulator. Also, they transformed the overall graphical network into a relationship graph of employers. If individuals are very related to each other in the network, then there is strong bonding in relationship with each other. Making progress to the same framework, Neunerdt et al. [3] proposed two algorithms for collecting and processing web comments in context of social blogging. Agarwal [1] proposed his extraordinary research work on "Prediction of Trends in Online Social Networks". He expended the "directed links of following" in the social media of Twitter to determine the flow of information. This approach directed a user's influence on others users that could decide if the topic is stylish or viral in the social networking world.

1.3 LinkedIn

If user can utilize Facebook, LinkedIn, Gplus, Twitter, or else some other online site for social networking, Internet banking or daily purchases, you must be responsive of messages and emails which are argued to be since these sites but actually the tricks may contain nasty content. I have received many emails that claim to be from my personal bank, but they are actually sent by a spammer. Spammers are there in the hopes of obtaining my users user id and password. Claiming of emails of Twitter and Facebook invitations is now most common. Emails and messages may still contain an attach RAR file or ZIP file that recipients may use to unlock to observe which user is invited them and made a flow to open the file. The attachment actually contains a worm; it may destroy the entire user's computer and user's reputation on personal and organizational level.

2 Research Background

The paper refers to the definition of information security as given by IMS for information security. It defines "securing the information from different threats in order to ensure business confidentiality, reducing business risk, and increase ROI and business opportunities" [4].

2.1 Finding from Short Survey

Information security is a technical problem but nowadays it is management problem as organizations are facing real financial losses and threat of reputation [7, 11]. Recent survey by CSI—Computer Security Institute—found that there are various risk levels to security (Table 1).

2.2 Finding from short survey chart

See Fig. 1.

3 Discussion and Conclusion

It is very important to keep awareness of social media among the employees and within the organization. There are many negative consequences for such exploring to social media. Due to such study and effect of information leakage and by previous studies, we have concluded that employees and other individuals are very

Table 1 The percentage of threat in real world when exploring personal information to social networking sites [6]

Social site	Uses	Risk percentage (%)
Facebook	Facebook allows posting of personal data	61
Twitter	Twitter creates business relations and connections	17
LinkedIn	Creates followers	4
Google Plus	Same as Facebook but with low risk due to its usability …	40
Myspace	User's space	18

There are biggest risk of security Facebook (61%), Twitter (17%), LinkedIn (4%), Google Plus (40%), and Myspace (18%)

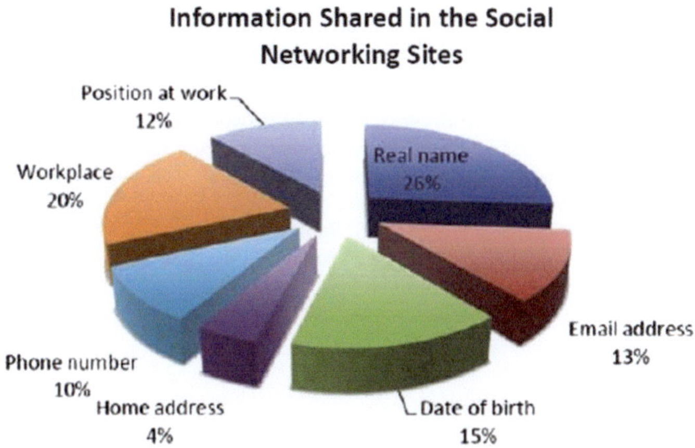

Fig. 1 The types and percentage of information shared on social media

well aware about the threat by leakage of organizational and personal information to the outer world, as mentioned issues and percentage of sharing information might lead to serious damages.

By considering the security problem caused by social networking sites, the suggestions must be implemented by organizations and individuals. Such considerations are more distinguished by SETA programs, with organizational policies [2, 12].

Based on above discussions, it can be said that many users are aware of the use of social media that is directly concerned with the security issues. However, organizations and many awareness programs in the society play important role to install this awareness to individual in order to protect them from leakage of valuable information of personal and professional information, which may cause serious security disaster.

References

1. Abdul Molok NN, Ahmad A, Chang S (2011) Disclosure of organizational information by employees on Facebook: looking at the potential for information security risks. In: 22nd Australasian Conference on Information Systems (ACIS2011), Sydney, Australia
2. Abdul Molok NN, Chang S, Ahmad A (2013) Discolsure of organizational information on social media: perspectives from security managers. In: 17th Pacific Asia Conference on Information Systems (PACIS2013), Jeju Island, South Korea
3. Agarwal P (2013) Department of Computer Science and Engineering, IIT Delhi. Prediction of trends in online social network
4. CSI (2007) 12th annual computer crime and security survey. Computer Security Institute
5. Eminagaoglu M, Uçar E, Eren S (2009) The positive outcomes of information security consciousness training in companies-A case study. Inf Secur Tech Rep 14:223–229

6. Neunerdt M, Niermann M, Mathar R, Trevisan B (2013) Focused crawling for building web comment corpora. In: The 10th Annual IEEE CCNC- Work-in-Progress, pp 761–765
7. Olsik J (2011) The ESG information security management maturity model. Enterprise Strategy Group, Milford, Massachusetts
8. PricewaterhouseCoopers (2010) Security for social networking. pwc.com.au, Australia
9. Radianti J, Gonzalez JJ (2007) A preliminary model of the vulnerability black market. Society
10. Rowe FM, Ciravegna F (2010) Harnessing the social web: the science of identity disambiguation. In: Web Science Conference
11. Sophos (2011) Security threat report: 2010. Sophos Group, Boston, Massachusetts
12. Star T (2012) Don't become an 'accidental' outlaw. In the Star Online

A Key Based Spiral Approach for DNA Cryptography

Ekta and Ajit Singh

Abstract The present paper provides the conceptual framework on DNA cryptography. A key based spiral technique is proposed which uses the concept of a key to generate a spiral transposition to provide more data security than the existing technique. The existing technique is not much robust against attacks and it uses a fixed spiral. Various attacks can lead to data access to unauthorized users. The proposed technique makes the transformation based on key. The performance comparison between the existing, i.e., DNA sequence dictionary method for securing data in DNA using a fixed spiral transposition and proposed technique, i.e., a key based spiral approach for securing the data, shows that the proposed technique is much better than the existing technique in terms of MSE, PSNR, and percentage of total bit changed and provides more security than the existing technique.

Keywords DNA cryptography · DNA structure · Spiral transposition
MSE · PSNR · Percentage of total bit changed · A, T, G, and C

1 Introduction

Nowadays, security of information has become very important with the growth of technical advancement and the use of internet spreading day by day at a very rapid rate. New technologies are emerging in IT sector which give invitation to the attackers and threats. Lots of things are affected by these threats and attacks like bank account, social security, etc. Information should be known to the receiver

Ekta (✉) · A. Singh
Department of CSE & IT, Bhagat Phool Singh Mahila Vishwavidyalaya,
Sonipat, India
e-mail: ektayadav956@gmail.com

A. Singh
e-mail: ghangas_ajit@rediffmail.com

M. U. Bokhari et al. (eds.), *Cyber Security*, Advances in Intelligent Systems
and Computing 729, https://doi.org/10.1007/978-981-10-8536-9_22

only, but because of the weak spots in the security system information gets vulnerable by exploiting the weakness of system as follows:

- The area where ciphers are stored,
- Strength of the used algorithm,
- Random number generator, etc.

Therefore, the main job of the designer who designs the security system is to diminish the chances of threats that attack our system and exploit the weakness. The modern cryptography algorithms like DES and MD5 are also in danger zone [1]. For this purpose, DNA computing provides helpful direction in solving different kinds of problems in cryptography and security. In DNA computing, DNA is used as an information shipper or carrier and modern technology of biology is used as a fulfillment tool. DNA cryptographic system is very powerful against attackers. DNA molecules are used for cryptography because of their massive parallels and extraordinary or vast information inherent capacity or density [2–4]. DNA becomes a perfect medium for data hiding because of its extraordinary storage capacity and the capability of synthesizing its sequence in any desirable length.

The chances of threats and attacks are increasing at a very rapid rate because of the rapid development in the technical advancement. So, the required security requirements are not satisfied with the traditional cryptography methods [5–7] DNA is a natural carrier of the information, which stores the data in the form of nucleotides. DNA can store any type of data whether it is image, text, audio, or video. The information stored in DNA can be any email, password, banking details, organization details, industry details, or any other personal or private information [8, 9, 4]. DNA cryptography provides security of data inherited in DNA in the form of nucleotides. It encodes the data or information in such an efficient way that it can be transmitted through any open environment in a secure and efficient way. So, two major issues present in the field of system security and cryptography are storage and security and both of these issues get resolved by the DNA cryptography [5, 3, 10, 11].

2 Existing Technique

The existing technique of DNA cryptography used a DNA sequence dictionary method using a fixed spiral for securing data [4]. The author used a five-stage method to encrypt the data using DNA sequence. The stages are shown in the flowchart given in Fig. 1. First, data is taken as an input. Then, this input data is converted into the binary form. After converting the data into the binary form, an 8×8 matrix is formed from this binary data. Then, a spiral transposition is done onto this matrix to get a new 8×8 transposed matrix. Spiral transposition changes the bit position in the matrix in such a way that it becomes very hard for the attacker to know what the actual data is. After spiral transposition, corresponding decimal value is given to the each 8-bit binary data. Then, the corresponding DNA sequence is given to these decimal values from the given dictionary table containing 64 values. But the main disadvantage of this approach is that it uses a fixed spiral; therefore, there is no flexibility in this approach [4].

3 Proposed Technique

The proposed technique is based on the concept of key based spiral approach for DNA cryptography where data as well as the key is taken as an input as shown below in the flowchart of Fig. 2. The data and the key both are converted into the binary form. After converting them into the binary form, compare the size of data bit with the size of key. If the size of key is less than the size of input data, then the key is repeated to get the size equal to the binary input data. Now, each bit of key is checked out. If the bit in the key is zero, then the new encrypted data have the same value as that of old data means no replacement is made. But if the key has 1 in the bit position, then the new encrypted data will have a new element, i.e., total data

Fig. 1 Flowchart of existing technique

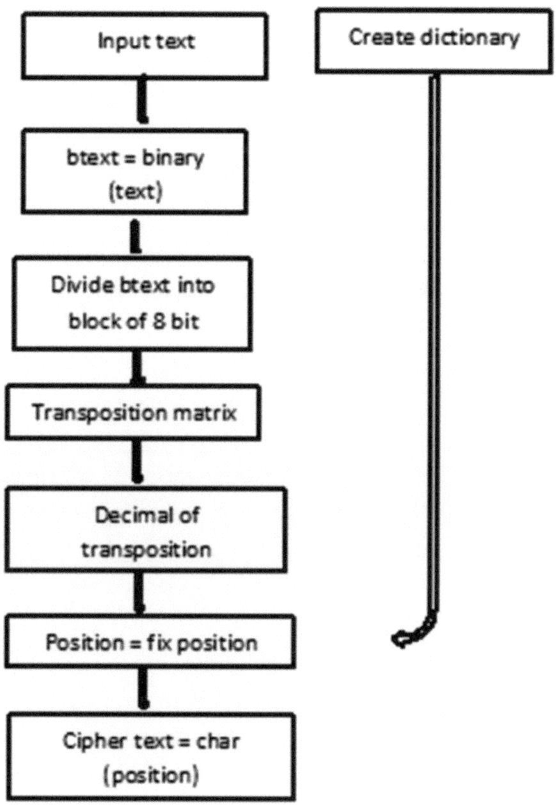

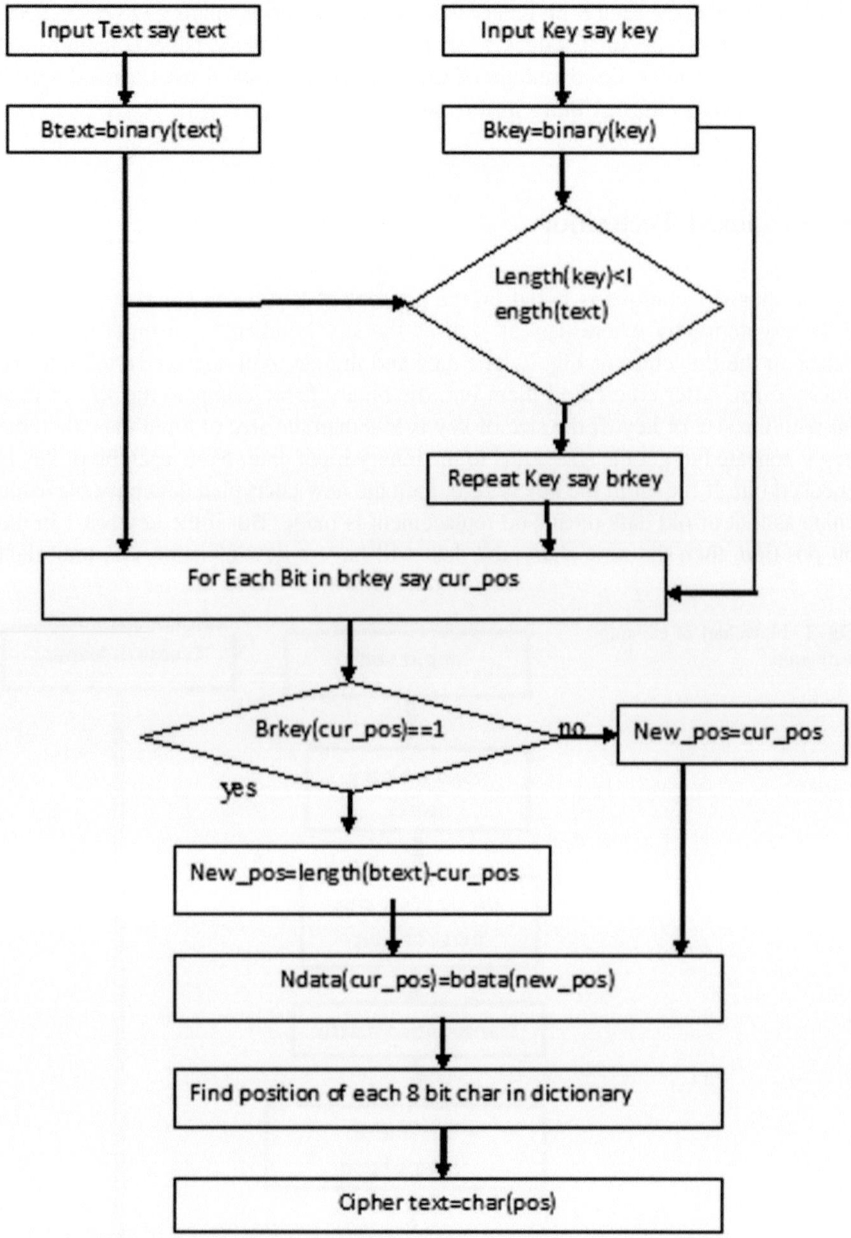

Fig. 2 Flowchart of proposed technique

length- key length. Suppose there are 100 elements in the input data. If we are checking the first bit of key and it is 0, then the new encrypted data have the same bit input as of old data. Suppose, now we are checking the second bit of key and it is 1, then @(100-1), i.e., 99th bit of the old data will go to the second position of the new encrypted data, and so on. Now convert this binary data into the decimal value and find the corresponding four-character-long DNA sequence into the dictionary.

3.1 Requirements of the Proposed Technique

The existing technique used a fix spiral transposition, so there was no flexibility. Once an attacker came to know about the technique used for encrypting the whole data, he could easily recover all the data. So, to enhance the security of information, a key based spiral is used, where the encryption of data is based upon key. This key based concept provides flexibility in encrypting the data because any key can be used to encrypt the data. So, first the attacker has to know about the particular key used in the encryption, and only then he can recover the original data.

3.2 Illustration of the Proposed Technique

The various steps involved are explained below:

(a) Step 1: Plaintext of 8 characters is taken as an input, i.e., "THURSDAY".
(b) Step 2: A key of four characters is also taken as input, i.e., "ABCD".
(c) Step 3: The plaintext "THURSDAY" is converted into its corresponding binary values (Table 1).
Now, the binary representation of the plaintext can be given into a matrix form (Fig. 3).
(d) Step 4: Key "ABCD" is also converted into its corresponding binary values (Table 2):

Table 1 ASCII input value to binary value

Character	ASCII value	Binary value
T	84	01010100
H	72	01001000
U	85	01010101
R	82	01010010
S	83	01010011
D	68	01000100
A	65	01000001
Y	89	01011001

0	1	0	1	0	1	0	0
0	1	0	0	1	0	0	0
0	1	0	1	0	1	0	1
0	1	0	1	0	0	1	0
0	1	0	1	0	0	1	1
0	1	0	0	0	1	0	0
0	1	0	0	0	0	0	1
0	1	0	1	1	0	0	1

Fig. 3 Binary value into matrix form

Table 2 ASCII key value to binary value

Character	ASCII value	Binary value
A	65	01000001
B	66	01000010
C	67	01000011
D	68	01000100

0	1	0	0	0	0	0	1
0	1	0	0	0	0	1	0
0	1	0	0	0	0	1	1
0	1	0	0	0	1	0	0

Fig. 4 Binary value of key into matrix

0	1	0	0	0	0	0	1
0	1	0	0	0	0	1	0
0	1	0	0	0	0	1	1
0	1	0	0	0	1	0	0
0	1	0	0	0	0	0	1
0	1	0	0	0	0	1	0
0	1	0	0	0	0	1	1
0	1	0	0	0	1	0	0

Fig. 5 Representation after repetition of key

Now, the binary representation of the key can be given in a matrix form (Fig. 4).

(e) Step 5: If the key size is less than the plaintext size, then repeat the key binary values to make the size of key equal to the size of plaintext. Therefore, repeat the binary key (Fig. 5).

(f) Step 6: Now make a spiral based upon the logic that if there is 0 at any bit position in the key then the new encrypted data has the same value as that of old data. But, if there is 1 in the key bit position, the data bit is replaced by a new data bit. Suppose there is 1 on the first position in the key and total data length is 64, then we will put (64-1) 63 element of the

0	0	0	1	0	1	0	1
0	0	0	0	1	0	0	0
0	1	0	1	0	1	0	1
0	0	0	1	0	1	1	0
0	0	0	1	0	0	1	1
0	1	0	0	0	1	0	0
0	0	0	0	0	0	0	0
0	1	0	1	1	1	0	1

Fig. 6 Representation after spiral

Table 3 ASCII equivalent of spiraled values

Binary value	ASCII value	DNA sequence
00010101	21	ATTA
00001000	8	AATC
01010101	85	TTTA
00010110	22	ATTT
00010011	19	ATAG
01000100	68	TAAC
00000000	0	CCCC
01011101	93	TTCA

old data into the first position of the new encrypted data. Therefore, a spiral based on this logic can be represented as (Fig. 6):

(g) Step 7: Now, the spiral's equivalent ASCII values and DNA sequence using the DNA sequence dictionary are shown in (Table 3):

Therefore, from the above illustration, the encrypted text for the plaintext "THURSDAY" using a key "ABCD" is "ATTAAATCTTTAATTTATAG TAACCCCCTTCA".

4 Performance Comparison

The performance comparison has been made between the existing and the proposed technique on the basis of PSNR, MSE, and percentage of total bit changed. It is clear from the results that the proposed technique is much better than the existing technique in terms of PSNR, MSE, and total percentage of bit changed. The proposed technique provides the low MSE and low total bit changed and high PSNR than the existing method.

4.1 Definition of Various Performance Terms

PSNR (Peak Signal-to-Noise Ratio): It is the measure of quality of picture with the comparison of cover image and stego image. If PSNR is higher, it means the performance of technique is also higher [12, 13].

MSE (Mean Square Error): It is defined as the square of error between the stego image and the cover image. It should be low for better results [14, 11].

Percentage of total bit changed: The total percentage of the bit change represents the amount of bits change in the cover data to get the stego data. The lower the bit change, the better is the technique [12, 13].

Various graphs generated using Matlab® and program codes are shown in (Figs. 7, 8, and 9).

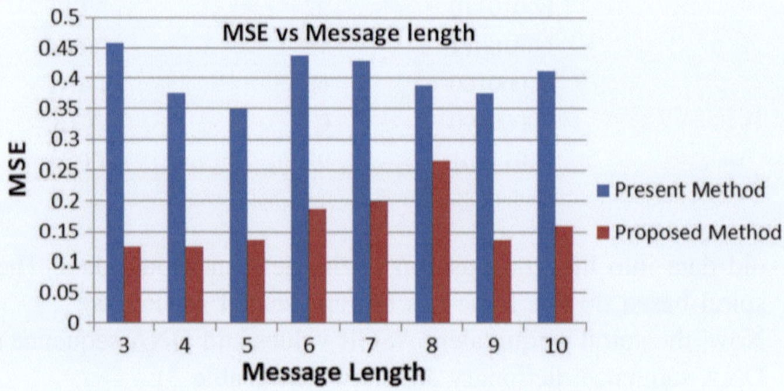

Fig. 7 MSE versus message length for proposed and existing technique

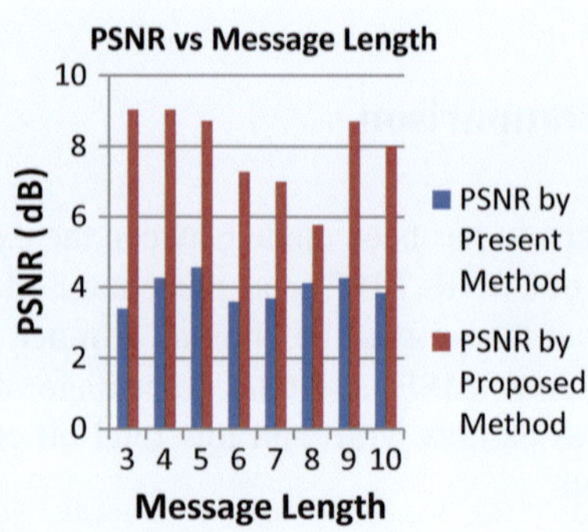

Fig. 8 PSNRS versus message length for proposed and existing technique

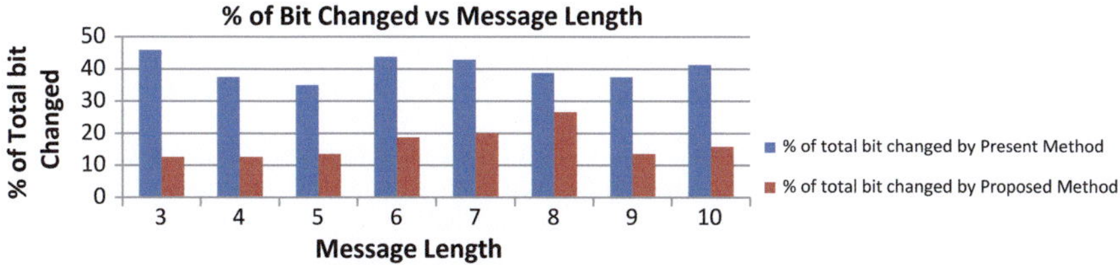

Fig. 9 Percentage of bit changed versus message length for proposed and existing technique

5 Conclusion

The existing technique is having a number of limitations such as use of fixed spiral, high MSE, low PSNR, and high percentage of total bit changed, due to which it doesn't fulfill the security requirements. Keeping in view to avoid such types of problems, the new technique is proposed which makes use of concept based on key based spiral transposition where the encryption is based upon key; different keys can be used to encrypt any type of data. Therefore, security is enhanced due to key flexibility system. The logic used in the key is based upon the existence of 0 or 1. If there is 1 in the key bit position, the data bit is replaced by a new data bit. Suppose there is 1 on the first position in the key and total data length is 100, then we will put (100-1), i.e., 99 elements of the old data into the first position of the new encrypted data. Therefore, the logic used here is better as compared to the earlier approach because it is based upon a key flexibility system, i.e., it can use a key or different keys to encrypt the data. The three main parameters, i.e., MSE, PSNR, and percentage of total bit changed also give us better results. The value of MSE is low; the lower the value of MSE, the better the result. The value produced by the PSNR is also high; the higher the value of PSNR, the better the results. The total number of bits changed also gets reduced so that the attacker cannot differentiate between the actual data, i.e., DNA and the encrypted data. Therefore, in comparison to the existing technique, this proposed technique has a good flexible key based encryption method and proposed method also produces lower MSE, higher PSNR, and total percentage of bits changed get reduced than the present method. Hence, the proposed technique is better than the existing technique. One other benefit of the proposed method is also the flexibility of key used.

References

1. Jacob G, Murugan A (2013) DNA based cryptography: an overview and analysis. Int J Emerg Sci 3(1):36–42
2. Chen J (2003) A DNA-based, bimolecular cryptography design. In: ISCAS'03 proceedings
3. Gehani A, LaBean T, Reif J (2004) DNA-based cryptography. Lecture Notes in Computer Science, Springer

4. Jain S, Dr. Bhatnagar V (2014) A novel sequence dictionary method for securing data in DNA using spiral method and framework of DNA cryptography. ICAETR
5. Soni R, Prajapat G (2013) A modern review on DNA cryptography techniques. Int J Adv Res Comput Sci Softw Eng 3(7)
6. Amin ST, Saeb M, El-Gindi S (2006) A DNA-based implementation of YAEA encryption algorithm. In: IASTED International Conference on Computational Intelligence
7. Pruthi Y, Dixit S (2014) A comparative study on DNA cryptography. IJARCEE 4(5)
8. Kahate A Cryptography and network security (3rd edn). McGraw-Hill
9. Shyam VMM, Kiran N (2000) A novel encryption scheme based on DNA computing. In: 14th IEEE International Conference, Tia, India
10. Borda ME, Tornea O (2010) DNA secret writing techniques. In: IEEE conferences
11. Kumar S, Chakraborty S (2011) Image steganography using DNA sequence. AJCSIT 1:2
12. Khalifa A, Atito A (2012) High-capacity DNA-based steganography. In: The 8th International Conference and informatics and Systems, IEEE
13. Torkaman MRN, Kazazi NS, Rouddini A (2012) Innovative approach to improve hybrid cryptography by using DNA steganography. IJNCAA 2(1)
14. Tulpan D, Regoni C, Durand G, Bellivean L, Leger S (2013) A hybrid stegano-cryptographic approach for data encryption using randomized error correcting DNA codes. HINDAWI 2013

Author Biographies

Ekta is currently pursuing PhD (2018) in Computer Science and Engineering from Bhagat Phool Singh Mahila Vishwavidyalaya, Haryana, India, a governement university.

Prof. Ajit Singh is working as Professor in Dept. of Computer Science and Engineering of Bhagat Phool Singh Mahila Vishwavidyalaya, Haryana, India, a governement university.

Permission-Set Based Detection and Analysis of Android Malware

Aditi Sharma and Amit Doegar

Abstract Smartphone industry has become one of the fastest growing technological areas in the past few years. The monotonic growth of Android share market and the diversity among various app sources besides official Google Play Store has attracted attention of malware attacker. To tackle with the problem of increasing number of malicious Android app available at various sources, this paper proposes a novel approach which is based on feature similarity of Android apps. This approach has been implemented by performing static analysis to extract the features from an APK file. Extracted features are useful and meaningful to make efficient training system. This paper proposes a permission-based model which makes use of self-organizing map algorithm. The implemented approach has been analyzed using 1200 heterogeneous Android apps. The proposed approach shows improved results for TPR, FPR, and accuracy.

Keywords Android applications · Android malware · Self-organizing map

1 Introduction

The shares of smartphone market are increasing day by day. Numbers of new smartphone companies are coming in market with new models having number of new and extra features. Although smartphone industry is a tough industry, if one wants to become a part of this industry, they have to come with little bit more that is just good. This can be provided by enhancing smartphone processor, operating system, battery life, storage capacity, screen resolution, and many more. In addition to this, smartphone has inbuilt apps which provide extraordinary features. Simultaneous execution of many app creates a burden on operating system for

A. Sharma (✉) · A. Doegar
Department of CS NITTTR, Chandigarh, India
e-mail: Aditi.cse@nitttrchd.ac.in

A. Doegar
e-mail: amit@nitttrchd.ac.in

M. U. Bokhari et al. (eds.), *Cyber Security*, Advances in Intelligent Systems and Computing 729, https://doi.org/10.1007/978-981-10-8536-9_23

faster execution. To handle this, a lightweighted operating system has been required. Android is lightweighted and open-source operating system. Lightweighted feature of Android operating system allows it to handle multiple requests efficiently. Open-source feature allows it to install apps from any source. It might be official Google Play Store or any third-party sources. In order to detect the threat in Android-based devices, two main techniques, static analysis and dynamic analysis, are used [1]. Static analysis based studies detect and analyze app without executing it. While in case of dynamic analysis, it usually detects and analyze app during execution or after the execution.

Today, for Android platform, there exist more than million of apps in official Google Play Store—targeted at a specific task and covering almost all area of our life. With diverse range of Android apps, Android smartphone penetrated deeper into our lives and became integral part of it [2]. The increased usage and popularity of Android smartphone attracted the attackers. Attacker not only affects the usage and popularity of Android smartphone but also created new possibilities for threats. Android malwares are growing with the same rate as Android smartphone market growing. Both are directly proportional to each other. This proportion creates a big challenge for us. The growth of Android malware generated a new area for research. To handle the challenge of growing rate of Android malware, we need to employ a novel approach which is also capable to detect new Android malware with improved accuracy.

2 Related Work

The number of concept and technique was proposed to reduce the growing amount of Android malware. To gain knowledge about malware propagation, a detailed study of related work is needed. A number of survey papers were written to pay attention on malware detection, analysis, and propagation with their cause and effect that was provided in studies of [3–6]. The Cooper et al. [3] Android apps was developing quickly for almost covering gaming, entertainment, adventure, education, social media, businesses, lifestyle, and other day-to-day activities. With quick development of these apps, developer had not provided more attention to security of these apps. Hence, a solid understanding of malware characteristics was needed. This helped to prevent many unwanted consequences present in the app. [4] told that malware was not only related to abnormal execution of a program. There were big incentives for writing malware [5]. Basic reason of all malware was to harm the users by any means. But all those malware were not shared similar characteristics. Based on malware characteristics, Android malware falls in 49 different malware families [6]. They gave first mobile malware survey and analyzed a total of 46 samples of iOS, Symbian, and Android with their incentives. Other Android-based analysis and detection approaches [7–9] were existed in literature. The authors utilized only permission set to detect and analyze the Android malware [7]. They developed a two-layered permissions-based detector. This detector utilized only requested features and used-features of Android apps [8]. They gave PUMA to detect Android malware also based on permission set [9]. They studied relationship of permissions requested by Android apps. This study was intended for non-malicious Android apps only.

3 Proposed Work and Methodology

To detect malicious apps, the proposed approach requires low-level feature visualization with high-level feature similarity that helps to determine typical indications of malicious activity. Many researchers implemented their approaches by knowingly class label in advance. To implement the proposed approach, we do not need any class label in advance, as we employed unsupervised clustering technique. The dataset has been collected from official Google Play Store [10] and androidsandbox.net [11]. The implementation process is as follows:

(a) **Android app reverse engineering**: In the first step, a Java-based APK tool has been used for automated reverse engineering of APK files. This tool provides readable Android Manifest.xml file, multiple Smali files, and other resource subfolders (Sect. 3.1).
(b) **Broad static analysis**: In the first step, given Android application is inspected and extracts different features from the Android manifest and Smali files (Sect. 3.2).
(c) **Embedding in vector space**: The extracted features have been mapped into a vector space separately for each model, where patterns and combinations of the features can be analyzed on the similarity bases (Sect. 3.3).
(d) **Self-organizing feature map based visualization**: Self-organizing feature map make cluster based on their feature similarity. The embedding of the features enables us to identify malware using SOM, which provides better visualization of features (Sect. 3.4).

3.1 Android App Reverse Engineering

The collected Android apps are in .APK format which are not directly readable to the users. To make these apps readable, we have to transform these apps into readable format. This transformation of APK files has been achieved by doing reverse engineering. APK tool [12] is used for transformation of APK files. APK tool transforms app nearly to its original form. One can modify the app and rebuild that app. It debugs Smali code step by step [15]. Generally, modifications are made to add some features. But attacker adds malicious code and rebuilds the app to harm the user.

3.2 Broad Static Analysis

All smartphones which are based on Android operating system have different capabilities, for example, some devices support cellular data networks while others only support Wi-Fi. Android deals with variety of features. The static analysis inspects given Android app without execution and extract as many as possible permissions. Every Android app must include a manifest file called as AndroidManifest.xml. This single file provides complete information that supports the installation and later execution of the application. Android app needs some functionality like reading SMS, sending SMS, making call, using camera, etc. It is mandatory to protect this functionality from unauthorized use. Android permissions have been created to protect these functionalities. Every app has a set of permission which user accepted at install time. The extracted permission has been helpful and meaningful to construct the model. The appropriateness of extracted features affects the result. The features have been extracted from Android manifest file of an app. For an example, if Android app wants to access the complete information of a network, the following is declared in Android manifest file:

<uses-permission android: name = “android.permission.ACCESS_NETWORK_STATE”/>

To declare a permission <uses-permission> tag is used.

3.3 Feature Embedment

The extracted features have been mapped into a vector space. An input vector has been made corresponding to an app permission set. The requested permission has been expressed in the form of a bit string. Every app permission has been stored in binary (0, 1) format. If feature vector is represented by F, then

$$F_i = \left.\begin{matrix} 1 \\ 0 \end{matrix}\right\} \begin{matrix} \text{if and only if the ith permission requested} \\ \text{otherwise} \end{matrix}$$

For example, an app is represented as the bit string [0, 0, 1, 1, 1] if it requested feature 3, 4, and 5 but not 1 and 2. The detailed description and construction of model are covered as follows:

Permission is the most recognizable security feature in Android apps. User cannot install an app until they will not accept permission because it is key factor to install app. Once user accepts permission, the particular app has been installed in user device. An attacker also needs user acceptance to get their app installed in user device. The malicious app looks like other non-malicious app, but attacker adds some additional features which affect the normal processing of an app. Hence, attacker adds additional non-related permissions in permission set to do harmful activity without user consent.

3.4 Self-organizing Feature Map Based Visualization

The permission-based model has been trained using Self-Organizing Maps (SOM). SOM is trained using unsupervised learning to produce a low-dimensional (typically two-dimensional) view of data [13].

SOM Algorithm [9]

Step 1: Initialize neuron weights $w_i = \left[w_{i1}, w_{i2}, \ldots, w_{ij}\right] \in R$. To initialize the Neuron weights, random numbers have been used.

Step 2: Load an input pattern $x = \left[x_1, x_2, \ldots, x_j\right] \in M$. Here, M can be any three models $M \in$ [Permission-based]. Distance between pattern x, and each neuron weight w_i, has been calculated and winning neuron or best matching neuron c has been identified as follows:

$$\|x - w_c\| = \min\{\|x - w_i\|\}$$

Euclidian distance is normalized to range [0, 1].

Step 3: Update weights all neighbor and of winning neuron c

$$w_i(t+1) = w_i(t) + h_{ci}(t)\left[x(t) - w_i(t)\right],$$

where

i	neighbor neuron index
t	integer, the discrete time coordinate
$h_{ci}(t)$	is a neighborhood kernel function of time and distance between neighbor neuron i and winning neuron c. $h_{ci}(t)$ defines the region of influence that the input pattern has on the SOM

$$h_{ci}(t) = \exp\left(\frac{||(r_c - r_i)||^2}{2\sigma^2(t)}\right)\alpha(t),$$

where

r_c and r_i	are positions of neurons and on the SOM grid
$\alpha(t)$	learning rate function
(t)	defines the width of the kernel

Both $\alpha(t)$ and $\sigma(t)$ decrease monotonically with time.

Step 4: Repeat steps 2–3 until the convergence criterion is satisfied.

The permission-based model has been trained with the help of SOM. SOM provides interesting pattern which helps to determine the maliciousness of an app. This interesting pattern occurred because SOM makes cluster on the basis of feature similarity.

3.5 Performance Measures [14]

To predict the accuracy of machine-learning based algorithms, there are several classifiers available in literature. In context to abovementioned problem, the performance measure is as follows:

Let $n_{\text{ben}\to\text{ben}}$ be the number of benign application correctly classified as benign

$n_{\text{ben}\to\text{mal}}$ be the number of misclassified benign applications

$n_{\text{mal}\to\text{mal}}$ be the number of malicious applications correctly classified as malicious

$n_{\text{mal}\to\text{ben}}$ be the number of misclassified malicious applications

$$\text{True Positive Ratio (TPR)} = \frac{n_{\text{mal}\to\text{mal}}}{n_{\text{mal}\to\text{ben}} + n_{\text{mal}\to\text{mal}}} \tag{1}$$

$$\text{False Positive Ratio (FPR)} = \frac{n_{\text{ben}\to\text{mal}}}{n_{\text{ben}\to\text{mal}} + n_{\text{ben}\to\text{ben}}} \tag{2}$$

Accuracy (ACC): The accuracy of a classifier refers to the ability of a given classifier to correctly predict the class label of new or previously unseen data.

$$\text{ACC} = \frac{n_{\text{ben}\to\text{ben}} + n_{\text{mal}\to\text{mal}}}{n_{\text{ben}\to\text{ben}} + n_{\text{ben}\to\text{mal}} + n_{\text{mal}\to\text{ben}} + n_{\text{mal}\to\text{mal}}} \tag{3}$$

4 Performance Evaluation

In order to verify the proposed approach, the constructed permission-based model has been verified against a collection of 400 samples, 200 from each category, i.e., benign and malicious. Result has been based on multiple numbers of tests. The evaluation of the permission-based model has been based on the performance measures. Performance measures are true positive rate, false positive rate, and accuracy as discussed in Sect. 3.5.

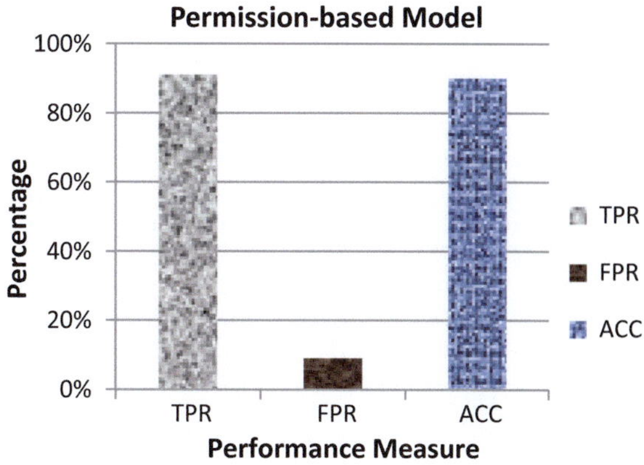

Fig. 1 Permission-based model

Figure 1 depicts the results that show the average detection rate for new Android malware by Android malware. The permission-based model achieved good detection rate. In permission-based model, filtering is done only on the bases of permission set which gives TPR, FPR, and ACC 91, 9, and 90%, respectively.

5 Conclusion

This paper proposes a novel approach for detecting potential Android malicious apps using Self-organizing Maps (SOM). Self-organizing map is an unsupervised clustering method; no prior information about class labels has been required. SOM detect and analyze new Android apps based on their feature similarity. The permission-based model has been investigated to detect malwares present in Android apps. In order to build the permission-based model, all the permissions have been extracted from a large number of benign and malicious APK files. APK files are not human readable file and feature cannot be directly extracted from these APK files. The APK tool has been used to transform the APK files into readable format and to extract features. The permission-based model has been constructed by extracting features from 400 benign apps and 400 malicious apps. To test permission-based model, total 400 apps (200 from benign dataset and 200 from malware dataset) have been used.

The evaluation of models is done using performance measures such as True Positive Rate (TPR), the False Positive Rate (FPR), and Accuracy (ACC). The TPR, FPR, and ACC of model are 91, 9, and 90%, respectively, which is better than existing approaches.

References

1. Idika N, Mathur AP (2007) A survey of malware detection techniques. Department of Computer Science, Purdue University, West Lafayette, IN 47907, pp 1–48, Feb 2007
2. Sharma A, Doegar A (2015) Review of malware detection and analysis for android environment using data mining techniques. In: Proceedings of national conference on computing technologies, national institute of technical teachers training and research, Chandigarh, CT31, pp 30–31, Mar 2015
3. Cooper VN, Shahriar H, Haddad HM (2014) A survey of android malware characteristics and mitigation techniques. In: Proceedings of 11th IEEE international conference on InfoTech: new generations, USA, pp 327–332
4. Thanh HL (2013) Analysis of malware families on android mobiles: detection characteristics recognizable by ordinary phone users and how to fix it. J Inf Secur (JIS) 4(4):213–224
5. Zhou Y, Jiang X (2012) Dissecting android malware: characterization an evolution. IEEE Symposium on Security and Privacy, San Francisco, pp 95–109
6. Felt AP, Finifter M, Chin E, Hanna S, Wagner D (2011) A survey of mobile malware in the wild. In: Proceedings of 1st ACM conference of security and privacy in smartphone and mobile devices (SPSM), USA, pp 3–14
7. Liu X, Liu J (2014) A two-layered permission-based android malware detection scheme. In: Proceedings of 2nd IEEE international conference on mobile cloud computing, services, and engineering, UK, pp 142–148
8. Sanz B, Santos I, Laorden C, Ugarte-Pedrero C, Bringas PG, Álvarez G (2013) PUMA: permission usage to detect malware in android. In: International joint conference, vol 189, no 1. Heidelberg, pp 289–298
9. Barrera D, OOrschot PCV, Kayacil HG, Somayaji A (2010) A methodology for empirical analysis of permission-based security models and its applications to android. In: Proceedings of the 17th ACM conference on computer and communication security (CSS), USA, pp 73–84, Oct 2010
10. Official Google Play Store. Online available: https://play.google.com/store?hl=en. Last accessed: 09 May 2015
11. Android Sandbox. Online available: http://www.androidsandbox.net/samples/01.2015/. Last accessed: 03 Dec 2014
12. APK Tool. Online available: https://code.google.com/p/android-apktool/. Last accessed: 22 Feb 2015
13. Self organizing map. Online available: http://en.wikipedia.org/wiki/Self-organizing_map/. Last accessed: 3 Mar 2015
14. Wu DJ, Mao CH, Wei TE, Lee HM, Wu KP (2012) DroidMat: android malware detection through manifest and API calls tracing. In: Proceedings of 7th Asia joint conference on information security, Tokyo, pp 66–69, Aug 2012
15. Performance Measures. Online available: http://en.wikipedia.org/wiki/Sensitivity_and_specificity/. Last accessed: 17 Jan 2015

Author Biographies

Aditi Sharma received the B.E. degree in Computer Engineering from Punjabi University Patiala, Patiala, India and M.E. in Computer Science and Engineering from Panjab University, Chandigarh, India. Research interest includes network security and malware analysis.

Amit Doegar received the B.E. degree in Computer Science Engineering from Karnatak University, Dharwar, India and M.E. in Computer Science and Engineering from Panjab University, Chandigarh, India. Research interest includes computer networks, image processing, virtual learning, and open-source technology.

Three-Level GIS Data Security: Conjointly Cryptography and Digital Watermarking

Monika Bansal and Akanksha Upadhyaya

Abstract Geographic Information System (GIS) plays a vital role in many applications especially in military operations as they need to be spatial in nature. Successful application of military operations demands for accuracy of information and quick decisions taking steps. GIS has now become the most powerful medium for sharing of military information to officers and commanders. In the era of digital communication, officers use GIS to deliver their strategic plans to intended officers [5]. GIS has proven to be an excellent tool for enforcement and deployment of security mechanisms in military applications and to deliver confidential information at distant locations. In our proposed system, we will introduce a new mechanism to protect GIS data carrying confidential and sensitive data for military and army purpose by combining two of the cryptography algorithms: Advanced Encryption Standard (AES) and RSA with digital watermarking techniques.

Keywords GIS · Cryptography · Digital watermarking · AES RSA

1 Introduction

Experts have long been recognized the importance of GIS in military and commercial application. The GIS data has two important properties. First, the effort it takes to put it in a suitable form for use in the GIS applications. This effort increases its cost. Second, GIS data contains confidential and sensitive information most of the time and it needs to be kept away from unauthorized users. Two possible threats for GIS data are as follows:

M. Bansal (✉) · A. Upadhyaya
Rukmini Devi Institute of Advanced Studies, Delhi, India
e-mail: monikabansal79@gmail.com

A. Upadhyaya
e-mail: akanksha0707@gmail.com

M. U. Bokhari et al. (eds.), *Cyber Security*, Advances in Intelligent Systems and Computing 729, https://doi.org/10.1007/978-981-10-8536-9_24

1. Illegal duplication and distribution—As GIS data is expensive and sensitive by nature, third parties used to make copies of this data by purchasing some layers of GIS and later sell them without taking any permission from original GIS data provider.
2. Unauthorized access—The act of accessing and tampering of data is done by intruder while information is being transmitted over untrusted communication channel.

The proposed system introduced in this paper is an attempt to solve these security problems in relation to GIS data.

2 Organization of Paper

Paper is organized into seven sections. Section 3 gives applications and limitations of cryptography and digital watermarking. In Sect. 4, we discussed security issues and threats while using GIS data with respect to the past work. We introduced and explained our proposed system with the help of flowchart in Sect. 5. At last, the paper is concluded by its future work.

3 Pros and Cons: Cryptography and Digital Watermarking

Cryptography, digital watermarking, and many other technologies have been used to handle security threats. Each of these technologies has its limitations and has been long used as a weapon to solve security and authentication problems related to data transmitted over network. Both of these have diversified applications and usage with different objectives.

Cryptography tries to take care of three important properties of information including confidentiality, authenticity, and integrity, while it is being transmitted over public network. It is the method of encryption of original data at sender side using key and algorithm before being transmitted over Internet and do reverse of the same process at receiver side. Encryption is the process of converting a readable or meaningful data in an unreadable and meaningless form. Many algorithms like AES, RSA, Hashing, etc. used for the same purpose. It is also used for the purpose of sharing secured data over unsecured network. The efficiency of cryptography depends on key management and its distribution and not on the algorithm used and this is one of the biggest security threats with this technique.

Digital watermarking is the method of hiding a digital information into digital signal like an image, audio, or video signal itself. One of the mostly used applications of digital watermarking is owner identification. To identify the owner of specific image or song, copyright information is embedded in the image or song itself. Other applications of digital watermarking include tampering detection, fingerprinting, broadcast monitoring, etc. [4].

The major limitation of digital watermarking is the manipulation of innocent image including cropping, color variations, rotations, lossy compression, etc. Moreover, some of the features of original image like color, texture, pixel's width, etc. get changed by digital watermarking to embed data or confidential information into it. Changing the features of image distorts the image, and many times it becomes very difficult to recover original image from the distorted image. Also, it cannot protect the GIS data and confidential information from access by unauthorized users.

A more secure system could be built by linking digital watermarking with cryptography. Security can be enhanced for broadcasting of such a sensitive and confidential data like GIS data by this method.

4 Related Work

From the past many years, GIS has been used by government agencies to transfer information. Earlier, professionals used to identify threats, plan resource deployments, and map potential action and contingency plans with the help of GIS. Also, for drawing and printing maps and for building of information desktop, applications were widely used. However, nowadays, the GIS platform allow users the ability to access confidential information and to use of maps in any easy manner in 24 × 7 from anywhere to anywhere and also on any network [3]. Being of its capability to deliver confidential and secret information, GIS is used by military forces in a variety of applications including terrorist activities monitoring, remote sensing, borderlines monitoring, order enforcement at battlefield, etc. The work that has been done in this area is mostly based on digital watermarking [6, 7]. Watermarking is a process of obtaining a digital watermarked file by embedding hidden information (watermarking pattern or watermark for simplicity) like copyright string in a dataset without producing perceptible changes in the data using a suitable watermarking algorithm [1].

5 Proposed System

The proposed algorithm is designed with an objective to provide a method for secure communication of confidential and sensitive information in the form of digital data like images including maps, shape files, etc. along with copyright messages over a network. The proposed model employs digital watermarking with cryptography having two levels of AES and one level of RSA. Several techniques are used for digital watermarking. Our proposed system uses least significant bit embedding technique in which any bit of integer part of the selected coordinates of

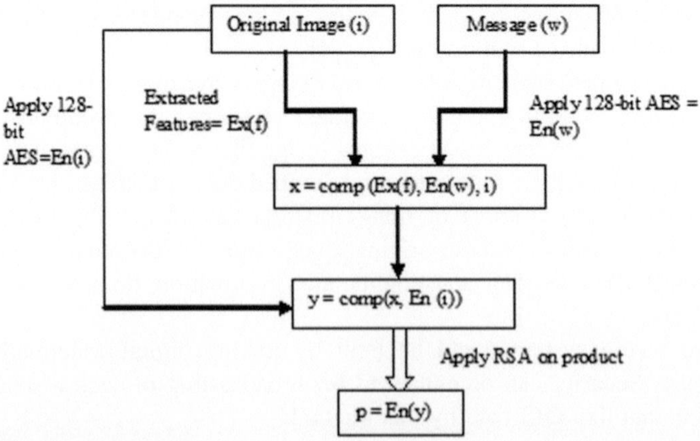

Fig. 1 Encryption at sender side

image is extracted and used [2]. The sequence of steps taken at sender and receiver side is shown as (Figs. 1, 2).

Encryption Algorithm (i,w)

```
Input: i = original image, w = original message
Step 1:
  1.1 Extract LSB from i using function Ex(f).
  1.2 Apply 128-bit AES on w by using encryption function, En(w).
Step 2: Apply composite function to embed encrypted message and extracted
features into image i, i.e.
       x = comp(Ex(f), En(w), i)
Step 3: Encrypt i using 128-bit AES encryption function, En(i).
Step 4: Apply composite function again on data structures obtained from
step 2 and 3.
      y = comp(x, En(i))
Step5: Obtain final message product p being ready to transmit over insecure
channel by encrypting y using RSA encryption function, i.e. p = En(y)
```

5.1 *Explanation*

The whole process of encryption and decryption passes through three stages of encryption at sender side and decryption at receiver side. At first stage, message which is to be sent by embedding it into an original image is encrypted using 128-bit AES algorithm in parallel extraction of least significant bits from original

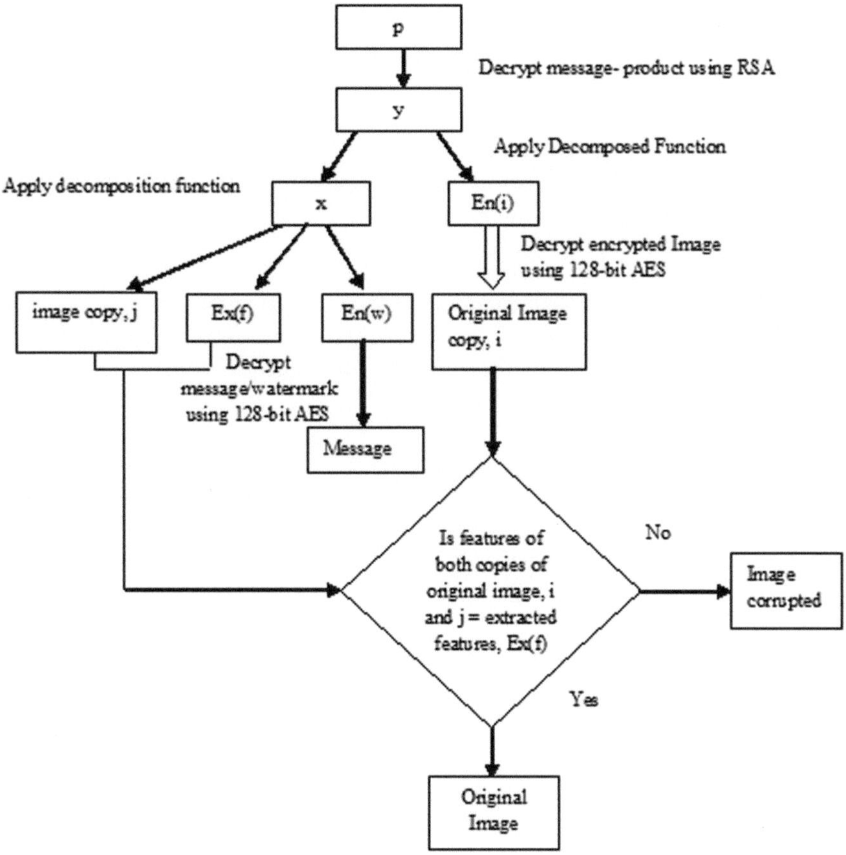

Fig. 2 Decryption at receiver side

image coordinates so that composition function can be applied over them. Extracting LSB helps in storing information of the image like checksum, compressed bits, etc.; here, in the proposed system checksum is stored in LSB for verification at other end. If at the other end the value of checksum founds to be different, then it can be identified that image has been tampered. After applying the composition function, comp(Ex(*f*), En(*w*), *i*), we get composite image, *x*, which is a combination of encrypted message, En(*w*), and extracted features (first bit of coordinates), Ex(*f*). In the second stage, complete product, *y*, gets obtained by combining the composite image with an encrypted original image being obtained after using 128-bit AES algorithm over it. Now, this envelope will hold composite image, *x*, and encrypted image, En(*i*). At last, the complete product will again get encrypted; using RSA algorithm, public key will be transmitted over the network for the user(s).

Decryption Algorithm (p)

```
Input: p = Encrypted message product received from insecure communication
channel
Step 1: Decrypt p using RSA algorithm, y = De(p).
Step 2: Apply decomposed function, decomp on the decrypted message product
y, obtained from step 1.
              (x, En(i)) = decomp(y)
Step 3: Obtain image i by decrypting En(i) using 128-bit AES algorithm and
in parallel apply decomposed function on x to get encrypted message En
(w),
extracted features Ex(f) and another copy of original image say j.
 i = De(En(i))
(j, En(w), Ex(f)) = decomp(x)
Step 4: Decrypt message using 128-bit AES algorithm, i.e. w = De(En(w)).
Step 5: Compare both copies of image stored in data structure i and j
respectively with extracted features Ex(f) and check whether the image has
been tampered or in the original form.
   If LSB(i) = LSB(j) = Ex(f)
   Then
              "Image not tampered"
   Else
              "Image tampered"
```

5.2 *Explanation*

Similarly, at receiver end decryption process will be applied. First, the complete encrypted product, *p*, gets decrypted using RSA and then decompose into two parts *x* and En(*i*) (selected bits of the coordinates). Now, *x* will be decomposed by applying decomposition function on *x*, and hence we will get Ex(*f*), En(*w*), and copy of original image, *j*. Next, both encrypted message, En(*w*), and encrypted image, En(*i*), get decrypted using 128-bit AES algorithm. This decrypted copy is an another copy of the same original image, say *i*. Now by comparing the extracted feature (bits) with features of both of these copies of original image, *i* and *j*, we can easily judge whether the image being received is distorted or not.

6 Conclusion

Under this research paper, we proposed a system that provides security at three levels. If an intruder is somehow able to decrypt the data at any of these levels, then it will be very difficult to decrypt at all levels. We have provided the security mix of symmetric and asymmetric cryptography that increases the security of the system. The proposed system can be used in the applications where sensitive information is needed to be transferred.

7 Future Scope

In this research paper, we have just proposed a system that could be implemented for providing efficient security to the organizations, businesses, military, medical, etc. Although the system provides security at three stages using symmetric as well as asymmetric algorithm, however, the use of other asymmetric algorithm for final stage could make system more secure, efficient, and accountable. Since the proposed system does not support any experimental data set, hence, it needs to be implemented for its actual result with strong mathematical foundation, comparing it with other algorithms on the basis of parameters like performance, efficiency, and complexity.

References

1. Abbas TA, Jawad MJ (2013) Proposed an intelligent watermarking in GIS environment. J Earth Sci Res (JESR) 1(1):1–5
2. Cox I, Miller M, Bloom J, Fridrich J, Kalker T (2007) Digital watermarking and steganography (2nd edn). USA: Morgan Kaufmann
3. Dakroury Y, El-ghafar IA, Tammam A (2010) Protecting GIS data using cryptography and digital watermarking. Int J Comput Sci Netw Secur (IJCSNS) 10(1):75–84
4. Wayner P (2008) Disappearing cryptography: information hiding: steganography & watermarking (3rd edn). USA: Morgan Kaufmann
5. White Paper (2014) GIS platform for national security. http://www.esri.com/library/whitepapers/pdfs/gis-platform-for-national-security.pdf
6. Wolthusen S (1998) On the limitations of digital watermarks: a cautionary note. Available at http://www.wolthusen.com/publications/SCI1998.pdf
7. Satyanarayana P, Yogendran S, Military applications of GIS. http://geospatialworld.net/Paper/Technology/ArticleView.aspx?aid=908

Digital Security: An Enigma

Avijit Dutta

Abstract The subject security has wide coverage and it is growing with every passing day. As civilization progressed from Agrarian to semi-industrialization, advanced industrialization and finally to present ICT (Information and Communication Technology) age, concerns for security are increasingly taking in all objects from physical to digital. It augmented apprehensions from losing material wealth to most abstract entities like wealth of knowledge in digital form. Today's technology allows wired and wireless access to tangible and intangible resource-built ups (material to digital), digitally, and steal the same if need arises. The riddle is to defend our own resources from the rapacious hand of ubiquitous computing and communicating technology evolved by us. The art and science of hiding and securing precious resources from possible predators in physical or digital forms make it complex and challenging. The enigma remains in the fact that predator uses same technology and at times also makes rule that prevails over others.

Keywords Collective intelligence · IoT (Internet of Things) · Ubiquitous computing · Web square

1 Introduction

Technology integration and its standardization have put civilization on fast track. From 'agrarian' to 'semi-industrialization', 'industrialization', 'advanced industrialization' and finally to 'digital age', the journey so far has been exciting. Innovations across different subject areas cooperate amongst themselves to make ways for new novelty. Weiser [1, 2] may have closely followed advances in computing hardware, system software and programming techniques during 90s to visualize the phenomena of ubiquitous computing, which now is a reality.

A. Dutta (✉)
NIC, New Delhi, India
e-mail: dutta_avijit@yahoo.com

M. U. Bokhari et al. (eds.), *Cyber Security*, Advances in Intelligent Systems and Computing 729, https://doi.org/10.1007/978-981-10-8536-9_25

Broadly, three factors have driven computing technology to ubiquity. First to name is 'Miniaturization', which is a trend to manufacture ever smaller mechanical, optical and electronic products and devices. Second to mention is 'Standardization', which is the process of developing and implementing technical standards that helps to maximize compatibility, interoperability, safety, repeatability or quality. Third to mention is 'Digital Communication', which evolved over packet switch networking technologies, mostly adhering to TCP/IP protocol standards. This allows data exchange between computing devices over wired or wireless network. At the advent of TCP/IP-related protocol like HTTP (Hypertext Transfer Protocol), World Wide Web (WWW) became a reality leading to web 1.0 paradigm, which allowed viewing vast amount of static information on web, advancing data disseminations practices, leading to dot-com era. Initial enthusiasm died down as viewers could not participate in the process, thus followed occurrence of dot-com burst. Web 2.0, which is interactive, revived web and took it to today's state of booming activities where everyone is keen to participate. In exponentially expanding web scenario, the exemplar that may follow web 2.0 is a subject of any one's guess now! To some, it is web 3.0, simply as next version standard, with more advanced technical facilities. For others, it is 'Web Square', the name and concept popularized by Tim O'Reilly and John Battelle. Progression of events allowed Tim O'Reilly, at a later date, to talk about IoT (Internet of Things) and collective intelligence [3]. He, during early years of twenty-first century, could visualize flooding of Internet usages with sensors and devices leading all to an era of nomadic and yet interactive WEB [1, 2, 4–6].

It was expected that the number of such devices would grow exponentially to guide technology to next-generation usages. These sensors and devices singularly termed as IoT are designed to add intelligence to everything from commonplace consumer items, home appliances, private or public utility systems, industrial items, healthcare system, education, agriculture and everything in between, even to railroad ties on big or small deals. 'IoTs' collects and broadcasts data across networks, enabling the data to be analysed on it or remote servers to add values and share. This approach changed the very way life and business processes were hitherto accomplished, leading to an archetype shift from physical to digital course of functioning [7–11].

Technology advances ushered era of first, second, third and fourth generations of computing. During this period, human–computer interactions shifted from 'One Machine many users' to 'One user One Machine' and finally to 'Many Machine Many User' setups. Digital computing stepped out from closed realm of scientists and academicians to arrive at the doorstep of common users. As discussed earlier technology integration, its standardization and digital communication steered us to the era of WWW and Internet. Broadly, evolutionary path of Internet can be viewed as follows—from years 1969 to 1995 it belonged to hardcore technocrats and scientists, from 1995 to 2000 it belonged to geeks, from year 2000 to 2007 it became Internet of masses, from 2007 to 2011 it turned as Internet of mobiles and from 2012 and days beyond it may evolve into the era of IoT. It may be opined that emergence of web 1.0 (static web) occurred during Internet of geeks and web 2.0

(interactive web) exemplar fructified during subsequent years of innovation and continues till date [12, 13].

In this process, our wealth perspective enlarged from physical to digital entities. Amongst all digital devices, smartphones captured imagination of most. Apart from calling facilities, it possesses seeing and listening capabilities embedded in it. With a smartphone, all life processes like socializing, shopping, banking, paying bills, acquiring medical advices, etc. are easily executable. It can also do video and static photography reasonably well. Being GPS enabled, it can collect and disseminate location information effectively. After sequential and object-oriented coding standard, mobile programming is the upcoming programming practice, which offers bigger provision for interactive programming in web 2.0 ages. The entire effort for a paradigm shift is to fulfil a very simple desire, to get and remain connected. But indiscriminate connectivity brings in the risks of security breaches. The brainteaser is to get and remain connected in a secured way. Present text dwells on this riddle and attempts to hold a collective view of entire scenario in the following section.

2 Collective Intelligence

The concept of data and the process of its collection, collation and dissemination have changed largely in the era of web 2.0 [7, 8]. Today, apart from texts, digits, audio and video, photographs too are taken to mean as data. Keyboard now is not the only means for data incorporation, interpretation and interaction with digital objects and Internet. Omnipresent smart devices can look, feel, sense, photograph objects and store them within a split second instruction at any desired location, really smartly [3, 6].

Technology miniaturization, standardization and large-scale product manufacture are bringing down the cost of computing and communicating. This has helped a wide range of computing and communicating devices in terms of size and performance like servers, desktop, laptop, palmtop, smartphones, wearable devices, etc. to be available in the market. These devices are also armed with seeing, listening, recording and storing capabilities, which cater to extensive range of data processing and disbursing needs, helping to bring most on board. These devices with an identity can be linked amongst themselves and numerous other small or large smart digital devices, termed singularly as IoT, as discussed earlier, over varied choices of connectivity options like broadband, Wi-Fi, R/F, Bluetooth, etc. [14, 15].

The depiction in Fig. 1 (IoT Scenario) attempts to present a window view of the situation arising out of the increasing presence of IoTs. This helped to enhance the mass base of smart devices usages. Digital devices are capable now to communicate intelligently amongst themselves and others in forms like M2M (Machine to Machine), M2I (Machine to Infrastructure) and M2E (Machine to Environment) in real time, process data at nodes or cloud deciding almost autonomously and present the most up-to-date information to us so that we can make the best decisions.

Benson Tao observes that present efforts towards building smart, connected, autonomous and contextually aware devices around the IoTs will prove to be catalyst for a change, leading to general betterment. As it turns out, IoT is a very broad concept, which includes all kind of wearable, carriable, attachable and implantable and everything in between devices that associates with us in our daily coir.

Interestingly, O'Reilly [3] envisaged today's Internet as a new born kid, who looks, touches and feels about the things around with the help of various sensors (being carried by us), like mobile phones and smart devices, to gather data in audio, video and text form and processes them to attain a higher state of awareness. It is increasingly getting intelligent with information gathered by sensors ubiquitously strewn around, in both static and mobile state and maturing incrementally like any living objects, though as a virtual entity. In return, it shares the collected data, information and knowledge whenever these are asked for, inform of an organized query, over digital network, establishing the concept of collective intelligence. Worldwide efforts are on to bring most on board, to enrich the process of collective intelligence and get maximum benefit out of it. Well, there is dark side of this process too, which is being discussed in following segments.

3 Emerging Challenges

In keeping with Mark Weiser's view of 'ubiquitous computing' concepts, one may find that Computing and Communicating (C&C) emerged as profound technology in this era, which has associated with our day-to-day life processes inseparably and continuing expansion process of its presence exponentially with smart devices termed as IoTs [1–3]. These phenomena are making fast inroads in our daily

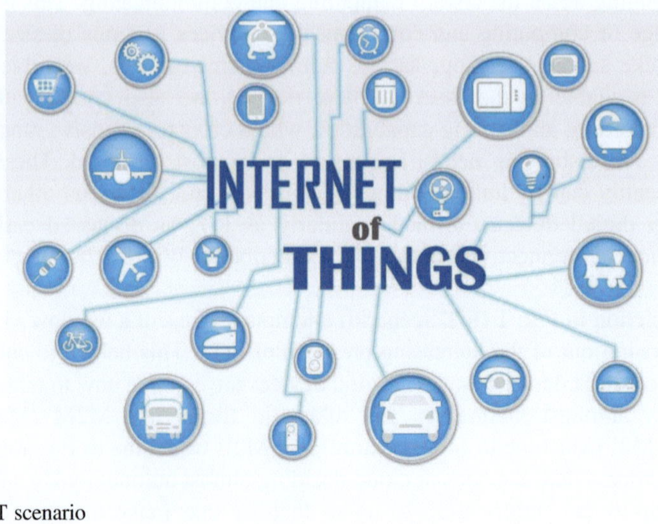

Fig. 1 IoT scenario

activities. Broadband routers offer Internet access to devices through Wi-Fi and Ethernet connections to make today's home network. Appliances like laptops, desktop computers and mobile devices, such as phones and tablets can get onto Internet through broadband router. With the IoTs finding their ways into the homes, innumerable new devices are produced that can connect to the same network. These devices are of two types; the first ones get connected through formal networking technologies as discussed earlier. Others may use different wireless technologies that suite device needs, conforming to lower energy consumption or ad hoc network coverage protocols. Nevertheless, everything is connected to the local network and can communicate freely with one another. Connections to the Internet are directed through a central router, which may (or may not) always contain basic firewall filtering functionality [9–11].

It may be known that connected version of different devices, participating in day-to-day activities, gets onto same network without essential security consideration. Despite increasing acceptance of IoTs, no standards have been planned so far for the use of these innumerable devices and sensors. They are almost on their own in the process of establishing connection, exchanging and processing information on instruction from numerous lawful or unlawful owners. Along with many goodies that computing ubiquity presents, the offered challenges lie in the fact that the 'IoT' today is an abstract collection of uses and products without common agreement or disagreement on mode of functioning. So, everyone does it their own way, often poorly, compromising security of connected devices as it greatly lacks an established concept of implementation and use. A study of security major like Symantec Corporation seems to have found that currently there is no single standard protocol in IoT and 'security' is not a word that gets strongly associated with this category of devices, leaving its consumers potentially exposed [9–11]. The 'enigma one' lies in the fact that these challenges are our own creation and we are forced to face them.

As information highway is being accessed by one and all, gradually concerns are gaining ground about the co-travellers with whom this highway is being shared! Symantec, after analysing 50 home devices, during year 2014, has observed that none of the devices used strong password, enforced mutual authentication practices or applied defence mechanism against brute-force attacks [10, 11]. It also has found mobile apps generally do not use Secure Sockets Layer (SSL) to encrypt communications to the cloud. The family of IoT devices possesses vulnerabilities, which are much in common. Potential weaknesses in authentication and traffic encryption could badly affect IoT systems. These facts though well known to the security industry, mitigation processes are not taken good care off.

It is generally felt that IoT vendors need to do more on security before marketing their product universally, leaving millions of people at risk of cyberattacks. This leads a feeling that 'IoT security is still a pipe dream' [9–11, 15]. The 'Enigma Second' lies in the fact that IoTs are being produced in large numbers with comprehensive knowledge about associated security hazards.

The digital security challenge mitigation begins with stopping innumerable entities approaching digital resources over data communication network, to verify their credentials and allowing passage, if found acceptable, denying it otherwise.

The process gets multifaceted as advancing objects grows in number and form, which taxes time and computing resources of approached entity. More often than not objects seeking access to resources are large, interactive and at times deceptive. Objects approaching resources constantly change form and advancing tactics to match the defence mechanism with the intent to crack the same. Real-time detection of specifics on attack vector is difficult and this leads to security breach. Authentication and authorization become important at such instances. Digital resources can be protected with cryptographic techniques and establishment of PKI (Public Key Cryptographic Infrastructure) system. Steganographic techniques allowing enveloped exchange of document also come handy for secured data exchange. Cryptography and steganography putting together can provide robust defence mechanism against predators during digital document exchange. Enigma Third' lies in the fact that for the defence of our ever evolving resources, eternally new mechanism needs to be explored. In the following section, collective effect of enigmas around 'Digital Security' is further discussed.

4 Enigma

Collectively, the digital security enigma lies in the fact that we are defensive against our own creation and in a way we are creating our own space for both security and insecurity. Adding to woes are the facts that lessons on computer hacking are included officially in course curriculum of many national and international universities. Today, the attacker and defender use same or equivalent technologies and at times they appear like either side of the same coin. Like for cryptography there is cryptanalysis, for steganography there is steganalysis and so on. Moving on one may even find that the perception of cybercrime is relative to geographical or political jurisdiction. The inherent view that hacking others network is fair, getting hacked is not, is scaring [8].

Financial sites of many institutions and well-offs are recurrently hacked by less fortunate for instant monetary gains using advanced C&C technologies. Scientific and Defence research sites of many advanced countries are being routinely intruded these days for a fast track course to new knowledge, while gainers appreciate the act, losers strongly denounce it. This has compelled many original equipment manufacturing countries to embed cyber sniffing tools, in both hardware and software systems, which are difficult to shake off, so as to pre-empt movement of cyber predators [9–11]. It ensures (!) security breach even with best defence mechanism up front as the attack can be initiated from either side of the system.

Fact remains that resourceful and militarily powerful countries cyber-snoops friends and foes including close allies, all alike. IoTs have made the process even simpler. These devices have made even our residential places vulnerable. Gartner research predicts that there will be more than 2.9 billion connected IoT devices in consumer smart home environments in 2015. These connected devices could provide a much larger surface for attackers to target home networks. IoTs are wearable,

Table 1 Scope for security lapses

1	Insufficient authentication/authorization	6	Insecure cloud interface
2	Insecure web interface	7	Insecure mobile interface
3	Insecure network services	8	Insufficient security configurability
4	Lack of transport encryption	9	Insecure software/firmware
5	Privacy concerns	10	Poor physical security

implantable, transferable and easily accessible, turning away complex defence technicalities. So these objects can be accessed and used by both predators and defenders with reasonable ease [10, 11].

It has been observed that most IoTs have very weak password management. This apart from some of these devices which are without keyboard, passwords are managed remotely. More often than not users continue to use default password making them vulnerable to cyberattack.

Proof of concept for most IoT attacks already exists, like remotely accessing onboard computer of an aircraft to alter scheduled flying course, a home network for permanent anchoring and to create unwarranted surprises, a pacemaker to affect health of person and the count goes on. Possibilities to derive financial objectives from such attacks are not very remote. Symantec list of Top Ten IoT Vulnerabilities is indicated by Open Web Application Security Project's (OWASP), which sums up most of the concerns and attack vectors surrounding this category of devices. These are given in Table 1 [8, 10, 11].

Enigma remains in the fact that at this backdrop demands for secured access to Internet, its usages are encouraged and number of people accessing digital network is growing with every passing day. To encourage it, further issues related to net neutrality is debated. Institutions controlling critical business operations are increasingly encouraging access to its functionalities over digital network shunning personal presence and activities in their premises. As Internet opens up rapidly to make more resources accessible, concerns grow for identifying the intention of the objects approaching resources. The paradigm shift makes life processes simple, though at times at the cost of individual and collective security, creating a dichotomy between security and accessibility that leads to a puzzle.

5 Analysis

The journey over Internet for knowledge and wisdom at this moment is open to all, which is expected to lead humanity to freedom from dogma, biases, short-sightedness, etc., the factors that slow down the process to become a superior entity. Plethora of web applications and mobile apps are being developed to ease the use of Internet; wherein, required technical knowledge of computing and communicating are minimal. Of late it is being observed that this freedom is being

Table 2 Cyber safety equation

Cyber safety	=	Cybersecurity/cyber insecurity
where		$0 \leq$ Security $\leq \infty$; $0 \leq$ Insecurity $\leq \infty$

used differently by a different stratum of humanity. The rulers, ruled, privileged, marginalized, scientists, technocrats, statesman, bureaucrats, etc., on right or wrong side of righteousness are using the priceless resource in line with their own agenda. As it is being deliberated that both 'security' and 'insecurity' scenarios are our own creation and since International Telecommunication Union (ITU) is producing measures of security one more measure 'Cyber Safety' may find place in present text in the following way (Table 2).

As strategic retreat, instead of attempting for an absolute secured environment in this milieu, effort could be made to make it safe, where security be more prevalent than insecurity. Increased security will enhance safety, and increased insecurity will reduce it. This is indicative of the fact that far from being deterministic, safety and security factors get probabilistic as technology advances in time, allowing **enigma** to seeps in. This in turn compels one to conceive a model on safety, leaving aside the path for absolute considerations. The analysis in this context follows next.

Deliberations so far underline the fact that advances in technology expected to associate increasingly more factors, both technical and non-technical, affecting digital safety and security, which may spice up existing enigma. Amongst these factors, data or digital communication expected to play a dominating role now and in near future as escalating indiscriminate digital connectivity presumed to dilute security considerations. Since computer network connects all and sundry across the globe, it will be quite interesting to assess broadly the association between 'Network Readiness' and 'Cybersecurity Preparedness Index'. Though both are abstract terms, in our journey to isolate factors affecting safety and security aspects the most, this text expected to open a small window view of challenges ahead.

ITU has produced security index as GCI (Global Cybersecurity Index) and cyber wellness measures for the year 2014. Global Information Technology Report (GITR) also has produced network readiness index for the same year. These are shown in 'Table 3' below in column **'A' and 'B'**. The analysis is done with limited scope presently, considering '**Network Readiness Index**' of top ten countries and their associated '**Cybersecurity Index**' as presented in **Table** 3. Values listed under column 'B' calculated to 10-point scale and listed under column **'B10'** to bring it at par with values listed under column **'A'** for comparison. The calculated value of **Correlation Coefficient** between these two parameters is presented next.

Correlation Coefficient: 0.9994697150416415. This indicates that there is high correlation between network readiness index and cybersecurity preparedness index. Thus, at this moment, to begin with, 'Network Readiness' may get maximum attention to be secured. It may be presumed that an enigmatic component has been identified.

Table 3 Network readiness and cyber security status of top 10 countries in the world

S. No.	Country Name	GITR Network Readiness Index (A)	ITU Cybersecurity Preparedness Index (B)	ITU Cybersecurity Preparedness Index on 10 Point Scale (B10)
1	Finland	6.04	0.618	6.18
2	Singapore	5.97	0.676	6.76
3	Sweden	5.93	0.647	6.47
4	Netherland	5.79	0.676	6.76
5	Norway	5.70	0.735	7.35
6	Switzerland	5.62	0.353	3.53
7	United States	5.61	0.824	8.24
8	Hong Kong SAR	5.60	0.618	6.18
9	United Kingdom	5.54	0.706	7.06
10	Korea Rep	5.54	0.706	7.06

Source [16, 17]

6 Conclusion

With a limited scope, deliberations so far have indicated that there is high correlation between 'Network Readiness Index' and 'Cybersecurity Preparedness Index'. Though absolute security is not achievable in today's scenario, mainly because of the fact that same technology and related standards are being used by both attackers and defenders, remaining oblivion to security issue may be catastrophic. Digital networks have been opening up precious resources to one and all at the backdrop of the debate on 'Net Neutrality'; thus, combinations of security options, with focus on digital network, may help in making a strong security module to enhance safety.

7 Future Scope

It has just been conceived that 'Digital Security' aspect increasingly getting probabilistic and security model needs to be evolved to control **'Enigma'** with an aim to establish enhanced safety. In this context, data from more countries needs to be included to make the study further accurate. Apart from factors like 'Network Readiness', associations of other factors like country-wise Knowledge Index (KI), knowledge economy index, ICT index, etc. with cybersecurity preparedness index, may be explored individually and collectively to evolve a reliable security/safety model that assures safe network usages.

Acknowledgements Contributions of theorists who can look into the future and guide science and technologies beyond horizon are deeply acknowledged.

References

1. Weiser M (1991) The computer for the 21st century. Scientific American, Sept 1991, pp 94–104
2. Weiser M, Brown JS (1996) The coming age of calm technology. Xerox PARC, 5 Oct 1996
3. O'Reilly T, Battelle J. Web squared: web 2.0 five years on; special report
4. Kleinrock L. Nomadic computing—an opportunity CCR 4/95
5. Burgin M, Eberbach E (2012) Evolutionary computation and the processes of life. ACM Publication
6. La Porta TF, Sabnani KK, Gitlin RD. Challenges for nomadic computing: mobility management and wireless communications. Bell Laboratories
7. Avijit D. Knowledge ubiquity in web 2.0 paradigm. Innovation in information system and technology. ITCDC '09 Macmillan Publications, pp 234–238
8. Avijit D. Digital security: a moving target. Int J Electr Electron Comput Sci Eng. Special issue —TeLMISR 2015. ISSN: 2348-2273
9. Barcena MB, Wueest C (2015) Insecurity in the Internet of Things. Symantec, security response, version 1.0, 12 March 2015
10. Symantec, ISTR, April 2015, vol 20
11. Symantec, Insecurity in Internet of Things, version 1.0, 12 March 2015
12. Cortada JW, Marc GAMLN How nations thrive in the information age. IBM Institute for Business Value, IBM Global Business Services
13. Kephart JO, Chess DM (2003) Autonomic computing. IBM Thomas J. Watson Research Center, IEEE Computer Society
14. https://bensontao.wordpress.com/2013/10/06/vivante-internet-of-things
15. http://securityaffairs.co/wordpress/34974/cyber-crime/iot-security-symantec.htm
16. INSEAD (2014) Global information technology report
17. ITU (2015) Global cyber security index & cyberwellness profile report
18. Lytinen K, Yoo Y. The next wave of nomadic computing: a research agenda for information systems research. Working papers on information systems, Sprouts. ISSN: 1535-6078
19. Cousins KC, Robey D. Human agency in a wireless world: patterns of technology use in nomadic computing environments. Information and Organization; Science Direct
20. Venkatasubramanian K, Gupta SKS (2006) Security solutions for pervasive healthcare. P1: Binaya Dash, 8 Dec 2006, vol 11:58, pp AU7921–AU7921˙C015
21. Kleinrock L. Nomadic computing. Computer Science Department, Los Angeles
22. Davis RM. Evolution of computers and computing. Science 195
23. Satyanarayanan M. Pervasive computing: vision and challenges. School of Computer Science, Carnegie Mellon University
24. TechTarget, Security Media Group. Information security, October 2014, vol 16, no 8
25. http://www.slideshare.net/MhaeLyn/iot-30545508

Author Biography

Avijit Dutta is an M.Sc. (Statistics), M.Phil. (Applied Mathematics/Statistics), and MBA (Finance and Marketing) graduate. He is associated with ICT for the last 34 years. During this period, he served both private and government institutions at various capacities in different projects. He retired from National Informatics Centre (NIC), New Delhi, Government of India (http://www.nic.in), as Scientist "F"/"Senior Technical Director" on December 31, 2018, after rendering 31 years and 2 months of coveted service. He continues to enjoy ICT thereafter on personal capacity.

ICMP Flood Attacks: A Vulnerability Analysis

Varun Chauhan and Pranav Saini

Abstract The increasing rate of cyberattacks based on the DDoS principle has created various new areas of concern for information security. It has also raised a pertinent question—Are we protected against such attacks? With significant rise in the number of attacks and resulting reports of high vulnerability to ICMP flood attacks, perhaps we need to reconsider and revisit the pros and cons of the ICMP protocol. In this paper, we mainly focus on giving readers a brief outline of DDoS attacks and its constituents, primarily the ICMP protocol. We also present a survey and the research findings that show the rising vulnerability to ICMP and subsequently DDoS.

Keywords Cybersecurity · ICMP attack · DoS attacks · DDoS attacks
Ping

1 Introduction

Denial-of-Service (DoS) attack and Distributed Denial-of-Service (DDoS) attacks appear to be similar, but they differ with respect to their scale of impact. In the case of a DoS attack, the impact is quite marginal as compared to mention of a DDoS attack, which in its essence is quite grand. Regardless of whether it is a DoS/DDoS attack, the attacker makes use of multiple computers. DoS attacks are mostly on the smaller end of this scale, while DDoS attacks lie on the higher end of it. Extensive DDoS attacks range from 100s to 1000s of systems. An attacker who is employing a DoS/DDoS attack technique has one simple goal in mind, i.e., to disrupt website

V. Chauhan (✉)
Knowledge Graph Department, Binary Semantics Pvt. Ltd., Gurgaon, India
e-mail: varunchauhan@google.com

P. Saini
Department of Information Technology, Bharati Vidyapeeth's College of Engineering, GGSIPU, New Delhi, India
e-mail: Pranav.saini94@gmail.com

M. U. Bokhari et al. (eds.), *Cyber Security*, Advances in Intelligent Systems and Computing 729, https://doi.org/10.1007/978-981-10-8536-9_26

performance. They disturb website performance by rendering it unable to respond to legitimate requests or disabling the website entirely, which makes it impossible for genuine users to gain access to the website. Such types of disruptions can be damaging to you and your business (Fig. 1).

A Denial-of-Service (DoS) attack comprises attackers sending messages to take advantage of certain vulnerabilities leading to the deviation or paralysis of business systems from normal operation, or sending a huge amount of standard messages quickly and repeatedly to a single node to choke system resources causing system failure [1]. As long as administrators keep on patching susceptibilities and focus on optimization of performance, the probable impact of a simple DoS attack is quite marginal.

Denial-of-service attack is considered to have taken place when several systems are flooded with data traffic, which clogs the targeted networks and makes them inaccessible to users. This kind of attack exploits the detectable vulnerabilities. Generally, they have very few hindrances to entry. The prowess of these attacks has also seriously affected giant technology firms such as Microsoft, Google, Apple, PayPal, Visa, and MasterCard, to name a few.

However, like numerous other cyberthreats, DDoS attacks have exhibited a more dangerous threat scenario. The number of such attacks has increased, motivations have become rewarding, and complex and targets are more vulnerable and abundant.

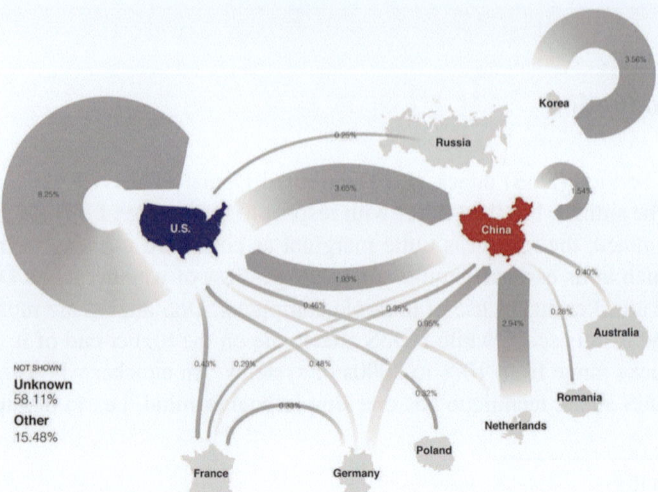

Fig. 1 A geography of who's hitting whom in denial-of-service cyberattacks. The large unknown reflects the difficulty of measuring the threat [7]

2 Related Work

Since the emergence of the Internet, Distributed Denial-of-Service (DDoS) attacks have shown a preferential trend among the cybercriminals. Naturally, this has led to a lot of research that seeks to understand and reduce the impact of such attacks. Douligeris and Mitrokotsa [2] presented a structural approach to the DDoS problem by "developing a classification of DDoS attacks and DDoS defense mechanisms. Furthermore, important features of each attack and defense system category were described and advantages and disadvantages of each proposed scheme was outlined." According to Eden [3], ICMP is a great hacking tool as it is versatile, mostly overlooked, and commonly misunderstood. The amount of information carried within the message could be used by attackers to exploit known vulnerabilities. Myers [4] strongly emphasized that while malicious consumption of resources is generally the chief purpose of a DDoS, different attackers might use different techniques that would generate traffic needed for realization of an effective DDoS attack. "A lone actor having a botnet at their disposal can use the botnet in order to choreograph such attacks."

3 Internet Control Message Protocol

The Internet Control Message Protocol (ICMP) is the means to give feedback about network troubles that is thwarting delivery of packets throughout the network. Upper protocols, like TCP, are able to understand that packets are not getting delivered, but ICMP provides a method for discerning more catastrophic problems, such as "TTL exceeded" and "need more fragments."

The ICMP protocol is used for sending various messages to convey network conditions. The majority of ICMP message types are necessary for proper operation of TCP, IP, and other such protocols. ICMP is not evil and should not be blocked.

3.1 CMP Flood Attacks

An ICMP flood is said to have happened when an attacker makes use of a botnet to send large amounts of ICMP packets to the target server in an attempt to exhaust any available bandwidth and prevent access to the legitimate users. This attack is considered "successful" when a huge number of sources are able to send sufficient ICMP traffic so as to consume and exhaust all available bandwidth of the victim's network.

One instance of this attack is the **"ping"** command. The "ping" command is primarily used to test network connectivity by checking whether your device is able to send and receive data to/from other device in the network, i.e., between two

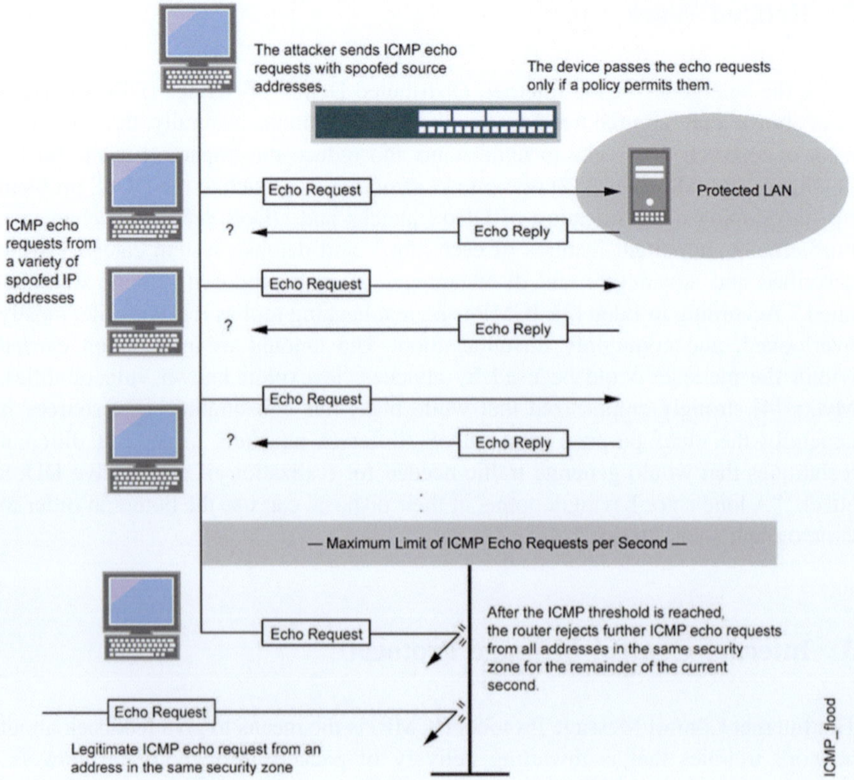

Fig. 2 ICMP flood attack

points in a network. However, this command can be given with different variables to make the ping larger in size and occur more often. Efficient application of such parameters and with adequate source systems initiating traffic will finally lead to the utilization of available system bandwidth (Fig. 2).

3.2 The Ping Utility—Packet Internet Groper

Everybody likes ping. It is simple. It is useful. And it also does precisely what the sonar-inspired name indicates.

Ping tells you if a remote computer is responding to network requests.

The ping utility was written by Mike Muuss, a senior scientist at the U.S. Army Research Laboratory [5]. It makes use of IP/ICMP ECHO_REQUEST and ECHO_REPLY timed packets in order to probe the "distance" to the target machine (Fig. 3).

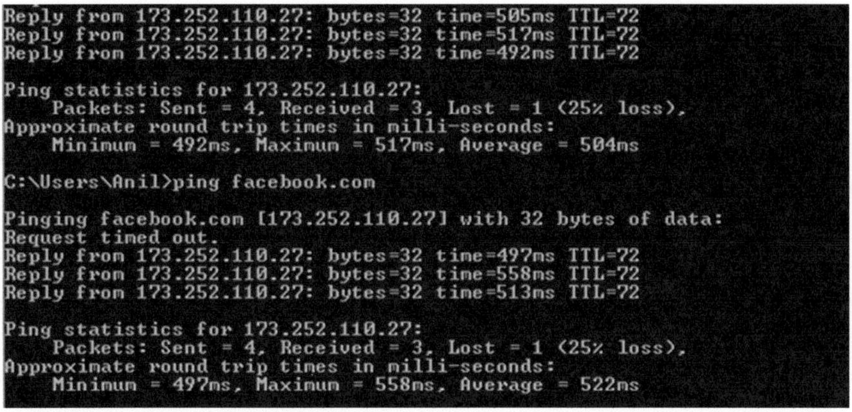

Fig. 3 Illustration of the ping command

4 Vulnerability Analysis

4.1 Survey on ICMP

A survey was conducted wherein data was collected about various websites vis-a-vis their vulnerability to ICMP.

Major categories of websites targeted:

- Social Networking Websites
- E-Commerce Websites
- Email Service Providers
- Search Engines
- Government Websites
- Private Enterprises

All the website and portals in these categories are privy to sensitive information and act as prime targets for attackers and hackers alike.

4.2 Survey Methodology

Step 1. A list of 100 top-most websites from each category was prepared and a database was maintained using MS-Excel.
Step 2. A range of parameters was decided, based on which results would be made and conclusions drawn. The parameters were as follows:

- Destination IP Address
- TTL, i.e., Time To Live

- RTT, i.e., Average Round Trip Time
- Were Packets Sent?
- Were Packets Received?
- Response IP Address

Step 3. Using the "ping" utility, ICMP scanning of these websites was done [6]. Each test had the following characteristics:

- Number of ICMP packets sent on a single "ping" = 4 (i.e., the default value in Windows OS)
- Size of each ICMP packet = 32 bytes (i.e., the default value in Windows OS)

Step 4. Results of each website were stored in the database.
Step 5. Finally, conclusions were drawn for each category (Fig. 4).

4.3 Research Findings

The results of the survey and the conclusions drawn are given below (by category):

1. **Social Networking Websites**: Approximately, 20% of websites have blocked ICMP requests and are therefore not vulnerable to such attacks. The remaining 80% of these though have allowed ICMP and are therefore vulnerable to such

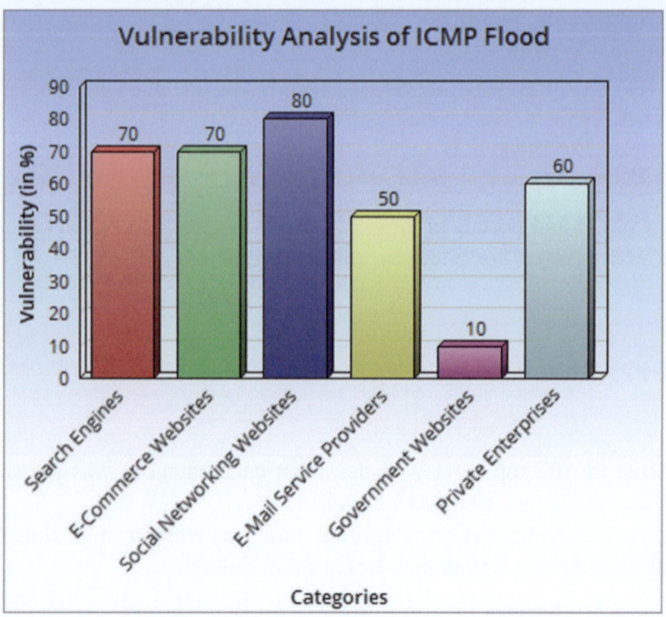

Fig. 4 Results of survey (values have been rounded up)

attacks. Some of these are namely, Facebook, Twitter, and LinkedIn which are privy to a huge amount of sensitive information.

2. **E-Commerce Websites**: Around 30% of such websites rejected ICMP echo and reply requests and are not vulnerable to such attacks. The remaining 70% though is highly vulnerable and can be brought down by such attacks in the future. These include sites like Flipkart, Snapdeal, and Jabong which are among the top e-commerce sites in India.
3. **Email Service Providers**: Here, we have a 50:50 ratio. 50% of such email providers are vulnerable to ICMP-based DDoS attacks. Hackers can gain sensitive knowledge that can lead to expensive losses. These include Gmail, Outlook, Hotmail, etc.
4. **Search Engines**: Only 30% of search engines have blocked ICMP requests, while the remaining 70% is highly vulnerable and sensitive to such attacks. These search engines can be manipulated to divert traffic which happened in the case of GitHub attack.
5. **Government Websites**: More than 90% of such websites that includes Indian and US Government websites are aware of such possibilities and have subsequently blocked an ICMP request on their servers and sites. The rest though are still highly vulnerable. These include the US Air Force and NASA.
6. **Private Enterprises**: 40% of private enterprises have blocked ICMP requests and hence are protected against this type of attack. The other 60% have allowed such requests and hence are vulnerable. These include Apple Inc., General Electric, Exxon Mobil, etc.

From the above results, we can conclude that around 47% of all website are vulnerable to such attacks. Therefore, these types of attacks need to be mitigated.

5 Conclusions

Through this paper, the most crucial terms with regard to DDoS and ICMP and the association between these terms have been explained. It has been shown—in particular regarding cybersecurity—that ICMP is a great hacking tool. Engineers, administrators, security officers, etc. need to be aware of the dangers. The data present within these messages can be misused by attackers to exploit known vulnerabilities in the system. We have seen all through this paper that ICMP can and has been used in many stages of an attacker's progress in a system compromise. We have also seen that ICMP is not just being used in the reconnaissance and probing phase which is most understood but it has also been used for exploiting systems as well as in certain occurrences as a covert passage for attacker's communication. Further, research should seek to test this vulnerability which has not been shown by this study. Practical implementation and testing can be done to further narrow down embedded vulnerabilities not detected in this research. Acceptance of these definitions and uniform use in the future would guarantee that research and development in the area of DDoS and primarily ICMP can progress more easily.

References

1. Website DDoS protection. Stop DDoS attacks against your website! https://sucuri.net/website-firewall/ddos-protection
2. Douligeris C, Mitrokotsa A (2003) DDoS attacks and defense mechanisms: classification and state-of-the-art, Greece
3. Eden L The truth about ICMP, global information assurance certification paper, SANS Institute
4. Myers L (2014) Guide to DDoS attacks, integrated intelligence center technical white paper, Center for Internet Security
5. Atwood J (2007) The story about PING. http://blog.codinghorror.com/the-story-about-ping/
6. ICMP attacks illustrated, SANS Institute InfoSec Reading Room
7. "The Internet's Aswarm in Denial of Service Attacks and It's Getting Worse." (2014) June 2014. http://www.forbes.com/sites/bruceupbin/2014/06/18/were-aswarmin-denial-of-service-attacks-and-its-getting-worse/

Statistical Approach Using Meta Features for Android Malware Detection System

Meenu Mary John and P. Vinod

Abstract In this paper, a static analysis malware detection system based on machine learning techniques and making use of features like hardware components, requested permissions, application components, and filtered intents are extracted from various applications. Prominent features are selected as a part of dimensionality reduction using GSS coefficient and mutual information. Experiment has been evaluated on 3000 malware samples from Drebin dataset and on 1631 benign samples collected from Google Play Store. High ROC curve of 0.998 has been obtained for model developed using individual attributes with overall scanning time of 1.49 s. However, when the optimal features extracted from each category of attributes were aggregated a remarkable improvement in *F*-measure, i.e., 0.996 was noticed with a low FPR value of 0.003 concluding the fact that the approach can be used to support commercial AV.

Keywords Android · Malware · Feature selection · GSS · Mutual information
Prominent features · Classifiers

1 Introduction

Smartphones installed with Android has gained its popularity over its counterparts like iOS, Blackberry, Symbian, and Windows. Due to increased popularity of Android devices, malware writers and hackers have found interest in identifying vulnerabilities and compromising these devices. This has given birth to malicious

M. M. John (✉) · P. Vinod
Department of Computer Science & Engineering,
SCMS School of Engineering & Technology, Ernakulum, Kerala, India
e-mail: meenumary12@gmail.com

P. Vinod
e-mail: pvinod21@gmail.com

M. U. Bokhari et al. (eds.), *Cyber Security*, Advances in Intelligent Systems and Computing 729, https://doi.org/10.1007/978-981-10-8536-9_27

apps in Google Play Store and in many third-party app stores. Traditional signature-based systems [1] have found to be incapable in the identification of zero-day malware. Exponential increase in growth of malware being repackaged with legitimate apps [2] has raised serious security concern. Many prior works in the domain of detection of malware are considered using single feature such as permissions, API, opcodes, etc. for identifying suspicious file. As such these methods did not scale in identifying unseen sample, there was a demand felt in the detection of files by composing different types of features in other words composing diverse optimal feature vectors. The main contribution of work includes the following: (a) Implementation of a malware scanner by incorporating static analysis using machine learning approach; (b) Classification of Android malware against benign with less classification overhead in minimum time; (c) High performance is achieved due to the application of GSS (Galavotti–Sebastiani–Simi) and mutual information feature selection methods; and (d) Composite (hereafter meta referred to as composite) feature space model results in high F-measure of 0.996 in 1.01 s. The remaining section is organized as follows: Sect. 2 introduces related work. Proposed framework is discussed in Sect. 3. Experimental results are covered in Sects. 4, and 5 concludes the paper with scope for future enhancement.

2 Related Work

In [3], feature sets from manifest file and dex code of different apps on Drebin dataset were analyzed. Authors in [4] rank permissions and determine a subset of critical permissions using sequential forward selection and PCA. In [5], probabilistic generative models ranging from Naïve Bayes to advanced hierarchical mixture models were utilized for scoring permissions. Proposed approach categorizes an app based on the usage of permissions, the function category of an app, and permissions requested by other apps in [6] to risky report if an app is malicious. A static analysis method is proposed in [7] for Android malware detection by extracting creator information from every app. MAST (Mobile Application Security Triage) architecture was proposed by authors in [8] to exhibit malicious behavior. In [9], Andromaly was proposed that monitors smartphone features and events contributing to 88 features to detect malware, whereas in [10] to detect maliciousness, Kirin looks for app permission and Stowaway in [11] detect overprivileged apps by analyzing API calls. Droidmat in [12] extracts API calls, intents, and permission to detect malware. API calls are extracted from decompiled source code for identifying malicious app in [13].

3 Methodology

To overcome the limitations of signature-based detection system, a static framework using multiple features extracted from.apk files is proposed and implemented. The proposed framework is evaluated using a benchmark dataset Drebin [14]. The architecture of the proposed framework is shown in Fig. 1.

3.1 Data Preprocessing

Malware samples are collected from Drebin dataset (5560 samples in 6 folders) in which three folders Drebin-0, Drebin-1, and Drebin-2 with a total of 3000 malware samples and 1631 benign samples downloaded from Google Play Store are used for experimentation. All input.apk files are disassembled using Androguard tool [15] to convert Android manifest file into human readable.xml format later used for feature extraction. The malware and benign samples are randomly divided into train set and test set in the ratio 60:40 resulting in three datasets for training and three for testing. The static features extracted from samples are depicted in Table 1.

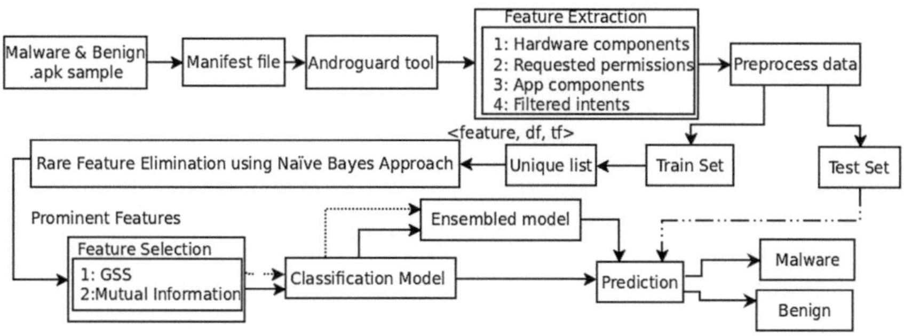

Fig. 1 Architecture diagram of proposed framework

Table 1 Static features extracted from android manifest file of various applications

Static features	Descriptions	Examples
Hardware components	Contains requested hardware components	CAMERA.FLASH, GPS, WI-FI
Requested permissions	Granted by user at the time of installation	SEND_SMS,READ_LOGS, WRITE_GMAIL
App components	Four components: activities, services, providers, and receivers	PACKAGE_INSTALL, DOWNLOAD_HIDE
Filtered intents	Contains action and category components	BOOTSERVICE, USER_PRESENT

Initially, from each feature set, rare attributes that are not relevant to be used for developing learned models are removed using Naïve Bayes approach. A unique list with feature, document frequency, and term frequency is used to eliminate irrelevant attributes using Eq. (1).

$$P(C_i|X) = P(X|C_i).P(C_i)|P(X), \tag{1}$$

where C_i denotes class [Benign (B) or Malware (M)] and X denotes a feature. Naïve Bayes score is calculated for each feature and is sorted in descending order. This would preserve the attribute that identifies a target class. Then, features with Naïve Bayes score greater than zero are extracted resulting in two feature lists: pruned malware and benign list of features. This initial pruning is repeated for all categories of feature from.apk samples and the pruned set is further given to feature selection techniques to obtain relevant features with minimum redundancy that is used for constructing learning models.

3.2 Feature Selection

In machine learning, a subset of relevant features is required to be used in the model construction. This is achieved by determining optimal feature vector. Feature selection is performed to achieve model simplification for easier interpretation, reduction in training time, and enhanced generalization by variance reduction. GSS coefficient (Galavotti–Sebastiani–Simi) and mutual information feature selection methods are applied to obtain significant attributes.

(a) **GSS (Galavotti–Sebastiani–Simi)**: GSS [16] is one of the simplified variants of chi-square statistics given by Eq. (2).

$$\text{GSS}(t_j, c_k) = P(t_j, c_k).P(\bar{t}_j, c_k) - P(\bar{t}_j, \bar{c}_k).P(t_j, \bar{c}_k), \tag{2}$$

where t_j represents feature and c_k represents class (B, M). $P(t_j, c_k)$ and $P(\bar{t}_j, c_k)$ represent joint probability of the presence and absence of a feature in a particular class [say c_k = M (Malware)]. $P(t_j, \bar{c}_k)$ and $P(\bar{t}_j, \bar{c}_k)$ represent joint probability of the presence and absence of a feature in alternate class [say $\bar{c}_k$ = B (Benign)]. The features are sorted in descending order of GSS score calculated using (2), and these significant attributes are involved in the preparation of malware and benign models.

(b) **Mutual Information (MI)**: Mutual information [17] measures arbitrary dependencies between a feature and a class. MI can be calculated as follows:

$$\mathrm{MI}(f, \mathrm{M}) = \frac{1}{P(\mathrm{M})} * \log \frac{P(f, \mathrm{M})}{P(f) * P(\mathrm{M})} \tag{3}$$

$$\mathrm{MI}(f, \mathrm{B}) = \frac{1}{P(\mathrm{B})} * \log \frac{P(f, \mathrm{B})}{P(f) * P(\mathrm{B})} \tag{4}$$

$$F_{\max} = \frac{\text{Larger MI}}{\text{Smaller MI}} \tag{5}$$

$F_{\max}$ is calculated using (5) and the result is sorted in descending order and subsequently used for preparing training models.

3.3 *Model Generation and Prediction*

Independent training models are constructed for features like action, activity, category, hardware components, requested permissions, content providers, broadcast receivers, and services. Each instance is represented in the form of a Boolean vector, where 1 denotes the presence and 0 denotes the absence of feature in the sample. The models are generated using three classification algorithms implemented in WEKA [18]. They are SVM [18] with linear, polynomial, radial, and sigmoid kernels; Random forest [18]; and rotation forest [18]. The accuracy, false positive rate (FPR), true positive rate (TPR), *F*-measure, and area under ROC (Receiver Operating Characteristic) curve (AUC) are measured at variable feature length during training phase. The model at optimal feature length is used to test the unknown samples. Subsequently, different category features of each optimal model are aggregated to form composite feature space, and this learning model is used to identify new samples that are not used in modeling.

4 Experiments and Results

Malware specimens are collected from Drebin dataset and benign samples from Google Play Store. Experiments were conducted on Ubuntu 14.04 platform with 8 GB RAM. The performance of the proposed framework is estimated using Eqs. 6–10.

$$F\text{-Measure}(F) = \frac{2(\text{Precision} * \text{Recall})}{(\text{Precision} + \text{Recall})} \tag{6}$$

$$\text{Precision}(P) = \frac{\text{TP}}{\text{TP} + \text{FP}} \tag{7}$$

$$\text{Recall}(R) = \frac{\text{TP}}{\text{TP} + \text{FN}} \tag{8}$$

$$\text{Accuracy}(A) = \frac{\text{TP} + \text{TN}}{\text{TP} + \text{FN} + \text{TN} + \text{FP}} \tag{9}$$

$$\text{AUC} = \text{area under the ROC curve} \tag{10}$$

Here, benign misclassified as malware is FP (False Positive). Benign correctly predicted as benign is TN (True Negative). Malware predicted as malware is TP (True Positive). Finally, malware misclassified as benign is FN (False Negative). An ideal malware detector should have high value of F-measure and AUC with minimum FPR.

4.1 Results

The effect of F-measure on independent models with linear SVM (L), random forest (Rdm), and rotation forest (Rtn) classifiers with GSS are shown in Figs. 2, 3, 4, 5, 6 and with mutual information in Figs. 7, 8, 9, 10, 11. D-0, D-1, and D-2 represent dataset-0, dataset-1, and dataset-2, respectively.

In Figs. 2. 3, 4, 5, 6, 7, 8, 9, 10, and 11, five independent training models out of eight models discussed in model generation and prediction using GSS and MI shows good results and is plotted. The results of linear SVM and random forest

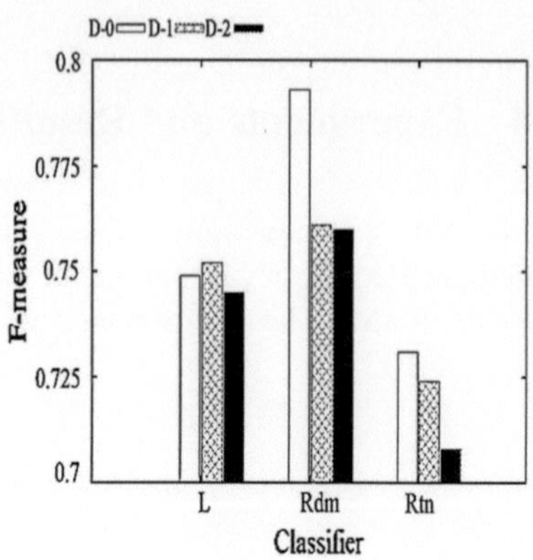

Fig. 2 Performance with action features using GSS

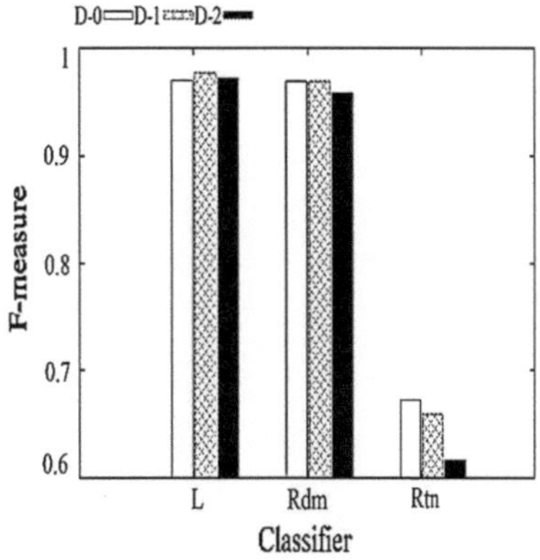

Fig. 3 Values of *F*-measure using activity with GSS

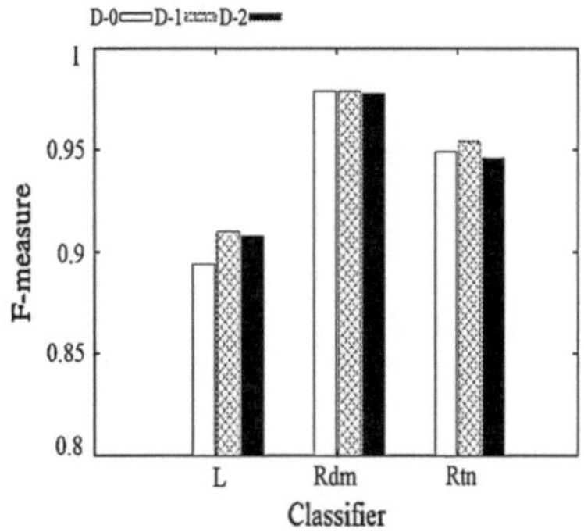

Fig. 4 Performance considering permission using GSS

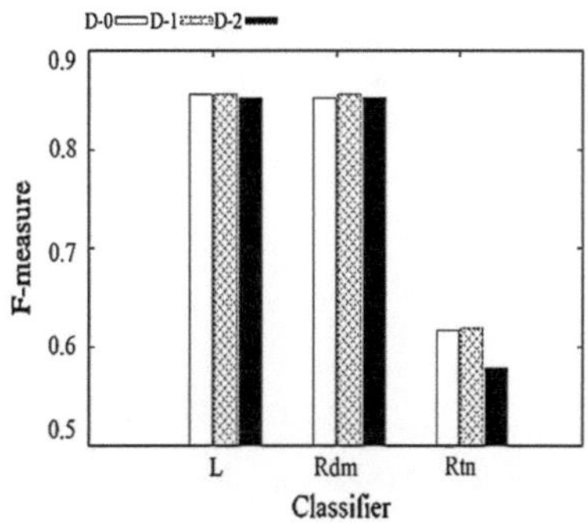

Fig. 5 Evaluation parameters with receiver attributes using GSS

classifiers are better than that of rotation forest. Malware model of GSS plotted above outperformed benign GSS model. In Fig. 2, GSS learning malware model of action using 236 features pruned out of 2727 features (236/2727), activity (1350/13,169) with linear SVM in Fig. 3 and permission (130/562) trained using random forest (refer Fig. 4) shows high *F*-measure of 0.793, 0.977, and 0.979. Receiver (390/2063) and service (340/1861) learning model depicted in Figs. 5 and 6

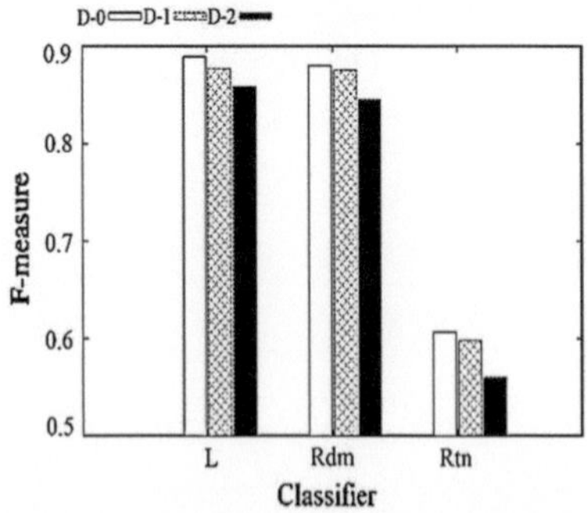

Fig. 6 Performance evaluated with service attributes using GSS

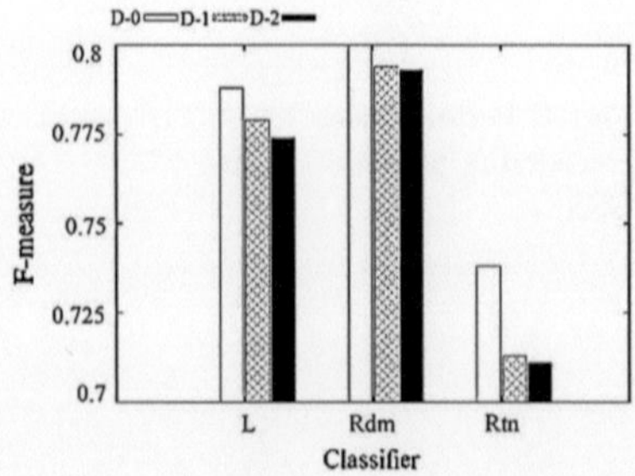

Fig. 7 Performance with action attributes using MI

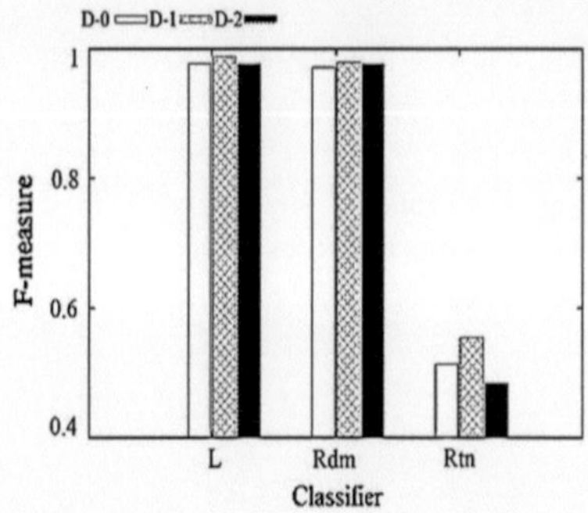

Fig. 8 Activity performance evaluation using MI

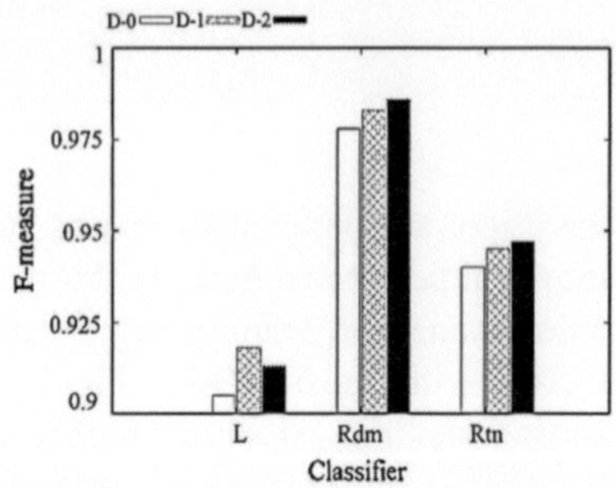

Fig. 9 Performance with permission attributes using MI

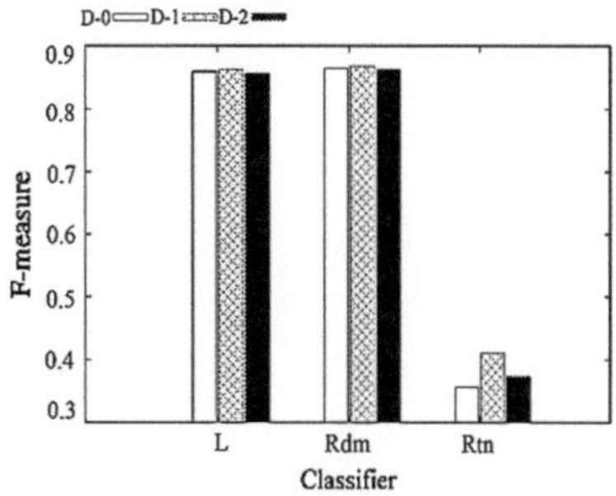

Fig. 10 Evaluate performance with receiver attributes using MI

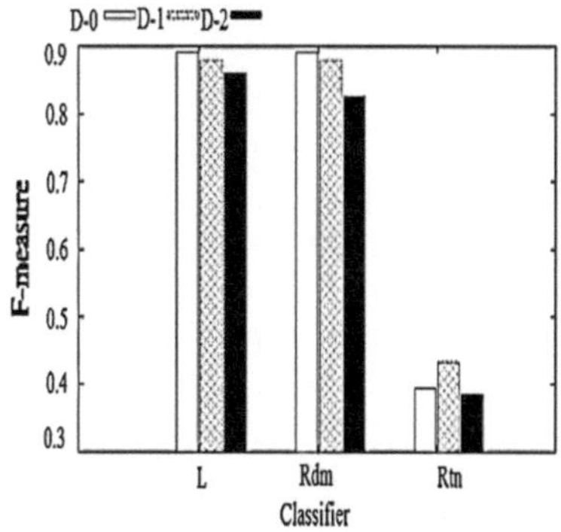

Fig. 11 Service attributes performance with MI

Table 2 Prediction of new samples for independent features in GSS using AUC

	Linear SVM			Random forest			Rotation forest		
Features	D0	D1	D2	D0	D1	D2	D0	D1	D2
Action	0.797	0.801	0.794	0.924	0.921	0.921	0.835	0.839	0.840
Activity	0.973	0.979	0.974	0.984	0.995	0.988	0.790	0.816	0.776
Permission	0.910	0.925	0.924	0.994	**0.996**	0.996	0.984	0.986	0.980
Receiver	0.875	0.875	0.872	0.891	0.890	0.888	0.729	0.739	0.735
Service	0.900	0.891	0.876	0.904	0.894	0.880	0.731	0.720	0.745

achieved F-measure of 0.856 and 0.889, respectively. MI learning model has obtained high F-measure of 0.988 and 0.986 with activity (12,550/13,169) and permission (559/565) model represented in Figs. 8 and 9. Graphs of action, receiver, and service training models plotted with F-measure against various classifiers are shown in Fig. 7 and in Figs. 10 and 11.

Table 3 Prediction of new samples for independent features in MI using AUC

	Linear SVM			Random forest			Rotation forest		
Features	D0	D1	D2	D0	D1	D2	D0	D1	D2
Action	0.825	0.819	0.816	0.939	0.936	0.941	0.833	0.829	0.813
Activity	0.980	0.989	0.979	0.997	**0.998**	0.998	0.723	0.517	0.751
Permission	0.920	0.931	0.929	0.994	0.996	0.997	0.980	0.983	0.976
Receiver	0.877	0.879	0.875	0.948	0.950	0.950	0.676	0.673	0.666
Service	0.902	0.892	0.877	0.955	0.951	0.872	0.658	0.657	0.644

Table 4 Composite feature space model

Dataset-0 (20,149 features)				Dataset-1 (19,664 features)				Dataset-2 (19,761 features)			
FPR	TPR	*F*1	C	FPR	TPR	F1	C	FPR	TPR	F1	C
0.23	0.995	**0.996**	L	0.34	0.995	0.995	L	0.003	0.998	**0.996**	L
0.23	0.994	0.993	R	0.11	0.997	**0.995**	R	0.001	0.992	0.995	R
2.50	0.940	0.950	T	1.25	0.936	0.957	T	0.020	0.926	0.946	T

In prediction phase, the results of AUC on effect of classifiers on different models using GSS and MI are shown in Tables 2 and 3. Out of all models, permission model using GSS shows AUC of 0.996, FPR 0.005, TPR 0.969, and accuracy 98.46% in 0.09 s with random forest. Activity model of MI obtained high AUC of 0.998 with random forest.

The composite feature space models in Table 4 show good result for 20,149 features with *F*-measure 0.996, FPR 0.23, and TPR 0.995 with linear SVM (L) classifier (represented as C) for dataset-0 in 1.15 s. For dataset-1, random forest (R) has high *F*-measure of 0.995 in 3.9 s. Linear SVM (L) shows high *F*-measure of 0.996, FPR 0.003, and TPR 0.998 with dataset-2 in 1.01 s. Following are the inferences from the study: (a) Composite feature space model shows better *F*-measure of 0.996 compared to individual models with linear classifier, (b) linear SVM works well with Boolean vector space model, (c) compared to linear SVM and random forest, rotation forest (T) has poor performance, and (d) less detection time shows effectiveness of model in real-time malware scanning. As the results obtained with linear SVM and random forest are comparable, an ensemble classifier can be created to improve the performance further.

5 Conclusion

Classification of Android malware against benign is conducted using static analysis. From higher dimensional space, relevant features are mined using GSS coefficient and mutual information. The overall *F*-measure of each classifier is compared and linear SVM is found to be the best classifier in case of composite feature space model. In future, experiments would be conducted on features extracted from .dex code (restricted and suspicious API calls, network addresses, used permissions, etc.) of applications, and ensemble classification approach would be looked on for obtaining better performance.

References

1. Grace MC, Zhou Y, Zhang Q, Zou S, Jiang X (2012) Riskranker: scalable and accurate zero-day android malware detection. In: MobiSys, pp 281–294. ACM
2. Zhou W, Zhou Y, Jiang X, Ning P (2012) Detecting repackaged smartphone applications in third-party android marketplaces. In: Proceedings of second ACM conference on data and application security and privacy, pp 317–326. ACM
3. Arp D, Spreitzenbarth M, Hubner M, Gascon H, Rieck K (2014) Drebin: effective and explainable detection of android malware in your pocket. In: NDSS. The Internet Society
4. Wang W, Wang X, Feng D, Liu J, Han Z, Zhang X (2014) Exploring permission-induced risk in android applications for malicious application detection. IEEE Trans Inf Forensics Secur 9 (11):1869–1882
5. Peng H, Gates CS, Sarma BP, Li N, Qi Y, Potharaju R, NitaRotaru C, Molloy I (2012) Using probabilistic generative models for ranking risks of android apps. In: ACM conference on computer and communications security, pp 241–252. ACM
6. Sarma BP, Li N, Gates CS, Potharaju R, Nita-Rotaru C, Molloy I (2012) Android permissions: a perspective combining risks and benefits. In: SACMAT, pp 13–22. ACM
7. Kang H, Jang J, Mohaisen A, Kim HK (2015) Detecting and classifying android malware using static analysis along with creator information. Int J Distrib Sens Netw, 479174:9
8. Chakradeo S, Reaves B, Traynor P, Enck W (2013) MAST: triage for market-scale mobile malware analysis. In: Proceedings of security and privacy in wireless and mobile networks, ACM
9. Shabtai A, Kanonov U, Elovici Y, Glezer C, Weiss Y (2012) Andromaly: a behavioral malware detection framework for android devices. J Intell Inf Syst 38(1):161–190
10. Enck W, Ongtang M, McDaniel PD (2009) On lightweight mobile phone application certification. In: ACM conference on computer and communications security, pp 235–245. ACM
11. Felt AP, Chin E, Hanna S, Song D, Wagner D (2011) Android permissions demystified. In: ACM conference on computer and communications security, pp 627–638. ACM
12. Wu D, Mao C, Wei T, Lee H, Wu K (2012) Droidmat: android malware detection through manifest and API calls tracing. In: AsiaJCIS, pp 62–69. IEEE
13. Cen L, Gates C, Si L, Li N (2013) A probabilistic discriminant model for android malware detection with decompiled code. In: Dependable and secure computing, IEEE
14. Drebin Dataset. http://user.cs.uni-goettingen.de/~darp/drebin/
15. Androguard. http://code.google.com/p/androguard/
16. Largeron C, Moulin C, Gry M (2011) Entropy based feature selection for text categorization. In: SAC, pp 924–928. ACM
17. Sebastiani F (2002) Machine learning in automated text categorization. ACM Comput Surv 34:147
18. Weka. http://www.cs.waikato.ac.nz/ml/weka

Composite Email Features for Spam Identification

Princy George and P. Vinod

Abstract An approach is proposed in this work to search for composite email features by applying a language-specific technique known as NLP (Natural Language Processing) in email spam domain. Different style markers are employed on Enron-spam dataset to capture the nature of emails written by spam and ham email authors. Mainly, features from five categories, consisting of character-based features, word-based features, tag-based, structural features, and Bag-of-Words, are extracted. Dimensionality reduction is applied subsequently using TF–IDF–CF (Term Frequency–Inverse Document Frequency–Class Frequency) feature selection method in order to choose the prominent features from the huge feature space. The experiments are carried out on individual feature as well as composite feature models. A promising performance is produced by composite model with an *F*-measure of 0.9935 and minimum *FPR* of 0.0004.

Keywords Email · Ham · Spam · Style markers · Dimensionality reduction Composite model

1 Introduction

Email is one of the most popular means of communication in the era of Internet. Spam, referred to as unsolicited commercial email (UCE) or unsolicited bulk email (UBE) [1], consumes most of the bandwidth. Moreover, it can also quickly consume server storage space. It is observed that the nature and the characteristics of spams change over time [2] and this demanded efficient approach for filtering unwanted emails. There are many techniques designed and developed to categorize

P. George (✉) · P. Vinod
Department of Computer Science & Engineering,
SCMS School of Engineering & Technology, Ernakulam, Kerala, India
e-mail: princyscms@gmail.com

P. Vinod
e-mail: pvinod21@gmail.com

M. U. Bokhari et al. (eds.), *Cyber Security*, Advances in Intelligent Systems and Computing 729, https://doi.org/10.1007/978-981-10-8536-9_28

emails. All these methods look for some known patterns or features (words) alone that usually appear in spam or ham messages, to classify the emails. These methods do not consider the syntactic and the semantic peculiarities of the messages. This was the primary motivating factor to discover varied features existing in the spam emails. Also, the studies done on author gender identification [3] by applying NLP [4, 5] became another inspiration behind this proposed work to investigate the contribution of tag-based features and other linguistic attributes in developing an email spam classification model with minimum *FPR*. Contributions of our approach are (a) prepared an efficient model for classification of spam and ham mails, (b) higher performance is obtained by applying feature selection method, (c) evaluated efficiency of each category of attribute set in spam categorization, and (d) an overall performance, i.e., *F*-measure of 0.9935 with a smaller *FPR* of 0.0004 justifying the applicability of our proposed approach in real-time spam filtering system.

The reminder of the paper is organized as follows. In Sect. 2, a review of the related works is done. The proposed mechanism is described in Sect. 3. Section 4 discusses details of experiments and the results of the study. Finally, inferences are included in Sects. 5 and 6 presents the concluding remarks of the study.

2 Related Works

In [3], an author gender identification technique was proposed and it could achieve accuracy of 85.1%. A new one-class ensemble scheme is put forward, which uses meta-learning to combine one-class classifiers in [6]. Blanzieri and Bryl [7] have discussed various machine learning applications for email spam filtering. Menahem et al. [8] implemented a new sender reputation mechanism based on an aggregated historical dataset. In [9], the authors designed a fusion algorithm based on online learners and experimented on TREC (Text REtrieval Conference) and other datasets. Comprehensive review on machine learning approaches to spam filtering is discussed in [10]. Drucker et al. [11] investigated the applicability of Support Vector Machines (SVMs) in classifying email as spam or legitimate mail. Three-layer Backpropagation Neural Network (BPNN) technique is implemented on datasets PU1 and Ling, resulting in 97 and 99% of classification accuracy with less execution time [12]. A three-way decision approach (accept or reject or further exam) is discussed and experiments on SpamBase dataset resulted in reduced misclassification rate in [13]. Wu [14] utilized spamming behaviors with a backpropagation neural network, employed on datasets from Hopkins, Reeber, etc. to achieve improved performance (*FPR* = 0.0063).

3 Proposed Methodology

Email spam detection process is carried out through different steps (refer Fig. 1) and evaluated over Enron-spam dataset [15, 16]. The following subsections introduce the proposed approach.

3.1 Preprocess Dataset

Email body is extracted from each email in the dataset. The resulted collection of extracted email body is partitioned into train and test (60:40 ratio). Style markers are treated as features in our approach. There are 31 characters, 38 words, 35 tags, 3 structural features, and 10,280 Bag-of-words extracted from mail body.

- ***Character-based features*** [3] include total number of characters (*C*), ratio of total number of lower case letters (a–z) and *C*, ratio of total number of uppercase characters and *C*, fraction of total number of digital characters and *C*, fraction of total number of white-space characters and *C*, ratio of total number of tab space characters and *C*, and fraction of number of special characters and *C* (25 special symbol features).
- ***Word-based features*** [3] consist of total number of words (*N*), average length per word, ratio of total different words and *N*, fraction of words longer than 6 characters and *N*, ratio of total number of short words (1–3 characters) and *N*, Guirad's *R*, Herdan's *C*, Rubet's *K*, Maa's *A*, Dugasts *U*, L. Janenkov and Neistoj Measure, Sichel's *S*, Yule's *K* measure, Simpson's *D* measure, Hapax Dislegomena, Hapax legomena, Honore's *R* measure, Entropy, and ratio of word length frequency distribution and *N*.

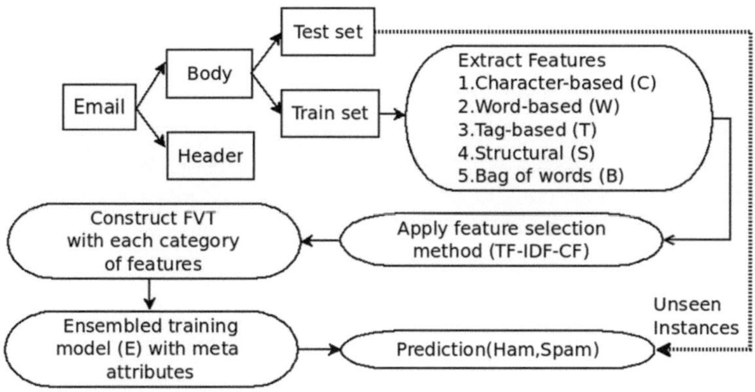

Fig. 1 Framework for email spam filtering

- ***Function words*** [3] (or grammatical words or tag-based features) are words that express grammatical relationships with other words within a sentence. Tags are extracted from email text using NLTK (Natural Language Tool Kit) [17] in python, and Part-of-Speech (POS) [18] tagging is done using Penn Treebank [5] tag set.
- ***Structural features*** [3] represent the way an author organizes the layout of a message. The main features are total number of lines, total number of sentences (S), and average number of words per sentence.
- In ***Bag-of-Words***, all sentences in each email body are tokenized into a set of words and frequency of every term is counted within each file (called as term frequency).

3.2 Application of Feature Selection Method

Feature selection determines optimal attributes from a huge attribute space without changing physical meaning of the attribute. The main benefits of dimensionality reduction (or feature selection) are (a) elimination of redundant features, (b) reduction in noise thereby increases accuracy of classifiers, (c) reduction of time complexity of classification, and (d) minimization of over-fitting of the training data.

A weighting method called TF–IDF–CF [19] is applied in our proposed approach. This method is developed based on TF–IDF (Term Frequency–Inverse Document Frequency). It says that if a term appears in more documents, then it becomes less important, and the weighting will also be less. A new attribute, called as class frequency, is introduced to assess the frequency of each term in every document within a specific class. A general form of TF–IDF–CF is shown in Eq. (1).

$$a_{ij} = \log(tf_{ij} + 1.0) * \log((N + 1.0)/n_j) * (n_{cij}/N_{ci}) \quad (1)$$

In Eq. (1), tf_{ij} indicates the term frequency of term j in document i, N is the total number of instances in the dataset, and n_j indicates the number of documents that term j occurs. The term n_{cij} represents the number of files within the same class c where document i belongs to and term j appears, N_{ci} gives the total count of documents within the same class c where document i belongs to. The algorithm for extracting significant words is given below.

Input: $W \leftarrow \{w_1, w_2, \ldots w_L\}$ where w_j is a word in feature space W such that $1 \leq j \leq L$
$C \leftarrow \{S, H\}$ where S is Spam and H is Ham class
$F \leftarrow \{f_1, f_2, \ldots f_N\}$, set of training files, where $N \leftarrow |S| + |H|$
Output: $SW[1{:}L]$, list of L features sorted in descending order based on TF-IDF-CF score

for each ***word*** $w_j \in W$ **do**
  $t_{1s} \leftarrow df_{w_j,S}/|S|)$ //last term of Eqn (1) for spam
  $t_{1h} \leftarrow df_{w_j,H}/|H|$ //last term of Eqn (1) for ham
  $t_2 \leftarrow \log((N+1)/(df_{w_j,S} + df_{w_j,H}))$ //middle term of Eqn (1)
  for each ***document*** $f_i \in F$ **do**
    $t_3 \leftarrow \log\left(tf_{f_i,w_j} + 1\right)$ //first term of Eqn (1)
    $tic_s[j] \leftarrow tic_s[j] + (t_3 * t_2 * t_{1s})$ //TF-IDF-CF score in spam class
    $tic_h[j] \leftarrow tic_h[j] + (t_3 * t_2 * t_{1h})$ //TF-IDF-CF score in ham class
  end for
end for
for each ***word*** $w_j \in W$ **do**
  $R[j] \leftarrow tic_s[j]/tic_h[j]$ //TF-IDF-CF score of word w_j
end for
$SW[1{:}L] \leftarrow sort(W, R)$ //$sort()$ function is invoked

3.3 Generation of Classification Models and Prediction

Feature selection produces a reduced feature vector table (FVT) which is taken as the input for training the classifiers. Multinomial Naïve Bayes (MNB) and support vector machine are used as classifiers in this investigation. Individual training models are created for each category of feature during training phase. The model with highest *F*-measure is chosen for prediction. Finally, the optimal models obtained from each category of features are aggregated to develop a composite feature space used for building spam and ham model, subsequently used for prediction.

4 Experimental Setup and Results

The experiment was performed on Ubuntu 14.04 platform with the support of Intel core 7 and 8 GB RAM. In this work, 12,045 ham and 4496 spam emails have been chosen from Enron-spam dataset. The classification models are generated by LibSVM (kernels *k0* (Linear), *k1* (Polynomial), *k2* (Radial), and *k3* (Sigmoid)), and Multinomial Naïve Bayes (MNB) in WEKA [20]. When a ham is misclassified as spam, a false positive (FP) occurs. If ham data is predicted as ham then it is known as true negative (TN), whereas if spam is correctly classified as spam data then it is true positive (TP). When a spam is wrongly taken as ham, it is considered as false negative (FN) [21, 22]. In this analysis, *F*-measure (also called as F_1-*score*) and

FPR are used as the significant evaluation parameters. The F_1*-score* can be interpreted as a weighted average of the precision and recall, and it ranges from 0 to 1. Precision (*P*) is a measure of the accuracy provided that a specific class has been predicted. Recall (*R*) measures the proportion of actual positives which are correctly identified as such.

$$F\text{-measure} = 2PR/(P+R) \quad (2)$$

$$P = \mathrm{TP}/(\mathrm{TP}+\mathrm{FP}) \quad (3)$$

$$R = \mathrm{TP}/(\mathrm{TP}+\mathrm{FN}) \quad (4)$$

$$\mathrm{FPR} = \mathrm{FP}/(\mathrm{FP}+\mathrm{TN}) \quad (5)$$

Figures 2, 3, and 4 depict *F*-measure, *FPR, and Time* parameters, respectively, obtained for six feature sets, represented as *C, W, T, S, B, and E* (refer Fig. 1) with five different classifiers (LibSVM-*k0, k1, k2, k3*, and mnb). The highest *F*-measure of value 0.9983 is produced in Bag-of-Words (*B*) (refer Fig. 2) with a smaller *FPR* of 0.0013 by linear SVM for a feature length of size 10,153 (refer Fig. 3), whereas the composite model could also achieve a very closer *F*-measure value 0.9935 (refer Fig. 2) with lowest *FPR* rate of 0.0004 (see Fig. 3) in comparison with all other models with linear SVM classification. From Fig. 4, it is clear that MNB takes less execution time but produces insignificant performance for various style markers.

The top ten features from character-based, word-based, tag-based, bag-of-words, and all three variables from structural attribute set are given in Table 1. These attributes are found to have higher variance in target classes thereby stands as representative features of writing styles adopted by email spammers [23, 24].

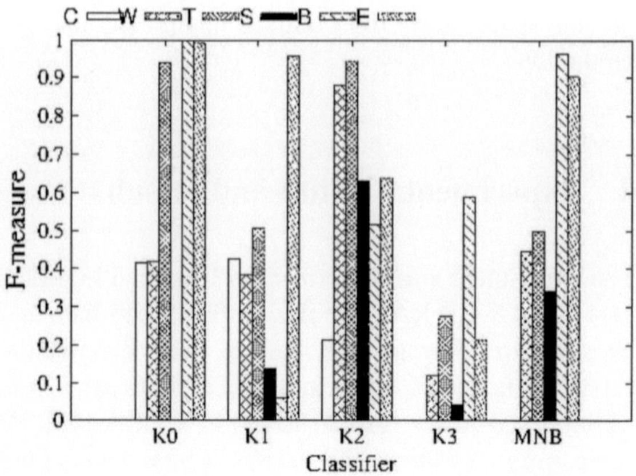

Fig. 2 *F*-measure versus classifiers

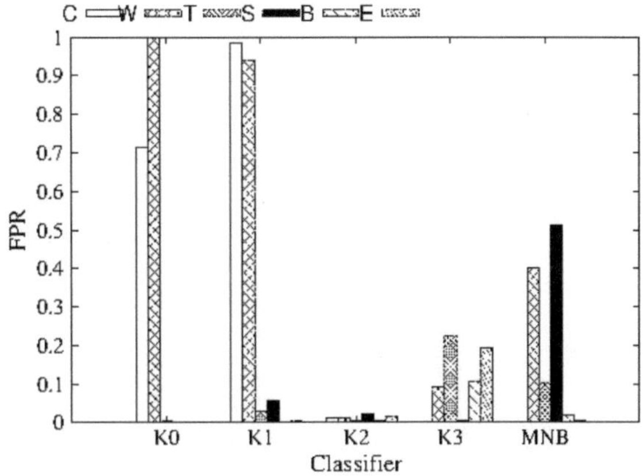

Fig. 3 *FPR* versus classifiers

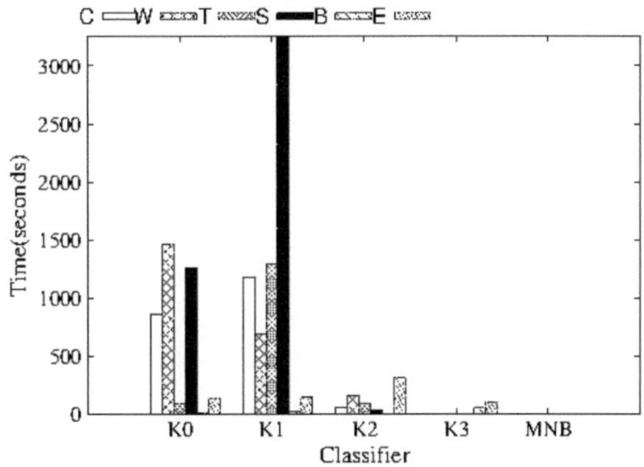

Fig. 4 Time versus classifiers

5 Inferences

It has been analyzed that SVM classifier performs well with large number of features, but it is computationally expensive. Performance is observed higher when stop words are removed from the text before model construction. Independent style markers with small number of features produced insignificant results in terms of *F*-measure, which is clearly visible for character-based, word-based, and structural features. Hence, these attributes are not sufficient enough to prepare an efficient spam filtering model independently. This is due to the absence of attributes having high correlation with target class. As the features in the feature space increase, the performance also improves, since relevant attributes contributing to the effective classification appear as a candidate in the optimal feature space. This is why bag-of-words produced a highest *F*-measure with larger feature space of size 10,153. Tag-based attributes and bag-of-words played an important role in the generation of composite model as they could produce lower *FPR* value and an

Table 1 Top features from each attribute category

Character	Word	Tag	Structural	BoW
|	Words with length 20	Foreign word	Total number of lines	Php
%	Words with length 18	-None-	Total number of sentences	Sex
_	Words with length 17	Adjective, superlative	Average number of words per sentences	Meds
}	Words with length 19	Noun, proper singular		Medications
=	Words with length 16	Adjective, comparative		Pill
+	Words with length 15	Adverb, comparative		Macromedia
$	Words with length 13	Adverb, superlative		Dose
{	Words with length 14	Pronoun, possessive		Mai
`	Words with length 12	Predeterminer		Tongue
*	Honore's R	Adverb		Wi

appreciating *F*-measure in its independent model generation. Therefore, ensemble of different sets of style markers resulted in better performance. Finally, it has been analyzed from the investigation that composite feature space could greatly reduce misclassification of ham messages as spam. This is proved by lowest *FPR* value (0.0004) produced by composite model along with a high *F*-measure (0.9935) compared to all independent models generated in our study. This makes our proposed meta-feature model a good detector system in the real-time applications.

6 Conclusion

In the investigation for email spam classification, TF–IDF–CF is the dimensionality reduction method, applied on various style markers such as character-based, word-based, tag-based, structural, and bag-of-words to choose relevant features from the large feature space. A vector space model for the relevant features was constructed and given to classifier through WEKA tool. The composite feature space generated an effective model for email spam classification, producing a very high *F*-measure (0.9935) and a very small *FPR* (0.0004) in linear support vector machine than independent models. The study can be extended in future to find out whether involvement of male or female community is more in email spam generation.

References

1. Zhu Y, Tan Y (2011) A local-concentration-based feature extraction approach for spam filtering. IEEE Trans Inf Forensics Secur 6(2):486–497
2. Wang D, Irani D, Pu C (2013) A study on evolution of email spam over fifteen years. In: Bertino E, Georgakopoulos D, Srivatsa M, Nepal S, Vinciarelli A (eds) CollaborateCom, pp 1–10. ICST/IEEE
3. Cheng N, Chandramouli R, Subbalakshmi KP (2011) Author gender identification from text. Digital Invest 8.1:78–88
4. Manning CD (1999) Foundations of statistical natural language processing. In: Schutze H (ed). MIT Press, Cambridge
5. Bird S, Klein E, Loper E (2009) Natural language processing with Python. O'Reilly Media, Inc.
6. Menahem E, Rokach L, Elovici Y (2013) Combining one-class classifiers via meta learning. In: Proceedings of the 22nd ACM international conference on information and knowledge management, ACM
7. Blanzieri E, Bryl A (2008) A survey of learning-based techniques of email spam filtering. Artif Intell Rev 29.1:63–92
8. Menahem E, Pusiz R, Elovici Y (2012) Detecting spammers via aggregated historical data set. Network and system security. Springer, Berlin, pp 248–262
9. Xu C, Su B, Cheng Y, Pan W, Chen L (2014) An adaptive fusion algorithm for spam detection. IEEE Intell Syst 29(4):2–8
10. Guzella TS, Caminhas WM (2009) A review of machine learning approaches to spam filtering. Expert Syst Appl 36(7):10206–10222
11. Drucker H, Wu S, Vapnik VN (1999) Support vector machines for spam categorization. IEEE Trans Neural Netw 10.5:1048–1054
12. Ruan G, Tan Y (2010) A three-layer back-propagation neural network for spam detection using artificial immune concentration. Soft Comput 14(2):139–150
13. Zhou B, Yao Y, Luo J (2010) A three-way decision approach to email spam filtering. In: Farzindar A, Keselj V (eds) Canadian conference on AI. LNCS, vol 6085. Springer, pp 28–39
14. Wu C-H (2009) Behavior-based spam detection using a hybrid method of rule-based techniques and neural networks. Expert Syst Appl 36(3):4321–4330
15. Bekkerman R (2004) Automatic categorization of email into folders: benchmark experiments on Enron and SRI corpora
16. The Enron-Spam Datasets. http://www.aueb.gr/users/ion/data/enron-spam/
17. Natural Language Tool Kit (NLTK). http://www.nltk.org/
18. POS tagging. http://textminingonline.com/dive-into-nltk-part-iii-part-of-speech-tagging-and-pos-tagger
19. Liu M, Yang J (2012) An improvement of TFIDF weighting in text categorization. In: International proceedings of computer science and information technology, pp 44–47 (2012)
20. WEKA-Data Mining Software in Java. http://www.cs.waikato.ac.nz/ml/weka
21. Han J, Kamber M (2005) Data mining: concepts and techniques. Kaufmann, San Francisco [u. a.]
22. Kibriya AM, Frank E, Pfahringer B, Holmes G (2004) Multinomial Naïve Bayes for text categorization revisited. In: Webb GI, Yu X (eds) Australian conference on artificial intelligence. LNCS, vol 3339. Springer, Berlin, pp 488–499
23. Metsis V, Androutsopoulos I, Paliouras G (2006) Spam filtering with Naïve Bayes-which Naïve Bayes? In: CEAS, pp 27–28
24. Bird S (2006) NLTK: the natural language toolkit. In: Proceedings of the COLING/ACL on interactive presentation sessions, association for computational linguistics

Role of Multiple Encryptions in Biometric Devices

Himanshu Gupta and C. Aka Assoua Anne-Marie

Abstract This paper debates about the role of multiple encryptions in biometric devices with a particular focus on the privacy and security benefits of biometric devices. This research paper is proposed to engage a larger number of data users to consider the beneficial role of multiphase encryption in biometric devices with enhanced security solutions. This paper discusses about how multiphase encryption can be promoted with biometric devices in order to overcome the present loopholes of the security devices. In current scenario, wireless security demands to provide an approach for securely verifying the user's identity, authenticating the data access and certifying the security applications. The security of data has nowadays become challenging issues that comprises areas like data encryption, protected communication channel, and reliable third party to preserve the databases. The immediate growth in the area of information technology, the super-secure communication of confidential data is highly required. Biometrics technology has been extensively used in user's verification and identification, but there are several security issues to provide adequate security. Therefore, using multiple encryption techniques in biometric devices, we can enhance the data security enormously.

Keywords Biometric encryption · Multiple encryptions · Security

1 Introduction

1.1 Biometrics

Biometrics can be defined as an approach which is based on automated methods for uniquely recognizition based on one or more basic physical or behavioral human

H. Gupta (✉) · C. A. A. Anne-Marie
AIIT, Amity University, Noida Sec-125, Uttar Pradesh, India
e-mail: himanshu_gupta4@yahoo.co.in

C. A. A. Anne-Marie
e-mail: Claumich2@yahoo.fr

M. U. Bokhari et al. (eds.), *Cyber Security*, Advances in Intelligent Systems and Computing 729, https://doi.org/10.1007/978-981-10-8536-9_29

traits for verification purposes. As the matter of fact, everyone in the world is unique and hence this uniqueness can be used for identity verification. In simple language, it can be stated that biometric technology is typically considered to examine human characteristics for identification and security purposes. The most common parameters which are measured under this technology are fingerprints, hand, eye, face, and voice. The fingerprints' identification systems have been installed as access control systems since 1960s. The biometric product based on the geometry of the hand was introduced during the 1970s in many access control applications. Eventually, the systems using biometric technology were enhanced and moved from the geometry of the hand to the characteristics of the eye. In the middle of 1980s, the system was executed to analyze the unique patterns of retina while parallel improvements were on to recognize the iris patterns.

1.2 Multiphase Encryption Technique

Multiphase encryption technique can be stated as a phenomenon through which the original data is encrypted multiple times with same or different secured encryption algorithms in each phase of encryption and this process will be occurred multiple times as per our requirements. Due to which the complexity of the encryption algorithm is increased to a larger extent [1].

Multiphase encryption algorithm has been proven more secure in comparison of traditional encryption algorithms such as DES (Data Encryption Standard), AES (Advance Encryption Standard), and DSS (Digital Signature Algorithm). Using this approach of encryption, we can ensure the integrity and security of the user's data over vulnerable wireless network as internet [2].

1.3 Brief Description of Encryption in Biometrics Devices

The biometric technology may use a two-dimensional image such as fingerprint, palm print, face recognition, iris, or retina. The subsequent digital key generated is used as a cryptographic key [2]. And as the common requirement of biometric technology, the system must comprise of distortion tolerance, discriminative, and secure. In this research paper, we are going to explain how the multiple encryption techniques can be implemented to safeguard data in biometric devices [3] (Fig. 1).

This picture explains briefly how the encryption should work in biometric devices. First, there is a key generator and a sensor that is at the applicant side. When the user wants to store its data, he just enters the required biometric input,

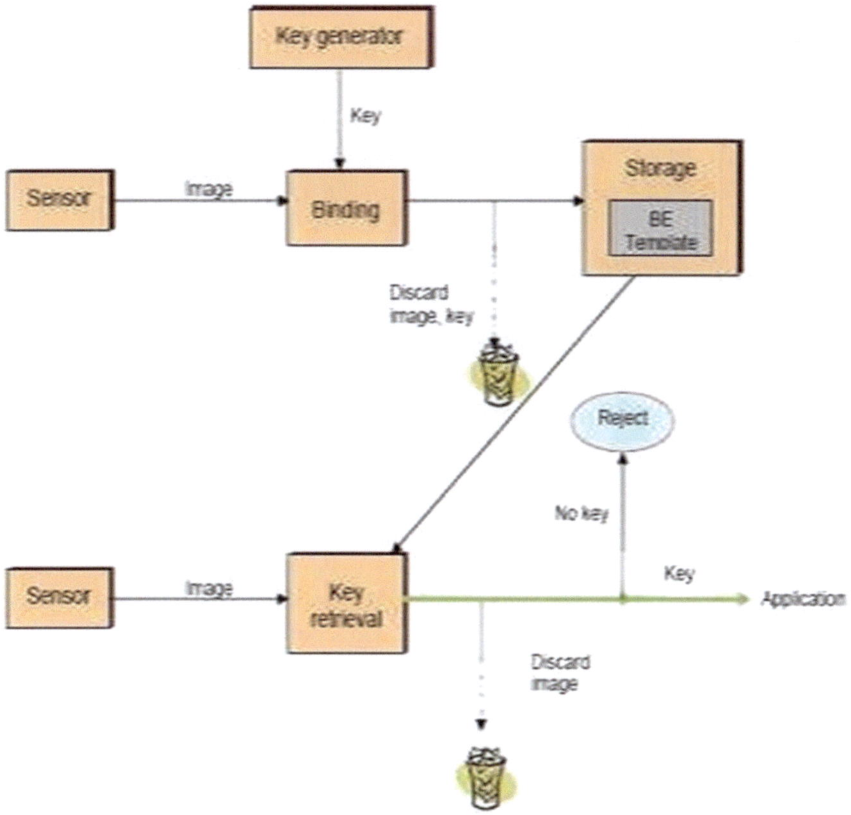

Fig. 1 Encryption process in biometric devices

that is, his eye, voice, fingerprint, or any biometric used for the security purpose. Then, an image of this metric is generated and a key as well. Both the key and the image are bind together and stored in the database. After this template has been saved, the key and the image are just destroyed. If the user wants to access its data from the database, again the biometric input will be checked with saved template. If the image matches, then the key is retrieved and the image is discarded. Now, the user can access the particular application as per his requirement. If the image does not match, the request is rejected [4, 5].

2 Proposed Model

In the proposed model, we recommend a strategy according to which the data within the biometric device is padded with random number. The method consists of two phases by default the enrolment phase and the retrieval phase.

2.1 Enrollment Phase

In the implementation of the enrolment phase, two different ciphertexts are used. For producing image by the sensor at the time of the enrolment phase, two different ciphers are used. The image produced at the enrollment time is duplicated. A copy is binded with a cryptographic key and a first biometric encrypted template is produced. A pseudo-random number (in bits format) is now generated and this activates the production of a second independent key. The second key is used to bind the second copy of the image and the first biometric encrypted template together. And the final encrypted template is produced which is finally stored as multiple encrypted data. The keys and the images were generated initially and discarded once the final image is developed and stored.

2.2 Retrieval Phase

When the user wants to access a desired application, two images are taken from the sensor device. The first image used to decrypt the first biometric encrypted image, and the second copy of the biometric image is used for verification purpose. The subsequent keys are retrieved and the user can access the application. If one phase fails, the process is rejected and access is denied (Fig. 2).

3 Conceptual Framework

3.1 Enrolment Phase

In the enrollment phase, we divide the inner work of proposed multiple encryptions into three stages:

In the first stage: P1 (a)

When the user wants to log in the first time to a particular application, he just registers with his biometric input with the help of a sensor. Suppose the biometric input is the fingerprint. The image of the fingerprint is taken from the sensor, and

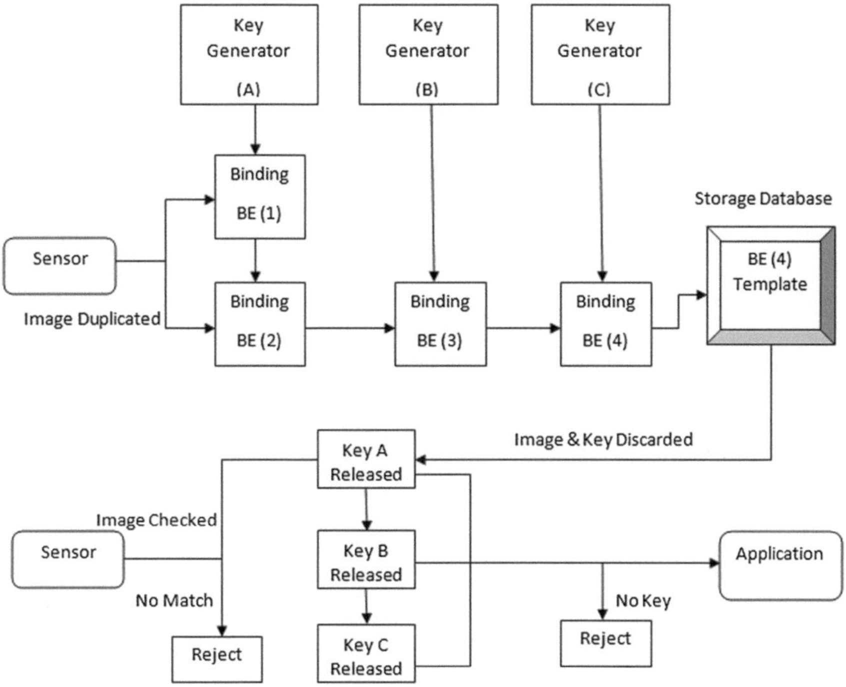

Fig. 2 Proposed scheme of the multiple encryption in biometric devices

then duplicate copy is generated and saved before being converted into binary format. Each sample of fingerprint image is called, respectively, as $F1(n)$ and $F2(n)$ where n is the metric. Then, a pseudo-random number Key(A) is generated and taken as a cryptographic key. This cryptographic key is a single digit between 0 and 9 that is converted into binary number and then in octal format.

The first function $F1(n)$ is matricized into matrix of $(m * m)$ size where maximum value of $m = 2$. Those matrices will be generated sequentially according to number of binary digits in a line and a column. If there is no enough digit for making a matrix, then the size of the matrix will be padded with NULL value (0), which should create a very less distortion (almost null according to the correlation algorithm).

The next step is doing a matrix multiplication between each and every matrices and the same Key(A). Results will be written sequentially according to initial position of matrix. The output from phase 1 is called as biometric encrypted template as BE(1) which is the first template and is binded with Key(A). One copy is stored in database for retrieval purpose. Now, the Key(A) input is discarded.

The output of the first part of stage P(1) as BE(1) will be used as the input of the stage P1(b). The second function that is nothing but the digitized and binary version of the input image $F2(n)$ is matricized into matrix of $(m * m)$ size where maximum value of $m = 2$. The same process as above is followed. Then, BE(1) is multiplied with each and every matrices produced with $F2(n)$ as $F2(n)$: $(m * m) * \mathrm{BE}(1) = \mathrm{BE}(2)$. The output is BE(2). The BE(1) input along with the function $F2(n)$ is discarded. One copy of BE(2) is stored in database.

In the second phase: P2

A pseudo-random number Key(B) is generated and taken as a cryptographic key. This cryptographic key is a single digit between 0 and 9 that is converted into binary number of 1 octet.

In this phase, output BE(2) is EXORed with the cryptographic key Key(B) (Fig. 3).

$$\mathrm{BE}(2)\,\mathrm{EXOR}\,\mathrm{Key}(\mathrm{B}) = \mathrm{BE}(3)$$

The output is a biometric encrypted template BE(3) which is bind with the cryptographic key, Key(B). Then, BE(3) is stored in database and key(B) is discarded.

In the last phase: P3

The third pseudo-random key, Key(C), is generated. In this encryption phase, an idea from Ceaser cipher technique of encryption will be followed.

The cryptographic key is taken as a three-digit octal number, and its value will predict the position to which it should be added. Suppose the PRNG number is 3

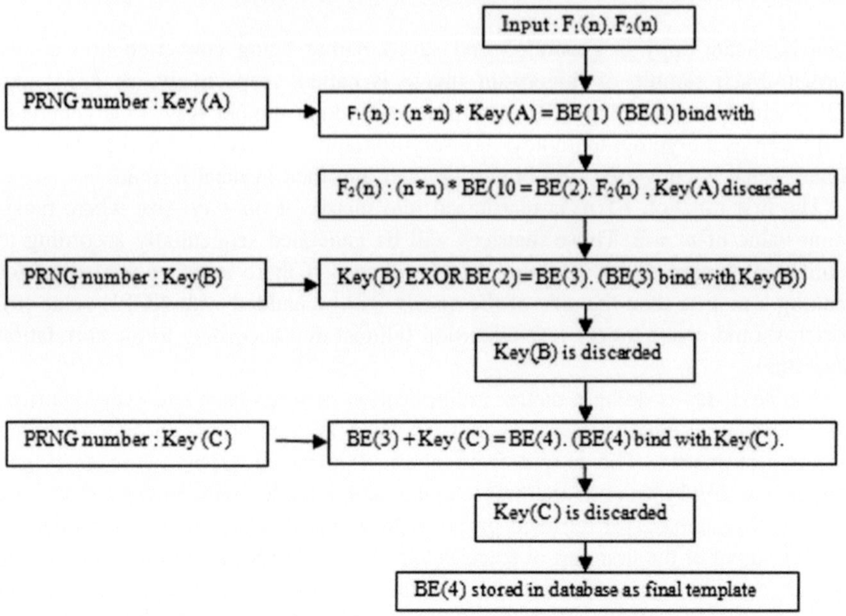

Fig. 3 Enrollment phase

and all numbers will be grouped into three digits. And 3 in octal system is 3 = 011. It means, 011 will be added to each 3th forward position in the list of numbers in BE(3). If in the first row, we have

$$\text{BE}(3): 10110101111010101100011101 0110\ldots$$

Every three bits will be grouped together so we get

$$101\ 101\ \underline{011}\ 110\ 101\ \underline{011}\ 000\ 111\ \underline{010}\ 110$$

To the 3th binary octet, then the 6th, then the 9th in a raw, and so on, we will add 011.

So BE(3) + key(C) = 1 0 1 1 0 1 ($\underline{0\ 1\ 1 + 0\ 1\ 1}$) 1 1 0 1 0 1 ($\underline{0\ 1\ 0 + 0\ 1\ 1}$) 0 0 0 1 1 1 ($\underline{0\ 1\ 0 + 0\ 1\ 1}$) 1 1 0... = 1 0 1 1 0 1 $\underline{1\ 1\ 0}$ 1 1 0 1 0 1 $\underline{1\ 0\ 1}$ 0 0 0 1 1 1 $\underline{1\ 0\ 1}$ 1 1 0... = BE(4)

The result is biometric encrypted template BE(4) which stored in database, bind with cryptographic key Key(C) and linked to the intended application. Key(C) is then discarded.

3.2 Retrieval Phase

The retrieval phase is a combination of correlation algorithm, that is, the basic algorithm in biometric encryption and also, some mathematical operations taken in a block as multiple encryption different levels. The objective of the retrieval phase is to allow the user to access a particular application after authentication and verification (Fig. 4).

At the retrieval phase, the biometric is taken as an input from the sensor. And this biometric image is digitized, binarized, and then every single bit is compared with $F1(n)$ copy that was stored in the database. Approximately, 99% match can be tolerated. If there is a match then the process is pursued, if not, the access is denied. Then, the Key(A) is released and input image A(n) is matricized as $F1(n)$ and multiplied with the cryptographic key Key(A). The result is called as BEr(1) and it is compared with BE(1); if there is a 99% match, then A(n) is discarded and go to the next phase. If not, process is rejected.

$F1(n)$ is now multiplied with BEr(1) and result is BEr(2). Then, BEr(2) is compared with BE(2). If there is a 99% match, then Key(B) is released, and BEr(1) is discarded. If not, the process is rejected. BEr(2) is EXORed with the key, Key(B), and produces a biometric encrypted BEr(3) sample. Then, BEr(3) is compared with BE(3).

If there is a 99% match, then Key(C) is released, and BEr(2) is discarded. If not, the process is rejected. BEr(3) is now Ceaser Ciphered with the cryptographic key Key(C) like in the enrollment phase. The result is called as BEr(4) and it is

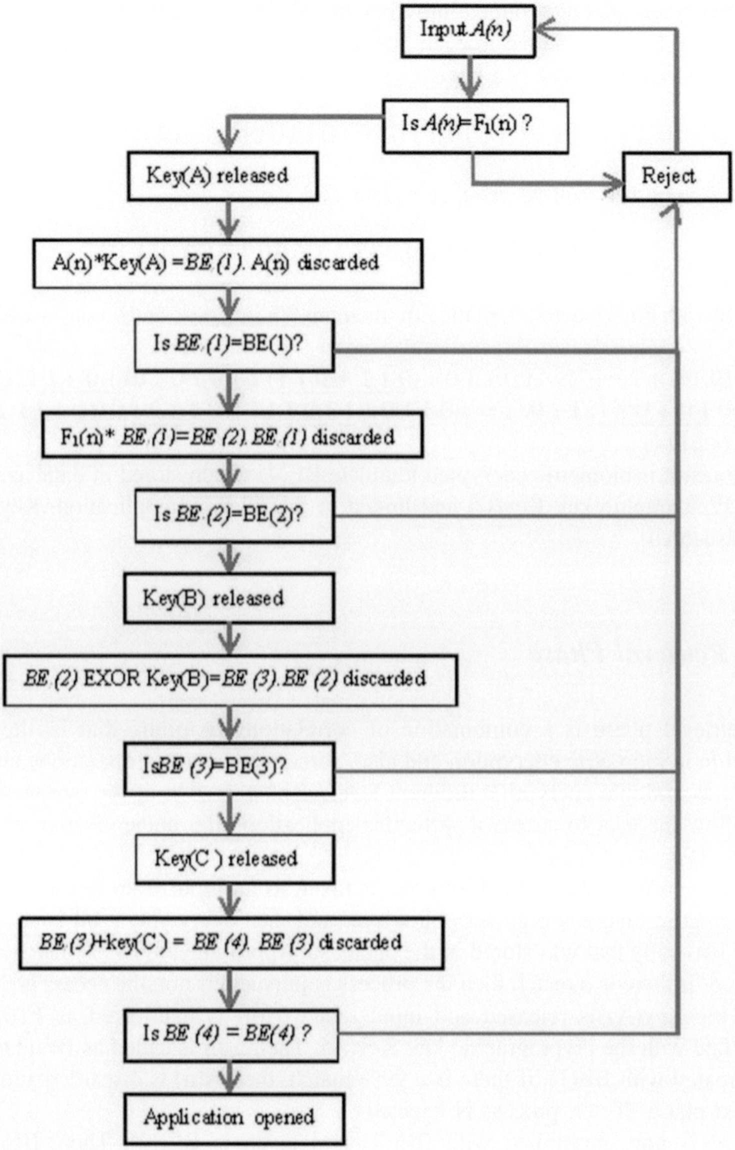

Fig. 4 Retrieval phase

compared with BE(4); if there is a 99% match, then the link to the application is activated and the user gets access to that application. After that, BEr(4) is discarded. If there is no match, the process is interrupted.

4 Future Work

After completion of this research paper, we came across some limitations such as

- Level of security implemented,
- Ease of application access,
- Availability of resources to implement the technology on a common platform, and
- Time management.

We are planing to work more effectively on the prior aspects of the biometric technology like enhancing more security. This research paper is only a theoretical one and we are not 100% sure that everything that we have proposed will effectively work in biometric devices. Everything proposed here will be implemented at software level. So the next step will be to create an application based on all above-given mathematical calculations.

5 Conclusion

Here, we proposed the implementation of multiple encryption technique with biometric technology to provide enhanced security solutions. However, the proposed algorithm also allows the user to produce several keys and random numbers which comprises of their unique biometric information. The execution of the multiple encryption technique offers numerous advantages over the current authentication methods. The proposed technique is convenient to the user and cannot be shared or forgotten by the user. Furthermore, the need of the unique cryptographic keys and the pseudo-random numbers is increasing rapidly as the growing concern about the possible attacks by the intruders.

References

1. Gupta H, Sharma VK (2013) Multiphase encryption: a new concept in the modern cryptography. Int J Comput Theory Eng 5(4):638–640
2. Wikipedia, Network security and cryptography. https://en.wikipedia.org/wiki/Network_security, 2017
3. Venkatachalam SP, Kannan PM, Palanisamy V (2009) Combining cryptography with biometrics technology for enhanced security. In: INCACEC 2009, pp 1–6, June 2009, ISBN: 978-1-4244-4789-3
4. Le C (2011) A survey of biometrics security systems. Weblink. http://www.cse.wustl.edu/~jain/cse571-11/ftp/biomet.pdf, 28 Nov 2011

5. Tomko G (1998) Biometrics as a privacy-enhancing technology: friend or foe of privacy? In: Privacy laws & business, 9th privacy commissioners/data protection authorities workshop, Spain

Author Biographies

Dr. Himanshu Gupta is working as a Senior Faculty Member in the well reputed Indian university Amity University Uttar Pradesh, Noida. He completed all his academic as well as professional education from reputed central university Aligarh Muslim University, Aligarh (Uttar Pradesh) India. He has visited Malaysia, Singapore, Thailand, Cambodia, Vietnam, Indonesia, Hong Kong, Macau and China for his academic and research work. He has delivered many Technical Sessions on "Network Security & Cryptography" in the field of Information Technology in various reputed International Conferences, World Summit and other foreign universities as an Invited Speaker. He has more than 60 Research Papers and Articles in the field of Information Technology, which have been published in various reputed Conference Proceedings and Journals.

C. Aka Assoua Anne-Marie is associated with Amity University, Noida as a research student and having her expertise in Network Technology & Management. She has been associated in many academic and research activities in the area of Network Technologies. She earned the CCNA Certification during her stay as a research student in the Amity University, Noida.

Buffer Overflow and SQL Injection: To Remotely Attack and Access Information

Mehak Khurana, Ruby Yadav and Meena Kumari

Abstract In today's electronic world where data is accessed through internet, intranet, and extranet, the security of the information is an important issue. Buffer overflow attack in software and SQL injection attack in web application are the two main attacks which are explained in this paper with the aim to make user understand that how unintentional flaws get injected, how these flaws lead to vulnerabilities, and how these vulnerabilities are exploited by the attackers. In this paper, the real-time attack example is also shown with its screenshots step by step.

Keywords Ethical hacking · Buffer overflow · SQL injection · Vulnerabilities

1 Introduction

In the electronic world, security is the major issue on the internet, intranet, and extranet. Ethical hacking is a term which is used to increase security by identifying and overcoming those vulnerabilities on the systems owned by third party. Attacker uses vulnerabilities as an opportunity to attack software and web application. Thus, system needs to be protected from attacker so that attacker cannot hack information and make it misbehave according to him/her. So, ethical hacking is a way to test and to identify an information technology environment for present vulnerabilities.

Software is used everywhere in the digital world. But due to the flaws in software, software fails and attacker takes this as an advantage and uses this opportunity to make software misbehave and use according to them. Flaws increase the risk to security. Some of the software developer manages the software risk by

M. Khurana (✉) · R. Yadav · M. Kumari
The NorthCap University, Gurgaon, India
e-mail: mehakkhurana@ncuindia.edu

R. Yadav
e-mail: rubyyadav@ncuindia.edu

M. Kumari
e-mail: meenakumari@ncuindia.edu

M. U. Bokhari et al. (eds.), *Cyber Security*, Advances in Intelligent Systems and Computing 729, https://doi.org/10.1007/978-981-10-8536-9_30

increasing the complexity of the code, but absolute security cannot be achieved. According to the literature survey, some of the software flaws which lead to security vulnerabilities are Buffer Overflow (BO), Incomplete Mediation (IM), and Race Condition (RC) [1].

The other class of vulnerabilities that exist in the web application can be exploited through SQL injection. Attacker takes advantage of the unintentional flaws in the input validation logic of Web components. SQL injection attack leads to high security risk to the web applications which allow attackers to access databases completely. These databases contain user information and if this information is accessed by the attacker, the confidentiality of the user will be leaked and thefts and frauds can take place. In many cases, attackers use an SQL injection vulnerability to take full control of web application and corrupt the system that hosts the Web application.

Buffer overflow and SQL injections are some of the vulnerabilities in the software and the web application, respectively, which are discussed in detail in this paper.

This paper gives an overview of one of the flaws that exist in the software, i.e., buffer overflow and how this flaw leads to the security vulnerabilities that can be exploited and what are the preventives measures that can be taken to protect it from the attackers. This paper also explains one of the famous attacker's techniques to access information from the database of the web application using Kali Linux. The SQL queries in Kali Linux that are used to retrieve information from the database of a web application are shown for a particular website. This paper provides description and example with screenshot of how these attacks can be performed and what will be the outcome.

2 Buffer Overflow

Buffer overflow is a software flaw which is introduced unintentionally by the programmer. For example, in a program, while writing a data to an allocated memory, if data is assigned to the memory which is not allocated, it overruns the boundary of the allocated memory. Most popular languages C and C++ also do not have built-in boundary check, i.e., they do not automatically check the data trying to access memory location of an array is outside the boundaries (total size) of an array, for example (Table 1).

Here, the total size of array is 10, but the data is assigned at location 30 which is outside the boundary of an array. Boundary check can eliminate vulnerability. Java and C # are the languages which have boundary checks but they have performance penalty for checking so the developer use C and C++ for coding [2]. These buffer overflow vulnerabilities can be exploited by attackers in many ways:

Table 1 Program with flaw

```
void main()
{
int buffer[10];
buffer[30] =45;
}
```

(a) Denial-of-Service Attack—Buffer overflow flaw may likely cause system crash, so attacker exploits this vulnerability to launch denial-of-service attack.
(b) Inject Attack Code—Attacker can manipulate the code to
  (i) Overwrite the system data.
  (ii) Overwrite the data in the memory in such a way that it transfers the code to malicious code, i.e., pointer points to injected malicious code. Buffer overflow vulnerabilities mostly dominate in the class of remote penetration attack.

Figure 1 shows the structure of memory organization of CPU. Here, text stores the code of the program, the data section consists of text and static variables, heap stores dynamic data, and stack section (shown in Fig. 2) stores the dynamic local variables, parameters of the functions, return address of the function call (where the control will be transferred after the function executes), stack pointer points to the top of the stack. Stack grows from high address to low address (while buffer grows from low address to high address).

Fig. 1 Memory organization

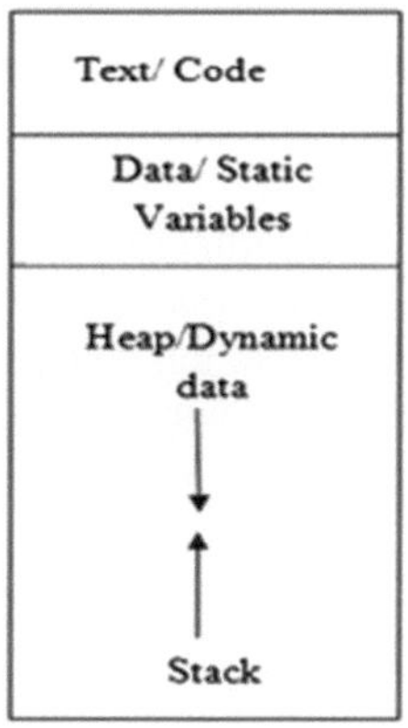

Fig. 2 Stack structure

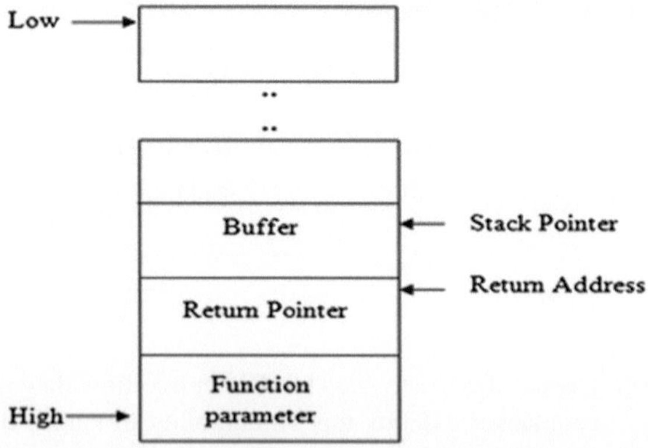

2.1 *Goals of Buffer Overflow Attack to Exploit Vulnerability*

The main goal of the attacker is to take buffer overflow as an advantage and to fetch the control of the privilege program by subverting the function of that program. Attacker tries to attack the root program and execute code similar to shellcode. To achieve this goal, two sub-goals need to be achieved [3].

(a) To alter the victim's program by making it to jump to random memory location, with suitable parameter loaded into register and memory.
(b) To alter victim's program by adding malicious code to victim's program address space to jump to address where malicious code is injected.

2.1.1 Jump to Random Memory Location

Attacker overwrites program with arbitrary sequence of byte with goal of corrupting the victim program. It is done by making the victim's pointer to point to random address.

According to Table 2, if attacker tries to use more memory (>10), buffer overflow will overflow into the space where the return address is located. Attacker can overwrite this return address with the random bits or random address; by this, the program will jump to random memory location after function execution [4] and may lead to program crash as shown in Fig. 3b.

Table 2 Source code

```
void area (int a, int b);
void main()
{
        area (2, 3);
}
void area (int a, int b)
{
        int buffer[10];
}
```

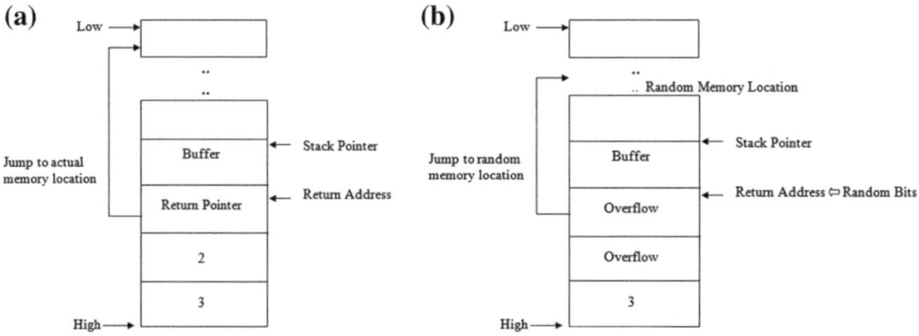

Fig. 3 **a** Jump to actual memory location. **b** Jump to random memory location

2.1.2 To Place Malicious Code in Victim's Program Address Space

Stack and heap are two areas of memory that a program used for reading and writing, i.e., buffer can be located in any of these two areas. Attacker provides data as input to the program to store in a buffer. This data is actually the instruction with the help of which attackers try to use victim program's buffer to store the malicious code of his/her choice.

Attacker injects this executable malicious code into the buffer and overwrites the return address with the address of this malicious code as shown in Fig. 4b. This return address can be chosen by hit-and-trial method.

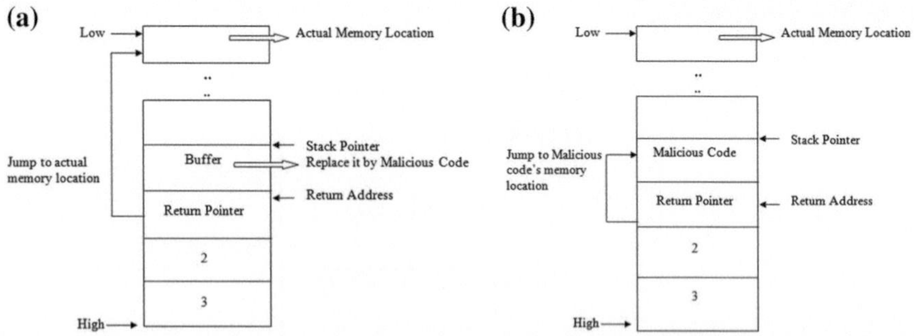

Fig. 4 **a** Malicious code can be inserted in buffer. **b** Return address jumps to malicious code

2.2 Challenges with Buffer Overflow

1.3.1 There are some difficulties with buffer overflow attack, they are [5]

(a) Attacker may not know the exact location of malicious code injected.
(b) Attacker may not know the exact location of the return address with malicious code starting address.

1.3.2 These difficulties can be overcome by different methods:

(a) First problem can be solved by injecting No Operation (NOP) before malicious code.
(b) Second problem can be resolved by inserting the return address repeatedly. This may overwrite the actual return address with attacker's return address and will make pointer jump to any NOP address which in turn may point to next NOP and after last NOP malicious code will be executed (Fig. 5).

Fig. 5 Insert NOP

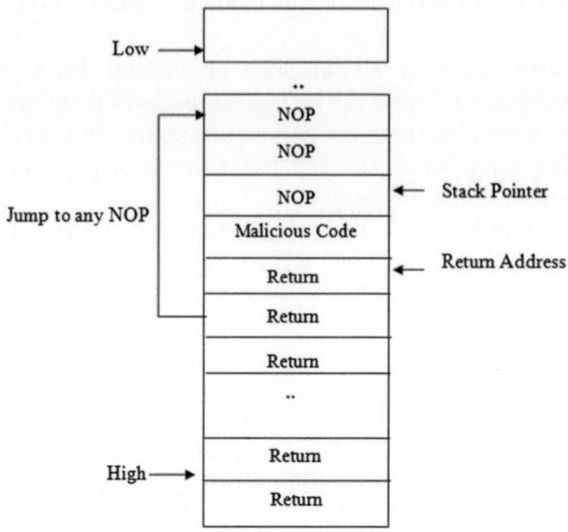

2.3 *Protection Against Buffer Overflow*

There are some ways to protect the software from buffer overflow:

(a) Brute force method—to write completely the correct code but to write an error-free code is not achievable. One of the ways to achieve near to error-free code is to introduce buffer overflow intentionally to search for vulnerable components in the program. The other way is to use debugging and analysis tools to find buffer overflow vulnerabilities. This method does not eliminate all the vulnerabilities but reduces them [6].
(b) Do not allow the code to execute on stack; stack is made non-executable by using No execute bit or NX bit (supported by some hardware); memory can be flagged so that code cannot be executed in a specified location.
(c) Safe program language—Java and C# have boundary check at runtime. They automatically check the arrays out of bound. These languages do not allow memory locations to be accessed which are out of boundary but have performance penalty for checking, due to which developer chooses C language. So in that case do not use unsafe function, use its safe alternative. Use safe functions such as fgets, strncpy, strncat, and snprintf instead of C unsafe functions gets, strcpy, strcat, sprintf, scanf, etc. [7].
(d) Runtime Stack Checking—Runtime stack checking can be introduced by pushing special value on the stack after return address. When return address is popped off stack, the special value can be used to verify that return address has not changed and in order to overwrite the return address, this special value also needs to be overwritten.

3 SQL Injection

SQL injection is one of the most famous attacks used in hacking. Every web application has its data stored in any database. These databases contain some sensitive and confidential data. Web applications accept the data from the users. This data is retrieved from the database through SQL queries. To insert, retrieve, update, and delete the data from database, SQL language is used. Using SQL injection attacker can have unauthorized access to the system. For example, there is any website let say Gmail that provides user an interface to enter his email id and password. The email id and password form the part of the internal SQL query. User enters his credentials, then these credentials are matched with the data stored in the database. So if the hacker gets the access to that database he can easily get your credentials and thus can attack your account like sending fake mails, deleting important data, or extracting private information from database. Thus, SQL injection is defined as a mechanism that allows hacker to inject SQL commands to allow them to gain access to the data held within your database. SQL injection uses the concept of duality of data and command to get information from database. In SQL injection, the hacker type SQL keyword to modify the structure of SQL query was developed by web programmer, and trick the SQL interpreter to execute unintentional orders. The SQL query is modified in such a way that the interpreter is unable to differentiate between the actual command and hackers input [8]. The interpreter is tricked to execute such unintended commands. For example, when we search any website, we write URL:

Original query: https://88keystoeuphoria.com/video.php?id='32'

Injected query: https://88keystoeuphoria.com/video.php?id='32''

This is translated into query—Select * from TABLE where id='32''

The hacker has intentionally modified the query and inserted an extra apostrophe after 32. It is syntactically incorrect, so our database will throw an error message that infers the information about table like table name. Therefore, he is able to extract information using wrong query.

3.1 *Testing Website for SQL Injection*

For SQL injection, first the hacker/attacker identifies whether a website is vulnerable or not. There are various tools to check vulnerability of website [9]

(a) Acunetix—It automatically checks the given web application for SQL injection and other vulnerabilities.
(b) Nesus—Nessus is the best unix vulnerability testing tool. It also runs on windows. Key features of this software include remote and local file security checks client/server architecture with a GTK graphical interface etc.
(c) Retina—It is an another vulnerability testing tool. It scans all hosts on a network and reports on any vulnerability found.
(d) Metasploit framework—It is an open-source penetration testing software tool with the world's largest database of public and tested exploits.

For example, let say we have a website say keystoeuphoria.com. Now we are going to exploit it using Kali Linux. Before starting, read the following disclaimer:

You may face legal action if you do not have the permission from the administrator of the website that you are testing for SQL injection. They can track your IP address. So it is advisable to try it only if access privilege is provided.

SQL injection includes four main steps [10]:

Step 1: Enumerate the database

Open the terminal window on Kali Linux and write the following command

Sqlmap—u "https://keystoeuphoria.com/video.php?id=32"—dbs;

Result—The command checks whether the typed URL website is vulnerable or not, and if it is vulnerable it will show you the list of various databases that exist over that website (Fig. 6).

(a)

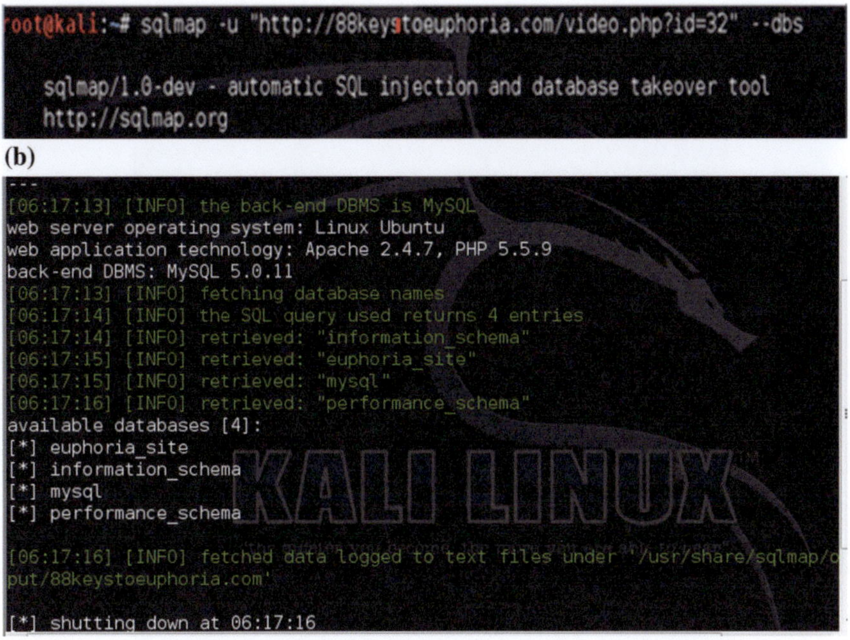

Fig. 6 **a** Query to retrieve database names. **b** List of database names retrieved

Step 2: Enumerate the table name

After having the details of various databases that exist over website *keystoeuphoria,* the attacker tries to find out the various tables that exist in the chosen vulnerable database. Following command is typed on the terminal:

Sqlmap—u "https://keystoeuphoria.com/video.php?id=32"—D *databasename* —tables

Sqlmap—u "http://keystoeuphoria.com/video.phpid=32"—D euphoriadb—tables (Fig. 7).

Step 3: Enumerate the column name

After obtaining different table names, we will choose the one that is most useful to us like admin table, as admin table might include user admin password details. If one is able to obtain the admin password, he can easily get the privileges of admin and do changes in site as per his wish. So before looking at the data, we have to find the different column names by enumerating the column name:

Sqlmap—u " *url* "—D *databasename*—T *tablename*—columns

Sqlmap—u "https://88keystoeuphoria.com/video.php?id=32"—D euphoriadb—T admin—columns (Fig. 8).

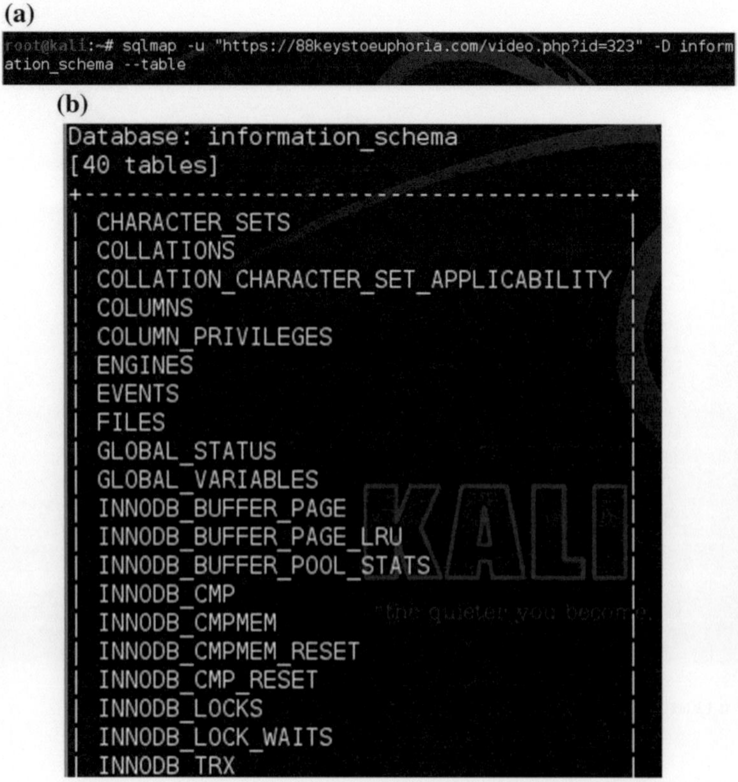

Fig. 7 **a** Query to retrieve table names. **b** List of table names retrieved

Step 4: Fetch Password/Column content:

After fetching the above information, we try to extract vulnerable information for exploitation like the admin password details by the following command.

Sqlmap—u " *url* "—D *dbname*—T *tablename*—dump (Fig. 9).

This example shows that the database information can be accessed that is been hosted on web application due to SQL injection vulnerabilities. This will lead to loss of information and confidentiality and will result in financial cost for recovery, downtime, penalties, etc.

Even if the sites are not storing user information in the web application database, they are also at risk of losing database integrity. SQL injection vulnerabilities allow the attacker to inject malicious code by taking advantage of persistent storage and dynamic page content generation. This may redirect the visitor visiting this vulnerable site to malicious site. By redirecting visitor to this malicious site, attacker can remotely access the visitor's system by exploiting his other system's vulnerability or system crash can take place [11].

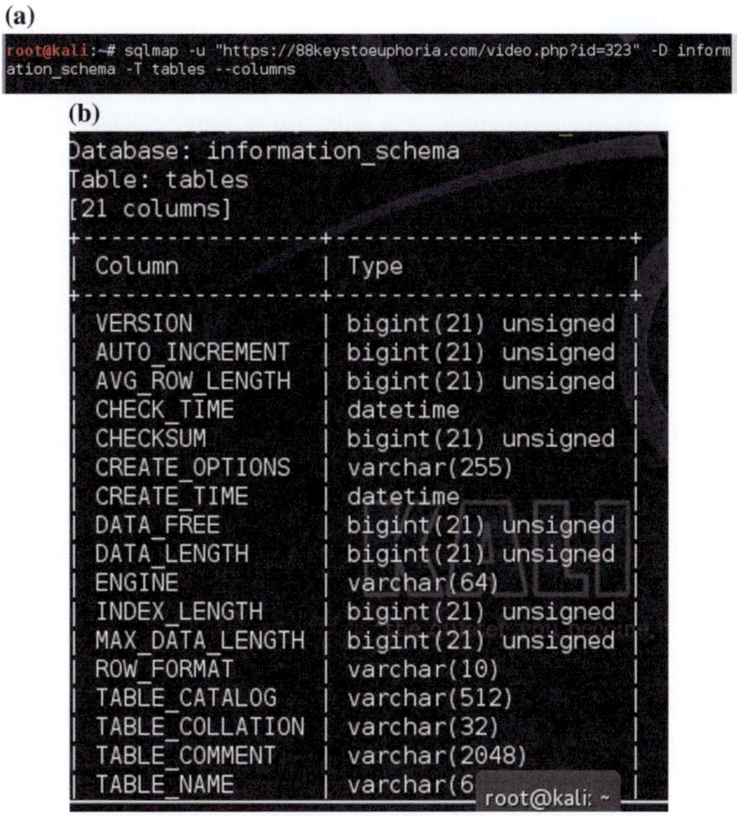

Fig. 8 **a** Query to retrieve column names. **b** List of column names retrieved

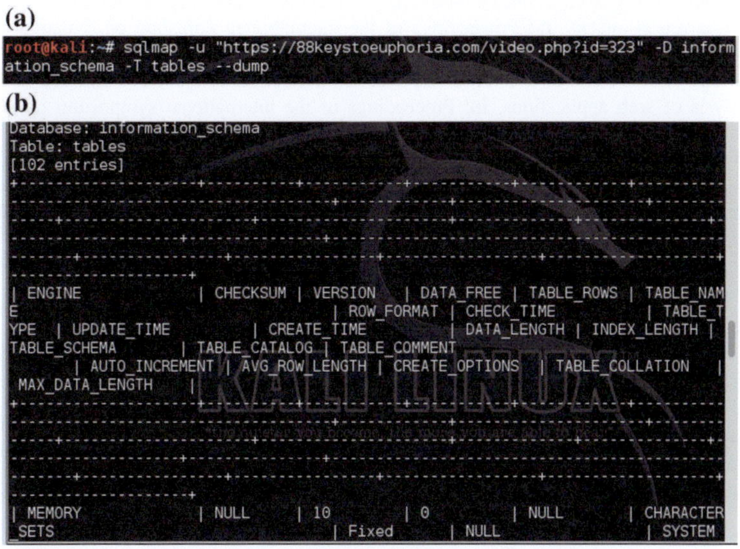

Fig. 9 **a** Query to retrieve dump. **b** List of dump retrieved

4 Conclusion

Buffer overflow and SQL injection are still biggest security problems in software and web applications, respectively, that will exist in future for long time due to large amount of legacy code. This paper explains buffer overflow attack vulnerabilities and the preventives measures that can be taken to protect it from the attackers. This paper demonstrates method with example for testing web applications for SQL injection vulnerabilities that attackers use to compromise a web application. These SQL queries can be tried on real-time application under administrative control.

Refrences

1. Stamp M (2006) Information security principles and practices. Wiley, Hoboken, NJ
2. Cowan C, Wagle P, Pu C, Beattie S, Walpole J Buffer overflows: attacks and defenses for the vulnerability of the decade. In: Proceedings of DARPA information survivability conference and expo (DISCEX)
3. Foster JC, Osipov V, Bhalla N, Heinen N (2005) Buffer overflow attacks detect, exploit, prevent. Syngress Publishing Inc., Rockland
4. Shaneck M (2003) An overview of buffer overflow vulnerabilities and internet worms. In: CSCI, 10 Dec 2003
5. Kak A (2015) Buffer overflow attack. In: Lecture Notes on Computer and Network Security, Purdue University, 2 April 2015
6. "Buffer-Overflow Vulnerabilities and Attacks", in Lecture Notes, Syracuse University. http://www.cis.syr.edu/~wedu/Teaching/CompSec/LectureNotes_New/Buffer_Overflow.pdf
7. Halfond WGJ, Viegas J, Orso A (2006) A classification of SQL injection attacks and countermeasures. In: Proceedings of the international symposium on secure software engineering, Mar 2006
8. Halfond WGJ, Orso A (2005) Combining static analysis and runtime monitoring to counter SQL-injection attacks. In: Proceedings of the international workshop on dynamic analysis (WODA), May 2005
9. Halfond WGJ, Anand S, Orso A (2009) Precise interface identification to improve testing and analysis of web applications. In: Proceedings of the international symposium on software testing and analysis (STA), July 2009
10. Boyd SW, Keromytis AD (2004) SQLrand: preventing SQL injection attacks. In: Lecture Notes in Computer Science, vol 3089. Springer, pp 292–302
11. Dougherty C (2012) Practical identification of SQL injection vulnerabilities, Carnegie Mellon University. Produced for US-CERT, a government organization, 2012

Author Biographies

Mehak Khurana is currently working as assistant professor in The NorthCap University in CSE and IT and has around 6 years of experience. She completed her M.Tech from USIT, GGSIPU in 2011 and B.Tech from GTBIT, GGSIPU in 2009. Currently she is also pursuing Ph.D in the field of Information Security and Cryptography at NCU. Her key areas of interest are Cyber Security, Ethical Hacking and Cryptography. She has contributed research papers in various national and international journals and conferences. She is lifetime member of Cryptology Research Society of India (CRSI).

Ruby Yadav has worked as Research Associate in The NorthCap University in CSE & IT dept. She has published papers in reputed international conferences and journals. She has completed M.Tech and B.Tech from MDU. She is lifetime member of Cryptology Research Society of India (CRSI).

Meena Kumari has worked as a professor, Dept of CSE & IT at The NorthCap University. She has also worked as Scientist ‘G’ at DRDO (Defence Research & Development Organization) and has 37 years of research experience in cryptology.

Prime Numbers: Foundation of Cryptography

Sonal Sarnaik and Basit Ansari

Abstract Prime number plays a very important role in cryptography. There are various types of prime numbers and consists various properties. This paper gives the detail description of the importance of prime numbers in cryptography and algorithms which generates large/strong prime numbers. This paper also focuses on algorithms which find prime factors and tests whether the entered number is prime number or not.

Keywords Prime numbers · Primality testing · Prime number generation

1 Introduction

Exchange of information or data plays a very vital role nowadays. There are various ways through which this data is exchanged. Today's most common way is to communicate through some electronic medium for exam Internet. We perform many important tasks through the internet such as online shopping, online banking, personal data share, etc. So it is very important to make this communication very secure so that an attacker will not be able to get access to the data. Currently, there are various security measures to make this communication secure one of the method is to use Cryptography [1–4]. Cryptography focuses on the concept that "security can be achieved by hiding the data or converting it into some unreadable form," so cryptography is the study of mathematical science which is used to convert the data in some incomprehensible form which gives security to the data [1–3], i.e., cryptography is the art of secret writing [4]. Secret writing is achieved by applying the key to the original data which converts original data into unreadable data (called as Encryption) and unreadable data to original data (called as Decryption) [1–4]. This

S. Sarnaik (✉) · B. Ansari
Marathwada Institute of Technology, Aurangabad, India
e-mail: sonalsarnaik141@gmail.com

B. Ansari
e-mail: basit.ansari@sycet.org

M. U. Bokhari et al. (eds.), *Cyber Security*, Advances in Intelligent Systems and Computing 729, https://doi.org/10.1007/978-981-10-8536-9_31

task is achieved by applying key at sender and key at receiver for encryption and decryption. Two types of keys are mostly used in cryptography, symmetric key and asymmetric key [3, 4]. The intensity of the security will completely rely on the type of key is used. An asymmetric key is much stronger then symmetric key as in asymmetric key two different keys are used one for encryption (encryption key is publically declared) and one for decryption (Decryption key is private only known to receiver) whereas in symmetric key, the same key is used to encryption and for decryption [1–4]. An asymmetric key is also called a public-key cryptosystem [3–5].

There are various algorithms which are used to provide security to the data. Basically, all the concepts of cryptography based on the modular arithmetic concepts, Number systems, Groups rings, Fields, etc [4, 5]. This paper focuses on the concepts of the number system and in which prime number which plays a vital role in Cryptography. If we consider about asymmetric key then the calculation of key completely depends on the prime number and its factors [3–5].

2 Prime Numbers

The numbers which are divisible by itself or by 1 are called as prime numbers and other numbers are called as composite numbers. Examples: 2, 3, 5, 7, 11, 13, 17, 19, etc., are prime numbers which are divisible by only one or by itself and rest of the numbers such as, 2, 4, 9, 10, 12, 14, etc., are composite numbers [4, 6–10]. The securities of cryptographic algorithms are depending on prime numbers and its length. There are various type of prime numbers such as Balance prime, Circular Prime, Long Prime, Mersenne Prime, Minimal Prime, Strong Prime, Palindromic Prime, Permutable Prime, Twin Prime, Unique Prime, Wilson Prime, Regular Prime, Integer Sequence Prime, Higgs Prime, etc. All these types of prime numbers have different properties and it is used in cryptography depending on its properties. The main type of prime numbers which plays a vital role in cryptography are strong prime numbers. A strong prime is a prime number with certain special properties. A number p is a strong prime number if it satisfies following conditions [2–4]:

- p is large prime number
- $p - 1$ must have large prime number factor, say $a1$ $q1$, where $p = a1 * q1 + 1$
- $q1$ must have large prime factors say $a2$ $q2$, where $q1 = a2 * q2 + 1$
- $p + 1$ must have large prime factors say $a3$ $q3$, where $p = a3 * q3 - 1$.

3 Importance of Prime Number in Cryptography

Strong primes are basically used in public-key cryptography to make encryption key and decryption key more secure. Algorithms such as RSA algorithms, Taher and ElGamal algorithms, elliptical curve cryptography, etc., uses strong prime numbers for the encryption key and decryption key generation [2–5]. For example, RSA algorithm uses two types of key, public key (also called as an encryption key) and private key (also called as decryption key) [2–4]. The public key is used to encrypt data; this key is publically declared and known to all [4, 5].

Private key is used to decrypt the data by the receiver, as the name suggests this key is private and no one else can use this key [4, 5]. The main security point in RSA is completely depending on two prime numbers chosen by the sender used for public-key generation and private-key generation [2–5, 11].

RSA algorithm:

Step 1: Sender selects two large prime number p and q
$n = p * q$
Calculate $\varphi(n) = (p - 1) * (q - 1)$

Step 2: Choose d such that it satisfies following condition.

- $\text{Gcd}(d, \varphi(n)) = 1$
- $\text{Max}(p, q)$
- d must be prime no

Step 3: Find e such that it satisfies:

- $e.\, d \equiv 1 \bmod \varphi(n)$
- $e > \log_2(n)$
- $\text{Gcd}(e, \varphi(n)) = 1$

Step 4: $C = M^{e} \bmod n$
Step 5: $M = C^{d} \bmod n$

Where M is original text, C is Ciphertext, p and q both are prime numbers, n is the product of two prime numbers, $\varphi(n)$ is Euler's totient function, e is the Encryption key, d is the Decryption key.

In above demonstration, we can easily understand that if p and q are sufficiently large then complexity other computations will be increased and so decryption key will be very difficult to find out by any third user. This has been shown in [11]. If encryption key and n are known then by applying various factorization methods it is very easy to find prime factors of n, through which decryption key is easy to find [11].

4 Primality Testing

There are various tests which will give us result that whether the entered number is a prime number or not. Methods such as Fermat little's theorem, Miller Rabin, Solovay Strassan [2–6]. An old method of primality checking on the given number is trial and error method, where number "n" will be divided by all possible m from 2 to n, if n gets divided by m then the number is not prime number else number is a prime number [2–5].

Example:
n = 13 then **m** = 2, 3, …12

n mod m =?	13 mod 7 = 6
13 mod 2 = 1	13 mod 8 = 5
13 mod 3 = 1	13 mod 9 = 4
13 mod 4 = 1	13 mod 10 = 3
13 mod 5 = 3	13 mod 11 = 2
13 mod 6 = 1	13 mod 12 = 1

In this example, n is not divisible by all possible m up to $n - 1$. Hence we can say that the given number n is called a prime number. This method is very much time consuming and hence it is not used. Following are the algorithms/Methods which are mostly used to identify whether the entered number is prime or not.

i. **Fermat little theorem**

A different method is used to check primality of a given number is Fermat little theorem. According to Fermat's Little Theorem any number "p" who is prime and any number "a", where $p \nmid a$ (a is not divisible by p), $a^{p-1} = 1 \pmod{p}$ [4].

Example:
$a = 15$, $p = 37$

$a^{p-1} = 1 \pmod{p}$.
$15^{37-1} \bmod 37 = 1$ $1 = 1 \bmod p$
so, 37 is a prime number.

ii. **Solovay–Strassen Algorithm**

This algorithm is based on Monte Carlo algorithm with error probability at most of half. It uses Legendre Jacobi symbol $\left(\frac{a}{n}\right)$, where n is the odd composite number which can be factorized. Instead of factorizing, it can be solved by using some concepts of number theory and some other properties [3, 4].

Properties such as

a. Legendre's Symbol: This property will be applicable only if n is prime number.

$$\left(\frac{a}{n}\right) = 0, \text{ if } m = 0 \mod n$$
$$\left(\frac{a}{n}\right) = 1, \text{ if } x^2 \bmod n = m \text{ but } m \neq 0 \mod n \; (x \text{ is some value})$$
$$\left(\frac{a}{n}\right) = -1, \text{ otherwise}$$

b. Bimultiplicativity:

$$\left(\frac{m1m2}{n}\right) = \left(\frac{m1}{n}\right)\left(\frac{m2}{n}\right) \text{ or } \left(\frac{m}{n1n2}\right) = \left(\frac{m}{n1}\right)\left(\frac{m}{n2}\right)$$

c. Invariance:

$$\left(\frac{m}{n}\right) = \left(\frac{m \bmod n}{n}\right)$$

d. Reciprocity: If, m and n are both odd positive numbers then

$$\left(\frac{m}{n}\right) = -1^{(m-1)(n-1)/4}\left(\frac{n}{m}\right)$$

e. Special Values:

$$\left(\frac{2}{n}\right) = -1^{\left(n^2-1\right)/8}, \left(\frac{1}{n}\right) = 1, \left(\frac{0}{n}\right) = 0$$

f. Euler's Theorem: If n is prime number then for any m,

$$m^{(n-1)/2} = \left(\frac{m}{n}\right) \bmod n$$

Input: Take any odd number "n"
Output: Number is prime of Not

Step 1: pick a random integer **"a"**,
Where **a** ≥ 1 and $a \leq n - 1$.

Step 2: $z = \left(\frac{a}{n}\right)$ —by using Legendre Jacobi Symbol
if $z = 0$, then write ("Entered number is composite")

Step 3:

$$y = a^{(n-1)/2} \bmod n$$

If $z \equiv y \bmod n$
Then
Write ("Entered number n is prime")
Else
Write ("Entered number n is composite")

Example:
Say n = 367

Step 1: **a = 21 where a is 1 < 21 < 366**
Step 2: $x = \left(\frac{a}{n}\right) = \left(\frac{21}{367}\right)$

$$\left(\frac{21}{367}\right) = \left(\frac{7*3}{367}\right) = \left(\frac{7}{367}\right) * \left(\frac{3}{367}\right) --- \text{By Bimultiplicativity propety} \tag{1}$$

$$\begin{aligned}
\left(\frac{7}{367}\right) &= (-1)^{(7-1)*(367-1)/4}\left(\frac{367}{7}\right) --- \text{By Reciprocity property} \\
&= (-1)\left(\frac{367}{7}\right) = (-1)\left(\frac{367 \bmod 7}{7}\right) \\
&= (-1)(-1) = 1 -- \text{By Invariance Property and Euler's Theorm} \\
\left(\frac{3}{367}\right) &= (-1)^{(3-1)*(367-1)/4}\left(\frac{367}{3}\right) --- \text{By Bimultiplicativity property} \\
&= (-1)\left(\frac{367}{3}\right) \\
&= (-1)\left(\frac{367\, mod\, 3}{3}\right) --- \text{By Invariance property} \\
\left(\frac{1}{3}\right) &= (-1) -- \text{By Special value property} \\
&= (-1)(1) = (-1)
\end{aligned} \tag{2}$$

Putting above values in Eq. 1,

$$x = \left(\frac{21}{367}\right) = \left(\frac{7*3}{367}\right) = \left(\frac{7}{367}\right) * \left(\frac{3}{367}\right) = (1)(-1) = -1$$

$$x = -1$$

Step 3:

$$\begin{aligned} y &= a^{\frac{n-1}{2}} \bmod n \\ y &= 21^{\frac{367-1}{2}} \bmod 367 \\ y &= 366 \quad (\text{Which is equal to} -1 \bmod 367 = 366), \text{so} \\ y &= -1 \end{aligned} \tag{3}$$

from Eqs. 2 and 3

$$x \equiv y \bmod n$$

Hence, 367 is a prime number.

iii. **Miller–Rabin Algorithm**

Input: **Any odd number "n"**
Output: **Number is prime of Not**
Step 1: $n - 1 = 2^i j$, where n and j both are odd.
Pick a random number **k**, Where, $k \geq 1$ and $k \leq n - 1$.
Step 2: **Calculate** $l = ka^j \bmod n$ if $l \equiv 1 \bmod n$ then write("Entered number is prime")
Step 3: for $m = 0$ to $j - 1$
do $l \equiv -1 \bmod n$
Then return ("Entered number is prime")
Else
$l = l^2 \bmod n$
Step 4: Write ("Entered number is Composite")

Example:
n = 131

Step 1: $n - 1 = 131 - 1 = 130 = 2^1 * 65$, So $k = 1$ and $m = 65$. Consider $a = 40$ where $1 \leq 40 \leq 130$

Step 2: $b = a^m \bmod n = 40^{65} \bmod 131 = 130$

$b \equiv 1 \bmod 131$, hence go to next step

Step 3: **for i = 0 to 1**

$$b \equiv -1 \bmod n$$

$$130 \equiv -1 \bmod 131$$

$$130 \equiv 130 \quad ---\text{condition is true hence 131 is prime}$$

5 Prime Number Generation Algorithm

If we consider the example of RSA algorithm we can say that security of RSA completely depends on the two prime numbers, but is very difficult to find such strong prime numbers because if a prime number is week then the decryption key will easily break [11]. Similarly, there are various algorithms in cryptography which uses the prime number in the process of key generation. To avoid this difficult to find large or strong prime number, there are various prime number generation algorithms which gives a strong/large prime number as output [4, 12]. Algorithms such as a naive incremental generator, Random search for a prime Product of Primes, Modular search method, Williams–Schmidt algorithm for finding strong primes, Gordon's algorithm for finding strong primes, etc [3–10, 12]. If we discuss Gordon's algorithm for finding strong primes then the following algorithm and its output shows how it produces large and strong prime number from two small prime numbers [12].

Input: Two prime numbers q, r.
Output: a strong prime p is generated.

Step 1: Pick an integer j_0. Calculate and pick the first prime number in the sequence of $2 * j * r + 1$, Where, $j = j_0, j_0 + 1, j_0 + 2 \ldots$ Denote this prime by $s = 2 * j * r + 1$

Step 2: Calculate $l_0 = 2(q * s - 2 \bmod s)\, q - 1$.

Step 3: Pick an integer k_0. Calculate and discover the first prime number in the sequence $l_0 + 2k * s * q$,
Where $k = k_0, k_0 + 1, k_0 + 2 \ldots$
Symbolize this prime by $p = l_0 + 2 * k * s * q$.

Step 4: Write (p).

Example:

First prime number	Second prime number	Generated prime number
5	7	349
13	23	5641
157	163	557663
1511	1523	186832127
9941	9973	3034530013
10039	10753	1858419679
1435139	1255361	90549882804427
3413857	4281313	11418127264703807
7646137	8378239	27535998464638019

6 Integer Factorization Algorithms

It is easy to find Prime factors of a small number, such as 35 = 7 * 5, but the same task becomes difficult if we try on very large numbers. In public-key cryptography, it is very important to get prime numbers through factorization from a large composite number [4, 5, 8, 13–17]. Various algorithms are there which performs the task of finding prime factors of a large composite number, such as Number Field sieve, Quadratic sieve algorithm, Pollard P-1 algorithm, Pollard's rho algorithms, etc [3–5, 8, 16, 17]. We can get the original odd composite number by multiplying Prime factors with each other. Consider the following example Where, 8633 is an odd composite number and 89, 97 are two prime factors, By multiplying these two factors, we can get the original odd composite number, 89 * 97 = 8633.

Example: **8633 = 89 * 97,** Here **n** 8633, **p** 89 and **q** 97

i. **Pollard's rho algorithm**:

Integer factorization algorithms can be differentiated in two terms, Special-purpose algorithm and general purpose algorithm, Pollard's rho algorithm is an example of special-purpose factoring algorithm, which is used to find small prime factors of a composite integer. It is basically useful to find nontrivial factors [3, 4].

INPUT: Consider any odd composite integer **n**.
OUTPUT: a nontrivial factor *d*.

1. Consider two numbers *i* and *j*, where *i* = 2, *j* = 2.
2. For *k* = 1, 2, . . .do the following:

2.1 Calculate $i = i$^2 + 1 mod n,

$j = j$^2 + 1 mod n,
$j = j$^2 + 1 mod n.

2.2 Calculate d = GCD ($i - j$, n).
2.3 If d is greater than 1 but less than n, Write (p) and terminate with success. (Second factor can be calculated by using $d1 = (n/d)$)
2.4 If d is equal to n then terminate the algorithm with failure

Here, p and q are the smallest prime factors of n. This algorithm uses polynomial function f with integer coefficient, i.e., $f(x) = x2 + c$, Where c can be any value from 1 but not $c \neq 0, -2$ [3–5, 13–17].

Example:

Odd composite number	First factor	Second factor
143	11	13
259	7	37
1927	41	47
391883	67	5849

ii. **Pollard p-1 algorithm**:

This algorithm is an example of special-purpose factoring algorithm to find used to find prime factors p and q from odd composite integer n. It uses smoothness bound concept which is calculated by $\sqrt{n}+1$ [3–5, 13–17].

INPUT: Consider odd composite integer n.
OUTPUT: A nontrivial factor of d.

Step 1. Calculate smoothness bound B.
Step 2. Pick random integer s, Where $2 \leq s$ and $s \leq n - 1$, Compute $d = gcd(s, n)$. If $d \geq 2$ hen write (d is first factor).
Step 3. For each prime $t \leq B$ do the following:

3.1 Compute $l = \left|\frac{\ln n}{\ln t}\right|$
3.2 Compute $s \leftarrow s^{tl}$ mod n

Step 4. Compute $d = gcd(s - 1, n)$.
Step 5. If $d = 1$ or $d = n$, then terminate the algorithm with failure.

Else, Write (d is the first factor). (Second factor can be calculated by using $d1 = (n/d)$)

Example:

Odd composite number	First factor	Second factor
87	3	29
553	7	79
2253	3	751
112579	103	1093

7 Conclusion

Prime number is a very important concept in cryptography. Because of its various features, it is used in almost all well-known algorithms of cryptography such as RSA, Taher and ElGamal, Diffie–Hell key exchange algorithms, etc. Also, various algorithms are there to generate prime numbers such as Gordon's algorithm for finding strong primes and various algorithms to check its primality. This paper focuses on such algorithms with various examples and its use in various cryptographic techniques.

Book References

1. Menezes B. Network security and cryptography: Cengage Learning, India, 2010, 432
2. Bose R. Information theory, coding and cryptography 2008, Tata Mc Graw hill
3. Menezes AJ, van Oorschot PC, Vanstone SA (2001) Handbook of applied cryptography, CRC Press, London, Oct 1996, 816
4. Stinson DR (2006) Cryptography: theory and practice, 3rd edn. CRC Press, London

Journal References

5. Rivest R, Shamir A, Adleman L (1978) A method for obtaining digital signature and publickey cryptosystem communications. ACM 21:120–126
6. Crandall R, Pomerance C (2001) Prime numbers, a computational perspective. Springer, New York
7. Joye M, Paillier P, Vaudenay S (2000) Efficient generation of prime numbers?, Springer-Verlag, 1965:34–354
8. Rivest RL, Silvermany RD. Are strong primes needed for RSA?
9. Agrawal M, Kayal N, Saxena N. Primes is in p
10. Wagsta SS Jr (2014) Is there a shortage of primes for cryptography?, 2(IX), Sep 2014, IJARET
11. Sarnaik S, Gadekar D, Gaikwad U. An overview to integer factorization and RSA in cryptography
12. Saouter Y. A (1995) new method for the generation of strong prime numbers, RR-2657, INRIA

13. Galbraith SD (2012) Towards a rigorous analysis of Pollard Rho. Mathematics of public key cryptography. Cambridge University Press, Cambridge, pp 272–273, ISBN 9781107013926
14. Yan Y (2008) Integer factorization attacks. Cryptanalytic attacks on RSA, Springer-Verlag, US, 255
15. Abubakar A, Jabaka S, Tijjani BI (2014) Cryptanalytic attacks on Rivest, Shamir, and Adleman (RSA) cryptosystem: issues and challenges, JATIT, Mar 2014, 61(1):37–43
16. Hawana B (2013) An overview and cryptographic challenges of RSA. IJERMT
17. Chalurkar SN, Khochare N, Meshram BB (2011) Survey on modular attack on RSA algorithm, IJCEM, Vol 14, Oct 2011, 106–110

Steganography: A Survey

Shilpa Pund-Dange

Abstract Due to the popularity of Internet and communication media, data security is one of the most focused areas of research. Cryptography and steganography are two important disciplines in the area of security. Image steganography is one of the techniques used to hide data inside an innocent image so that it is not visible to an eavesdropper while communication. This is a very useful technique when we transmit data from sender side to the receiver side. Many steganographic methods are suggested by the researchers struggling for good embedding capabilities and imperceptibility. This paper describes a survey on various image steganography techniques in spatial domains with their strengths and weaknesses.

Keywords Steganography · Stego-image · Spatial · Transform

1 Introduction

In recent years, the security and confidentiality of sensitive data have become very important due to the fast growth of internet and communication technologies. Therefore, how to protect this secret data from the unauthenticated user during transmission become an important issue nowadays. The well-known techniques which are used to provide security are Cryptography and Steganography. Cryptography is often used to protect information secrecy making message scramble so that it cannot be understood. Steganography means hiding information in digital media such that no one should be aware of the existence of information.

S. Pund-Dange (✉)
Department of Computer Science, Modern College, Shivajinagar,
Pune 411005, India
e-mail: shilpashlok24@gmail.com

M. U. Bokhari et al. (eds.), *Cyber Security*, Advances in Intelligent Systems and Computing 729, https://doi.org/10.1007/978-981-10-8536-9_32

The components of a basic framework of Steganography are as follows:

1. Cover object
2. Stego key
3. Stego object.

The sender embeds the secret message into the cover object by using the stego key. The same stego key will be used at the receiver's end to extract the secret message.

2 Steganography Techniques

There are three different ways to hide a digital message in a digital cover.

Injection: In injection method, the secret message is directly embedded in the host medium. This increases the file size and hence sometimes the changes can be easily detectable.
Substitution: In this method, the actual data is substituted with the secret data. This creates a little change in the size of the cover object. However, the quality of the cover object can degrade depending on the type of cover object and the amount of data embedded.
Generation of New Files: In this method, a cover is specially generated for the purpose of concealing a secret message [1].

2.1 Types of Steganography

There are two basic types of Steganography:

Technical Steganography: Technical steganography uses special tools, devices, or scientific methods to hide a message. In technical Steganography, hiding places in the cover object are found out to embed the secret message. Various computer-based methods are used for embedding and extracting process.
Linguistic Steganography: Linguistic steganography is used to hide the message within the text in such a way that no one should aware of the presence of a secret message. It is not perceptible to the human eye.
Steganographic systems can be grouped by the type of covers used (text, image, audio, video, or executables) or by the techniques used (Fig. 1).

This paper focuses on image steganography. In this technique, pixel intensities are used to hide the information. Image steganography can be carried out by two techniques:

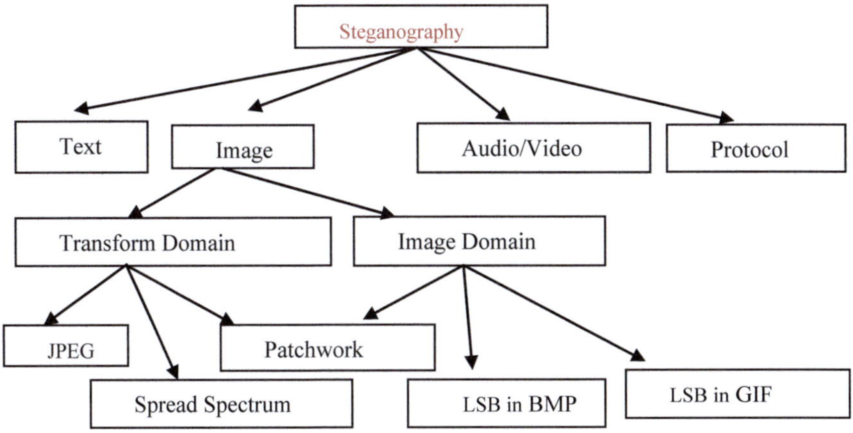

Fig. 1 Types of covers

1. Transform Domain (Steganography in the image frequency domain)
2. Image Domain (Steganography in the image Spatial Domain).

Here focus is on Spatial Domain Technique.

2.2 *Spatial Domain Methods*

There are many versions of spatial steganography. In all these methods, some of the bits in the image pixel values are directly changed for data hiding. Least significant bit (LSB) steganography is one of the simple techniques that hide a secret message in the least significant bit of the pixel value. As the only LSBs are changed, there is no distortion in the image and the change is not perceptible to the human eye. Some spatial domain methods are listed below:

1. Least significant bit (LSB)
2. Edges-based data embedding method (EBE)
3. Pixel value differencing method (PVD)
4. Pixel intensity-based method
5. BPCS steganography
6. Mapping pixel to hidden data method
7. Labeling or connectivity method
8. Random pixel embedding method (RPE)
9. Texture-based method
10. Histogram shifting methods [2, 3].

Generally, image steganography is categorized into the following aspects.

Capacity: Maximum data can be embedded into the image.
Imperceptibility: After embedding process, the perceptual quality of the stego-image will not be degraded.
Robustness: After embedding, even if an image undergoes different transformations like filtering, cropping, etc., still data should be intact.
Temper Resistance: Once the message has been embedded into stego-image, it should not be altered.
Computation Complexity: Computational cost for embedding and extracting a message must be less [2].

3 Literature Review

As the focus is on Spatial Domain Method, some of the methods are explained below:

In LSB method, a digital media like audio, video, or image, there is a large amount of space which we can use for steganography. Digital data consists of bytes. Each byte contains 8 bits. These 8 bits makes a color of a pixel. The MSB plays important role in the different shades of color. The LSBs have less impact on color. So if we make a change in the Least Significant Bit, it changes the value by +1 or −1 which is not perceptible to the human eye. So by taking the advantage of human perception, LSB steganography works.

For example, following is the bit representation of the digital cover

11000001 10010110 10000001 11001101 01101001 01110101 01001110 10100110

We want to embed a message which is a secret code, suppose 207. The binary representation of 207 is **11001111**.

Now by using the LSB method, the message is embedded as follows:

1100000***1*** 1001011***1*** 1000000***0*** 1100110***0*** 0110100***1*** 0111010***1*** 0100111***1*** 1010011***1***

To embed 8 bit of data we need to change only five bits. This change will create a very small or no noticeable difference in the cover image. Hence, if the digital cover is in several kilobytes or megabytes then we can embed huge amount of data within.

In Pixel Value Differencing (PVD) method [4], the cover images having the maximum intensity value 256. Two neighboring pixels $p1$ and $p2$ are read and the difference value d in between them is computed. The reading of two neighboring pixels of the cover image is carried out through each of the rows of the image in a zigzag manner. Let the gray values of two adjacent pixels are g_1 and g_2 then $d = g_2 - g_1$. Take the absolute value of d which may be in the range from 0 to 255.

All values of d are in the range 0–255 say D_i. The width of D_i is calculated which is always taken as a power of 2. The secret message is embedded according to the range of D_i and is replace with another difference value d. The difference 'n' between the old and the new difference values is calculated. And accordingly, the new pixel values are calculated as g_i-ceiling ($n/2$) and g_{i+1} +floor ($n/2$). The message bits are extracted by calculating the difference between the new difference value and the lower bound of the range block.

In ELSB [5], all the edge pixels in an image are used. Here, the masked image is created by masking two LSBs in the cover image. Then, find out the edge pixels by using the Canny Edge detection method and then hide the secret message in the LSBs of the edge pixel. In this way, the stego-image is formed.

At the receiver, the stego-image is again masked as the same. Then by using canny edge detector, the edge pixels are identified. We will get same edge pixels. The secret message is extracted from the two LSB bits of the identified edge pixels.

BPCS [6, 7] by Eason, overcomes the limitations of LSB technique. As compared to the above techniques, BPCS Steganography has very large embedding capacity. In LSB technique, data is embedded in LSBs. But in BPCS technique data can be embedded in planes in the complex region.

An image consisting of n-bit pixels. Convert all pixel intensity values in binary. If $n = 8$, then every pixel is 8 bits. Then decomposed the image horizontally into 8-bit planes. Therefore, img = [PL7 PL6 PL5 PL4 PL3 PL2 PL1 PL0] where PL7 is the Most Significant Bitplane and PL0 is the Least Significant Bitplane. For each bit plane, the complexity of the image is determined. Accordingly, an image is segmented into the informative region and noise-like region. An informative region is having a simple pattern while noise-like region having a complex pattern. Here, data embedding takes place in the noise-like region. Thus, BPCS steganography is not perceptible to the human vision system.

Pixel Intensity Based method [8], uses 24-bit RGB image. So, Three pixels (Red = 255, Green = 255 and Blue = 0) are generating Yellow color. If we change (Blue = 16) still it generates Yellow color. If both yellow colors are comparing, both have almost the same visibility. So, the idea is that if we change the lower intensity pixel value it has less visual degradation quality effects. So here we can use 4 LSBs for data embedding.

4 Observations

LSB method

- LSB work well with grayscale as well as color image.
- LSB method is easy for implementation.
- Changes in the image are not perceptible to the human eye.
- But once notice suspicious, easy to crack the message.

Pixel Value Differencing Method

- A little distortion is possible at the edges of the image.
- At the time of extraction, there is no need referencing a cover image.
- Only grayscale images are used for the experiment.
- The method is using an indexing technique on the pixel difference values *d*.
- If the range widths are from 8 to 128 with the power of 2, then the embedding capacity is more. If the range widths are from 2 to 64 with the power of 2, then the embedding capacity is less.
- The value of PSNR (peak Signal-to-Noise ratio) is less for the range widths 8–128 whereas it is more for the range widths 2–64.
- The value of RMSE (root mean square error) is more for the range widths 8–128 whereas it is less for the range widths 2–64.
- The method is easy to implement.
- But if the image undergoes any transformation like cropping, then the bits of the secret message is lost.

ELSB Method

- It is an improvement over LSB method. In LSB bits are hidden in each and every pixel of the image. Once it observes suspicious, the message can crack easily. Hence in ELSB, secret data gets embedded on the edge pixels.
- Only grayscale images are used for the experiment.
- The change in the image is not perceptible to the human eye.
- But the data hiding capacity is less as compare to LSB.

BPCS

- Very large data hiding capacity.
- Image quality is maintained. The changes in the images are not perceptible to the human eye.
- Once the data is embedded, it is difficult to alter.
- But the computational cost is more.

Pixel Intensity-Based method

- All bytes of the cover image is used for data hiding.
- The data hiding capacity is large.
- It works for the color images.

5 Conclusions and Future Work

This paper describes different techniques and types of steganography. Also, it gives a survey on different steganographic methods for the image in spatial domain with some observations and limitations. The next plan is to develop a hybrid steganographic method using the existing methods or a new one which satisfies steganography aspects mentioned above.

References

1. Kipper G (2003) Investigator's guide to steganography. crc press
2. Hussain M, Hussain M (2013) A survey of image steganography techniques. Int J Adv Sci Technol 54
3. Kale P, Bartere M (2015) A survey on image steganography technique. Int J Pure Appl Res Eng Technol 3(9):143–152
4. Wu DC, Tsai WH (2003) A steganographic method for images by pixel-value differencing. Pattern Recogn Lett 24(9–10):1613–1626, Elsevier
5. BrahmaTeja KN, Madhumati GL, Rao KRK (2012) Data hiding using EDGE based steganography. Int J Emerg Technol Adv Eng 2(11). Website: www.ijetae.com. ISSN 2250-2459
6. Eason RO, Kawaguchi E (1998) Principle and applications of BPCS steganography. Proc SPIE 3528:464–473
7. Bhattacharyya S, Khan A, Nandi A, Dasmalakar A, Roy S, Sanyal G (2011) Pixel mapping method (PMM) based bit plane complexity segmentation (BPCS) steganography. In: 2011 world congress on information and communication technologies, IEEE
8. Hussain M, Hussa M (2010) Pixel intensity based high capacity data embedding method 978-1-4244-8003-6/10 ©2010 IEEE

Author Biography

Shilpa Pund-Dange is basically a science graduate and completes her Masters of Computer Application from Amravati University, Amravati, Maharashtra in 2000, perusing Ph.D. From SSPU, Pune. She has total experience of 15 years. Presently she is working as Assistant Professor, Dept of Comp. Science at Modern College of Arts, Science and Commerce, Shivajinagar, Pune-5, Maharashtra. Her research area includes network security, Cryptography, Steganography.

Comprehensive Methodology for Threat Identification and Vulnerability Assessment in Ad hoc Networks

Richa Tyagi, Naveen Kumar Sharma, Kamini Malhotra and Anu Khosla

Abstract Ad hoc networks are self-configuring wireless networks without any centralized management. These days, such networks are useful in military application owing to the ease of deployment. The inherent characteristics of these networks introduce new security threats and vulnerabilities that lead to more security attacks as compared to wired and wireless infrastructure networks. For threat identification, a hybrid threat identification methodology is proposed which combines the "Asset centric and Attacker centric" approaches. It takes into account the critical assets present in the network and the adversary capability required for compromising these assets. Further, a vulnerability assessment methodology is proposed under which the network vulnerabilities are analyzed at different levels—Host, Routing Protocol, Node Behavior, and Crypto Algorithms. The proposed methodology has been examined using two different types of scenario-emulated network and real network.

Keywords Threat model · Vulnerability assessment · Malicious node
Asset- and attacker-centric model · Black hole · Wormhole

R. Tyagi (✉) · N. K. Sharma · K. Malhotra · A. Khosla
SAG, DRDO, Metcalfe House, New Delhi, India
e-mail: richa.drdo@yahoo.co.in

N. K. Sharma
e-mail: nksharma97@gmail.com

K. Malhotra
e-mail: kaminimalhotra@sag.drdo.in

A. Khosla
e-mail: akhosla@sag.drdo.in

M. U. Bokhari et al. (eds.), *Cyber Security*, Advances in Intelligent Systems and Computing 729, https://doi.org/10.1007/978-981-10-8536-9_33

1 Introduction

Ad hoc networking [1, 2] is one of the emerging areas of research in wireless communication. Such a network is a collection of wireless nodes (or routers), dynamically forming a temporary network without any centralized administration. The network has a dynamic topology that may change rapidly and unpredictably. The network may operate in a standalone fashion or may connect to infrastructured wireless or wired network.

These networks have inherently very different properties as compared to conventional wired and wireless infrastructure networks. Features like auto-configuration and adaptivity make them highly useful for communicating in environments where no previous infrastructure exists in a cost-effective way. These existing features of the ad hoc networks are essential in several communication situations like military operations, disaster recovery operations, and networking of sensors deployed in remote areas.

Owing to the unique characteristics of these networks, there exist numbers of security risks that make the security design of these networks very challenging [2]. While designing a security solution for these networks, it is essential to assess all the threats and vulnerabilities existing in such networks so as to mitigate them effectively [3–8]. In this paper, a comprehensive methodology is proposed for threat identification and vulnerability assessment to make the existing network less prone to attacks and security breaches.

Section 2 covers the methodology developed for Threat identification in ad hoc networks under three categories: Host, Network, and Application Services. Section 3 describes the methodology for Vulnerability Assessment of ad hoc networks. Finally, Sect. 4 presents the conclusion based on the proposed work and some directions for future research.

2 Threats in Ad hoc Networks

Threat to a network is any potentially malicious occurrence that can disrupt the operation, functioning, integrity, or availability of the network or system [1, 7, 8].

There are three general approaches to threat identification: (a) **Attacker-Centric** approach views it from an attacker's point of view–their goals, motivations, and how they might achieve them; (b) **Design-centric** approach starts from the design of the system looking for types of attacks against each element (c) **Asset-Centric** approach starts from assets entrusted to a system [9].

Ad hoc networks require customized threat model in contrast to threat model of traditional networks. Therefore a hybrid threat identification methodology was developed which combines the '*Asset centric and Attacker centric*' approaches that take into account the critical assets present in the network and the capabilities of the adversary required to compromise these assets.

2.1 Critical Assets in Ad hoc Networks

Ad hoc network deployment and functioning require a set of resources that are shared among nodes. These can be described as assets. Although the network has a number of assets, only those critical assets have been chosen that are fully owned by the ad hoc layer [10] and are discussed below.

(a) **Algorithm Processing**: These are resources deployed in a node for calculating, maintaining, and processing ad hoc networking.
(b) **Algorithm Storage**: The space required to store algorithms for the node that are loaded on booting time or on request.
(c) **Network and User Information**: This refers to information shared between nodes to aid in routing and contains information such as node location, power availability, node speed, direction, radio profiles, user profiles, etc. This also includes the information about the routing tables stored on a node.
(d) **Network Topology and Node Roles**: This refers to information about the topology of a network, its behavior, and function of individual nodes and their routing loads.
(e) **Payload Messages**: These are messages containing the control information and user data which is carried on behalf of an application.
(f) **Routing Messages**: These are route discovery, update, and reporting messages that are critical for an ad hoc network to successfully maintain connectivity and routing capabilities.

2.2 Adversary's Capabilities in Ad hoc Networks

As the physical layer is wireless in ad hoc network, the adversary can exploit it in many ways and disrupt the network functions [6–8]. The adversary's capabilities can be characterized as

(a) **Passive and Active**: A *passive* adversary listens and records all the messages including the routing updates in an unauthorized way. This information can be used for traffic analysis. An *active* adversary prefers to interfere in some way, e.g., by modulating packet, forwarding, injecting, replaying packets, etc.
(b) **External and Internal**: An *external* adversary carries out attacks by nodes that do not belong to the network. It causes congestion, sends false routing information or unavailability of services. An *internal* adversary mounts attacks as compromised nodes that are part of the network.
(c) **Static and Mobile**: A *static* adversary has the capability to set the corrupted nodes only once. A *mobile* adversary has the capability to change the set of corrupted nodes from period to period.

(d) **Computational Bounded and Computational Unbounded**: In the *computational bounded* environment, an adversary mounts limited traffic analysis and break weak cryptographic algorithms easily. In *computational unbounded* environment, eavesdrop traffic is relayed back to high-performance supercomputing network for analysis and mounting further attacks even on strong crypto algorithms.
(e) **Byzantine**: In *Byzantine* scenario, an adversary compromises intermediate node or a set of intermediate nodes that work in collusion and carry out attacks such as creating routing loops, routing packets on non-optimal paths and selectively dropping packets.
(f) **Deployment Capability**: It describes the capability of an adversary to deploy single or multiple and external or internal compromised nodes that can achieve a degree of physical to the network under attack.

These attributes can be used in combination, e.g., attacker may be active, internal, and mobile.

2.3 *Threat Identification*

In the proposed solution, threats have been categorized under following three categories:

(i) *Host-based threats*, (ii) *Network-based threats*, (iii) *Application-based threats*.

And for each category threat identification was carried out taking into account the targeted assets and required attacker's capabilities [11]. The security parameter breach by the adversary has also been considered.

The first step of the methodology was to classify critical assets under these three categories. Table 1 categorizes the assets of ad hoc network.

The developed threat identification method was applied to each category. It gives a list of threats and possible attacks under individual threat, the impact of the threat on the critical assets, attributes of the adversary's capability required for specific threat and security parameter breached by the adversary. Threats against network-based assets are described in Table 2. The major threats affecting the network are Eavesdropping, Manipulation of data packets, Routing protocols threat, Misdirecting traffic, DoS, and Masquerading.

Threats against Host-based assets are described in Table 3. The major threats affecting the hosts are DoS, Modification, and Information leakage. Threats against Application-based assets are described in Table 4. The major threats affecting the applications are Manipulation of application protocols and services, DoS and Repudiation of Services.

Table 1 Critical assets classified under three categories

SI	Host systems	Network components	Applications
1	**Algorithm processing** (Resources required by each host to communicate in ad hoc mode)	**Algorithm processing** (Resources required by a network to calculate, process and maintain routing)	**Algorithm processing** (Resources required to run the applications)
2	**Algorithm storage** (Storage required by each host to load algorithms on boot or communication time)	**Network topology and node roles** (Topology of a network and its behavior and functions)	**Algorithm storage** (Storage required to run application services)
3	**Network and user information** (Information about host location and its profile, power availability, speed, and direction)	**Payload messages** (Control information data propagating in the network)	**Network topology and node roles** (Topology of a network and services running on the nodes)
4	**Payload messages** (User data propagating between host systems)	**Routing messages** (Maintaining and updating routing fields and connectivity)	**Payload messages** (Custom applications and Security-Related applications data)

Table 2 Threats against network-based assets

Threat's name and possible attacks	Critical assets affected and threat's description	Attributes of adversary's capability required	Security parameter breached
Eavesdropping	**Network topology and node roles**: Unauthorized nodes gather routing messages to extract worthwhile information from unencrypted or weakly encrypted data	Passive, external, static, computational bounded/ unbounded, deployment capability	Confidentiality Anonymity
Manipulation of data packets	**Payload messages and routing messages**: Malicious modification and replay of routing data packets possible	Active, external/internal, static/mobile, deployment capability	Integrity

(continued)

Table 2 (continued)

Threat's name and possible attacks	Critical assets affected and threat's description	Attributes of adversary's capability required	Security parameter breached
Routing protocol threats (i) Routing table (RT) overflow (ii) RT poisoning (iii) Packet replication (iv) Route cache poisoning (v) Rushing attack	**Routing messages**: Aim to disrupting the operation of the network by modifying routing information (i) Adversary advertises routes and prevents creation of new routes to authorized node (ii) Compromised nodes send fictitious routing updates (iii) Adversary node replicates stale packets (iv) Poison the route cache (v) Adversary rapidly spreads routing message in the network. In each route discovery, acts as one of the intermediate node	Active, external/internal, static/mobile, deployment capability	Availability integrity
Misdirecting traffic (i) Black hole (ii) Gray hole (iii) Wormhole (iv) Byzantine	**Routing messages & payload messages**: Redirect traffic to a different destination (i) A malicious node falsely advertises good path then intercepts and discards all packets (ii) A malicious node has the ability to forward some routing packets and discard others (iii) A tunnel is generated between two colluding attackers and redirects the traffic through this (iv) Set of compromising nodes works in collusion to create routing loops, nonoptimal routing paths and dropping packets	Active, internal, static/mobile, computational bounded/unbounded, Byzantine, deployment capability	Integrity Availability
Denial of service (i) Jamming (ii) Flooding	**Algorithm processing and network topology and node roles**: Adversary attempts to	Active, external/internal, static/mobile, deployment capability	Availability

(continued)

Table 2 (continued)

Threat's name and possible attacks	Critical assets affected and threat's description	Attributes of adversary's capability required	Security parameter breached
(iii) Distributed DoS	prevent legitimate users to access network services (i) Adversary transmits high power signal of same frequency at which node is receiving signal (ii) Adversary floods the network with false routing messages (iii) Several adversaries that are distributed throughout the network collude and prevent legitimate user from accessing the services		
Masquerade (i) Spoofing (IP, MAC) (ii) Sybil (iii) Session hijacking	**Network topology and node roles**: Adversary assumes the identity and privileges of an authorized node (i) Adversary modifies address information in packets and adopts an authenticated identity in the network (ii) Adversary represents multiple false identities (iii) Adversary takes control over a session between nodes	Active, external/internal, static/mobile, deployment capability	Authentication Confidentiality Integrity Anonymity

Table 3 Threats against host-based assets

Threat's name and possible attacks	Critical assets affected and threat's description	Attributes of adversary's capability required	Security parameter breached
DOS Physical destruction, environmental attacks (heat, RF, power, and other resources attack)	**(i) Algorithm processing**: The resources required for operation/processing of a node may not be available **(ii) Payload messages**: Nodes may not be able to participate in communication	Active, external/internal, static/mobile, byzantine, deployment capability	Availability

(continued)

Table 3 (continued)

Threat's name and possible attacks	Critical assets affected and threat's description	Attributes of adversary's capability required	Security parameter breached
Modification Data corruption, node malfunction, node replication	**(i) Algorithm storage**: Algorithms may be read or altered at the node's storage **(ii) Network and user information**: nodes or user specific information might be modified	Active, external/ internal, deployment capability	Integrity Authenticity Confidentiality Anonymity
Information leakage Traffic monitoring and analysis	**(i) Network and user information**: Node or user specific information might be readable **(ii) Payload messages**: Unauthorized capture of transmitted data might be possible	Passive, external, static, computational bounded/ unbounded, deployment capability	Confidentiality Anonymity

Table 4 Threats against application-based assets

Threat's name and possible attacks	Critical assets affected and threat's description	Attributes of adversary's capability required	Security parameter breached
Manipulation of application protocol in direct and covert communication	**Payload messages**: Compromised application protocols and leak or modify sensitive information	Active, external/ internal, deployment capability	Confidentiality Integrity
Side channel leakage	**Network topology and node roles**: Side channels may be used by clients to infer about network communication	Passive, external/internal, deployment capability	Confidentiality
Manipulation in time services	**Payload messages**: Actively insert the jitter in security protocol and other services	Active, internal	Integrity
Manipulation in security-related services (i) Reputation-based approach	**Network topology and node roles and payload messages**: Set of compromised nodes communicating misleading information	Active, internal, Byzantine, deployment capability	Availability Integrity

(continued)

Table 4 (continued)

Threat's name and possible attacks	Critical assets affected and threat's description	Attributes of adversary's capability required	Security parameter breached
(ii) Environmental (iii) Service collusion threat	(i) In this approach, collusion by set of nodes to isolate a target (ii) In distributing sensing services, environmental corruption of the sensed information may prompt the derivation of a misleading inference (iii) Set of nodes compromised and gives misleading information to services (sensing)		
Denial of service (i) Resilience thrashing (ii) Resources consumption (buffer limit, computational power)	**Network topology and node roles, algorithm processing, and storage**: Services running at node may be subjected to DoS attack (i) In resilience services, MANETs should be dynamically reconfigurable and services may be dynamically relocated. By clever manipulation, adversary causes a system to repeatedly reconfigure (ii) Adversary needs to send appropriately timed requests to deny service availability to legitimate users. It also sends service requests that are highly computationally intensive	Active, external/internal, mobile, deployment capability	Availability
Repudiation of a service	**Payload messages**: Denial of service by an adversary node involved in communication	Active, external/internal	Non-repudiation

3 Vulnerabilities of Ad hoc Networks

Vulnerability is an inherent weakness in design, configuration, or implementation of a network or system that renders it susceptible to an attack. Ad hoc networks are more vulnerable than wired and wireless infrastructure networks due to their inherent characteristics of (i) Sharing broadcast wireless channel, (ii) No central controlling infrastructure, (iii) Absence of authentication mechanism, (iv) Insecure operational environment, (v) Resources constraint, (vi) Node as router, (vii) dynamic network topology, and (vii) Scalability [1, 2]. These characteristics introduce several vulnerabilities which can be exploited by an adversary.

In addition to these vulnerabilities, the network also share the vulnerabilities of wired and wireless infrastructure network, such as (i) Analysis of message flow, (ii) Hijacking of medium or network connection, (iii) Manipulation of data, (iv) Masquerading, (v) Flooding of data, etc., to be enumerated. Because of these additional vulnerabilities, they are more prone to security attacks. Many existing security solutions for conventional networks are ineffective and inefficient for this environment. Consequently, researchers have been working in the past decade on developing new security solutions or changing current ones to be applicable to ad hoc networks [4–6, 12–16].

To develop a methodology to assess the vulnerabilities of these networks, it is important to understand the nature of these vulnerabilities and subsequent security risks they pose.

3.1 Proposed Methodology for Vulnerability Assessment

To assess vulnerabilities in large-scale networks two different network scenarios were considered:

1. Nodes were connected directly without access point in ad hoc mode using 802.11 (WiFi) technologies and kept 30 m apart.
2. Ad hoc network was emulated using EXata Cyber Software with four real nodes mapped to simulated nodes.

Vulnerabilities were analyzed at the following levels:

(i) *Vulnerability of Host*, (ii) *Vulnerability of Routing Protocol*, (iii) *Vulnerability of a node becoming malicious*, (iv) *Vulnerability of Crypto Algorithm.*

3.1.1 Vulnerability of Host

Host system vulnerabilities arise due to implementation gaps in OS, misconfigurations of OS/Applications, open vulnerable services and ports. Vulnerability scanning tool, 'Nessus' was used to scan the vulnerabilities present in each node or host. Host-based scanning provided information about a total number of hosts connected to the network, open default ports, and services running on those ports, operating systems of the host and presence of firewall if any. A report containing a list of vulnerabilities, criticality of vulnerability, and multiple numbers of solutions to mitigate that particular vulnerability is compiled. These vulnerabilities can lead to DoS, Unauthorized access, and Unauthorized acquisition of system attacks.

3.1.2 Vulnerability of Routing Protocol

One of the major sources of vulnerabilities in ad hoc networks is the routing protocol, which may be exploited by malicious nodes to disrupt the normal routing behavior. A variety of routing protocols have been developed but many of these proposed routing protocols have inherent security flaws. The proposed methodology depends on the various fields of the routing protocol. Vulnerabilities of the two most commonly used unsecured routing protocols, Dynamic Source Routing protocol (DSR), and Ad hoc On-Demand Distance Vector Routing protocol (AODV) were assessed. The manipulation of the following features leads to vulnerabilities:

(i) Modification in fields of routing protocol—Modify RREQ or RREP packets to cause DoS, Generate false RRER packets to increase routing delay, Modify hop count and distance sequence to redirect traffic.
(ii) Impersonations of network IP address posing as a legitimate node thus redirecting or dropping the packets.
(iii) Flooding of routing packets to disrupt the normal routing behavior.
(iv) Eavesdropping and manipulation of routing information easily due to wireless broadcast communication.
(v) Host vulnerabilities affecting routing protocols.

These vulnerabilities may lead to Black hole, Gray hole, Information disclosure, DoS, Snooping, Manipulation of network traffic, and Routing attacks.

To assess the Routing Protocol vulnerability, the Wireshark Packet sniffer tool was used to find out the details of routing protocol, routing packets, and data packets that were present during transmission in the given ad hoc network. Routing data packets and its fields' information (number of Route Request packets, Route Reply packets, Route Error packets, hop count, destination sequence number, etc.) were collected using sniffers for analysis.

3.1.3 Vulnerability of a Node becoming Malicious

The possibility of a node becoming malicious is very high and is the second major source of vulnerability in the ad hoc networks. A node can become malicious when it breaches any of the security principles and start behaving in one or more of the following ways:

(i) A node drops the packet fully or partly.
(ii) A node wastes the battery, storage, and bandwidth by performing unnecessary operations.

(iii) A node becomes a part of the network without authentication and starts disrupting the normal behavior of the network.
(iv) A node starts injecting stale packets and creates confusion in the network.

These vulnerabilities lead to Wormhole, Byzantine, Resource consumption, Impersonation, Session Hijacking, and DoS attacks.

3.1.4 Vulnerability of Crypto Algorithm

Crypto algorithm forms the core of security in ad hoc networks. The security parameters—authentication, confidentiality, and integrity of data should be taken care during design of the network. The strength of the cryptographic algorithms used should be high and match with the level of secrecy required in communication. Inappropriate and weak crypto algorithms can be exploited by an adversary to compromise a node or data and routing protocol communication and become a source of vulnerability. These vulnerabilities lead to unauthorized access to the network, system, and data and cause message tampering, stealing information, and DoS attacks.

4 Conclusion

In this paper, a comprehensive methodology for threat identification and vulnerability assessment is presented. For threat identification, a hybrid methodology based on Asset-centric and Attacker-centric approaches is proposed which followed by the proposed vulnerability assessment methodology, which analyzes the vulnerabilities at four levels: Host, Routing Protocol, Node Behavior, and Crypto Algorithms. To mitigate these vulnerabilities several security solutions for ad hoc networks have been proposed in the literature. The host-specific vulnerabilities can be mitigated using cryptographic techniques like Password-Based Group Systems and Threshold Cryptography. Similarly, the ad hoc routing protocols vulnerabilities can be avoided by using security aware routing protocols. Detection of malicious nodes is possible by using Wireless Intrusion Detection System (WIDS). Security in ad hoc networks is a very complex and challenging task and the methodology proposed will help in further development of security solutions.

References

1. Murthy CSR, Manoj BS (2004) Ad hoc wireless networks architectures and protocols. Published byPearson Education (ISBN 81-297-0945-7)
2. Sarkar SK, Basavaraju TG, Puttamadappa C (2008) Ad hoc mobile wireless networks principles, protocols, and applications, 22. Aurebach Publications, Taylor & Francis Group

3. Sen S, Clark JA, Tapiador JE (2010) Security threats in mobile ad hoc networks. J Dept Comput Sci, Univ. of York, UK, 32
4. Goyal P, Parmar V, Rishi R (2011) MANET: vulnerabilities, challenges, attacks, application. JCEM, 11:32–37
5. Sangwan S, Jangra A, Goel N (2011) Vulnerabilities and solutions: mobile ad hoc networks for optimal routing and security. J GRCS 2(5):8–12
6. Yau P-W, Mitchell CJ (2003) Security vulnerabilities in ad hoc networks: research programme of the virtual centre of excellence in mobile & personal communication. In: Proceeding of the 7th ISCTA, 99–104
7. Spiewak D, Engel T, Fusenig V (2006) Towards a threat model for mobile ad hoc networks. In: Proceeding of the 5th international conference on information security and privacy, 35–40
8. Clark JA, Murdoch J, McDermid JA, Sen S, Chivers HR, Worthington O, Rohatgi P (2007) Threat modelling for mobile ad hoc and sensor networks. In: ITA conference
9. Information Security Provider and Research Centre (2011) Threat modelling. www.Praetorian.com
10. Martin A (2006) A platform independent risk analysis for mobile ad hoc networks. In: Boston university conference on information assurance and cyber security
11. Chidambaram V (2004) Threat modelling in enterprise architecture integration. SETLabs briefings. EABC 2(4)
12. Saini R, Khari, M (2011) Defining malicious behavior of a node and its defensive methods in ad hoc networks. JCA, 20(4)
13. Chayal D, Rathore VS (2011) Assessment of security in mobile ad hoc networks (MANET). J GlobResComp Sci, 2(6)
14. Kayarkar H (2012) A survey on security issues in ad hoc routing protocols and their mitigation technequies. Int. J. Adv Netw Appl 03(05):1338–1351
15. Sen S, Clark JA (2007) Intrusion detection in mobile ad hoc networks: In guide to wireless ad hoc network. InGuide to Wireless Ad Hoc Networks, 53:427–454. Springer Publication, London
16. Marti S, Giuli TJ (2000) Mitigating routing misbehaviour in mobile ad hoc networks. In: Proceedings of the 6th ACM international conference on mobile computing and networking (MobiCom), pp 255–265

Hardware Trojans: An Austere Menace Ahead

Anupam Tiwari and Chetan Soni

Abstract Hardware Trojans, a relatively unheard threat viz-a-viz the typical software-based malwares and virus attacks that keep betiding across is being realized gradually by the IT security domain including the users, the IT Security professionals, and the corporate sector who all of a sudden discern the immense threat they might already be living in with. A distinctive dormant Hardware Trojan threat can be so flagitious that the victim does not even know if he is effectuated when he might already be. Hardware Trojans are evolving threats that can shake the roots of any set and constituted government or corporate giant for that matter. Unlike Software virus/malware threats, Hardware Trojans are pertinacious in nature. This paper brings out an overview of these threats including classifications, mechanisms they work on and the current set of countermeasures being researched upon.

Keywords Integrated circuits · Hardware · Trojans · Threats · Networking threats IC fabrication · Backdoors · System on chip · Trojan side channel

1 Introduction

We all are purview to the City of Troy story wherein few hundred years back, Greek soldiers undertook many attempts but unsuccessfully to capture the city of Troy. Eventually, they departed, leaving behind a large wooden horse, ostensibly as a gift. The citizens of Troy were too happy to accept the wooden horse but as it had to come about; a group of Greek soldiers came out of the horse late night handily and opened the gates for their paisanos, who easily dismissed the quiescent city.

A. Tiwari (✉) · C. Soni
National Informatics Centre, Ministry of Defense, New Delhi, India
e-mail: anupam.tiwari@nic.in

C. Soni
e-mail: chetan.soni@nic.in

M. U. Bokhari et al. (eds.), *Cyber Security*, Advances in Intelligent Systems and Computing 729, https://doi.org/10.1007/978-981-10-8536-9_34

Come to present, Trojan [1] as a term today is synonymous more with the IT Security incidents that have seen a phenomenal increase over a decade. For over a decade now, the IT Security domain loyalists have dedicated their energies, resources, domain knowledge, brainstorming sessions and investments into ensuring that the security is ensured for the user. And so the market today got an overplus of options too, viz., antivirus solutions, Firewalls, Internet Security Editions, UTMs, and the list goes on. These may be different technically in operating but there is one common thing in all these options that they all have a mechanism to detect the threats which are all software based. They have no way, no mechanism to thwart, or even think to detect a threat which is embedded deep inside the IC hardware. A threat is so obliterated to be seen, so unthinkable that for the panic struck solution providers it is like where to start from? How to do? What to do?

2 Defining Hardware Trojan

A Hardware Trojan [2] is a designed alteration of an IC ensuing in the undesired conduct of an electronic device when desired to be in operation with a malicious intent without the knowledge of the user. This undesired conduct in the IC may take any of the forms, viz., Logic Modification which might involve placing an additional logic gate with an optional activation programmed to give unlooked-for output signal leading to overall error result or it can be an Electrical modification that would falsify the timing characteristics of IC by doing Extra capacitive loading on a circuit path.

2.1 Hardware Trojans: Origin and Penetration

Hardware Trojan came into being primarily imputed to outsourcing the fabrication and design to third parties attributed to the huge scales of requirements and economies involved. Now, this small modification can be in place anywhere of a corporate house infrastructure, household chores appliances, or even military and defense COTS equipment.

2.2 Hardware Trojan Security Significations

The austere consequences of Hardware Trojans are well left to the imagination of what holds on to be excluded today in the increasing scenario where dependence on IC and SoC is only increasing. The key heads affected and vulnerable to such attacks may include Logistics Systems and Support domain, viz., Transport infrastructure, Traffic Control, Metro/Rail monitoring and control, Civil critical applications, viz., Banking, Stock market IT infrastructure, Military Systems viz Weapon control systems, Satellite controls, Radar systems, Surveillance Systems, Decision support systems, Aviation and Aeronautics industry or Miscellaneous domains like Data centers IT infrastructure, Personal info stored in Clouds, Government systems in critical setups, etc.

2.3 Hardware Versus Software Trojans

As brought out from the above about HT, the comparison between severity viz-a-viz Software Trojans allows HT to take leaps out-front lead. It empathizes that the software threats that exist with us over decades now are yet to get a stable and an assured solution by any means and this HT threat has just arrived in the fora. A mini comparison [3] between the two is bought out in the figure below:

Attribute	Hardware Trojans	Software Trojans
Agency involved infecting	Prefabrication embedding in the hardware IC during manufacturing or retrofitted later	Resides in code of the OS or in the running applications and gets activated whilst execution
Mode	Third-party untrusted agencies involved to manufacture ICs in various stages of fabrication	Downloading malicious files from the Internet or via social engineering methods executing malicious files or commonly sources USB, etc.
Current Remedial measure available	Currently none, since once embedded there is no way to remove the same other than destroying	Signatures released by antivirus companies and software patches based on behavioral pattern observed

3 Hardware Trojan Systematics

A hardware Trojan to operate needs ground and power supply which can be low or high depending on the design it is based on. A Trojan that requires a low-end power supply will have low chances of being detected whereas a Trojan requiring higher power supply would invariably be at a larger chance of detection by a sensor if placed. Hardware Trojans have a range of classification based on various characteristics and modes they work in. The classification keeps on evolving as more newfangled approaches and dimensions of attacks are detected. A form of classification based on the activation mechanism of triggering the attack that can be Digital or Analog. Analog will typically get activated based on any analog input type like Temperature, Pressure, time-lag etc. whereas digital will be based on some kind of Boolean logic function [4] has classified the same in another manner as shown in Fig. 1. The classifications as shown are to some degree perceivable by

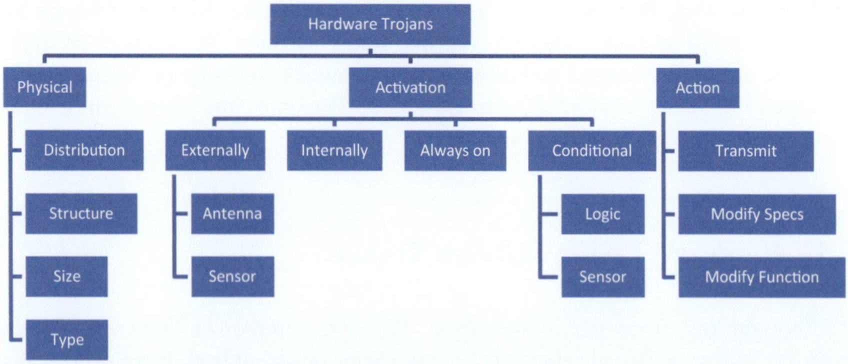

Fig. 1 Taxonomy of Hardware Trojans [1]

their names and depict a very basic and broad classification of the HTs. Another classification [5] divides Hardware Trojans into two types that include Parasite-Based HTs and Bug-based HTs. A parasite based HT hides in the original circuit without altering it and is not involved to lose any set and defined functionalities in the circuit whereas a Bug-based HT not only alters the circuit but also causes it to lose its set and configured functionalities. Of the two parasites HTs become more difficult to be detected through owing to hidden nature and is actually untraceable in specified specs as well as testing.

4 Nemesis Framework

Hardware Trojans insertion would actually gain a large mileage and suit to bestow maximum scathe in a typical supply chain which essentially consists of unalike and miscellanea of insertion points. Hardware Trojan-infected hardware would be more apt for a larger organization and a huge victim base since it will allow a deeper penetration in terms of the scale of victims.

4.1 Hardware Trojan Structure and Mechanics

A typical HT will have primarily two components including a Trigger and a Payload [6]. The trigger part is used to set off the malicious action while the payload is the malicious part that really accomplishes the vicious action. Before a triggering action takes place in an IC, the Hardware Trojan lies peacefully abeyant without any activity and pings anywhere.

Vide [6], the triggering action for a Network Hardware Trojan is shown associated with the LED light of Ethernet controller acts as a method to interpret the packet timings. The activity LED light seen in general flicking gives a broad indication of the current network traffic presently user is involved with. The [6] has taken the RTL88111E chip for the study which deciphered that there is 160 ms delay between the LED Light to cycle on and off and it is this 160 millisecond delay during which there is no network activity. This timing behavior of this LED activity is used as a trigger for the Hardware Trojan.

Further to this [7], demoed the payload execution with the ENW02A-1-BC01 Gigabit Ethernet PCI-Express card. The network hardware Trojan was shown degrading the network services using noise injection in chips clock circuitry of the Ethernet controller in the form of a bias voltage. The demonstration included desynchronizing the clock of the Ethernet controller chip owing to changes in the affected bias voltage that lead to the changes in the resonant frequency on the external crystal. Vide [8], HT can be an elementary alteration to the original IC. This refers to an insertion of two input AND gates wherein while the HT is inactive the IC gives the desired output unaffected while the same gives an always zero output irrespective of the input given. They referred this particular example as *Stuck at Zero* Trojan, i.e., SAZ.

5 HT Insertions

Hardware Trojans can actually get inserted at various stages of their life cycle typically during design and manufacturing process or maybe even retrofitted to an existing Hardware IC.

5.1 Design and Manufacturing Process

Economic inducements have goaded the semiconductor industry to dissever the design of IC from fabrication. This has allowed potential vulnerabilities from suspicious circuit foundries to covertly embed malicious HT into the erstwhile original design. In the typical design process involved in Application-specific integrated circuit (ASIC), the semiconductor intellectual property core (IP core), i.e., the reusable unit of chip layout design which is an intellectual property of one party or may be licensed to another and Standard model cells wherein low-level very-large-scale integration (VLSI) layout is encapsulated into an abstract logic representation are often considered untrusted [9].

5.2 CAD Tools for Modification of RTL

CAD tools can be periled appositely tapping software vulnerabilities to alter RTL [10] without the intercession and intent of the designer and once compromised, it would be a herculean task to detect. Besides, the concept of SoC based on recyclable hardware is a permeating praxis in the semiconductor industry today owing to the huge diminution in cost and time attributes involved. Sadly here, only the supply and demand factors are being addressed, i.e., the user is only interested in getting his functionalities right and the seller may just be involved to ensure the same reaches the customer at the right time but the malicious untrusted third party in the process may butt in something unknown to either that can be a reason for chaos later.

5.3 Malicious Reprogramming of FPGA

A typical customer holds a bare manufactured IC and configures the same with the help of a field-programmable gate array. The FPGA configuration is generally specified using a hardware description language (HDL), similar to that used for an application-specific integrated circuit (ASIC).

5.4 Side-Channel Attacks

MOLES [11] aka Malicious Off-chip Leakage enabled by Side channels engineered to leak information below the effective noise power level of the device. Vital and critical data vide Moles can be retrieved with the assistance of spread spectrum technology, i.e., a type of wireless communications in which the frequency of the transmitted signal is designedly altered [12] and since the signal of the reduced information vanishes in the noise, it becomes arduous of what data has been transferred [13]. HT based on this actually is a novel way to designedly leak out information.

5.5 Malicious Processor

n advantageously contrived and implanted backdoor at an untrusted fabrication facility involved in manufacturing the typical pc processor can be victimized by a software antagonist at a later scheduled timeline. Such backdoors are ordinarily designed to be out of action during booting or activated under uncommon predetermined stipulates or can get activated with a singular rare input condition that is ascertained by the malevolent intender [14]. This kind of a backdoor in a processor will never be divulged by the run of the mill or state of the art antivirus versions predominately available COTS.

6 Known Cases of HT in Recent Times

It comes as a surprise though that such a severe threat that is currently the topic of various forums, discussions, conferences, and research work has no such case studies to know the impact. Whatever heard and read is all discredited and only suspected, for e.g., Operation Orchard [15] wherein a Syrian nuclear reactor was subjected to Israeli Airstrike, seems to have been worked out via a hidden kill-switch function in the radar infrastructure. This functionality was then thought to be used to disable the Syrian radars for the short duration of the attack.

Mi-grade FPGA chips, e.g., ACTEL have been a suspect of containing a backdoor function that's equivalent of admin debug designed into the JTAG functionality of the subject chip IC. The subject IC Actel/Microsemi ProASIC3 chips could be used for accessing FPGA configuration using this backdoor. The researchers confirmed that this backdoor was not present in the original firmware loaded with the chip [16].

7 Measures to Detect Hardware Trojans

Vide above basic introduction we can see the kind of potent threat this brings along and the worst part till date is no formal or assured methods exist to detect any such threats. A typical hardware Trojan threat can actually exist in an IC as a 5–6 line code that gets activated under predefined conditions as a set. Though at present the severity of the threat being realized is finally forcing IT security domain to look and seek ways to resolve. Few good but only prelim measures include the following.

7.1 Embedded Systems Challenge

Polytechnic Institute of New York University based at USA every year organizes this competition by the name of Embedded Security Challenge (ESC) that bids two teams in a contest wherein one team designs target system hardware and the other team tries to identify and exploit the vulnerabilities in the target hardware [17].

7.2 Trust in ICs

This concept aims at a secure cycle of IC design and manufacturing primarily comprehending insertion points including chip authentication, IC design, IP protection, and manufacture [18]. Defense Advanced Research Project Agency backs the SHIELD [19] (Supply Chain Hardware Integrity for Electronics Defense) program that proposes to build trust in the typical supply chain that involves Design, Manufacturing, Testing, Integration, packaging, and finally distribution. The SHIELD root of trust as proposed would be able to avow the provenance of an IC as it goes through the typical Supply chain processes.

7.3 Golden Model Fabrication

One way of ensuring a Hardware Trojan free IC is a fabrication of the complete IC in a trusted plant with no third parties involved and no outsourcing involved. Once fabricated, this IC can be used as a reference model for "Integrated Circuits under Test" for behavioral and performance deviations [20].

8 Countermeasures to Detect Hardware Trojans

Probably, as we see above, these are only too prelim measures to counter Hardware Trojans perhaps a long way to go before a 100% trusted IC checks in before us. Ideally any malevolent modification to any IC should be perceptible during tests and inspections whilst pre-silicon manufacturing or post-silicon testing but that is not an easy thing to do since the complex ICs today, with so many multiple agencies involved at various echelons of manufacturing and design, will unlikely have a golden model of the intact IC. Moreover, if the antagonist decides to taint only a minuscule percentage of the complete batch of ICs being manufactured, the complexness to detect only step-ups further. Another way out for detection involves Nanometer physical inspection [21] which is for one very complex from point of conduct but also is mostly not economically viable. Vide [22], the countermeasures for HT as concentrate on three panoptic categories of countermeasures for protection against HT. These include Runtime monitoring, Design for security and Trojan Detection approaches which attempt to arrest any kind of malicious embedding of HT at prefabrication stages using pre-silicon test approaches or using non destructive techniques at post-silicon manufacturing test stage. The Run *Time Monitoring* approach is based on online monitoring while the circuit is in operation. The *Design for Security* approach essays to make the insertion of HT at any stage hard or facilitate detection ease during pre/post fabrication whereas the *Trojan Detection* approach can be logic testing based on generating set and predefined test patterns and side-channel analysis for HT. Between these, *Design for Security* approach may not be a very effective way to resolve the HT threat owing to the diversity of threat classification discussed above whilst *Runtime Monitoring* may be more effective since this approach can be applied for real-time monitoring.

8.1 Destructive Versus Nondestructive Detection Technique

Once the IC is fabricated and boxing concluded for use by the end user, there remains very restricted ambit and visibility to endeavor to detect any kind of HT presence. However, destructive reverse engineering resolves to an extent in such cases. It involves depackaging the IC, acquiring microscopic images of each layer, trust validating the same after rebuilding the design of the end product. This approach uses a sample of the infected batch of ICs, thus it would be judicious to apply this wherein infection or insertion of the HT is limited to a small percentage. Scanning Electron Microscopy (SEM) is used to destructively delayer one chip wherein all of the transistors and connections can be averred. Also, this approach makes the IC under test unusable further, that's why the name destructive came to the fore. It takes from weeks to maybe months depending upon the complexity of the IC under detection for giving a 100% assurance of an HT free IC. Nondestructive methods relate to ways of detection that keeps the chip usable after the test. Between the two, Destructive detection technique is more effective viz-a-viz nondestructive detection technique.

8.2 Homomorphic Encryption/Decryption

One of the countermeasures against Hardware Trojans proposed by Aliyu and Bello [23] is the use of Homomorphic Encryption and Decryption which offers brilliant security boasts since it allows operating on data without revealing the contents being worked at. Homomorphic encryption is a type of encryption which allows processing of data on ciphertext and generates an encrypted result which on decryption is valued equally to the one processed with plain text. This certainly is an advantage plus for handling Hardware Trojans. Homomorphic encryption may be Partial or Full where Partial Homomorphic proffers to do either multiplication or addition on ciphertexts without unwrapping the original plaintext data while Full Homomorphic appropriates efficacious rating of a capricious depth circuit compiled of multiplications and additions.

9 Conclusion

IC is the basic core component of the diverse range of electronic systems being exploited across various domains pan globe today and the growing dependence makes it essential to ensure these ICs faithfully and sincerely perform the tasks they are designed and fabricated for. Hardware Trojans being inserted or retrofitted at any stage in these ICs are thus a grave threat that stands as a serious challenge today for the IT security domain. The software industry which has been campaigning in all gears put into ascertaining a malware/virus free application or an OS, over decades now, is yet to reach anywhere as daily various zero days keep getting deciphered which might be existing in an unknown quantified figure. The HT threat actually adds to the excruciation since this is indeed indecipherable with the present set of researches and studies did across. The future researches have a wide domain to work on starting to explore the emerging attacks on these ICs, developing trust validation standards for ICs being manufactured in the electronic industry and come out with inexpugnable apt approaches to counter such threats.

References

1. Trojan at https://en.wikipedia.org/wiki/Trojan_horse_%28computing%29
2. Mitra S, Wong HSP, Wong S (2015) Stopping Hardware Trojans in their tracks
3. Bhunia S (2014) Hardware trojan attacks: threat analaysis and counter measures
4. Karri R (2010) Trustworthy hardware: Identifying and classifying Hardware Trojans. IEEE Comput 43(10)
5. Wang X, Plusquellic J (2008) Detecting malicious inclusions in secure hardware: challenges and solutions. In: Proceedings of the 2008 IEEE international workshop on hardware-oriented security and trust, Washington
6. Zhang J (2014) DeTrust- defeating hardware trust verification with stealthy implicitly-triggered Hardware Trojans
7. Shield J, Hopkins B (2015) Hardware Trojans—a systemic threat
8. Shield J, Hopkins B (2015) Hardware Trojans—a systemic threat, p 47, Para 5
9. Shield J, Hopkins B (2015) Hardware Trojans—a systemic threat, p 49, Para 5.3
10. Aliyu A, Bello A (2014) Hardware Trojan model for attack and detection techniques
11. Rad R, Plusquellic J, Tehranipoor M (2010) A sensitivity analysis of power signal methods for detecting Hardware Trojans under real process and environmental conditions
12. Wu TF, Wong HSP, Wong S, Mitra S (2015) TPAD-hardware trojan prevention and detection for trusted integrated circuits
13. Lin L, Burleson W (2009) MOLES—malicious off-chip leakage enabled by side-channels
14. Spread Spectrum at http://searchnetworking.techtarget.com/definition/spread-spectrum
15. Hardware Malware book By Edgar Weippl (2013) Adrian Dabrowski, Heidelinde Hobel, p 67, para 4.2
16. King ST, Tucek J, Cozzie A, Grier C, Jiang W, Zhou Y (2008) Designing and implementing malicious hardware. In: Proceedings of the first USENIX workshop on large-scale exploits and emergent threats(LEET)
17. Adee S (2008) The hunt for the kill switch. IEEE Spect 45(5):34–39

18. Skorobogatov S (2012) Breakthrough silicon scanning discovers backdoor in military chip. In: Cryptographic hardware and embedded systems (CHES'12), vol 7428. Springer, Berlin, pp 23–40
19. The Embedded Systems Challenge at https://csaw.engineering.nyu.edu/
20. DARPA Trust in IC at http://www.darpa.mil/program/trusted-integrated-circuits
21. Shahrjerdi D, Rajendran J (2014) Shielding and securing integrated circuits with sensors
22. Hardware Malware book By Edgar Weippl (2013) Christian Krieg, Adrian Dabrowski, Heidelinde Hobel, p 67, para 4.2
23. Aliyu A, Bello A (2014) Hardware Trojan model for attack and detection techniques

Author Biographies

Anupam Tiwari is an IT Security enthusiast and an incisive learner, holds rich experience and qualifications in the demesne including CDAC & GFSU Certified Cyber Security Professional, Certified Ethical Hacker with B.E and M.Tech in Computer Science from JNTU Hyderabad. He also holds three post graduation qualifications in Information Security, ERP and Operations & Systems and presently pursuing his research in the world of cryptocurrencies. He is a senior member and regular contributor to articles in leading defence and engineering journals. He has been a regular participant in National and International Seminars as a guest speaker and He is working with the Min of Defence wherein he has variegated experience of service in IT security implementations and conduct of Cyber Audits.

Chetan Soni is an cyber security follower. He holds vast experience and qualifications in field of cyber security. He is B.E. in computer science and holds two PG Diploma in field of Information security and Aeronautical engineering. He has done various certifications in field of Information Security including CEH. He has ten years of experience in domain of Information Security. His area of interest is implementation of firewalls and network security. He is presently working with Min of Defence where he has implemented various cyber security measures and conducted Information Security audits in his organization.

Cybersecurity for Supervisory Control and Data Acquisition

Sahebrao N. Shinde and Reena P. Shinde

Abstract SCADA stands for Supervisory Control and Data Acquisition, a communication technology which collects data from distant facilities and sends control signals to actuators. A number of factors exist that increases the risk allied with SCADA systems. SCADA components are considered to be profoundly privileged targets for cyberattacks through which hackers can easily hit the nation's critical infrastructure and economy. This paper investigates security issues of SCADA communication protocols. In order to protect the SCADA networks, we focus on the protocols as they were not designed with inherent security features. This paper emphases on the security system through protocol hardening. The objective is to modify the structure of such protocols to provide more integrity and authentication. In the proposed structure, two algorithms are used to enhance the security and integrity of the payload. They are discussed further in the next six sections.

Keywords SCADA · Data link layer protocol · CRC · Cybersecurity Industrial network

1 Introduction

SCADA is critical infrastructure to provide the services to real-time system such as traffic control, electric power generation, power grid, waste treatment, etc. It collects facts from distant services and sends signals to actuators. These SCADA systems [1] were introduced for local systems and its applications have been expanded to wide area networks as technology evolves. Proprietary controls and limited security issues made SCADA to some extent secured. As a result of

S. N. Shinde (✉)
Department of Computer Science, C.M.C.S. College, Nashik, India
e-mail: Sns110@gmail.com

R. P. Shinde
Department of Computer Science, Sinhgad College of Science, Pune, India
e-mail: reena.pingale@gmail.com

M. U. Bokhari et al. (eds.), *Cyber Security*, Advances in Intelligent Systems and Computing 729, https://doi.org/10.1007/978-981-10-8536-9_35

increased commercial grid and internet, this network is considered vulnerable to computer-generated outbreaks. These systems were primarily designed with the thought for functionality and performance and little thought toward security.

Later on, commercial grid and internet have connected to SCADA [2] which introduces cybersecurity threats. It could pose a threat to the economy of country and life of citizens. If intruders attack SCADA components through which they can shake the nation's critical infrastructure and economy. These types of attacks have a potential to obstruct. The essential operations of the nation such as disrupt financial service, shut down power systems.

Along with opportunities like improved response to electric system, optimization of performance-generating stations and resilience to failure, modern communication control systems, and computing also render the physical processes and systems susceptible to deliberate attacks from core or outer parties.

2 Industrial Network

SCADA has advanced prerequisite with reference to reliability, uptime, and inactivity as compared to the IT systems, so it is impossible to constantly apply security measures to the information technology organization. Confidentiality, Integrity, and Availability is the main concern for both the systems. The top priority for SCADA systems is Availability whereas Confidentiality is for IT system. It is required to analyze various threats and vulnerability that affects the SCDA system operation.

The topic covered in this paper is the core of automation and Industrial grids that constitute Critical National Infrastructure. Traditionally, such systems were installed standalone and did not interface with the outside world. SCADA [3] components are considered to be privileged targets for cyberattacks through which hackers can easily hit the nation's critical infrastructure and economy. Such attacks can potentially shut down power systems, interrupt financial service and, therefore, obstruct the essential operations of the nation. While modern communications, computing and control systems bid remarkable openings to expand response of the power-driven system, optimize generating station performance, and offer resilience to failure, they also render the physical processes and systems prone to purposeful attacks.

Protecting the SCADA systems which perform the monitoring and control functions of utility infrastructure, such as electricity, gas, water, etc., is critical for national security. Any vulnerability in these systems can pose serious threats and can bring down operations of a utility. In critical applications, the appropriate control strategy to block execution and any unknown or malicious behavior.

Security risk analysis and development of precise safety keys will help us to understand, how this can be protected from attacks.

The protocols used in SCADA [4, 5] systems traditionally have been built with little thought given to security. Security of SCADA system by means of protocol hardening is a plausible solution to address such threats.

DNP3 protocol is used to communicate between the Master and Outstation by critical infrastructure. Securing DNP3 is an active research topic. The third version of Distributed Network Protocol is applied by SCADA to converse amongst the Outstation and Master. DNP3 protocol optimizes the conduction of acquiring data and control commands within the main units and slave units. It is different than the protocols found for email transmission, hypertext forms, and SQL. It is highly suitable for SCADA applications.

3 Industrial Network Protocol (DNP3)

DNP3 [6, 7] is a permitted, robust, efficient modern SCADA protocol. Remote computers found in the field are denoted as outstation and the control centers as masters. This protocol optimizes the conduction of acquiring data and control commands within the main units and slave units.

DNP3 [8] is a simplified 3 layer standard (application, data link and physical) initially proposed by the International Electrotechnical Commission but later on, Enhanced Performance Architecture (EPA) enhanced the architecture of DNP3 by introducing an additional layer, a pseudo transport layer enabling message segmentation.

3.1 Application Layer

It provides customized utilities like data formats, the efficient spread of acquired data, features, and control commands [9]. This layer provides service to send/receive messages to/from DNP3 devices. A fragment is a block of octets containing request or response information transported between a master and an outstation. Application layer fragment structure is of two types:

- Request fragment
- Response fragment

In request fragment, the application request header is of 2 bytes: Application control (1 byte), Function code (1 byte).

In response fragment, the application response header is of 4 bytes: Application control (1 byte), Function code (1 byte), and Internal Indication (2 byte).

3.2 Pseudo Transport Layer

It allows message segmentation, by breaking down the long fragment of Application layer to the size of the data unit of Data Link layer (Transport function) at transmission time and amalgamate it at receiving site. The Transport function adheres header (1 octet) and application data (1–249 octets).

3.3 Data Link Layer

It transports data across a communication channel to destination device bi-directionally. This layer performs several functions like encapsulation, error detection, source, and destination addresses. It encodes data received from pseudo transport application layers with fixed sized data link header.

The encoded data is sent over a communication channel for transmission. The DNP3 data link frame has fixed length header block (10 octets) followed by optional data blocks. Each block ends with a 16 bit CRC. Frame length may be long as 292 octets.

3.4 Physical Layer

It is topmost level, responsible for transferring messages on physical media.

4 Security Issues in Industrial Network

4.1 Issues Related to Device Security MTU/RTU

The device in industrial networks are sometimes located in remote places and therefore device security takes a high priority in design and deployment of these devices.

4.2 Issues Related to Protocol Security

Integrity and authentication are of utmost importance in the industrial network as unauthorized data manipulation by adversaries can have disastrous consequences. In the absence of integrity and authentication measures, one can attack or replay the attack in the direction of the network.

4.3 Mod-Based Security

The intense growth of liabilities has become one of the key challenges for security personnel, who not only need to consider the increasing amount of attacks, but also identify how these attacks could be combined in complex ways. Clearly, a methodology must exist, but it is not significant. For instance, a company may identify their competitor using industrial spies against them, but the company may judge this as nonexistent for specific parts of their infrastructure. For example, an outlying control station operating with 10-year-old technology is less prone to threats. The severity of the threat must be determined by allocating resources properly.

Few business experts treat SCADA as usually customized for particular sector's application, which requires a good precise knowledge of a certain system and industry to attack it. Furthermore, specialized knowledge requirement will reduce the number of attackers, concluding why SCADA attacks are diverse from the attacks on other computer networks. Although SCADA attacks are infrequently effective, the oppositions showcase its curiosity.

There are a number of ways using which we can perform a security analysis of a given network based on protocol application and topology.

Fault Tree Analysis (FTA) is a tool used for security and reliable evaluation for demonstrating the failure paths in a system. It does system-level risk evaluations using a tree structure. It is almost 50 years old and is extensively utilized. The failure in the system is exhibited in a visual fault tree. The simple set of logic rules and symbols within the tree structure make a qualitative and quantitative evaluation of complicated systems. Fault trees are simple to design, but it is difficult to solve complex tree structure. All the features of fault tree and additional capabilities are exploited by the Attack trees.

Like fault trees, Attack trees (AT) are also representations of reality, providing a simplified representation of complex real-world drivers. The accuracy underlying the drivers and future analysis is determined by the time or effort spent in learning and norms made.

The attacks on the target is represented by an upside-down tree structure with the goal as the root node, the sub-goals are different ways of achieving that goal and leaf nodes as the lowest level tasks. The leaf nodes contain user-defined values called indicator values to store attributes of that leaf node.

Leaf nodes can have Boolean value (true/false), explicit value (1-low to 4-high), or continuous value (cost: 0 to any dollar amount). There can be additional options for continuous node too. In the attack tree, some part of the openly accessible attack data is used as indicator values. A complex tree can have numerous attack scenarios only if all possible paths are covered to reach the root. A threat agent profile helps to reduce the number of tree attacks. Attack tree consists of physical/cyberattacks and illustrates touch points amongst them.

5 Proposed Solution Industrial Network Security

This work deals with communication security aspects of DNP3/SCADA. Our work enhances the security of the DNP3 protocol to alleviate the threats. The most important focus is on the redistributes the bytes of the protocol, on the augmentation of the CRC algorithm and Blowfish algorithm for better security aspect. Traditionally DNP3 protocol has only CRC is used for detecting transmission error [10, 11]. We provide the security in following ways:

- Encrypting DNP3 Packet.
- Modify the internal structure of protocol.

Out of 292, it uses 34 bytes of the DNP3 link protocol data unit for integrity and security. We redistribute these bytes to enhance the payload range and security of the DNP3 protocol with the help of following rearranges fields:

- New LH Header
- Sequence Number
- Original LH Header
- Payload Data
- Enhanced CRC

In this proposal, the message is protected by encryption using Blowfish and our algorithm for authentication as shown in Fig. 1.

- In this ZA protocol, the message is protected by the following two algorithms.
- Blowfish encryption algorithm: Blowfish provides the confidentiality to the data by encrypting the data.
- Enhanced CRC algorithm for data authentication in the protocol: CRC helps in the authentication of the data at both sides. In the enhanced CRC technique, it uses only 4 bytes of DNP3 protocol.

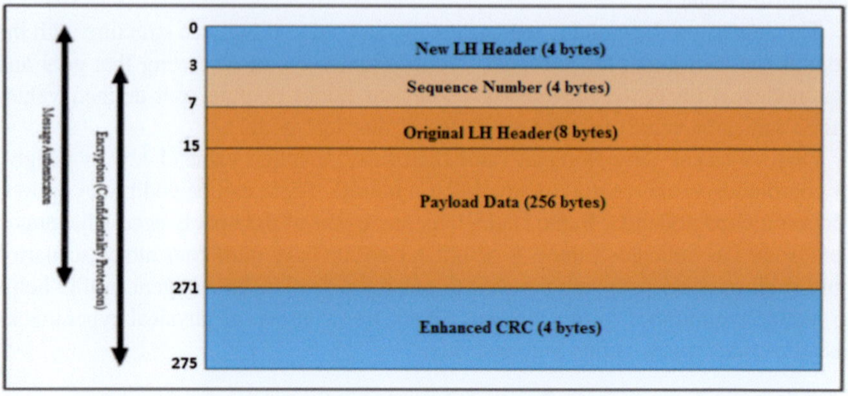

Fig. 1 Message Protection using Blowfish and Proposed Algorithm

Enhanced CRC Algorithm for Message Authentication and Blowfish Encryption Algorithm

CRC helps in the authentication of the data at both sides. In the enhanced CRC technique, it uses only 4 bytes. Blowfish helps in confidentiality of the payload.

Blowfish [12] is a variable length keyed symmetric block cipher. It was developed in 1993 by Bruce Schneier. This algorithm contains Key Expansion and Data Encryption Part. In key Expansion part, inputted key value up to 448 bit is converted into a number of sub-array keys of total 4168 bytes. Data Encryption contains network which consists of 16 rounds. Every round has a key-dependent permutation and key and data-dependent substitution.

In this scenario, payload data, original header, key sequence number and enhanced CRC are encrypted with the help of Blowfish encryption algorithm as shown in Fig. 2. The total 272 bytes are under Blowfish encryption algorithm. It is a symmetric block cipher and each block is 64 bits. This cryptography's secret key ranges from 32 to 448 bits. It is a strong encryption algorithm to provide security in the SCADA protocols to use the generator polynomial. The generator polynomial is used to divide the message to find out the remainder as CRC [13, 14]. The degree of generator polynomial should be r, to compute an r-bit CRC checksum.

The remainder polynomial is generated when sender appends r 0-bits to the message of m-bit and divides the resulting polynomial by the generator polynomial. The data transmitted is the original m-bit message followed by the r-bit CRC. The CRC [15, 16] method treats the message as a polynomial in GF (2). At the receiver side, the receiver uses the same generator polynomial to divide received the message. If the remainder generated after dividing the received message is zero, then no error occurred in the message, otherwise, an error occurred.

In ZA protocol, below polynomial can be used to represent the original message:

$$P(z) = a_{N-1}z_{N-1} + a_{N-2}z_{N-2} + \cdots + a_0$$

Original message is represented in a binary form

$$[a_{N-1}a_{N-2}...a_0]$$

Here a_{N-1} represents the MSB whereas a_0 is LSB.

For CRC computation generator polynomial is all times associated, and we use generator polynomial $G(z)$ of M degree which can be denoted in a polynomial:

$$G(z) = g_M z_M + g_{M-1}x_{M-1} + \cdots + g_0$$

And binary representation is

$$[g_M, g_{M-1}\cdots g_0].$$

In our enhance algorithm we divide the original message of N bits

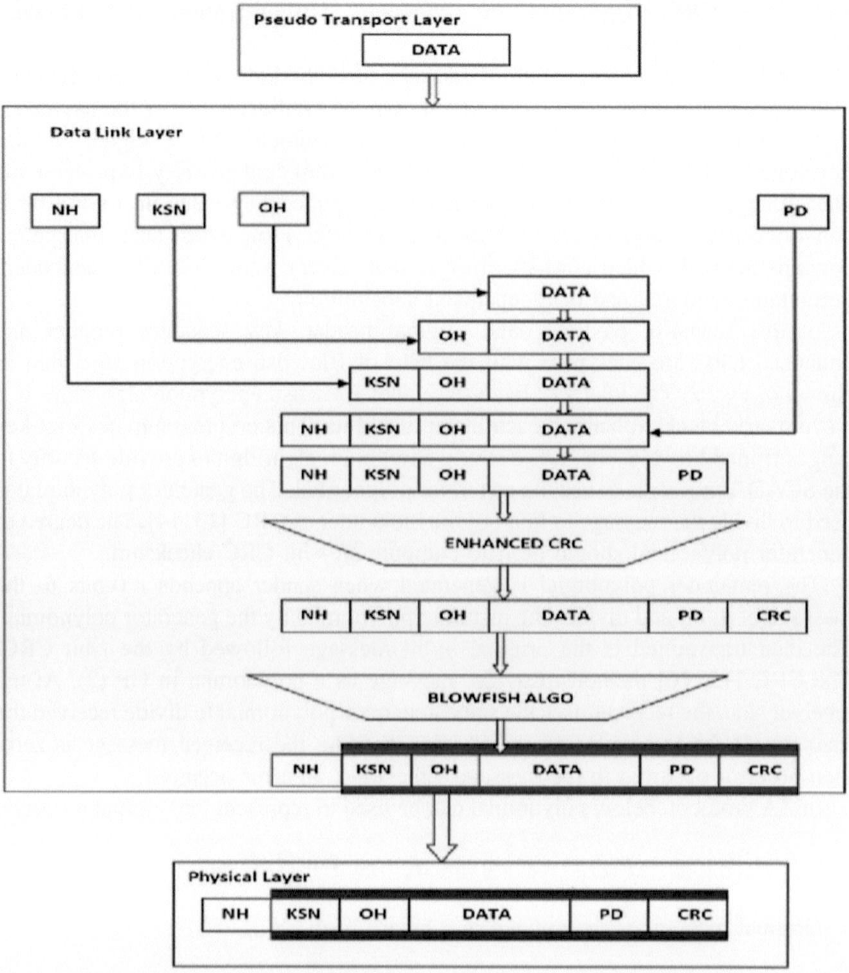

Fig. 2 Internal Structure of ZA Protocol

$$[a_{N-1}a_{N-2}a_{N-3}\ldots a_0] \text{ into } n \text{ chunks of } M \text{ size}$$

Without loss of generality, $N = nM$, where original message of N bits, M bits size of chunk, n is integer. For example message of 272 bytes is divided 68 chunks of 4 bytes as shown in Fig. 3.

Here $W_i(z) = a_{(i+1)M-1}z_{M-1} + \cdots + a_{iM}$. Then original message will be

$$P(z) = W_{n-1}z_{N-1} + W_{n-2}z_{N-2} + \cdots + W_0 \tag{1}$$

And $W_i(z)$ is the ith chunk of the original message

Consider,

Fig. 3 Enhanced CRC

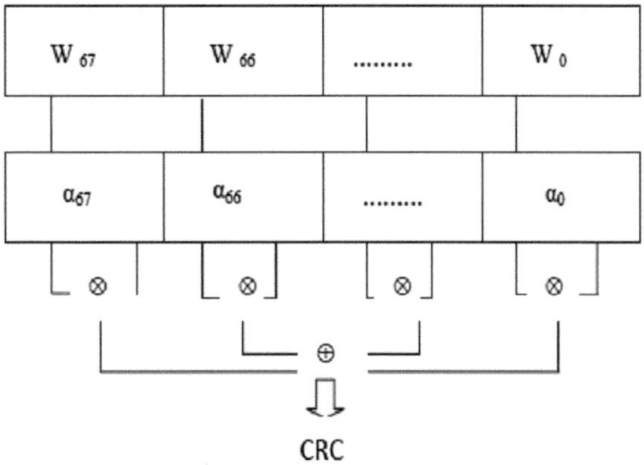

$$P(z) = \text{Original message}$$
$$G(z) = \text{generator polynomial}$$

To calculate the CRC, affix M zeroes next to LSB and then divide the affixed message by $G(z)$. Then correspondingly:

$$\mathrm{CRC}[P(z)] = (P(z)z_M) \bmod G(z) \tag{2}$$

From the Eq. (2) and congruence property, CRC computation on segmented message (1):

$$\mathrm{CRC}[P(z)] = W_{n-1}(z)\, n_M \bmod G(z) + \cdots + W_0 z_M \bmod G(z).$$

Here, the modulo of $W_i(z)$ by $G(z)$ will be $W_i(z)$, i.e., $W_i(z)|G(z)| = W_i(z)$.

$$W_i(z)z_{(i+1)M}|G(z)| = W_i(z) \bmod G(z)z_{(i+1)M} \bmod G(z),$$
$$\text{for } i = 0, 1, 2, \ldots, n-1.$$

Note: For each chunk, the degree of $W_i(z) < M$.
Let us define α coefficient,

$$\alpha_i = z_{(i+1)M} \bmod G(z) \quad \text{for } i = 0, 1, \ldots, n-1.$$

Now CRC can be computed as:

$$\mathrm{CRC}\ [P(z)] = W_{n-1} \otimes \alpha_{n-1} \otimes W_0 \otimes \alpha_0$$

By the help of the $G(z)$, we calculate α.
To compute α factor, consider

$$\alpha_0 = z_M \bmod G(z) = \{g_{M-1} + \cdots + g_0]$$
$$\alpha_1 = z_{2M} \bmod G(z) = [\alpha_0 \otimes \alpha_0]$$
$$\ldots$$
$$\alpha_n = z_{nM} \bmod G(z) = \alpha_{0n}$$

After ($\alpha_0\ \alpha_1\ \ldots\ \alpha_n$) is computed, then CRC is computed as

$$\mathrm{CRC}(\beta(z)) = W_{n-1} \otimes \alpha_{n-1} \otimes W_0 \otimes \alpha_0$$

The operation $\otimes$ and $\oplus$ are Galois Field multiplication and addition over GF (2^M), respectively.

Now enhanced CRC algorithm is presented as:

(i) Put original message of N bits and divide it into n chunks $[W_{n-1}W_{n-2}\ \ldots\ W_1W_0]$ and for every chunk size is M bit ($N = nM$).
(ii) Initially take generator polynomial $G(z)$ and its degree M and at the same time calculate α coefficient (as discussed above).
(iii) Perform the n-pair Galois field multiplication in parallel and then XOR the products which give the CRC result.

Here original message divided into small 68 chunks of 4 bytes. These chunks are undergoing CRC algorithms to provide message authentication. It is used to provide integrity of the message in SCADA protocol. Here 4 bytes are used in the CRC out of 20 bytes and the remaining bytes are reserved for future work. So the protocol is providing authentication and integrity by using blowfish and enhanced CRC. Through this approach, we rearranged bytes of the DNP3 protocol to enables confidentiality, integrity, and authenticity. In this protocol, we have done modification in the protocol to reserve the bytes and provide security. The Payload data and original LH header are encrypted by Blowfish algorithm to provide the confidentiality to the message. The 4 bytes of our proposed CRC is used to provide message authentication.

6 Conclusion

This paper investigates security issues of network communication protocols. In order to protect the SCADA networks, we focus on the protocols as they were not designed with inherent security features. The aim is to modify the structure of such protocols to provide more integrity and authentication. In the proposed structure, two algorithms are used to enhance the security and integrity of the payload. We have freed 16 bytes in the frame for future enhancements and possible modifications. The aim is to increase the security of such protocol to alleviate threats.

References

1. Saquib Z, Patel D, Rajrajan R (2011) A configurable and efficient keymanagement scheme for SCADA. Int J Res Rev, June 2011, 1(2):16–24
2. Saxena A, Pal O0, Saquib Z, Patel D (2010) Customized PKI for SCADA systems network. Int J Adv Networking Appl 01(05):282–289
3. Mahboob A, Zubairi J (2010) Intrusion avoidance for SCADA security in industrial plants. Collab Technol Syst (CTS), Proc. CTS 2010, 447–452, IEEE Digital Library
4. Bhagaria S, Prabhakar SB, Saquib Z (2011) Flexi-DNP3: flexible distributed network protocol version 3(DNP3) for SCADA security. Recent Trends Inf Syst, 293–296, 21–23 Dec 2011
5. Saiwan S, Jain P, Saquib Z, Patel D (2011) Cryptography key management for SCADA system an architectural framework. Adv Comput Control Telecommun
6. Dawson R (1997) Secure communication for critical infrastructure control system. University of Queensland
7. Majdalawieh M, Parisi-Presicce F, Wijesekera D (2006) DNPSec: Distributed network protocol version 3 (DNP3) security framework. Adv Comput Inf Syst Sci Eng, 227–234, Springer, Dodrecht
8. DNP3 Application Note AN2003-001, http://www.dnp.org/
9. Distributed Network Protocol (DNP3). In: IEEE Standard for Electric Power Systems Communications 2012
10. Rogaway P, Bellare M, Black J (2006) OCB a block—cipher mode of operation for efficient authenticated. ACM Trans Inf Syst Secur
11. Bellare M, Rogaway P (1994) Entity authentication and key distribution. In: Advances in cryptology (CRYPTO'93). Lecturer notes in computer Science. Springer, Berlin
12. Schneier B (1994) Description of a new variable-length key, 64-bit block cipher (Blowfish), fast software encryption. In: Cambridge security workshop proceedings. Springer, Berlin, pp 191–204, Vol 809, FSE 1993, Lecture Notes in Computer Science
13. Ji HM, Killian E (2002) Fast parallel CRC algorithm and implementation on a configurable processor. In: IEEE 2002, vol 3
14. Feldmeier DC (1995) Fast software implementation of error detection code. IEEE/ACM Trans Networking, IEEE/ACM Trans. on Networking, 3(6), Dec 1995, 640–651
15. Joshi SM, Dubey PK, Kalpan MA (2000) A new parallel algorithm for CRC generation, communication. In: ICC IEEE international conference
16. Sarwate DV (1988) Computation of cyclic redundancy checks via table lookup. Commun ACM 31(8)

k-Barrier Coverage-Based Intrusion Detection for Wireless Sensor Networks

Jaiprakash Nagar and Sandeep Sharma

Abstract Wireless sensor networks (WSNs) is an egressing technology having various applications such as in military for surveillance and reconnaissance, in health care for patient monitoring, environmental monitoring, weather monitoring, etc. These networks are vulnerable to different types of security threats such as intrusion. Therefore, intrusion detection is the main issue in sensor networks. It is assumed that mobility of sensors can be advantageous to get improved coverage performance. In this work, we discuss an intrusion detection technique in mobile sensor networks. The performance of the network is analyzed in terms of probability, such as k-barrier coverage probability versus moving intruders. Then, the effect of number of sensors, sensing range of sensors, and the speed of sensors and intruder on the probability of *k*-barrier coverage is analyzed. Finally, this work proves that the performance of the network can be improved up to a significant order with mobile sensors as compared to that of static sensors.

Keywords Intrusion · *k*-barrier coverage · Sensors · Field of interest

1 Introduction

A sensor network is a group of small sensors called nodes having low-power operational characteristics. This technology has many attracting features (e.g., unattended network operation, low installation cost, etc.); therefore, wireless sensor networks are being deployed for many applications like reconnaissance missions and surveillance for military, in health care for patient monitoring, for industrial monitoring, to monitor environmental and physical phenomena, such as wild fire,

J. Nagar (✉) · S. Sharma
School of Information and Communication Technology,
Gautam Buddha University, Greater Noida 201308, Uttar Pradesh, India
e-mail: jpnagar91@gmail.com

S. Sharma
e-mail: sandeepsvce@gmail.com

M. U. Bokhari et al. (eds.), *Cyber Security*, Advances in Intelligent Systems and Computing 729, https://doi.org/10.1007/978-981-10-8536-9_36

wildlife, water quality, earthquake, ocean, and pollution; to monitor manufacturing machinery performance and industrial sites, such as building safety and in houses to detect burglary, and so on [1].

Since wireless sensor networks have no switches or gateways to supervise the flow of information, the security of such networks is a significant issue [2]; particularly for the applications where concealment has main importance, hence intrusion is one of the major issues in sensor networks. In [3], intrusion is defined as "any set of actions that attempt to compromise the integrity, confidentiality, or availability of a resource" and intrusion prevention techniques such as authentication, encryption, secure routing, access control, etc., are presented as the initial line of security against intrusions. Therefore, in order to operate wireless sensor networks in a secure way, any type of intrusions must be detected before the intruders can affect the network. Many intrusion detection approaches have been proposed by researchers [4, 5]. In [6], the authors proposed a cross-layer approach for intrusion detection in MANETs and IDSs for mobile ad hoc networks in [7, 8]. Some of the applications deploy stationary sensors to monitor the field of interest, while the others deploy mobile sensors to improve surveillance quality that can be provided by a network.

Many works take a static sensor network, in which sensors are kept static after the initial spread, hence the covered region remains covered and the uncovered region remains uncovered throughout the network's lifetime. Thus, the coverage performance of these networks is primarily ascertained by the initial confirmation of network and the deployment strategy of sensors. Once the sensing characteristics and the deployment strategy of sensors are recognized, the coverage performance can be calculated and persist the same throughout the network lifetime. On the other hand, many applications deploy mobile sensors to monitor the field of interest such as in border surveillance. In [9], the patrol operations at American borders, tried UAVs having sensors along with the preexisting static sensor networks along the American/Mexican borders. The mobility of sensors helps to cover the uncovered regions, thus mobile sensor networks provide time-varying coverage to the field of interest, which increases the probability of hidden intruder detection. Therefore, the coverage provided by a mobile sensor network counts not only on the starting network conformation but also on the mobile characteristics of the sensors. Sensors can move in a highly coordinated manner or independently. Here, it is assumed that sensors move independently having no coordination between them.

A sensor network is considered to give k-barrier coverage, if every intruder course crossing the breadth of the area is detected by leastwise "k" sensors consecutively. In this work, we compute the performance of the network having mobile sensors in terms of k-barrier coverage probability and analyze the effect of network parameters on k-barrier coverage.

Organization: This paper is arranged as follows: In Sect. 2, we discussed various intrusion detection-related works and how they are helpful to improve the performance of the wireless sensor networks. Section 3 explains the network model along with the mobility model considered in this work and their assumptions and limitations. Section 4 summarizes the intrusion detection formulation in an MSN.

Section 5 discusses the various results and their analysis. Finally, Sect. 6 concludes the paper.

2 Related Work

Recently, researchers started working on coverage-related issues in sensor networks. It has been analyzed that system and network parameters like the sensor's sensing range, sensor count, velocity of sensor, sensor deployment strategies, etc., [10, 11] affect the performance of the sensor networks. Various deployment methods such as Gaussian distribution, uniform distribution, random distribution, etc., are used to deploy sensors for different coverage requirements [12] and the performance of the networks is computed in terms of barrier coverage. In [9], the authors determined the mobility characteristics of intrusion detection technique in mobile sensor networks and showed that the velocity of sensors, sensing range, and sensor density improve the barrier coverage performance of WSNs up to a significant level. In [13], the authors compared the performance of uniformly distributed and Gaussian-distributed wireless sensor networks under various network parameters like sensing range of sensors, sensor count, maximum allowable intrusion distance, intruders starting point, etc., and showed that Gaussian distribution gives better detection performance at a point and uniform distribution gives better performance in large areas with equal chances of detection. The mobility patterns of intruder and sensors play a major function in the detection capability of mobile sensor networks. In [14], the authors explained that mean detection time of intruder can be minimized when sensors select their direction of motion uniformly and randomly between $[0, 2\pi]$ and an intruder can increase its detection time by being stationary. The density of sensors also affects the coverage performance of the WSNs. In [15], the authors concluded that using percolation method, when sensor count per unit area is less than 2ln2, in every condition there exists a crossing route that cannot be discovered by sensor network and when the sensor count per unit area is larger than 2ln2, it is highly probable that there is no crossing path which cannot be detected by sensors. Moreover, many works show that increase in the node density improves the performance of the network.

Transmission range of the sensors also affects the intrusion detection probability, broadcast reachability, and network connectivity. In [16], the authors showed that the broadcast reachability and network connectivity increase sharply with the increase in the transmission range of sensors and reach at a particular threshold. It is observed that the network connectivity increases at a slower rate than the broadcast reachability with the increase in transmission range. This work is very helpful for selecting critical network parameters and helps in designing heterogeneous and homogeneous WSNs. In addition, it has been analyzed that the intrusion path also affects the detection probability of the WSNs. In [17], the authors proposed a mobility pattern in which an intruder follows a sinusoidal path to gain access to the network. The author studied the effect of different routes on intrusion detection probability using k sensing and single sensing in a given WSNs. Moreover, it has been shown that the amplitude and frequency of a sinusoidal course affect the probability of intrusion detection significantly while the change in phase value has a negligible effect on multiple-sensing and single-sensing detection. Hence, the author concluded that in order to avoid detection by sensors, intruder should follow a sine-curve path.

3 Mobility and Network Model

In this part, we explain the mobility and network model and discuss the concept of barrier coverage to evaluate the performance of networks having mobile sensors. We assume a two-dimensional rectangular area in which an MSN is deployed having *S(A)* mobile sensors as shown in Fig. 1. This region is considered to have an area A and width W, and initially, it is assumed that the mobile sensors are spread through uniform distribution independently. Under random deployment consideration, the location of sensors can be calculated with the help of a stationary Poisson process in two-dimensional having density η_A. Therefore, the total number of sensor in the region A will be given by

$$\boldsymbol{P_r(S(A) = k) = \frac{e^{-\eta_A|A|}.\eta_A|A|}{k!}} \quad (1)$$

3.1 Mobility Model

Various mobility models are available which defines the motion of sensors; here it is assumed that the motion of sensors is independent on each other and having no coordination between them. Speed and direction of motion of sensors characterize

Fig. 1 Intrusion detection scenario in MSNs

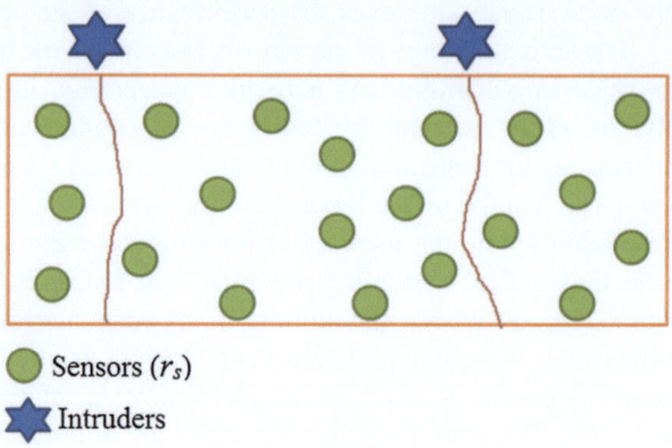

their movement. Sensor chooses its direction of motion randomly from $\emptyset \in [0, 2\pi]$ according to the distribution with PDF $P_r(\emptyset)$. Sensor also chooses its speed from $\upsilon_s \in [0, \upsilon_s^{max}]$ according to PDF $P_{\upsilon s}(\upsilon_s)$. A sensor travels to walls of the region with selected speed and direction after reaching the edge, the sensor bounces back and chooses another direction, this process keeps repeating. This model is referred to the mobility model with the random direction [18]. It is assumed that an intruder follows a crossing path from one parallel boundary to another which is taken as a line segment.

3.2 Sensing Model

It is assumed that r_s is the sensing range of each sensor. Each sensor senses the surrounding area and detects the events within its range of sensing. In this work, an intruder is considered a point that must be discovered by sensors as it penetrates the boundary. An intruder is considered to be detected by a sensor, when it has been found within the sensing range of sensors. This model is the basic sensing model for a sensor and is known as disc-based sensing model.

3.3 Coverage Measures

In this section, the coverage of the intruder traveling path is defined in terms of *k*-barrier coverage. A sensor network is considered to render *k*-barrier coverage, when the intruder track traversing the breadth of the area is cumulatively discovered leastwise *k* moving sensors. The mobile sensor network performance is measured in terms of *k*-barrier coverage probability, i.e., $P_r(\Delta \geq k)$. Where Δ is the cumulative coverage count by moving sensors for any intruder way. Another coverage parameter known as the uncovered distance is defined as the mean distance traveled by the intruder between the consecutive coverage. In addition to the uncovered distance, the frequency of coverage is defined as sensor coverage count per unit time (coverage rate) and is also computed dividing the intruder speed by uncovered distance.

4 Intrusion Detection in an MSN

Intrusion detection in a Mobile Sensor Network (MSN) is analogous to the kinetic theory of gas molecules, especially the theory of mean free path. An intruder is taken as an electron and a sensor is considered as a gas molecule. The mean distance covered by an intruder among consecutive coverage by moving sensors is deduced from the kinetic theory of gas molecules. The mean distance traveled by an intruder among consecutive coverage is denoted by mean uncovered distance C_s. The k-barrier coverage probability $P_r(\Delta \geq k)$ in mobile sensor networks is achieved by modeling the sensors coverage rate θ_s and the uncovered distance λ_d.

Let us assume that sensor is stationary having sensing range r_s initially, coverage cross section can be formulated with the help of a circle of radius r_s as shown in Fig. 2. The mean uncovered distance can be computed by dividing intruder-covered distance by the number of sensor coverage, or it can be computed by dividing the intruder speed by coverage rate C_s.

$$C = 2r_s + \frac{\pi r_s^2}{\upsilon_i t} \tag{2}$$

The mean uncovered distance for a stationary sensor will be

$$\lambda_d = \frac{1}{\eta_A \left(2r_s + \frac{\pi r_s^2}{\upsilon_i t}\right)} \tag{3}$$

where $C = 2r_s + \frac{\pi r_s^2}{\upsilon_i t}$ is the stationary sensor's coverage cross section and η_A is sensor density respectively. Average uncovered distance in a MSN will be calculated by modeling the mean relative velocity of moving sensors with respect to intruders. The relative velocity is formulated in terms of intruder and sensor velocity vector as shown in Fig. 3. To calculate the coverage rate of sensor, the velocity of intruder (υ_i) will be replaced by average relative speed of the mobile sensors in the area of interest. Mobile sensors $\overline{\upsilon_{rel}}$. Then the coverage of sensor per unit time is given by $\eta_A \cdot c \cdot \overline{\upsilon_{rel}}$ where C is the coverage cross section between mobile sensors and intruders.

Theorem 1 *Sensors coverage rate is given by*

$$\theta_s = \eta_A \cdot C \cdot \overline{\upsilon_{rel}} \tag{4}$$

Proof Let us assume that intruder j has some probability to be detected by some moving sensors $i \in \forall$ for $i \in \forall S(A)$ having cross section C_i and density of sensors η_i, hence

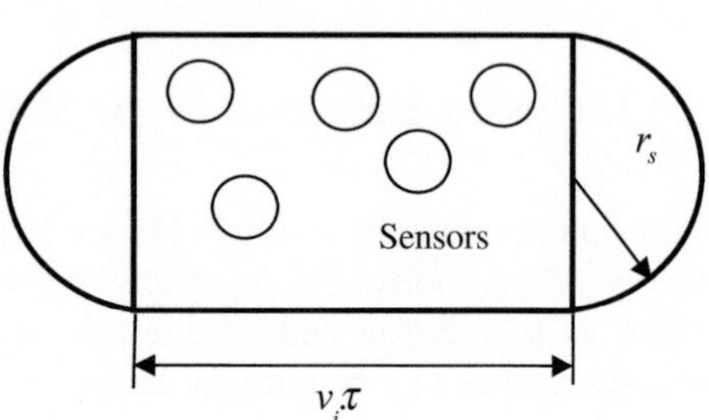

Fig. 2 Covered area with sensing range r_s at $t = \Gamma$

Fig. 3 Intruder speed proportional to moving sensors changes with the angle among their respective directions of motion only

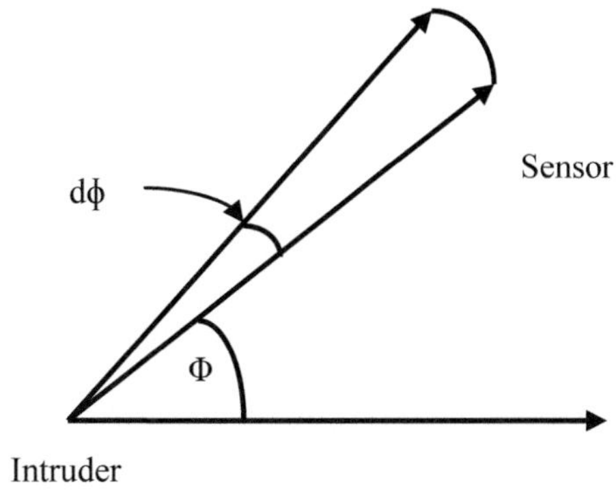

$$\theta_s = \overline{\upsilon_{rel}} \cdot \sum\nolimits_{i \in \forall S(A)} \eta_A \cdot C_i$$
$$\theta_s = \eta_A . C . \overline{\upsilon_{rel}}$$

Uncovered time duration is the inverse of coverage rate.

4.1 Barrier Coverage in a Sensor Network

Since the *k*-barrier coverage probability depends on coverage rate of sensors and uncovered distance.

Theorem 2 *The k-barrier coverage probability is given by*

$$P_r(\Delta \geq k) = 1 - \sum_{n=0}^{k-1} \left(\frac{e^{(-\theta_s \cdot t)} (\theta_s \cdot t)^n}{n!} \right) \tag{5}$$

Proof Suppose each sensor has coverage rate (θ_s), then the probability that an intruder will have n sensors coverage exactly on its traveling way with breadth W is given by

$$P_r(\Delta = n) = \frac{e^{(-\theta_s \cdot t)} (\theta_s \cdot t)^n}{n!} \tag{6}$$

Therefore, the probability that an intruder will be detected by leastwise *k* sensors while crossing the track with breadth *W* is given by

$$P_r(\Delta \geq k) = 1 - \sum_{n=0}^{k-1} \left(\frac{e^{(-\theta_s \cdot t)} (\theta_s \cdot t)^n}{n!} \right)$$

Here, the generalized concepts of coverage are discussed having no specific mobility model.

4.2 Average Relative Speed

An intruder speed relative to moving sensors changes with the angle between their respective motion directions as shown in Fig. 3. The entire moving sensors move randomly in all possible directions, a fraction $\mathrm{d}\phi/2\pi$ of them move in the direction that is with an angle ϕ of the intruder (υ_i) direction. In this section, we calculate the mean relative speed taking random direction mobility model which is given by

$$\overline{\upsilon_\mathrm{rel}} = \frac{1}{2\pi}\int\limits_0^{2\pi} \upsilon_\mathrm{rel}\mathrm{d}\phi \tag{7}$$

from Fig. 4

$$\upsilon_\mathrm{rel}^2 = \upsilon_\mathrm{i}^2 + \upsilon_\mathrm{s}^2 - 2\upsilon_\mathrm{i}\upsilon_\mathrm{s}\cos\phi$$
$$\overline{\upsilon_\mathrm{rel}} = \frac{1}{2\pi}\int\limits_0^{\pi}\sqrt{\upsilon_\mathrm{i}^2 + \upsilon_\mathrm{s}^2 - 2\upsilon_\mathrm{i}\upsilon_\mathrm{s}\cos\phi\mathrm{d}\phi}$$

Due to symmetry of ϕ the relative speed will be

$$\begin{aligned}\overline{\upsilon_\mathrm{rel}} &= 2\frac{(\upsilon_\mathrm{i}+\upsilon_\mathrm{s})}{\pi}\int_0^{\pi/2}\sqrt{\left(1-\frac{4\upsilon_\mathrm{i}\upsilon_\mathrm{s}(\sin\phi)^2}{\upsilon_\mathrm{i}^2+\upsilon_\mathrm{s}^2+2\upsilon_\mathrm{i}\upsilon_\mathrm{s}}\right)}\mathrm{d}\phi \\ &= 2\frac{(\upsilon_\mathrm{i}+\upsilon_\mathrm{s})}{\pi}E(\chi).\end{aligned} \tag{8}$$

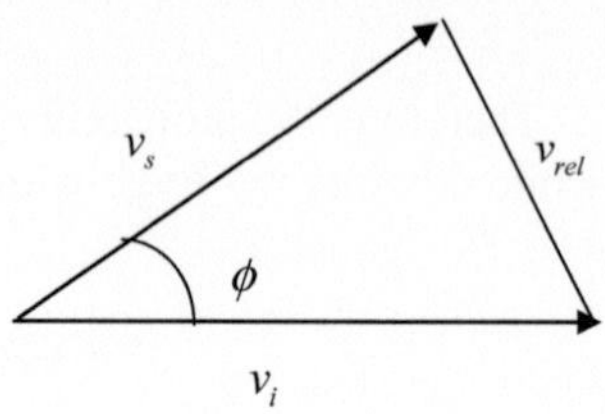

Fig. 4 Relative speed of sensors

$$E(\chi) = \int_0^{\pi/2} \sqrt{\left(1 - \chi.(\sin\phi)^2\right)} \mathrm{d}\phi \tag{9}$$

$$\chi = \frac{4\upsilon_i\upsilon_s}{(\upsilon_i + \upsilon_s)^2}. \tag{10}$$

5 Result Analyses

In this section, we investigated various analytical results through simulation and study the effect of different network parameters on the probability of intrusion detection. In this work, we evaluated the performance of the network in terms of *k*-barrier coverage probability. All the results are obtained by simulating the scenarios on MATLAB simulation tool by varying different network parameters. MATLAB provides all the necessary components and features, which can help to simulate the different analytical models and to obtain the results. The various results are simulated with MATLAB tool under the specified network parameters such as: area of simulation is considered as rectangular area having dimensions 50 m × 100 m, sensing range one, random direction mobility model. Effect of other parameters such as node density and sensor to intruder velocity ratio on *k*-barrier coverage probability is also studied. Moreover, the effect of increasing *k* on the *k*-barrier coverage probability is also analyzed.

5.1 *Effect of Node Density on* k-*Barrier Coverage Probability*

The probability that an intruder will be detected by leastwise *k* sensors while crossing the belt area increases as the number of mobile sensors increase and reach to one quickly with an increase in number of sensors as shown in Fig. 5. Theoretical concepts also validate the simulation results because when mobile sensors are increased in the region of interest, there are more chances that the intruder will be discovered by more sensors. Therefore, *k*-barrier coverage probability tends to one with an increase in the number of mobile sensors.

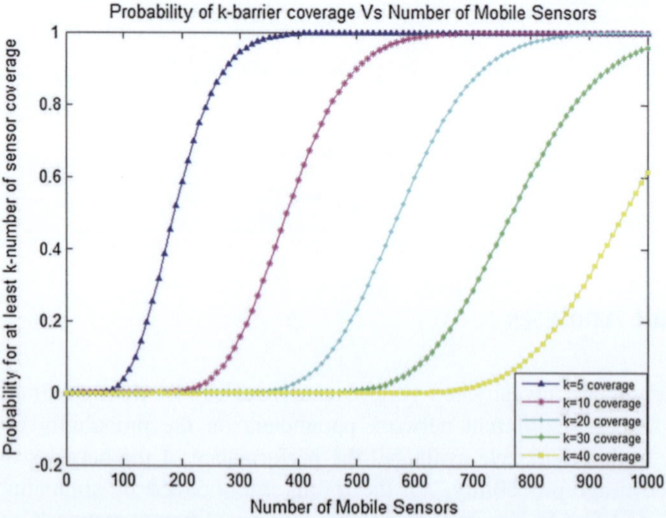

Fig. 5 Effect of mobile sensor density on *k*-barrier coverage probability at different values of *k*

5.2 *Effect of Sensor to Intruder Velocity Ratio on* k*-Barrier Coverage Probability*

It has been observed that *k*-barrier coverage probability increases as the ratio of the velocity of the sensor to the velocity of intruder increases and reaches to its maximum value at a certain value of the ratio for different *k*-barrier coverage requirements as shown in Fig. 6. Theoretical calculations also validate simulation results as the velocity of the sensors increases they can cover a large area in less time and provide full coverage to the every intruder crossing path.

5.3 *Effect of Varying on* k*-Barrier Coverage Probability at Various Number of Moving Sensors*

The *k*-barrier coverage probability decreases by increasing *k* at a different number of mobile sensors as shown in Fig. 7. Simulations results verify analytical results. As the number of moving sensors increase, the *k*-barrier coverage probability reaches to zero for large values of *k* because the requirement of *k*-barrier coverage for large values of *k* will be compensated by the increase in the number of sensors. Increase in the value of *k* means that intruder must be detected by more sensors which put a limitation on the detection probability of the network. Increase in the required *k* sensor coverage can be compensated by deploying more moving sensor in the region of interest.

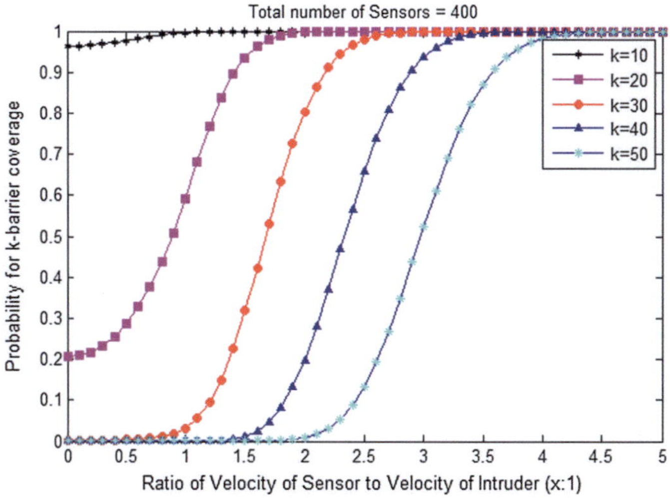

Fig. 6 Effect of sensor to intruder velocity on *k*-barrier coverage probability at different *k*

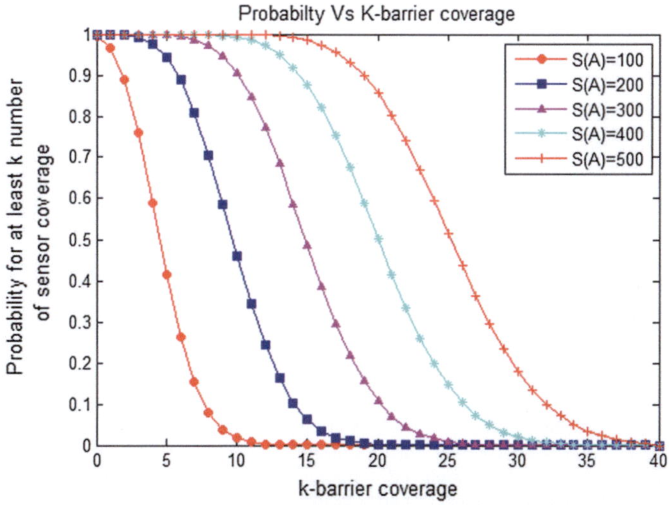

Fig. 7 Effect of increasing *k* on *k*-barrier coverage probability at various numbers of mobile sensors

6 Conclusions

This work analyzes the performance of a mobile sensor network in terms of intrusion detection capability, which is measured in terms of *k*-barrier coverage probability. The *k*-barrier coverage probability depends on the different system and network parameters such as sensor density, sensing range, the speed of the sensors, and intruders.

Novelty of this work is that, instead of having variable velocities of sensors, we considered the constant velocity of every sensor which remains same throughout the simulation time. In this paper, we simulated various performance metrics in terms of k-barrier coverage probability. The probability of k-barrier coverage reaches to unity at a specific value of k as the number of moving sensor increase as shown in Fig. 5. For example at $k = 10$, the k-barrier coverage probability reaches to one when number of moving sensors is 700. Again, the probability of k-barrier coverage improves as sensor to intruder velocity ratio increases as shown in Fig. 6. For example, at $k = 20$ barrier requirement, the k-barrier coverage probability reaches to unity when the velocity ratio is 2.5. Moreover, for a given number of sensors, the k-barrier coverage probability decreases as the k-barrier requirement increase as shown in Fig. 7. For instances, when 200 sensors are spread in the field of interest, the k-barrier coverage probability reaches to zero at $k = 20$ sensor requirement. Hence we can conclude that mobility improves the performance of sensor networks.

References

1. Akyildiz IF, Su W, Sankarasubramaniam Y, Cayirci E (2002) A survey on sensor networks. IEEE Commun Mag 40(8):102–114
2. Nakul P (2013) A survey on malicious node detection in wireless sensor networks. IJSR. 2 (1):2319–7064
3. Zhang Y, Lee W, Huang YA (2003) Intrusion detection techniques for mobile wireless networks. J Wireless Networks 9(5):545–556
4. Farooqi A, Aslam F (2009) Intrusion detection system for wireless sensor networks: a survey. FGCN/CAN CCIS 56:234–241
5. Rasam MA, Maarof MA, Zainal A (2012) A survey of intrusion detection schemes in wireless sensor networks. AJAS 1636–1652
6. Sharma S, Mishra R (2014) A cross layer approach for intrusion detection in MANETs. IJCA 93(9):34–41
7. Butun I, Morgera SD, Sankar R (2013) A survey of intrusion detection systems in wireless sensor networks. IEEE Commun Surv Tutorials
8. Anand Babu GL, Shekhar Reddy G, Agarwal S (2012) Intrusion detection techniques in mobile ad hoc networks. IJCSIT 3:3867–3870
9. Keung GY, Zhang BLQ (2012) The intrusion detection in mobile sensor network. IEEE/ACM Trans Networking 20(4):1152–1161
10. Wang Y, Lun Z (2011) Intrusion detection in a k-Gaussian distributed wireless sensor network. J Parallel Distrib Comput 1598–1607
11. Gaur B, Kumar P (2013) Wireless sensor deployment using modified discrete binary PSO method. IJIREEICE 1(3)
12. Peng M et al (2011) Impacts of sensor node distributions on coverage in sensor networks. J Parallel Distrib Comput 1–14
13. Wang Y, Fu W, Agrawal DP (2013) Gaussian versus uniform distribution for intrusion detection in wireless sensor networks. IEEE Trans Parallel Distrib Syst 24(2):342–355

14. Liu B, Dousse O, Nain P, Towsley D (2013) Dynamic coverage of mobile sensor networks. IEEE Trans Parallel Distrib Syst 24(2):301–311
15. Li J, Jiang S, Pan Z (2009) Strong barrier coverage for intrusion detection in wireless sensor network. In: Proceedings of the second symposium international computer science and computational technology (ISCSCT'09), pp 62–65
16. Wang Y, Wang X, Xie B, Wang D, Agrawal DP (2008) Intrusion detection in homogeneous and heterogeneous wireless sensor networks. IEEE Trans Mob Comput 7(6):698–711
17. Wang Y, Leow YK, Yin J (2009) Is straight-line path always the best for intrusion detection in wireless sensor networks. In: 15th ICPDS, pp 565–571
18. Camp T, Boleng J, Avies V (2002) A survey of mobility models for ad hoc network research. Wireless Commun Mob Comput 2(5):483–502

Performance Analysis of Vulnerability Detection Scanners for Web Systems

Shailendra Singh and Karan Singh

Abstract Much work is done in the area of vulnerability detection. However, it is still not sufficient to detect all the vulnerabilities present in a web application. Vulnerability detection scanners are an automated way to check for these vulnerabilities. But even after many improvements their detection rate is very low. In most cases, averaging to 40% detection of vulnerabilities. This rate can be increased when we provide favorable situations to scanners, increasing its detection rate. This work deals with such situations. The selection of best scanner for a given situation. So that detection of vulnerabilities is fulfilled in a more efficient way.

Keywords Security · Vulnerability · Scanners · Detection

1 Introduction

Internet is full of information and data. It is the backbone of today's working environment [1]. Internet together with its hypertext data and information is called *World Wide Web,* commonly known as WWW or just Web. Users interact with the web using the web application and browsers [2]. A web application is a combined system of a server, a website hosted by the server and a back-end database. Web applications are used to serve user's different needs in a convenient and efficient manner. Because of this, web applications are increasing in numbers. But with an increased number of web applications, a number of attacks on these applications also increased. In the Figure, Cisco Annual security report [3] shows the increased number of security alerts in the year 2012–13.

S. Singh (✉) · K. Singh
School of Computer & Systems Sciences, Jawaharlal Nehru University,
New Delhi 110067, India
e-mail: shaile91scs@jnu.ac.in

K. Singh
e-mail: karancs12@gmail.com

M. U. Bokhari et al. (eds.), *Cyber Security*, Advances in Intelligent Systems and Computing 729, https://doi.org/10.1007/978-981-10-8536-9_37

To tackle the growing number of alerts, we use automatic vulnerability scanning tools. These scanners use black-box approach, i.e. they do not need a code of the application. These tools scan web applications to find potential web vulnerabilities. Later these vulnerabilities are corrected to make the application more secure. Our work focuses to increase detection of these vulnerabilities by favoring one scanner to another in different conditions. This paper is organized as follows. Section 2 explaining the related work done. Section 3 explains the proposed work. Section 4 discusses about the performed experiment and results. Section 5 concludes the paper.

2 Related Work

Many research works are done on the topic of vulnerability.

Sili et al. [4] explained in their research that, most current browsers have a monolithic architecture which does not maintain a clear separation between its modules. All modules work in one process, hence vulnerability in one module can lead to whole system corruption. To overcome this, some browsers used a modular approach to increase the security (like chrome) but they are also not fully secure. Chrome itself, covering most security concerns, has some loopholes which question its security aspect, which when exploited can be used to attack other sites.

Johari and Sharma [5] have suggested in research that in all the potential web attacks, the major ones are SQL injection (SQLi) and cross-site scripting (XSS). These types of attacks are done by manipulating the vulnerabilities present in the code application or script. SQL Injection possessed more risks because it affects the underlying database which is of utmost importance for any organization.

Fonseca [6] have suggested in their research, that half of the SQLi attacks are done using the numeric field exploitation, i.e., Input Fields meant to get data from users are the most Vulnerable spots if taken input is not properly sanitized.

Duraes and Madeira [7] have proposed many ways to detect and prevent vulnerabilities present in the system. According to his study, Fault injection approach is the most efficient way for detecting and correcting vulnerabilities. Fault injection approach uses the fact that major portion of vulnerabilities falls under a small category of faults. So, we can use this knowledge to write better codes.

Avancini and Ceccato [8] have suggested a method for detecting input parameter vulnerabilities by focusing on structural constraints corresponding code responses. By using Taint analysis, they try to spot the Vulnerability. A Vulnerability is present when a tainted value is used in a sink statement. They have obtained improved results with the use of genetic algorithms. The major drawback of this method is that the majority of vulnerabilities can only be detected in run time, because input values define the flow of code and in a different situation, a code can behave differently.

Wang [9] have proposed a method for detecting underlying vulnerability in a web application by using hidden web crawlers. They have used information gathered by hidden web crawlers to effectively craft the attack string, which greatly unfolds the vulnerability present in the system. The search area is increased when used in conjunction with Access Authentication database table (AADT).

Dessiatnikoff [10] have extended the Xin Wang methodology [9] and suggested a method to predict the vulnerability present in the code. The authors have classified the response pages into three clusters based on the distance of normalized change in their responses. Since a response is always associated with a request and vice versa. Hence it is enough to check the responses. Based on these clusters, the author is able to predict the Vulnerability present in the system with a greater accuracy than other scanners present.

Damjanovic and Djuric [11] have suggested that by using domain knowledge of a particular web application in conjunction with functional programming paradigm and Model-Driven Architecture, we can draw the attack model. It is possible to model the attack using this knowledge in the form of attack tree, with a global goal of attack the system. Analyzing this tree unfolds the vulnerability present in the system. Later further gained knowledge through this attack model can also be incorporated into the system to enhance the method's effectiveness.

Buja et al. [12] used Four-layer approach to Prevent and Detect a Vulnerabilities in the web system. In his model, he used Boyer–Moore string matching algorithm which reduced the time in matching the pattern in brute-force approaches. This algorithm is mostly used to detect virus Detection where large data is analyzed in a short time. It improved the detection speed in quite a number.

Many researchers are trying to improve the detection capability of a scanner. Since many of the best scanners are only having detection capability of around 40% which is not a very good upper limit. Our goal is to choose scanners such that this upper limit is increased. This can be done by using problem-specific scanners, i.e. use of different scanners based on the criteria or problem at disposal.

3 Proposed Work

Since the advent of Web applications, users have now power to do many things such as E-commerce, Online Banking, etc. For this purpose, application store and send confidential data to server. Now, since applications are prone to Vulnerabilities. Hence these vulnerabilities are used to attack on web applications. Which later results in the compromise of confidential data and manipulation of system. To obliterate these attacks probability, we tend to find the underlying vulnerabilities in initial states so that it will not make system Vulnerable in later stages. With all our best efforts 100% detection of vulnerabilities is not possible. So one best alternative is that we deploy the web application. After that, we scan it for potential vulnerabilities and rectify them as we encounter them making it a part of maintenance. However, many vulnerabilities are only surfaced when they are deployed in the real world. Also, some vulnerabilities do not even lead to a successful attack and hence investing unnecessary power is not a good thought.

For this purpose, we use vulnerability detection scanners to detect the vulnerabilities present in the system. They use the Black-Box approach to detect the vulnerabilities, i.e., they do not need the code of the application to work.

3.1 Vulnerability Scanner Working Mechanism

Web application contains Vulnerabilities which are used to attack the application in order to compromise the security of system. Vulnerability scanners are used to detect those vulnerabilities. After successful detection, we can rectify these vulnerabilities from the system. Hence making the system more secure. All of Vulnerability scanners use the following basic procedure to detect the vulnerabilities present in the system.

Figure 1 shows the typical working of a scanner. Every phase uses information generated by its component to successfully complete the task. Different scanners deploy these components in a different manner and hence greatly changing the efficiency of the scanner.

3.2 Tools

In this proposed work, we are trying to set a benchmark for some well known open-source scanners. Our work is focused on evaluating their performance based on different parameters such as time taken in scan, Number of Vulnerabilities detected, etc. For this, we have chosen three well-known open-source Vulnerability scanners. Table 1 shows the list of Scanners used for this purpose.

These scanners are top in their league with most downloaded scanners by penetration testing users.

3.3 Data Sets

For this Dissertation work, we have used following vulnerable applications:

Application shown in Table 2 are some standard applications meant to check the working of a scanner listed in OWASP directory Project [13]. Since in real-life attacking, a web application is both illegal and punishable offense. These datasets are hosted by different commercial scanner developers to either test their scanner or use it as research data. There are many possible development languages for web application. However, in this work we chose application written in PHP only. By confining to only PHP-written code, it is easy to demonstrate the relative

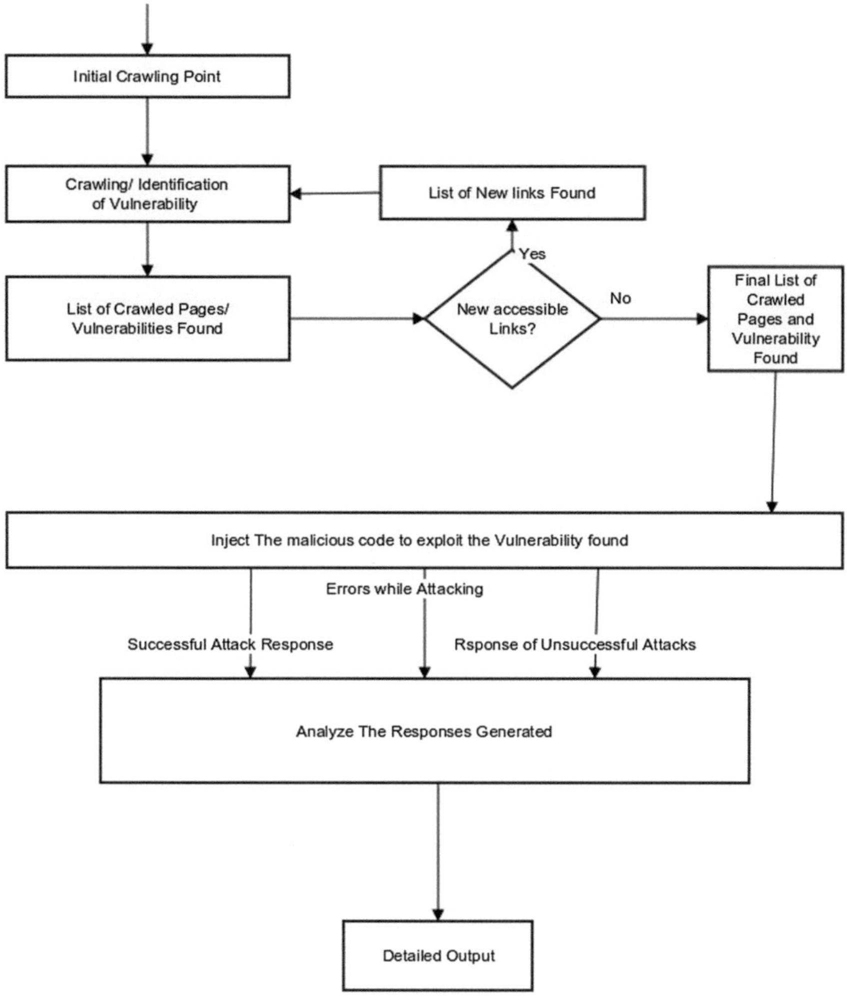

Fig. 1 Work flow diagram of a scanner

Table 1 Vulnerability scanners

S. no.	Scanner	Creation year	Language	Interface	Version
1	Wapiti	2006	Python	Command-line	2.3.0
2	W3af	2007	Python	Command-line and GUI	1.6.45
3	ZAP	2010	Java	GUI	2.4.0

comparison statics for the scanner tools. In this work, we have fed these vulnerable web applications as Input data to scanner tools. The output results are analyzed to show the different comparison statistics of vulnerability scanners.

Table 2 Data sets

S. no.	Project name	Type	Web-link	Language
1	Acuart	Online	http://testphp.vulnweb.com/	PHP
2	Vicnum Project	Online	http://vicnum.ciphertechs.com/	PHP
3	Web Scanner Test Site	Online	http://www.webscantest.com/	PHP
4	Zero Bank	Online	http://zero.webappsecurity.com/	PHP

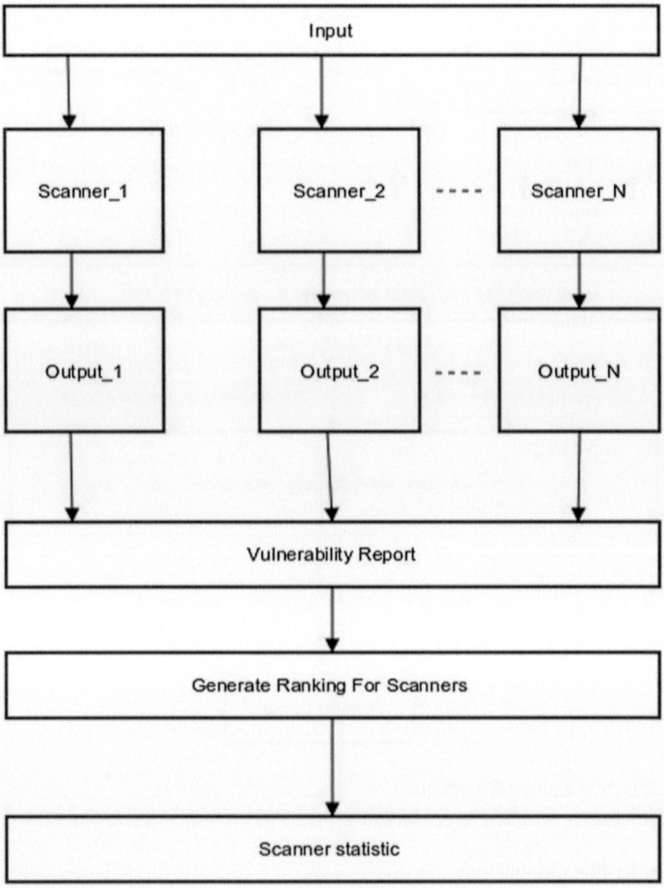

Fig. 2 Evaluation procedure

3.4 Working Procedure

We are proposing a vulnerability detection approach for web applications. The proposed approach depends upon the report generation of scanners and its own scanner ranking phase. The evaluation procedure of the proposed work is given in Fig. 2. In this work, the first task is to generate the vulnerability detection report using the different scanners available. In this model, we used three open-source scanners available to users. Applying these scanners to datasets available online we are able to produce scanner outputs, i.e., vulnerability detection reports for each data set. After that, the proposed work is applied on these generated reports. By applying the proposed algorithm to the generated reports, different analyses are done based on criteria specified. According to specified criteria, a scanner is ranked. For different criteria, different scanners get the high rank. The final generated reports show the efficient scanner according to criteria specified.

Proposed Algorithm: In this proposed work, the algorithm works in two different phases. The first phase is to generate scanning reports produced by vulnerability detection scanners. Next phase uses these reports to generate the ranking of scanners. The algorithm in pseudocode is as follows:

Phase 1: Report Generation

BEGIN

Step 1: Take Dataset i where i = 1 to n;

Step 2: Take Scanner j where j = 1 to m;

Step 3: Scan Dataset i by using Scanner j;

Step 4: Save Generated report as Output[i][j];

END

Phase 2: Ranking Phase

BEGIN

Step 1: Take Output[][];

Step 2: Initialize scanner rank[] = 1 ;

Step 3: Initialize Criteria[] = criteria of ranking ;

Step 4: For each Criteria[k] repeat step 5-7;

Step 5: Analyze Output[][]; Step 6: if Output[j][i] < Output[j][i+1] than increment scanner rank[i+1]; else increment scanner rank[i];

Step 7: Repeat step 6 and 7 for each scanner i for each dataset j.

Step 8: Generate Report according to Criteria[].

END

Example: For initial working explanation can be given as follows.

We take two scanners like wapiti and w3af. We use these scanners on some vulnerable web applications. In this case, we choose online vulnerable application like vicnum project [15]. Scanning this web application using the specified scanners, respectively, we generate vulnerability detection report. Successful generation of reports leads to the main phase of the algorithm. Where these reports are analyzed according to different criteria set, i.e., time, performance for a particular vulnerability, etc. In this case, two reports are analyzed for the same web application. For the comparison of the criteria, let us take time as criteria. The algorithm will show the efficiency of these scanners time-wise, i.e., which is taking less time to finish the scan. Algorithm will rank these scanners based on this criteria. Change in criteria will also lead to change in ranking of the scanners.

4 Experiment and Results

This section explains the experiment performed and result obtained. A detailed explanation is also given for the result obtained.

4.1 System Requirements

The system configuration for the experiment to perform is listed below. Some are Compulsory as to run the scanners used.

The Hardware configuration for this experiment is which allowed successful and efficient execution of the experiment.

- Processor: Intel Core i7 (3.4 GHz)
- Main Memory:1 GB Minimum
- Hard Disk Space: 20 GB Minimum
- Input Device: Keyboard and Preferred Mouse

Software Requirement for this work is as follows:

- Operating System: Ubuntu 14.04—Tools and IDE used: Latex, Gummi editor.

4.2 Experimental Results

Using the experimental setup, when the proposed algorithm is run. We obtained Different results based on the criteria we specified.

First Run: For our first run, we chose the Criteria as "Total number of vulnerability detected". In this run, we are interested to find the scanner which is capable of generating most number of vulnerability detection alerts.

Figure 3 shows the alerts detected when performing scans on the data sets. An alert is a potential vulnerability in the web application. It is evident from the figure that ZAP detected more alerts than the rest of the two scanners. This is because of two main reasons:

1. Since ZAP includes the Top 10 vulnerability profiles standardized by OWASP, it is more efficient to detect the vulnerability since it has pre-information about them.

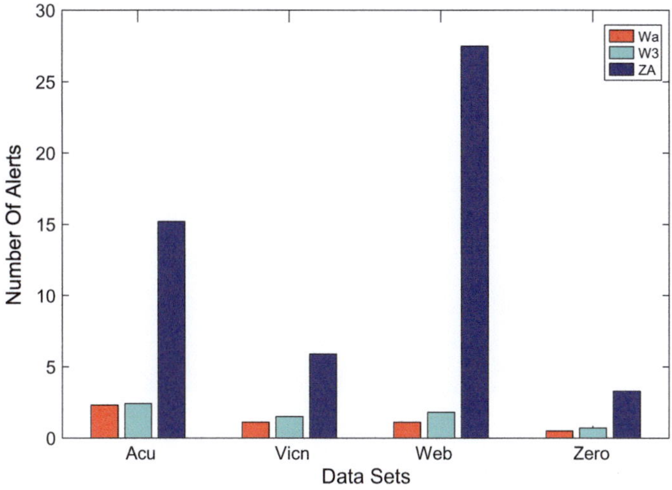

Fig. 3 Alert detected

2. Usually, a request has multiple responses and hence ZAP has multiple alerts for the same request. Hence, the high number of alert detection.

It may look that ZAP is accumulating unnecessary alerts unlike the rest two. But in many situations, a vulnerability is often surfaced when certain conditions are met by generating as many as alerts, ZAP increases its coverage area. So, considering this point ZAP is able to generate more possible vulnerable points than rest of the two.

So, for our first criteria, we can see that ZAP has higher performance and hence higher ranking.

Second Run: For this run, we chose the criteria as "Shortest time taken in one scan". When we apply the proposed algorithm, we get the result as shown in Fig. 4.

In this case also ZAP has shown the most efficient performance, which took the least time in all of the scanners to finish the scan. On an average, ZAP was 167% faster than w3af and 236% faster than Wapiti. In short, ZAP is efficient in the manner of time taken to complete a scan. This duration may differ as enabling different plug-ins affect the time to scan drastically. But the algorithm is able to show the comparison for each dataset.

It is interesting that Wapiti is taking more time than others. Prime cause of this is that when Wapiti is executed without any specific setting it runs all its modules one by one, and hence takes more time whereas W3af and ZAP run only the basic module configuration. So time duration differs in greatly by the plug-ins and modules configured.

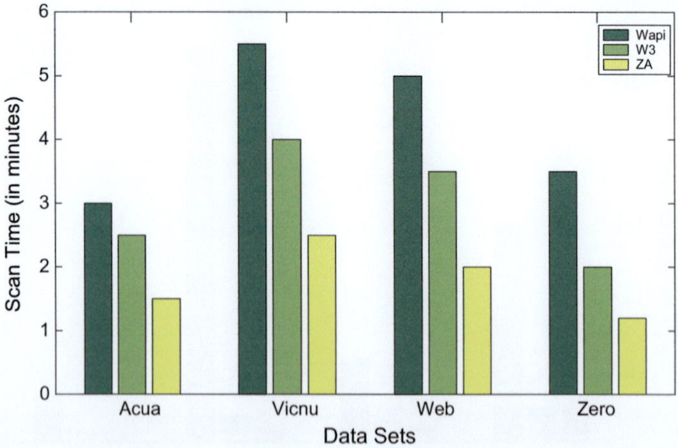

Fig. 4 Time laps in one scan

Third Run: In this Run, we set criteria as "Severity of Vulnerability", i.e., High, Medium and Low severity vulnerabilities. The proposed algorithm generates the following reports.

Figure 5 shows the report for Acuart dataset [14]. As we can see, in this case ZAP stands out by generating more number of alerts in each section. Whereas Wapiti and W3af have comparatively the same performance.

Figure 6 shows the same report for dataset 2, i.e., Vicnum project [15]. Which also shows the same results as in case of dataset Acuart. But what is interesting in this is that although ZAP generated high number of alerts in other category. The High-risk factor is almost the same in each of the scanner statistics. If we would have chosen criteria based on only High-risk Vulnerability, the output would have ranked all the scanners with the same rank.

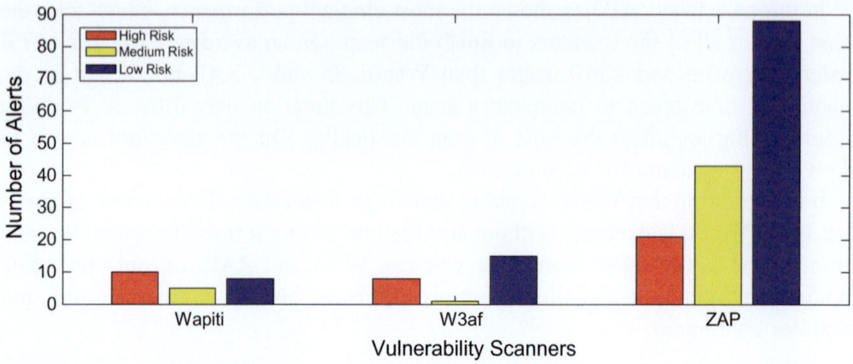

Fig. 5 Risk Distribution For Acuart

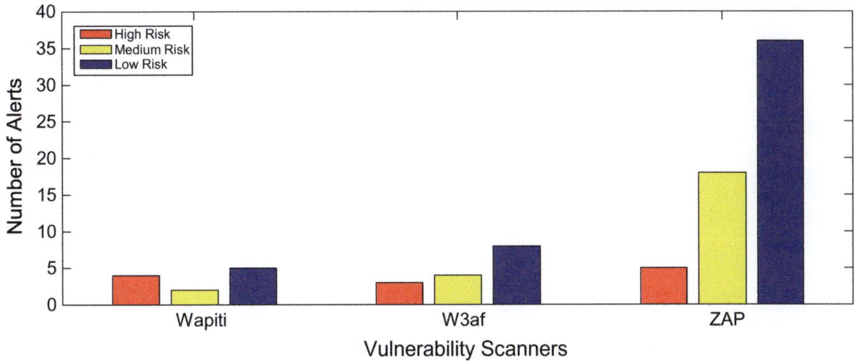

Fig. 6 Risk distribution for vicnum project

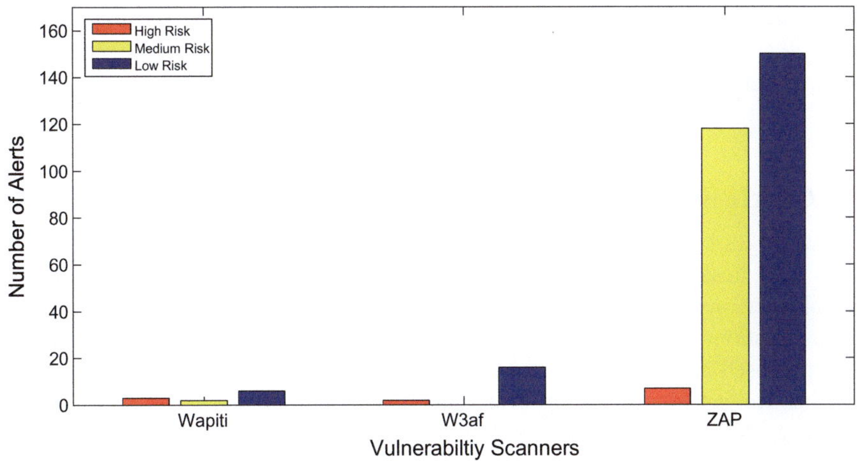

Fig. 7 Risk distribution for web scanner test site

Figure 7 shows the report for dataset 3, i.e., for Web Scanner Test suite [16]. A similar report has been generated for the dataset Zero Bank [17]. It is shown in Fig. 8.

These two reports have rather interesting factors associated with them. For Fig. 7, if we consider medium risk vulnerability alerts it is zero for W3af, and High-risk type are very less which may be due to unable to bypass ther authentication page, which reduced the number of detected vulnerabilities. Since our algorithm uses the scanner report as input it also affects the working of algorithm, ranking a scanner incorrectly. Hence for better ranking, it should be desirable to have a good scanning result. As For Fig. 8 results are changed, as we can see in other results ZAP is prominently ranked but in this result ZAP is unable to detect a high-risk vulnerability which in turn is detected by W3af in high number. Hence,

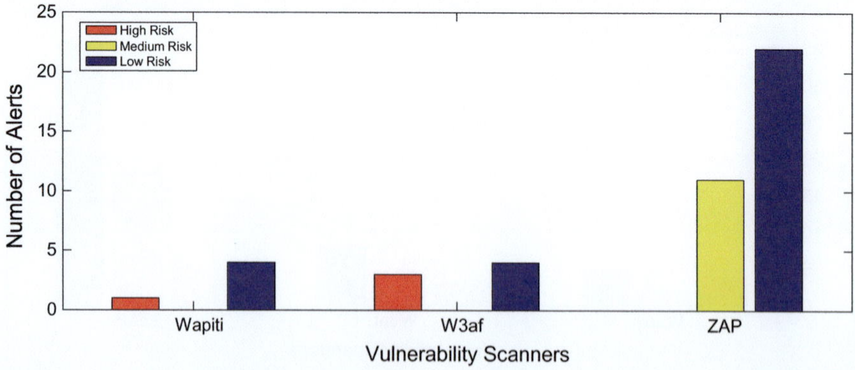

Fig. 8 Risk distribution for Zero Bank

our algorithm would have ranked W3af as efficient if we would have chosen the criteria only for high-risk vulnerability. These results show that if we choose different criteria different ranking is given to the same report.

5 Conclusion

This work deals the issue of how to prioritize Web vulnerability scanners in different situations. However, these scanners work well in some situation and poor in some situations. Hence, it is crucial to adaptively use them as the scenario arrives. The proposed algorithm tries to deal this issue by analyzing the scanner's output. By this, we can roughly estimate that, in which criteria which scanner to be used. We here showed that for the criteria being the "scan time" or "severity of alerts" will produce different statistics. Based on these, the proposed algorithm tries to rank vulnerability detection scanners. As with every work, this algorithm also is far from being perfect. Ambiguous ranking may possible if reports are biased or erroneous. Algorithm does not have the capability to predict similarity between reports, which when added, will enable the algorithm to rank scanners more accurately. Future work includes addition of this functionality to improve the results so that better results can be obtained.

References

1. Kern C, Kesavan A, Daswani N (2007) Foundations of security: what every programmer needs to know. In: Paperback, 14 Feb 2007
2. Tanenbaum AS, Wetherall DJ. Computer networks, 5th edn. Prentice Hall, Upper Saddle River

3. Cisco.com (2015) Cisco annual security report. http://www.cisco.com/web/offer/gist_ty2_asset/Cisco_2014_ASR.pdf
4. Sili M (2010) Security vulnerabilities in modern web browser architecture. In: MIPRO, Opatija, Croatia, pp 1240–1245
5. Johari R, Sharma P (2012) A survey on web application vulnerabilities (SQLIA,XSS) exploitation and security engine for SQL injection. In: International conference on communication systems and network technologies, pp 453–458. https://doi.org/10.1109/csnt.2012.104
6. Fonseca J (2014) Evolution of web security mechanisms using vulnerability and attack injection. IEEE Trans Dependable Secur Comput 11(5):440–453
7. Duraes JA, Madeira HS (2006) Emulation of software faults: a field data study and a practical approach. IEEE Trans Software Eng 32(11)
8. Avancini A, Ceccato M (2011) Security testing of web applications: a search based approach for cross-site scripting vulnerabilities. In: 11th IEEE international working conference on source code analysis and manipulation, pp 85–94. https://doi.org/10.1109/scam.2011.7
9. Wang X (2010) Hidden web crawling for SQL injection detection. In: Proceedings of IC-BNMT2010. IEEE, pp 14–18
10. Dessiatnikoff A (2011) A clustering approach for web vulnerabilities detection. In: 17th IEEE Pacific rim international symposium on dependable computing, pp 194–203
11. Damjanovic V, Djuric D (2010) Functional programming way to interact with software attacks and vulnerabilities. In: Third international conference on software testing, verification, and validation workshops. IEEE, pp 388–393. https://doi.org/10.1109/icstw.2010.53
12. Buja G, Jalil KBA, Mohd Ali FBH, Abdul TF (2014) Detection model for SQL injection attack: an approach for preventing a web application from the SQL injection attack. In: IEEE Symposium on Computer Applications & Industrial Electronics (ISCAIE), Penang, Malaysia, pp 60–64
13. Owasp.org (2015) OWASP vulnerable web applications directory project—OWASP. https://www.owasp.org/index.php/OWASP_Vulnerable_Web_Applications_Directory_Project
14. Acuart, http://testphp.vulnweb.com/
15. Vicnum Project, http://vicnum.ciphertechs.com/
16. Web Scanner Test Site, http://www.webscantest.com/
17. Zero Bank, http://zero.webappsecurity.com/

Performance Evaluation of Multicast Source Authentication Scheme

Yogendra Mohan, C. Rama Krishna and Karan Singh

Abstract Multicast is a one to group communication. The applications of multicast are broadcasting stock quotes, videoconferencing, and software distribution. The deployment of efficient and secure communication mechanism is hindered because of the lack of security. There are various schemes such as simple hash scheme, hash tree scheme, and hash tree signature scheme. But these existing approaches also suffer from communication overhead and computation overhead. To solve the major problem of security concern is solved with support of source authentication mechanism. The purpose of our work is to evaluate the performance of multicast source authentication. The objectives of the proposed work are to reduce the communication overhead and computation cost of multicast communication system. The proposed work is implemented in QualNet 5.1.2.

Keywords Multicast communication · ECDSA · Source authentication
ECCSA · Elliptic curve cryptography · Hash tree · Non-repudiation

1 Introduction

The large-scale development of Internet and use of electronics meant for communication resulted the new digital era of communication. The data or information can be sent to various network like unicast, broadcast, multicast, etc. In the case of

Y. Mohan (✉)
CSED, NERIST, Nirjuli 791109, Arunachal Pradesh, India
e-mail: yogendra.mohan@gmail.com

C. R. Krishna
NITTTR, Chandigarh 160019, India
e-mail: rkc_98@hotmail.com

K. Singh
School of Computer & Systems Sciences, Jawaharlal Nehru University,
New Delhi 110067, India
e-mail: karan@mail.jnu.ac.in

M. U. Bokhari et al. (eds.), *Cyber Security*, Advances in Intelligent Systems
and Computing 729, https://doi.org/10.1007/978-981-10-8536-9_38

unicast, there is one-to-one communication, while in case of broadcast one-to-all communication and in case of multicast the communication is between one source to a group of destinations. The demand of multipoint communications (multicast) among various parties is increasing. Unicast communications are overheaded and underutilized. Multicasting is increasing day by day for various applications such as video on demand (VoD), IPTv, broadcasting, and stock quotes. The multicast IP address is well known as class *D*. That is why, there are many security obstacles present in multicast. There is a need to maintain security goals to provide security at source and group ends. In multicast network, the source is not necessarily member of the group, so untrusted source may cause the rescuer deployment of the multicast services. Hash and digital signatures are the used for integrity [1], authentication, and non-repudiation. However, these mechanisms is used to design for point-to-point [2] transmission, and embedded in multicasting.

Multicast communication suffers from various challenges such as congestion, security threats, and addressing and the security threat is a biggest challenge in the multicast. This challenge is handled by source authentication and group authentication. Source authentication is main objective of proposed work. The researchers [3–9] have provided the mechanism for source authentication. The authors have used RSA [10, 11] for digital signature to achieve the source authentication [12], but existing mechanisms suffered from computation overhead and communication overhead. To solve these problems, we are proposing source authentication mechanism which is based on Elliptic Curve Cryptography Digital Signature Algorithm (ECDSA) [13, 14] for multicasting. The proposed approach is known as Elliptic Curve Cryptography Source Authentication (ECCSA).

2 Related Works

The literature possess several approaches and models for providing source authentication in multicast communication. The issues and challenges in the area of multicast security are described in this section existing multicast source authentication protocol such as simple off-line chaining, tree chaining, EMSS, and HMSA are described with their advantages and disadvantages.

In Hash chaining [9] scheme, the working of sender and receiver are described below into the blocks [15] then the hash of the first block is computed and signs the hash of the first block. The technique of the hash chaining scheme, sender first divides message *M* into 4 blocks $\{B_1, B_2, B_3, B_4\}$ then computes the hash of the first block, signs it, and transmit to each receiver.

In tree chaining [16, 17] scheme each packet carries the required authentication information so that each can be individually verifiable. In other words, even if $n - 1$ out of n packets are lost the authenticity of the single received packet can be verified. The stream is signed block by block.

Efficient Multi-chained Stream Signature (EMSS) [18, 19] scheme each packet of the stream is hash linked [20, 21] to many target packets. Even if some packets are lost;

a received packet is verifiable if it remains a hash-link path that relates the packet to a signature packet. For a given packet, the EMSS chooses target packets randomly.

Jin et al. [22] proposed a hybrid approach (HMSA) in which hash tree and hash chaining scheme are combined. In this approach, the author has targeted on the main disadvantage that occurs with both the scheme.

This section explained the existing multicast source authentication protocol with non-repudiation [11] and their advantages and disadvantages. There is no scheme which will satisfy all the requirements for multicast source authentication. In the next section, a novel multicast source authentication with non-repudiation protocol hash redundancy mitigation scheme for multicast source authentication [23] is proposed which makes a tradeoff between communications overhead [24] and robustness [25] against the packet loss.

3 Proposed Method

Multicast communication suffers from various attacks such as distributed denial of service (DDoS) [26, 27], Message modification [25], replay attacks [28], and eavesdropping [29]. The attacker uses the source as data transmitter or it works as a source of data because multicast IP address [30] are well known to everyone. There is a need to provide a mechanism which protects the source of multicast communication and mechanism is known as multicast source authentication (MSA). This subsection is providing the procedure for packet generation procedure [31] and packet verification [32] procedure as follows:

Sender Side

Packet Generation Procedure: M is a message of any size and message is divided into blocks. The block size may be 2, 4, 8, 16, 32, 64, and 128(packets) (Fig. 1).

Hash Generation: The main arguments of the proposed work are based on following procedure.

- Sender generates H_{ij} (i = 1 and j = 1to 8) of first block root hash [H_{118}] by using packet hashes H_{11}, H_{12}, H_{18} and hashes of the internal node. Similarly for others blocks.
- Sender signed over root hash of the first block.
- Sender sends signed hash of first block root to each receiver
- Sender sends first packets P_{11} of block one with packet ID, sibling hashes of current packet path to root (H_{12}, H_{134}, and H_{158}) and second block root hash [H_{118}].
- Sender sends the second packet with only first packet hash value h_{11}. Because it uses to generate root hash of the value H_{11}. Because it is used to generate root hash of the sender side.
- Now, Sender sends the P_{13} with H_{14} and H_{12} only and uses the stored values to generate the root of the first block.

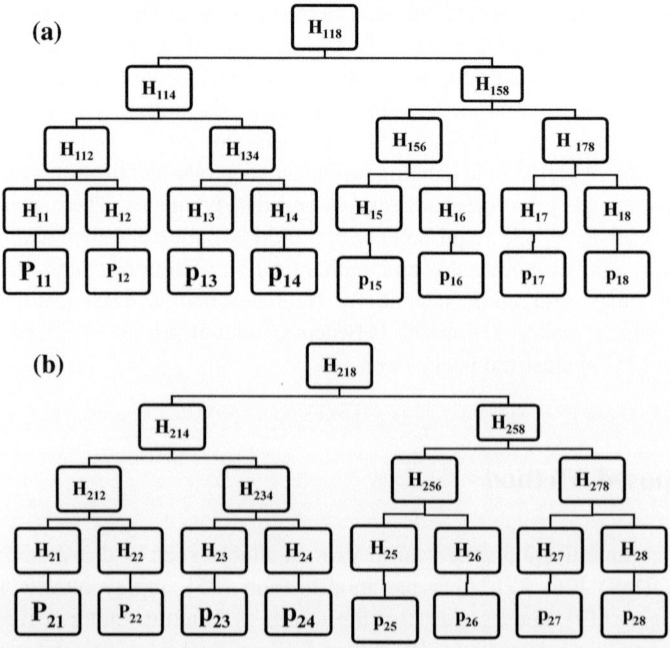

Fig. 1 **a** Hash generation process for block 1. **b** Hash generation process for block 2

- Sender sends the P_{14} with only H_{13}.
- Now, sender sends packets P_{15}, P_{16}, P_{17}, and P_{18} according to step 4, 5, 6 and 7. So sender sends P_{15} with a sibling ($H_{16,}$ H_{178}, H_{118}) with second block root [H_{118}], P_{16} with H_{15} and P_{17} with H_{18}+H_{156}.
- Repeat all steps for $n - 1$ block and with last block no need to send the signature root packet.

Signature Generation & Distribution: Associate the root hash (*H*) of packet *Pi* with signature and does the following:

- Choose a random number *k* (integer) between 1 to $N - 1$.
- Generate Hash (*P*)
- Generate the curve point $k \cdot G = (a, b)$
- Generate $e = a \bmod N$. If $e = 0$ then go back to step 1
- Generate $d = (k^{-1})(h_l + ed_a) \bmod N$. if $d = 0$, then go to step 1.
- Sender's signature for the root hash of packet *Pi* is the pair of integers (*e*, *d*).

Receiver Side

To verify Sender signature (*e*, *d*) on *H*: Receiver associated with public key C_a does the following:

- Verify that e and d are integers between 1 to $(N - 1)$
- Generate $h = H(m)$
- Generate $t = (d^{-1}) \bmod N$
- Generate $v1 = h_l t \bmod N$ and $v2 = et \bmod N$
- Generate curve point x $v1G + v2\ C_a$
- If $a = 0$, then reject the signature, $v = a \bmod N$
- Accept the signature if $v = e$.

Digest Regeneration and Verification of Root Hash

- Receivers first receive the signed hash root of the first block.
- Receivers unsigned the root hash and store it.
- Receivers receive packet P_{11} and compute H_{11}.
- Now regenerate the hash root of the first block with help of H_{12}, H_{134}, H_{158} and computed first block root hash $[H_{118}]$.

Receivers verify the authentication of P_{11}, H_{12}, H_{134}, H_{58} and second block hash of root, if stored root hash of block one is identical with the computed root hash of block one (Fig. 2).

- Receivers store the value H_{12}, H_{134}, H_{156}; second block root hash $[H_{118}]$.
- Receivers get P_{12} along with previous packet hash, i.e., H_{11} then it computes the hash [33] of packet P_{11} and generates first block root hash with the help of store hashes. If computed first block root hash H_{118} is identical with stored first block root H_{118}, so source is authentic along with packet P_2.
- Same way receiver received packet P_3, P_4 and with the help of stored value of hash to generate the first block root hash H_{118}. The proposed work flow chart is given in Fig. 3.

4 Result Analysis and Discussion

We use QualNet simulator version 5.0 to simulate our work. QualNet simulator provides wide a variety of simulations

A platform that can predict wireless wired and mixed platform network and networking device performance.

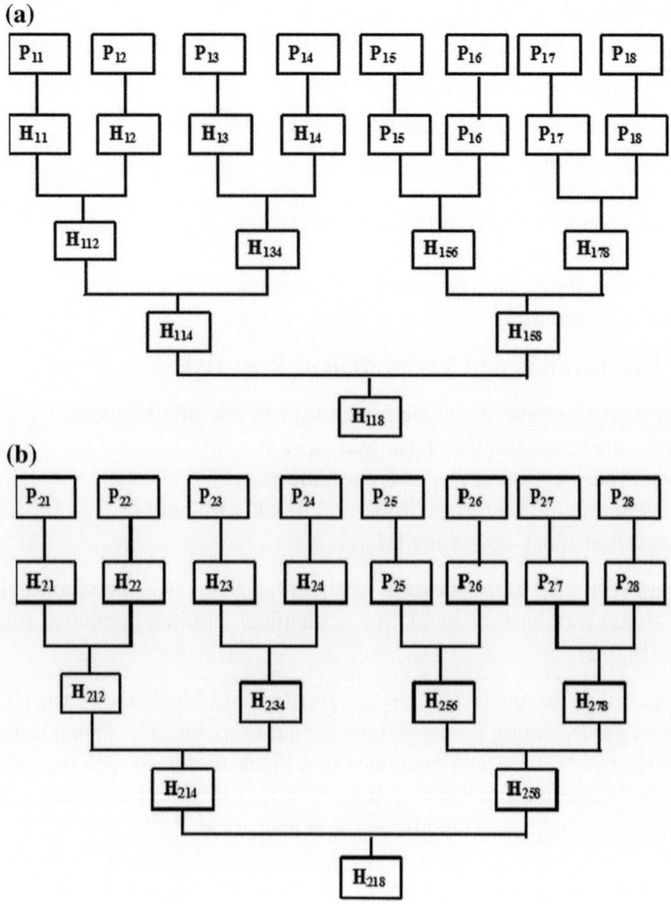

Fig. 2 **a** Hash verification process of block 1. **b** Hash verification process of block 2

4.1 *Parameters Used*

There are following parameters used for implementation of the work are shown in Table 1.

4.2 *Experimental Topology*

The general scenario of multicast is shown in Fig. 4. In this topology, there is one source and there are eight receivers. Source needs to send packet only once then in the network cloud there are many numbers of routers which makes a copy of the

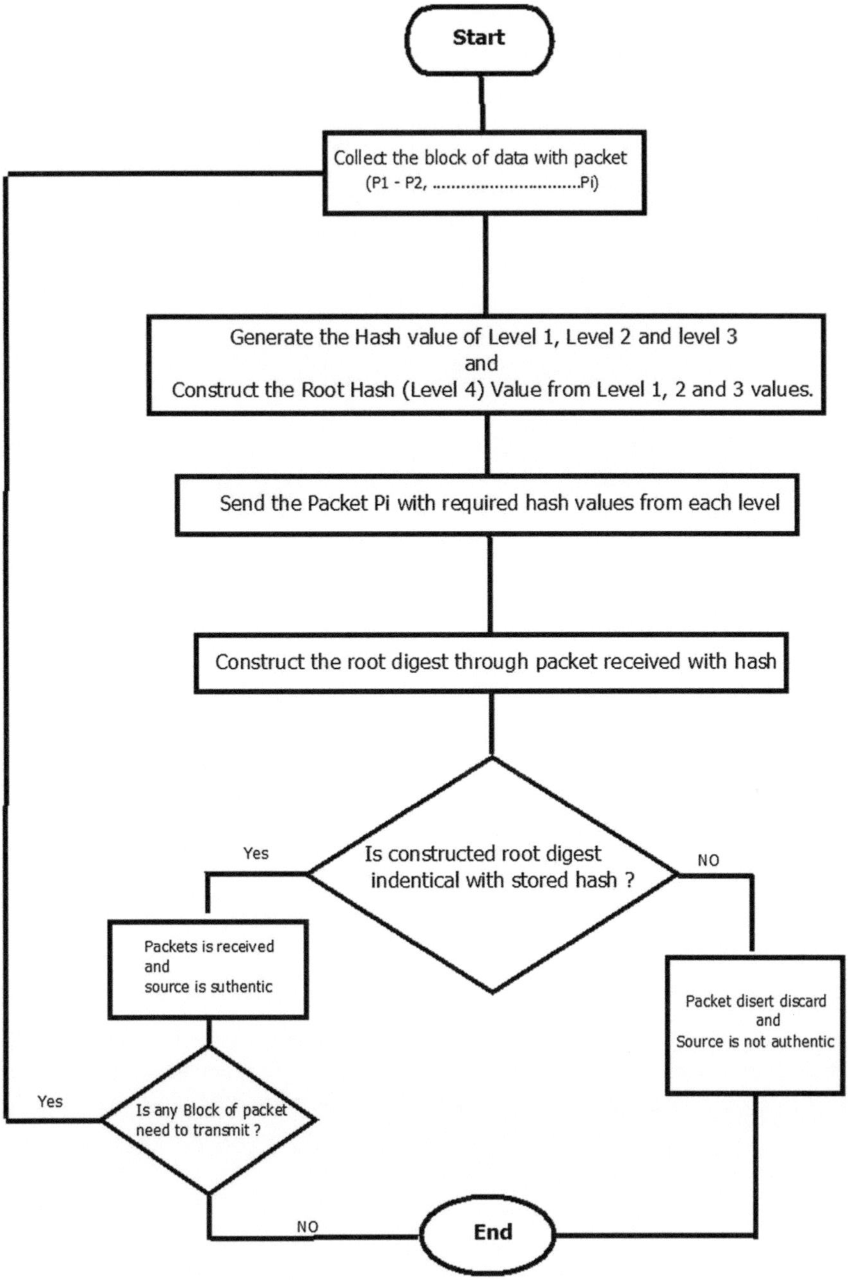

Fig. 3 Flowchart of the proposed work

Table 1 List of implementation parameters

Implementation parameters	Assumed values
Block size	2, 4, 8, 16, 32, 64 (No. of packets)
Packet size	64, 128, 256, 512 (Bits)
Size of SHA-1	20 byte
Size of ECC signature	128 bits
Buffer size	2 block
Simulation time	60 s

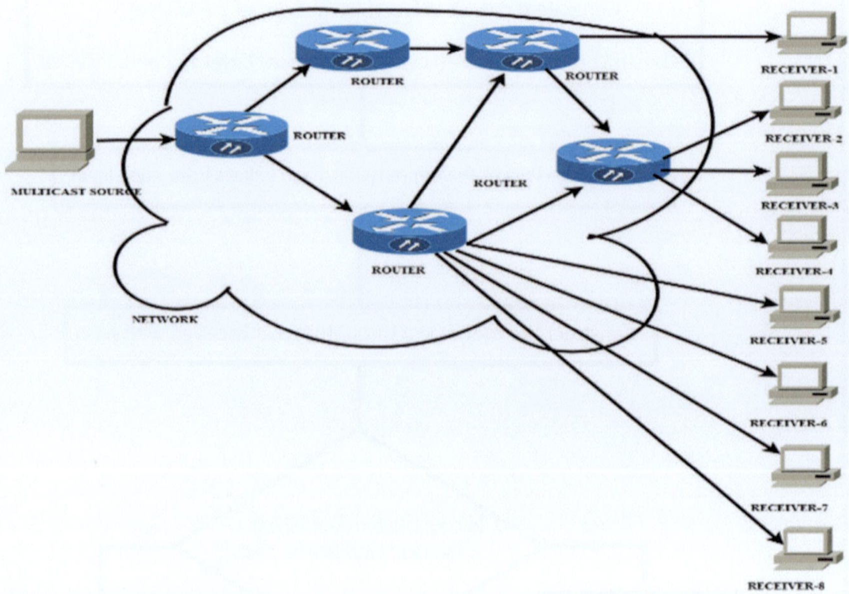

Fig. 4 Experimental topology

packet and send to its neighbor routers. Finally, packet is reached to the end router which makes many copies of packet as the number of receivers in a particular multicast group then transmit the packet to that entire receiver.

4.3 *Result Analysis*

There are many schemes [34, 35] discussed in literature survey and they used the RSA for source authentication for multicasting. According to NIST recommendation, achieving 128-bit security means that the RSA key should be at least 3072 bits although the same security can be provided using Elliptic Curve Cryptography

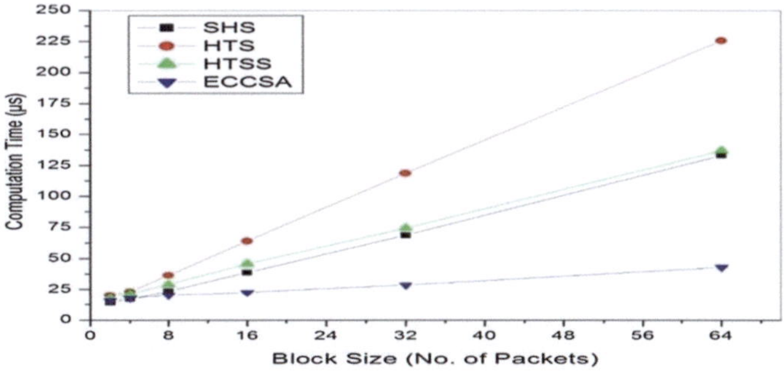

Fig. 5 Block size versus commutation time

Digital Signature Algorithm (ECDSA) [36] with the key of 256 bits. Hence the key size has been reduced.

Effect of Packet Size on Computation Time

It can be observed from the Fig. 5 that the computation time in case of HTS is highest and computation time SHS and HTSS are approximately equal and greater than ECCSA scheme.

Effect of Packet Size on Computation Time

It can be observed from the Fig. 6 that the computation time in case of HTS is highest and computation time SHS and HTSS are approximately equal and greater than ECCSA scheme.

Effect of Packet Size on Communication Overhead

It can be observed from the Fig. 7 that the communication overhead is less than SHS, HTS, and HTSS.

Effect of Packet Size on Verification Rate

It can be observed from the Fig. 8 that the verification rate of ECCSA is greater than the HTS [37] but less than HTSS and SHS. The verification rate is a little bit less but the other advantage of ECCSA schemes is less communication overhead because the ECCSA scheme did not send the redundant data through the channel.

Effect of Packet Size on Communication Overhead

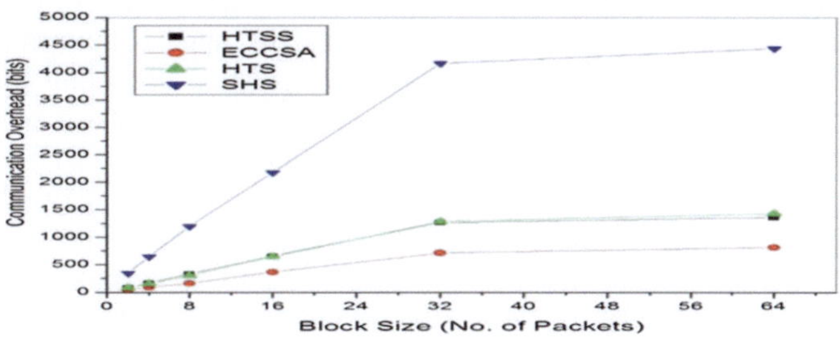

Fig. 6 Block size versus communication overhead

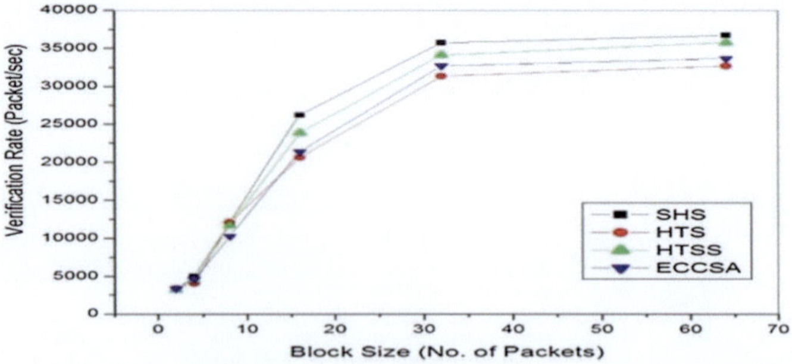

Fig. 7 Block size versus verification rate

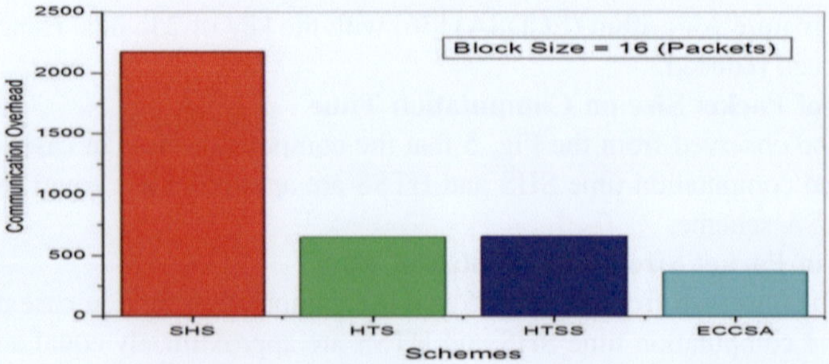

Fig. 8 Schemes versus communication overhead

Figure 8 shows the comparative result of existing schemes and purposed scheme. The base of comparison is communication overhead on block size 16 (packets). It can be observed from the graph that the communication overhead is less than the SHS, HTS and HTSS.

5 Conclusions

The multicast source authentication technique known as Elliptic Curve Cryptography Source Authentication is proposed. This approach is a combination of two different algorithms which perform its operation according to network conditions. This scheme is used to reduce the computation overhead and communication overhead and the scheme have less communication overhead as compared to SHS, HTS, and HTSS.

The proposed work is for wired multicast communication model but rapid growth of wireless communication and wireless-based application like military application, software updates, audio, video conferencing, intelligent houses etc.

force us to deploy the techniques for multicast source authentication with non-repudiation which can efficiently work on wired as well as wireless (heterogeneous) environment.

References

1. Challal Y, Bettahar H, Bouabdallah (2004) A taxonomy of multicast data origin authentication: issues and solutions. IEEE Comm Surveys Tutorials 6(3):34–57
2. Wang Q, Nahrstedt K (2009) Time valid one-time signature for time-critical multicast data authentication. In: IEEE INFOCOM, Rio de Janeiro
3. Balasubramanian K, Roopa R (2012) HTSS: hash tree signature scheme for multicast authentication. IJCA proceedings on international conference in recent trends in computational methods, communication and controls (ICON3C), no 6, pp 28–32, Apr 2012
4. Berbecaru D, Albertalli L, Lioy A (2010) The forward diffusion scheme for multicast authentication. IEEE/ACM Trans Netw 18(6):1855–1868
5. Perrig A, Canetti R, Song D, Tygar J (2001) Efficient and secure source authentication for multicast. In: Proceedings of network and distributed system security symposium (NDSS-2001), vol 1, pp 35–46
6. Park JM, Chong E, Siegel H (2002) Efficient multicast packet authentication using signature amortization. In: Proceedings of the IEEE symposium on research in security and privacy, pp 227–240
7. Lin IC, Sung CC (2010) An efficient source authentication for multicast based on Merkle hash tree. In: Proceedings of international conference on intelligent information hiding and multimedia signal processing (IIH-MSP-2010), pp 5–8, Oct 2010
8. Perrig A, Tygar JD, Song D, Canetti R (2000) Efficient authentication and signing of multicast streams over lossy channels. In: IEEE Symposium on Security and Privacy, pp 56–73
9. Perrig A, Tygar JD et al (2001) Efficient and secure source authentication for multicast. In: Internet society network and distributed system security, pp 35–46
10. ElKabbany GF, Aslan HK (2012) Efficient design for the implementation of Wong-Lam multicast authentication protocol using two-levels of parallelism. IJCSI Int Comput Sci Issues 9(3, 1), May 2012
11. Hou A, Yang S et al (2009) Secure elliptic curve generating algorithm over GF. Comput Eng 23:138–140
12. Park JM, Siegel JM et al (2002) Efficient multicast packet authentication using signature amortization. In: IEEE Symposium on Security and Privacy
13. Chan A (2003) A graph-theoretical analysis of multicast authentication. In: 23rd international conference on distributed computing systems
14. Shiv kumar S, Umamaheswari G (2014) Certificate authority schemes using elliptic curve cryptography, rsa and their variants simulation using Ns2. Am J Appl Sci 11(2):171–179
15. Sridevi J, Mangaiyarkarasi R (2011) Efficient multicast packet authentication using digital signature. Int J Comput Appl® (IJCA). In: International Conference on Emerging Technology Trends (ICETT)
16. Jin-xin, Zhou ZG et al (2007) A hybrid and efficient scheme of multicast source authentication. In: Eighth ACIS international conference on software engineering, artificial intelligence networking and parallel/distributed computing, vol 2, pp 123–125
17. Suri SS, Varghese G (2001) A lower bound for multicast key distribution. In: Proceedings of IEEE INFOCOM, pp 422–431, Apr 2001

18. Eltaief H, Youssef H (2010) RMLCC: recovery-based multi-layer connected chain mechanism for multicast source authentication. In: 35th annual IEEE conference on local computer networks, Colorado
19. Wong CK, Gouda M, Lam SS (1998) Secure group communications using key graph. In: Proceedings of the ACM SIGCOMM'98, Canada, pp 68–79, Sept 1998
20. Boneh D, Franklin M et al (2001) Lower bounds for multicast message authentication. Eurocrypt, LNCS (2045):437–452
21. Borella M, Swider D, Uludag S, Brewster G (1998) Internet packet loss: measurement and implications for end-to-end Qos. In: International conference on parallel processing, Aug 1998
22. Gennaro R, Rohatgi P (2001) How to sign digital streams. Inf Comput
23. Pannetrat A, Molva R (2003) Efficient multicast packet authentication. In: Proceedings of the ISOC network and distributed system security symposium, pp 251–262, Feb 2003
24. Qing-Hai A, Lu X et al (2012) Research on design principles of elliptic curve public key cryptography and its implementation. In: International conference on computer science and service system 2012
25. Perrig A, Canetti R, Tygar JD, Song D (2004) Efficient authentication and signing of multicast streams over lossy channels. In: Proceeding IEEE symposium on security and privacy (SP '00), pp 56–75, Feb 2004
26. Solum E, Chakravarthy R (2009) Modular over-the-wire configurable security forlonglived critical infrastructure monitoring systems. In: Proceedings of 3rd ACM international conference on distributed event-based systems (DEBS 2009), Nashville, TN, July 2009
27. Choi S (2005) Denial-of-service resistant multicast authentication protocol with prediction hashing and one-way key chain. In: Seventh IEEE international symposium on multimedia (ISM '05), Dec 2005
28. Bergadano F, Crispo B et al (2002) Individual authentication in multiparty communications. Comput Secur 21(8):719–735
29. Canetti R, Pinkas B et al (1999) Multicast security: a taxonomy and ecient constructions. INFOCOM
30. Hauser CH, Thanigaina than Manivannan et al (2012) Evaluating multicast message authentication protocols for use in wide area power grid data delivery services. In: 45th Hawaii international conference on system sciences
31. Zhou Y, Fang Y (2007) Multimedia broadcast authentication based on batch signature. IEEE Comm Magazine 45(8):72–77
32. FeiJia and Mario Gerla (2010) Group-based secure source authentication protocol for VANETs. Workshop on Heterogeneous, Multi-hop Wireless and Mobile Networks, IEEE
33. Challal Y, Bouabdallah A (2004) A taxonomy of multicast data origin authentication: issues and solutions. IEEE Commun Surv Tutorials—COMSUR 6(1–4):34–57
34. Bergadano F, Crispo B (2000) Individual single source authentication on the MBone. In: IEEE international conference on multimedia and expo
35. Fuloria F, Alvarez F (2010) The protection of substation communications. In Proceedings of SCADA security scientific symposium, Jan 2010
36. Bai Z, Yang H, Zhang W (2011) Study on fast implementation of prime-field ECC. Commun Technol 12(87–89):92
37. Pang S, Liu S, Cong F, Yao Z (2011) An efficient scalar multiplication algorithm on montgomery-form elliptic curve. Acta Electronica Sinica 04:865–868

Author Biographies

Yogendra Mohan has completed his ME (Computer science and Engineering) and is currently working as Assistant Professor in the Department of Computer science and Engineering, North Eastern Regional Institute of Science and Technology (deemed to be university—MHRD, Government of India), Nirjuli, Itanagar, Arunachal Pradesh, India. Before he joined NERIST, he worked as Assistant Professor in various colleges of AKTU, Lucknow, for more than 10 years. He also worked as software developer for 2 years. His areas of research are computer network security and cloud computing.

Dr. Rama Krishna received B.Tech. from JNTU, Hyderabad; M.Tech. from Cochin University of Science and Technology, Cochin; and Ph.D. from IIT Kharagpur. He is Senior Member, IEEE, USA. Since 1996, he is working with the Department of Computer Science & Engineering, National Institute of Technical Teachers' Training & Research, Chandigarh, and currently holding the position of Professor and Head. His areas of research interest include computer networks, wireless networks, cryptography and cyber security, and cloud computing. To his credit, he has more than 80 research publications in referred international and national journals and conferences. He acted as Associate Editor for International Journal of Technology, Knowledge and Society. He is a member in advisory/technical committees of many national and international journals and conferences and also chaired many technical sessions. He is a reviewer of Elsevier Journal of Vehicular Communications, Elsevier Journal of Computers & Security, Elsevier Journal of Information and Software Technology. He has 20 years of experience in organizing more than 100 training programs in the upcoming areas of CSE and IT for the faculty of engineering colleges, polytechnics, and industry professionals. He is instrumental in launching various initiatives at NITTTR Chandigarh toward paperless office.

Dr. Karan Singh has completed his B.Tech. (Computer Science & Engineering) from Kamala Nehru Institute of Technology, Sultanpur, in 2004 and M.Tech. (Computer Science & Engineering) from Motilal Nehru National Institute of Technology, Allahabad, UP, in 2006. He has completed his Ph.D. (Computer Science & Engineering) from Motilal Nehru National Institute of Technology, Allahabad, UP, in 2010. He has more than 10 years of experience in research and teaching. Currently, he is associated with School of Computer and Systems Sciences, JNU, New Delhi, India. His research areas are computer network and information security. He supervises 23 research candidates. He has more than 40 research papers (journal, IEEE conferences, national and international conferences) and 2 are accepted. He is the reviewer of conference and journal papers. He worked as General Chair of 9th International Conference, QShine 2013. He was an organizer of the workshop with ICUM Conference, Russia, and trying to open a research platform in India. He had taught more than 10 subjects to PG/UG classes. He was involved in many administrative activities. He has designed a computer laboratory. He is a professional/life member of various bodies such as Association for Computing Machinery (ACM), New York; Computer Science Teachers Association (CSTA), USA; Computer Society of India (CSI), Secunderabad, India; Cryptology Research Society of India (CRSI), Kolkata, India; Institute of Electrical and Electronics Engineers (IEEE), USA; International Association of Computer Science and Information Technology (IACSIT), Singapore; Institute for Computer Sciences, Social-Informatics and Telecommunications Engineering (ICST), America; International Association of Engineers (IAENG), Hong Kong; Association of Computer Electronics and Electrical Engineers (ACEEE), India; Internet Society (ISOC), USA; Academy & Industry Research Collaboration Center (AIRCC).

Design and Implementation of a Secure Hierarchical Trust Model for PKI

Sarvesh Tanwar and K. V. Prema

Abstract Public-Key Infrastructure (PKI) provides the authenticity of the public keys for a particular user. The public key is embedded in Digital Certificates. Therefore we tried to develop a specialized Hierarchical Trust Model. In this digital certificates are created using RSA of 2048 bits for key generation and combination of symmetric and asymmetric cryptography for the purpose of the security. As RSA is not suitable for large message encryption, we used AES-128 bit symmetric key for signing the information. The private key is stored locally on Machine, that is why sensitive information is stored as attributes of an Object. The object of a class is converted into Byte Array. This Byte Array is stored in BLOB data type of the database. The data is retrieved from MySQL database from BLOB data type field. This Byte Array is then converted into an object. The required data is extracted from the object.

Keywords RSA · MySQL · Object · Byte array

1 Introduction

Organizations need enhanced security for data and strong credentials for identity management. Digital certificates are used for secure data and proper authentication from users and computers both within and outside the organization. Most commonly used certificates are Digital Certificates, which are part of the public key infrastructure (PKI). A PKI is the combination of software, hardware, key gener-

---

S. Tanwar (✉)
Department of CSE FET, Mody University of Science & Technology, Laxmangarh, India
e-mail: s.tanwar1521@gmail.com

K. V. Prema
Department of CSE, Manipal Institute of Technology, MAHE, Manipal, Karnataka, India
e-mail: drprema.mits@gmail.com

M. U. Bokhari et al. (eds.), *Cyber Security*, Advances in Intelligent Systems and Computing 729, https://doi.org/10.1007/978-981-10-8536-9_39

ation, encryption technologies, certificate generation processes, and services that enable an organization to secure its communications and business transactions. PKI enables secure communications and business transactions by the exchanging digital certificates between authenticated users and trusted resources [1].

2 Trust Model

A trust model provides a framework for building a trust relationship among the entities. The implementation of a PKI requires ensuring the trust relationship among the end entities for a secure communication over the unsecured channel. The awareness of the trust relationships leads to the establishment of a trust model that the PKI enforces [2].

2.1 Hierarchical Trust Model

The hierarchical trust model is like an upside-down tree structure, root is the starting point of trust [3]. All nodes of the model have to trust the root CA, and keep a root CA's public-key certificate [4]. The Root CA's self-signed certificate is used for signing other CA certificates and its subordinate CA's certificate. It can be a public trusted company such as Verisign.

In hierarchical trust model, CAs are assembled under a common root CA, which issues certificates to Sub CAs. The hierarchy can have an arbitrary number of levels, usually, it has two levels: Root CA and certificate issuing CAs [5]. It has a single root CA and is holding all certificates; all end-users refer to and trust it for all transaction. Hierarchical Model can also have Registration Authorities (RAs) which are the initial processing points of user's identification and issues key pairs. RA produces flexibility for smaller groups by allowing them to have their own local and customized services.

(a) **Root CA**
Root CA is trust anchor for all the users like Controller of Certifying Authorities (CCA). All nodes have to trust the root CA, and keep the root CA's public key certificate. Root CA do the cross certification between two users to communicate. It generates certificates for the intermediate/Sub CAs, which in turn generates certificates for the leaf CAs, and the leaf CAs generate certificates for the end entities (users, network devices, applications). Root CA is self-certified and generates certificate for the CA containing the entity's identity and public key [6]. The generated certificate is signed by the Root CA. Its public keys must be distributed to all entities that trust on its certificate. The level of trust that a Root CA has depends on the level of acceptance that other entities have in that Root CA [2].

(b) **Sub CA/RA**
CA can assign some of his tasks to RA/SubCA. SubCA can issue/sign certificates on behalf of the CA. Most importantly, an RA is delegated, with the CA's explicit permission, the authority to perform tasks on behalf of the CA [7]. A typical function of an RA is to interrogate an end entity's certificate request by examining the name, validity dates, applicable constraints, public key, certificate extensions, and related information. The RA may also be responsible for performing due diligence tests on the end entity [1].

(c) **End user**
An end user/entity is any user, computer or node that needs a digital certificate to identify and doing secure communication among other user or entities. An end entity first gives a request for a certificate including all the information required for generating a certificate and send it to its SubCA or RA (Fig. 1).

3 Problem Statement

A certificate represents a trust from the CA to the owner of the certificate [8]. The advantage of the hierarchical structure is a short and definite path and is easily traceable back to a trusted node. Our main objective is to integrate security principles in a hierarchical model. This model implements authentication (digital certificates), confidentiality (encryption), and integrity (SHA 512) non-repudiation (digital signature).

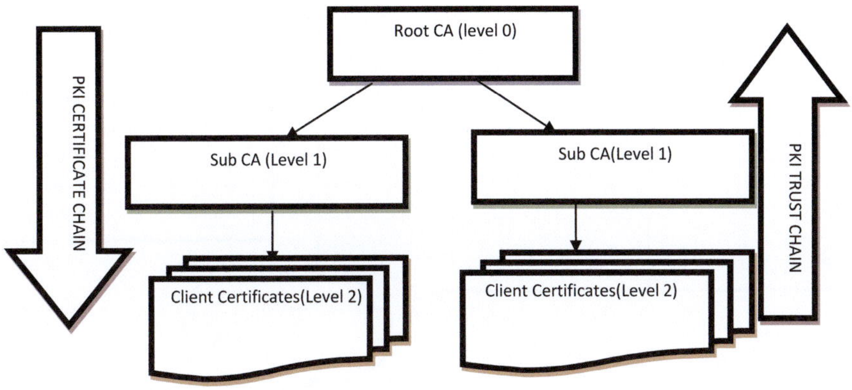

Fig. 1 Hierarchical trust model in PKI

4 Proposed Approach

We proposed an approach to implement a hierarchical trust model to be more secure. Any CA/user can trust on Root CA that is responsible for CA to whom he has issued certificates. This work as follows:

1. Creation of Trust model.
2. When a company wants to do communication with another, it, first of all, checks its certificate and CA.
3. If both are having certified by the same CA, no issues and they can trust each other and make transactions.
4. Certificates are stored in Archive or Database for future reference.
5. RFC 2527 and RFC 3280 standards are followed (Fig. 2).

5 Implementation

This approach is implemented on java jdk1.7 version with Xampp for My SQL and Apache Server. Digital Certificate is a most important module, which is signed by CA/Sub CA to sign the certificates and request. For generating digital signature we used a hybrid approach of cryptography.

Symmetric key encryption—Message Digest (MD) is calculated using an instance of SHA-512. Then MD is encrypted with a shared key. For security purpose, the shared key is encrypted with the receiver's public key so that key cannot be decrypted by anyone else who does not possess the matching private key and also ensure that the public key is associated with the user.

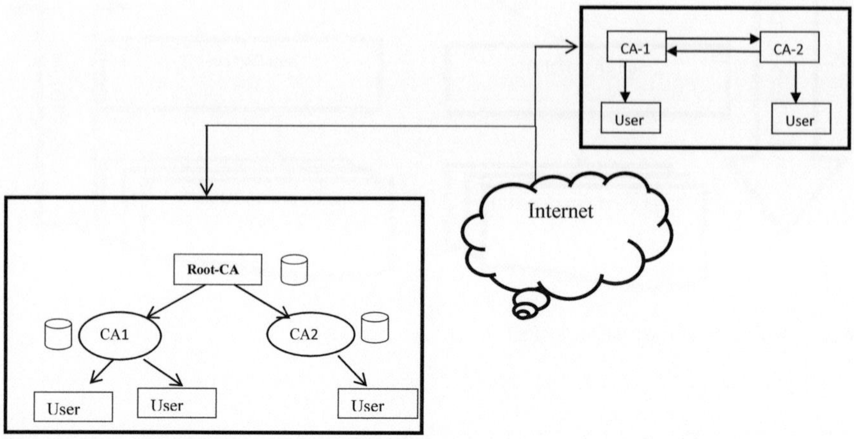

Fig. 2 Proposed approach

Digital signatures—Encrypted MD is signed with the sender's private key and can be verified by anyone who has access to the sender's public key. This verification proves that the sender has access to the private key, and the public key is binding in the certificate. This also ensures that the message has not been tampered/altered with, as any manipulation of the message will result in changes to the encoded message digest, which otherwise remains unchanged between the sender and receiver.

AES symmetric key algorithm is very secure fast and conventional encryption algorithm, for encrypting the MD, the result is ciphertext. Once the message is encrypted with this key then AES key is encrypted by the recipient's public key. This public key-encrypted AES key is transmitted along with the ciphertext to the recipient.

Decryption works in the reverse order. The receiver uses his or her private key to recover the AES key, which he/she uses to decrypt the encrypted ciphertext.

5.1 Steps for Generating Digital Certificate and Signature

1. Root CA is self-certified by generating aself-signed certificate by using RSA for key generation.
```
keyPairGenerator.initialize(2048);
privkey = pair.getPrivate();
pubkey = pair.getPublic();
```
2. Sub CA send certificate request to Root CA, so that it will be certified by Trusted Root Server like Controller of Certifying Authorities (CCA).
3. String
```
concat1=srno+oo.getFname()+oo.getLname()+oo.getCity()+oo.getState()+oo.getOrgunit()+oo.getOrg()+oo
.getEmail()+oo.getCountrycode()+oo.getMobileno()+oo.getIssuedBy()+oo.getIssuedTo()+oo.getValidto()+
oo.getValidfrom()+publickey.toString();
System.out.println("Fingerprint="+msgdigest);
msgdigest=new sha512().sha512(concat1);
oo.setDigest(msgdigest);
byte[] b=new byte[1024];
    b=concat1.getBytes();
msgdigest=sh.new Digest().digestIt(b);
```
4. Root CA Generate symmetric key by creating the instance of AES-128 bit algorithm.
5. Encrypt the hashed data which is send by the Sub CA in the form of certificate request with symmetric key that was generated in the step 4.

$$E_{symkey}[H(biologicalinformation + \quad receive\ \ public - key)]$$

6. Encrypt the symmetric key with public key of CA, so that only recipient that is having private key (private/public key pair) can only decrypt the symmetric key.

$$E_{pubkey}[E\_symkey]$$

```
byte [] bbskey= certWrt.getSemkey();
System.out.println("Symetric key in encrypted mode (byte array form) "+bbskey);
```
7. Digital Signature and encrypted key is send to Sub CA e.g created in previous step. Encrypted symmetric key is also stored in CA's database in BLOB format.

5.2 Digital Signature Verification

1. Connect to Root CA server.
2. Sub CA extract private key from its database that is stored in BLOB format.
3. Calculate message digest on the personal information and public key that is send to CA for certificate generation (digisign1).
4. Extract encrypted symmetric key and decrypt it by its own private key and
```
byte[] bb = se.decryptData(bbskey,ownprikey,"RSA/ECB/PKCS1Padding");
System.out.println("Symetric key in decrypted mode (byte array form)  "+bb);
convert it into key format.
byte[] bb = se.decryptData(bbskey,ownprikey,"RSA/ECB/PKCS1Padding");
System.out.println("Symetric key in decrypted mode (byte array form)  "+bb);
```
5. Decrypt encrypted hash value with the key that is received in step 4 (digisign2).
```
ddgg[]=se.decryptData(cipherText,key2,"AES");//RSA/ECB/PKCS1Padding");
System.out.println("Digital Sing in decrypted form byte array   "+ddgg);
```
6. If digisign1== digisign2, Digital signature is verified.
7. After verification of the digital signature, there will be handshake between the Root CA and Sub CA by sending a hello message that is encrypted with the Root CA's public key and send this message to Sub CA.
```
data1 = bos.toByteArray();
final byte[] cipherText1= se.encryptData(data1,pubkey,"RSA/ECB/PKCS1Padding");
hobj.setMsg(cipherText1);
toClient.writeObject((HandShake)hobj);
System.out.println("received message from CA ");
```
8. Root CA decrypts that message with its own private key.
```
byte []bb= se.decryptData(hobj.getMsg(),privkey,"RSA/ECB/PKCS1Padding");
ByteArrayInputStream bais1 = new ByteArrayInputStream(bb);
```
9. Root CA again encrypts the message with Sub CA's public key and sends back it to Sub CA, so that only Sub CA can decrypt it.
10. CA decrypts it with its own private key and successful handshake is done between Root CA and Sub CA. The same steps will also be repeated for making communication between CA and Sub CA.

6 Results

As the information is stored in the form of objects in the database, it is difficult to intercept the database. Nobody changes the information in the database (Fig. 3).

6.1 Public-Key Directory

Each CA and sub CA have a public key database in which all the public key of the issuer and issue is stored in the form of an object by taking its data type as BLOB (Figs. 4, 5, 6, 7 and 8).

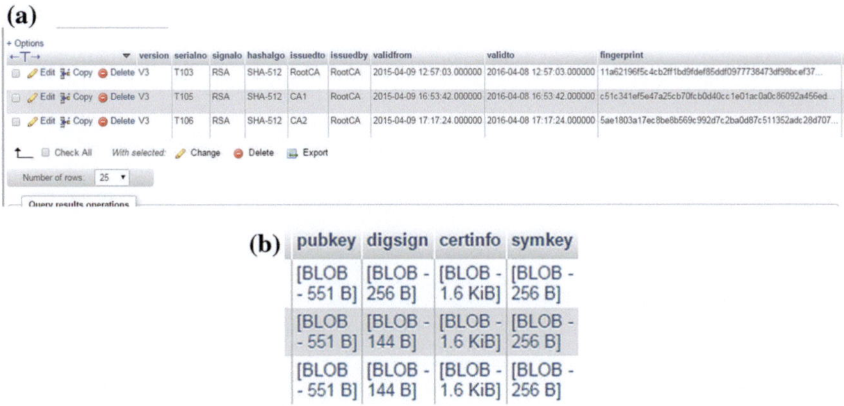

Fig. 3 **a** Database of Root CA. **b** Database of Root CA

Fig. 4 Public-key directory

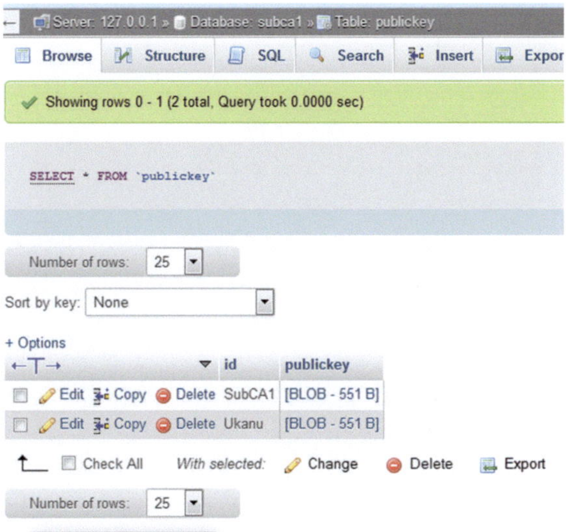

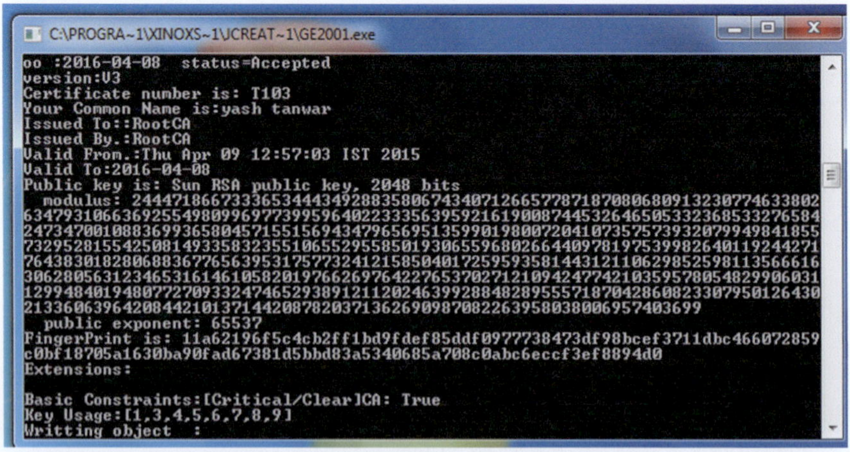

Fig. 5 Self-signed certificate of Root CA

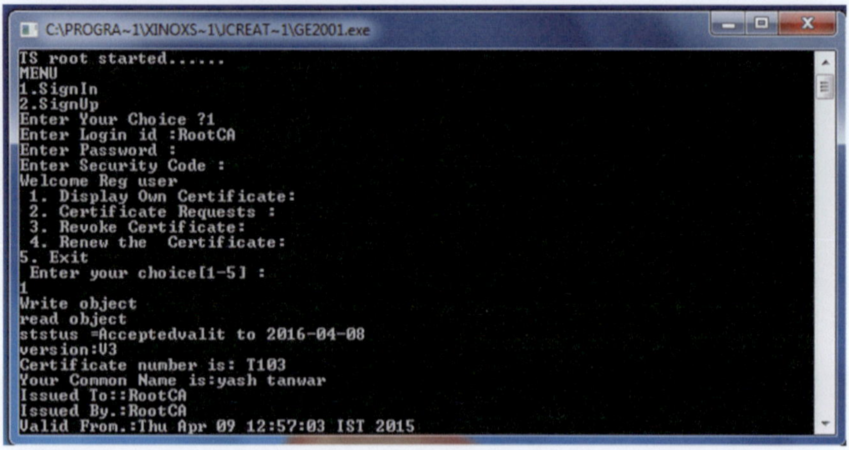

Fig. 6 Services provide by Root CA

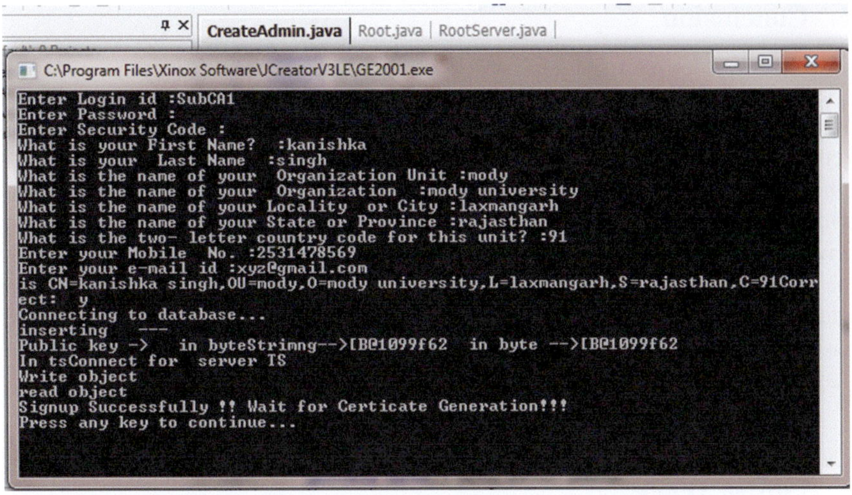

Fig. 7 Certificate request sent by SubCA to Root CA

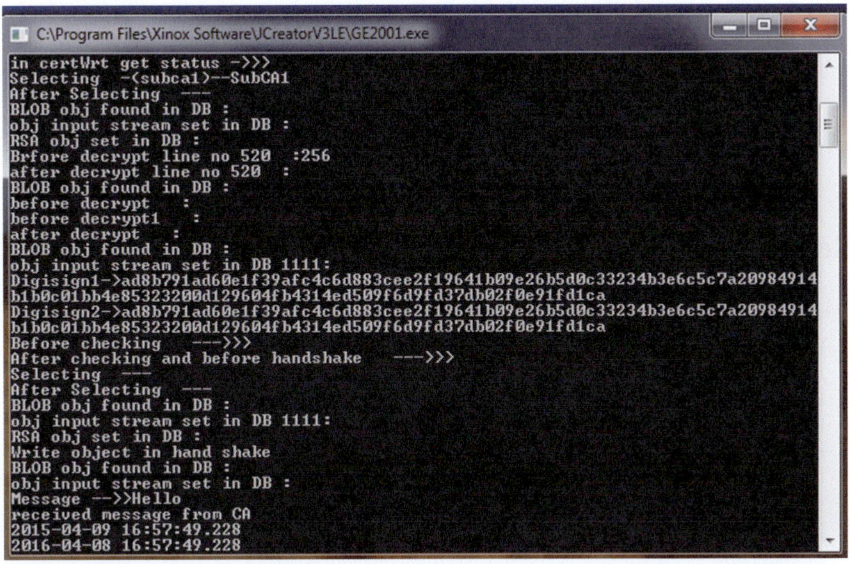

Fig. 8 Certificate generated by SubCA

7 Conclusion

The hierarchical trust model designed by us is secured than the existing one. We have created a digital certificate for 2048 bits and use the hybrid approach for generated the digital signature. As the use of encryption and then storage of Java objects in BLOB enables confidentiality and message integrity. Hence, the system will enable secure communication and provide proper authentication. Password, private key, issuer public key, message and other sensitive information is stored in the BLOB form and hence is highly secure both from client's side attack, back-end attack and also during transmission over internet. The application is completely based on OOPs concept and hence can be implemented in any kind of organization may it be academics, government, public sectors, banks, etc.

8 Future Work

This model is implemented in Java. One can implement it with more public key size such as 4096 bits and SHA 1024 bit key. It would be more secure as the long key is secure. One can also simulate it on simulators such as MATLAB or OPNET simulator. The model can then be applied to two distinct working organizations having separate policies. Policy mapping rules can be made to verify certificates of each other.

References

1. Yanchao Z et al (2005) AC-PKI: anonymous and certificateless public-key infrastructure for mobile ad hoc networks. In: 2005 IEEE international conference on communications, 2005, ICC 2005, vol 5, IEEE
2. Liming H et al (2006) Fast authentication public key infrastructure for mobile ad hoc networks based on trusted computing. In: International conference on wireless communications, networking and mobile computing, 2006, WiCOM 2006, IEEE
3. Gong HX, Hui ZW, Hao L, Lv XY (2014) Based on improved CAN PKI trust model. J Chem Pharm Res 6(3)
4. Liping H (2011) Research on trust model of PKI, IEEE
5. Jarupunphol P, Mitchell C (2003) PKI implementation issues in B2B E-commerce. In: Gattiker UE (ed) EICAR conference best paper proceedings. EICAR, 2003, Copenhagen, p 14. ISBN: 87-987271-2-5
6. Nicusor V (2010) Public key infrastructure for public administration in Romania. In: 2010 8th international conference on communications (COMM). IEEE
7. Garcia C, Carlos L, Perez-Leguizamo C (2011) An autonomous decentralized public key infrastructure. In: 10th international symposium on autonomous decentralized systems (ISADS), IEEE

8. Audun J (2013) PKI trust models. In: Theory and practice of cryptography solutions for secure information systems

Author Biographies

Sarvesh Tanwar is a Research Scholar with Department of Computer Science & Engineering in College of Engineering & Technology (CET), Mody University of Science & Technology, Lakshmangarh (Rajasthan), India. She received her M.Tech Degree from Maharishi Markendeshwar University (MMU), Mullana with Distinction and is doing Ph.D from Mody University of Science & Technology (MUST), Lakshmangarh. Her research areas are Cryptography and Ad hoc networks. She has around 11 years of teaching experience.

Dr. K. V. Prema is currently working as Professor, Department of Computer Science & Engineering MIT, MAHE, Manipal, Karnataka, India. Her research areas are Network Security, Computer Networks, Neural Networks and Pattern Recognition. She has around 26 years teaching experience and has published around 100 research papers in National/International Journals/ Conferences. She is also on the editorial board of some journals.

Encryption and Decryption Technique Using Java

Ankur Saxena, Neeraj Kaushik and Nidhi Kaushik

Abstract In today's communication era, sharing of data is increasing significantly. The data being transmitted is vulnerable to several approaches. Consequently, the information security is one of the most challenging facts of communication. This research will represent a view on the modern state in the field of encryption, in particular on private key block ciphers which are widely applied for bulk data and connection encryption. Encryption is the contrivance of converting plain text into the cipher text in which plain text is taken the input for the encryption process, and cipher text is considered as the output. Decryption is the mechanism of changing cipher text into the plaintext. This technique runs on any web server or application server. The core thought is to encrypt secret information before transmitting it to interested websites. A J2EE information model is employed to test the integrity of the mechanism.

Keywords Encryption · Decryption · Java · AES · DES · Tomcat

1 Introduction

Every person stores huge amounts of data like e-mails, contacts, calendars, documents, photos, and on the net. To cover and protect the privacy of online delicate data is another system. This requires that you know which computers will be attached to each other so that the key can be present on each one. It is same as a secret code that each of the computers must know in order to translate the information [1].

A. Saxena (✉) · N. Kaushik · N. Kaushik
Amity University, Noida, Uttar Pradesh, India
e-mail: asaxena1@amity.edu

N. Kaushik
e-mail: nkaushik1@amity.edu

N. Kaushik
e-mail: nkaushik2@amity.edu

M. U. Bokhari et al. (eds.), *Cyber Security*, Advances in Intelligent Systems and Computing 729, https://doi.org/10.1007/978-981-10-8536-9_40

Java: It is one of the most robust, mainly used, and perfect programming languages for creating enterprise applications. Over the years, Java development has evolved from applets run on a web browser (Chrome, Mozilla) to large enterprise distributed applications run on multiple servers. Presently, Java has three different flavors, and each addresses certain programming requirements [2].

Encryption: A practice of changing simple text into secret message text is called as Encryption. Encryption technique is used by cryptography to send secret messages through at mid-channel. The encryption processes require two parts key and algorithm.

Decryption: It is just an antipole process of encryption of text.

Plain Text: It is the main message that somebody wants to broadcast with the other end is mentioned as plain text. For example, Neeraj sends "Dear Ankur, Welcome" message to the Ankur. In this, "Dear Ankur, Welcome" message showed.

Cipher Text: The message that is not easily known or useless is what treated as cipher type text. By the technique of cryptography, the early message is converted into non-readable form before the broadcasting of the actual message. Like "Ank172#@81ukl8*^5%" is a cipher text show "Hello Ankur how are you" [3].

Hashing: It is used to build, search or delete data from the hashtable. Hashing is so commonly used in computing that one might expect that there is no dearth of programmer to understand well hash functions and that choosing a suitable function not be a difficult task [4] (Fig. 1).

Fig. 1 Flow of cryptography

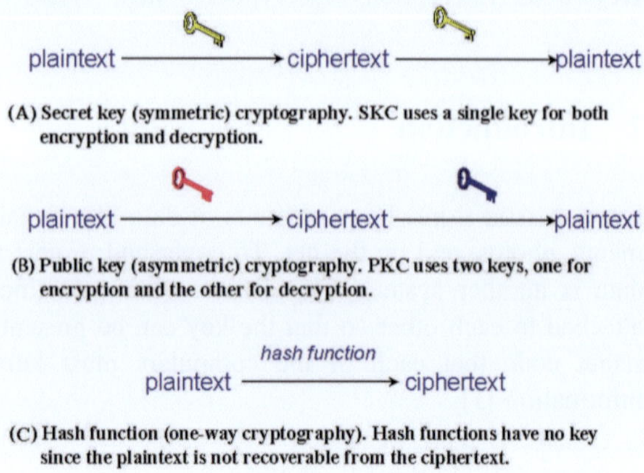

1.1 Symmetric-Key Cryptography

Symmetric-key cryptography glances to encryption methods in which all the source and destination claim the same key. It is implemented in two ways as block and stream ciphers. The block cipher enciphers input data in blocks of plaintext whereas stream cipher used individual characters as input form. The data encryption standard and the advanced encryption standard are generally block cipher layouts which have designate cryptography by the USA.

Advanced Encryption Standard (AES) algorithm is not for security as well as for high pace and its hardware and software operation are fast and quick. New encryption standard was approved by NIST to displace DES. Encrypts data slabs of 128 bits with in 10, 12, and 14 round calculate on size of the key. This can be applied to separate platforms mainly in gadgets devices, and it is very rigorously tested using many applications [5].

1.2 Data Encryption Standard (DES)

This algorithm plan is to implement a typical method to cover commercial enterprise and unorganized information. In this, the similar key is used for encryption and decryption process [6]. DES algorithm has been explained with this flowchart (Fig. 2; Table 1).

1.3 Public-Key Cryptography

The symmetric key uses the similar key for message encryption and decryption process; still, a message can include a distinct key than others. The drawback of symmetric cipher is the central management necessary to use them soundly. Any specific pair of conveying parties need, elegantly, shares a distinct key, and may be each of the cipher text. The number of keys needed increases as the second power of the number of network members, which very quickly need critical key management scheme to controlling form and secret keys. The Diffie and Hellman's research sparked widespread efforts to finding public-key encryption [7] (Fig. 3).

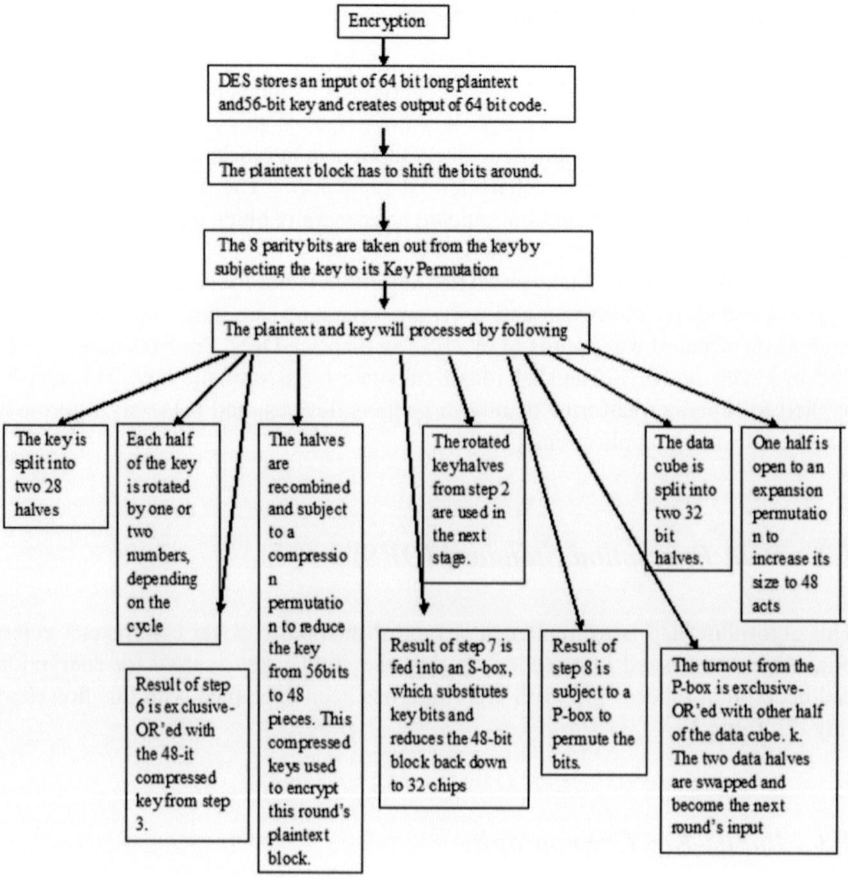

Fig. 2 Flow of DES technique

Table1 Comparison between AES and DES techniques

Factors	AES	DES
Developed	2000	1977
Size	128, 192, 256 bits	56 bits
Block size	128 bits	64 bits
Encryption	Faster	Moderate
Decryption	Faster	Moderate
Security	More	Less
Hardware and software implementation	Faster	Better in hardware than in software
Rounds	14	16

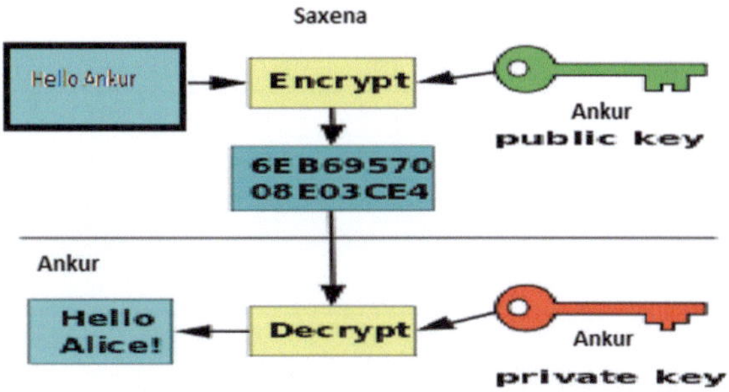

Fig. 3 Flow of public-key cryptography

2 Review of Literature

2.1 The Round Number

This encryption technique depends on the capacity across the shortcut encounter, which is more active than the brute force process. Along the block duration and 128 bit key length for AES algorithm, it has not found to six or even more trolls on an interpreted version of the usage of shortcut encounters [8].

User study three sets of initial keys only one bit difference after ten round expansions with the round key technique which chosen by random, in Table 2 through them, the first set key has variation in 16th built, the second in 128th, and last in 40th. The big divergence of this key variation after ten rounds is show in Table 3 [9].

2.2 Byte-Rotation Encryption Technique

The BREA algorithm has the following key features:

1. It is a symmetric key block cipher algorithm.
2. Each block size is 16 bytes.

Table 2 Initial key—three sets

	key1	A0 B2 CC AA 34 C2 BB 77 23 12 45 A2 A1 23 31 A4
1	key2	A0 B3 CC AA 34 C2 BB 77 23 12 45 A2 A1 23 31 A4
	key1	01 01 01 01 01 01 01 01 01 01 01 01 01 01 01 02
2	key2	01 01 01 01 01 01 01 01 01 01 01 01 01 01 01 03
	key1	12 34 56 78 90 0A 0B 0C 0D 0E 0F 01 02 03 04 05
3	key2	12 34 56 78 91 0A 0B 0C 0D 0E 0F 01 02 03 04 05

Table 3 Bit difference change (BD)

Rounds		0	1	2	3	4	5	6	7	8	9	10
BD	1	1	4	18	30	43	38	47	36	37	28	31
	2	1	9	29	49	47	63	59	75	66	71	58
	3	1	3	14	36	37	64	59	57	58	59	54

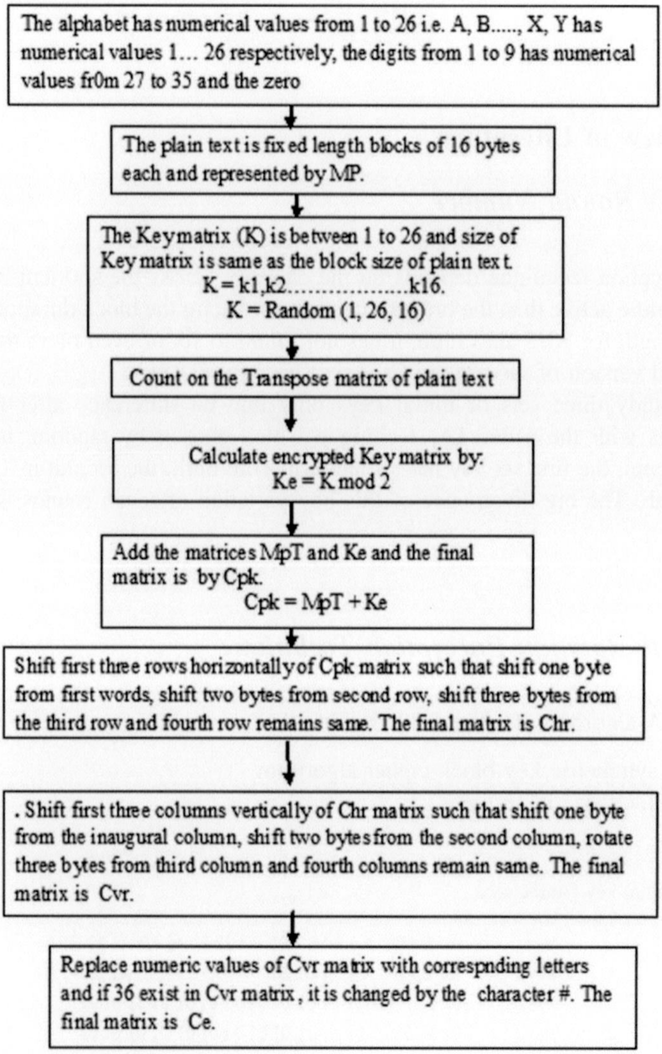

Fig. 4 Byte-rotation encryption technique flow

3. Size of key matrix is 16 bytes.
4. Values of key matrix are randomly selected and ranging from 1 to 26.
5. Mono-alphabetic substitution concept is followed.
6. Byte-Rotation technique is used.

Byte-Rotation Encryption Technique Flow [10]: (Fig. 4)

3 Methodology

The encryption user must use a secret key with a technique. In this process, user uses a technique called advanced encryption standard 128 and the string bytes “AnkurSaxena” as the secret key. Advanced encryption standard technique can use a key of 128 bits, so programmer selected that key.

```
package Ankur;
import java.security.*;
import java.security.spec.InvalidKeySpecException;
import javax.crypto.*;
import sun.misc.*;
public class AESEn {
private static final String ALGO = "AES";
   private static final byte[] keyValue =  new byte[] { 'A', 'n', 'k', 'u', 'r', 'S', 'a', 'x, 'e', 'n', 'a' };
public static String encrypt(String Data) throws Exception {
      Key key = generateKey();
      Cipher c = Cipher.getInstance(ALGO);
      c.init(Cipher.ENCRYPT_MODE, key);
      byte[] encVal = c.doFinal(Data.getBytes());
      String encryptedValue = new BASE64Encoder().encode(encVal);
      return encryptedValue;
   }
public static String decrypt(String encryptedData) throws Exception {
      Key key = generateKey();
      Cipher c = Cipher.getInstance(ALGO);
      c.init(Cipher.DECRYPT_MODE, key);
      byte[] decordedValue = new BASE64Decoder().decodeBuffer(encryptedData);
      byte[] decValue = c.doFinal(decordedValue);
      String decryptedValue = new String(decValue);
      return decryptedValue;
   }
   private static Key generateKey() throws Exception {
      Key key = new SecretKeySpec(keyValue, ALGO);
      return key;
}
}
```

The generateKey() method to generate a key for advanced encryption standard technique with a given key.

This program demonstrates the above encryption technique.

```
package Ankur;
public class Checker {
public static void main(String[] args) throws Exception {
String password = "Saxena";
String passwordEnc = AESEn.encrypt(password);
String passwordDec = AESEn.decrypt(passwordEnc);
System.out.println("Plain Text : " + password);
System.out.println("Encrypted Text : " + passwordEnc);
 System.out.println("Decrypted Text : " + passwordDec);
 }
}
```

The following output is got from the above test; user clearly shows that the original text is replaced with decryption:

Plain Text: Saxena
Encrypted: sbhCap4urE50a/d
Decrypted: Saxena (Fig. 5)

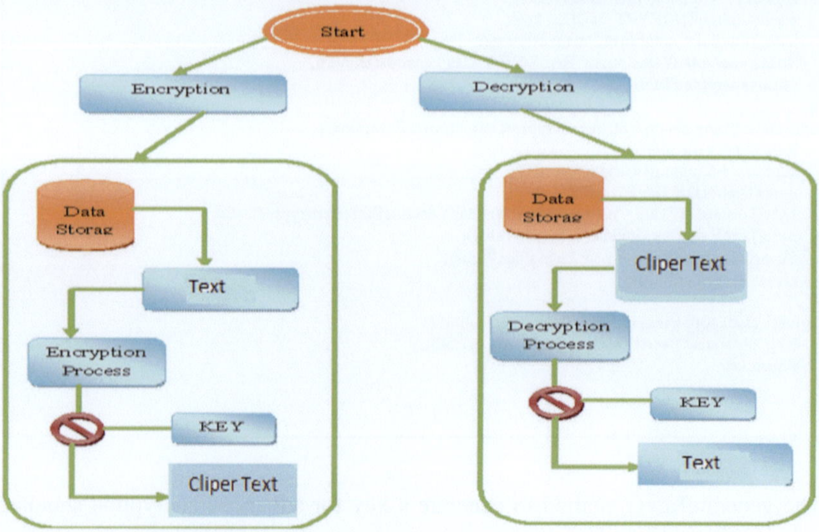

Fig. 5 The graphical representation of encryption system

4 Conclusion

Encryption technique plays a key role in network security. This work reviewed the competence of encryption, AES techniques, AES with Java over tomcat web server or application host. Roots on the text files are used and the technical outcome, it was achieve that AES technique utilize least encryption. It is also observed that decryption of AES technique is safer than various other techniques. By using simulation result, it is calculated that AES algorithm is a better than DES technique. Our future research will target on compared and analyzed cryptographic encryption like AES, DES. It will incorporate experiments on audio, image, and video encryption or decryption, and the target will be to advance encryption and decryption velocity or time.

References

1. Saxena A, Jakhmola R (2011) Securing confidential data using Java/J2EE. Int J Sci Technol Manag 2(3):54–59
2. DSarkar D, Jaiswal A, Saxena A (2015) Understanding architecture and framework of J2EE using web application. Int J Comput Sci Inf Technol 6(2):1253–1257
3. Thambiraja E, Ramesh G, Umarani R (2012) A survey on various most common encryption techniques. Int J Adv Res Comput Sci Softw Eng 2(7):226–233
4. Saxena A, Chaurasia (2014) Key and value paired data using java hash table. Int J Eng Manag Res 4(1):81–89
5. Mahajan P Dr, Sachdeva A (2013) A study of encryption algorithms AES, DES and RSA for security. Glob J Comput Sci Technol Netw Web Secur 13(15):15–22 Version 1.0
6. Prashant G, Deepthi S, SandhyaRani K (2013) A novel approach for data encryption standard algorithm. Int J Eng Adv Technol (IJEAT) 2(5):264
7. Agarwal V, Agarwal S, Deshmukh R (2014) Analysis and review of encryption and decryption for secure communication. Int J Sci Eng Res (IJSER) 2(2):1–3
8. FIPS PUb 197-the official AES standard. http://www.techheap.com/cryptography/encryption/fips-197.pdf
9. Chen† Q, Tang Z, Li Y, Niu Y, Mo J (2011) Research on encryption algorithm of data security for wireless sensor network. J Comput Inf Syst 7(2):369–376
10. Bhati S, Bhati A, Sharma SK (2012) A new approach towards encryption schemes: byte—rotation encryption algorithm. In: Proceedings of the world congress on engineering and computer science 2012, vol II WCECS 2012, October 24–26

Author Biographies

Ankur Saxena is currently working as Assistant Professor in Amity University Uttar Pradesh (AUUP), Noida. He has 12 years of wide teaching experience at graduation and post-graduation level and 3 years of industrial experience in the field of Software Development. He has published 10 books with international repute publication. He has published many research papers in reputed national and international journals. He is editorial board member and reviewer for a number of journals. His research interests are Cloud Computing, Big Data, evolutionary algorithms, software framework, design & analysis of algorithms, biometric identification.

Neeraj Kaushik Presently working as Assistant Professor (Computer Science) in Amity University Uttar Pradesh. He has compeleted MCA from Guru Jambheshwar University in 2002. He has 15+ years of teaching experience. He has earlier worked in institutes like University College, Kurukshetra and Department of Management, Kurukshetra University Kurukshetra. His research endeavors are mainly in areas like Cryptography, Information Security, cloud computing and Big data Analytics. His manuscripts are published in ACM and Springer.

Nidhi Kaushik Presently working as Assistant Professor (Computer Science) in Amity University Uttar Pradesh. She has compeleted MCA from Kurukshetra University in 2004 and presently pursuing PhD from Mewar University. She has 13+ years of Teaching experience. She has earlier worked in National Institute of Technology, Kurukshetra. Her research endeavors are mainly in areas like Software Reliability, Optimization Techniques, Cryptography, Information Security and Big data Analytics. Her manuscripts are published in ACM and Springer. She contributed as Co-editor of a reputed book titled "Rising India…an echo".

Detection and Removal of Security Attacks Using ALARM Protocol in WSN Environment

Seema Rawat, Praveen Kumar and Bhawna Dhruv

Abstract A mobile ad hoc network comprises many mobile wireless nodes. MANET is a self-configuring network and such network can be organized easily without any base station. MANET can be very efficiently used in salvage-related area, military, and law enforcement. But it faces the issues of security and confidentiality, especially when used in susceptible areas. Safe routing protocols have been refined to provide protection and confidentiality at various levels, e.g., ALARM protocol (Anonymous Location-Aided Routing) provides both privacy features and security, which include data virtue, node verification, and obscurity. This network focuses on achieving the major security objectives which are confidentiality, authentication, authorization, and integrity. In this paper, we have proposed ALARM protocol in WSN environment which uses network time protocol synchronization and removes the malicious node from the network, hence preventing the network from attacks.

Keywords MANET · ALARM · Security attacks · Wireless sensor network

1 Introduction

Wireless networking is an automation field in which two or more systems interact with each other using typical network protocol without using any cable. Such networks are of two types: infrastructure or infrastructure less. In infrastructure

---

S. Rawat (✉) · P. Kumar · B. Dhruv
Amity University Noida, Noida, India
e-mail: srawat1@amity.edu

P. Kumar
e-mail: pkumar3@amity.edu

B. Dhruv
e-mail: bdhruv8@gmail.com

M. U. Bokhari et al. (eds.), *Cyber Security*, Advances in Intelligent Systems and Computing 729, https://doi.org/10.1007/978-981-10-8536-9_41

network, the interaction takes place among the wireless nodes and few access points. Ad hoc network is a type of infrastructure less and decentralized type wireless network which basically means, there is no actual infrastructure such as router devices or access points in wireless networks. In routing process, each node involves itself by forwarding data to and for all the nodes [1].

In ad hoc network, the regulation of which node to forward data is made dynamically on the basis of network design and connection. Essentially, it is a network which is generally used in emergency situations. A fixed infrastructure is not required such types of networks. Nodes which are in close radio range, interact directly which each other using the wireless links whereas the nodes which are far from each other take the help of intermediate nodes so that relay message can be passed. Wireless networks are the networks which make use of radio waves or microwaves in order to establish interaction between the devices. In such network, all the nodes act as router.

MANET is mobile ad hoc network. It is self-establishing network which is infrastructure less in nature. In MANET, different mobiles are associated through different wireless links. Every mobile node can freely move, which further means that there is no central control available. In MANET, mobile nodes can join or leave the network at any instance [2]. MANET is used in some crucial applications such as emergency salvage, vehicular network, military, and law prosecution. There are various problems in MANET like security concerns, transfer issue, etc. Due to same reason, there are different types of attack which are provoked in MANET. These attacks can be of different types, such as:

- Eavesdropping is a type of attack which takes place in the mobile ad hoc networks. Eavesdropping is executed to obtain any information which is secret in nature and is kept classified during entire communication.
- Gray-hole attack's other name is routing misbehavior attack. It leads to message dropping.
- Replay attack is a type of attack in which the attacker executes a replay attack that is repeatedly retransmitted. The actual data that has been captured by the network is repeatedly transferred. This attack spots the route novelty and brings out the poor security design.

To isolate these attacks from interaction path in the network, there are different techniques which we will be discussed further. In this proposed mechanism, we tried to prevent these attacks (replay attack) by using mutual authentication among the nodes in the entire network. For this, we used authentication-based protocol called ALARM using cryptographic mechanism of digital signature in the wireless sensor network.

2 MANET

MANET is a type of mobile ad hoc network. This is a self-configuring and infrastructure less network. In this network, many mobile nodes are connected through wireless link. There is no central controller available in this network. The types of MANET are as follows:

(1) Wireless sensor network: A wireless sensor network is a group of devices which are sensing in nature and are used for monitoring and recording the physical condition while passing the information to central location.
(2) Wireless mesh network: This network works upon mesh topology. This network comprises gateway, routers, and clients. The traffic in this network is forwarded by routers from gateways. This is not connected to the Internet.
 The absence of infrastructure in the ad hoc network proves to be a huge challenge in these networks. All the mobile nodes share the power to accept as well as route the traffic to further nodes. MANETs work upon limited bandwidth and mobility of the nodes; therefore, there is a need to have energy efficiency hence making the whole communication very unreliable. The protocols of ad hoc routing are as follows:

 - Zone routing protocol (ZRP)
 - Ad hoc on demand distance vector (AODV)
 - Wireless routing protocol (WRP)

In MANET, the topology changes very dynamically. This type of network does not have fixed infrastructure. This network has typical following characteristics: changing topology, limited bandwidth, and energy inefficient.

A. Types of MANET
 The different types of MANETs are discussed below:

 - Vehicular ad hoc network: This type of network is used for communication in the mobile vehicles. The communication does not come to halt even if the vehicles are moving in different or opposite direction.
 - The data intelligently and allows further data communication.
 - Intern-based mobile ad hoc network: In such type of network, the routing algorithms cannot be directly deployed. This network uses fixed nodes for data interaction.

3 Alarm Protocol

ALARM: It is defined as Anonymous Location-Aided Routing in MANET. The nodes which are used in this protocol indicate the current location and are used to forward the data to other nodes for communication. ALARM is highly recommended because this serves the purpose of both authentication and security. It is also to prevent the network from the active and passive attacks.

This basically follows two schemes, i.e., initialization and operation.

A. Initialization

- The group manager is the head of the entire network. He is the one who adds all the nodes in the network as the group members. During this phase, every group member is assigned a private key that is unknown to anyone. This key is required to implement the valid group signatures for security purpose [3]. Every group member has a public key as well which is only known to the group manager. The group manager is only responsible for every group signature and verifies all the signers.
- The group manager is responsible for adding or deleting the group member [4]. The GM must check whether joining or joining is feasible for the network or not.

B. Operation

- The time duration is divided into equal parts. While beginning process, every node member generated a temporary public–private key combination.
- Every stop will let us know about the location of the node through GPRS.
- The GPRS would contain its location, time stamp as well as the temporary public key.
- When a new "Location Announcement Message" is received, every node member will check that the same LAM has not been received by them before [5]. When this is verified, the time stamp with group signature is checked. If all the entities are verified, the node forwards the LAM to its neighboring node.
- Whenever a node wishes to interact with the other location, it asks if the other node already exists there or not and generates a session key if there is no node at that particular location.
- Then, the message is forwarded to the nodes. The path is chosen based upon shortest path or other path computing algorithms.

4 Proposed Work

The protocol ALARM is used majorly for mutual authentication among the nodes. Having read the assumptions like location and time, we get to know that clocks of the mobile nodes are weakly synchronized. When the clocks are weakly synchronized in any network, then the possibility of replay attack becomes more, making the data transmission among the nodes very unreliable. In this work, we will isolate the replay attack in the mutual authentication using ALARM protocol in wireless sensor network. Using NTP, we can ensure strong clock synchronization among the nodes. The term "strongly synchronized" refers to that if the data is transferred from one node to other, the processing speed is very fast [6]. If there exists trust relationship among the nodes, no replay attack is possible in the network because there is no waiting time for the data transfer during communication.

Due to weak synchronization, the confidential information from the network may be lost. But while using NTP, mutual authentication among the nodes takes place and malicious node is removed from the network (Fig. 1).

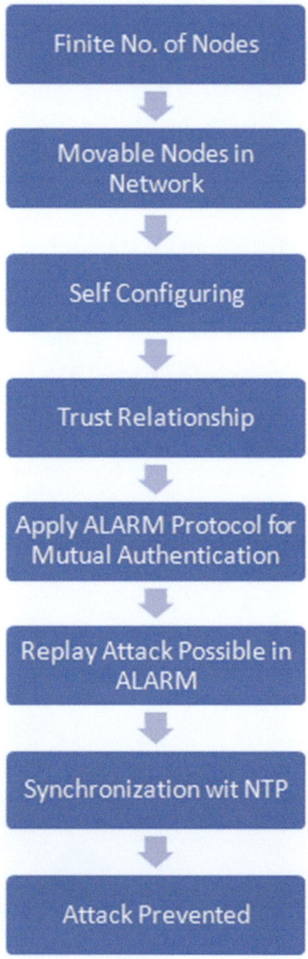

Fig. 1 Flowchart of proposed methodology

5 Result

In this figure shown below, it can be seen that the flood messages move to the monitor node which then identifies the malicious node and finds the best suitable path for further data transmission (Fig. 2).

In the figure shown below, it is seen that the source node gets reply message from each node for carrying forward the data communication. In this way, the interaction among the nodes is stopped, and a new path is established (Figs. 3, 4).

In the figure shown above it is clear that, due to the new proposed algorithm, whenever a malicious node is detected in the network, we find the best suitable path hence removing the malicious node from the entire network.

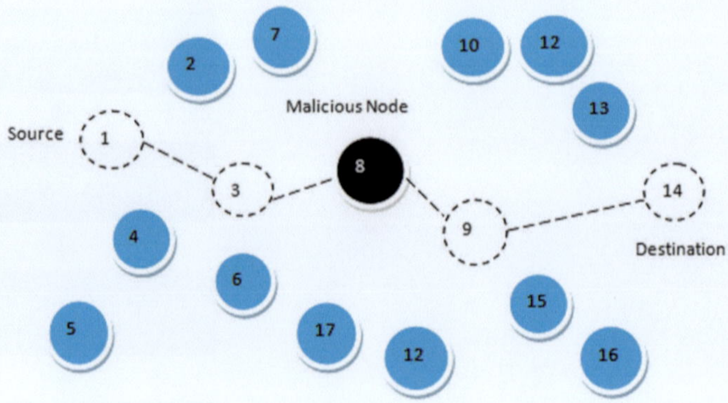

Fig. 2 Malicious node detection

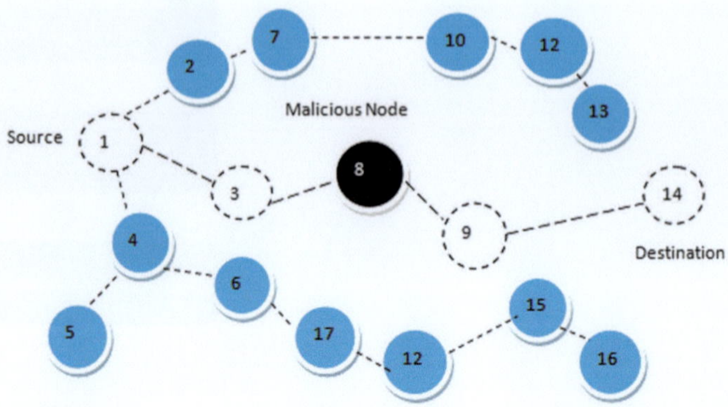

Fig. 3 New path identified

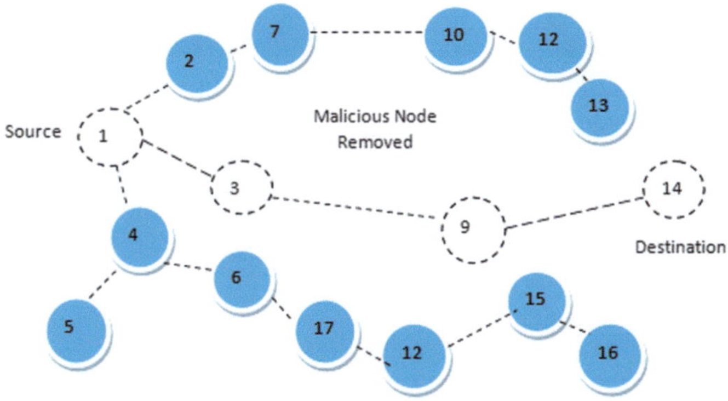

Fig. 4 Removal of malicious node

Packet loss:
The two axis of the graph represents different entities; *X* being the time and *Y* being the packet loss. As in this network, the replay attack takes place resulting in higher packet loss due to delayed transmission of the data packets. The graph basically represents that earlier there was huge packet loss which is in green color and now it has been majorly reduced by which is depicted by red line. This is only possible due to the isolation of the malicious node (Fig. 5).
Network throughput:
Throughput can be defined as the average rate per unit time. In this case, it can be defined as the average rate of packets delivered successfully in per unit time. The throughput of any network should always be high. But in this case, due to replay attacks, it is very low. On the contrary, we see that the network throughput increases rapidly after isolation of the malicious node. In this graph shown below, the red line represents the throughput of the network while replay attack is being taking place. Whereas the green line depicts the new throughput which is very high after the isolation of the malicious node (Fig. 6).

6 Conclusion and Future Scope

In this work, we can conclude that due to major properties of the mobile ad hoc network, various attacks are possible. These properties are open channel, infrastructure less network, and variably changing topologies. These attacks can be prevented by different authentication protocols. In our work, different types of attacks and their detection, isolation, and impacts on the network are well analyzed. The main aim of security is that the packet transmission in the entire network from one location to another should be reliable and verified. In the network, all the nodes should follow strong trust relationship because any type of malicious node can

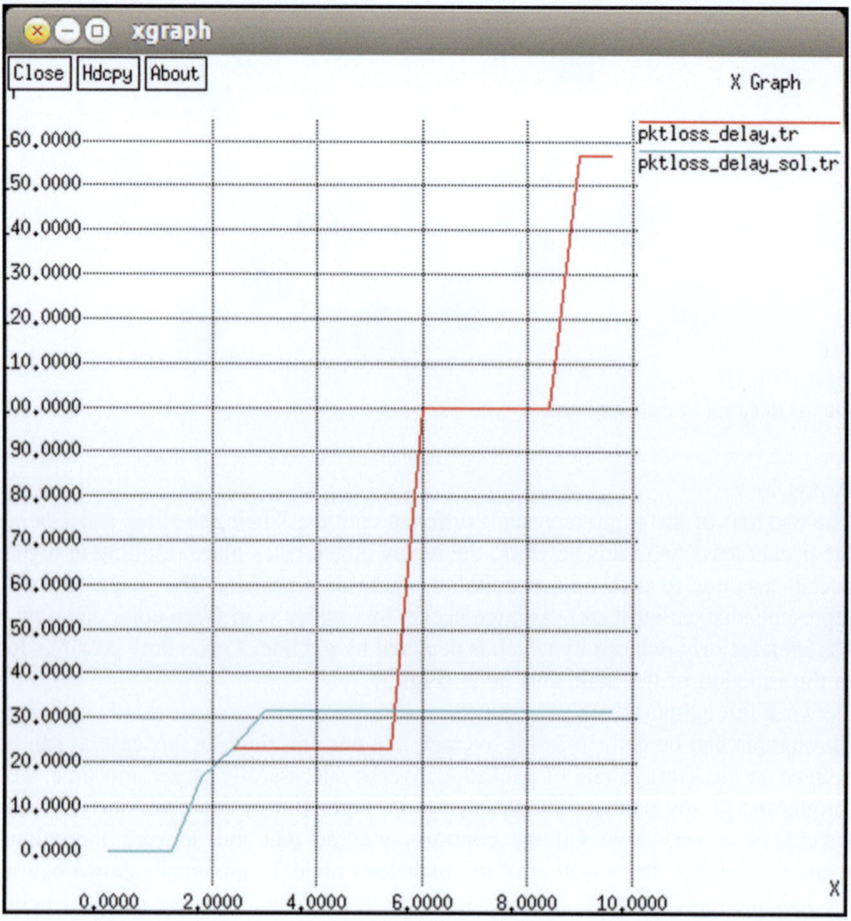

Fig. 5 Packet loss

attack the network, modifying or fabricating the information which is very important.

We have reviewed the ALARM protocol in the WSN environment which has increased security as well as privacy in the networks. In our proposed algorithm, we detect and isolate any malicious using network time protocol which supports strong synchronization of the nodes in the network, reducing the packet loss and increasing the network throughput. In future, we can also produce the latest version of ALARM protocol for reducing the packet loss.

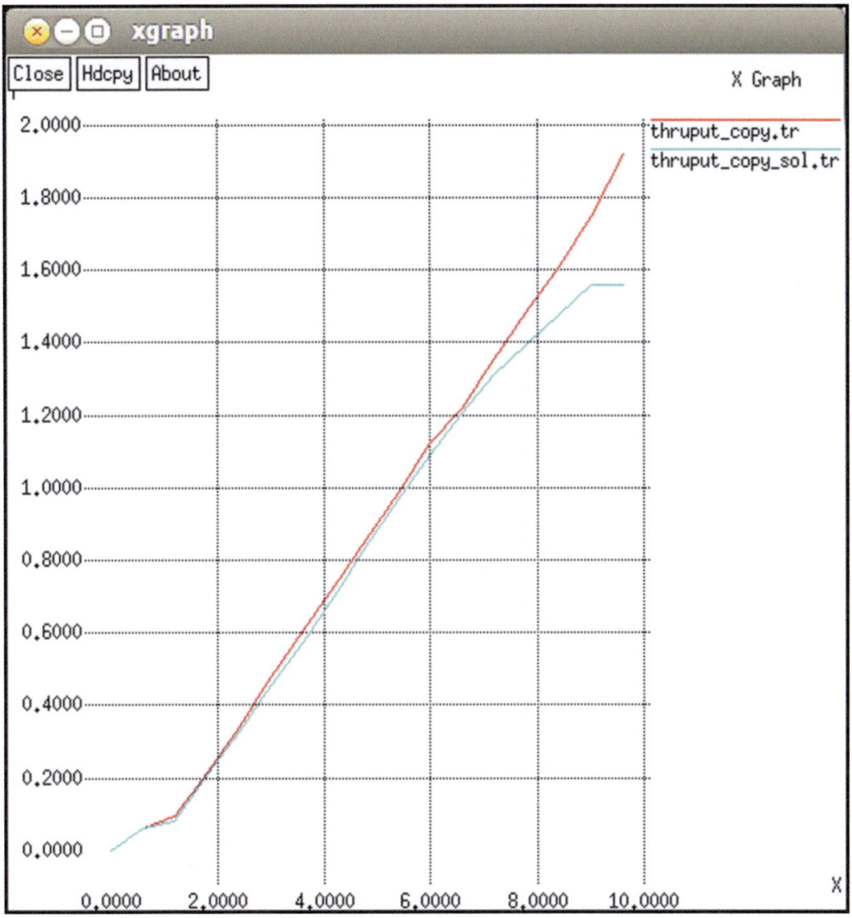

Fig. 6 Network throughput

References

1. Levya Mayorga I (2014) Performance analysis of a non preemptive hybrid WSN protocol in mobile environment. In: 28th international conference on advanced information networking and applications workshop, IEEE, pp 486–491, May 2014
2. Shen H, Zhoa L (2013) ALERT: anonymous location based efficient routing protocol in MANET. IEEE Trans Mob Comput 12(6) June 2013
3. Agarwal P, Ghosh RK (2008) Cooperative black and gray hole attacks in mobile Ad hoc network. In: 2nd international conference on ubiquitous IMC, Korea
4. El Defrway K, Tsudik G (2011) ALARM: anonymous location aided routing in suspicious MANET. IEEE Trans Mob Comput 10 Sept 2011

5. Cheng Y, Agarwal D (2005) Distributed anonymous secure routing protocol in wireless MANET. OPNETWORK
6. Koulali MA, Kobbane A (2012) Optimal distributed relay selection for duty cycling wireless sensor network. In: Global communication conference, IEEE, pp 145–150, Dec 2012

Seema Rawat is working as Assistant Professor at Amity University Uttar Pradesh Noida. She is M.Tech in Computer Science and B.Tech in Information Technology. She has 12.3 years of experience in academics. She has a number of patents and copyright to his credit and published more then 70+ research paper in International Journals and Conferences (Scopus Indexed). She is a member of IEEE, IACSIT and IAENG. Her primary research area includes Cloud Computing, Data mining and Artificial Intelligence.

Encryption Technique Using Elliptic Curve Cryptography Through Compression and Artificial Intelligence

Subhranil Som

Abstract This paper is an algorithmic approach to a compression scheme followed by an encryption of the compressed input stream using Elliptic Curve Cryptography (ECC) over prime field. The compression is an Artificial Intelligence (AI) approach where the input stream is fully read, and the repetitive groups in input stream are replaced by some unused character set. Elliptic curve has been chosen as it requires very less key size. The cryptanalysis to find back the private key requires discrete logarithmic approach. In the encryption scheme, first, the required parameters have been chosen to satisfying the equation $[4a^3 + 27b^2 \neq 0 \bmod p]$, where a prime number "$p$", which defines the cardinal number of the set. Each "$p + 1$" elements of the set has been evaluated. Each distinct character in the input stream is reflected to a point over the elliptic curve to deduce a point (x_A, y_A) using an integer value (K) which has been agreed by both sender and receiver. The receiver of the cipher text chooses a point from the set as the generator point generates public key set using key and is distributed among all the senders. This public key set has used in conjunction with the sender's private key and the point (x_A, y_A) to generate the cipher text which has been passed over to the intended recipient. The receiver takes up the cipher text and uses private key to find back the (x_A, y_A). The actual character from (x_A, y_A) using K and the original input stream has been evaluated.

1 Introduction

Early computer applications had no or very less security. People understood that data on computers are tremendously important feature of modern life. That is why many areas in security began to gain eminence [1]. As outcome researchers are still at work in the area in cryptography to develop the security more effectively [2].

S. Som (✉)
Amity Institute of Information Technology, Amity University,
Uttar Pradesh, India
e-mail: ssom@amity.edu; subhranil.som@gmail.com

M. U. Bokhari et al. (eds.), *Cyber Security*, Advances in Intelligent Systems and Computing 729, https://doi.org/10.1007/978-981-10-8536-9_42

In this paper a new technique has been proposed, where an algorithmic approach to a compression scheme followed by an encryption of the compressed input stream, using Elliptic Curve Cryptography (ECC), over prime field, has been cascaded. The compression is an Artificial Intelligence (AI) approach where the input stream is fully read and the repetitive groups in input stream are replaced by some unused character set. In the encryption scheme, first, the required parameters have been chosen to satisfying the equation [$4a^3 + 27b^2 \bmod p \neq 0$] and a prime number "$p$", which defines the cardinal number of the set. Each "$p + 1$" elements of the set are evaluated. Each distinct character in the input stream is reflected to a point over the elliptic curve, to deduce a point (x_A, y_A), using an integer value (K) which has been agreed by both sender and receiver. Receiver of the cipher text by choosing a point from the set of Generator points generates public key set, using private key and is distributed among all the senders. This public key set is used in conjunction with the sender's private key and the point (x_A, y_A) to generate the cipher text which has been passed over to the intended recipient. Receiver takes up the cipher text and uses private key to find back the point (x_A, y_A). Lastly, the actual character from (x_A, y_A) using K and the original input stream has been evaluated.

In Sect. 2 of this paper, the proposed technique has been discussed, Sect. 3 the Performance and Analysis are discussed. The conclusion is given in Sect. 4 followed by References.

2 The Proposed Technique

The technique has been described in the following subsection:

2.1 *Select Appropriate Elliptic Curve (EC) Equation and Produce the Field GF(q)*

To grow a field through p^m elements, it has been indicated as Galois Field [GF(p^m)], polynomial $f(x)$, (degree m) *irreducible* over GF(p). An elliptic curve (EC) and finite field GF(q) have chosen in following ways:

(a) Finite field, an efficient illustration of field elements have been chosen in a way that the processes are easily executed.
(b) The other representations of curve (projective, etc.) have been taken into consideration.
(c) Number of points on the curve, #E(GF(q)), has been divisible by large prime "n".
(d) #E(GF(q)) $\neq q$, where q = #GF(q) (field order).

The following equation of EC has been chosen:
y^2(mod p) = x^3 + ax + b(mod p) over field Zp = {0, 1,…, p − 1}
Where a and b are in Zp; x, y are also in Zp and $4a^3 + 27b^2$ [1]0 mod p
Let the Equation be: $\mathbf{y^2 = x^3 + x + 6}$.

2.2 Key Generation

Let us suppose that, "p" is a prime number = 11. Then the cardinal number of the set of point is (11 + 1).

For $x = 0, 1,\ldots, 10$, compute $z = x^3 + x + 6 \bmod 11$

z has been checked whether is a quadratic residue by

Legendre symbol (z/p) = z^(p − 1)/2 mod p = z^5 mod p

If YES, compute two square roots: $\pm z^{(p+1)/4} \bmod p = \pm z^3 \bmod p$

Hence, the points are: (2,4),(2,7), (3,5),(3,6), (5,2),(5,9), (7,2),(7,9), (8,3),(8,8), (10,2), O.

Let the generator point in (2, 7) represented by ***G***.

Compute the 2G, 3G, … as follows:

$xR = s2 - xP - xQ$ and $yR = s(xP - xR) - yP$ where $s = (yP - yQ)/(xP - xQ)$ if $P \neq Q$, $s = (3xP2 + a)/(2yP)$ if $P = Q$

For user A: User A has chosen random number to generate **private key** (Ak) = 7

"Ak" is multiplied with G to obtain the public key as follows:

Ak*G = 7*(1, 5)

This has been done as follows:

G + G = 2G

Hence, 7 * G = 2(2G + G) + G = (7, 2) (Let this point be denoted by G_A).

Thus, the total public key pair is [G, G_A].

Each user issues their public key.

2.3 Encryption of the Plain Text

Encryption of the text has been done in 3 phases.

a. **Public Key validation:**
   Public key validation is done as follows:

   (a) Verify that $Q = \infty$.
   (b) Verify that x_Q and y_Q *has been* correctly represented elements of Fq (for example integers interval (o, q − 1) where Fq is prime field and m bits strings of length, if Fq is binary which is field of order 2 m).

(c) Authenticate, Q satisfies EC equation has been defined by a and b.
(d) Authenticate, that $n_Q = \infty$.
(e) If verification has been failed, return "Invalid", otherwise, return "Valid".

b. **A character has been compressed of text to be encrypted to a point in the EC:** Method has been chosen for representing each character of plain text to be a point in the EC:
Steps:

(i) Pick an EC Ep(a,b).
(ii) Let, E has N points on it.
(iii) Let alphabets consists of digits 0–9 and the letters A–Z has been coded as 10, 11,…, 3.
(iv) This alters messages into series of numbers within 0–35.
(v) An auxiliary base has been chosen for parameter, example $k = 20$ (Both parties need to be agreed on this).
(vi) Each number, let, mk take x = mk + 1 and attempts to solve y.
(vii) Another way to try x = mk + 2 and then x = mk + 3 up until solving for y.
(viii) In exercise, find y prior hit x = mk + $k - 1$. After point (x,y) has been taken. Number m has been converted as a point on the EC. On this method, sequence of points has been generated from entire message.

Decryption:
Point (x,y) has been considered as each point and set "m" to greatest integer which has been $<(x - 1)/k$. The point (x,y) has been decoded to symbol m.
Example:
Let, $p(751)$, $a(-1)$, $b(188)$, $n(727)$ has been treated as parameter of curve.

(a) Let plain text is "B".
(b) "B" has been encrypted as 11.
(c) x = mk + 1 that is 11*20 + 1 = 221 not to be solved on behalf of "y" such that,
$y2 = x3 + ax + b$ mod p
(d) Need to solve for x = mk + 2, $x = 222$, y not exists. x = mk + 3, $x = 223$, y not exists.
(e) x = mk + 4, so, $x = 224$ can be solved for y and $y = 248$.
(f) The (224,248) $\approx$ (x_m, ym) point has been encrypted and decrypted as message.

c. **Encryption Scheme:**
In this part of the technique, the point (x_m, ym) has obtained after compressing the text into an elliptic curve which is encrypted by the user using public key and the public key of the receiver. Let, user B wants to send a cipher text to user A. The cipher text is:
[GB, (x_m, ym) + b*G_A]

2.4 Decryption of Cipher Text

Decryption of the cipher text has been done in two steps:

Step 1: Cipher text has decrypted first to the compressed point. This was done as follows:
User A multiplies private key with public key of User B
$Ak * G_B$
The resultant is subtracted from cipher text point:
$\{(x_m, ym) + b*G_A\} - Ak * G_B$

Step 2: The original character decompression from the point is done as follows:

(a) (224,248) point has been encrypted and decrypted to message.
(b) On the way to decrypt compute $(x - 1)/k = (224 - 1)/20 = 223/20$ that is 11.15.
(c) Above equation returns 11 as plaintext.
(d) The number 11 has been decoded to character "*B*".
(e) The possibility which has failed to find square and hence has been failed to associate m to a point, which is about $1/2k$ [3].

2.5 Compression of Text Prior to Encryption

(a) Example of plain text to be compressed

Let, the plain text is:

"ANAMIKA SENGUPTA IS A GIRL. SRI PRABIR SENGUPTA IS HER FATHER'S NAME. SMT SOMA SENGUPTA IS HER MOTHER'S NAME. LISTENING TO MUSIC IS HER HOBBY"

(b) The substitution technique for compression

Here, searches for every repeating group of characters and replace them with a binary number. Here in this text, first repeating group is "A SENGUPTA IS"; this will be replaced by $(1)_2$.

So the text becomes:

"ANAMIK $(1)_2$ A GIRL. SRI PRABIR SENGUPTA IS HER FATHER'S NAME. SMT SOM $(1)_2$ HER MOTHER'S NAME. LISTENING TO MUSIC IS HER HOBBY."

Next repeating group is "IS HER"; this will be replaced by $(11)_2$.

"ANAMIK $(1)_2$ A GIRL. SRI PRABIR SENGUPTA $(11)_2$ FATHER'S NAME. SMT SOM $(1)_2$ HER MOTHER'S NAME. LISTENING TO MUSIC $(11)_2$ HOBBY."

Like this searching and replacing algorithm carries on till all the repeating group of characters are replaced. The replacement has been done if the total size of the repeating string is more than the size of binary number, which replaces the string.

3 Performance Analysis Is Compared

In this section, the proposed algorithm has been analyzed for time complexity performance in contrast to RSA and Triple-DES. This performance analysis has been done over text files (*.TXT), and executable files (*.EXE). The analysis has been done over the parameters "Encryption time", "Decryption time", "Character Frequency", and "chi-square values". Java programming languages have been used for developing the programing implementation of the technique.

3.1 *Time Complexity Studies on Text Files*

Ten different text files sizes have been taken for experiment. The encrypted time, the decrypted time, and source file sizes have been noted for Triple-DES, RSA, and proposed technique. Tables 1 and 2 has been shown the encrypted and decrypted time of growing size of .txt files for proposed, T-DES, and RSA techniques. The proposed technique has been taken higher time to encrypt or decrypt compared to Triple-DES and RSA for any file size. Figure 1 shows the pictographic representation of the same.

Table 1 Comparative study of file size and encrypt time for text files (for proposed, RSA, and T-DES algo)

File name (.TXT)	File size (in bytes)	Encrypt Time (in s)		
		RSA	Triple-DES	Proposed Algo
adcajavas.txt	629	~0	~0	3.21
license.txt	7168	1	2	21.87
oledbjvs.txt	10,240	1.68	2.56	38.76
nerohistory.txt	17,408	1.99	2.96	40.65
nero.txt	33,792	3.76	4.54	50.43
whatsnew.txt	69,632	6.87	7.32	60.87
new.txt	94,208	7.21	7.98	63.99
c text.txt	132,096	7.97	9.87	65.43
9.txt	540,672	10.65	12.90	68.98
incidia.txt	1,190,912	14.89	15.98	71.65

Table 2 Comparative study of file size and decrypt time for text files (for proposed, RSA, and Triple-DES algo)

File name (*.TXT)	File size (in Bytes)	Encrypt time (in s)		
		RSA	Triple-DES	Proposed Algo
adcajavas txt	629	~0	~0	2.98
license.txt	7168	1	1.9	20.51
oledbjvs.txt	10,240	1.65	2	36.87
nerohistory.txt	17,408	1.99	2.65	39.65
nero.txt	33,792	3.77	3.54	48.87
whatsnew.txt	69,632	6.80	7.01	55.87
new.txt	94,208	7.01	8	60.43
c text.txt	132,096	7.54	9.31	61.08
9.txt	540,572	10.65	13.01	65.72
incidia.txt	1,190,912	14.12	15.99	69.43

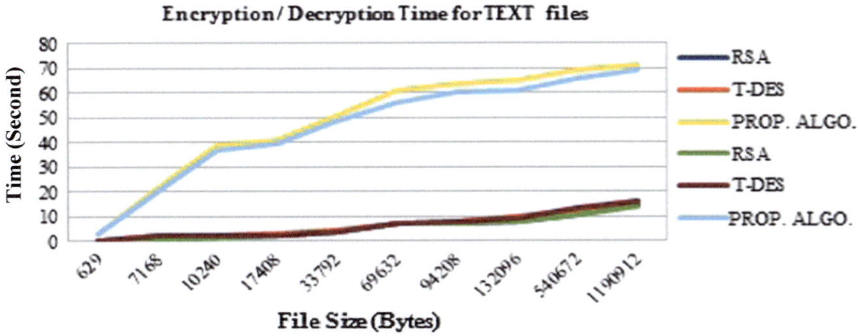

Fig. 1 Encrypt and decrypt time for proposed Algo, RSA, and Triple-DES techniques for .TXT files

3.2 *Time Complexity Studies on Executable Files*

Ten different sizes of .exe files have been taken for experiment. Comparative studies of time complexity have been done for these files to encrypt and decrypt using proposed, RSA, and Triple-DES Technique. Experimental results have been noted down in Tables 3 and 4. From the data of Tables 3 and 4 depicts the proposed technique has taken more time to encrypt and decrypt in comparison to Triple-DES and RSA technique for any size of the executable files. The pictographic representations of the same have been given in Fig. 2.

Table 3 Comparative study of file size and encrypt time for EXE files (for proposed, RSA, and Triple-DES algo)

File name (*EXE)	File size (in bytes)	Encrypt time (in s)		
		RSA	Triple-DES	Proposed Algo
1.exe	28,672	2	4	35
2.exe	96,256	3	6	41
3.exe	130,048	7	9	50
4.exe	175,104	13	17	57
5.exe	292,364	14	19	61
6.exe	355,328	19	23	67
7.exe	613,376	29	34	78
8.exe	775,168	35	41	81
9.exe	1,307,648	49	58	98
10.exe	1,835,003	61	67	102

Table 4 Comparative study of file size and decrypt time for .EXE files (for proposed, RSA, and Triple-DES algo)

File name (*EXE)	File size (in bytes)	Decrypt time (in s)		
		RSA	Triple-DES	Proposed Algo
1.exe	28,672	2	4	33
2.exe	96,256	4	6	40
3.exe	130,048	8	10	45
4.exe	175,104	15	18	55
5.exe	292,864	16	21	58
6.exe	355,328	21	23	62
7.exe	613,376	33	39	73
8.exe	775,168	41	43	79
9.exe	1,307,645	53	61	91
10.exe	1,835,008	66	72	96

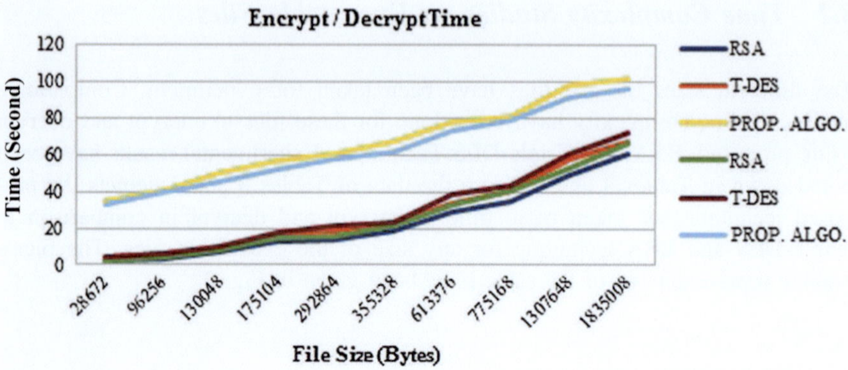

Fig. 2 Encrypt and decrypt time for proposed technique, RSA, and Triple-DES techniques for .EXE files

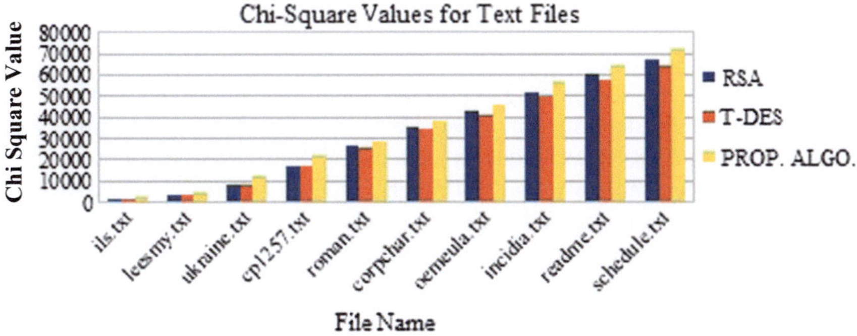

Fig. 3 Pictorial representation of chi-square values for RSA, proposed algo, and Triple-DES

Table 5 Comparison of chi-square values in RSA, Triple-DES, and proposed Algo for text files

File name (text file)	Chi-square values		
	RSA	Triple-DES	Proposed Algo
1.txt	2035.20	1925.98	2192.76
2.txt	4021.59	3835.10	5045.89
3.txt	3758.46	8250.29	119.54
4.txt	17,421.28	17,511.096	21,988.32
5.txt	26,322.44	25,761.70	28,635.97
6.txt	35,324.74	34,432.70	37,982.87
7.txt	44,382.20	42,563.22	45,872.89
8.txt	51,524.99	49,327.87	56,674.01
9.txt	61,235.54	58,929.74	63,999.52
10.txt	67,092.13	65,203.10	71,896.89

3.3 Parametric Test for Non-homogeneity

The well-recognized chi-square parametric tests have been done for non-homogeneity among encrypted and source files. The higher chi-square values endorse heterogeneity of the encrypted and source files. To perform the experiment text file has been taken. Chi-square test has been done using encrypted and source files for proposed, RSA, and Triple-DES techniques. The increased value of the chi-square proves the non-homogeneity for increasing file size. Ten different text file sizes are taken for experiment. The high chi-square value ensures non-homogeneity among encrypted and source files. The good degree of non-homogeneity is detected in all three cases of implementation. It has been concluded that proposed technique has ensured optimum security in communication. Graphical depictions of chi-square values have been given below (Fig. 3) (Table 5).

4 Conclusion

The main attraction of the proposed algorithm is that, compared to RSA, it provides more or less similar security for a lesser bits size, thereby dropping processing overhead. The proposed technique is perfect for constrained situation such as PDAs, cell phones and smart cards. Though proposed technique has taken more time for encryption and decryption as compared to T-DES and RSA, it has shown good result in chi-square test. It has been seen that encrypted file using proposed algo has high chi-square value. This high value is indicating good security.

References

1. Atul K (2005) Cryptography and network security. Tata McGraw-Hill, New Delhi. ISBN 0-07-049483-5
2. Som S, Mandal JK (2008) A session key based secure-bit encryption technique (SBET). In: National conference (INDIACom-2008) on computing for nation development, New Delhi, India, 08–09 Feb 2008
3. Al-Vahed A, Sahhavi H (2011) An overview of modern cryptography. World Appl Program 1 (1):3–8. ISSN: 2222–2510
4. Certicom (2000) Standards for efficient cryptography, SEC 1: elliptic curve cryptography, Version 1.0, Sep 2000
5. Certicom (2000) Standards for efficient cryptography, SEC 2: recommended elliptic curve domain parameters, Version 1.0, Sep 2000
6. William S Cryptography and network security, principles and practice
7. Anoop MS (2015) Elliptic curve cryptography—an implementation guide. URL: http://www.infosecwriters.com/text_resources/pdf/Elliptic_curve_AnnopMS.pdf. Last accessed on April 2015
8. Darrel H, Alfred M, Scott V (2003) Guide to elliptic curve cryptography. Springer, Berlin. ISBN 0-387-95273-X
9. Henri C, Gerhard F, Roberto A (2005) Handbook of elliptic and hyper-elliptic curve cryptography. Chapman and Hall/CRC. ISBN: 978-1-58488-518-4
10. Jadhav A (2011) Implementation of elliptic curve cryptography on text and image. Int J Enterp Comput Bus Syst 1(2): ISSN (Online): 2230–8849. http://www.ijecbs.com, July 2011
11. Kumar R, Jaiswal UC (2011) Experimental investigation of image encryption technique using public key. Int J Tech 1(1):12–14
12. Sharma RD (2011) Quantum cryptography: a new approach to information security. Int J Power Syst Op Energy Manag (IJPSOEM) 1(1)

Author Biography

Dr. SubhranilSom received his Master degree in Computer Application in 2003, and his Ph.D. in Computer Science and Engineering from government university, University of Kalyani, West Bengal, India in the year of 2012. He is currently Associate Professor in internationally reputed Amity University, UP, India. He is empaneled Ph.D. supervisor in the Amity University. He holds a distinction in Physics and Mathematics in Graduation from Jadavpur University, Kolkata, WB, India. His fields of interest include Cryptography and Network Security, e-Health, Robotics, Core Java, C++, C, etc. He was attached with a WHO's International Research Project on "e-Health for Health Care Delivery", University of New South Wales, Sydney, Australia. He has visited Malaysia, Singapore, Thailand, UAE, and Australia for his academic and research work. He has finished several courses related to computer application, object-oriented analysis and design, software engineering, and project management. He has more than 15 years of teaching and research experiences.

A Robust Server-Side JavaScript Feature Injection-Based Design for JSP Web Applications Against XSS Vulnerabilities

Shashank Gupta and B. B. Gupta

Abstract Cross-Site Scripting (XSS) attack vectors are well-thought-out selected as a serious infection for contemporary HTML5 websites. In this paper, a novel server-side JavaScript feature injection-based design is proposed that relies on the concept of inserting the features of JavaScript in order to discover the variation between the stored and observed features in the HTTP response. In addition to this, injection of context-sensitive sanitization functions has also adopted by our design to detect the XSS attack vectors in HTML websites. The prototype of our design will be developed in Java as a server-side framework, and the experimental results of our proposed design on JSP websites will also be evaluated as further extension.

Keywords Cross-site scripting (XSS) attacks · Script injection vulnerabilities JavaScript · Context-Sensitive sanitization routines · HTTP

1 Introduction

XSS is accredited as the most harmful category of web application vulnerability [1–6]. This could be executed as follows: The attacker visits the Vulnerable Web Application (VWA) and posts a comment containing malicious JS code [13–16]. The victim visits the web application and logs in through the web browser. The credentials of the victim get stored on the victim's browser record and login through a cookie file sent by the web server [17–20]. If the victim clicks on the attacker's malign link, the script gets executed by JavaScript interpreter and victim's cookies

S. Gupta (✉)
Department of Computer Science and Information System, Birla Institute of Technology and Science, Pilani, Vidhya Vihar, Pilani 333031, Rajasthan, India
e-mail: shashank.csit@gmail.com

B. B. Gupta
Department of Computer Engineering, National Institute of Technology Kurukshetra, Kurukshetra 136119, Haryana, India
e-mail: gupta.brij@gmail.com

M. U. Bokhari et al. (eds.), *Cyber Security*, Advances in Intelligent Systems and Computing 729, https://doi.org/10.1007/978-981-10-8536-9_43

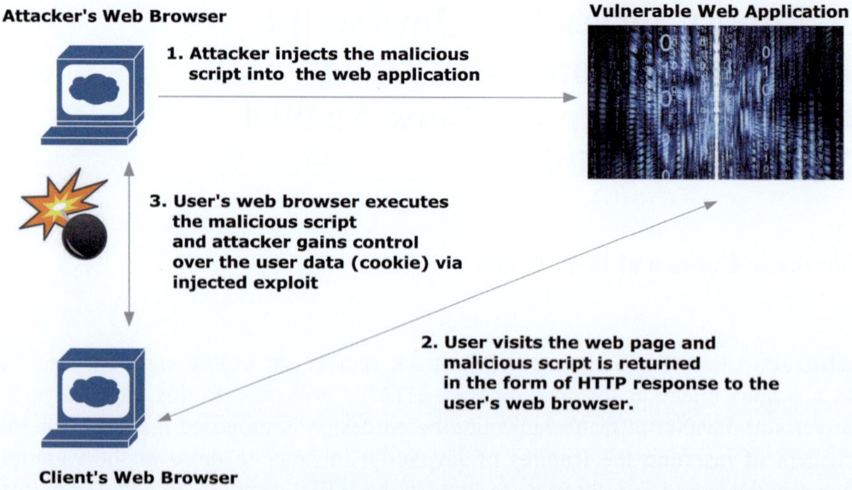

Fig. 1 An instance of injection of suspicious script code on JSP websites

get imported to attacker's system. Figure 1 describes a typical cookie-stealing scenario by injecting the XSS worm on the web applications.

2 Proposed Defensive Framework

The authors suggested a server-side JavaScript feature injection-based design is proposed that rely on the concept of inserting the features of JavaScript in order to discover the variation between the stored and observed features in the HTTP response. The idea of injecting the context-sensitive sanitization routines has also adopted by our design to detect the malicious XSS payloads in JavaScript code. The defensive server-side design regularly creates the rules, incorporates the feature content, and automatically injects context-sensitive sanitization routines with the key goal to detect the presence of XSS attack vectors.

The design of the proposed server-side XSS defensive framework (shown in the Fig. 2) operates in two phases: JavaScript feature injection and auto-context-sensitive sanitization. In the first phase, our design presents a novel idea of feature injection that consists of arbitrarily created tokens as well as features of legitimate JavaScript code w.r.t. the quantity of attributes/tags. Feature injection is the procedure of injecting a JavaScript comment that cannot transform the anticipated behaviors of the response. Such comments are calculated for detecting the presence of XSS attack payloads for differentiating between the benign and injected JavaScript. Subsequently, Rule Extractor component is accountable for retrieving possible features of data as well as holding such features in some shape of precise rules. Such component is also accountable for producing a variety of precise rules that are created on the added features as well as saves such rules in the Rule-Based Feature Repository module. Once, the initial HTTP response is produced on web server, it has to pass through the Rule-Based Variance detector, which detects some deviation among the actual stored features and observed features. Even, slight dissimilarity detected would be deliberated as suspicious injected code and finally, the appended features will be extracted from the code of JavaScript before entering into the second phase of Auto-Context-Sensitive Sanitization. The second phase, Auto-Context Sensitive Sanitization performs a practice of automated sanitizer assignment via evaluating and discovering the chunk of injected code. However, assignment of sanitizer is stationary as well as occasionally deviates to dynamic whenever it is necessary. The key objective of such module is to determine some inputs related to sanitization on the path of source code of JavaScript.

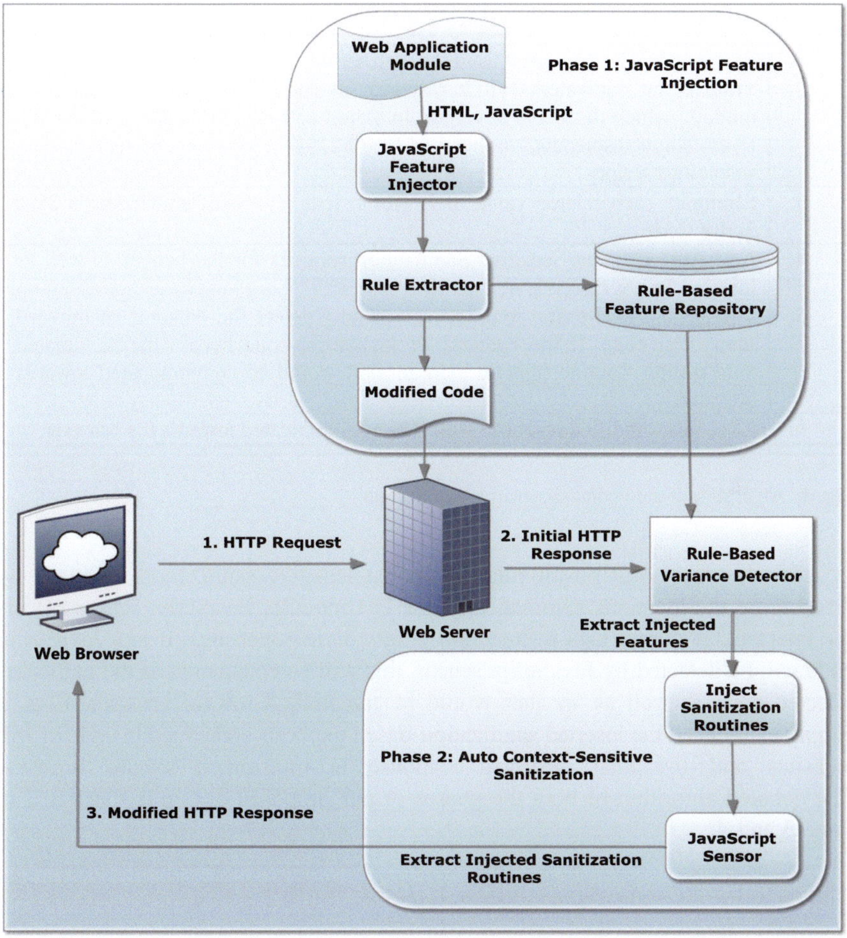

Fig. 2 Design of proposed server-side XSS defensive framework

Algorithm: Phase 1: JavaScript Feature Injection	
1.	Retrieve the possible Injection Points IP_i (for i = 1, 2, 3, -------n) from the source code of HTML and JavaScript.
2.	Append the Features F_i (for i=1, 2, 3,-----n) of JavaScript in their extracted source code with some random value of token R_i (for i=1,2,3,-----n)
3.	Transmit the extracted values of F_i to the Rule Extractor component, which generates some well-defined policies based on these extracted features. Such policies are stored in the Rule-Based Feature database.
4.	Lastly, the modified code is transmitted on online server.

Fig. 3 Algorithm of JavaScript feature injection

Algorithm: Phase 2: Auto-Context Sensitive Sanitization	
1.	Extract the HTTP Request from the web server.
2.	Transfer an equivalent HTTP response to Rule-Based Variation Detector module, which discovers deviation in stored and injected features of scripts. Even, slight discrepancy noticed in (F1, F2, ---- Fn) would be remarked as suspicious scripts.
3.	Eliminate each related value of F_i (for i=1, 2, 3, -----n) embedded in Java Script Code.
4.	Add Auto Context Sensitive Sanitization routines for the benign as well as injected JavaScript code in a manual way.
5.	The JavaScript Sensor component will now detect the contents of injected JavaScript code. If the contents of JavaScript code bypass the Automated Sanitization Routine Injector then an alert would be communicated towards browser.
6.	Else, final modified response would be communicated towards the browser.

Fig. 4 Algorithm of auto-context-sensitive sanitization

After the successful positioning of context-sensitive sanitization functions by discovering the locations automatically, the last module, JavaScript sensor detects the injected JavaScript tags in injection points of JSP websites. If any JavaScript code will be detected by JavaScript sensor, this will be considered as the malicious injected code as well as an alert would be transmitted toward browser. Else, it simply extracts all the inserted sanitization-based methods embedded in code of JSP websites and the final reformed response is transmitted toward browser. The detailed algorithm of both the phases of our proposed design is illustrated in Figs. 3 and 4.

3 Discussion

Usually, XSS attacks involve that the web servers, which are controlled by an attacker, has to initiate a communication with the compromised web pages. Here, the authors suggested an innovative framework, which is highly inspired by the current literature works as mentioned in [11, 12]. Our proposed design is reliant upon the notion of incorporating features of script data in order to discover the variation between the stored and observed features in the HTTP response. In addition to this, the notion of incorporating the context-sensitive sanitization functions has also adopted by our design to detect the XSS attack vectors embedded in JSP websites. The benefits of our design versus other two recent related XSS defensive techniques [11, 12] include: (1) it possesses capability for noticing suspicious JavaScript function invocation. (2) It is based on the automated preprocessing technique of insertion and abstraction of script features and sanitization methods embedded in JSP websites. (3) It did not incorporate the valid script as this could again create the prospect of comprising distant JavaScript file in the related anchor tag. (4) Our technique consumes tolerable time in detecting XSS attack vectors as the authors suggested a programmed procedure of insertion of script features and related sanitization functions.

Our framework simply senses association among the deposited features and incorporated ones embedded in JSP web platforms. Hence, we could not assure that our technique can alleviate the attack vectors that circumvent certain conditions that were present in rule-based repository. In addition, the entirety and correctness of mined features of script data could not be guaranteed. The authors preferred to scrutinize the functions for automatic confirmation of retrieved script data features. However, we considered that our proposed design presents a reasonable assurance that it will detect certain attack vectors with small percentage of false positives and incurs tolerable runtime overhead. We will implement the prototype of our design in Java as a server-side framework. Throughout the course of experimental evaluation, we will test and assess the XSS attack recognition proficiency of our server-side design on the following JSP websites (i.e., JAuction [7]; JVote [8], MeshCMS [9] and Easy JSP Forum [10]).

4 Concluding Remarks and Further Scope

The authors suggested a server-side JavaScript feature injection-based design that deals with these issues by incorporating an innovative concept of feature injection declarations as well as automated assignment of sanitization methods. The proposed design discovers deviation between the stored and observed features in the HTTP response message produced on server-side. In addition, the technique detects the malicious JavaScript attack vectors via a programmed assignment of context-sensitive sanitization methods. In future, the authors will implement our server-side design in Java and would assess the suspicious scripts recognition proficiency of proposed design on JSP websites. In addition, we will also utilize the HTML5 websites for introducing the concept of inserting the features of script data and incorporate context-sensitive sanitization routines in their source code.

References

1. Klein A (2002) Cross site scripting explained. White Paper, Sanctum Security Group, June
2. Gupta S, Gupta BB (2016) XSS-secure as a service for the platforms of online social network-based multimedia web applications in cloud. Multimed Tools Appl 1–33
3. Gupta BB, Gupta S, Gangwar S, Kumar M, Meena PK (2015) Cross-site scripting (XSS) abuse and defense: exploitation on several testing bed environments and its defense. J Inf Priv Secur 11(2):118–136
4. Gupta S, Gupta B (2015) PHP-sensor: a prototype method to discover workflow violation and XSS Vulnerabilities in PHP web applications. In: 12th ACM International Conference on Computing Frontiers (CF'15), Ischia, Italy
5. Chaudhary P, Gupta S, Gupta BB, Chandra VS, Selvakumar S, Fire M, Goldschmidt R, Elovici Y, Gupta BB, Gupta S, Gangwar S. Auditing defense against XSS worms in online social network-based web applications. In: Handbook of research on modern cryptographic solutions for computer and cyber security, vol 36, pp 216–245, 16 May 2016
6. Gupta S, Gupta BB (2014) BDS: browser dependent XSS sanitizer. Book on cloud-based databases with biometric applications, In: IGI-global's advances in information security, privacy, and ethics (AISPE) series, 31 Oct 2014, pp 174–91
7. JAuction-0.3. http://sourceforge.net/projects/jauction/
8. JVote. Accessed from http://sourceforge.net/projects/jspvote/
9. MeshCMS. http://cromoteca.com/en/meshcms/
10. Easy JSP Forum. http://sourceforge.net/projects/easyjspforum
11. Shaihriar H, Zulkernine M (2011) S2XS2: a server side approach to automatically detect XSS attacks. In: Ninth international conference on dependable, automatic secure computing, IEEE, (2011), pp 7–17
12. Shaihriar H, Zulkernine M (2011) Injecting comments to detect javascript code injection attacks. In: Proceedings of the 6th IEEE workshop on security, trust, and privacy for software applications, Munich, Germany, July, pp 104–109
13. Gupta S, Gupta BB (2015) Cross-site scripting (XSS) attacks and defense mechanisms: classification and state-of-the-art. Int J Syst Assur Eng Manage 1–19
14. Gupta S, Gupta BB, Chaudhary P (2017) Hunting for DOM-based XSS vulnerabilities in mobile cloud-based online social network. In: Future Generation Computer Systems. 12 June 2017
15. Gupta S, Gupta BB (2016) Alleviating the proliferation of JavaScript worms from online social network in cloud platforms. In: 2016 7th international conference on information and communication systems (ICICS), IEEE, pp 246–251
16. Gupta S, Gupta BB (2016) An infrastructure-based framework for the alleviation of JavaScript worms from OSN in mobile cloud platforms. In: International conference on network and system security 28 Sep 2016, pp 98–109. Springer International Publishing
17. Gupta S, Gupta BB (2016) XSS-immune: a Google chrome extension-based XSS defensive framework for contemporary platforms of web applications. Secur Commun Netw 9(17):3966–3986
18. Gupta S, Gupta BB (2016) Alleviating the proliferation of JavaScript worms from online social network in cloud platforms. In: 2016 7th International Conference on Information and Communication Systems (ICICS), IEEE, pp 246–251

19. Gupta S, Gupta BB (2017) Smart XSS attack surveillance system for OSN in virtualized intelligence network of nodes of fog computing. Int J Web Serv Res (IJWSR) 14(4):1–32
20. Gupta S, Gupta BB (2016) JS-SAN: defense mechanism for HTML5-based web applications against JavaScript code injection vulnerabilities. Secur Commun Netw 9(11):1477–1495

Author Biographies

Dr. Shashank Gupta is currently working as an Assistant Professor in Computer Science and Information Systems Division at Birla Institute of Technology and Science, Pilani, Rajasthan, India. He has done his Ph.D. under the supervision of Dr. B. B. Gupta in Department of Computer Engineering specialization in Web Security at National Institute of Technology Kurukshetra, Haryana, India. Recently, he was working as an Assistant Professor in the Department of Computer Science and Engineering at Jaypee Institute of Information Technology (JIIT), Noida, Sec-128. Prior to this, he has also served his duties as an Assistant Professor in the Department of IT at Model Institute of Engineering and Technology (MIET), Jammu. He has completed M.Tech. in the Department of Computer Science and Engineering Specialization in Information Security from Central University of Rajasthan, Ajmer, India. He has also done his graduation in Bachelor of Engineering (B.E.) in Department of Information Technology from Padmashree Dr. D.Y. Patil Institute of Engineering and Technology Affiliated to Pune University, India. He has also spent two months in the Department of Computer Science and IT, University of Jammu for completing a portion of Post-graduation thesis work. He bagged the 1st Cash Prize in Poster Presentation at National Level in the category of ICT Applications in Techspardha'2015 and 2016 event organized by National Institute of Kurukshetra, Haryana. He has numerous online publications in International Journals and Conferences including IEEE, Elsevier, ACM, Springer, Wiley, Elsevier, IGI-Global, etc. along with several book chapters. He is also serving as reviewer for numerous peer-reviewed Journals and conferences of high repute. He is also a professional member of IEEE and ACM. His research area of interest includes Web Security, Cross- Site Scripting (XSS) attacks, Online Social Network Security, Cloud Security, Fog Computing and theory of Computation.

Dr. B. B. Gupta received PhD degree from Indian Institute of Technology Roorkee, India in the area of Information and Cyber Security. In 2009, he was selected for Canadian Commonwealth Scholarship and awarded by Government of Canada Award ($10,000). He spent more than six months in University of Saskatchewan (UofS), Canada to complete a portion of his research work. He has published more than 70 research papers(including 01 book and 08 chapters) in International Journals and Conferences of high repute including IEEE, Elsevier, ACM, Springer, Wiley Inderscience, etc. He has visited several countries, i.e. Canada, Japan, China, Malaysia, Hong-Kong, etc. to present his research work. His biography was selected and publishes in the 30th Edition of Marquis Who' s Who in the World, 2012. He is also working principal investigator of various R&D projects. He is also serving as reviewer for Journals of IEEE, Springer, Wiley, Taylor & Francis, etc. He is serving as guest editor of various Journals. He was also visiting researcher with Yamaguchi University, Japan in 2015 and with Guangzhou University, China in 2016, respectively. At present, Dr. Gupta is working as Assistant Professor in the Department of Computer Engineering, National Institute of Technology Kurukshetra, India. His research interest includes Information security, Cyber Security, Mobile/Smartphone, Cloud Computing, Web security, Intrusion detection, Computer networks and Phishing.

PHISH-SAFE: URL Features-Based Phishing Detection System Using Machine Learning

Ankit Kumar Jain and B. B. Gupta

Abstract Today, phishing is one of the most serious cyber-security threat in which attackers steal sensitive information such as personal identification number (PIN), credit card details, login, password, etc., from Internet users. In this paper, we proposed a machine learning based anti-phishing system (i.e., named as PHISH-SAFE) based on Uniform Resource Locator (URL) features. To evaluate the performance of our proposed system, we have taken 14 features from URL to detect a website as a phishing or non-phishing. The proposed system is trained using more than 33,000 phishing and legitimate URLs with SVM and Naïve Bayes classifiers. Our experiment results show more than 90% accuracy in detecting phishing websites using SVM classifier.

Keywords Phishing · SVM · Bayes classifier · Machine learning URL

1 Introduction

Phishing is one of the major security threats faced by the cyber-world and could lead to financial losses for both industries and individuals. In this attack, criminal makes a fake web page by copying contents of the legitimate page, so that a user cannot differentiate between phishing and legitimate sites [1]. Life cycle of phishing attack is shown in Fig. 1. According to anti-phishing working report in the first Quarter of 2014, second highest number of phishing attacks ever recorded between January and March 2014 [2] and payment services are the most targeted by these attacks. The total number of phishing attacks notice in Q1 (first quarter) of

A. K. Jain (✉) · B. B. Gupta
Department of Computer Engineering, National Institute of Technology Kurukshetra, Kurukshetra 136119, Haryana, India
e-mail: ankit.jain2407@gmail.com

B. B. Gupta
e-mail: gupta.brij@gmail.com

M. U. Bokhari et al. (eds.), *Cyber Security*, Advances in Intelligent Systems and Computing 729, https://doi.org/10.1007/978-981-10-8536-9_44

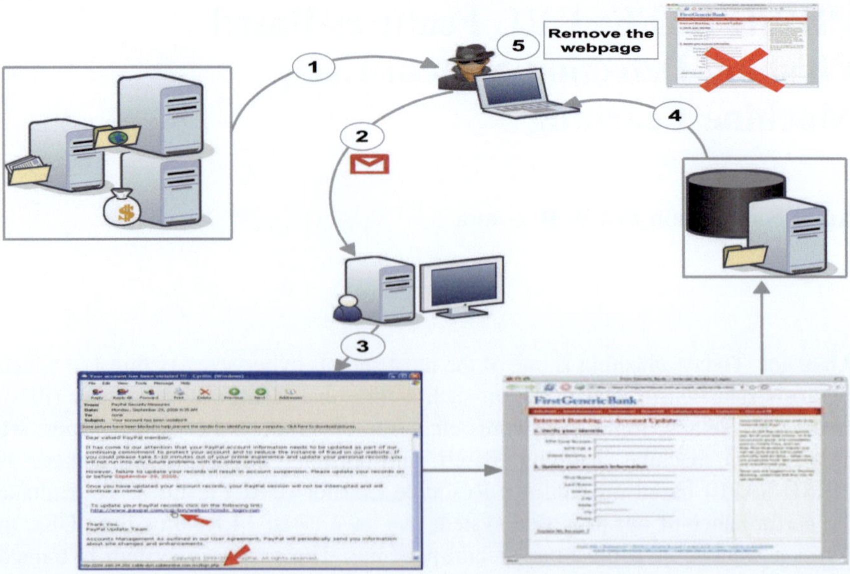

Fig. 1 Phishing life cycle: (1) phisher copies the content from legitimate site and constructs the phishing site; (2) phisher sent link of phishing URL to Internet user; (3) user opens the link and fills personal on fake site; (4) phisher steals the personal information of user; (5) phisher deletes the fake web page

2014 were 125,215, a 10.7 percent increase over Q4 (fourth quarter) of 2013. Existing solution like heuristic based, visual similarity based take features from the web page content so they take a lot of time to take decision. The phishing URL classification scheme based only on investigative the suspicious URL and speed up the running time of system. Therefore, in this paper, we proposed a machine learning based phishing detection system which uses the URL features and analysed it using naive Bayesian and SVM classifiers. Moreover, it does not require any information from the e-content of the suspicious web page.

The remainder of this paper is organized as follows. Section 2 describes the background and state-of-art techniques, its advantages and limitations. Section 3 describes our proposed phishing detection system in details. Evaluation of the proposed system with results is discussed in Sect. 4. Finally, Sect. 5 concludes our paper and discusses the scope for future work.

2 Related Work

There have been several techniques given in the literature to detect phishing attack in last few years. In this section, we present an overview of detection approaches against phishing attacks. Phishing detection approaches are broadly classified into two types: user education based techniques and software-based techniques.

Software-based detection is further classified into heuristic based, blacklist-based and visual similarity based techniques.

User Education based approaches: To classify phishing and non-phishing email, Kumaraguru et al. [3] developed two embedded training designs to teach users. After this training, users can identify phishing emails by themselves. Sheng et al. [4] proposed an educational interactive game "Anti-Phishing Phill" that educates good habits to keep away from phishing attacks.

Softwar-based approaches: Software-based detection is further classified into following sub-categories:

(a) Blackl-based approaches: In this type of approaches, the suspicious domain is matched with a predefined phishing domain called blacklist. The negative aspect of this scheme is that it usually does not cover all phishing websites because a freshly launched fraud website takes some time to add to the blacklist record. Sheng et al. [5] depicted that blacklists are typically add in the record at diverse frequencies, approximate 50–80% of phishing domains added in blacklist after performing some financial loss.
(b) Heuris-based approaches: In this type of approaches, the heuristic design of suspicious websites matches with the feature set, which are generally found in phishing websites [6]. Zero-day attack (i.e., attacks that were not seen before) can be identified using heuristic approach. Zhang et al. [7] proposed a content-based phishing detection technique called CANTINA, which take a rich set of feature set from various field of a web page.
(c) Visual similarity-based approaches: Visual similarity-based approaches compare the visual appearance of a suspicious website and its corresponding legitimate site. Visual similarity-based techniques use features set like text content, HTML Tags, Cascading Style Sheet (CSS), image processing, etc., to make decision. Chen et al. [8] proposed an anti-phishing approach based on discriminative key-point features in a web page.

Based on the abovementioned approaches proposed in the literature, we found that there exists no single technique that can detect various types of phishing attacks. Moreover, Blacklist/White-list based approaches cannot detect zero-day attacks. Heuristic-based techniques can detect the zero-day attack but fail to detect attack if embedded object present in the web page and false positive is also high in these approaches. Moreover, visual similarity-based approaches can detect the embedded objects present in the web page but they fail to detect the zero-day attacks. Therefore, in this paper, we have proposed a machine learning based anti-phishing system (i.e., named as PHISH-SAFE) based on Uniform Resource Locator (URL) features which can able to detect variety of phishing attacks efficiently.

3 Proposed Phishing Detection System

In this section, we will discuss our proposed phishing detection system which can detect a phishing page before user inputs personal information. Total 32,951 phishing URLs are taken from phishtank.com to evaluate the performance of the proposed system. Following features are used for the phishing detection:

- **IP Address**: A phisher uses the IP address in place of domain name to hide the identity of a website.
- **Sub Domain**: Phishing sites contain more than two sub-domains in URL. Each domain is separated by dot (.). If any URL contain three or more than three dots, then the probability of the suspicious site is more. In our experiment, we found that 12,904 sites contain three or more number of dots.
- **URL contains "@" symbol**: the presence of "@" symbol in the URL ignore everything previous to it. In our dataset, out of 32,951 phishing URL, 569 sites contain @ symbol.
- **Number of dash (-) in URL**: To looks like genuine URL, phisher adds some prefix or suffix with the brand name with dash, e.g., www.amazon-india.com. We found that 42.5% of phishing URLs contain "dash" symbol.
- **Length of URL**: To hide the domain name, phisher uses the long URL. In our experiment, we found the average length of URL is 74. We found that 7406 phishing sites contain length between 14 and 40 characters. 10,466 phishing sites are having length between 41 and 60 characters. 6602 phishing URL contain length between 61 and 80 character and 8475 sites contain length between 81 and 2205 characters.
- **Suspicious words in URL**: Phishing URLs contain suspicious words such as token, confirm, security, PayPal, login, signin, bank, account, update, etc., to gain the trust on website. We have taken these nine frequently occurred words in phishing sites.
- **Position of Top-Level Domain**: This feature checks the position of top-level domain at proper place in URL.
  Example—http://xyz.paypal.com.accounts.765issapidll.xtmll.ebmdata.com.
- **Embedded Domain in URL**: It checks this by checking for the occurrence of "//" in the URL.
- **HTTPS Protocol**: HTTPS protocol is used for security. Phishing does not start with https while legitimate URL provides security. (In our phishing dataset, only 388 phishing sites contain https protocol).
- **Number of times http appears**: In phishing websites, http protocol may appear more than one time but in genuine site, it appear only one time.
- **Domains count in URL**: Phishing URL may contain more than one domain in URL. Two or more domains is used to redirect address.
- **DNS lookup**: If the DNS record is not available then the website is phishing. The life of phishing site is very short, therefore; this DNS information may not be available after some time.

- **Inconsistent URL**: If the domain name of suspicious web page is not matched with the WHOIS database record, then the web page is considered as phishing.
- **Age of Domain**: If the age of website is less than 6 month, then chances of fake web page are more.

Training and testing of the proposed system are performed using following classifiers:

(a) Naïve Bayes: Naïve Bayes is the probabilistic classifier, based on Bayes' theorem with "naive" independence supposition. This classifier, used in text categorization, can be an earning-based variant of keyword filtering. The rules for decision making are explained below:

$$\emptyset_{k|y=1} = p\left(x_j = k|y = 1\right) = \left(\frac{\sum_{i=1}^{m}\sum_{j=1}^{n_i} 1\left\{x_j^{(i)} = k \text{and} y^{(i)} = 1\right\} + 1}{\left(\sum_{i=1}^{m} 1\{y^{(I)} = 1\}n_i\right) + |V|}\right) \quad (1)$$

$$\emptyset_{k|y=1} = p\left(x_j = k|y = 0\right) = \left(\frac{\sum_{i=1}^{m}\sum_{j=1}^{n_i} 1\left\{x_j^{(i)} = k \text{ and } y^{(i)} = 0\right\} + 1}{\left(\sum_{i=1}^{m} 1\{y^{(I)} = 1\}n_i\right) + |V|}\right) \quad (2)$$

$$\emptyset_{y=1} = \frac{\sum_{i=1}^{m} 1\{y^{(i)} = 1\}}{(m)} \quad (3)$$

$\emptyset_{x|y=1}$ estimates the probability that a particular feature in a phishing URL will be the k-th word in the dictionary. $\emptyset_{x|y=0}$ estimates the probability that a particular feature in a legitimate URL will be the k-th word in the dictionary. $\emptyset_y$ estimates the probability that any particular URL will be a phishing URL. m is the number of URLs in our training set. The entire dictionary contains V words or the entire URLs are V in number. For training, $\emptyset_{x|y=0}$, $\emptyset_{x|y=1}$, $\emptyset_y$ are calculated and for testing, $p(x|y = 1)\ p(y = 1)$ is compared to $p(x|y = 0)\ p(y = 0)$. To avoid underflow error, logarithms are used. An email is classified as spam or phishing according to the following equation:

$$\log p(x|y = 1) + \log p(y = 1) > \log p(x|y = 0) + \log p(y = 0) \quad (4)$$

Support Vector Machine: Support vector machine (SVM) is supervised learning models frequently used classifier in phishing attack detection. SVM worked based on training examples and a predefined alteration θ:Rs → F, it makes a map from features set to produce a transformed feature space, storing the URL samples of the two classes with a hyperplane in the transformed feature space.

Table 1 Experiment results

URL instances	Classifiers	
	Naive Bayes (%)	SVM (%)
10,000	64.74	76.04
25,000	76.87	91.28

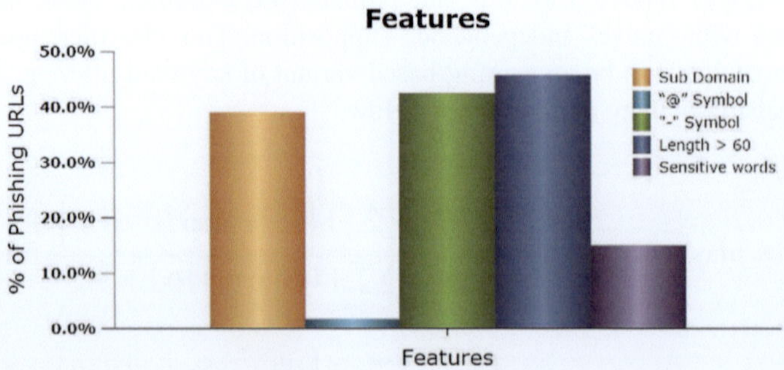

Fig. 2 Features contain by phishing URLs

4 Results and Discussion

In this section, we will discuss the tools and datasets used for implementation and experiments results. The phishing detection using machine learning is classification problem where system learns using various features of phishing and legitimate URLs. After learning the system takes decision automatically based on training. We have recognized various features of phishing and legitimate URLs discussed in the previous section. We have collected 32,951 phishing URLs, taken from PhishTank [9] and 2500 legitimate URLs taken from various sources.

Dataset Used: The dataset for phishing URLs is downloaded from PhishTank. On 20th March 2015, a set of 32,951 phishing URLs were downloaded from PhishTank. The datasets for non-phishing URLs are downloaded from Yahoo Directory by using LinkKlipper from Chrome and DMOZ open directory.

Experiment Results: The feature extraction algorithm is implemented in Java and the features of the URLs are stored in rows of a Sparse Matrix. A set of 15,000 training data (14,000 phishing URLs and 1000 non-phishing URLs) produced an accuracy of 76.04%. A set of 25,000 training URLs (23,000 phishing URLs and 2000 non-phishing URLs) produced an accuracy of 91.28%. Phishing URL detection using Naïve Bayes and SVM classifiers produced the results shown in Table 1. From Table 1, it is found that when the size of the training set increases, SVM performs better than Naïve Bayes classifier to detect phishing URL. Figure 2 shows the features contain by phishing URLs.

5 Conclusion and Future Scope

This paper presented our proposed phishing detection system based on machine learning. We have used 14 different features that distinguish phishing websites from legitimate websites. Our experiment results show more than 90% accuracy in detecting phishing websites using SVM classifier. In future, more features can be added to improve the accuracy of the proposed phishing detection system. Furthermore, other machine learning techniques can be used to increase the efficiency of the proposed system.

References

1. Almomani A, Gupta BB, Atawneh S, Meulenberg A, Almomani E (2013) A survey of phishing email filtering techniques. IEEE Commun Surv Tutor 15(4):2070–2090
2. Anti Phishing Work Group (2014) Phishing attacks trends report. http://docs.apwg.org/reports/apwg_trends_report_q2_2014.pdf
3. Kumaraguru P, Rhee Y, Acquisti A, Cranor LF, Hong J, Nunge E (2007) Protecting people from phishing: the design and evaluation of an embedded training email system. In: CHI 2007: proceedings of the SIGCHI conference on human factors in computing systems, ACM, New York, pp 905–914
4. Sheng S, Magnien B, Kumaraguru P, Acquisti A, Cranor LF, Hong J, Nunge E (2007) Anti-phishing phil: the design and evaluation of a game that teaches people not to fall for phish. In: SOUPS 2007: proceedings of the 3rd symposium on usable privacy and security, ACM, New York, pp 88–99
5. Sheng S, Wardman B, Warner G, Cranor LF, Hong J, Zhang C (2009) An empirical analysis of phishing blacklists. In: CEAS 2009
6. Almomani A, Gupta BB (2013) Phishing dynamic evolving neural fuzzy framework for online detection zero-day phishing E-mail. IJST 6(1):122–126
7. Zhang Y, Hong JI, Cranor LF (2007) Cantina: a content-based approach to detecting phishing web sites. In: Proceedings on WWW, ACM, New York, pp 639–648
8. Chen K-T, Huang C-R, Chen C-S (2010) Fighting phishing with discriminative key point features. IEEE Internet Community
9. Phishing URLs Dataset available at: https://www.phishtank.com

Author Biographies

Ankit kumar Jain is presently working as Assistant Professor in National Institute of Technology, Kurukshetra, India. He received Master of technology from Indian Institute of Information Technology Allahabad (IIIT) India. Currently, he is pursuing PhD in cyber security from National Institute of Technology, Kurukshetra. His general research interest is in the area of Information and Cyber security, Phishing Website Detection, Web security, Mobile Security, Online Social Network and Machine Learning. He has published many papers in reputed journals and conferences.

B. B. Gupta received Ph.D. degree from Indian Institute of Technology Roorkee, India in the area of Information and Cyber Security. He published more than 100 research papers (including 02 books and 14 book chapters) in International Journals and Conferences of high repute including IEEE, Elsevier, ACM, Springer, Wiley, Taylor & Francis, Inderscience, etc. His biography was selected and published in the 30th Edition of Marquis Who's Who in the World, 2012. Dr. Gupta also received Young Faculty research fellowship award from Ministry of Electronics and Information Technology, government of India in 2017. He is serving as associate editor of IEEE Access and Executive editor of IJITCA, Inderscience, respectively. He is also serving as guest editor of various reputed Journals. He was also visiting researcher with Yamaguchi University, Japan in January 2015. At present, Dr. Gupta is working as Assistant Professor in the Department of Computer Engineering, National Institute of Technology Kurukshetra India.

Semantic Security for Sharing Computing Knowledge/Information

Mamta Narwaria and Sangheeta Mishra

Abstract Due to the wide deployment of Internet and information technology for storage and processing of data, the ever-growing privacy concern is the major obstacle for information sharing. In the present digital scenario, the information security is of prime concern. With hundreds of terabytes or even Petabytes of data/ information floating over around, it is important to have the access to the private sensitive data only to authorized users. The explosive increase in the amount of data/information leads to the growth of data mining techniques, a significant resource for information security. The data mining is the extrication of relevant patterns/ knowledge of information from bulk of data. It provides the variety of applicable techniques, in accordance with the different security issues aroused, to achieve a desired level of privacy. This paper provides a wide survey of the emerging issues in the security field and various privacy-preserving techniques PPDM techniques that can be used to mitigate the increasing security risks and threats. It also centers on analyzing the problem of computation on private information developing new concepts and techniques to deal with emerging privacy issues in various contexts security of information while sharing and exchange using Differential Privacy. Finally presents the challenges and techniques for differential privacy as a trusted path to achieve privacy and discuss some of the theoretical and practical challenges for future work in this area.

Keywords Data mining · Privacy-preserving data mining · Information security Differential privacy

M. Narwaria (✉)
School of Computer Science & Engineering, Galgotias University, Greater Noida, India
e-mail: mamta2410@gmail.com

S. Mishra
Department of Computer Applications, BSSS, Bhopal, India
e-mail: sangheeta.mishra@gmail.com

M. U. Bokhari et al. (eds.), *Cyber Security*, Advances in Intelligent Systems and Computing 729, https://doi.org/10.1007/978-981-10-8536-9_45

1 Introduction

Data mining is to extract required data from high dimensional databases. The big databases are introduced by data mining application that are spread over the business applications, which helps in predicting future trends, analyzing the data to implement proactive decisions. The widespread availability of digital data in the age of information, data analysis which goals at efficient and accurate discovery of pattern and securing the private data at the same time, is the crucial task to be performed. Differential privacy is one of the important techniques for releasing statistical data without compromising the individual's privacy. It reveals the queries output from database at maximum accuracy while minimizing the chances of identifying the individual private data.

2 Literature Review and Related Work

Differential privacy has acknowledged much attention over some of the previously used privacy algorithms, especially concentrates on the interactive setup for minimizing the additive noise magnitude and checking the level of feasibility of differentially private technique.

Barak et al. [1] discuss the technique which ensures that the non-negative marginal count value and their sum are consistent for the problem of marginals of a contingency table. Xiao et al. [1–38] and others address privelet, a wavelet transformation-based approach for reducing the noise magnitude in the released data to ensure differential privacy for multidimensional matrix. Hayes et al. [1–15] specify a method one-dimensional dataset-based differentially private histograms. Rastogi et al.*{} design the mechanism for data perturbation which follows differential privacy. Machanavajjhala* et al.*{} proposed the technique for synthetic data generation.* **{LAP 1}**.

The concept of differential privacy is first given by Dwork et al. [22] which is extended to the precise literature with McSherry. Micheal Schroeder coined the term "differential privacy". Dwork and Naor [24] then formulate the impossibility of the semantic security. Composition and group privacy for(€,0)–differentially private method is given by Dwork et al. [22]. Composition for(€,δ) –differential privacy was addressed by Dwork et al. [20] and then by Dwork and Lei [21]. Mironov proposed a mitigation against the vulnerability of the DP to inappropriate implementation of real numbers.

3 Differential Privacy

This is aimed at that there must be no difference in the response to the query containing any particular individual or not. That is any adversary should unable to frame or learn anything about the individual by querying the database. The two ways for collecting and publishing data in the sanitized form are:

- Interactive
- Noninteractive

In the interactive approach, the data miner provides an interface to access the dataset. The data miner queries the database holder using some private mechanism. This is also referred as privacy-preserving distributed data mining (PPDDM).

In case of noninteractive setup, the data collector brings out an anonymized version of data for analysis, which is collected as a result of applying sanitization algorithm like permutation, subsampling and aggregation, identifier removal, etc. In this approach, the horizontally partitioned data from different sources is securely integrated without revealing the sensitive information. This approach gives more flexibility than the former one.

Differential Privacy proposed by Dwork [19] is cryptographically motivated. It ensures that the attacker cannot gain information about any data item in database by simply querying the database. The approach imposes confidentiality by giving perturbed query responses from database and provides a more robust privacy guarantee. It is the framework which enables the analysis of privacy-sensitive datasets and also ensures the privacy of individual-specific information. It is flourishing as an area of research, including domains like computer security and programming languages, statistics, databases, medical informatics, law, social science. One of the research efforts is to reduce the error value that must be added to query and analysis output keeping differential privacy. The other is to extend the valuable existence of data for differentially private analyses.

3.1 €-Differential Privacy

It guarantees that considering probabilistic approach, any individual tuple has a negligible effect on the released statistical response, considering two databases D_A D_B differ in exactly one element. The response R of a given query on both the database is indistinguishable using masking function *M* applied on the outcome of query, satisfying the probability distribution P_R [2, 39]:

$$\frac{P_R[M(D_A) = R]}{P_R[M(D_B) = R]} < = e^{€} \tag{1}$$

where

P_R is the probability of the perturbed query outcome of D_A and D_B,
M is the privacy granting function (Perturbation) on the query response from database D_A and D_B,
R is the Perturbed query response from database D_A and D_B, and
$e^{€}$ is the exponential e epsilon value. € > 0, is public and specified by data owner.

The technique provides a stronger privacy guarantee with the lower value of €. Typically, the differential privacy is achieved by calibrating magnitude of noise to the response of the query according to the sensitivity of the function. Where the sensitivity is the maximum variation in the value due to addition or removal of a single row.

Sensitivity:

$$S(f) = \mathrm{Max}_{\text{where } D_A, D_B} \| f(D_A) - f(D_B) \| \tag{2}$$

For the given function f: $D \rightarrow R^d$ Over an arbitrary domain D.

€-differential privacy can be achieved by the following methods.

3.1.1 Laplace Mechanism

For the given function f: $D \rightarrow R^d$ Over an arbitrary domain D. Satisfies €-differential privacy by adding independently

$$M(X) = f(X) + \mathrm{laplace}(S(f)/€))^{\mathbf{d}} \tag{3}$$

where Laplace function is a random variable sampled from Laplace distribution.

3.1.2 Exponential Mechanism

Let q:($D \times T \rightarrow R$) Over an arbitrary domain D. Chooses an output t with probability proportional to the value exp(eu(D,t)/2Δq) satisfies €-differential privacy.

Mc sherry and Talwar [1–31] proposed the exponential mechanism that takes as input a dataset D and output range T chooses t € T which is close to the optimum value w.r.t utility function q which assigns a real-valued score to every output t. The better utility is achieved by higher score. The exponential mechanism is applied where we chose the "best" response but adding noise directly to the computed quantity which completely destroys its value. While in the Laplace mechanism, we estimated the counts and reported the noisy maximum.

3.2 (€,δ)—*Differential Privacy*

It is the non-strict variation of €-differential privacy technique in which very small probabilistic values δ equivalent privacy breaches are allowed. It can thus implemented in the areas where €-differential privacy found impossible to enforce and provides lower data utility. Dworks et al. [] extend the concept for the temporal input set and recomputation of the outcome of the randomized algorithm based on that temporal input.

4 Key Characteristics of Differential Privacy

Differential privacy provides protection from arbitrary risk. It also neutralizes the linkage attacks automatically by including all the operations or information over temporal dataset. Differential privacy technique has a measure of privacy loss and also permits the analysis and its control incurred by groups. It compares a number of techniques to find which technique provides better accuracy and privacy. The behavioral properties of the differential privacy method under the composition make it more complex than the other. Differential privacy is resistant to the post-processing that is the analyst cannot computes the outcome of the function from the differentially private algorithm and cannot increase the loss of privacy without additional knowledge about the private database.

5 Research Methodology

See Table 1.

Table 1 Comparision of three privacy model in terms of data format and data size

		K-anonymization	De-identification	Differential privacy
Data format	Structured	Y	N	Y
	Semi-structured	N	Y	N
	Un-structured	N	Y	N
Data size required	Single record	N	Y	N
	Dataset	Y	Y	Y
	Double dataset	N	N	Y

6 Conclusions

The study identifies the up-growing and promising areas of research where data mining can be applied to accomplish protection of the information. The survey literature also discusses the hottest trends and direction of research and relevance of data mining in the safekeeping of information to improve the effectiveness of privacy preserving/anonymization of data. The main aim of this study is to incorporate the recent DM techniques to remove the curbing in the privacy preservation methodology. The adoption of data mining to secure the information which is the vital resource is helpful to improve the performance in privacy preservation.

References

1. Barak B, Chaudhuri K, Dwork C, Kale S, McSherry F, Talwar K (2007) Privacy, accuracy and consistency too: a holistic solution to contingency table release. In: PODS
2. Friedman A, Schuster A (2010) Data mining with differential privacy. In: KDD, pp 493–502
3. Beimel A, Kasiviswanathan SP, Nissim K (2010) Bounds on the sample complexity for private learning and private data release. In: Theory of cryptography, Springer, Berlin, pp 437–454.
4. Bhaskara A, Dadush D, Krishnaswamy R, Talwar K (2012) Unconditional differentially private mechanisms for linear queries. In: Karloff HJ, Pitassi T (eds) Proceedings of the symposium on theory of computing conference, symposium on theory of computing, NewYork, USA, 19–22 May 2012, pp 1269–1284
5. Blum A, Dwork C, McSherry F, Nissim K (2005) Practical privacy: the SuLQ framework. In: Li C (ed) Principles of database systems, ACM, pp 128–138
6. Blum A, Dwork C, McSherry F, Nissim K (2005) Practical privacy: the sulq framework. In: Principles of database systems
7. Blum A, Ligett K, Roth A (2008) A learning theory approach to non-interactive database privacy. In: Dwork C (ed) Symposium on theory of computing, Association for Computing Machinery, pp 609–618
8. Blum A, Monsour Y (2007) Learning, regret minimization, and equilibria
9. Casti JL (1996) Five golden rules: great theories of 20th-century mathematics and why they matter. Wiley, NY
10. Hubert Chan TH, Shi E, Song D (2010) Private and continual release of statistics. In: Automata, languages and programming, Springer, Berlin, pp 405–417
11. Chaudhuri K, Hsu D (2011) Sample complexity bounds for differentially private learning. In: Proceedings of the annual conference on learning theory (COLT2011)
12. Chaudhuri K, Monteleoni C, Sarwate AD (2011) Differentially private empirical risk minimization. J Mach Learn Res JMLR 12:1069
13. Chaudhuri K, Sarwate A, Sinha K (2012) Near-optimal differentially private principal components. Adv Neural Inf Process Syst 25:998–1006
14. Chen Y, Chong S, Kash IA, Moran T, Vadhan SP (2013) Truthful mechanisms for agents that value privacy. In: Association for computing machinery conference on electronic commerce
15. Dandekar P, Fawaz N, Ioannidis S (2012) Privacy auctions for recommender systems. In: Internet and network economics, Springer, Berlin, pp 309–322
16. De A (2012) Lowerbounds in differential privacy. In: Theory of cryptography conference, pp 321–338

17. Dinur I, Nissim K (2003) Revealing information while preserving privacy. In: Proceedings of the association for computing machinery SIGACTSIGMOD-SIGART symposium on principles of database systems, pp 202–210
18. Duchi JC, Jordan MI, Wainwright MJ (2013) Local privacy and statistical minimax rates. arXiv preprint arXiv:1302.3203
19. Dwork C (2006) Differential privacy. In: Proceedings of the international colloquium on automata, languages and programming (ICALP), vol 2, pp 1–12
20. Dwork C, Kenthapadi K, McSherry F, Mironov I, Naor M (2006) Our data, ourselves: privacy via distributed noise generation. In: EUROCRYPT, pp 486–503
21. Dwork C, Lei J (2009) Differential privacy and robust statistics. In: Proceedings of the 2009 international association for computing machinery symposium on theory of computing (STOC)
22. Dwork C, McSherry F, Nissim K, Smith A (2006) Calibrating noise to sensitivity in private data analysis. In: Theory of cryptography conference'06, pp 265–284
23. Dwork C, McSherry F, Talwar K (2007) The price of privacy and the limits of lp decoding. In: Proceedings of the association for computing machinery symposium on theory of computing, pp 85–94
24. Dwork C, Naor M (2010) On the difficulties of disclosure prevention in statistical databases or the case for differential privacy. J Priv Confid 2(1):93–107
25. Dwork C, Naor M, Pitassi T, Rothblum GN (2010) Differential privacy under continual observation. In: Proceedings of the association for computing machinery symposium on theory of computing, Association for Computing Machinery, pp 715–724
26. Dwork C, Naor M, Pitassi T, Rothblum GN, Yekhanin S (2010) Pan-private streaming algorithms. In: Proceedings of international conference on super computing
27. Dwork C, Naor M, Reingold O, Rothblum GN, Vadhan SP (2009) On the complexity of differentially private data release: efficient algorithms and hardness results. In Symposium on theory of computing '09, pp 381–390
28. Dwork C, Naor M, Vadhan S (2012) The privacy of the analyst and the power of the state. In: Foundations of computer science
29. Dwork C, Nikolov A, Talwar K (2014) Efficient algorithms for privately releasing marginals via convex relaxations. In: Proceedings of the annual symposium on computational geometry (SoCG)
30. Dwork C, Nissim K (2004) Privacy-preserving datamining on vertically partitioned databases. In: Proceedings of cryptology 2004, vol 3152, pp 528–544
31. Dwork C, Rothblum GN, Vadhan SP (2010) Boostingand differential privacy. In: Foundations of computer science, pp 51–60
32. Dwork C, Talwar K, Thakurta A, Zhang L (2014) Analyze gauss: optimal bounds for privacy-preserving pca. In: Symposium on theory of computing
33. Fleischer L, Lyu Y-H (2012) Approximately optimal auctions for selling privacy when costs are correlated with data. In: Association for computing machinery conference on electronic commerce, pp 568–585
34. Ghosh A, Ligett K (2013) Privacy and coordination: computing on databases with endogenous participation. In: Proceedings of the fourteenth ACM conference on electronic commerce (EC), pp 543–560
35. Ghosh A, Roth A (2011) Selling privacy at auction. In: Association for computing machinery conference on electronic commerce, pp 199–208
36. Groce A, Katz J, Yerukhimovich A (2011) Limits of computational differential privacy in the client/server setting. In: Proceedings of the theory of cryptography conference
37. Gupta A, Hardt M, Roth A, Ullman J (2011) Privately releasing conjunctions and the statistical query barrier. In: Symposium on theory of computing'11, pp 803–812
38. Gupta A, Roth A, Ullman J (2012) Iterative constructions and private data release. In: Theory of cryptography conference, pp 339–356
39. Dwork C, Roth A (2014) the algorithmic foundations of differential privacy. Found Trends Theor Comput Sci 9(3–4):211–407

Paradigmatic Approach to Cloud Security: Challenges and Remedies

Rana Majumdar, Hina Gupta, Sakshi Goel and Abhishek Srivastava

Abstract Cloud computing is an amalgamation of resources over the Internet which dynamically allocates capacity and resources without setting up a new physical environment. Enterprises understand the convincing monetary and operational profits provided by cloud computing. Virtualization and usage of pooled IT resources in the cloud environment, provided to the organizations, makes them realize noteworthy cost savings and speeds up deployment of new applications. On the contrary, the valuable benefits of business cannot ajar without comprehending the challenges of data security. This work emphasis on the practices that can be incorporated into the cloud environment to provide enhanced security. It highlights a set of control-based technologies and protocols to provide regulatory consent and protect information, infrastructure, and data applications associated with the use of cloud. This work proposes a design which can be used to control the data, authenticity, and security at all the levels to solve the problem of security in cloud computing environment.

Keywords ENISA · CSA · DES · RCA · SAAS · PAAS

R. Majumdar (✉) · H. Gupta · S. Goel · A. Srivastava
Amity School of Engineering & Technology, Amity University, Noida, India
e-mail: rmajumdar@amity.edu

H. Gupta
e-mail: guptahina189@gmail.com

S. Goel
e-mail: goel.sakshi.aries@gmail.com

A. Srivastava
e-mail: asrivastava8@amity.edu

M. U. Bokhari et al. (eds.), *Cyber Security*, Advances in Intelligent Systems and Computing 729, https://doi.org/10.1007/978-981-10-8536-9_46

1 Introduction

The word cloud computing was once a catchphrase around the globe, but now it has become a mainstream. Cloud offers a platform to the user to use the application, save the data, and access it when needed. It can be defined as the separation of the applications from the system. Although the cloud provides a lot of benefits such as ease of usability, flexibility, and accessibility but the major challenges associated with cloud is the issue of security. Security is a prime obligation for cloud to work as a strong and viable solution [1]. A similar thought has been also shared by researchers' corporate people [2], government organization [3, 4] and academics [5]. Virtualization helps cloud providers to take off the control from the client and manage their data. The user although has a security from other user's but the data is completely under the control of the service provider whose authenticity cannot be verified by the cloud users. This poses a great threat to the data which is of utmost importance. This issue has impacted the model's creditability and popularity. The cloud providers have to deal with security that requires a lot of expenses and resources. The cloud security can be attained by implementing the three main aspects namely:

- *Strong protection to data,*
- *Complete control over the data, and*
- *Investment control.*

If the trio is achieved by any means, then the threat to the security in cloud can be surpassed. The efforts of identifying the risks and vulnerabilities have been done by ENISA (European Network and Information Security Agency) [3] and the Cloud Security Alliance (CSA) [4]. The documents of the two organizations present a surfeit of security issues, recommended solutions dealing with privacy of data to infrastructural arrangement.

2 Review of Literature

In literature review, authors showed concerns about various cloud-related security issues, on the basis of cloud's architecture, service delivery, cloud characteristic, and the role of cloud stakeholder. Mohamed et al. [6] analyzed the different techniques of cryptography that were used earlier to secure data in the cloud. Their study showed that the AES algorithm was the fastest and secure algorithm used for securing cloud data amongst other algorithms like DES, 3DES, two-fish, blowfish, RC-4, and RC-6.

Mohamed et al. [7] emphasized on the security vulnerabilities and threats that are open and most significant issues in cloud computing. The author has illustrated the relationship between the vulnerabilities and threats. They have also presented the methods to deal with the vulnerabilities and threats related to cloud computing. The various countermeasures discussed in the paper are of utmost importance.

Mahalle and Shahade [8] have highlighted that using a combination of two algorithms AES and RSA, two different files can be shared securely from data transmission point of view.

Ficco et al. [9] in their work highlighted the effect of intrusion detection attack on cloud environment and also explained the method for its prevention. The paper focused on dynamic structure of the cloud. The model proposed here uses collaborative intrusion detection and prevention technique which basically works on distributed cloud where the attacks are detected externally as well as internally.

It is quite evident that previous researches only focused on individual aspects of cloud computing environment form security point but none of them used collaborative approach which is essential and works for infrastructure layer of cloud (IaaS). In this paper, authors reveal the importance of collaboration rather than tackling individual security issues at a time.

3 Problem Conceptualization

In cloud environment, as cloud provides services based on users requirements, so it is quite obvious that users have no control over their data. In this computing environment, private data is completely under the control of the service provider whose authenticity cannot be verified by the cloud users. This poses a great threat to the user's data which is of utmost importance. This issue has impacted the model's creditability and popularity. The cloud providers have to deal with security that requires a proper trusted strategy and pool of resources. This paper emphasized on the following features for attainment of cloud security, they are namely

- *Robust data security,*
- *Thorough control over the data, and*
- *Proper control mechanism.*

3.1 Methodology

As a result of the increasing interest in cloud computing, there is an enhanced effort to evaluate the prevailing trends and technology dealing with the problem and providing solutions [10]. In the above section, authors recommended cloud security implementation mechanism by implementation of policies for a complete security solution. The solution for providing security in cloud computing environment should deal with aspects mentioned in Table 1.

Table 1 Security aspects

1	Security of network	Agreement and legal issues
2	Interface	
3	Security of data	
4	Virtualization	
5	Control	

3.1.1 Cloud Security

Researchers showed various mechanism and techniques to handle security issues in cloud environment but unfortunately, they are not sufficient because of their individual efforts and lack of collaborative and central policies. So definitely, security solution is not proposed by their work as discussed in the previous section. This work categorizes the solution for providing security by identifying factors using historical data and case studies from various aspects; they are summarized as follows:

- *Security of network,*
- *Interface,*
- *Security of data,*
- *Virtualization,*
- *Control, and*
- *Agreement and legal issues.*

While identifying factors, the following questioners were prepared to combat cloud-related concerns:

1. *Is the data secured on cloud?*
2. *Is the confidentiality of data maintained?*
3. *Are the security measures in compliance with government organizations?*
4. *What will happen if the attacker brings down the application hosted on cloud?*

The information security is based on CAI triad as shown in Fig. 1.

Fig. 1 Information security

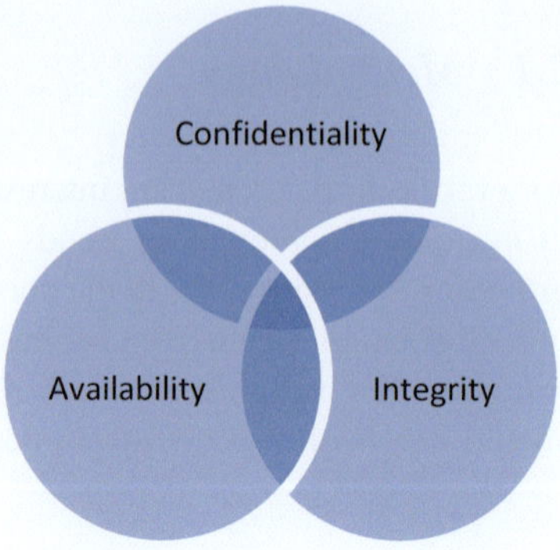

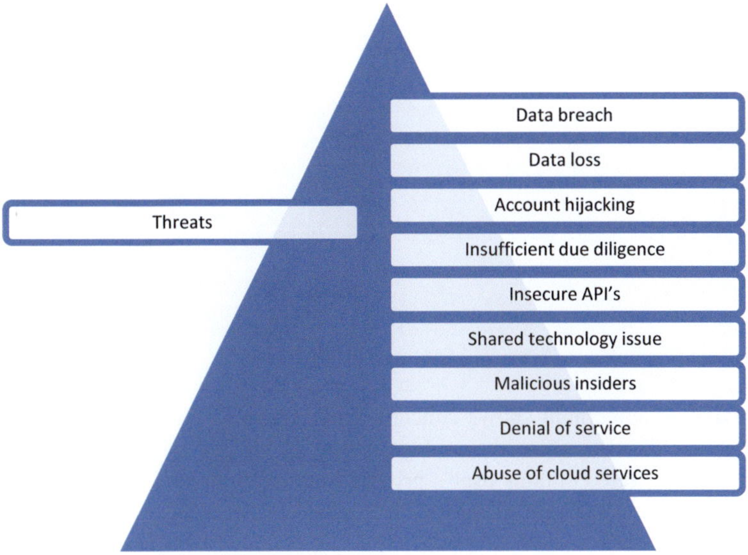

Fig. 2 Threats associated with cloud

The cloud security thus focuses on multi-tenancy, velocity of attack, information assurance, data privacy, and ownership. The various threats related to the cloud are (Fig. 2).

The security measures should deal with the following three features: privacy, agreement, and architecture.

4 Proposed Work

For achieving greater security the following observations helps to achieve that to a great extent. The security should be managed from outside to inside. Here authors investigate security issues from both service providers and users point of view and suggested a concentric circular approach as a security factor (Fig. 3).

Figure 3 states that the security of data on cloud depends on the features provided by the cloud provider. At the first level, the architecture of cloud should be considered that encompasses security of the network, virtualization, and interfaces. The second aspect to be considered is related to the agreement between the cloud user and cloud service provider. It encompasses the services provided to the user and services to be provided by the provider. The third level to be considered is related to privacy of data. This is considered to be the most crucial layer from user's

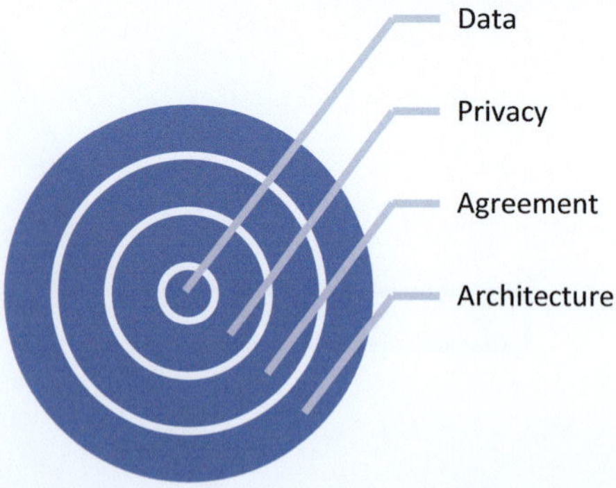

Fig. 3 Concentric circular approach

perspective as agreement shows concern about agreed policies and regulations. It encompasses the data security and legal issues associated with the same. Finally, the innermost circle contains user's private, confidential data.

4.1 Architecture

The outermost circle named architecture should deal with security of network, interfaces used, and virtualization. So the basic responsibility of this layer is to group security, interface, and virtualization. The major issue concerning network communication is the infrastructure of cloud. The solution provided should extend customer's present network structure [11]. It should utilize the existing local security measures of the customer and enhance them to the network of cloud [12]. Following considerations should be made regarding architecture

- *Security of data in transit*: The channel used for transmitting the data should be protected against spoofing, man-in-middle attack, sniffing, etc.
- *Use of Firewall*: As the firewalls are used at a small scale to provide security, it should be extended to prevent denial of service attacks, and detect peripheral security evaluation procedure.
- *Security agreement*: The protocols and technologies used at various levels in cloud should be configured properly without hampering the privacy of data and performance.

The proposed solution should also deal with issues related to the customer interface, service provider interface, and the cloud interface.

4.2 Agreement

It deals with the norms and the requirements to provide service and availability of data. It also deals with the kind of services provided and audit to be done by customer, third party, and service providers regarding the cloud.

4.3 Privacy

It deals with security of data and the legal issues associated with it. The security of data is provided by the technique of cryptography is used to encrypt the data [13]. A check should also be kept on data redundancy to ensure integrity and availability of data. Legal issues include the location at which the data of the user reside, the management of how the hardware is shared, and the privileges that are provided to the user. The following diagram illustrates the proposed remedies in detail with stepwise explanation.

Step 1:
Complete data about the client should be collected and what data he is willing to store on cloud.

Step 2: Architecture

1. The data should be collected regarding which deployment or delivery model he is willing to use.
2. On which server is the client hosting the application (on his own private server or a third party server).
3. A check should be made by cloud provider for the server on which the data needs to be stored.
4. Good authorization technique must be used.
5. A boundary for each user's data should be designed and checked against intrusion of data by unauthorized user.
6. The firewall should be checked to prevent DoS attack and evaluate peripheral security

Step 3: Agreement

Safe and good techniques must be used for identity management.
Some security measures should be designed for virtualization manager.
An audit should be done by service provider, customer, and third party.

Step 4: Privacy

Data should be encrypted while being stored.
Data that is flowing over the network should also be encrypted using network traffic encryption technique such as secure socket layer and transport layer security.
When the data is being stored, it should be replicated for backup.
A proper strategy should be planned for business continuity and disaster recovery.
Data transactions should be safe and data integrity should be maintained.
Routing of data should be monitored.

5 Comparison of the Proposed Approach to the Existing Approach

The framework that has been proposed in our work provides a trade-off to the existing approaches. The proposed work consists of the layered structure or shell structure. The security check is levied on all the layers which apprehend the security of the cloud architecture. Since the check is done layer after layer and no direct access to the innermost layer, the vulnerability associated with the cloud security is reduced to a great extent. The main objective of the security mechanism is to provide ample measures to protect the stored data, data in transit, modified encryption techniques are all enforced in our work. All the new features that have been incorporated and realized in this work make it more secured measure as compared to the existing approaches. As data is the king, so handling sensitive or business-critical facts outside the organization will certainly lead risk because any subcontracted service evades an organization's in-house security panels easily. This work investigates security in terms of risk and with cloud; one possible approach will be to have a compatible control with preestablished dedicated service with service providers. Organizations should try to learn about provider's position for greater control so that, it may not know exactly where its data resides or have any ability to influence changes to the location of data. Most providers store data in a shared environment, introduces security risk. No one security method will solve all these data protection problems so it is important to consider multiple layers of defense.

When adopting cloud services, among other critical factors we work on the basics of where my data is, and how to handle new security threats?

Nowadays, security is no longer a source of worry. It has simply become another reflection of hazard controlling policies and procedures.

6 Conclusion

Security is an essential facet for providing a trustworthy infrastructure where a user or a business process can move its data to cloud and use it as and when required. The diagrammatic representation provided in this work has a holistic security flow which needs to be followed by the organizations. This work illustrates a framework through concentric circles and demonstrated the concept through pictorial representation using tabular form. In future, authors will definitely provide mathematical illustration through case studies.

References

1. IDC (2009) An IDC. Update.slideshare.net/JorFigOr/cloud-computing-2010-an-idc-update
2. HP's (2009) Hurd dings cloud computing, IBM, CNET news
3. Catteddu D, Hogben G (2009) Technical report. European network and information security agency, benefits, risks and recommendations for information security, Enisa
4. Security Guidance for Critical Areas of Focus in Cloud Computing (2009) Technical report, Cloud Security Alliance
5. Rimal BP, Choi E, Lumb I (2009) A taxonomy and, survey of cloud computing systems. In: Fifth international joint conference on INC, IMS and IDC, NCM
6. Mohamed EM, Abdelkader HS, EI-Etriby S (2012) Enhanced data security model for cloud computing. In: 8th international conference on INFOrmatics and Systems (INFOS2012)
7. Mohamed EM, Abdelkader HS, EI-Etriby S (2011) A quantitative analysis of current security concerns and solutions for cloud computing
8. Mahalle VS, Shahade AK (2014) Power, automation and communication (INPAC): enhancing the data security in cloud by implementing hybrid encryption algorithm (Rsa&Aes). In: 2014 international conference on encryption algorithm
9. Ficco M, Tasquier L, Aversa R (2013) Security issues in cloud computing. In: Eighth international conference on P2P, parallel, grid, cloud and internet
10. Ibrahim AS, Hamlyn-Harris J, Grundy J (2010) Emerging security challenges of cloud virtual infrastructure. In: Proceedings of APSEC 2010, cloud workshop, Sydney, Australia
11. Tompkins D (2009) Security for cloud-based enterprise applications
12. Jensen M, Schwenk J, Gruschka N, Iacono LL (2009) Technical security issues in cloud computing. In: IEEE international conference on cloud computing
13. Muttik I, Barton C (2009) Cloud security technologies. Elsevier, Amsterdam

Author Biography

Rana Majumdar completed his M.Tech in 2009 in CSE from Amity University. He has been working as Assistant Professor in the Department of Information Technology, ASET, Amity University Noida from 2009 till date.

The Digital Signature Schemes Based on Two Hard Problems: Factorization and Discrete Logarithm

A. B. Nimbalkar

Abstract This paper gives the survey of digital signatures, which are based on two hard problems: (1) factorization (FAC) and (2) discrete logarithms (DL). In 1994, L. Harn developed digital signature which is based on this two hard problems. Z. Shao showed the drawback of L. Harn's scheme and proposed his new scheme. There are various schemes which are based on these two hard problems, because attacker cannot solve both the problems simultaneously.

Keywords Factorization · Discrete logarithm · Cryptography · Digital signature

1 Introduction

Cryptography is used to implement confidentiality, data integrity, authentication of entity and data origin. Information exchange over a network is said to consist mainly of two technical processes, namely, encryption and decryption of the message. The encryption is used to encode the message which is essentially conversion of plain text into cipher text and the decryption is the reverse process of encryption.

There are techniques based on symmetric key cryptosystems such as DES, AES, and Blowfish. In the symmetric key cryptosystem, same key is used for both encryption and decryption. There was some problem with symmetric key like secret key transportation. A secret key cannot be transmitted over the insecure channel. This problem is solved by public key cryptosystem, i.e., asymmetric cryptosystem. It uses two different keys; the key used for encryption is kept public the so-called public key. The key used for decryption is kept secret and called as private key. In 1976, Diffie and Hellman [1] invented the first public key cryptography scheme. The practical implementation of this scheme was done by Rivest, Shamir, and Adleman (RSA) in 1978 [2]. Based on the Diffie–Hellman method of computing

A. B. Nimbalkar (✉)
A.M. College, Pune, Maharashtra, India
e-mail: nimbalkar_ab@yahoo.com

M. U. Bokhari et al. (eds.), *Cyber Security*, Advances in Intelligent Systems and Computing 729, https://doi.org/10.1007/978-981-10-8536-9_47

DL, ElGamal [3] invented new signature in 1985, which is used for message confidentiality and digital signature schemes In 1985 elliptic curve cryptography was invented which uses points of elliptic curve as group.

As asymmetric cryptosystem solve the repudiation problem, it is used to design the digital signature schemes. A digital signature is a mathematical scheme for validating the authenticity of a digital document. The digital signature has three main phases. First phase is key generation. It includes the choice of two large prime numbers and generates two keys, public and private keys. The second phase is digital signature generation in which the message, keys, and modular arithmetic are used to form the signature. The third is signature verification phase, where the message is checked against the original message using the verification equation, if equation satisfies then verifier believes that message is indeed an authenticated message, else message is considered to be altered.

The digital signatures were developed using both the hard problems. In 1994, Harn [4] designed new digital signature scheme based on FAC and DL. After this, there were various schemes based on both the hard problems. Extensive research has been done to show that without knowing private key, attacker can forge the signature.

2 Review of Digital Signatures

2.1 *L. Harn*

There are several public key cryptosystems which are based on single cryptographic assumption, such as factoring or discrete logarithms. In May 1994, Harn [4] designed new scheme which is based on two hard problems, namely, FAC and DL. To break this scheme attacker requires to solve Diffie–Hellman problem in a subgroup of $\mathbb{Z}_p^*$ as well as factoring a specific integer into product of two primes, both of these problems are difficult. His scheme is based on two different cryptographic assumptions for increasing the security and also maintaining the efficiency of development. L. Harn maintains the computational time of the signature implementation that is maximum of RSA and ElGamal scheme.

2.2 *He and Kiesler*

The schemes which are based on single hard problem are not secure. It is known that ElGamal scheme is less secure than RSA because computation of DL is easier than the factorization. RSA schemes are efficient because it has message expansion is one while in ElGamal message expansion is two. In July 1994, He and Kiesler [5] designed two new signature schemes which are based on both the hard problems that enhance the security. The message expansion in first version signature is two but in second it is three.

2.3 N. Y. Lee and Hwang

In 1996 Lee and Hwang [6] showed that there is probability that the attacker can forge the signatures of L. Harn schemes if he can solve DL modulo large prime number. They showed that even if use of hash function there is possibility of attack.

The attack can be avoided if the condition that s' is not allowed to equal to $p'q'$. They proposed a modified L. Harn scheme which is based on both the hard problems.

2.4 Z. Shao

Shao [7] designed two digital signature schemes in 1998. The security of these signatures was equal to ElGamal and L. Harn signature schemes. There were some drawbacks of ElGamal Scheme that are the size of public key is large, more modulation was used, and every user uses his own public modulus. The substitution attacks work on L. Harn signature scheme if one does not use one-way hash function. On L. Harn scheme homomorphism attack gives private key x although forging signature is not possible. If one wants to forge the signature then it is necessary that one should able to find the cubic root modulo $p - 1$.

The Z. Shao scheme resists substitution and homomorphism attack. The efficiency of Shao scheme is same as ElGamal and L. Harn scheme. In Z. Shao's scheme, only thing is that message expansion is three.

2.5 N. Y. Lee

The public key cryptographic algorithms are secure because there is no good algorithm to solve the FAC and DL. Lee [8] in 1999 showed that the signatures proposed by Z. Shao are not secure as he claimed. The security of Shao's schemes depends on only FAC and not DL. N. Y. Lee not proposed any scheme.

2.6 Z. Shao

Shao [9] in 2002 showed that there is forgery attack against Wei-Hua He's signature scheme. If the attackers solve DL they can easily forge signature without knowing private key of signer and this does not depend upon hardness of both FAC and DL as claimed by Wei-Hua He. The task of designing new scheme based on two hard problems was an open problem.

2.7 Shimin Wei

Wei [10] in 2004 tried to attack He–Kiesler's scheme and showed that He–Kiesler scheme does not resist his message attack. Based on this attack he designed new scheme which resists such an attack and security based on two hard problems FAC and DL. In 2007, Wei [11] improved Shao's schemes [7] using quadratic residues theory and proposed two new schemes based on two hard problems. Wei claimed that his signatures resist Li_Xiao attack. The problem-solving quadratic equation is equally hard as solving the FAC.

2.8 J. Zheng, Zuhua Shao, S. Huang, T. Yu

Zheng et al. [12] in 2008 showed that attacker can forge the Shimin Wei signature schemes (2007). They showed that in Wei's scheme, the universal forgery attack can be possible and the two different messages (m) have same signature. Using Wei's scheme if we obtain the signature of one message then it is easy to obtain signature of second message. This drawback can be remove by demanding $0 < m < p/2$. They showed that universal forge attack can be done in less computation than that of legal signer does. Also they showed that one can forge signature scheme for arbitrary message without knowing private keys. Hence the security of Shimin Wei scheme is fails.

2.9 Ismail, Thate, Ahmad

Ismail et al. [13] designed a new scheme in 2008, which provides better security by using hash function. The main aim of designing the scheme was to increase the security using FAC and DL. They showed five different attacks that were resisting their signature. But time complexity in verification phase of signature was increased.

2.10 Swati Verma, Birendera Kumar Sharma

In the year 2012, Swati Verma modified the Wei [10] scheme. The security of their scheme depends primarily on two things: Use of one-way hash functions and the intractability of solution to both DL and FAC simultaneously. They claimed that this is more secure than earlier Wei [10] scheme.

3 Table of Comparison of Digital Signature Based on FAC and DL

Scheme	Signature	Secret key	Public key	Signing equation	Verification
Elgamal [3]	$\{m(r, s)\}$	x is $< p$	$y = \prec^x \bmod p$	$m = xr + ks \bmod (p - 1)$	$\prec^m \equiv y^r r^s \bmod p$
Harn Scheme [4]	$\{m(k, r, s)\}$	x is $1 \le x \le p - 1$	$y = \prec^x \bmod p$	$m^1 - ks^1 + X_1 r \bmod p_A - 1$	$\prec_A^{m^1} = r^{s^1} {y_A}^T \bmod p_A$
He and Kiesleirs [5]	$\{m(r, s, c)\}$	x_1 is $1 \le x_1 \le n$ $x = {x_1}^2 \bmod (p - 1)$	$y = g^{x^2} \bmod p$	$m = xr + ts \pmod{p - 1}$	$g^{m^2} = y^{r^2} \cdot r^{s^2} \cdot g^{2rx^2} \bmod p$
Shao Scheme [7]	$\{m(k, r, s)\}$	$x = 1 < x < (p_1 q_1/2)$	$y = g^{x^2 + x^{-2}} \bmod p$	$x^{-1}s + xr = mt^{-1} + kt (\bmod p_1 \cdot q_1)$	$y^{(s^2 + x^2)} = r^{m^2 + k^2} \cdot g^{4(mk - sx)} \bmod p$
Shao [9]	$\{m(r_1, r_2, s)\}$	$R = p_1 q_1$ x is god $((x + x^{-1})^2, R) = 1$	$y = g^{(x + x^{-1})^2} \bmod p$	$(x + x^{-1}) = s(t + t^{-1}) + f(r_1, r_2, m)\,(t + t^{-1})^{-1} \bmod R$	$y \equiv r_1^{s^2} \cdot r_2^{f^2(r_1 r_2, m)}$ $g^{2sf}(r_1, r_2, m) \bmod p$
Wei's Scheme [11]	$\{m(r_1, r_2, s)\}$	x is $1 < x < n$	$y = g^{x^2} \bmod p$	$mt^{-1} = xr_1 + ts^2 \pmod{(p - 1)}$	$r_1^{s^4} \cdot r_2^{m^2} = y^{r^2} \cdot g^{2ms^2}$
Ismail et al. [13]	$\{m(k, R, s)\}$	x is $0 < x < n$	$y = g^x \bmod p$	$s = \left(xh(m) + Rh(m)^4 + kh(m)^r\right)^d \pmod p$	$g^{s^c} \equiv y^{h(m)} K^R R^k \pmod p$
Swati Verma [10]	$\{m(r_1, r_2, s)\}$	x is $1 < x < n$	$y = g^{x^2} \bmod p$	$h(r_1, r_2, m)T^{-1} = xr_1 + Ts^2 (\bmod p - 1)$	$r_1^{s^4} \cdot r_2^{h(r_1 \cdot r_2 \cdot m)^2} = y^{r_1^2} \cdot g^{2h(r_1 \cdot r_2 \cdot m)s^2}$

4 Conclusion

The digital signatures based on single hard problem either Factorization or Discrete Logarithm may not secure in future because computation can be possible. L. Harn and He-Keisler gives the idea that if we combine these two problem then security become more. Then there are many signature based on this two hard problem. Some of signature can be forge without solving the hard problem. We make the comparative analysis of all digital signature schemes which are based on two hard problems like Factorization and Discrete Logarithm. As security increases the Time complexity also increases. The RSA signature has message expansion 1. ElGamal has message expansion 2 and L. Harn has message expansion 3, as he uses both hard problems for enhancing the security.

References

1. Diffie W, Hellman ME (1976) New directions in cryptography. IEEE Trans Inf Theory 22:644–654
2. Rivest RL, Shamir A, Adleman L (1978) A method for obtaining digital signatures and public key cryptosystems. Commun ACM 21:120–126
3. ElGamal T (1985) A public key cryptosystem and a signature scheme based on discrete logarithms. IEEE Trans Inf Theory IT-31(4):469–472
4. Harn L (1994) Public-key cryptosystem design based on factoring and discrete logarithms. IEE Proc Comput Digital Techn 141:193–195
5. He J, Kiesler T (1994) Enhancing the security of ElGamal's signature schemes. IEE Proc Comput Digital Technol 141:249–252
6. Lee NY, Hwang T (1996) Modified Harn signature scheme based on factoring and discrete logarithms. IEE Proc Comput Digital Tech 143:196–198
7. Shao Scheme Z (1998) Signature scheme based on factoring and discrete logarithms. IEE Proc Comput Digital Tech 145(1)
8. Lee NY (1999) Security of Shao's signature schemes based on factoring and discrete logarithms. IEE Proc Control Theory Appl 146(2)
9. Shao Scheme Z (2002) Digital signature scheme based on factoring and discrete logarithms. Electr Lett 38(24), 21 Nov 2002 (Online No: 20021093)
10. Wei S (2004) A new digital signature scheme based on factoring and discrete logarithms. Progr Crypt Int J Ser Eng Comput Sci 769:107–111
11. Wei S (2007) Digital signature scheme based on two hard problems. Int J Comput Sci Netw Secur 7(12)
12. Zheng J, Shao Z, Huang S, Yu T (2008) Security of two signature schemes based on two hard problems. In: Proceedings of the 11th IEEE international conference on communication technology, pp 745–748
13. Ismail ES, Thate NMF, Ahmad RR (2008) A new digital signature scheme based on integer factorization and discrete logarithm. J Math Stat 4(4):222–225. ISSN 1549-3644

Gaussian Tendencies in Data Flow in Communication Links

Rudra Pratap Ojha, Dharm Raj, Pramod kumar Srivastava and Goutam Sanyal

Abstract We have modeled data flow in communication link using random motion of a particle, which results in a Gaussian pattern of traffic flow over a period of time. The varying degrees of spectral deviation present a coherent model of data flow for wired links. We have considered multiple link systems and presented an n-dimensional representation of traffic model using a Gaussian function governed by n-parameters. The model opens new insights toward analyzing and predicting bandwidth requirements in communication links and their prospective failure.

Keywords Random walk · Gaussian distribution · Failure analysis
Reliability analysis

1 Introduction

Data flow model in communication link is of fundamental importance in understanding the bandwidth requirement and failure analysis. Existing models use Poisson distribution to model traffic flow. Poisson distribution fails to make accurate prediction about traffic flow density as it assumes a uniform probability of occurrence of data bits within a given period of time. Poisson modeling fails to properly capture the characteristics of traffic flow [1, 2]. Some packets are skipped in case of Poisson random variable [3]. Another aspect of Poisson distribution is

R. P. Ojha (✉) · D. Raj · P. K. Srivastava
Galgotias College of Engineering & Technology, Greater Noida, India
e-mail: rpojha@gmail.com

D. Raj
e-mail: dharmraj4u@gmail.com

P. K. Srivastava
e-mail: pramod_pooja59@rediffmail.com

R. P. Ojha · G. Sanyal
National Institute of Technology, Durgapur, India
e-mail: nitgsanyal@gmail.com

M. U. Bokhari et al. (eds.), *Cyber Security*, Advances in Intelligent Systems and Computing 729, https://doi.org/10.1007/978-981-10-8536-9_48

that it takes into account variation of traffic density with time. Gaussian distribution can take into account spatial variation in traffic density across various locations along a network.

Several economic and technological decisions are driven by model of data flow. Sometimes, the data flow shows an exponential increase over a period of time leading to extensive development and increase in channels. A drop in the requirement has negative consequences on communication industry particularly when the related investment has been made. This happened in the context of telecom crisis of 2002 when it was assumed that the exponential rise in traffic flow would continue for several years [4]. A correct data flow model might have averted the crisis.

2 Random Walk and Data Flow

Random processes show random motion. Data flow between communication links is random which implies that we can model it in terms of random motion. We consider two data nodes *A* and *B* connected by a wire with a sensor *S*. The sensor *S* generates a value 1 when data is transferred between *A* and *B* and 0 if there is no

Fig. 1 Random walks Gaussian distribution

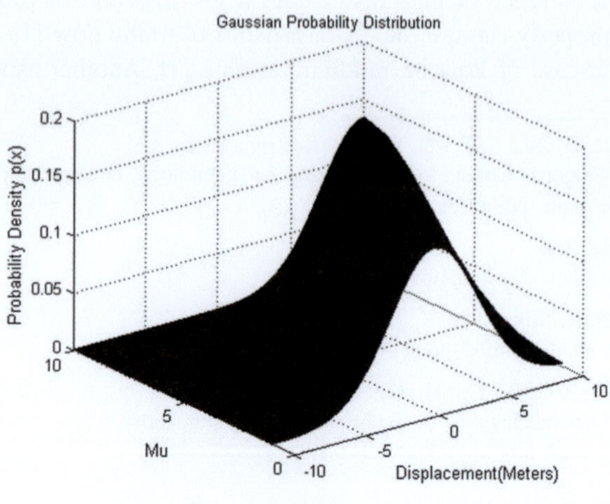

Fig. 2 Gaussian distribution profile in three dimensions

data flow every second. We consider the density of 1 s and 0 s between A and B. On carrying out a brief computational simulation of the process, we get a Brownian motion as shown in Fig. 1, which shows a Gaussian distribution.

3 Gaussian Model of Data Flow

Random walk within a set of fixed constraints shows Gaussian distribution which is given by the following equation [5]:

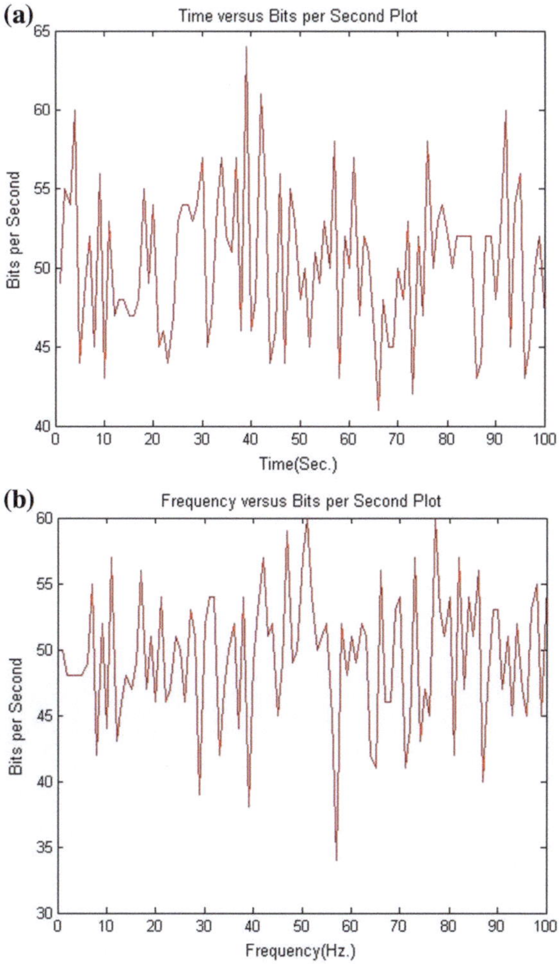

Fig. 3 **a** Gaussian density profile of random bits with time; **b** Gaussian density profile of random bits with frequency

$$p(x) = \frac{1}{\sigma\sqrt{2\pi}} e^{-\frac{(x-\mu)^2}{2\sigma^2}} \quad (1)$$

$p(x)$ is the probability density of a random variable, σ is its spectral deviation, "μ" is the mean, and x is the dimension along which Gaussian distribution is being measured. The graph shown in Fig. 2 is a plot of Eq. (1).

When we consider the data flow over a period of time between two nodes, we get a Gaussian model. Figure 3a shows the graph of temporal traffic density with respect to time, and Fig. 3b shows its Fourier representation.

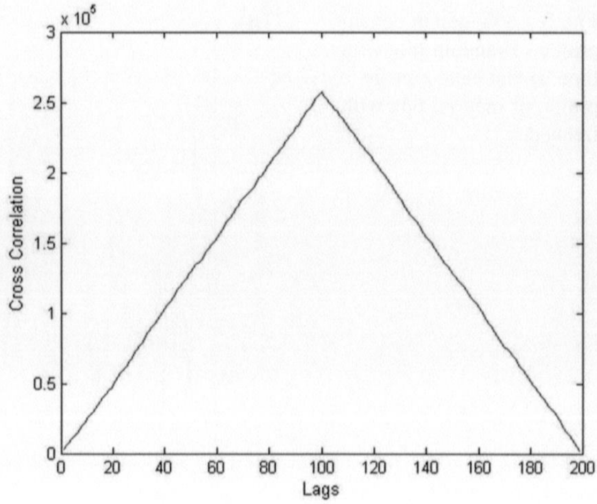

Fig. 4 Correlation between time domain and frequency domain plots of traffic density showed in Figs. 3a, b

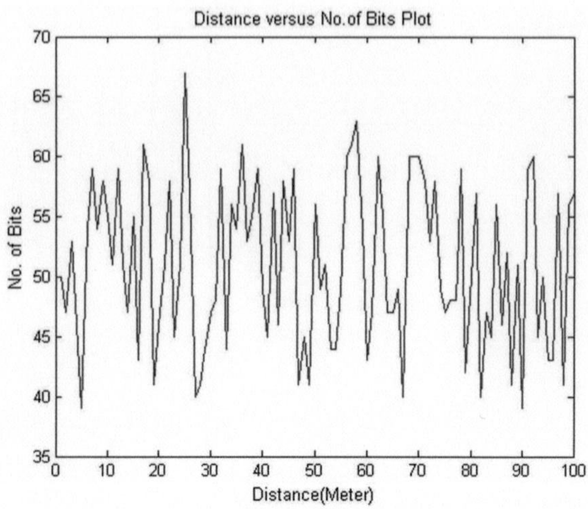

Fig. 5 Gaussian density profile of random bits with time

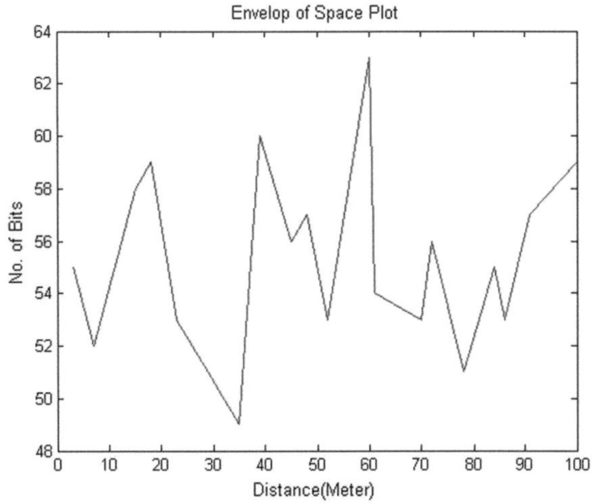

Fig. 6 The peaks of Gaussian data points are plotted separately showing a set of Gaussian envelopes

Find the correlation between time domain and frequency domain shown in Fig. 4. This also shows Gaussian nature.

4 Spatial Gaussian Distribution

Gaussian distribution can also be spatial in nature. The density of traffic along a route can vary in a Gaussian manner at a particular instant of time. This is evident in general traffic network when the density of vehicles in high at the crossroads and is sparse at distances away from the main traffic junctions. Figure 5 shows a simulation of traffic density along a network line. The same graph shows the Fourier Transform.

The peaks of Gaussian distribution are taken and plotted in Fig. 6 which shows a set of Gaussian envelopes.

5 Correlations to Existing Models

Figure 7 shows Traffic density along a network with time in Network Traffic of Tata Communications Ltd., which shows a Gaussian distribution. The two sets of data points are plotted and the envelope of the traffic density is similar to the graph shown in Fig. 6 in distribution.

The Gaussian property is of more prominent nature. Although the empirical data shows temporal distribution, the spatial distribution should have a similar profile.

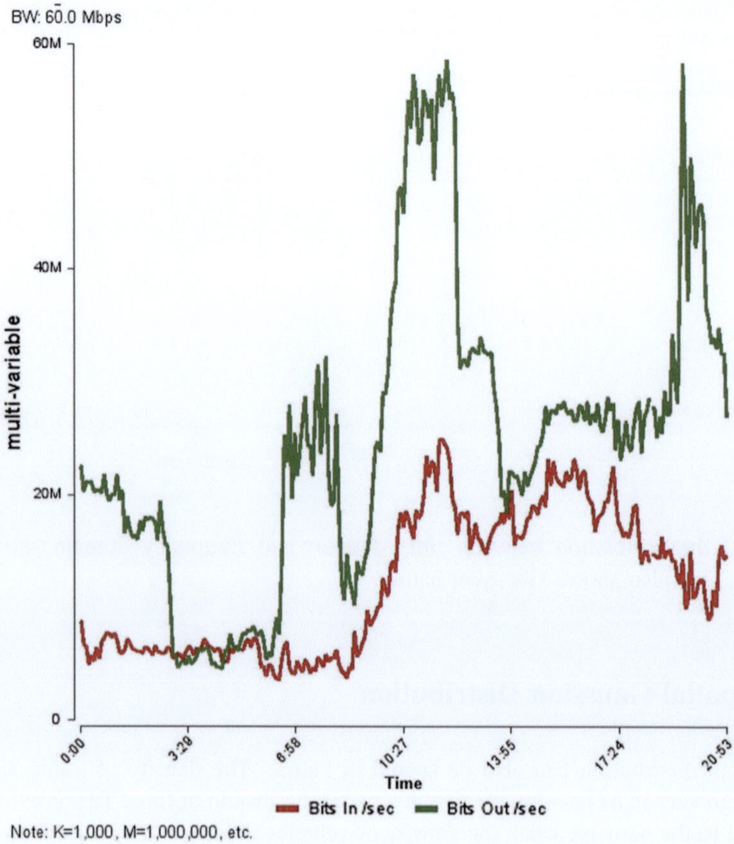

Fig. 7 Traffic density along a network with time in network traffic

6 Conclusion

We have modeled data flow using random motion and Gaussian curve, which reflects the detailed physical behavior of traffic in a communication link. We considered various drivers which influence data flow and change the topography of the Gaussian curve. The work started with computational models and finally, the results were verified through empirical data.

The model can help in making a more accurate forecast about requirements of data in communication link and help in failure analysis. The model can also be used in exploiting low-density points along the network nodes. There are times when the spectral deviation starts decreasing and the Gaussian curve for a certain link starts taking the form of an impulse function. When the rate of change of spectral deviation starts varying at a rate beyond a cut off value, the prospects of link breakdown or traffic jamming would go up. Thus, a Gaussian angle of traffic density can open new dimensions in traffic analysis. In future, the failure analysis helps in the study of reliability of the system.

References

1. Sunita K, Mukta N, Jiten M, Shilpa S (2001) Traffic characterization for heterogeneous applications. ECPE 6504
2. Moore AW, Zuev D (2005) Internet traffic classification using Bayesian analysis techniques. In: Proceedings of the 2005 ACM SIGMETRICS international conference on measurement and modeling of computer systems, pp 50–60
3. Hohn N, Veitch D (2003) Inverting sampled traffic. In: Proceeding ACM internet measurement conference, Miami, USA, pp 222–233, Oct 2003
4. Coffman KG, Odlyzko AM (2001) Internet growth: is there a"Moore's law "for data traffic?". In: Abello J, Ardalos PMP, Resende GC (eds) Handbook of massive data sets. Kluwer
5. Reif F Fundamental of statistical and thermal physics

Author Biographies

Rudra Pratap Ojha is working as an Assistant Professor in Department of Information Technology at Galgotias College of Engineering & Technology, Greater Noida. His qualifications are BTech, MTech from Motilal Nehru National Institute of Technology, Allahabad, and PhD (pursuing) from National Institute of Technology, Durgapur. He has published more than ten journals and conferences research papers. His areas of interest are wireless sensor network, real time system, mathematical modelling and simulation.

Dharm Raj is working as an Assistant Professor in Department of Information Technology at Galgotias College of Engineering & Technology, Greater Noida. His qualifications are BTech, MTech from IIIT, Allahabad, and PhD (pursuing) from Gautam Buddha University, Greater Noida. He has published journals and conferences research papers. His areas of interest are NLP, Image processing, mathematical modelling and simulation.

Pramod Kumar Srivastava is designated as an Assistant Professor in Department of Mathematics. His qualifications are BSc, MSc, and PhD. He has published more than 15 journals and conference research papers and ten books. He has experienced of 15 years in teaching and research and along with PhD guidance. His areas of interest are wireless sensor network, mathematical modelling and simulation.

Goutam Sanyal is designated as a Professor and Dean in Department of Computer Science and Engineering. His qualifications are Bachelor's of Engineering, Master's of Technology, PhD (Engineering), FIE (India), and MIEEE. He has more than 150 journal and research papers. He has a work experience of 29 years in teaching and research and along with PhD guidance. His areas of interest are wireless sensor network, computer architecture, computer graphics, computer vision, image processing, VLSI, mathematical modelling and simulation.

MIX
Papier aus verantwortungsvollen Quellen
Paper from responsible sources
FSC® C105338

If you have any concerns about our products,
you can contact us on
ProductSafety@springernature.com

In case Publisher is established outside the EU,
the EU authorized representative is:
Springer Nature Customer Service Center GmbH
Europaplatz 3, 69115 Heidelberg, Germany

Printed by Libri Plureos GmbH
in Hamburg, Germany